# The Asian financial crisis

MANCHESTER
UNIVERSITY PRESS

# The Asian financial crisis

*Crisis, reform and recovery*

Shalendra D. Sharma

Manchester University Press
Manchester and New York

distributed exclusively in the USA by Palgrave

*Published by* Manchester University Press
Oxford Road, Manchester M13 9NR, UK
*and* Room 400, 175 Fifth Avenue, New York, NY 10010, USA
www.manchesteruniversitypress.co.uk

*Distributed exclusively in the USA by*
Palgrave, 175 Fifth Avenue, New York,
NY 10010, USA

*Distributed exclusively in Canada by*
UBC Press, University of British Columbia, 2029 West Mall,
Vancouver, BC, Canada V6T 1Z2

*British Library Cataloguing-in-Publication Data*
A catalogue record for this book is available from the British Library

*Library of Congress Cataloging-in-Publication Data applied for*


ISBN    0 7190 6602 6 *hardback*
        0 7190 6603 4 *paperback*


First published 2003

11  10  09  08  07  06  05  04  03      10 9 8 7 6 5 4 3 2 1

Typeset in 10/12 pt Times
by Graphicraft Limited, Hong Kong
Printed in Great Britain
by Bookcraft (Bath) Ltd, Midsomer Norton

# Contents

# List of tables and figures

## Tables

## Figures

# Acknowledgements

This project has incurred debts of gratitude too numerous to mention. Nevertheless, I would like to thank a number of colleagues who graciously took time from their busy schedules to comment on the whole manuscript or the various chapters. All these individuals have made indelible impressions on this study and improved this work immeasurably. I wish to express my appreciation to Barbara Bundy, Rudiger Dornbusch, Barry Eichengreen, Hartmut Fischer, Tetteh Kofi, Richard Kozicki, Michael Lehmann, Man Lui-Lau, Charles N'Cho, Bruce Wydick and numerous colleagues at the IMF, the World Bank, and the Asian Development Bank, and also to the anonymous reviewers for Manchester University Press. Colleagues and friends at Bank Indonesia, the Bank of Thailand, the Reserve Bank of India, Bank Negara Malaysia and the Singapore Monetary Authority opened doors for my research and provided me with many useful contacts and logistical support. None of these individuals bear any responsibility for the flaws in my analysis, albeit they deserve much of the credit for that which proves useful.

I would also like to acknowledge the inspiring leadership of Stanley Nel, Dean of College and Arts and Sciences at the University of San Francisco. Dean Nel has not only single-handedly established a supportive environment for excellence in research and teaching at the college; his guidance, stern encouragement and mentoring has made an invaluable contribution to my professional and intellectual development. I could not have completed this project without his consistent support. Thanks also to Tony Mason, Richard Delahunty and the entire team at Manchester University Press for their professionalism and high standards and for shepherding the manuscript into a book. The fact that this book is published by the distinguished Manchester University Press makes my many months of toil on this project worthwhile. My profound thanks also to my mother, sister and brothers for the boundless support and encouragement they have given me over the years. Regretfully, my father, who made a lifetime of sacrifices for his children's education did not live to see this book. My greatest debt, however, is to my wife Vivian and our son Krishan. They have seen this book's long journey from the beginning to the end. However, they never wavered once in their support. It is safe to say that without their support and love this book would never have been written. I dedicate this book to them.

# 1

# Introduction:
# issues, debates and
# an overview of the crisis

In his celebrated *Manias, Panics and Crashes*, Charles Kindleberger (1978)
predicted a historical average of at least one financial crisis per decade.
Yet, in Gerard Caprio's (1997, 79) memorable phrase, the 1990s have been
a period of boom in busts. A financial crisis every twenty-four months –
beginning in 1992–93 with the speculative attacks against several currencies
in the Exchange Rate Mechanism (ERM) of the European Monetary System, followed by the sudden collapse of the Mexican peso in December 1994,
and more recently, the Asian financial crisis that was set off when the Bank
of Thailand devalued the baht on July 2, 1997.[1] The unexpected meltdown
of the Thai economy and the contagion (the so-called Asian flu) spread with
unprecedented ferocity, and, by the end of August 1997, the currencies of
three of Thailand's neighbors, Malaysia, Indonesia and the Philippines, had
all been devalued substantially (see Table 1.1), despite vigorous efforts by
these governments to stop their currencies from falling.[2]

During September and October, the currencies of Taiwan and Singapore came under intense pressure. While both countries managed to avoid

**Table 1.1** *Rate of currency depreciation 1997–98 (local currency per US dollar)*

|  | 2 July 1997 | End Sept. 1998 | Rate of dep. (%) July 1997–Sept. 1998 |
| --- | --- | --- | --- |
| Philippine peso | 26.38 | 43.80 | 66.10 |
| Indonesian rupiah | 2,341.92 | 10,638.30 | 354.30 |
| Thai baht | 24.40 | 38.99 | 59.80 |
| Malaysian ringgit | 2.57 | 3.80 | 47.80 |
| Korean won | 885.74 | 1,369.86 | 54.70 |

*Source*: OECD (1999, 249).

1

full-blown financial crises, both were, nevertheless, forced to engage in competitive devaluations by floating their currencies rather than losing reserves by trying to stabilize the exchange rate.[3] Nevertheless, Singapore, in spite of its strong economic fundamentals (huge foreign exchange and fiscal reserves, and a solid financial sector), saw its currency depreciate by 15 per cent and its stock market fall by 13 per cent. Similarly, Taiwan, despite its strong economic fundamentals (consistent current account surpluses and large foreign reserves), saw its currency, the New Taiwan dollar, come up against strong speculative attack. Between 1989 and July 1997, Taiwan had pursued a *de facto* pegging of the New Taiwan Dollar to the American dollar, with the exchange rate being held within a narrow range of NT$26–27 to US$1. After the crisis broke, Taiwan's central bank initially widened the band to about 28.7, with occasional interventions in the foreign exchange market to keep the rate steady. Yet, in the face of unrelenting battering, the Taiwanese central bank was forced to intervene extensively in the currency markets – spending some US$5 billion defending the value of the currency. However, the New Taiwan Dollar was abruptly floated on October 17, 1997 – after which it depreciated by 7 per cent. By October 20, the US dollar had broken through the NT$30 barrier for the first time in ten years.

Taiwan's depreciation led to speculation that the Hong Kong SAR dollar would be devalued as well – since Taiwan and Hong Kong are competitors in export markets.[4] Moreover, speculators reasoned that if Taiwan, with its enormous foreign reserves (about US$90 billion at the time), could not defend its *de facto* peg, neither could Hong Kong. Given this, even Hong Kong SAR, with its current account surpluses, budget surpluses that consistently averaged 2 per cent of GDP per year, large foreign reserves (US$92.8 billion at the end of 1997), and a currency firmly linked to the US dollar (at about 7.80 Hong Kong SAR dollars = US$1.00), since 1983 through a currency board, came under sustained attack. Indeed, the attack on Hong Kong's seemingly impregnable currency board system came as a surprise to many.

Specifically, Hong Kong's currency board system is based on a linked exchange-rate system that requires the monetary base (the sum of banknotes in circulation and bank balances with the central bank) to be fully backed by the foreign currency to which the domestic currency is linked. Thus, any change in the monetary base has to be matched by a corresponding change in the amount of US dollar reserves held by the Hong Kong Monetary Authority (HKMA). In effect, under Hong Kong's currency board system, the currency issued was fully (i.e. 100 per cent) backed by foreign reserves, and the exchange value of the Hong Kong dollar *vis-à-vis* the US dollar was fixed at the intervention/official rate.[5] The 100 per cent back-up requirement meant that one could not use the existing Hong Kong dollar currency to exhaust the official reserve. Thus not only was the money supply disciplined and demand-determined, but the monetary and exchange-rate system in

Hong Kong was far more stable than the "fixed" exchange rate system in the crisis-affected countries.

Yet these impressive fundamentals failed to provide immunity to Hong Kong. In the week beginning October 20, hedge funds and other speculators mounted a massive onslaught on the Hong Kong dollar. To pre-empt an all-out assault on the Hong Kong dollar, the HKMA raised its interest rate.[6] By October 23, the HIBOR (Hong Kong Inter-Bank Offered Rate) was pushed to an unprecedented intra-day high of 280 per cent, while the three-month inter-bank rate shot up to 37 per cent (Yam 1998). This in turn prompted local banks to raise their prime lending rates. The sharp rise in interest rates allowed speculators to amplify the impact of their short selling of shares and speculative selling of stock futures on the stock index. That is, speculators were engaged in "double play" by selling short both foreign exchange and stocks.[7] This caused the Hang Seng Index to plunge 1,700 points, or 14.6 per cent – the largest point drop and the third largest percentage loss in its history. Overall, the Hang Seng Index fell steadily from a high of 15,447 points in July 1997 to 7,225 points by August 1998 (Tan 2000, 131). Although Hong Kong managed to maintain its exchange rate peg to the dollar (despite strong speculative attacks), it suffered a 20 per cent drop in share prices, a sharp decline in property prices, and a precipitous fall in the stock market – triggering a worldwide fall in stock prices.[8]

The depreciation of the Taiwan dollar also drew attention to the vulnerability of South Korea, which is closely competitive with Taiwan. Since Taiwanese products compete closely with Korea's in the global markets, the move in undercutting the price competitiveness of Koran goods would sooner or later put enormous pressure on the Korean currency, the won. In fact, by early November 1997, the crisis had spread to Republic of Korea – the world's eleventh largest economy. The Korean won came under increasingly heavy selling pressure, with the US dollar exchange rate rising from 870 in the first quarter of 1997 to over 1,100 in the fourth quarter of 1997. With the won under growing pressure, foreign banks ran down their claims on Korean banks and on their foreign branches – forcing these banks to buy dollars with which to repay their debts. The central bank came to their aid by selling them dollars directly and by depositing dollar reserves with their foreign branches. As a result, Korea's foreign reserves, net of deposits, began to deplete rapidly: from US$30 billion to less than US$15 billion by the third week of November. Moreover, the sharp depreciation of the won not only greatly reduced Korea's competitive edge, but also exacerbated its credit crunch problem in the international capital markets.[9] This crunch in turn caused a currency crash and a liquidity crisis in an economy with unhedged and short-term foreign liabilities. Since the Korean economy is the third largest in Asia, the fall of the won implied a real depreciation that negatively affected the competitive position of the other countries in the region. Indeed, the fall of the won resulted in further competitive devaluation throughout

**Table 1.2**   *Changes in real GDP (%)*

|                  | 1996 | 1997 | 1998  |
|------------------|------|------|-------|
| Indonesia        | 8.0  | 4.5  | −13.7 |
| Korea            | 6.8  | 5.0  | −5.8  |
| Malaysia         | 8.6  | 7.5  | −7.5  |
| Philippines      | 5.8  | 5.2  | −0.5  |
| Singapore        | 7.6  | 8.4  | 0.4   |
| Thailand         | 5.5  | −1.3 | −10.0 |
| China            | 9.6  | 8.8  | 7.8   |
| Hong Kong (SAR)  | 4.5  | 5.3  | −5.1  |
| Taiwan           | 5.7  | 6.8  | 4.8   |
| Japan            | 5.0  | 1.6  | −2.5  |
| USA              | 3.7  | 4.5  | 4.3   |

*Source*: World Bank (2000).

East Asia. Faced with such mounting problems, the Korean government initially approached Japan for financial aid, but the request was turned down. In desperation, the Korean authorities (on November 20) widened the band in which the won was allowed to fluctuate – and the won fell quickly to the edge of the new band. The very next day, the Korean government turned to the IMF for help. On December 4, an IMF-led support package of US$57 billion was announced, and two days later the won was allowed to float.[10] However, in spite of all these measures, Korea was, nevertheless, plunged into a deep recession.

Indeed, the crises turned out to be so severe that, in a matter of weeks, East Asia's high-performing "tiger economies," accustomed to annual growth rates of anywhere between 6 per cent and 10 per cent were reduced to "whimpering kittens."[11] As Table 1.2 shows, Indonesia's economy (measured in real GDP) contracted by 13.7 per cent in 1998 and Thailand's by 10 per cent and Hong Kong, Malaysia, and South Korea each contracted by between 5 per cent and 8 per cent. Such sharp swings in GDP are of the same order of magnitude as what occurred in the United States during the Great Depression in the 1930s (Gilpin 2000). Indeed, like the Great Depression, the financial crisis took a heavy socioeconomic toll. A fall in output of the severity described above was invariably accompanied by massive job losses, as bankruptcies and cutbacks in production multiplied. This led to a sharp rise in both unemployment and underemployment. According to the World Bank (2000, 103), at the end of 1998, unemployment in Indonesia, Thailand and Korea had reached some 18 million, compared to 5.3 million in 1996. Moreover, the rise in inflation in the context of a greatly weakened labor market extracted a further toll in terms of falling real wages and incomes.

The combined effects of growing unemployment, rising inflation, and the absence of a meaningful social safety-net system, pushed large numbers of displaced workers and their families into poverty.

In economic terms, 1997 began on a positive note for the long-beleaguered Russian economy. The gradual decline in inflation and successful exchange-rate management were promising signs. Moreover, the stock market was on the rebound, and output actually rose slightly (by 0.8 per cent) for the first time in over a decade. While the budget deficit remained uncomfortably high, at 7 per cent of GDP, the domestic and foreign attractiveness of government bonds led the Yeltsin administration to conclude that Russia would need no further IMF funds after the full disbursement of the current loan (Gould-Davies and Woods 1999, 16). However, by October 1997 Russia began to feel the first waves of Asian contagion. As Asian banks with losses on lending at home sold their holdings of Russian high-yielding bonds to improve their liquidity position, this placed great pressure on the ruble and on the bond market. According to one account roughly US$2 billion invested by Southeast Asian businesses fled Russia between January and March 1998 (Illarionov 1999, 69). Furthermore, a sharp drop in the price of the country's biggest export commodity, gas and oil (a drop of 31 per cent between January and July 1998), coupled with Russia's inadequate (and grossly unfair) tax base, a large and growing fiscal imbalance financed by short-term ruble-denominated T-bills (or GKOs), widespread corruption and the failure of the authorities to come to grips with the long-standing fiscal problems made Russia particularly vulnerable to changes in investor sentiment.

Russia responded to the growing economic pressure by raising interest rates. However, this only increased the already heavy burden of interest repayments on loans – inexorably pushing the country further into debt. In an effort to stop this deadly downward spiral, the government redoubled its effort at revenue (tax) collection, including empowering the authorities to seize and sell off assets of tax debtors. Such measures (supported by the IMF), only served to bring stiff opposition from the entrenched vested interests, especially the powerful business interests of the oligarchs. The continuing revenue shortfalls, the high debt-service burden and the international flight to quality finally pushed the authorities to appeal for foreign assistance. Under pressure from the United States Treasury, the International Monetary Fund on July 20, 1998 approved its portion (US$11.2 billion) of a US$22.6 billion loan package to strengthen Russia's economic program and help stabilize the ruble.[12] Although US$4.8 billion was spent almost immediately to defend the ruble, this failed to bolster confidence in the financial markets.[13] As asset prices and foreign currency reserves continued their free fall, the government devalued the ruble by 34 per cent on August 17 and unilaterally imposed controls on capital flows and a 90-day moratorium on the repayment of Russia's foreign financial liabilities. Such arbitrary actions led to further depreciation of the ruble, bringing in its train Russia's loss of access to international capital markets, a virtual collapse of the banking sector and the accumulation of large external arrears.[14] The widespread expectation among market participants that Russia would receive a rescue package because it was "too big to fail" turned out to be wrong. Indeed, the speed of the Russian collapse brought home the message that no country (not even a nuclear power) was too big to fail.

The Russian default was particularly traumatic, sending investors throughout the world scrambling for cover and inflicting heavy losses on a number of large financial institutions. In fact, so severe was the impact of the Russian crisis that interest rate spreads widened significantly, seriously straining the financial markets in the United States and other industrialized countries. With the Russian experience still fresh, investor confidence made another sharp *volte-face* in perception of sovereign risk. Inevitably, this triggered a new round of large-scale capital outflows from emerging markets, including Brazil, the world's ninth largest economy (after the G-7 and China), and the other country once deemed too big to fail. Although Brazil's ambitious inflation stabilization program, the *Plano Real* (introduced in July 1994), had made exemplary progress towards restoring price stability and productivity growth and reducing inflation between 1994 and 1998 (after decades of out-of-control inflation), it failed to contain the fiscal deficit adequately. The fiscal deficit, estimated at 8 per cent of GDP in 1998, also contributed to a widening of the external current account deficit to 4.5 per cent of GDP in 1998.[15]

These substantial fiscal and trade deficits and the structure of public debt (which makes the government's finances extremely sensitive to changes in short-term interest rates and the exchange rate), made Brazil highly vulnerable to changes in investor sentiment – in particular, the widespread sentiment in financial markets that Brazil's crawling peg was simply not sustainable. To stem the huge outflows of US$12 billion in August and another US$19 billion in September 1998, the Brazilian authorities increased official interest rates to more than 30 per cent in September 1998 and to more than 40 per cent in October, and announced several fiscal measures, including substantial spending cuts, to stabilize the *real* (IMF 1999, 49). However, this brought only temporary relief. By late September, Brazil's foreign reserves had dwindled to US$45 billion, below the level of its short-term debt. As the *real* came under renewed pressure from speculators the Brazilian government sought external assistance.[16] In November the IMF announced a US$41.5 billion multilateral loan package (with the IMF contributing US$18.1 billion under a three-year Stand-By Arrangement), to sustain the value of the *real* and help Brazil with its balance of payments problem.[17]

However, the calming effects of the IMF program were short-lived. The failure by the authorities to reach political agreement on the fiscal adjustment program prevented Brazilian congressional approval and further undermined investor confidence. In December 1998 the Brazilian congress again failed to pass a critical component of the fiscal package (pension reform legislation), and in early 1999 the important state of Minas Gerais threatened to suspend servicing its debt to the federal government. Market concerns were immediately reflected in increased capital outflows, and spreads on Brazil's external debt rose to about 1,000 basis points.[18] By early January 1999 Brazil had about US$36 billion in reserves compared to US$70 billion in August 1998. The Standard and Poor's ratings agency downgraded Brazil's foreign debt rating, and the *Bovespa*, Brazil's leading stock index, fell by 27 per cent in a week. As reserves continued to decline, the government was forced to abandon its exchange-rate policy and float the beleaguered *real* on January 15, 1999 – just two weeks after President Cardoso's second inauguration.[19]

For the G-7 nations and their OECD partners, acting in concert with the IMF, the World Bank and other multilateral financial institutions, managing the crises has been both frustrating and extremely costly.[20] If the Mexican rescue package cost an unprecedented US$52 billion (with the IMF and the United States contributing US$17 billion and US$20 billion respectively),[21] between August 1997 and December 1998 the G-7 and its partners had already pledged just over US$200 billion to support Indonesia, South Korea, Thailand, Russia and Brazil – with the IMF contributing an unprecedented US$65.3 billion.[22] This amount does not include the additional US$30 billion pledged by Japan under the Miyazawa Initiative.[23]

The frequency and severity of the crises, the enormous size of the rescue packages and the realization that such bailouts could not be continued indefinitely finally forced a reality-check on the complacent G-7 leaders.[24] President Clinton, who in November 1997 dismissed Asia's financial woes as "a few small glitches in the road," a few months later characterized the Asian/global crises as "the greatest financial challenge facing the world in the last half century."[25] The urgent task facing the global community, President Clinton, the other G-7 leaders, their finance ministers and senior bureaucrats now argued, was to fix the potential flaws and to create a more equitable, sustainable and stable international financial and monetary system.[26] Their collective *esprit de corps* was lucidly captured by the self-effacing, then United States Treasury Secretary, Robert Rubin, who in his inimitable manner stated that the task before the global community was to construct a "new international financial architecture" that was "as modern as the markets."[27]

Rubin's pithy epigram has generated a veritable cottage industry. An ever-growing list of architects have come up with proposal after proposal on how to reform the existing economic regime and construct a new international financial architecture. Indeed, collaborative initiatives have already been unveiled to reduce susceptibility to financial crisis, and to deal with it more effectively when and where they occur. While there is broad consensus on the motherhood and apple-pie issues such as the need to strengthen the global financial system via more intensive surveillance and monitoring of capital markets and country financial sectors (in particular, the banking system), timely dissemination of financial information under internationally agreed standards, greater transparency in both public and private sector activity, including greater private-sector burden-sharing in order to eliminate (or at least keep within permissible limits) the problems associated with asymmetric information and moral hazard, there is also much disagreement.[28] Policy-makers, financial analysts, academic economists and others have been engaged in intense and usually instructive debates regarding the pros and cons of trade liberalization, capital controls, fixed versus floating exchange rate regimes, currency boards, dollarization, the role of the IMF, among other issues.

However, before much of the reforms envisioned in the new financial architecture had had a chance to be implemented, Asia was already in the midst of making a remarkable economic recovery – defying even the most optimistic predictions, which predicted the lapse of at least a decade before any meaningful recovery could take place. In this light, the IMF triumphantly noted that "the financial crises that erupted in Asia beginning in mid-1997 are now behind us and the economies are recovering strongly."[29] Major factors behind the recovery include strong exports (partly due to depreciated exchange rate levels), the rebuilding of foreign reserves (partly because of collapsing imports in 1998), fiscal deficits and low interest rates stimulating aggregate demand, reforms to the financial system resulting in foreign direct investment inflows, expansionary monetary and fiscal policy, and an improvement in the global economic environment – at least until September 11, 2001.

## The focus and organization of the study

Why did an apparently localized currency crisis in Thailand soon engulf a number of countries long considered economic miracles? If the economic fundamentals were seemingly sound, why was the crisis so severe, and not a relatively mild correction? If the warning signs of an impending economic slowdown were there, why did no one predict the crisis? What has been the socioeconomic and political impact of the crisis? How effectively did the governments of Thailand, Indonesia and Korea respond to the crisis prior to the conclusion of agreements with the IMF? What were the deficiencies in domestic policies that contributed to the onset of the crisis? How did the international community, especially the IMF, respond to the crisis? What was the content of the IMF policies, and how did it affect the economies under the IMF programs? What has been the nature of the economic recovery in the crisis countries, and what explains the relatively quick recovery? How valid is the claim that the IMF policies are largely responsible for the recovery? What explains why Hong Kong, Singapore and Taiwan came through such a severe region-wide economic contraction relatively unscathed? On the other hand, what explains why the People's Republic of China (PRC), which suffers from many of the problems responsible for the crisis, remained conspicuously insulated from the turmoil raging around it? More conceptually, did the Malaysian capital controls work? What type of exchange regime is most suitable in this era of free capital flows? And last, but not least, what types of reforms are envisioned in the new international financial architecture, and what implications does it hold for emerging economies in Asia and elsewhere?

The aim of the study is to provide answers to these complex and inter-related questions. Already a large and ever-growing body of literature (academic, policy-oriented and journalistic) has emerged addressing some of these issues – with the question dealing with why the crisis occurred receiving most of the attention. However, much of this literature remains either too general or too country-specific, with the country-specific usually being highly technical and specialized. This study moves beyond the existing literature by highlighting that it was the interactive conjunction of many factors – domestic political and macroeconomic policies, as well as international economic forces – that caused the crisis. Yet it is not always easy empirically to distinguish the various interrelated factors. This study will attempt to make sense of the causes by highlighting what I term the "vulnerability" and "precipitating" factors up to mid-1997. Such an approach requires a broad political-economic framework. Indeed, one of the major strengths of this study is that it adds substantially to the emerging scholarship by providing a broad comparative political-economic perspective on the Asian financial crisis and its aftermath.

Chapters 2, 3, 4 and 5 are detailed case studies of individual countries, Thailand, Indonesia, South Korea and the PRC in turn. The chapters on Thailand, Indonesia and South Korea not only examine the factors behind the crisis, but also highlight the underlying similarities and the fundamental differences between the individual cases. Specifically, the chapters illustrate that inappropriate macroeconomic policy responses to large capital inflows, weaknesses in domestic financial intermediation and poor corporate governance resulted in the build-up of vulnerabilities, while banking fragility, high leverage and currency and maturity mismatches made these economies highly susceptible to reversals in capital flows. However, these weaknesses remained unnoticed as long as these economies were growing. Despite these similarities, each country also suffered from its own unique sets of problems, and varied in its response to the crisis. Also, since the most common criticism of the IMF prescriptions was that they were indiscriminately applied, without taking account of the unique problems faced by each country, such detailed case studies provide a useful approach to assessing critically the validity of these criticisms and the overall efficacy of the IMF programs. Chapter 5, with detailed illustrations from the PRC, documents why it escaped the worst of the crisis. The aim of Chapter 6 is twofold: first, to provide a review of the competing perspectives on the new international financial architecture; and second, to document the emerging consensus on a number of fundamental issues and its implications for emerging market economies. For example, a detailed review of the Malaysian capital controls is provided to discuss the pros and cons of capital account liberalization. The Conclusion examines the reasons behind Asia's remarkable economic recovery, and the challenges that lie ahead.

## Competing perspectives on the Asian crisis

As has just been noted, the Asian financial crisis was caused by many factors and the conjunctural interactions among them. These mutually overlapping and at times competing perspectives can be roughly divided into three broad categories, viz. those that see the crisis as mainly the result of: (1) investor panic coupled with the intrinsic volatility of international capital markets – which can quickly transform a modest liquidity problem into a full-blown financial crisis; (2) unanticipated exogenous shocks and unfavorable external economic developments; and (3) structural weakness and mismanagement of the domestic economies. Because no single variable is likely to have caused the crisis, the issue is the degree to which each of these different factors contributed to its onset and severity. The following section provides an overview of the various perspectives.

### *Investor panic and the instability of international financial markets*

There are generally two strands to this argument. An asymmetric information view of financial crises defines a financial crisis as being a non-linear disruption to financial markets in which the asymmetric information problems of adverse selection and moral hazard become so severe that financial markets are unable to channel funds efficiently to those who have the most productive investment opportunities. According to Frederic Mishkin (1999), foremost among financial market imperfections is that there are endemic problems of asymmetric information (or differential information among different stakeholders) in international lending that reduce the efficiency of financial markets, and often contribute to overshooting and instability.[30] In particular, it is argued that international lenders have limited and poor information about local borrowers. Indeed, in emerging markets, information on the financial positions of banks and corporations is far less adequate than in the markets of advanced countries. Problems associated with asymmetric information are amplified in these economies, resulting in investor assessments that swing from periods of excessive optimism or euphoria to periods of excessive gloom and panic. This, in turn, often leads to adverse selection, where lenders over-extend credit, often to unsound and poorly-managed local banks and companies, as well as to panic withdrawals at the first sign of trouble.

Indeed, asymmetric information and the resulting adverse selection problem can lead to credit rationing, where some borrowers are denied loans even when they are willing to pay a higher interest rate. Moreover, the widely held belief that there are implicit guarantees by governments to maintain fixed exchange rates and to bail out local borrowers reinforces this process. At the same time borrowers are also encouraged by the same beliefs with regard to exchange rates and government bail-outs in time of crisis. As economic theory tells us: financial intermediaries who receive implicit guarantees will rationally choose investments that would otherwise be too risky. Moreover, implicit guarantees provide adverse incentives to international lenders to lend without implementing adequate supervisory, control and risk-management systems. These market failures not only increase the risks of international lending, but also make the market vulnerable to periodic crises. In such an environment it becomes rational for individual lenders to follow the herd when tell-tale signs of a crisis emerge. According to Mishkin (1999), in the case of Asia this herding phenomenon generated a self-fulfilling panic that led to market overreactions, which were not necessarily warranted by the economic fundamentals.[31]

The other related view, articulated by Furman and Stiglitz (1998), argues that although some macroeconomic and other fundamentals may have worsened in the Asian economies in the mid-1990s, the extent and depth of the crisis cannot be attributed to a deterioration in fundamentals, but rather to the panicky reaction of anxious domestic and foreign investors. In a similar vein, Radelet and Sachs (1998; 1998a) argue that in Asia the problem was one of liquidity rather than insolvency. That is, banks were not insolvent by any standard. Rather, East Asian financial institutions had incurred a significant amount of external liquid liabilities that were not entirely backed by liquid assets.[32] Compounding this problem was the fact that a large proportion of foreign borrowings by corporates and banks were unhedged because of the prevailing expectations of stable exchange rates. When these expectations were disappointed, the scramble to repay these foreign currency loans created a massive market imbalance. In mid-1997, countries that relied on short-term capital inflows were caught in a liquidity crisis when investors refused roll-over lending. For example, in Indonesia, when available foreign exchange reserves were insufficient to cover short-term foreign liabilities, a sudden loss in investor confidence led to a rush for the exits by foreign investors, leading to a dramatic collapse of the rupiah. Many corporations, which would otherwise have been profitable, were made insolvent because over-depreciation of the rupiah increased the domestic value of their foreign debts to unsustainable levels.

11

Thus, the East Asian countries were victims of a shift in investor expectations that became self-fulfilling.[33] Radelet and Sachs support their claims by showing that, up until the third quarter of 1997, optimism about the region was expressed by international bankers (as shown by low and falling risk premia attached to loans to East Asia), credit ratings agencies (as shown by ratings that remained unchanged throughout 1996 and the first half of 1997), and securities firms (as shown by their published forecasts). On the other hand, clear evidence of a collapse in investor confidence can be seen in the dramatic reversal of capital flows. In 1996, the capital inflow to the five Asian crisis economies (Korea, Thailand, Indonesia, Malaysia, the Philippines) was US$93 billion. In 1997, the figure was a minus US$12.1 billion, a swing of US$105 billion. This dramatic reversal represented 11 per cent of the combined GDP of the five countries (IMF 2000a). Similarly, quarterly Bank of International Settlements (BIS) data on banking flows show that international bank lending to the five crisis-affected countries was positive, at almost US$50 billion, in the first half of 1997, but swung to minus US$40 billion in the third quarter of 1997, thereafter averaging close to minus US$100 billion for the three quarters that followed (BIS 1999). For Radelet and Sachs (1998a), there is no other way to explain such a swift and massive outflow of capital once the crisis broke except as a classic bank run – where commercial banks and portfolio investors suddenly seized with panic demanded immediate payment, thereby forcing financial intermediaries to liquidate at great loss.[34] Compounding the problem of investor panic were the overly harsh fiscal and monetary policies prescribed by the IMF. Radelet and Sachs note (1998a, 4–5):

> The [Asian] crisis is a testament to the shortcomings of the international capital markets and their vulnerability to sudden reversals of market confidence . . . In this sense, the Asian crisis can be understood as a crisis of success caused by a boom of international lending followed by a sudden withdrawal of funds. At the core of the Asian crisis were large scale foreign capital inflows into financial systems that became vulnerable to panic . . . A combination of panic on the part of the international investment community, policy mistakes at the onset of the crisis by Asian governments, and poorly designed international rescue programs have led to a much deeper fall in (otherwise viable) output than was either necessary or inevitable.

Radelet and Sachs make a compelling argument. Certainly, the revolutionary advances in computing and other communications technology have enabled investors to access information on macroeconomic data, asset prices and exchange rates at the push of a button. Today, global capital markets operate around the clock searching for the highest rate of return, and financial transactions can occur instantaneously. Among other things, this has made bank and currency runs both easier and faster. Large depositors and other banks can withdraw funds almost instantaneously. Indeed, the highly competitive and globalized financial world has created individual market participants that are huge enough to mobilize, often with the help of leverage, financial resources larger than the GDP of smaller economies. They can build up dominating positions in the markets of smaller economies and influence short-term market movements singly or through acting in concert. Even small depositors no longer need to line up physically at banks to withdraw their funds. They can transfer their funds to other banks by telephone, computers and automatic transaction machines (ATMs). Not only can funds be withdrawn faster and more cheaply; runs can start upon the receipt of any adverse news about the financial health of financial institutions and countries. Thus, in a world of integrated, securitized and electronically linked capital markets, where in-depth information is expensive to obtain, it may be rational for investors to react to even small news – and move funds in and out of markets with a click of the computer keyboard. Arguably, relatively small bad news can lead to a major speculative attack, even if the news is not related to any important change in economic fundamentals. Thus Calvo (1996) argues that emerging markets are vulnerable to a herd mentality among investors. Since it is too costly for investors to address the state of each economy, it is optimal for them to pull out of a group of related markets simultaneously when they spot signs of trouble in any one of them. Similarly, Masson (1998) argues that small triggers can be precipitating factors for investors, leading to across-the-board loss of confidence and a higher perceived risk of holding investments in a set of countries. As investors follow each other and pull out their funds, the herd behavior pushes these countries into financial distress.

The comprehensive study by Kaminsky and Schmukler (1999) analyzes the twenty largest one-day swings in stock prices (in US dollars) in Hong Kong, Indonesia, Japan, South Korea, Malaysia, the Philippines, Singapore, Taiwan and Thailand since January 1997 to see what type of news moves the markets in days of extreme market jitters. Of special interest was whether news in one country would affect markets in another, and if so, what type of news. The authors classified news into seven different categories: news related to agreements with international organizations, the financial sector in each country, monetary and fiscal policies, credit-rating agencies, the real sector and political announcements. Their study found that some of the biggest one-day downturns cannot be explained by any apparent substantial news, but seem to be driven by herd instincts of the market itself. Similarly, Goldfajn and Baig (1998) construct dummy variables to represent good and bad news. They find that news in one crisis country affects exchange rates and stock markets in the others, suggesting contagion. Thus there appears to be an element of pure contagion effect at work – that is, a sudden and massive shift in market sentiment unrelated to market fundamentals.[35] Their study reinforces the view that, in this era of mobile capital, even countries with otherwise exemplary macroeconomic environments (in Asia, countries such as Singapore, Taiwan and Hong Kong) can become victims of market contagion.

There is no doubt that a currency crisis in one country can worsen market participants' perception of the economic outlook in countries with similar characteristics and trigger a generalized fall in investor confidence. Since financial market turbulence can spread from one country to another via three main channels – monsoonal effects, spillovers and pure contagion effects – the study by Goldfajn and Baig (1998) of financial market developments in Malaysia, Indonesia, the Philippines, Thailand and South Korea from July 1997 to May 1998 provides evidence of high correlations between sovereign spreads across the five countries. This indicates that markets felt that the probability of private debt default increased dramatically in these countries, and nervousness about one market was transmitted to other markets readily. As a consequence, global investors demanded higher risk premiums for all countries. Moreover, in Asia, the rapid downgrading of the region's sovereign ratings by international rating agencies further fueled the shift in market sentiment, triggering panic selling of foreign-owned local assets. Also, we now know that the most severely affected crisis countries experienced external liquidity crises as investors came to doubt that adequate reserves were available to service maturing foreign debts. As this doubt became widespread, panic set in, soon to be followed by a stampede – to borrow Sachs's apt metaphor. On the one hand, local residents rushed to buy foreign exchange to cover their dollar liabilities, thereby intensifying exchange-rate pressures. On the other hand, instinctively risk-averse and with a low tolerance for uncertainty, the fickle international financial markets and their managers did what they had done in Mexico in 1994 – fleeing the region as fast as they had entered. Seen in this light, Asia's punishment was in a sense disproportionate to the crime – it became a helpless victim of irrational panic and investor stampede.

Yet external shock by itself need not have caused a crisis of the magnitude that Asia experienced – if only its domestic economic and political structures had been robust. Confronted with a contagious external shock the highly integrated economies of Thailand, Indonesia, Malaysia and Korea, with their embedded inefficiencies and weak financial systems, could not withstand the impact.[36] The domino effect of the weakening currencies first adversely affected the financial sector, and then the real sector of the national economies. Furthermore, an important component of vulnerability is the credibility of the government with regard to its ability to suffer (or inflict) pain in defense of the currency. A combination of weak banking systems and low reserves can undermine a country's ability to defend the currency. If a country with low reserves cannot tolerate capital flight, weak banking systems make interest rate defenses more costly. The moral of the story is rather simple: it is difficult to point to any emerging market economy that experienced a financial crisis, but did not suffer from some fundamental weaknesses. In Asia, the rapid capital withdrawal greatly exacerbated the underlying weakness.

Furthermore, it is hard to overlook the contagion stemming from the growing financial integration within the region. As Masson (1998) notes, a crisis in one country may affect the economic fundamentals of a group of countries to which it is closely associated through trade and financial links. For example, depreciation in the value of the currency of one country can affect the price competitiveness of other countries through spillover effects. Financial interdependence can also contribute to the transmission of a crisis, as initial turmoil in one country can lead outside creditors to recall their loans elsewhere, thereby creating a credit crunch in other debtor countries. Also, any major trading partner of a country in which a financial crisis has induced a sharp currency depreciation could experience declining asset prices and large capital outflows or could become the target of a speculative attack as investors anticipate a decline in exports to the crisis country, and hence a deterioration in the trade account. In the case of Asia, the initial baht devaluation certainly affected investor confidence in the Asian region, just as the decline in the Indonesian rupiah made Korean investors suffer large losses. In order to make up the losses, Korean investors started to sell Russian and Brazilian securities, thereby depressing their bond prices. Overall, the deepening recession in the worst-affected countries pulled down their neighbors, further weakening regional economic growth. Indeed, there is substantial evidence that trade linkages are an important reason for the spread of crises.[37]

### Unfavorable external economic developments

These included China's devaluation in 1994, Japan's prolonged recession and the appreciation of the US dollar, which worked in tandem to make the Asian economies highly vulnerable to shocks.

#### China's devaluation

Central to China's economic growth has been the liberalization of the foreign trade and investment regime, and the adoption of an ambitious open-door strategy. Prior to the introduction of the Deng reforms, China remained a backward and closed economy, with foreign trade amounting to a minuscule 7 per cent of GNP. However, the liberalization of the foreign trade and exchange-rate regime, followed by further wide-ranging reforms introduced in 1988 (which included increased retention of foreign exchange and easier access to foreign exchange adjustment centers established in 1986), enabled businesses, in particular the enterprises, to buy and sell foreign exchange at a depreciated rate known as swap rate, and thus greatly helped to boost exports. By the early 1990s, foreign trade had grown to an unprecedented $200 billion, or roughly 40 per cent of GNP (Cerra and Dayal-Gulati 1999).

On January 1, 1994 China unified its exchange rate by bringing the official rate into line with the prevailing swap-market rate, resulting in a depreciation in the official rate by about 50 per cent (in effect, the yuan was devalued by 50 per cent).[38] China's pre-emptive devaluation, even as it led to a real exchange appreciation for the dollar-pegged currencies in Southeast Asia (sharply undercutting their export competitiveness), created an export boom for China.[39] Moreover, reform measures such as (a) the abolition of the retention quota system for foreign exchange; (b) the revision of the tax system to allow a zero value-added tax (VAT) rating for exports by domestic firms and the newly established foreign-funded enterprises;[40] (c) further relaxation of China's open-door policy towards foreign direct investment, including the provision of special tax incentives to foreign investment in technology-intensive industries; and (d) generous tariff concessions (including lower income tax rates and tax holidays) to firms operating in the coastal special economic zones only served further to enhance China's international competitiveness and helped it to expand its export markets greatly. Between 1990 and 1997, Chinese exports to industrialized countries have grown at an average rate of 15.5 per cent per annum, and for the period 1995–1997, which saw a decline in world trade growth, China's exports to the United States grew by 8 per cent, while Japanese exports declined by 2.4 per cent. Also, China's share of garment exports exceeded the total from the five Asian crisis economies (Indonesia, Korea, Malaysia, the Philippines and Thailand), rising from 37 per cent in 1990 to 60 per cent in 1996, and its share of electronics exports increased from 12 per cent to 18 per cent over the same period. Overall, since the start of the reform period, China's share of world trade has almost quadrupled.[41] Yet some analysts, while admitting that the Chinese devaluation caused a deterioration in the competitiveness of the East and Southeast Asian nations' economies, maintain that the perceived shift after 1994 in the regional competitive advantage towards China has been exaggerated. They note that while the yuan did depreciate in nominal terms, its *real* depreciation was eroded by the fact that China's inflation rate since 1995 was higher than those of its trading partners. Also, it should be noted that Thailand, Indonesia and Malaysia experienced a gradual erosion in the competitiveness of their export industries as a result of rising domestic costs, especially wage costs, against the backdrop of an industrialization process that was not very effective in shifting from labor-intensive industries to higher levels. Thus, it can be concluded that the Chinese devaluation was "at best a contributing factor to the Asian financial crisis, not the primary cause" (Liu *et al.* 1998, 1).

### The Japanese recession

Japan, the world's second largest economy – suffering from what has been described as the "world's slowest economic crisis" – has inadvertently played a significant role in the emergence and spread of the Asian crisis.[42] Japan's monetary problems began with the currency agreements of 1985 (the Plaza Agreement) and 1987 (the Louvre Agreement), when the G-7 countries attempted to establish more predictable foreign exchange intervention and target bands for exchange rates between the leading currencies. Under these agreements the Japanese agreed to buy US dollars in the foreign exchange markets, the domestic counterpart being the creation of yen. This derailed Japanese monetary growth as measured by M2+CDs from its long success-ful growth path of about 8 per cent per year, causing money growth to accelerate to about 12 per cent per year. This was the origin of the bubble in equity prices and in real estate sectors in the late 1980s. Specifically, when the manufacturing sector no longer required significant amounts of new credits, the banks turned to the "bubble sectors" such as construction, real estate and non-bank finance to build their loan book. Soon this resulted in a number of famous anomalies, including the three-quarters of a square mile plot of land under the Imperial Palace in Tokyo, which was supposedly worth more than the entire state of California, and the fact that the market capitalization of Nippon Telegraph and Telephone (NTT) was worth more than the capitalization of entire markets such as Germany (Mera and Renaud 2000, 66–7).

The Japanese economy first showed signs of serious strain in the late 1980s, when the bubble economy of the 1980s – the speculative boom that generated hundreds of billions of dollars in bad debt – burst.[43] Since the collapse of the asset-price bubble, economic growth in Japan has stagnated. Over the period 1987 to 1995, the Nikkei index declined by more than 49 per cent. Real estate prices have also declined by more than 50 per cent since 1990. Real invest-ment spending, which had been growing at 20 per cent per annum in 1989, plummeted to less than 1 per cent in 1992 (Tan 2000, 41). From 1992 to 1996, annual real growth in Japanese GDP has averaged less than 1 per cent compared to 2.6 per cent in the United States over the same period. More broadly, real GDP growth in Japan averaged just 1.4 per cent during 1991–2000, one-third the average growth rate recorded during 1981–90.[44] Japan's performance during 1991–2000 also compared poorly with average growth rates of 3.4 per cent for the United States and 2.1 per cent for the EU.

The collapse in asset prices dealt a significant blow to Japan's financial institutions, as Japanese banks were allowed to use 45 per cent of the mar-ket value of their equity holdings to meet the Bank of International Settle-ments (BIS) reserve requirements. The decline in stock prices reduced their reserves, while their real estate loans became problem loans. According to one estimation, the collapse of asset prices has caused a significant contrac-tion of individual wealth. The total decline in the Japanese people's wealth caused by the collapse of real estate prices amounts to 1,000 trillion yen, twice Japan's annual GNP.

Despite prime minister Hashimoto's call for a "big bang" approach to financial reform in November 1996, the Japanese financial system deteriorated further in the second half of 1997. The large increase in consumption tax in April 1997 (implemented to address Japan's large fiscal deficit), caused the economy to lapse deeper into recession. Real growth over the four quarters of 1997 amounted to minus 0.4 per cent, unemployment and bankruptcies increased, and the country remained trapped in recession throughout 1998. In response to the deepening contraction and a growing credit crunch, the Japanese government approved yet another (the thirteenth) broad fiscal stimulus package totaling 17 trillion yen in April 1998, a further 17 trillion yen in 1999, including 6 trillion yen in tax cuts (Horiuchi 2000, 30–1). So far, these measures have failed to resolve the roots of Japan's economic malaise: the US$800 billion to US$1 trillion in non-performing loans.[45] As the next section illustrates, Japan's long recession has had a significant impact on the crisis-hit countries in the region.

During the late 1980s and 1990s, with the very rapid and sustained appreciation of the yen, Japanese manufacturers recognized that they needed to transfer a large proportion of Japan's manufacturing production (particularly at the low end of the technology spectrum) to the lower-labor-cost countries in Asia and elsewhere. This circumstance enabled the Japanese banks (which were then among the world's largest financial intermediaries), substantially to increase their global presence. Japanese banks were not only too happy to service Japanese companies that were increasingly involved in foreign direct investment, but also to re-cycle capital – given Japan's position as the world's pre-eminent source of surplus capital. Foreign direct investment (FDI) from Japan tripled in the decade to 1997, rising from US$22.3 billion in 1986 to US$66.2 billion in 1997. While the United States and Europe remained important destinations for Japan's FDI, the Asian share showed the largest rise, increasing from around 10 per cent of the total in 1986 to 25 per cent in 1997 (Grenville 1999, 3). Moreover, an added impetus to lend came when, in order to revive the Japanese economy from deep recession, the Japanese government reduced the discount rate to 1 per cent in April 1995. Thus, facing virtually non-existent interest rates at home, Japanese banks sought higher returns through aggressive, large-scale lending, in particular, to the fast-growing East and Southeast Asian economies. Among other reasons, the East and Southeast Asian countries eagerly sought Japanese FDI because it enabled them to engage in the profitable "yen-carry-trade."[46] Japan's total international investments, consisting of foreign direct investment, portfolio investment (such as equity securities, debt securities, money market instruments and financial derivatives), and other investments, including loans, trade credits, foreign currencies, foreign deposits and other assets, increased sharply – "from a net asset position of 29 trillion yen in 1986 to 124 trillion yen in 1997, of which 75 per cent was accounted for by the private sector (banking and other sector) and the balance by the public sector ... these investments have provided the financing needs of both the private, government and banking sectors in Asia, particularly in

**Table 1.3**   *Asia's foreign bank borrowing as of June 1997*

| Borrowing country | Total foreign loans (US$B) | Total from Japanese banks (US$B) | % of Total from Japanese banks |
|---|---|---|---|
| Indonesia | 59 | 23 | 39 |
| Malaysia | 29 | 10 | 34 |
| S. Korea | 103 | 24 | 23 |
| Thailand | 69 | 38 | 55 |
| Total | 260 | 95 | 37 |

*Source*: Bank for International Settlements (1998).

the NIEs and ASEAN economies" (Daquila 1999, 94–5). By mid-1997, Japanese banks accounted for more than one-third of the cross-border loans by foreign banking institutions to customers in the high-performing Southeast Asian countries alone (see Table 1.3). By comparison, US banks had lent only US$21 billion or 8 per cent of foreign loans to Indonesia, South Korea, Malaysia and Thailand (Alexander 1998, 17–18).

However, the bursting of the asset bubble left Japanese banks with deteriorating asset quality, while the stagnant economy further weakened the already over-leveraged banks, culminating in the failure of several large institutions. For example, in 1996, Nissan Life Insurance, a major insurance company, collapsed. In November 1997, one of Japan's ten large nation-wide city banks, Hokkaido Tokushoku Bank (popularly known as Takugin) went bankrupt despite the effort to rescue it through a merger with the Hokkaido Bank. It was revealed that Takugin's capital adequacy ratio (CAR) was less than zero, as against its reported figure of 9.34 per cent. Also in November 1997, Sanwa and Yamaichi Securities went bankrupt (Landers and Biers 1998, 98–105). By the end of 1997, the profitability of the financial sector had fallen sharply, resulting in the need for more write-offs of bad loans.[47] As the crisis deepened, many of the banks suffered capital losses and were forced to re-balance their loan portfolios in adherence to capital adequacy standards.[48] Since the capital adequacy requirement is higher for international than for national lending, many banks chose to recall foreign loans and contain the magnitude of the domestic lending squeeze. At the same time, banks and financial institutions in East and Southeast Asia that had borrowed from Japan were hit by the currency shocks and the financial outlook of Japanese banks and securities firms correspondingly deteriorated. On the basis of Japanese banks' reports of their financial outlook for the fiscal year ending in March 1999, the 17 largest Japanese banks suffered a net combined after-tax loss of 3.6 trillion yen (US$29.5 billion at US$1: 22 yen). Moreover, even after spending 10.4 trillion yen to dispose of non-performing loans in the 12 preceding months, the total non-performing loans at these banks stood at over 20.9 trillion yen. It is estimated that the bad loans of the major Japanese banks alone total about 7 per cent of GDP. This figure far exceeds the amount of government resources spent (2.5 to 3 per cent of GDP) to resolve the Savings and Loan crisis in the United States.[49]

Thus, Japan suffers from its own economic crisis – characterized by severe deflationary pressure and prolonged undervaluation of its currency. Overall, the prolonged recession in Japan has greatly reduced Japan's demand for imports from the rest of Asia. In the first quarter of 1998, imports from Southeast Asia to Japan had fallen by 26 per cent from the previous year, while Japanese tourism to the Asian region dropped by 50 per cent from June 1997 to June 1998.[50] Moreover, Japanese manufacturers sharply reduced the pace of direct investments into Asia (which had been concentrated in areas such as automobiles and electronics), as existing capacity dwarfed the reduced size of regional demand for these products. Also, as the Nobel economics laureate Merton Miller has noted, Japan in trying to export its way out of its long recession has significantly contributed to the regional downturn (Vines 2000, 14). Clearly, Japan's ability to act as a catalyst for regional recovery has been severely limited. This is in sharp contrast to the US role in the Mexican peso crisis of 1994–95. In the latter, an expanding US economy was able to absorb the shocks and guide Mexico towards recovery. However, Japanese banks, faced with the deterioration in their balance sheets, became the first to pull out of Asia, calling in their loans and exposures to the region.

Indeed, Japanese banks were not only forced to cut losses by refusing to roll over existing loans, they also refused to extend new ones, a decision that extended to closing foreign branches and selling parts of their overseas operations. According to the Monetary Authority of Singapore (2001), Japan added a total of US$69 billion in net liquidity to East and Southeast Asia during the second half of the 1980s – a figure based on the aggregate of trade, foreign direct investment, portfolio investment and bank credit flows. However, this net liquidity inflow turned to a net outflow of US$126 billion during 1991–95, and an even larger net outflow of US$374 billion during 1996–2000. These actions have contributed significantly to the vicious spiral of illiquidity and the resultant insolvency and regional credit crunches. Fred Bergsten (1998, 1–2) notes:

> Japan, which accounts for three quarters of the Asian economy, has plunged into recession and is already close to a "lost decade" . . . The crisis countries must put their own houses in order but, even if they do everything right, they cannot resume satisfactory growth until Japan does so. The "flying geese" formation, whereby the rest of Asia follows the lead of Japan, may become a flock of dead ducks for a prolonged period – whereas rapid growth and open

markets in the United States enabled Mexico to bounce back from its 1995 crisis after only one year.

*The US dollar appreciation*

Before the crisis, Thailand, Indonesia, Malaysia, Singapore, South Korea and the Philippines all adopted a currency basket system. However, the fact that the US dollar had a high weight in the basket meant that all had *de facto* pegged their currencies' nominal exchange rates to the US dollar. One of the benefits of such fixed but adjustable exchange rate regimes was to provide macroeconomic discipline by maintaining the prices of tradable goods in line with foreign prices. These regimes contributed to the relative stability of the real exchange rate until mid-1995. The currency stability *vis-à-vis* the US dollar was instrumental in bringing in direct and portfolio investment. In particular, the dollar-pegged regime attracted Japanese foreign direct investment and helped the governments to promote export-led growth.[51]

Following the 1985 Plaza Accord, the G-7 countries (USA, UK, Germany, Italy, France, Canada and Japan) undertook a major currency market intervention to realign exchange rates. One major effect of this was the appreciation of the Japanese yen and the depreciation of the US dollar. Hence, the Plaza Accord is known for bringing down the value of the US dollar and ushering in a new era of the appreciating yen. Between 1985 and 1988, the yen almost doubled in value *vis-à-vis* the dollar and other Asian currencies tied to the dollar. More broadly, by 1988, the yen was almost 30 per cent above its average for the 1980–85 period on an inflation-adjusted, trade-weighted basis. Overall, in the decade 1985 to 1995, the yen had appreciated dramatically against the US dollar, from about 238 to 80. This had major consequences for Japanese industry, as many firms found it increasingly unprofitable to export from Japan. For example, it was reported that for every 1 yen movement in the $US/Yen exchange rate, the profits of the Toyota motor car company experienced a change of 12 billion yen (Tan 2000, 27). Not surprisingly, many Japanese firms began moving their operations offshore – where wages were much lower and the exchange rate was more favorable. Japanese foreign investment, which totaled about US$9 billion in 1985, jumped to US$68 billion by 1989. By the mid-1990s, 40 per cent of the total output of major Japanese electronics companies was produced offshore, while for medium-sized electronics companies the ratio was 60 per cent. The high-performing ASEAN countries (especially Indonesia, Malaysia and Thailand) were the major beneficiaries of Japanese investments.[52] As Tan (2000, 28) notes, "between 1985 and 1990, Japanese foreign investment in ASEAN countries doubled (from US$11 billion to US$21 billion), much of it going into labor-intensive industries such as textiles and electronics component manufacture. By 1991, some 400,000 workers in ASEAN countries were working in Japanese-owned companies. By the early

21

1990s, the Sony Corporation was making more color television sets in Malaysia than in Japan."

However, by the mid-1990s the era of the strong yen was over. The third external shock that has contributed to the Asian financial crisis has been the sharp appreciation of the dollar that began in 1995, especially its appreciation *vis-à-vis* the yen. As the dollar rose relative to the yen in the months before the crisis, the currencies of the crisis countries rose in comparison with the yen also. In some cases the crisis countries followed the dollar very closely; in others the link was looser, because they used a basket peg but still gave the dollar substantial weight.[53] This system of a *de facto* peg or quasi-peg against the dollar conferred competitive advantage on these countries when the dollar was relatively weak in the international currency market. However, from April 1995, when the dollar began to appreciate against the yen, the real effective exchange rates of most of the region's currencies started to appreciate. Since these East Asian economies exported a substantial proportion of their goods to Japan, the resultant loss in export competitiveness contributed to a deterioration in the current account of the Japanese balance of payments.

Specifically, after hitting a historic high of 80 yen to the dollar in June 1995, the yen experienced a downward trend, falling to 127 yen to the dollar in April 1997 – just before the Asian crisis broke. The yen's sharp depreciation led to a marked deterioration in East and Southeast Asia's export performance and current account imbalances in 1996, paving the way for the currency crisis. For example, in the case of Thailand, although the baht had edged down by about 4 per cent against the dollar in the two years leading up to the July 2, 1997 devaluation, its real effective exchange rate (trade-weighted) had appreciated by about 15 per cent over the same period. This largely reflected its sharp appreciation of approximately 35 per cent against the yen. As a result, export growth decelerated sharply, from over 20 per cent in 1995 to virtually zero in 1996, with the current account deficit reaching 7.9 per cent of GDP. The exchange-rate policy of pegging to a basket of currencies in which the dollar was weighted heavily had constrained the government from allowing the baht to depreciate against the dollar at a faster rate to stimulate exports. Similarly, other Asian countries that had also pegged their currencies loosely to the dollar suffered a sharp slowdown in exports on the back of the weakening yen. The depreciation of the yen against the dollar also affected capital flows. It increased the capital inflow through interbank short-term borrowing, notably from Japan – since depreciation of the yen against the dollar under a *de facto* dollar-pegged exchange-rate regime was equivalent to the appreciation of the crisis-affected countries' own currencies against the yen. This prompted banks as well as non-banks in Thailand, South Korea and Malaysia to borrow from Japan in order to invest in high-yielding risky foreign bonds, real estate and consumer loan services. Most of these investments turned into non-performing loans in these countries after the bubble burst in 1997.

Thus, since Asian countries have substantial trade relationships with Japan, the yen depreciation relative to the US dollar meant that these countries on a *de facto* dollar peg became less competitive *vis-à-vis* Japan. Korean firms lost ground to Japanese firms as the yen depreciated in 1995–96. Thai firms that lost competitiveness when China *de facto* devalued its currency in 1994, lost further competitiveness as the yen depreciated *vis-à-vis* the US dollar in 1995–96. Therefore the yen depreciation from 1993 to April 1995 produced the boom in Asia, while the yen appreciation from April 1995 to 1997 depressed economic activity. Clearly, the business cycles in Asia are fundamentally correlated with the yen/dollar cycle. While these three external factors did not trigger the crisis, they cumulatively contributed to its severity and duration.

### Domestic structural weakness and mismanagement

The fact that no one predicted the crisis is hardly surprising. The celebrated "tiger economies" of Southeast and East Asia were long viewed as the "miracle economies," with seemingly impeccable economic fundamentals and constituting a model for others to emulate. Between 1965 and 1990 the economies of Japan, the four original tigers (Hong Kong, Korea, Singapore and Taiwan), and the three emerging tigers, or the newly-industrializing economies of Southeast Asia (Indonesia, Malaysia and Thailand) grew more rapidly than any other group of economies in the world, averaging 7 per cent per year growth rates in real terms since the mid-1970s, and over 9 per cent per year since the late 1980s.[54] This meant that the fast-growing Asian economies were doubling their real GDP approximately every 7 years during the 1960s and 1970s, and roughly every 7 to 10 years during the 1980s (World Bank 1993). All these economies also experienced dramatic increases in real per capita incomes. In South Korea and Singapore, for example, real per capita income grew more than 700 per cent between 1965 and 1995. Over the same period Taiwan and Hong Kong logged a 400 per cent increase, while Malaysia, Thailand and Indonesia each experienced real per capita income growth of over 300 per cent (Crafts 1999). South Korea's unprecedented growth in per capita GNP (6.9 per cent over 1960–81 and 8.5 per cent over 1980–94) increased incomes from US$1,700 in 1981 to US$8,260 in 1994. Equally impressively, Indonesia's per capita GNP rose from US$90 in 1972 to US$880 in 1994, Thailand's from US$220 to US$2,410 and Malaysia's from US$450 to US$3,480.[55]

Not surprisingly, a spate of popular books, including Jim Rohwer's (1995), *Asia Rising: Why America will Prosper as Asia's Economies Boom* and John Naisbitt's (1995) bestseller, *Megatrends Asia*, not to mention a growing list of academic tomes, projected the inexorable shift in power towards the

Asia-Pacific economies – besides showering laudatory praises on the virtues of the so-called East Asian-style state-guided capitalism. The region's self-styled gurus, such as the Malaysian strongman, Mahathir Mohamad, and Singapore's patriarch, Lee Kuan Yew, found the semiotic imagery of Asian-style capitalism congenial, as it suggested that their leadership played a critical role. Predictably, they confidently asserted that Asia's exuberant growth was destined to continue long into the next millennium. The World Bank (1993), along with a growing number of leading economists such as Columbia's Jagdish Bhagwati (1996), concurred with the sanguine assessments. Indeed, the World Bank's (1993) influential study, *The East Asian Miracle: Economic Growth and Public Policy*, praised the prudent role of the state in Asia's economic development, claiming that the miracle was due to the state's adherence to the market-friendly policies epitomized by the so-called "Washington Consensus." That is, by adopting liberalized capital accounts, open trade and foreign investment policies, a single competitive exchange rate and a commitment to the principles of comparative advantage, economic integration and export-led growth, Asia was able to build an economy on solid foundations. In other words, an economy based on both the accumulation of factors of production (especially the massive investment in physical capital), and increases in total factor productivity, measured in terms of improvements in technology and efficiency.

In those halcyon days the lone dissenter was the iconoclastic economist, Paul Krugman. In a provocative article published a few years before the Asian crisis (in 1994), he argued that East Asia's economic growth, impressive as it was, could be explained by basic economic factors such as high savings rates, investment in education and job creation. In other words, growth was achieved as a result of increased inputs, not as a result of increased total factor productivity. Indeed, Krugman likened the experience of the fast-growing economies of East Asia to the former Soviet Union, which grew rapidly in the 1920s and 1930s through large increases in the employment of capital and labor, rather than increases in total factor productivity. Krugman called this working harder, not smarter – growth as a result of "perspiration rather than inspiration." This finding prompted him to refer to the high-performing economies of East Asia as a collection of paper tigers. Since there are inevitable limits to expanding growth by raising savings rates, labor force participation, etc., Krugman predicted that East Asia's growth rates were bound to decline over time. However, Krugman's model predicted "diminishing returns" or a gradual loss of economic growth, not a sudden and precipitous financial crash.[56]

As is usually the case, there is always much wisdom after the fact. Before the dust had even settled from the wreckage of the crisis, a veritable cottage industry sprang up virtually overnight to describe and analyze the many ills afflicting the Asian model of development. The one that caught the popular imagination was crony capitalism. Many now argued that the Asian development model was in fact infected with the virus of cronyism and patronage. Rather than operating on the principles of free market economics, there was widespread political interference with the market process. This included such practices as patronage appointments of relatives and cronies to state-owned enterprises and other businesses, granting lucrative government contracts to political allies, allocating credit to favored firms and industries without prudential oversight, promoting those with nepotistic, factional and personal ties to the well-connected, and engaging in predatory rent-seeking and other activities geared towards embezzlement and self-aggrandizement. Krugman (1998, 74) describes the workings of the insidious crony capitalism in evocative prose:

> how Asia fell apart is pretty familiar . . . the region's downfall was a punishment for its sins. We all know now what we should have known even during the boom years: that there was a dark underside to "Asian values," that the success of too many Asian businessmen depended less on what they knew than on whom they knew. Crony capitalism meant, in particular, that dubious investments – unneeded office blocks outside Bangkok, ego-driven diversification by South Korean *chaebol* – were cheerfully funded by local banks, as long as the borrower had the right government connections. Sooner or later there had to be a reckoning.

The following chapters will illustrate that cronyism and corruption was indeed a big problem and played a significant role in undermining economic development. The lack of transparency in economic management, besides fostering moral hazard in the form of expectations of government guarantees to politically connected lending, also resulted in the fatal mis-allocation of investment, falling returns to investment and growing fragility in the financial system. In each crisis-affected country, the connections between politicians and certain private enterprises created a moral hazard problem, whereby these enterprises were seen as carrying an implicit guarantee against insolvency. Thus there was a strong incentive for financial institutions to lend to these enterprises, regardless of the soundness of their operations. The moral hazard problem arose even more directly when banks and finance companies themselves had close political connections. In some countries, particularly Indonesia, these problems were made worse by direct political interference and official malfeasance in the allocation of credit and in creating monopolies in certain activities.

Yet this study departs from the exceptionally sweeping view of crony capitalism in two important regards. First, the case studies will show that *both* the statist or *dirigiste* policies that most Asian governments had followed for so long, *and* the more recent policy shift towards financial deregulation and liberalization were conducive to rent-seeking and cronyism. As is well known to area specialists, the economic success of many Asian economies was built on a particular kind of economic strategy that emphasized export-orientation, centralized coordination of production activities, and implicit (and in some cases explicit) government guarantees of private investment projects. Moreover, there also existed a close operational relationship and interlinked ownership between banks and firms. Hailed as the "Asian developmental model," this strategy allowed firms to rely heavily on bank credit. Not surprisingly, by international standards, firms in the crisis-affected countries were highly leveraged. Indeed, the pervasive role of government in the selective promotion of industries and in the coordination of investment, including state control over the allocation of credit and capital account transactions, spawned a government–private sector nexus with an affinity for rent-seeking behavior. Second, the evidence unequivocally demonstrates that crony capitalism did not trigger the crisis, albeit it greatly exacerbated it.

### Towards a synthesis of the macroeconomic perspective

When the bubble burst in 1997, a twin crisis emerged in Asia – meaning that the currency crisis was accompanied by a crisis in the banking and financial sector. Soon a vicious cycle emerged, as the depreciation of the currencies exacerbated weaknesses in the financial sector, which in turn fueled further capital outflows and pressure on the exchange rates. The subsequent pages will show that weaknesses in the private sector (in the banking, financial and corporate sectors) were at the heart of the Asian crisis. Specifically, weak corporate structures (where the focus too often was on increasing scale and market share rather than on economic returns), weak regulation of the financial system, connected and directed lending, and implicit and explicit guarantees of financial institution liabilities created an unprecedented degree of moral hazard. The banking sectors in the crisis-hit countries were characterized by poor regulatory supervision, lack of bank transparency and excessive short-term, unhedged foreign currency borrowing. All suffered from liquidity shortages and escalating levels of non-performing loans. In fact, their balance sheets exhibited growing maturity and currency mismatches in the period leading up to the crisis. This meant that they were vulnerable to sharp swings in interest rates resulting from external shocks. Eventually borrowers – whether public (as in Mexico or Russia), or private (as in Asia) – were unable to roll over short-term debt, often denominated in foreign currency and held by a large number of creditors.

The roots of this problem date back to the all-too-swift liberalization of the financial sector (a) without having the appropriate prudential supervision and regulation in place, and (b) in conditions such that even where formal rules were in place (for example, legal lending limits, capital adequacy ratios), weak enforcement impeded the development of a healthy banking sector. In this environment, liberalization included reduction of barriers to entry for banks and non-bank financial institutions, deregulation of interest rates, relaxation of directed credit and reserve requirements on banks, promotion of new financial markets and instruments and the liberalization of the external dimensions of the financial sector. Moreover, some variations among countries notwithstanding, liberalization permitted local residents and non-resident foreign entities to open accounts with commercial banks in either national or foreign currencies. It also permitted banks to extend credit in foreign currencies in the domestic markets; bank and non-bank private sector corporations to borrow abroad; foreigners to own shares listed by national companies on domestic stock exchanges; the sale of securities on international stock and bond markets by national companies; the sale of domestic monetary instruments such as central bank bills and treasury bills to non-residents; and the establishment of offshore banks – which were also allowed (in some cases) to borrow broad and lend domestically.

However, the rapid liberalization of the financial and banking sectors created problems. First, many banks were established with very small capital bases. Second, as economic theory suggests, while lower reserve requirements (which allowed the banking industry to maintain a lower degree of liquidity), may be desirable on efficiency grounds, they can also directly exacerbate international illiquidity and increase the possibility of financial runs. Third, banks incurred excessive risks by being overly dependent upon short-term funds to finance long-term investments, many of doubtful viability. This is was not simply due to lack of oversight. Rather, state banks were routinely encouraged to lend imprudentially to questionable state enterprises and to priority projects of various ministries. As Iwan Azis (1999, 80) notes, "too often, governments in the region played favorites. A few highly leveraged and well-connected groups were given special, often non-transparent, access to credit. These private businesses could obtain loans from state banks without difficulty at interest rates that were much lower than the market rate, and under more lenient conditions. This spelled trouble for the lending banks, as the probability of default on such loans was relatively high." Similarly, private banks, which usually had close relationships with particular business groups, routinely broke prudential rules in terms of amounts and conditions of loans to related companies. In some cases, the large conglomerates set up new banks primarily to serve their own often risky projects. In these so-called banks, lenient disclosure rules and poor banking regulations aggravated bad credit analysis and distorted investment decisions. Compounding all this was excessive lending – which fueled asset price inflation, while the corporate sector overstretched itself by engaging in risky or unproductive projects.

Fourth, poor risk management on the part of banks meant that alarm bells did not go off until the situation got out of control. Ineffective banking supervision, political interference and a critical lack of transparency prevented disciplinary mechanisms from operating properly. To make matters worse, both the banking and the corporate sectors were taking excessive currency risks by borrowing in foreign currencies (which had much lower interest costs than domestic currencies) to fund projects that could only generate income in domestic currencies. Implicit government guarantees on exchange-rate stability eroded awareness of the risks arising from currency and maturity mismatches between the banking and corporate sectors.[57] Last but not least, weak regulation of financial intermediaries and poor governance in corporate and government sectors induced excess domestic and external debt financing and made these countries extremely vulnerable to changes in capital market sentiment. In fact, this combination of financial system and corporate sector vulnerabilities and weaknesses contributed to the crises and magnified the negative impact of exchange-rate devaluations and foreign capital withdrawals on financial institutions.

How did this problem develop; why was it allowed to fester? How did it manifest itself (if at all), and what measures were taken to deal with them? Although the following chapters will flesh out in more detail the similarities and differences across countries, it is useful to sketch out some of the salient features – many of which were common across the crisis-affected countries and beyond. Briefly, three forces interacted to leave a number of countries in the region, notably Thailand, Korea, Indonesia and Malaysia, vulnerable to external shocks. These included: (a) the globalization of financial markets and the easy availability of private capital, especially short-term capital; (b) macroeconomic policies, in particular, haphazard capital account liberalization that permitted capital inflows to fuel a credit boom; and (c) increasingly liberalized, but insufficiently regulated financial markets that were growing too rapidly.

Since the post-war period, capital flows to developing countries have undergone some significant changes. From the end of the Second World War until the mid-1970s, the flow of resources into developing countries was dominated by official development assistance (ODA). The oil embargo and the recycling of petrodollars that began in earnest in 1974 gave rise to a new investment regime. The ready availability of funds allowed developing countries either to augment or to replace ODA and direct investment with large-scale bank lending. In 1981, more than half the resource flows to developing countries consisted of private lending. The option of borrowing from private banks abruptly came to an end in 1982, when Mexico declared a moratorium on the payment of its foreign debt, thereby ushering in the era of the debt crisis. It is now recognized that the debt crisis came about because the accumulation of foreign-currency-denominated sovereign banking debt had reached unsustainable levels.[58] At the end of 1973 the non-OPEC developing countries carried a stock of net external foreign currency bank debt of US$4.5 billion. By the end of 1982 the figure had reached US$145.9 billion, an increase of US$141.4 billion (Lamfalussy 2000, 2).

With the onset of the debt crisis there was a sharp decline in capital inflows to developing countries – from US$30 billion in 1977–82 to under US$9 billion in 1983–89 (IMF 1995, 33). However, the liberalization of cross-border financial transactions in the late 1980s and early 1990s dramatically reversed this trend. The international diversification of institutional portfolios (mutual funds, insurance companies, pension funds, proprietary trading of banks and securities houses) and the progressive integration of global capital markets led to a dramatic revival and expansion in capital inflows to developing countries. Private capital flows to developing countries increased sixfold over the years 1990 to 1996. Between 1990 and 1994, net capital surges to developing countries skyrocketed to US$524.2 billion, with a disproportionate share going to the Asian economies, which received some US$260 billion, or roughly 50 per cent of all the total capital flows (IMF 1995, 3). Although private capital flows comprise a wide range of instruments, including bank deposits and credits, equities, direct investments, corporate bonds and government securities, what was significant about this new surge was the sharp rise (in terms of both absolute levels and the share of total inflows) in short-term portfolio capital flows in the form of short-term interbank loans (which can be readily withdrawn), commercial bank debt, tradable bonds and equity shares.[59] For developing countries as a whole aggregate private portfolio capital flows increased from $6.6 billion from the base years 1983–89 to $218 billion between 1990 and 1994 to an all-time high of $167 billion in 1996.[60]

Propelling this expansion was an aggressive search by global capital markets (which operate around the clock) for ever higher returns to capital.[61] Large private capital flows to emerging markets were driven in part by low interest rates in Japan, Western Europe and the United States, along with international investors' imprudent search for high yields. Developed country banks and financial institutions, often trapped in slow-growing but highly competitive home markets, scanned the globe for investment opportunities. Emerging markets, especially in Asia, were booming, and offered greater profitability than investments in the developed countries. Indeed, to facilitate the capital inflows, many Asian countries (with some pressure from the United States) opened their money and capital markets and removed foreign-exchange controls. Indonesia and South Korea gained IMF Article 8 status in 1988, Thailand in 1990, the Philippines in 1995 and China in 1996 – obliging these countries to remove restrictions on current account payments.[62] In addition, South Korea opened its securities market in January 1992 (when it permitted non-residents to invest directly in Korean stocks as part of its plan to promote the gradual expansion of its capital market), and was required to submit a schedule of capital liberalization in preparation for admission to the OECD. China, on the other hand, was required to liberalize trade and foreign-exchange regulations in expectation of securing membership in the World Trade Organization (WTO). Other Asian countries earnestly opened offshore markets in order to develop their domestic financial markets and facilitate overseas fund-raising. By the late 1980s, Hong Kong and Singapore were already established as major international financial centers. In 1990, Malaysia established the Labuan market, and in March 1993 Thailand established the Bangkok International Banking Facility (BIBF) to raise funds abroad. In fact, so determined was Thailand to become a leading financial center in Asia that the BIBF was characterized by looser regulations with regard to interest rates, reserve requirements, withholding taxes on interest and foreign-exchange controls than its onshore counterparts.[63] Likewise, although Indonesia's capital account had been opened since 1972, liberalization of the domestic banking system began in 1988, when domestic banks and Indonesian corporations were permitted new entries in the banking system and given much more freedom in their methods of raising financing. Thus, the number of banks increased from 111 in 1998 to 240 by March 1994. Twenty Indonesian foreign-exchange banks also opened branches in 14 countries, including offshore banking units in the Cayman and Cook Islands.

The fast-growing Asian economies quickly emerged as the most important destination for private capital flows. International commercial and investment banks, mutual fund managers, securities firms, stock brokers, portfolio investors, currency traders and others in competitive marketing-sales – given their voracious appetite for commissions enthusiastically sold (if not, oversold) the opportunities in Asia's emerging economies. As R. Johnson (1997) notes, "from the early 1980s on, it was an article of faith that Asia was a miracle . . . for years, strong economic performance and rising asset prices inspired investors, commentators and economists to uncover more evidence of good news about Asia wherever they looked. This process of mutual reinforcement continued into 1997." Indeed, the very economic success of Asia and its seemingly unbound potential made it an ideal investment location. According to a World Bank report (1998a, 6–7):

> East Asia generally absorbed nearly 60 per cent of all short-term capital flows to developing countries. In the mid-1990s, much of the short-term private capital came from Japanese banks as they followed their corporate foreign investors into Korea and Southeast Asia. The Europeans soon followed in an aggressive search for profits. By 1996, the Bank for International Settlements (BIS) reported that European Union (EU) banks' outstanding bank loans amounting to US$318 billion; the Japanese banks had US$261 billion; and the US banks had US$46 billion.

No doubt, capital flows between countries can yield what Larry Summers (2000) has termed "enormous socioeconomic benefits." The efficiency gains from the reallocation of capital from industrial to developing countries can improve living standards by mobilizing global savings to finance investments in countries where the marginal productivity of investments is relatively high. Capital flows also allow investors to diversify their risks and increase returns from more productive foreign projects, and allow residents of recipient countries to finance investments, and individual countries to smooth consumption. Portfolio capital flows consisting of international placements of tradable bonds, issues of equities in international markets, and purchases by foreigners of stocks and money market instruments (in particular, securities and mutual funds) can greatly benefit emerging economies by fostering financial integration and improving the returns on investments through knowledge/skills spillover, enhanced competition and market efficiency effects.

However, these benefits can be offset by various capital market imperfections, often caused by a lack of information. In the case of herd behavior, foreign investors may react to the actions of others whom they believe to have access to better information. Also, the allocation of savings may be biased owing to incomplete information about proposed projects. Thus adverse selection may take place, as lenders base the cost of credit on the average perceived creditworthiness of borrowers. Moreover, the high volatility of short-term capital flows may negate their beneficial impact. Feldstein (1994) notes that a surge in capital inflow may also increase imports and thereby dampen domestic production and investment. Surges tend to affect a country's macroeconomic stability by causing inflationary pressure and an increase in the current account deficits. The real exchange rate tends to appreciate in the capital-receiving country, while the traded goods sector of the economy loses competitiveness in international trade. The increase in the current account deficit and the appreciation of the real exchange rate also make the economy more vulnerable to shocks. When the inflow of foreign capital is interrupted, the economy has to go through reverse adjustments in the current account and real exchange rate. On the other hand, sudden outflows may disrupt local financial markets, forcing the authorities to choose between higher interest rates and a depreciation of the exchange rate. Therefore empirical studies have found that capital flows pose fewer problems if they are long-term, in the form of direct investment, propelled by the growth prospects of the economy, and invested in physical assets, rather than consumed and domestically induced.[64]

However, many of the capital inflows to emerging markets (including Asia) have been described as arbitrage capital flows. That is, capital flows into emerging economies were a reflection not so much of the investors' confidence in the economic performance of these economies, as of the ability of the governments to guarantee abnormal rates of return. The chain of guarantees included the commitment to a nominal exchange rate target as well as the implicit guarantee of deposits and solvency to the domestic banking system. In Asia (as in Mexico), the crisis erupted when the perception regarding the governments' capacity to honor the guarantees changed. Thus, short-term capital inflows can be a mixed blessing. In other words, short-term, yield-sensitive and liquid private capital inflows are not a costless lubricant, especially if the flows are large relative to GDP. When investors borrow short-term, they may fall into maturity mismatch difficulties – which arise when the assets backing short-term debt obligations are longer-term, and therefore less liquid than their liabilities.[65] These disparities imply that, when debts are not rolled over, assets must be liquidated at a discount to cover short-term obligations. Moreover, short-term capital inflows that often show up as an expansion in liquid short-maturity bank deposits are highly sensitive to cyclical fluctuations in domestic or international interest rates. Thus they exhibit high levels of volatility, with sudden outflows potentially resulting in balance of payments problems or widespread financial crises. Indeed, Eichengreen (1999) cites short-term borrowing as a major source of financial fragility, and demonstrates that the ratios of short-term debt to reserves are robust predictors of financial crises. In Asia, the ratio of short-term debt to foreign reserves (a rough measure of a country's ability to meet its current obligations from its own liquid resources) rose sharply from 1994 to 1997 (see Table 1.4). In the three most severely affected countries, Korea, Thailand and Indonesia, short-term debt-to-reserves ratios had risen to over 150 per cent by June 1997 – or just before the baht's devaluation (World Bank 1998a, 8).

The unprecedented volume of capital inflows fueled a domestic credit boom (Table 1.5), and this in turn played a critical role in fueling the rapid growth of the banks' and other financial intermediaries' balance sheets.

Compounding these were the macroeconomic policies adopted by governments – policies that inadvertently created incentives for private agents to take advantage of the easy access to international capital markets. To many analysts the most glaring policy error was hasty capital account liberalization. Some have explicitly argued that the root cause of the Asian crisis

**Table 1.4** *Short-term external debt and international reserves pre-crisis: 2nd quarter of 1997*

| Economy | Short-term debt ($ billions) | International reserves ($ billions) |
|---------|------------------------------|-------------------------------------|
| Korea | 70.18 | 34.07 |
| Indonesia | 34.66 | 20.34 |
| Malaysia | 16.27 | 26.59 |
| Philippines | 8.29 | 9.78 |
| Singapore | 196.60 | 80.66 |
| Thailand | 45.57 | 31.36 |
| Taiwan | 21.97 | 90.02 |

*Source*: ADB (1999, 26).

**Table 1.5** *Domestic credit and growth-rates*

| Country | Credit (% of GDP) | | CAGR[a] (%) |
|---|---|---|---|
| | *1991* | *1997* | *1991–97* |
| Indonesia | 50.3 | 65.4 | 21.5 |
| Korea | 94.5 | 137.9 | 19.0 |
| Malaysia | 116.7 | 165.4 | 19.9 |
| Thailand | 96.3 | 147.7 | 19.1 |

[a]CAGR: Compound Annual Growth Rate.
*Source*: Shirazi (2000, 84).

was the accelerated deregulation and liberalization of the capital account (A. Singh 1999). This important issue needs some elaboration.

Macroeconomic theory tells us that free capital movements contribute to efficient allocation of capital and provide opportunities for both foreign investors and domestic residents. For lenders, the advantages include increased portfolio diversification and higher returns from more productive foreign projects. Similarly, borrowers can gain in several ways. They can obtain resources to finance cyclical downturns and balance-of-payments disequilibria, thus allowing them to smooth out consumption. Emerging economies can augment savings available from domestic sources and finance projects with higher social returns. When combined with the liberalization of entry for foreign banks and brokerages, an open capital account can support reform and competition in the financial sector. Also, by reducing the scope for discretionary policy at home, openness to international capital markets can impose fiscal and monetary discipline on domestic policy-makers. Yet it is also recognized that benefits can be offset by various capital market imperfections, often caused by a lack of information. Moreover, free capital flows have the potential to affect a country's macroeconomic stability. Unimpeded capital flows can lead to real exchange-rate appreciation and current account deficits, and force authorities to engage in sterilization operations in an attempt to retain control of the money supply. Sudden outflows can disrupt domestic financial markets, forcing authorities to choose between higher interest rates and a depreciation of the exchange rate. Thus, the Janus-faced capital flows have the capacity to both improve and to destabilize an economy.

Till recently, most Asian economies kept their financial systems relatively closed. Foreign borrowing was limited and capital inflows controlled. The controls ensured that the financial sectors remained generally immune from external shocks, despite their domestic fragility. Most importantly, the controls prevented domestic fragility from being translated into external vulnerability in the form of short-term, unhedged foreign debt. All this began to change, beginning in the late 1980s and early 1990s, as the Asian economies gradually opened and deregulated their capital and domestic markets. Bhagwati (1998) blames the "Wall Street–Treasury Complex which commands tremendous influence over financial institutions like the IMF" for inappropriately pushing for capital account liberalization, without taking into consideration the costs associated with "the inherently crisis-prone nature of freer capital movements." In a nutshell, the argument is that rapid domestic and external financial liberalization in the crisis-affected Asian economies led to increased competition in the banking system – reducing the franchise value of banks and inducing them to pursue risky investment strategies. Furthermore, the rapid expansion of non-banking financial institutions (NBFIs) was an additional important source of competition for banks, especially in Korea and Thailand. Since the NBFIs were generally less regulated and subject to weaker supervision than banks, their rapid growth exacerbated the overall fragility of the financial system.

Clearly, managing an economy with open capital accounts is a difficult challenge in this era of financial globalization. Yet this study will show that capital account liberalization by itself was not the problem. Singapore, Hong Kong and Taiwan, which adhered to transparently market-based policies and maintained well-regulated financial systems guided by independent central banks, were able to respond more effectively to the shocks than those with poor prudential surveillance and poor financial sector transparency. However, in the hard-hit countries the problem was that supervision and regulatory oversight did not keep up with liberalization. Specifically, inappropriate sequencing of capital account liberalization and premature deregulation made the financial sector extremely vulnerable to shocks. Indeed, a study of 53 countries from 1980 to 1995 by Demirguc-Kunt and Detragiache (1998) finds that financial liberalization (understood as the deregulation of interest rates) is strongly correlated with a fall in the bank's liquidity (measured by the ratio of liquid to total assets), and the likelihood of banking crises. However, that probability decreases if the institutional preconditions for liberalization and market discipline, in terms of contract enforcement, relative lack of corruption and bureaucratic interference, and respect for the rule of law are in place.

An equally serious policy error was the implicit insurance of the fixed exchange rate – which signaled a guarantee against exchange rate loss. That is, investors and borrowers mistook the stability of the exchange rate for the absence of exchange-rate risk. This not only encouraged both domestic borrowers and foreign lenders to increase the flow of funds; it also motivated excessive risk-taking, including large foreign-exchange risks that were passed on to the rest of the domestic economy. Also, the maintenance of domestic interest rates that were significantly higher than the world market rate, coupled with high domestic funding costs and market segmentation, added to the incentives to borrow abroad – besides being a further lure for capital inflows. In Thailand, during the period 1991–96, domestic financial intermediation costs accounted for 28 per cent of the nominal baht interest cost (World Bank 1998a, 8). The domestic cost of funds was significantly higher than the costs of borrowing offshore, even after taking into account exchange-rate risks, which only added a further incentive to borrow foreign funds. Since this access to foreign markets was only available to the largest and best credit corporations, these firms and banks enjoyed a market advantage, and undoubtedly used their access to political leaders to protect their position – making it more difficult for regulators to limit offshore borrowing to prudent levels. This was compounded by the creation of offshore financial markets in which local corporations could (because of regulatory and tax advantages), obtain lower-cost finance than in domestic markets. As was noted earlier, this trend was at its most severe in Thailand.

Ironically, the large-scale capital inflows that helped fuel the rapid credit expansion led to the build-up of external and domestic financial imbalances, besides lowering the quality of credit and distorting investments. First, in all the crisis-affected countries, short-term borrowing was used to finance long-term projects. This created a sizeable maturity mismatch in the balance sheets of domestic financial institutions. Second, domestic banks lent to domestic firms in local currency, while borrowing short-term in foreign currencies without hedging.[66] In addition, while investments were made in non-tradeables, such as land, buildings and infrastructure, which generated returns in local currency, the repayments, however, had to be made in foreign currency. These created a significant currency denomination mismatch. Third, the rapid reforms to liberalize the financial sector and to remove barriers to the entry of foreign capital without the development of the institutions or practices that characterize a mature financial market created what Eichengreen (1999) has aptly termed "an explosive mix." Fourth, the easy availability of credit was not only associated with inefficient intermediation, but also fueled investments in increasingly risky assets, besides powering speculative booms. In fact, the investment boom was concentrated in: (a) sectors with already excessive capacity (in part through government direction); (b) narrowly specialized industries, such as electronics and other prestigious projects; and (c) non-traded sectors, particularly real estate. For example, in the case of Korea, Borensztein and Lee (1999) find that credits were systematically allocated to sectors with poorer economic performance. In Thailand, total advances to manufacturing expanded ten-fold between 1985 and 1996, but credit to the real estate sector increased twenty-two-fold during the same period (A. Islam 1999, 55). In Thailand, Indonesia and Malaysia, excessive intergroup lending practices often resulted in resources not being put to their most productive use.[67]

Rather, in all three countries much of the lending went to finance equity purchases and land. Not only was there overinvestment caused by excessive lending (as many projects with negative net present value were financed), but the prices of local assets rose beyond their true economic value, leading to overvaluation of asset prices. For example, in an environment where "large sums of money were invested in buildings in every major city in the region: whether it was Seoul, Taipei, Hong Kong, Singapore, Beijing, Shanghai, Bangkok, Kuala Lumpur or Jakarta . . . real estate investment was a tangible expression of these cities' success and pride" property values in Bangkok, Seoul, Kuala Lumpur and Jakarta rose at double-digit rates through 1996 (Mera and Renaud 2000, 12: also World Bank 1998a, 7). Rising asset prices provided greater collateral to banks and led to greater lending, which further increased collateral values, and so on. As long as growth remained high, this became a "virtuous and self-reinforcing cycle." All this created an appearance of high returns, not only in real estate, but also in the stock market. In what seemed like a permanent boom, stock market investors became accustomed to high rates of return. Until 1996, these expectations were self-perpetuating. When the market began to collapse in response to a realization that many firms could not generate earnings growth to justify stock values, many investors were literally shocked. As Corsetti, Pesenti and Roubini (1998) argue, these over-investment and overvaluation may have given the appearance of spectacular economic growth potential in Asia. Indeed, a cross-country comparison by La Porta, Lopez-de-Silanes and Shleifer (1998) suggests that relatively weak accounting standards in East Asian countries may have allowed firms in crisis-affected countries to cloak their actual financial position and continue in business even after they were no longer financially viable.

Paradoxically, the macroeconomic policy mix used to deal with the over-heating pressures and capital inflows in the 1990s added an impetus for further inflows, particularly for the accumulation of short-term unhedged external liabilities. In particular, exchange-rate policies played a large role in motivating capital flows. Specifically, although the appropriate policy response to capital inflows is to allow greater flexibility in exchange rates – implying appreciation in nominal exchange rates during periods of large inflows and depreciation during periods of outflows – the Asian governments opted for a stable exchange rate, for a number of reasons.[68] First, the prevention of appreciation in the nominal exchange rate following large capital inflows was seen as a policy priority with a view to maintaining the competitiveness of exports and inviting FDI inflows. It should be noted that the informal dollar pegs had not only insulated all these countries from each other and from beggar-your-neighbor devaluations; the pegs had also successfully anchored their domestic (wholesale) price levels during their remarkable rapid growth in the 1980s through to 1996. Second, there was concern that once the currency was allowed to float, it might become highly volatile, inhibiting not only capital inflows but also trade transactions. Third, a stable exchange rate was seen as an effective anchor against inflation in the domestic economy. And fourth, governments saw their ability to maintain a stable exchange rate as an indicator of their policy credibility. However, a fixed or highly stable exchange rate regime is inherently vulnerable to speculative attacks, particularly when there are expectations that devaluation is likely. As long as Asian governments appeared certain to protect the fixed dollar peg, investors could be comfortable in the knowledge that there was little foreign-exchange risk. Thus the predictable nominal rates encouraged unhedged external borrowing, thereby rendering financial institutions highly exposed to a variety of external threats, including declines in asset values and exchange-rate devaluations. Also, the informal pegging of domestic currencies to the US dollar encouraged capital inflows, owing to the large interest-rate differentials. As was noted earlier, as the yen depreciated against the US dollar throughout much of 1996, so the pegged currencies lost competitiveness against the important yen market.

It is important to note that although capital inflows to Asia surged in the 1990s, most of the economies managed to avoid the substantial exchange-rate appreciations that have often been associated with large capital inflows, particularly in Latin America. Through a combination of tight fiscal policy and monetary policies aimed at sterilizing the monetary impact of these inflows, they avoided large appreciations against the US dollar.[69] However, tightening monetary policy in an effort to sterilize inflows and curtail credit expansion increased domestic interest rates, as well as the differential between domestic and foreign rates. That is, sterilized intervention (a combination of foreign-exchange intervention and domestic open-market operation to keep the monetary base constant in proportion to GDP), will in theory keep the interest rate level; but in practice, the interest rate may rise.[70] In Asia, the sterilization of capital inflows raised interest rates on domestic deposits, while the apparently durable fixed exchange rate regime led market participants to neglect the possibility of a devaluation. This had the perverse effect of creating further incentives for investors to borrow abroad to make local investments.[71] Moreover, the increase in short-term interest rates as a result of sterilization discouraged long-term investment demand, as the cost of capital rose, while returns on less risky assets, such as government paper, became more attractive. Sterilization, therefore, had the unintended effect of changing the composition of capital flows away from long-term to short-term. It is hardly an exaggeration to note that the monetary policy stance created a severe moral hazard problem by implicitly guaranteeing the dollar returns of foreign investors.

Many of the capital inflows and associated investment booms were intermediated through weak domestic financial institutions that were often undercapitalized and poorly regulated. The inflows also fed into a system of corporate finance that increased risks from abrupt changes in interest or foreign-exchange rates. Therefore, the patterns of indebtedness varied across countries. In Thailand, finance companies and banks, availing themselves of extremely low-interest yen-denominated loans, borrowed through government-sanctioned channels to invest in real estate. Specifically, the Bangkok International Banking Facility (BIBF), established in 1993, greatly facilitated foreign borrowing by residents. Predictably, financial institutions' net foreign liabilities rose from 6 per cent of domestic deposit liabilities in 1990 to 33 per cent by 1996 (World Bank 1998a, 8). Korean banks also increased their exposure to foreign borrowing, as regulations favored short-term foreign borrowing by financial institutions and strongly discouraged corporations from borrowing abroad directly. In Indonesia, corporations became the primary borrowers from foreign sources, with much of it coming from offshore.

In retrospect, the banks were able to grow their risky loans this rapidly, in part, because they were not fully exposed to market discipline until the governments' explicit or implicit guarantees lost their credibility. We also now know that the regulations necessary to intermediate capital inflows were not in place, nor were weak firms operating with a high degree of risk sufficiently disciplined through competition and monitoring by shareholders or creditors – foreign as well as domestic. The problem was not simply the failure to develop adequate systems to monitor the extent of borrowing and its term structure; such oversight also created a blind-spot that prevented the growing problem of over-leveraged, unhedged short-term borrowing to be perceived early enough. Thus many firms were allowed to operate while their losses continued to mount. We now know that the licensing and supervision regulation of merchant banks in Korea permitted groups of companies to own both banks and the same groups of firms to whom they were lending. In fact in Korea, many conglomerates (or *chaebols*) had ownership links that were not confined to non-bank financial institutions: the larger *chaebols* were often linked with a major bank. Many of these enterprises could continue to borrow, and the banks could continue to overlook the rise in bad loans. In Indonesia, the number of banks expanded very rapidly in the 1990s, but the supervisory authorities failed to carry out prudential screening of applicants to check out their creditworthiness. Rather, in Indonesia, where roughly 50 per cent of banks belonged to a narrow circle of business groups, and the other 50 per cent were state-owned, the system allowed Suharto family members and their cronies preferential access to resources. In this environment, supervisory and regulatory frameworks could hardly stop the well-connected borrowers from getting access to funds, and in the process becoming even more highly leveraged. Similarly, in Thailand (where a small number of families owned both banks and corporations), the scope of finance companies' activities greatly expanded in the 1990s without commensurate improvement in their prudential supervision.

The cozy collaborative relations between governments, financial institutions and borrowers, the weaknesses in bank and corporate governance coupled with poorly enforced prudential regulations (not to mention the fact that creditors' rights were weakly enforced because the judicial systems in these countries were underdeveloped), encouraged fiscal indiscipline and excessive risk-taking. Krugman (1999a) has called this the "Pangloss equilibrium" – where implicit (and implausible) guarantees offered by governments were believed by investors. In this environment, banks with insufficient capital adequacy ratios, inadequate asset classification systems, weak accounting standards, especially for loan valuation and disclosure practices, lack of adequate deposit insurance schemes and an overall poor provisioning for possible losses flourished. Claessens and Glaessner (1998) add that the limited role of foreign banks in the local Asian markets reduced the ability of banking systems to absorb shocks, and more generally, inhibited the institutional development of the banking sector. All these, together with the removal of controls over the allocation of credit, increased the channeling of funds into fueling of asset bubbles. Over time these weaknesses contributed to growing systemic fragility in the financial and non-bank corporate sectors. Combined with export slowdown, falling property and stock values, and ultimately the massive loss of confidence in international financial markets when the seeds of doubt were first sowed with the onset of the Thai currency crisis, they triggered large-scale capital flight from the region. They also greatly compromised the ability of these economies to withstand the shock of the large-scale outflow of foreign capital.

## A political economy of the crisis

Behind the complex economic causes of the crisis lie the broader political factors. First, why did the so-called Asian model of development, which generated such high economic growth and equity for several decades, succumb to the crisis so quickly? The distinctive Asian model of development and the so-called "developmental states" it spawned were built around close business–government relations. This relationship had many positive features. For example, Alice Amsden (1989) in *Asia's Next Giant: South Korea and Late Industrialization* attributed Korea's phenomenal export-led economic modernization that began in early 1960 under the authoritarian Park Chung Hee regime to the collaborative relationship or "pragmatic synergy" between a highly centralized, interventionist and fortuitous developmental state and the large private conglomerates (the *chaebols*) it created. Endowing itself with exclusive authority over the coordination of fiscal, monetary and trade policies, Korea's administrative state kept a watchful eye over the *chaebols*, while at the same time nurturing them with generous subsidies and protection from competition in return for utilitarian performance standards necessary to meet the stringent requirements of export-oriented industrialization. The state–*chaebol* alliance became indispensable to South Korean development. Working closely together, they were seen as formidable partners, with an uncanny ability to follow market signals, to respond pre-emptively to externalities and to broker relations with foreign investors and creditors. In Korea and in the rest of the high-performing Asian economies, it was believed that such close government–business relationships helped improve the flow of information between the public and private sectors and helped spur rapid capital accumulation. In the banking sector, the so-called "relationship banking" was seen as having several advantages, including the capacity to manage efficiently short-term credit and investment flows. Indeed, the high-performing Asian states' alleged need to actively mobilize citizens and corporations behind a coherent market-based development strategy became the principal justification of authoritarian rule. Ruling elites and advocates of "Asian democracy" argued that Western-style democracy often leads to undisciplined and disorderly behavior – which are inimical to rapid economic development. On the other hand, a regime insulated from conflicting societal demands and guided by prudent technocratic decision-making was seen as ideally suited to providing the requisite order and promoting economic development.

It is now clear that the efficacy of the Asian developmental model was greatly exaggerated. The custodians of Asia's development states (like state elites elsewhere) confirm Naim's (1997, 309) apt observation that "while economic fundamentals eventually force governments to adopt painful corrections, political calculations make their imprudent postponement all too frequent." Governments everywhere exhibit politically-induced learning disabilities. The evidence unambiguously indicates that ineffective policy responses and indecisiveness on the part of a paternalistic authoritarian regime (Indonesia under Suharto), a "semi-authoritarian regime" (Malaysia under Mahathir Mohamad), and the two newly established democratic governments (Thailand under Chavalit Yongchaiyudh and Korea under Kim Young Sam) played a big role in generating market uncertainty and eventually a disastrous loss of investor confidence – both domestically and internationally.[72] Compounding this problem were the deep socio-structural and institutional weaknesses, and the much-touted close business–government relationship banking – which in the critical months prior to the crisis served to weaken the independence of central banks and regulatory authorities and slowed their ability to respond to early warning signals. The country case studies will show that the implicit government guarantees to private risk-taking contributed much to the onset and the depth of the crisis. Specifically, the long-standing patterns of business–government relations created a domestic version of moral hazard. In Thailand, Korea, Indonesia and Malaysia the pervasive involvement of government in the financial and corporate sectors created expectations that banks and firms would be protected against failure. However, over time such relationships generated widespread corruption and cronyism. This only served further to undermine the capacity of governments to respond to emerging economic problems, including the ability of the central banks and regulatory authorities to enforce whatever rules of prudential regulation and supervision did exist on the books. This lack of transparency in business–government relations was less of a problem when the Asian economies were relatively closed, but became a serious problem following liberalization and deregulation in the late 1980s and early 1990s.

For example, in Suharto's Indonesia the line between the public and the private had long become blurred as Suharto governed as the quintessential patriarchal ruler, granting extravagant patronage and protection to loyalists and cronies, and meting out harsh punishment to dissenters. Eventually, the capriciousness inherent in personalism – in particular, the lax distinction between public and private funds and the arbitrary use of state resources for personal aggrandizement – took its toll. Moreover, the complete absence of representative institutions and institutionalized forms of political mediation and accountability in Indonesia further exacerbated the problems of corruption, cronyism and nepotism.[73] Yet, what about Indonesia's famed economic technocrats (the so-called Berkeley Mafia), who were known to have Suharto's ear, and enjoyed privileged access and influence, especially during times of economic troubles. Why did they not intervene (as they had done in the past) and guide the economy in a more sustainable direction? Like everything else in Suharto's Indonesia, the technocrats not only lacked an independent power base, their influence "depended entirely on their relationship with Suharto" (Pincus and Ramli 1998, 729). Clearly, over the years this relationship had soured. It seems that in the months before and during the crisis, the respected technocrats were politically isolated and powerless, their influence seemingly eclipsed by Suharto's children and cronies. In fact, during the height of the crisis, Suharto reneged on implementing the much-needed economic and legal reforms because such policies would hurt the vast economic interests held by his children and cronies. In the end, Suharto's erratic policy announcements only served to unnerve investors. Given the fact that power was so heavily concentrated in Suharto's hands, any perceived weakness in his willingness or ability to respond expeditiously (whether real or perceived), resulted in a disastrous loss of investor confidence, both domestically and internationally.

In the case of Malaysia, under the ostensible rationale for ethnic redistribution of resources, Mahathir and the Malay political elite built up an increasingly centralized political system based on patronage and cronyism. In their insightful study, *Malaysia's Political Economy: Politics, Patronage and Profits*, Gomez and Jomo (1999) note that the emergent class of *bumiputera* (Malay) capitalists are neither authentic entrepreneurs nor industrial managers. Instead, they function as financial manipulators, engaged in deal-making and asset stripping and as collectors of rents of various kinds, including financial subsidies, lucrative non-competitive contracts from the state and protection from foreign competition. As a group they have failed to contribute to the efficiency, productivity, diversification or international competitiveness of the Malaysian economy. Compounding this problem was Mahathir's "big growth push" policy to propel Malaysia to developed-country status by the year 2020. The ever-growing list of extravagant megaprojects designed to facilitate Mahathir's "Vision 2020" included the Bakun dam (Asia's largest hydroelectric dam, costing an estimated M$15 billion), Kuala Lumpur's showpiece, "Petronas," or the world's tallest "twin towers," built at a cost of some M$2 billion, a super-modern airport (estimated at M$9 billion), a new administrative capital for the state of Sarawak in Borneo, and, the most audacious, a M$20 billion national administrative capital near Kuala Lumpur aptly called *Putrajaya* (or "city of kings"), to be built as a tribute to Mahathir Mohamad himself. Such ambitious projects resulted in massive public investment expenditure and rapid credit expansion.[74] Besides the big projects, not only was much of the credit directed to the property sector, which "eventually weakened the financial position of the banks, as this lending led to a property glut," but bank-lending increasingly took "the form of 'connected' (state-directed) lending rooted in the long-standing intimate link between the government and business" (Athukorala 1998, 92–3).

Thus, instead of responding appropriately when the financial crisis struck (for a start, limiting the self-aggrandizing projects and connected lending), Mahathir's first reaction was to find scapegoats. In a fiery speech on 20 September 1997 (before a joint World Bank–IMF annual meeting in Hong Kong), he argued that "currency trading is unnecessary, unproductive and immoral" and that it "should be stopped and made illegal" (Jomo 2001, 14). A few days later Mahathir suggested that there might be an international Jewish conspiracy to financially cripple his predominantly Muslim country. He lashed out against foreign currency traders with a Jewish heritage, in particular, the financier George Soros, branding him as a moron and criminal (Tan 2000, 17–18). As Gomez and Jomo (1999, 189) note, "the ringgit probably fell much further than might otherwise have been the case, as a result of international market reaction to Mahathir's rhetorical and policy responses to the unfolding crises." The discussion in Chapter 7 will show that the Malaysian government's subsequent policy responses further aggravated the crisis.

What about the two democracies, Thailand and Korea? Suffice it to note that scholars have long distinguished between two forms of democratic governance. Under *procedural* forms of democracy, a minimum set of democratic rules and rights are observed, including free and fair electoral competition based on universal suffrage, guaranteed freedoms of expression and association, an independent media, court and judiciary, and accountability through the rule of law. However, a *substantive* democracy meets more than the basic procedural requirements: citizens in such settings are also broadly included in the political arena, because democratic norms and values are highly institutionalized and routinized (Karl and Schmitter 1991). Clearly, Thailand and Korea (like most new democracies) have hardly solved the chronic institutional deficit in their polities: the exercise of democratic governance remains imperfect in both countries. Yet if we accept minimalist procedural definitions of democracy, which emphasize competition for national offices (that is, regimes that are freely elected are democratic), then Thailand and Korea crossed this threshold before the outbreak of the crisis, and Indonesia during the outbreak (or in the midst) of the crisis.

At the time of the crisis, the deeply fragmented democratic governments in Thailand and Korea – incessantly pulled in all directions by interest groups and legislative and electoral pressures – or what Haggard (2000, 49) has termed "different veto gates" – delayed dealing with the mounting problems in the financial sector.[75] Similarly, according to Wade (2001, 69–70), "in Thailand and South Korea, new civilian democratic regimes corrupted the central policy-making technocracy and lost focus on *national* economic policies. Government–bank–firm collaboration came to be steered more by the narrow and short-term interests of shifting coalitions. Their experience is bad news for the proposition that more competitive politics yield better policies." In the case of Korea, it has been argued that political gridlock and the "immature and unconsolidated nature of Korean democracy" made for poor economic policy-making. Specifically, "policy gridlock was frequent because of a traditional political culture and weak democratic institutions, which were most pronounced in the legislative process. First, the system of legislative bargaining was not firmly established. Despite its constitutional mandate, the National Assembly continued to be subordinate to the executive branch in the policy-making process. Nor did the bureaucracy provide a stable mechanism of interest intermediation. As a result, disputing parties did not have a place in which to negotiate" (Mo 2001, 468). Compounding these problems were the growing divisions within the ruling party, and the impending general elections (in December 1997) made the government highly sensitive to pressures from corporations and the well-organized working class. Under pressure, the ruling party legislators backed away from introducing the necessary policy reforms, or indeed any policy measures they deemed would damage their chances in the upcoming elections.

In the case of Thailand, an incoherent and deeply fragmented party system produced an undisciplined coalition government subject to factionalism, blackmail and policy incoherence. As Haggard (2000, 52) notes, "all of the democratically elected governments [in Thailand] before the crisis . . . were constructed from a pool of approximately a dozen parties, and cabinet instability was a chronic problem. As leader of the governing coalition, the prime minister was vulnerable to policy blackmail by coalition partners threatening to defect in pursuit of better deals in another alliance configuration." Indeed, weak party discipline made political parties and governments highly sensitive to demands from powerful business constituents. For example, the Finance Minister Amnuay Virawan and the Central Bank Governor Rerngchai Marakanond found that their efforts to close down ten ailing finance companies came to nothing because determined opposition from within the government vetoed their measure. Not surprisingly, under such inauspicious conditions, the Thai government proved slow in reacting to early warning signals before the crisis struck, and had great difficulty in formulating a coherent response once it did.

While both democratic and authoritarian regimes in Asia proved equally susceptible to the economic crisis, democracies have, nevertheless, demonstrated a remarkable ability to respond more effectively to the crisis. Specifically, the following chapters will illustrate that the democratic governments in Thailand (under Chuan Leekpai, November 1997–January 2001), in Korea (under Kim Dae-Jung, January 1998–) and to a lesser extent, in Indonesia, first under the "quasi-democratic" interim Habibie regime (May 1998–October 1999) and later under the democratic Abdurrahman Wahid government (October 1999–July 2001), were quite successful in exploiting their new popular mandates (not to mention their honeymoon periods), to implement some important reforms, including taking action against the previously favored vested interests. Thus the crisis opened a maximum window for reform – and given the substantial popular expectations that the new leaders quickly repair the economic damage – helped to empower these governments with a mandate to carry out macroeconomic reforms. This suggests that democracies not only provide legitimacy, moral authority and credibility to a regime, but that, at particular critical junctures, they may also demonstrate a remarkable capacity to formulate and implement significant political and economic reforms.

### The role of the IMF

The principal responsibility for dealing with the Asian crisis at the international level was assumed by the International Monetary Fund. Soon this relatively unknown multilateral financial institution was put into the global spotlight as never before. Its every official utterance and policy move became the subject of intense public scrutiny and scathing criticism – from both the right and the left. With the benefit of hindsight, it is clear that the IMF's record in dealing with the Asian financial crisis has been mixed. According to the IMF's former deputy managing director, Stanley Fischer (1998a, 106), "the basic approach of the IMF to these crises has been appropriate – not perfect, to be sure, but far better than if the structural elements had been ignored or the Fund had not been involved." The subsequent chapters will present a more nuanced picture of the IMF's policies and its socioeconomic impact. At this stage, it is useful to understand better the role of the IMF, especially what the organization can and cannot do under its mandate, as well as to outline the basic components of, and the controversies surrounding, the IMF-led rescue packages in Asia.[76]

Under the institution's Articles of Agreement, the 182 member countries who are signatories to the charter have committed themselves to promoting global trade and deepening economic integration by maintaining a stable international monetary system.[77] This goal is to be achieved by maintaining orderly exchange arrangements among members, to avoid competitive exchange depreciation, and allowing individual national currencies to be exchanged for foreign currencies in the marketplace without restriction (currently only 117 members have agreed to the full convertibility of their currencies). Member countries are obliged to keep the IMF informed of any changes in their financial and monetary policies that may adversely affect fellow members' economies, and expeditiously to modify or reform national policies on the advice of the IMF in order to facilitate international trade. Nevertheless, as an international organization whose members are sovereign nations, the IMF cannot examine a country's financial books without explicit permission from the country's authorities. In fact, the IMF is not even allowed to send a mission to a country unless it has been formally invited by the country's authorities.[78] In effect, the Fund operates much like a credit union for the member countries, serving as a manager of their common pool of financial resources, estimated to be over $220 billion in 2001.[79] As in a credit union, member countries are entitled to withdraw their contributions almost at will. Nevertheless, the resource base allows the Fund to establish a stable value for each currency, and to provide confidence to members by making the general resources temporarily available to them, thus providing them with the opportunity to correct maladjustments in their balances of payments without resorting to measures destructive to national or international growth. The Fund's capital comes almost entirely from "quota subscriptions" or membership fees, assessed on the basis of members' economic size. For example, the United States, with the world's largest economy, contributed about 18 per cent (approximately $38 billion in 1997) of the total quota, followed by Japan and Germany, which contributed 5.67 per cent each. Quotas are reviewed every five years, allowing member countries either to increase or to lower their contributions. The size of quotas not only determines what a country can borrow in time of need, but also the voting power of the member country. For example, in 2001, the US executive director held 17.1 per cent of the votes, and Japan's director was second, with 6.1 per cent of the votes, followed by Germany, with 6.0 per cent of the votes. On the other hand, a director from South Africa representing twenty-one African countries held 3.2 per cent of the votes, the Egyptian director, representing thirteen Arab countries, held 2.9 per cent of the votes, and Brazil, representing nine Latin American nations, held 2.4 per cent of the votes.

Members can approach the IMF for financial assistance when they experience balance of payments difficulties. Although payments and receipts for imports and exports and long-term private capital flows across national boundaries rarely balance completely, the resulting imbalances are typically covered by short-term capital. However, serious imbalances may result in balance of payments difficulties. The problem may be resolved by large-scale use of foreign currency reserves – although a country's ability to sustain an external imbalance in this way is obviously limited by its holdings of foreign reserves. At, or close to, the point where reserves are exhausted, a country has little choice other than to devalue substantially, or to float its exchange rate. This was the circumstance that confronted a number of Asian countries in 1997 and 1998. Initially governments attempted to defend their exchange rates by resorting to their own means of foreign exchange management. They began their defense against the currency onslaught by way of intervention in the foreign-exchange market, in line with their adherence to a pegged system of foreign-exchange management – a rigid pegged system in the case of Thailand and Korea, and a managed float in the case of Indonesia. After losing substantial reserves in market intervention, particularly in the first two countries, one by one the three abandoned their pegged systems and allowed their currencies to float. As was noted earlier, the massive currency depreciations that followed had severe effects, as large volume of existing foreign-currency borrowing had not been hedged against exchange-rate risk. This made many borrowers, including many banks, insolvent overnight. Just before they called on the IMF for assistance, Thailand and South Korea had perilously low reserves, and were on the verge of debt default. Specifically, although the baht was floated on 2 July 1997, it continued to depreciate, forcing the Thai authorities to request IMF assistance on 5 August 1997. The Bank of Korea announced its decision to stop defending the won at the exchange rate of 1,000 won per US dollar on 17 November 1997. The Korean authorities requested IMF assistance on 21 November 1997. On 14 August 1997, Indonesia announced that the trading band for the rupiah was being abandoned. It formally sought IMF support on 8 October 1997 – after the rupiah was already excessively depreciated. Thus, it is important to note that these three economies were already deep in crisis when they called the IMF to "restore confidence."

IMF financing can only be provided if the member country's authorities commit to necessary policy changes and reforms, and to maintain these policies and reforms on track – adjusting them only if the circumstances dictate. This is called "IMF conditionality." It involves commitments on both sides. On the one hand, conditionality provides assurances to the country that as long as it implements the agreed-to policies, it will continue to receive IMF financing. On the other hand, conditionality provides safeguards to the IMF that the funds it has lent are being used for the intended purpose and that the member country will be able to repay what it has borrowed from the Fund. Generally, IMF support is organized under a number of facilities. In 1963, the Fund established the *Compensatory*

*Financing Facility* (CFF) to help countries overcome shortfalls in export earnings. In the 1970s and 1980s several new facilities were created. Today, regular IMF facilities include the *Stand-by Arrangements* (SBA), the *Extended Fund Facility* (EFF), created in 1974, the *Supplementary Financing Facility* (1979), and the *Structural Adjustment Facility* (1986), the expanded *Compensatory and Contingency Financing Facility* (1988), and the *Enhanced Structural Adjustment Facility* (1998).[80] The SBA is designed to provide short-term balance of payments assistance for deficits of a temporary or cyclical nature; these arrangements are typically for 12 to 18 months. The drawing of funds is phased on a quarterly basis, and their release is conditional upon meeting performance criteria and the completion of periodic program reviews. The rationale for such phasing is that it maintains incentives for the authorities to continue implementing the policies agreed under the program.[81] The EFF is designed to support medium-term programs that generally run for three years – with the particular aim of overcoming balance of payments difficulties stemming from macroeconomic and structural problems. In the case of Asia, much of the IMF's support was organized under the *Emergency Financing Mechanism* (EFM) and the newly created *Supplemental Reserve Facility* (1997). These mechanisms, with a greatly reduced period of negotiation, review and IMF board approval, permitted the programs to be put in place very quickly. This meant that they forced exceptionally quick analysis and negotiation, and important decisions at times had to be made on "more-than-usually incomplete information" (Lane *et al.* 1999, 6). Letters of Intent and "Memoranda of Economic and Financial Policies" (or the IMF "conditionality") laid out the strategies and sequencing of the IMF-supported programs.[82] According to the then IMF Managing Director, Michel Camdessus (1998):

> As soon as it was called upon, the IMF moved quickly to help Thailand, then Indonesia, and then Korea to formulate reforms programs aimed at tackling the roots of their problems and restoring investor confidence. In view of the nature of the crisis, these programs had to go far beyond addressing the major fiscal, monetary, or external balances. Their aim is to strengthen financial systems, improve governance and transparency, restore economic competitiveness, and modernize the legal and regulatory environment.

The conditions that the IMF imposed on Thailand, Indonesia and Korea in exchange for IMF-led rescue packages consisted of *three* basic components. The *first* concentrated on macroeconomic policy reform, in particular (a) the introduction of tight fiscal and monetary policy (i.e. an increase in interest rates and the adoption of strict limits on the growth of money supply), in order to produce current account surpluses and to stabilize the value of the currency by slowing currency depreciation; and (b) the maintenance of high interest rates to stem (or reverse) the capital outflows. It was believed that such a strategy would improve the current account and the balance of payments, halt the depreciating exchange rate, reduce money growth and inflation and reduce the government budget deficit. The *second* component focused on structural reforms of the financial sector. It is important to note that structural reforms come within the purview of IMF supported programs when tackling them is essential to solve a country's macroeconomic problems. And the *third* consisted of non-financial microeconomic policies such as the removal of trade barriers, the elimination of monopolies, enterprise reform and restructuring, creating competitive factor markets and curtailment of government budgets – in particular, the elimination of subsidies. It was presumed that all these measures could be implemented without significantly harming the real economy.[83]

However, the following chapters will show that the initial results of the Fund-supported programs in Indonesia, Korea and Thailand were not what had been hoped. Specifically, the programs were not successful in quickly restoring confidence. On the contrary, capital continued to exit and the currencies continued to depreciate after the IMF-supported programs had been adopted. Moreover, the economies sank deeper into recession, contrary to initial projections of only a mild slowdown. Why was this the case? One of the IMF's sternest critics, the Harvard economist Jeffrey Sachs (1999, 1997a, 1997c) has asserted that the IMF's unimaginative "one model fits all" prescriptions actually made Asia's financial turmoil worse. He argues that the problems in the Asian economies were "far from fatal." On the contrary, the economies had deep strengths, such as high rates of savings, budget surpluses, flexible labor markets and low taxation. Hence, "there is no fundamental reason for Asia's financial calamity except financial panic itself." In effect, "the crisis is a testament to the shortcomings of international capital markets and their vulnerability to sudden reversals of market confidence." This problem was made worse by the Fund's callous overdose of unnecessary conditions: notably, pressing beleaguered governments to raise the existing budget surpluses still higher and to tighten domestic bank credit by increasing interest rates, including the imprudent closing down of several weak (but viable) banks. For Sachs, such ill-advised policies only served to prolong asset-price deflation in real estate and to erode investor confidence further. This resulted in a "stampede mentality," with resultant capital flight and economic contraction.

In their more comprehensive study, Radelet and Sachs (1998) argue that the IMF's fiscal and monetary tightening undermined confidence by contributing to the economic downturn and raising fears of insolvency – thereby adding to downward pressures on exchange rates. They claim that given the huge deflationary shock caused by the massive outflow of capital, fiscal tightening was the wrong policy response. Furthermore, in view of the low levels of government debt and the fact that the balance of payments deficits had not been caused by loose fiscal policy in the first place, fiscal tightening was as unnecessary as it was damaging. Instead, the appropriate policy response should have been one of loose money and low interest rates, and an orderly working out of arrangements in which the "debtor country" would fall under IMF protection, which would facilitate negotiations between the debtor and private sector creditors to restructure the repayment program. To the extent that structural reforms were needed, they should have been undertaken more gradually, and only as the economy recovered from the effects of the crisis; not, as the IMF insisted they were, in the midst of the crisis (Radelet and Sachs 1998, 73–5).

Similarly, according to Furman and Stiglitz (1998), the IMF in raising interest rates greatly worsened the condition of corporate balance sheets, thereby prompting further capital flight and depreciating the exchange rate. In addition, they argue that structural reforms were a distraction in that they imposed heavy costs on economies already under strain. Thus fiscal and monetary tightening undermined confidence by contributing to the economic downturn and raising fears of insolvency. Yoshitomi and Ohno (1999) concur, arguing that monetary and fiscal policies should if anything have been eased, not tightened. In a similar vein, Corsetti, Pesenti and Roubini (1998) and Wade (2001) have argued that the sharp interest rate hikes were ineffective in slowing down currency depreciation. Rather, they claim the policy only worsened the extent of the crisis by leading to widespread banking and corporate bankruptcies. Indeed, the effects of these policies have been described in terms of a vicious cycle. That is, the credit crunch imposed severe financial losses on otherwise solvent companies and the widespread fall in profitability translated into higher levels of non-performing loans and credit risk, exacerbating the crisis-induced recessions and, in turn, causing a further contraction in the supply of credit. For the critics the failure of the currency and equity markets to make the expected quick recovery was clear evidence that the Fund's policies made the contraction deeper than necessary.

The following chapters will show that some of these criticisms are quite valid – especially in the case of South Korea.[84] However, some are problematic. For example, contrary to Sachs, we now know that the crisis-hit Asian economies were not simply mere victims of the sharp shifts in capital flows, but suffered from serious financial sector weaknesses and external-imbalance problems, not to mention non-existent prudential supervision and regulation. In its response to the critics, the IMF has argued that "before the Asian crisis broke, the IMF had warned Thailand of potential problems, but the government took no action. The IMF's staff also warned governments about financial sector weaknesses in several of the countries that were subsequently badly hit in the crisis" (Fischer 1998d, 5). Second, the fund has argued that, although it failed to foresee the virulence of the contagion effects produced by the widening crisis, the IMF-mandated programs introduced in Thailand, Indonesia and Korea were initially unsuccessful in restoring macroeconomic stability because the reform programs failed to bolster private sector confidence, and private sector capital out-flows far exceeded program projections (Fischer 1998, 1998a; Mussa 2000). The IMF has also correctly pointed out that when Thailand, South Korea and Indonesia approached it for funds they already had perilously low reserves, and the Indonesian rupiah was excessively depreciated. Thus, under these circumstances, the IMF had a difficult call. On the one hand, economic recovery may be imperiled if the currency does not stabilize. Fur-ther depreciation may generate capital losses to foreign investors, thereby discouraging their return, and cause further bankruptcies in domestic firms with foreign-currency exposure. One the other hand, the costs of keeping domestic interest rates high after a currency collapse may prove to be very high. Rising or maintaining high interest rates under crisis conditions may so weaken the economy that it may destabilize the exchange rate, causing it to depreciate further, thereby raising the risk premium or the probability of default on credit.

Following standard textbook macroeconomics, the IMF made the decision that the first order of business was to restore confidence in the currencies. In order to achieve this interest rates had to be temporarily increased – even if the higher interest costs complicated the situation of weak banks and corporations. Indeed, the IMF was fully aware that in the crisis-hit coun-tries, where corporations had high debt-equity ratios, with much of that debt being short-term, sharply higher interest rates could threaten much of the private sector with bankruptcy. Nevertheless, the Fund reasoned that restoring confidence and preventing a currency free fall required a period of high interest rates, and that, once confidence was restored, interest rates could return to more normal levels. Yet, as Sachs asks: why not operate with lower interest rates and a greater devaluation? For the IMF, the answer was twofold. First, the level of devaluations was already excessive, and second, the Asian economies needed to avoid further devaluations and sustain capital inflows to finance their current-account deficits and their large stock of short-term debt – much of it denominated in foreign currency. On the basis of its past experiences, the IMF was well aware that once the market loses confidence in a currency, raising interest rates is the only way to support the currency (Fischer 1998a; 2000; Mussa 2000). Also, it is not clear that low interest rates would have worked any better in a panic situation. If the authorities failed to raise rates and instead allowed their currencies to fall, banks and firms with large foreign-currency denominated liabilities would find their solvency threatened by the increase in the do-mestic currency cost of servicing foreign debts. Therefore, considering the severe balance sheet problems in Asia, the IMF concluded that sharper currency depreciation would exact a higher cost than the temporarily high interest rates.

The Fund has also maintained that some period of tight monetary policy was inevitable to prevent the depreciation–inflation spirals and the contagion they threatened. Given the high levels of private external debt in the crisis-affected economies, exchange-rate depreciation had a direct and extremely debilitating impact on the health of companies and banks, as well as on their access to financing. Under these circumstances loose monetary policies in the early stages of a currency crisis would have only contributed to exacerbating the extent of the depreciation and increasing the burden of foreign currency-denominated liabilities issued by banks and firms. Moreover, in the presence of large external net liabilities, a monetary expansion could actually produce financial distress and bankruptcies, setting in motion the same vicious circle described earlier. In addition, the IMF has contended that loose fiscal policies at the onset of the crisis would have raised doubts about the policy-makers' commitment to reducing the outstanding current account imbalances, jeopardizing the credibility of the plans. Finally, the IMF has claimed that the fiscal tightenings were relatively slight (1.5 per cent in the case of Thailand), and that it was necessary to pay for the cost of restructuring the financial sector. According to the IMF's Stanley Fischer (1998, 2), "the fiscal programs vary from country to country." In each case, the IMF asked for a fiscal adjustment that would cover the carrying costs of financial sector restructuring – the full cost of which is being spread over many years – and help to restore a sustainable balance of payments. Thus, *pace* to the critics, the IMF has repeatedly stated that it adopted a flexible policy in regard to fiscal targets – loosening them when the economic downtown proved to be more severe than anticipated (Lane *et al.* 1999; Mussa and Savastano 1999, 23–7). Indeed, the following country case studies will show that the IMF did modify some aspects of its program. In all three crisis-hit countries, the original targets of budget surpluses of 1 per cent or 2 per cent of GDP for 1998 were changed to budget deficits of similar range. In Indonesia, the IMF also agreed to let the government continue to subsidize some basic foodstuffs.

Yet, having noted this, the subsequent chapters will show that the IMF made mistakes in the fields both of crisis prevention and of crisis management. While the Fund's most damaging mistake was in its insistence on fiscal surplus for the crisis-stricken countries, this study will also show that the targets and tactics of the IMF did not remain unchanged over time. As the initial results of the Fund-supported programs in Indonesia, Korea, and Thailand proved not to be what had been hoped, and as the situation in Asia progressively deteriorated, the requests of the IMF became less and less restrictive over time. The Indonesian case provides a good example of such changes. The first IMF package of October 1997 encompassed strict fiscal discipline, while the agreement of June 1998 allowed the Indonesian authorities to limit the budget deficit – as opposed to targeting a budgetary surplus – to below 8.5 per cent of GDP. Yet the following pages will also show that the IMF was slow in revising its approach to fiscal policy. It was only when recessions rapidly materialized in the course of 1998 that the

IMF progressively loosened its fiscal conditions to allow for cyclically adjusted fiscal deficits. As Corsetti, Pesenti and Roubini (1998, 3) aptly note, "to some observers, such evolution represents an unequivocal sign of flexibility and open-mindedness. For others, these changes occurred too late."

With regard to the question of interest rates, the IMF has steadfastly maintained that a significant rise in interest rates was necessary to restore confidence in currencies that had suffered huge depreciations, and to arrest the spiral of competitive devaluations.[85] While acknowledging that such a policy would impact negatively on domestic firms with high debt, the IMF opined that it was still a better option than a failure to stabilize currencies. The reasoning behind this was that with so many firms carrying high levels of foreign short-term debt, an easing of their debt burden through a recovery of the exchange rate would do more to minimize insolvency than the maintenance of low interest rates. Furthermore, the rise in interest rates need only be temporary, since it could be reversed once confidence is restored in the currency market. Critics, on the other hand, have argued that this IMF medicine, inappropriately dispensed, hardly worked to restore confidence (Kristov 1998; Krugman 1998a; Sachs 1999). On the contrary, high interest rates only strengthened the deflationary pressures, besides having a profound effect on the credit crunch and corporate bankruptcies in these highly leveraged countries. The negative effect was exacerbated because stabilization policies were imposed in conjunction with rapid financial restructuring. To this the IMF has responded by claiming that several factors contributed to weak confidence, including half-hearted program implementation and growing political uncertainties, especially in Indonesia.

The *second* component of the IMF agreements focused on structural reforms of the financial sector. Given the IMF's view that lax prudential rules and financial oversight (which permitted the quality of banks' loan portfolios to deteriorate sharply), was at the root of the crisis, the reform measures included (a) the immediate closure of insolvent or weak financial institutions to stem further losses, and (b) the restructuring and recapitalization of potentially viable financial institutions, often with substantial government assistance. Further, to prevent a recurrence of the fragilities that had led to the crisis, the program required the implementation of institutional reforms, such as instituting effective bankruptcy laws, strengthening the regulatory framework and increasing the transparency of financial and corporate governance. These measures, seen by the IMF as addressing the root causes of the crisis, were deemed critical to restoring market confidence and the resumption of sustainable growth. However, the critics have argued that the IMF's "ill-conceived" closure of banks and finance companies (together with the unduly contractionary macroeconomic policies, with their insistence on reduced spending, high taxes and even higher interest rates) was directly responsible for the bankruptcy of otherwise viable firms and the overall economic slowdown (Radelet and Sachs 1998). Indeed, in the case of

Indonesia there is compelling evidence that the bank closures were carried out in an *ad hoc* manner, ignoring issues such as deposit insurance, thereby leading to panic withdrawals of funds and undermining investor confidence. Also, there is little doubt that the long lists of structural reforms imposed heavy costs on the already strained economies. There is general agreement that, to the extent that structural reforms were needed, they should have been undertaken more gradually, and only as the economy recovered from the effects of the crisis.

The *third* component consisted of non-financial microeconomic reform policies, such as an overall reduction of the role of government in the economy, the break-up or the abolition of monopolies, privatization of government corporations, deregulation of labor markets, and the removal of barriers to trade. This third *tranche* of measures marked a significant departure from past IMF practices, where the conditionalities had been mostly confined to macroeconomic policy – especially in its major area of competence, monetary and fiscal policy. While not questioning the need for such reforms, critics have argued that the timing of such unduly intrusive measures was inappropriate and not necessary for economic recovery. For example, Martin Feldstein (1998) has argued that the IMF's intrusive policies greatly aggravated the crisis. Instead of focusing on balance-of-payments adjustment, the IMF stepped out of bounds (since its charter provides no such mandate) when it began to meddle arbitrarily in the domestic economic affairs of sovereign countries. Insisting on structural reforms that lie beyond its traditional competence in macroeconomic adjustment, the Fund's misguided domestic structural and institutional reform measures had adverse consequences – turning a temporary liquidity problem into a country-wide and later region-wide financial meltdown. Feldstein (1998, 25) notes that Asian economies had prospered for decades despite the structural problems in their economy, and the IMF's intrusive measures (which included among other things "specifying in minute detail such things as the price of gasoline and the manner of selling plywood") were not a prerequisite to economic recovery. It is not difficult to argue that the IMF went overboard in its demands, especially in Indonesia, where the Fund's demands skyrocketed from 15 bullet points in November 1997 to 50 bullet points by the time the second deal was signed on January 14, 1998, to 115 bullet points by the third deal in April 1998.

Why did the IMF pursue such a radical surgery? The prevalent view within the Fund was that in this era of high capital mobility and market integration, it was impossible to fix the international financial system without simultaneously fixing the domestic microeconomic structures of crisis-affected countries. Hence, stabilizing a country's financial system necessitated institutional reforms that extended well beyond the traditional monetary, fiscal and exchange-rate policies (Mussa 2000). Also there was concern, since the international financial markets now knew about the pervasive structural problems, whether market confidence would be regained without the affected countries' agreeing to implement transparent auditing and accounting practices, improve corporate governance and reform (if not dismantle) their shaky banks, finance companies and government monopolies.[86] The IMF has argued that, without its determined intervention, it was highly unlikely that Thailand and Indonesia would close their insolvent banks and finance companies or that South Korea would rein in its greatly over-leveraged and out-of-control *chaebols*, or that Indonesia would dismantle the corruption-ridden and inefficient government monopolies in plywood and clove. Thus, in response to Radelet and Sachs (1998), who claim that the IMF's misguided three-pronged approach only exacerbated the panic by giving investors the misleading impression that something was fundamentally wrong with these economies, the IMF has argued that to the extent that the Asian crisis was attributable to structural problems rather than the traditional macroeconomic imbalances, an effective reform strategy had to address the "structural problems that lie at the heart of the economic crises in the three countries" (Fischer 1998a, 103). That is, IMF bailout packages would have served no purpose if the weaknesses of the financial sector were not corrected by the appropriate structural reforms, not to mention the fact that half-hearted reforms would not have helped to re-establish market confidence. As Fischer (1998a, 103) notes, "to ignore the structural issues would invite a repetition of the crisis."

Beyond these policies, IMF bailouts are seen as creating *moral hazard*. "Moral hazard" refers to a situation where people can reap the rewards from their actions when things go well, but do not suffer the full consequences when things go badly. Hence investors do not have to exercise due diligence, since they would expect a bailout in the case of default, or for that matter, debtor countries can choose to pursue risky economic policies with the expectation that they will not have to pay the full costs of their debts and investors will not lose the full amount invested if a financial crisis occurs. According to this reasoning, the history of IMF bailouts, especially the bailout of Mexico following the peso crisis (where the IMF and the G-7 effectively guaranteed in full the dollar-denominated Mexican government securities, the so-called *tesobonos*), convinced lenders that they would be able to get their money back regardless of whatever happens in a borrowing country.[87] Jeffrey Sachs (1998, 16) comments on "the failings of recent IMF bailout loans, in which private sector creditors walked away with the IMF money while debtor countries in effect nationalized the private sector debts . . . the IMF money went out to foreign creditors as fast as it arrived to the debtor governments." Thus the IMF, by cushioning the losses of imprudent lenders and borrowers with generous bailout packages, only encourages reckless behavior – with Asia and Russia being the most recent cases in point.[88]

It is undeniable that IMF bailouts have created the problem of moral hazard – after all, despite weak underlying fundamentals, investors purchased large amounts of Russian government securities under the expectation that geopolitical and security concerns would prompt the G-7 and the IMF to provide funds – and they were not wrong. Yet, it is important to note that not all investors in emerging market securities escaped losses as a result of the Mexican and Asian rescues. It is almost impossible for investors to ignore the fact that IMF financial support, even when exceptionally large, tends to be much smaller than what would be needed to imply a full and credible guarantee.[89] Nevertheless, it is critical that market participants do take a bigger hit (or receive a bigger haircut) to ensure that they do not escape all losses as a result of multilateral assistance for the crisis country. Also, in all fairness, the IMF cannot exclusively be held responsible for creating moral hazard. Bailing out the foreign holders of *tesobonos* and letting the Russians sell ruble-denominated treasury bills to foreigners had the strong support of the IMF's main shareholders, the G-7 countries. Finally, it should be noted that, unlike other forms of insurance, disbursements of IMF resources are not a cash payoff. Rather they are loans, to be repaid with interest. Thus, if investors are eventually bailed out of crises, it is not by the Fund, but by debtor countries themselves – that is, any "bailout" is funded by a member's own savings flows, as reflected in its external current account. This study will show that (a) moral hazard is a far more complex problem, and (b) it was not as pervasive or as severe as some have made it out to be. The study will also critically assess the IMF's efforts to reduce moral hazard.

## Notes

1  During 1992–93, the countries of the European Monetary System spent US$150–200 billion on intervention in foreign-exchange markets in an unsuccessful effort to stave off the devaluation of 10 European currencies. The crisis brought down the ERM, and forced the United Kingdom and Italy out of the system.

2  Prior to its floating, the baht was pegged to a dollar-dominated basket for almost 13 years. On July 11, less than two weeks after the baht was set free to float, the Philippine central bank widened the band within which the peso was allowed to fluctuate. Three days later, the Philippines became the first crisis-hit Asian country to receive financing from the IMF. The Bank of Indonesia widened its intervention bands from 8 per cent to 12 per cent in July 1997. However, on August 14, 1997 the rupiah was floated and immediately went into a free fall. In Malaysia, the central bank (Bank Negara) also intervened in order to prevent the ringgit from depreciating too quickly. In July 1997, following the devaluation of the baht, the ringgit fell 2 per cent to 2.25 against the dollar. Bank Negara spent 10 per cent of the country's foreign reserves propping up the ringgit. On July 14, the ringgit was de-linked from its dollar-denominated currency and allowed to float.

3  Under competitive devaluations, exports of countries whose currencies undergo a devaluation become more competitive in world markets as against the exports

of countries whose currencies do not undergo a devaluation to the same extent. This puts tremendous pressure on countries with stable currencies to devalue in order to make their exports competitive in world markets.

4  By end of 1997, the New Taiwanese dollar had depreciated by 15 per cent, while the stock market fell by 30 per cent.

5  The design of the currency board and linked exchange-rate system in Hong Kong is as follows. The three note-issuing banks in Hong Kong can surrender a certain amount of US dollars to the Exchange Fund of the Hong Kong government in exchange for an equivalent amount (at the official exchange rate of 7.8) of Certificates of Indebtedness – which will entitle them to print the said amount of Hong Kong dollars. With the Certificate of Indebtedness, the three note-issuing banks can use the same amount of Hong Kong dollars to redeem the equivalent amount of US dollars. According to the design, any discrepancy between the market and official exchange rates would be removed by cash arbitrage. However, in actual practice, the HKMA sells US dollars and buys Hong Kong dollars whenever the market exchange rate comes close to the intervention rate of 7.75. Thus, the currency board system operates with a self-adjustment mechanism to restore exchange-rate stability when it comes under pressure. That is, when there is an outflow of funds and the domestic currency is sold to the currency board, the monetary base will contract and interest rates will rise automatically. For details, see Yam 1998a.

6  The HKMA was sharply criticized for relying on this single tool, the interest rate, to defend the Hong Kong dollar. However, what is not always recognized is that the currency board's automatic adjustment mechanism would require local interest rates in the interbank market to go up in the event of a capital outflow – which would take the form of Hong Kong banks' selling Hong Kong dollars to the HKMA for US dollars at the fixed exchange rate. Moreover, the Hong Kong authorities also took several other steps, such as asking banks to limit loans to the speculative property and stock markets, strengthening prudential standards for non-performing loans of banks, increasing bank reporting requirements, and insisting on greater transparency of the banking sector.

7  According to theory, any speculative attack that bid up the domestic interest rate would attract capital inflows (thereby bringing the domestic interest rate back to the US level), making speculative attack unprofitable. However, such a process did not materialize. The huge gap between the Hong Kong dollar and US dollar interest rates was due to the so-called "Asian Risk Premium." Also, it should be noted that while the speculative attack on the forward currency market was the prime mover of the crisis, most of the profits came from the speculative selling in the stock futures market. For example, a fall of the Hang Seng Futures Index by 1,000 points would mean half-a-billion Hong Kong dollars' profit for every 10,000 contracts. If speculators altogether sold 50,000 contracts and gained 4,000 points in the futures index, the profit would be HK$10 billion.

8  On October 23, 1997, stock prices in Hong Kong fell by 10.4 per cent, a larger fall than what occurred following the Tiananmen incident. However, nothing better illustrated the crisis in Hong Kong than the spectacular collapse of Peregrine Investment Holding. This regional investment house, known for its risk-taking, fell because of its unsound investment in the ironically named Indonesian taxi company, Steady Safe. On the eve of its collapse, Peregrine held $270 million in

promissory notes, denominated in US dollars, from Steady Safe – or about one-third of its capital assets. In addition, it held an estimated US$400 million in other Indonesian debt securities. Because of the sharp decline of the value of the Indonesian rupiah and its failure to hedge against currency risk, Peregrine's investment became worthless virtually overnight.

9 Since Singapore and Taiwan competed directly with Korea in a wide range of export products, the fact that both had allowed their currencies to depreciate put Korea at a serious competitive loss.

10 Since 1990, South Korea had operated a managed floating system known as the "market average rate system (MARS)." Under this system the Bank of Korea would intervene actively if exchange-rate fluctuations exceeded the permitted plus or minus 2.25 per cent band against the preceding day's closing price.

11 The Malaysian Prime Minister Mahathir Mohamed lamented that "the financial turmoil had reduced the Asian Tigers into whimpering kittens, and . . . that the massive damage to their economies will take decades to restore": *Singapore Straits Times*, March 3, 1998, p. 11.

12 According to Gopinath (1999, 82), "Nowhere was the US influence more evident than in the decision to bail Russia out. The Clinton administration wanted to keep President Boris Yeltsin and his so-called economic reformers in office. The IMF staff, including Michel Camdessus and Russia expert John Odling-Smee, were reluctant because they worried they wouldn't be able to monitor how the money would be used. But with its largest donor urging it to go ahead, the IMF had little choice but to agree to pledge $11.2 billion to a $22.6 billion Russian rescue." Also see Bueno de Mesquita *et al.* (1999, 27), and *IMF Survey*, vol. 27, no. 17, August 31, 1998, pp. 275–6.

13 Illarionov (1999) argues that the refusal by the Duma (Russian Parliament) to accept key fiscal measures in the modified economic program worked out by the IMF and the Russian government in early July 1998 was the final straw.

14 The devaluation exposed the insolvency of the banks by leaving them with dollar obligations on forward contracts many times greater than their capital. For details, see *IMF Survey*, vol. 28, no. 15, August 2, 1999, pp. 241–3. Also see IMF 1999, 55–8.

15 See *IMF Survey*, vol. 27, no. 23, December 14, 1998.

16 In October 1997, speculators attacked the Brazilian *real* with the aim of profiting from an expected devaluation by selling the currency "short" – that is, borrowing the currency and selling it with the hope of repurchasing it more cheaply before repaying the lender. While this strategy is usually not sufficient to force a devaluation, it can put tremendous pressure on a currency. The outcome depends on the government's response. It can defend its currency by selling reserves and/or raising interest rates, or it can allow the devaluation to occur.

17 For details, see *IMF Survey*, vol. 27, no. 21, November 16, 1998; *IMF Survey*, vol. 27, no. 23, December 14, 1998; *IMF Survey*, vol. 28, no. 6, March 22, 1999.

18 Also, on January 6, 1999, when Itamar Franco, governor of the state of Minas Gerais, announced a moratorium on debt payments owed to the federal government (totaling US$15 billion), market confidence in the success of Brazil's fiscal stabilization plan waned further. And when a number of other Brazilian states joined the request of Minas Gerais, the net outflow of capital intensified.

19  The disorderly exit from the peg caused the *real* to overshoot (the *real* lost over 50 per cent of its value in a few months), hurt economic activity, and propelled unemployment to a decade-high 8.3 per cent in February 1999. For details, see *IMF Survey*, vol. 28, no. 3, February 8, 1999.

20  The G-7 (or Group of 7) countries comprise the United States, Great Britain, Germany, Japan, France, Canada and Italy. The OECD countries include the G-7 plus 15 other major economies of the world.

21  The US$20 billion was funded through a conditional collateralized loan funded from the US Treasury's Exchange Stabilization Fund.

22  Prior to Mexico, the largest IMF stand-by credit arrangement was the US$4 billion agreement with the United Kingdom in 1977. It is important to note that while the IMF and other multilateral institutions provided the rescue packages to ailing Asian economies quickly, the amount and timing of disbursements depended on the countries' performance under IMF-agreed reform programs. Between August 1997 and October 1998, Thailand received some 60 per cent of the financing committed for that period by the IMF and the World Bank. Korea received almost 90 per cent of the financing committed in the very early stages of the crisis. By contrast, official lending to Indonesia was held up, after an initial disbursement of US$3 billion in early November 1997, owing to the slow implementation of reforms. IMF disbursements resumed only in May 1998, and stepped up during the summer, after major political reforms took place in the country. For details on IMF lending, see *IMF Survey*, vol. 28, no. 5, March 8, 1999.

23  The Miyazawa Initiative announced by the Japanese government on October 3, 1998 was designed to help the crisis-affected countries restructure corporate debt, reform financial systems, strengthen the social safety net, increase employment and ease businesses' financial constraints. To achieve this quickly, the initiative provided for US$15 billion in short-term swap arrangements and the rest for medium and long-term use. Japan's Export–Import Bank was selected to guarantee loans to Southeast Asian nations as well as purchase bonds issued by their governments. In fact, an important element of this initiative is that it allows official Japanese institutions to guarantee bond money raised by crisis-hit Asian countries at rates available to the Japanese government. As of April 2000, only US$6.75 billion remain unused.

24  Gilpin (2000, 145) notes that "as early as the spring of 1997, Japan urged joint action to prevent a crisis, but the Clinton Administration, fearing a negative domestic reaction, failed to act." He adds that "the Clinton Administration was very slow in recognizing the serious nature of the unfolding crisis; indeed, as late as the November 1997 Asia-Pacific Economic Cooperation (APEC) Summit in Vancouver, the President dismissed the crisis as a few small glitches on the road" (p. 146).

25  Quotations cited in CPER (1998, 2), Gilpin (2000, 143) and Council on Foreign Relations (1999, 23). According to Tan (2000, 207), "one possible reason for the lack of interest and concern on the part of the Americans was the fact that US banks were the least exposed to countries affected by the currency crisis. At the end of 1996, total lending by US banks to Thailand, Malaysia, Indonesia and South Korea was US$22 billion. This was only about a quarter of the total lending of Japanese banks (US$92 billion), or European banks (US$82.3 billion) to these countries."

26  At the Birmingham summit in May 1998 the G-7 leaders and finance ministers stressed the need for reforming the international monetary system.

27  Robert Rubin, "Strengthening the Architecture of the International Financial System," public statement delivered at the Brookings Institution, April 14, 1998.

28  The terms "moral hazard" and "asymmetric information" will be elaborated later.

29  IMF, 2000d. "Recovery from the Asian Crisis and the Role of the IMF," IMF Issues Brief, June.

30  "Asymmetric information" emerges when one party to a financial contract does not have the same information as the other party.

31  "Herd behavior" suggests that investors' decisions are not always rational.

32  As is well known, even well-managed banks or financial intermediaries are vulnerable to panics, because they traditionally engage in "maturity transformation." That is, banks accept deposits with short maturities (up to three months) to finance loans with longer maturities (up to one year or longer). Under normal conditions banks should have no problem managing their portfolios to meet expected withdrawals. However, if all depositors decided to withdraw their funds from a given bank at the same time (as during a panic), the bank would not have enough liquid assets to meet its obligations – threatening the viability of an otherwise solvent financial institution.

33  Radelet and Sachs (1998, 4) note that there is "a critical distinction between illiquidity and insolvency. An insolvent borrower lacks the net worth to repay outstanding debts out of future earnings. An illiquid borrower lacks the ready cash to meet current debt servicing obligations, even though it has the net worth to repay the debt in the long term. A liquidity crisis occurs if a solvent, but illiquid, borrower is unable to borrow fresh funds from the capital market in order to meet current debt servicing obligations."

34  Implicit in the Radelet and Sachs (1998) account is the view that investor behavior was irrational. It should be kept in mind that when the currency crisis is analyzed as a bank run, investor behavior does not have to be irrational. Given that other creditors are withdrawing funds, it is rational for an investor to withdraw funds. In fact, it may be rational to be first in line.

35  "Contagion" refers to the spread of market disturbances from one country to another, which is observed through movements in exchange rates, stock markets and interest rates. Empirical examination of the evidence for contagion consists of four types of tests. The first estimates correlation coefficients of financial variables. According to this approach, a marked increase in correlations among markets of different countries is regarded as evidence of contagion (Calvo 1996). Eichengreen and Rose (1998) define contagion as a case where knowledge of a crisis elsewhere increases the probability of a crisis at home. The third type of tests estimates levels of volatility among financial markets. This approach examines whether conditional variances of financial markets are related to each other during the crisis period (Edwards 1998). Finally, a fourth type of test examines whether foreign news affects financial variables at home (Kaminsky and Schmukler 1999a).

36  Fratzscher (1998) has found that the financial markets in Southeast and East Asia are highly integrated, meaning that the financial channel of contagion is highly influential. While Fratzscher also found that Asian economies are close

trade competitors in terms of the similarity of export structures and export destination (including intra-regional trade), the size and significance of the coefficients in his econometric equations however suggest that the financial link was the most important channel of contagion in the Asian crisis.

37 Various factors may account for crises spreading across countries. First, simultaneous crises may be triggered by a change in the external environment such as increases in international interest rates. Second, crises can spread through trade and financial linkages. Portfolio reshuffling by investors in response to developments in one country may affect another country's access to flows. Third, the similarity of fundamentals with affected countries, such as geographical proximity or common development strategies, can lead to contagion.

38 At the time the official rate of the RMB (renminbi = yuan) was at 5.8 RMB per US dollar versus the 8.7 RMB per dollar at the swap center.

39 For a discussion of how China's pre-emptive devaluation contributed to the Asian financial crisis, see Corsetti, Pesenti and Roubini (1998).

40 The tax change meant that exporters could claim a refund of the VAT paid on inputs.

41 Data compiled from World Bank (1998, 1996), IMF (1997) and *Zhongguo Jinrong Nianjian 1997* (1997).

42 The quotation is from Mattione (2000, 185).

43 The classic bubble economy is one in which real estate prices continue to rise well beyond levels justified by the productivity of the assets. However, so long as the prices continue to rise, existing investors are rewarded and collateral is created for new loans to finance further investment, and so on – until the inevitable crash.

44 For the first four decades following the Second World War, Japan's overall economic growth was spectacular: a 10 per cent average in the 1960s, a 5 per cent average in the 1970s, and a 4 per cent average in the 1980s. For details, see Posen (1998).

45 Until the outbreak of the Asian financial crisis, the Japanese authorities had managed to cover up the seriousness of the banking crisis by a series of government-sanctioned takeovers of smaller failed banks by larger banks under the so-called "convoy system." Why has Japan failed to address its loan problem effectively? According to Lincoln (1998), politics is at the root of the problem. That is, Japanese politicians have incestuous relations with borrowers and the banking community. For example, investment banks commonly lend money to politicians to buy a particular stock and then ramp up stock prices, allowing the politicians to sell out, repay the loan, and make a profit. If the non-performing loan problem were cleared up, many such illegal transactions would come to light, causing embarrassment to those involved.

46 Grenville (1999, 3) notes that "the interest differential between the major industrial countries and the emerging market economies was the greatest for Japan – hence, the rise of the yen-carry trade – borrowing at low interest rates in yen, and on-lending at high returns in other countries, particularly in Asia. When local-currency borrowing rates were around 20 per cent (which was the case, for example, in Indonesia), yen-based interest rates seemed extraordinarily attractive."

47 Dobson (1998, 153) notes that "in 1996, only three out of twenty major Japanese banks recorded positive rates of returns on equity, and the rest had negative

rates ranging from −19.4 per cent to −3.15 per cent. In 1995, 13 trillion Yen of loan write-offs and loan loss provisions more than offset the operating profits of all Japanese banks, which led to a net loss of 3.8 trillion Yen."

48  The Basle Accord, an international agreement that set common standards by which to evaluate capital adequacy, was introduced in 1988. In order to create a "level playing-field" it requires that all internationally active banks satisfy the same two (minimum) risk-based capital ratios.

49  See "Japanese banks and market discipline" in *Chicago Fed Letter*, no. 144, August 1999 (publication of The Federal Reserve Bank of Chicago).

50  "Asia Trembles Again," *The Economist*, June 20, 1998, pp. 81–2.

51  Japanese investors did not need to worry about risk associated with overvaluation of a host country's currency as long the authorities succeeded in keeping inflation rates in line with the appreciation of the dollar.

52  Japanese manufacturing companies also shifted their production to North America, partly to avoid trade conflicts and partly to prepare for the North American Free Trade Area (NAFTA).

53  A study by Frankel and Wei (1994) on the exchange-rate policy of nine East Asian countries during the period 1979 to mid-1992 has shown that the weight that was attached to the US dollar in the currency baskets of most East Asian countries ranged from 0.9 to 1.0. The only exception was the Singapore dollar, which assigned slightly more weight to the yen. A study by Kwan (1995) further confirmed the dominant position of the dollar in East Asian currency baskets.

54  The only exception was the Philippines, which during 1991–95 posted a mere 2.2 per cent annual growth rate.

55  Within a broader historical perspective, the fast-growing Asian economies were doubling their average incomes approximately every 11 years. On the other hand, it took Great Britain about 60 years to double its average income after 1780; the United States took about 50 years to double its average income after 1840; and Japan took roughly 35 years to double its income after 1885 (Tan 2000, 23).

56  Krugman's findings have been questioned. According to Sarel (1997), Singapore, Malaysia and Thailand all had a TFP (total factor production) growth of 2 per cent to 2.5 per cent between 1978 and 1996, compared with only 0.3 per cent in the United States.

57  When private investors borrow short-term, they may fall into maturity mismatch difficulties. Maturity mismatch difficulties arise when the assets backing short-term debt obligations are longer-term, and therefore less liquid than their liabilities. Illiquid assets (such as real estate) cannot be sold quickly at fair value.

58  That is, governments in the developing world (especially, Latin America), which had borrowed heavily from foreign commercial banks during the 1970s (encouraged by very low real interest rates and by high prices for their commodity exports), were unable to service their debts when real interest rates rose sharply at the end of the 1970s, and a world-wide recession reduced demand for developing country exports.

59  Since the 1990s, the international bond market has been the largest provider of net financing to emerging markets. It has also served as the mainstay of external financing for sovereign borrowers (in marked contrast to the 1980s, when syndicated bank lending performed this role).

60 The 1996 figure is from the World Bank (1996a, 11–12). The other figures are from the IMF (1995, 2–4).

61 Calvo, Leiderman and Reinhart (1993) found that declines in US interest rates were correlated with increases in proxies for capital inflows (foreign reserve accumulation and real exchange rate appreciation) to Latin America in the early 1990s. Fernandez-Arias (1996), who studied a broader sample of emerging markets, estimated that global interest rates accounted for nearly 90 per cent of the increase in portfolio investment flows for the "average emerging market" in 1989–93.

62 Hong Kong, Japan, Singapore and Malaysia were accorded IMF Article 8 status as early as the 1960s.

63 Nidhiprabha (1998, 195) notes that "by the end of 1995, the short-term debt through the BIBF amounted to $41 billion, out of a total debt of $80 billion."

64 Lipsey (2001) finds that direct investors, especially those who operate manufacturing facilities in foreign countries, are much more likely to ride out economic crises than those involved in foreign bonds, equities, bank loans and other forms of investment. The major reason for this appears to be that much of the direct investment is bound up in enterprises that, in times of instability, can redirect sales from a country's local markets to export markets. Lipsey also credits the direct investors with being more willing to hang tough in the midst of seeming chaos. For example, he finds foreign direct investors operating in Asia "to be much less skittish than other investors in responding to the crisis."

65 Illiquid assets cannot be sold quickly at fair value. One common example of an illiquid asset is real estate – where it takes some time to locate a buyer willing to purchase the asset at its fair value.

66 There are a number of different instruments and approaches that can be used to manage currency risk in international trade transactions. These include (1) forward foreign-exchange contracts, (2) structural or balance-sheet hedges, (3) invoicing in local currency, and (4) use of foreign-exchange option contracts. A *forward foreign-exchange contract* involves contracting today to buy or sell a foreign currency at a future date at an exchange rate agreed today. Thus, for example, exporters can contract today to sell the foreign-exchange proceeds they expect to receive at a future date so as to insulate themselves from fluctuations in the exchange rate in the interim. Generally, the forward exchange rate on a given day will not be the same as the spot rate. The difference stems directly from the interest rate differential between the two currencies. However, it is also the case that forward contracts are generally favored for shorter-term hedging of trade flows, while borrowing or lending in foreign currencies is normally seen as a way to establish a *long-term structural hedge*. One reason why forward contracts are used to establish shorter-term hedges is their relative flexibility. Contracts can readily be rolled forward, or closed out according to the firm's view of the exchange rate. Also, forward contract maturities can be managed flexibly, through the use of swaps contracts. For example, a common practice for a firm is to enter into a spot contract immediately it sees a favorable opportunity in the market. Later, by executing a swap contract, the spot contract can be turned into a forward contract, with a maturity date that matches the underlying export receipt or import payment date.

The arrangements under which banks will deal with firms in foreign exchange, including in forward contracts, are also more flexible than those under which they will establish debt facilities. The documentation and security that banks require to support a foreign exchange dealing line often are less demanding than those required for debt facilities. For these reasons, managing foreign-exchange risk by managing the currency composition of the balance sheet through foreign currency borrowing tends to be limited to large corporations with the financial strength and profile to access offshore debt markets, or with offshore operations that can fund themselves directly in the markets in which they operate. *Invoicing in local currency* is another possible way to manage exchange-rate risk by passing it to the trading counter-party. However, invoicing in local currency does not of itself provide complete protection against exchange-rate risk. What matters, therefore, is not just the currency of invoicing, but the ability to negotiate a pricing arrangement (either in foreign currency or local currency), that leaves the effect of exchange-rate changes with the trading counterpart. Another hedging possibility available to local exporters and importers facing foreign exchange risk is *foreign exchange options.* As the name suggests, an option contract differs from a forward contract in that it gives the holder the right, but not the obligation, to buy or sell one currency in exchange for another at a specified exchange rate, and at an agreed point in the future. Under a forward contract the holder must buy or sell on the agreed date; with an option the holder has the choice.

67  Of course, in Mexico, the capital inflows fueled a consumption boom.

68  The underlying rationale is that the flexibility in exchange rates would introduce some uncertainties that might discourage purely speculative and highly reversible inflows. It also allows the monetary authorities a greater degree of independence in exercising control over monetary aggregates as they become relatively free from preoccupation with the stability of the exchange rate.

69  Intervention can be sterilized or left unsterilized. Unsterilized intervention will increase the monetary base, resulting in lower interest rates. The stimulating effect of lower interest rates may cause inflation if the economy is already at the full capacity of production – which is often the case for emerging market economies that attract massive capital inflows.

70  Suppose the initial capital inflows were in the form of FDI. The domestic end of sterilization is most likely effected in the short-term money market. Then, the short-term interest rate may increase, while the long-term interest rate will decline. The higher short-term interest rate will invite more capital inflows in the form of portfolio investment. Hence, sterilized intervention may increase capital inflows.

71  Montiel and Reinhart (1997) argue that the sterilization policies followed by the host (capital inflow) countries played an important role in setting the stage for the subsequent crisis. Specifically, sterilization operations kept domestic interest rates in the host countries higher than would otherwise have been the case, thereby inducing both larger net inflows and a high share of interest-sensitive short-term flows.

72  The Malaysian political system is sometimes referred to as "semi-authoritarian" or "semi-democratic" because it contains features of both systems. That is, although the constitutional framework of the Malaysian political system is essentially democratic (elections have been held regularly, the government is responsible to

an elected parliament and the judiciary is constitutionally independent), the democratic framework is accompanied by a wide range of authoritarian controls that greatly limit the scope for effective political opposition. The controls also makes the defeat of the ruling party at the polls almost impossible.

73 As Max Weber (1947) noted long ago, inherent in personalism is "patrimonial bureaucracy" with a penchant for official malfeasance and outright corruption.

74 Athukorala (1998, 89) notes that "public investment expenditure surged, pushing the total investment to GDP ratio to 46% in 1997, the highest in the region."

75 Haggard (2000, 49) defines a veto gate as an institution that has the power to veto a policy proposal, thus forcing a reversion to the status quo. Veto gates can include the president, the legislature, a second chamber of the legislature, a committee within a legislature, or the courts. In authoritarian governments, they may include the military. The preferences of these veto gates may be more or less closely aligned: thus the president and the legislature may represent distinct veto gates, but may either be of the same party (unified government) or of different parties (divided government).

76 The IMF's mandate is outlined in the charter of rights and obligations. This is contained in its constitution or "Articles of Agreement." The IMF's purpose is to promote international monetary cooperation, exchange-rate stability and the expansion of international trade by serving as a short-term lender, providing liquidity for member countries with short-term balance of payments problems. On the other hand, the World Bank's role is to provide longer-term development finance. Although the total size of the IMF's quotas increased from about US$9 billion at its creation in 1944 to nearly US$200 billion in 1997, it has declined relative to almost all relevant global economic indicators, whether the size of world trade, international reserves, or international financial flows.

77 The IMF has 182 members as of June 30, 2001.

78 Under Article IV of the IMF's Articles of Agreement, the IMF holds bilateral discussions with member countries, usually every year. An IMF staff team visits the country, collects economic and financial information and discusses with government officials the country's economic policies. On return to headquarters, the staff prepares a report – which forms the basis for discussion by the IMF Executive Board. At the conclusion of the discussion, the Managing Director, as chairman of the Board, summarizes the views of the Executive Directors, and this summary is than forwarded to the country's authorities.

79 However, much is in the form of currencies not readily used in international financial transactions. That is, once we take into account the fact that 75 per cent of country quota subscriptions are in domestic currency, and that approximately half the money on the IMF balance sheet cannot be used, the $215 billion figure does not look very large.

80 The other facilities include the Systemic Transformation Facility (STF), which is a temporary facility designed to extend financial assistance to transition economies, and the Structural Adjustment Facility (SAF) and the Enhanced Structural Adjustment Facility (ESAF), designed to assist the low-income and least-developed member countries.

81 However, in a capital account crisis such phasing may be problematic, since the authorities do not have the funds up front to counter capital outflows – and

indeed, owing to conditionality, it is not certain that they will ever have access to this money.

82 Conditionality is the mechanism whereby the IMF ensures that countries implement the necessary adjustments. The provision of the IMF's assistance is contingent on a government's agreement to a program of specific policies, and its subsequent adherence to that program. Credit is disbursed in periodic installments as a government fulfills its obligations – otherwise a program can be suspended or altogether terminated.

83 For details, see Michael Mussa (2000), who at the time was economic counselor and director of the Department of Research at the IMF.

84 There is agreement that South Korea got into trouble in mid-1997 because its financial sector had incurred short-term foreign debts that far exceeded its foreign-exchange reserves. Korea's problem was one of unsustainable corporate debt and the resultant temporary illiquidity, rather than insolvency. In such a context the IMF's demand for a fundamental restructuring of the Korean economy was not very prudent.

85 As Stanley Fischer (1998a, 104–5), notes, "the first order of business was to restore confidence in the currencies." To achieve this, countries have to make their currencies more attractive, which requires increasing interest rates temporarily – even if higher interest costs complicate the situation of weak banks and corporations.

86 Nellor (1998) notes that in the absence of comprehensive reforms, it would not have been possible to restore investor confidence in the crisis economies.

87 Specifically, the IMF and the G-7 extended the Mexican government loans that permitted it to pay off the holders of the *tesobonos* in full.

88 The fact that the strategy of investing in Russian debt securities in 1997–98 was referred to as the "moral hazard play" suggests that the international community's repeated resort to financial rescue packages influenced investor behavior. The community's official decision not to avert a Russian default in August 1998, and its bail-in efforts in Ukraine and Ecuador, were an attempt to moderate this expectation.

89 Holders of equities and long-term debt securities, especially those who sold at the height of these crises, took significant hits.

# 2

# Thailand:
# crisis, reform and recovery

During the period of economic growth, we were too complacent. In good
times we forgot many important truths and neglected many important tasks;
we opened up our economy, but our stated plans to pursue discipline were not
followed up; we attracted massive flows of cheap foreign capital, which we did
not always spend or invest with enough prudence . . . we did not examine the
fundamentals of our politics and governance or tackle issues such as bureaucratic inefficiency, lack of transparency and lack of accountability . . . naturally
we were quickly and severely disciplined by the market (Chuan Leekpai, Prime
Minister of Thailand, in a speech on March 11, 1998).[1]

When Thailand, the paradigmatic economic success story, fell victim to
the crisis, many analysts were dumbfounded – instinctively blaming the
pervasive cronyism and corruption for the country's troubles. However, as
it turned out, cronyism, corruption, clientelism and weak corporate governance were only part of the problem. After all, these problems existed
while Thailand notched up impressive growth rates for more than a quarter-
century before the financial meltdown in July 1997. Rather, this chapter
argues that it was the volatile convergence of a mounting current account
deficit, a sharp export slowdown, currency and maturity mismatches
among Thai commercial banks, the maintenance of a rigid exchange rate, a
rapid build-up of private short-term foreign-debt liabilities, an overheated
investment bubble in real estate and stock markets, and an external environment that unexpectedly turned sour in 1996–97, that led to the crisis.
All that this convergence needed was a trigger. The trigger was provided
by a loss of confidence on the part of the owners of short-term capital
in the Bank of Thailand's capacity to maintain its fixed exchange rate. Most
tragically, this convergence was neither foreordained nor sudden – but
had been building up since mid-1996, roughly one year before the baht's
devaluation.

Why was this explosive convergence allowed to persist for so long? The answer lies in the political economy of Thailand in the 1990s. Specifically, it is well known that the governments of Chuan Leekpai (September 1992–June 1995), and especially, those of Banharn Silpa-archa (July 1995–November 1996) and Chavalit Yongchaiyudh (November 1996–November 1997) were notoriously unstable multi-party coalitions and unable to formulate (let alone implement) a coherent macroeconomic policy. Lauridsen (1998, 157) notes that when the Banharn and Chavalit governments intervened, "it was in a too-little-too-late fashion, with strong policy formulation usually followed by weak policy implementation."[2] Yet what about the role of Thailand's highly influential and respected technocrats in the finance ministry and at the Bank of Thailand (BOT), the country's central bank?[3] As Siamwalla (1998, 9) states, "in a country in which corruption is rife, the Bank of Thailand is considered to be the only institution where it was unthinkable that any corrupt practices could be found. This reputation of incorruptibility gave it considerable moral authority and prestige and allowed it to enjoy *de facto* autonomy, overriding its *de jure* subservience to the Minister of Finance." Moreover, the BOT had a well-earned reputation for prudent macroeconomic management. Throughout the 1980s and early 1990s, the BOT conducted extremely cautious monetary policies (running a small surplus almost every year), a non-inflationary monetary policy, and a fixed exchange rate that was quickly adjusted whenever necessary.[4] Finally, the governments of successive prime ministers since the mid-1980s, including those at the helm in the years just before the crisis, were dominated by ministers, advisers and consultants from the financial and the business world. Given this, the Thai crisis has generated an interesting debate as to whether it was the technocrats or the politicians who should be held responsible for the policy failure?

Obviously, the answer is that both are responsible – albeit the wrongs of the politicians have received much more attention in the literature.[5] Analysts have raised questions regarding how much real autonomy the BOT really enjoyed in policy formulation and implementation. There is little doubt that the autonomy of the BOT as well as that of the Ministry of Finance (and related agencies) had gradually declined since the early 1990s. As Christensen and Siamwalla (1993, 7) note, during the many years of military rule, "the technocrats would not encroach on the sectoral and microeconomic mismanagement which benefits the political masters, while the latter would allow the technocrats to keep control over the macro economy." However, under both the Banharn and Chavalit administrations, the BOT and the finance ministry were "pushed and pulled by politicians" with increasing interference in the workings of these institutions from the prime minister's office (Lauridsen 1998, 157). During the sixteen-months-long Banharn administration, the heads of the BOT, the Ministry of Finance and Securities and Exchange Commission were summarily dismissed. In fact, there were three different finance ministers during this period. Such actions greatly undermined the autonomy and oversight capacity of the central bank and severely disrupted the formulation and implementation of prudent macroeconomic policy.

Yet, once one has noted this, the BOT must also take its share of the blame. Indeed, the Nukul Commission, a blue-ribbon panel consisting of prominent economists, financiers and civil servants and headed by a former central bank governor, Nukul Prachuabmoh, has shed disturbing light on those entrusted with regulating the country's financial system.[6] In fact, the 205-page Nukul Report has pinned the greatest blame for the mismanagement of macroeconomic policy squarely on the shoulders of Rerngchai Marakanond, the central bank governor from July 1996 to July 1997. Likewise, a recent World Bank study notes that "the Bank of Thailand, once considered a pillar of strength, no longer deserved its old reputation as a monitor of the economy and enforcer of financial discipline. The regulations and supervision practices the bank followed to ensure the soundness and safety of the financial sector had not kept pace with the rapid growth of financial institutions. The bank's staff was poorly trained and stretched thin" (Nabi and Shivakumar 2001, 11). What were the bank's policy errors? This chapter will argue that the BOT made two egregious policy blunders. First was the futile and costly defense of the baht during late 1996 and the first half of 1997, and second the bleeding of the Thai government's Financial Institutions Development Fund (FIDF) to prop up failing financial institutions, while neglecting to take actions to remedy the underlying structural problems in the financial and banking sector. The puzzling question is why Thailand's well-trained and highly professional technocrats made such serious policy errors. Drawing on the Bank of Thailand's published materials, this chapter suggests that Thailand's long period of economic boom had lulled the technocrats into complacency. Thinking that the sun would never set on the good times, they threw caution to the winds, becoming prisoners of what Charles Kindleberger (1978) long ago termed "disaster myopia" – a mindset whereby policy-makers and investors suffer from an inability to imagine any fiscal contraction, let alone a financial crisis. The policy prescriptions Thailand's technocrats enunciated to correct the macroeconomic misalignment under conditions of free capital mobility and fixed exchange rates can only politely be termed "inappropriate." Indeed, Thailand's economic technocrats as well as many observers remained unduly sanguine about the Thai economy despite mounting evidence of macroeconomic disequilibrium. In their "irrational exuberance" they erred in failing to read and correct the tell-tale signs of an impending economic slowdown.[7] This chapter illustrates the fact that such irrational exuberance suited the weak Thai coalition governments and politicians and an array of business constituents who had their own reasons for preserving the status quo.

## The emergence of the "fifth tiger"[8]

For a country that in the 1950s was ranked as one of the world's poorest, with an unpromising future, Thailand's economic performance has been nothing short of miraculous. In a pattern almost unique among oil-importing countries, Thailand's real output per head of population had not experienced a single year of negative growth since 1958. Between 1965 and 1996, the average annual growth rate of Thailand's real GNP per person was well over 5 per cent, as against an average of 2.4 per cent for low- and middle-income countries. Between 1986 and 1996, the Thai economy was the fastest-growing in the world, notching up an unprecedented real GDP growth of 10.4 per cent per annum (Warr and Nidhiprabha 1996, 1–3). Even more remarkable was the stability of this growth. Between 1988 and 1996, the growth rate of real exports was 14.5 per cent, inflation averaged a low 5.3 per cent and gross domestic savings as a percentage of GNP rose from 17 per cent in the early 1980s to over 30 per cent in the late 1980s. The growth in GNP per capita rose to about 8 per cent per annum in the first half of the 1990s. On the eve of the crisis in 1997, Thai GNP per capita had reached US$2,740 compared to the GNP per capita of US$220 in 1972 and US$870 in 1987 (Jomo 1997, 56–7). The rapid economic growth not only reduced poverty levels from over 57 per cent in the mid-1960s to 30 per cent in the mid-1970s and to about 13 per cent by 1996, but basic social indicators in terms of life expectancy, infant mortality, literacy and human resource development all also showed significant improvements (World Bank 1997, 1–4). The surge in growth also transformed the composition of production as Thailand moved from a predominantly agrarian to an industrialized economy. From 1980 to 1996, agriculture's share in GDP fell from 23 per cent to 11 per cent, while manufacturing's share increased from 22 per cent to 28 per cent. These changes also transformed Thailand financial system. By the mid-1980s, the Thai economy had become highly monetized, and the financial system was disproportionately deep compared to those of other emerging markets with similar per capita income. As of 1987, Thailand's formal financial system consisted of commercial banks, finance companies, *crédit foncier* companies, Government Savings Banks, private and government insurance companies and a number of sectorally specialized financial institutions. However, commercial banks were the central players in the system, absorbing 80.9 per cent of deposits and accounting for 73.1 per cent of total financial system assets, followed by the finance companies, which provided about 20 per cent of all the credit in the country (Alba *et al.* 1999, 8). With such impressive economic achievements, Thailand soon became the developmental showcase, the so-called "fifth Asian tiger" and the model for other emerging nations to emulate. What explains Thailand's phenomenal economic growth? What explains the economy's precipitous collapse in July 1997? What lessons does Thailand provide?

### The investment and export-led boom

If large and sustained rates of economic growth, to quote Paul Krugman (1994), are usually the result of both "inspiration" and "perspiration," in Thailand's case they took a lot of perspiration from both the civil society and the state.[9] The Thai government has long used policy instruments to influence the direction of economic activity. For example, the Board of Investment (BOI), created in 1959, used a combination of various investment-promotion schemes, tariff policies, tax regimes, and trade and price controls to direct the pattern of private investment, besides supporting extensive public investment in infrastructure. During the 1960s and early 1970s, industrial policies strongly supported capital-intensive import-substitution industrialization (ISI). Import tariffs were sharply raised to protect local industries, with special incentives for the production of final goods based on imported intermediate and capital goods. Indeed, as Christensen *et al.* (1997, 354) note, "the BOI's most significant power was over imports. It could exempt particular firms or industries from import duties on machinery, components, and raw materials, as well as imposing bans and surcharges on competing imports."

The officially stated emphasis on ISI was shifted towards the promotion of exports with the passage of the Investment Promotion Act of 1972. Local businesses responded eagerly to these opportunities, both on their own and through joint ventures with foreign firms – investing in agro-processing industries, trade, banking and other activities centered on the domestic market. In the late 1970s, the Thai government introduced a further series of measures designed to speed up the growth of manufactured exports. These included industrial export incentives, such as tax and tariff rebates and preferential interest rates on short-term loans. In the early 1980s, the Thai government implemented another round of export incentives, including tax incentives and currency devaluations in 1981 and 1984. For example, the BOI gave priority to export projects, granting numerous exemptions to export-oriented projects, including duties and business taxes on imported raw materials or components, business taxes on domestic input, export duties, and certain deductions from taxable corporate income.[10] The government also reformed the customs procedures and removed cumbersome regulations to help exporters expedite their processing and shipments. In addition, it established export processing zones (EPZs) – where businesses enjoyed exemption from import/export duties and business taxes. EPZ firms and factories also benefited from good infrastructure, and were entitled to get a 20 per cent reduction in their energy bills. All domestic exporters received concessionary credits and marketing assistance.[11]

Finally, a major incentive to export came from the changes in the real exchange rate. Specifically, throughout the 1960s and 1970s, the baht was tied to the US dollar, with occasional minor adjustments. While this policy served Thailand well during the era of fixed exchange rates, it became problematic once the major currencies began to float following the collapse of the Bretton Woods system. Linking the baht to the dollar led to an increase in the real effective exchange rate in the early 1980s, despite the 8.7 per cent devaluation against the dollar in 1981. In response, the Thai government changed the real exchange rate in 1984 by tying the baht to a basket of major currencies – albeit the US dollar weighed heavily in the basket. The aim of the new managed float was to maintain the baht–dollar parity within a somewhat wider band. The new exchange rate resulted in an immediate 15 per cent devaluation of the nominal exchange rate against the dollar – providing Thai firms with a real incentive to export.[12]

Nevertheless, a prolonged slump in world commodity prices saw overall export growth, especially exports of natural resources and some semi-manufactures, decline during the period 1980–86. Export growth recovered after 1986, but this recovery was not led by either exports of natural resources or semi-manufactures, but by a rapid growth of manufactured goods, such as clothing, textiles, office machinery, integrated circuits, and telecommunications and computer components. Indeed, Lall (1999) notes that this high export growth was based on a shift in the structure of the export sector – where complex activities began to replace simple production. The sector encompassed four types of technologies: resource-based (food processing), low (textiles, footwear, leather and plastics), medium (the automotive industry), and high (complex electronic and electrical products). Between 1985 and 1996, the share in exports of products manufactured using medium and high technology rose from among the lowest in the region (20 per cent) to the highest (50 per cent). Thailand's medium- and high-technology product export shares exceeded those of China, Hong Kong and Indonesia.

What explains the change in the pattern of exports? Generally, the production of manufactured exports requires higher levels of worker skills. Yet human resource development, particularly education levels and worker skills development (as measured by average years of adult schooling), remained weak in Thailand. In fact, although Thailand's investment in physical capital as a ratio of GDP has long been one of the highest in the world, not enough resources have been devoted to human capital or skill formation. Thus Thailand's secondary and tertiary school enrollment as a percentage of population have consistently been much lower than those of other high-growth Asian economies, including Indonesia and Malaysia, and have also lagged behind low-income countries such as India.[13] Rather, the impetus for the expansion of manufactured exports in Thailand came from outside – in the form of foreign capital. Indeed, in the 1980s capital inflows doubled, rising to US$4.5 billion per year, and between 1990 and 1996 they tripled to US$14 billion per year (Mahmood and Aryah 2001, 256). First, Thailand needed foreign capital, since its domestic savings were not high enough to finance the high level of investments necessary for rapid growth. Second, there was the appreciation of the yen *vis-à-vis* the weakening US dollar after the 1985 Plaza Accord, during which time the baht was effectively pegged to the dollar at a rate of roughly 25 baht per US dollar.[14] Third, as Japan, South Korea, Hong Kong and Taiwan faced sharply rising labor costs and protectionist barriers, this increased the cost advantage of exports from Thailand, Malaysia and Indonesia. Fourth, and most importantly, export expansion was fueled by massive inflows of foreign capital from Japan and the other newly industrializing countries, searching for lower labor costs and lower protectionist barriers in importing countries. For example, Taiwanese investors saw Thailand as "a key linkage between Asia and Europe, comprising abundant raw materials as well as good quality staff, reasonable land prices and wages, together with accommodative government policies" (Mahmood and Aryah 2001, 257). Similarly, for the Japanese, Thailand offered all the above, in addition to fulfilling their need to spread production bases overseas and to take advantage of Thailand's unfulfilled quotas under the Multi-fibre Arrangement (MFA), as well as to utilize the privileges under the Generalized System of Preferences (GSP) to which Thailand was entitled as a developing country.[15] Indeed, by the late 1980s, Thailand was one of the chief recipients of Japanese FDI, and by 1988 Thailand attracted more FDI than the four Asian newly industrialized countries combined.

As Tables 2.1 and 2.2 show, by the late 1980s capital flows (mostly in the form of private sector borrowing) increased dramatically, fueling a rapid expansion of exports of labor-intensive manufactured goods. Indeed, the two were intimately related, as much of the foreign investment was in the labor-intensive manufacturing sector – producing everything from textiles (in particular, garments), to wood products, rubber products, processed foods, canned goods, plastic goods, toys, shoes, leather products and confectionery, as well as medium and high-tech products such as computer components, electronics, automobile parts, telecommunications and sound equipment, machinery and electrical goods.[16] By the end of 1996, the manufacturing sector employed more than 4 million workers, accounted for 29 per cent of GDP and more than 70 per cent of export earnings (OECD 1999a, 22). In terms of export growth, between 1988 and the end of 1995 export growth averaged an extraordinary 28 per cent per annum, and as a share of GDP exports increased from 23 per cent in 1988 to 34 per cent in 1995 (Warr and Nidhiprabha 1996). Leading the expansion were technology-intensive exports:

> High-technology industry has grown rapidly in Thailand during the 1990s. Technology-intensive exports increased on average by 31% per year between 1992 and 1995, accounting for 54% of the total manufactured exports in 1996, up from 42% in 1992. The development of high-technology industry in Thailand was built on foreign capital, foreign technology and foreign product designs; final products, moreover, relied significantly on foreign markets. For

**Table 2.1** *Capital inflows (% of GDP, period averages)*

|                | 1980–86 | 1987–92 | 1993–96 |
| -------------- | ------- | ------- | ------- |
| Public sector  | 2.4     | −0.3    | 0.4     |
| Private sector | 2.6     | 8.1     | 9.7     |
| Total          | 5.0     | 7.8     | 10.1    |

*Source*: BOT (1998).

**Table 2.2** *Structure of Thai exports, 1981–93 (percentage of total exports)*

|                                | 1981 | 1985 | 1988 | 1990 | 1993 |
| ------------------------------ | ---- | ---- | ---- | ---- | ---- |
| **Agriculture**                |      |      |      |      |      |
| Rice                           | 17   | 12   | 9    | 5    | 4    |
| Tapioca                        | 11   | 9    | 5    | 4    | 2    |
| Total                          | 48   | 38   | 26   | 17   | 12   |
| **Labor-intensive manufactures**[a] |      |      |      |      |      |
| Textiles and garments          | 10   | 14   | 16   | 16   | 14   |
| Jewelry                        | 3    | 4    | 6    | 6    | 4    |
| Footwear                       | 0    | 1    | 2    | 3    | 3    |
| Total                          | 15   | 21   | 29   | 31   | 27   |
| **Medium/High technology manufactures** |  |   |      |      |      |
| Machinery and appliances[b]    | 0    | 1    | 4    | 8    | 10   |
| Electrical                     | 0    | 1    | 2    | 6    | 7    |
| Electrical circuitry[c]        | 4    | 4    | 7    | 6    | 8    |
| Vehicles and parts             | 0    | 0    | 1    | 1    | 2    |
| Total                          | 5    | 7    | 15   | 22   | 30   |
| Manufactures as percentage of total exports | 36 | 49 | 66 | 75 | 80 |

*Notes*: [a]Agriculture has been omitted. [b]Mainly computers and parts. [c]Mainly integrated circuits.
*Source*: Jomo (1997, 69).

example, the electronics sector absorbed nearly 40% of foreign direct invest-ment in manufacturing in Thailand between 1995 and 1997. On average, imported contents accounted for 80% of the value of high technology exports (OECD 1999a, 23).

The massive surges of capital inflows fueling export-promotion found a hospitable environment in Thailand. Long before it was fashionable (in the early 1980s), Thailand, in sharp contrast to most developing economies, already had relatively open current and capital accounts – although exchange controls still applied to the repatriation of interest, dividends and the principal of portfolio investment. In 1984, the government embarked on an ambitious stabilization program, including measures to liberalize further both the current and capital account transactions. As was noted earlier, the baht, which had been pegged to the dollar since the mid-1950s, was devalued by 15 per cent in nominal effective terms and then pegged against a basket of currencies that were weighted heavily (about 80 per cent) towards the US dollar.[17] The Exchange Equalization Fund, chaired by the deputy governor of the Bank of Thailand, determined the exchange value of the baht each working day in accordance with fluctuations of major currencies. With regard to portfolio investment, in 1986 the authorities reduced tax impediments to portfolio flows, in particular, for purchasing Thai mutual funds.

The acceptance of Article 8 of the International Monetary Fund (IMF) Agreement by the Bank of Thailand on May 20, 1990 served as a catalyst to further financial liberalization. The acceptance required Thailand to observe three conditions: (1) to allow unrestricted payments and transfers with respect to international current transactions; (2) to refrain from preferential treatment regarding international payments, including the use of a multiple exchange rate system; and (3) to accept local currencies of other member countries through current transactions. The period 1991–92 saw the liberalization of financial controls, the lifting of ceilings on interest rates, substantial relaxation of exchange controls, and major improvements in the tax treatment of dividends, royalty payments, capital gains and interest payments on foreign debentures.[18] By the end of 1992, the repatriation of investment funds, interest and loan repayments by foreign investors was fully liberalized. With regard to foreign direct investment, in addition to amendments in the Investment Promotion Act to promote more foreign investment, the government authorized (in 1991) 100 per cent foreign ownership of firms that exported all their output, while direct investment by Thai residents was gradually liberalized between 1991 and 1994. In April 1991, most controls related to capital account transactions were lifted. This meant that for the first time unincorporated Thai entities could open foreign-currency accounts, provided that the funds originated offshore. With the establishment of the Export–Import Bank of Thailand (EXIM Bank) in 1993, exporters not only had access to direct loans, loan guarantees and export insurance, but were also allowed to accept baht payments from non-resident baht accounts without prior approval from the central bank and to use their export proceeds to service external obligations. By early November 1994 all foreign-exchange restrictions on current account transactions were eliminated.[19] Now, commercial banks were able to freely extend credits and accept deposits in foreign exchange to and from foreigners, and foreign nationals could hold and operate non-resident baht accounts to facilitate international trade and investment. Thai citizens were now allowed to transfer up to US$5 million abroad for direct foreign investment purposes.

The passage of the Securities and Exchange Act in May 1992 marked a major step towards the establishment of a unified legal and institutional framework for the development of the capital market. The Act established the Securities and Exchange Commission (SEC) as an independent agency responsible for supervising capital market activities, including equities, bonds and derivatives, and permitted, for the first time, companies access to direct finance by issuing common stock and debt instruments.[20] The Securities and Exchange Act was a driving force for issuance for common stocks and debt instruments, and resulted in the rapid expansion of the Thai capital market. For example, new capital raised in the Stock Exchange of Thailand (SET) surged from 17.5 billion baht in 1990 to 55 billion baht per year between 1991 and 1993 and to approximately 130 billion baht per year during 1994–95. Market capitalization expanded rapidly, from 29.4 per cent of GDP in 1990 to 85.9 per cent in 1995. The SET index rose from 612.9 in 1990 to a peak of 1,682.9 in 1993 (Vajragupta and Vichyanond 1999, 44). Also, in keeping with the advances in information technologies, the Bank of Thailand (BOT) instituted improved clearing and settlement systems such as the BAHTNET and THAICLEAR (established in 1993), which greatly reduced transaction costs and facilitated business expansion. Also in 1993, the government established Thailand's first credit-rating agency, the Thailand Rating and Information Service (TRIS). This agency helped to promote the issuing of bonds and other debt instruments of private companies and public enterprises to private and institutional investors.

Finally, liberalization also allowed Thai banks and non-banks greater access to international financial markets for funds. In March 1993, an offshore banking center, the Bangkok International Banking Facilities (BIBF) was established, (1) to facilitate the growth of international banking business in Thailand by encouraging foreign-currency denominated bank loans into Thailand (out–in loans) to meet the funding needs of Thai firms and to finance domestic infrastructure development, and (2) to attract foreign banks with international reputation, technology and know-how to Bangkok in order to introduce more competition into the banking system and to transform Bangkok into a major financial center that could rival Hong Kong and Singapore. In February 1994, all foreign exchange restrictions related to outward direct investment and travel expenditures were removed. Given the fact that Thailand's capital account was fully open on the inflow side and there were no restrictions on foreign borrowing by the private sector, the creation of the BIBF led to rapid expansion in the number of financial institutions that could borrow and lend in foreign currencies, both on- and offshore. The government granted generous incentives to BIBF operations.

These included reduction in corporate income taxes from 30 per cent to 10 per cent, exemptions from specific sales taxes, exemptions from special business tax (including municipal tax), exemptions from stamp duties, reduction of withholding tax on interest on foreign loans for countries without double-taxation agreements with Thailand from 15 to 10 per cent, and exemptions from taxation on the permanent establishment of offices in Thailand (BOT 1998, 18). On top of all this, the facility enabled Thai investors to borrow in foreign currency at rates lower than the domestic interest rate.[21] Thai businesses shifted their foreign borrowing from loans to BIBF, and some capital inflows, particulary from Japan, were rebooked under the BIBF category so as to gain access to tax privileges, and then lend at low rates to Thai institutions through the BIBF. Overall, the establishment of the BIBF greatly helped to expand the volume of foreign bank loans into Thailand.

Initially, 46 BIBF licences were granted to 15 Thai banks, 11 foreign banks that already had branches in Thailand and 20 new banks from overseas. By December 1996, 49 banks had been granted BIBF licenses, including Thai commercial banks and foreign banks with and without local branches in Thailand (BOT 1998, 18). While BIBF banks were allowed foreign investment in Thai securities markets, and permitted to engage in other standard offshore banking activities such as loan syndication and foreign-exchange transactions in third-country currencies, the Thai authorities would have liked the BIBF to generate a balance between out–out and out–in activities. However, as it turned out, a large part of the BIBF activities was in "out–in" transactions – or borrowing from abroad and lending domestically. As Blustein (2001, 59–60) notes, "the officials who concocted the BIBFs evidently assumed that much of the money would be relent outside of the country; instead, most of it ended up being lent to Thai businesses and converted into baht."

Predictably, the BIBF's out–in transactions doubled in the first year of its operation, from 197 billion baht in 1993 to 456.6 billion baht in 1994 to 1.4 trillion baht in 1997 (BOT 1998a, 12). Initially, this expansion in part reflected a shift in FDI to BIBF lending as intra-company loans (a component of FDI) were replaced by BIBF loans, thus indicating a rebooking of FDI through BIBF. However, as BIBFs were permitted to lend in virtually unlimited amounts to residents, their lending exposures grew rapidly. This was especially the case with the new BIBFs, which believed that volume growth would qualify them for an upgrade to a full-branch status. In January 1995, the authorities further expanded the offshore banking business by granting 37 licences for the Provincial International Banking Facilities (PIBF) to 22 commercial banks in order for them to operate outside the greater Bangkok area. Just prior to the crisis, 30 PIBF offices were already in operation in the 5 provinces: Chiang Mai in the Northern region, Chonburi and Rayong in the Eastern region, Ayutthaya in the Central region and Songkhla in the Southern region. It should be noted that while the PIBF's and the BIBF's funding had to be from overseas, the PIBF could extend credit in both baht and in foreign currencies, but the BIBF could only extend credit in foreign currencies (BOT 1998, 18–19).

As was noted earlier, all these changes helped to deepen significantly Thailand's financial system (given the country's level of income), besides causing a rapid growth in the domestic money supply. The ratio of M2 to GDP increased from 62.2 per cent in 1987 to 74.7 per cent in 1992 to 79.5 per cent in 1996.[22] Even more impressive, the ratio of M3 to GDP rose from 73.2 per cent in 1987 to 107.6 per cent in 1996 – reflecting a more active role of finance companies and *crédit fonciers* in tapping domestic savings.[23] Moreover, the liberalization of the capital account coupled with the liberalization of interest rates in 1992 led to a lending boom. Total credit outstanding grew on average 22 per cent per annum in real terms over 1985 to 1996. The loan portfolio of finance companies grew at an even faster pace – on average 30 per cent in real terms per annum (Alba *et al.* 1999, 26).

Thailand's adoption of such market-friendly measures promoted massive capital inflows. Domestic borrowers were only too eager to borrow offshore, because the lower interest rates made such borrowing cheaper. Domestic corporate borrowers discovered that they could borrow at an interest rate of 5 per cent to 8 per cent instead of paying more than 13 per cent when borrowing domestically.[24] They could earn money simply by borrowing from abroad and depositing baht in Thailand. Domestic borrowers saw none of the problems that a strategy such as Thailand's fixed exchange-rate policy (which encouraged foreign borrowing denominated in US dollars) carried, as it gave the impression of carrying little or no exchange risk. In the absence of a well-developed domestic debt market, the stability of the baht exchange rate together with lower interest rates abroad encouraged Thai investors to tap foreign funds aggressively and without hedging, and then to speculate in local real estate, securities and other baht-denominated assets. For external investors, Thailand's exchange-rate stability (given the fact that the baht was pegged to the dollar) and booming growth rates offered a profitable venue for interest arbitrage and speculation. As Gilpin (2000, 145) notes, "anticipating strong economic growth and believing that their investments were secure, foreign banks, hedge funds, and other financial institutions were only too delighted to flood Thailand and other emerging markets with money."

Beginning in the late 1980s, foreign direct investment increased dramatically. From annual rates of inflow varying between US$100 and US$400 million over the previous fifteen years, the annual rate of inflow rose more than fivefold, to over US$2 billion per year, and remained at roughly these levels over the next eight years. In fact, between 1988 and 1996 Thailand was the recipient of the largest capital inflows relative to GDP in the world. According to the Bank of Thailand, between 1988 and 1996 Thailand received a staggering cumulative amount of US$100.3 billion, about 55 per cent of

1996 GDP, or 9.4 per cent of GDP on average per annum. Between 1987 and 1990, inflows increased to some US$11.1 billion. In 1994, but especially in 1995, capital inflows surged to over US$21 billion, but declined sharply in 1996 (Alba *et al.* 1999, 21). Banks and finance companies not only played the key role in intermediating the capital inflows, they also borrowed heavily (in US dollars and yen) in the world interbank market, to a total of some US$69 billion by June 1997.[25] Of this, about US$46 billion was in maturities of between 30 days and one year, although the reported official foreign exchange reserves stood at US$31 billion – of which (as we now know) a substantial fraction had already been committed to the forward market (Cooper 1999, 19). Also, many Thai firms who could not directly access overseas capital markets were now able to borrow from BIBF Thai banks. As a result, foreign bank loans through the BIBF soared from US$8 billion in 1993 (its first year of operation) to US$50 billion in 1996 (Alba *et al.* 1999, 23). Indeed, according to the World Bank, the Thai economy was transformed from one that was "partially integrated" in 1985–87 to one of the most integrated emerging market economies by 1994 (Alba *et al.* 1999, 3).

## Capital inflows and policy responses

Such massive inflows of foreign capital carry important macroeconomic implications. Under fixed exchange-rate regimes rapid capital inflows can be inflationary, as prices of domestic tradeables are bid up in the wake of capital surges. Emerging economies may have difficulty allocating the capital to productive uses. Massive surges of inflows may quickly enlarge the current account deficit and aggravate the balance-of-payments problem. As economic theory maintains, financial liberalization means more competition, and ideally a more efficient use of funds; but it also reduces the ability of monetary authorities to adjust interest rates. Domestic interest rates become subject to international market fluctuations, while new financial instruments mean that monetary aggregates such as M2 reflect the actual state of the economy less accurately.

In the case of Thailand in 1994, M2 growth fell to 12.9 per cent per year from its previous rate of 18.4 per cent – although both inflation and the current account deficit were on the rise, from 5.6 per cent of GDP in 1994 to 8.0 per cent in 1995 and 8.5 per cent in 1996 (Vajragupta and Vichyanond 1999, 52). Indeed, the Thai monetary authorities were aware of the growing problem. For instance, the Bank of Thailand in its 1993 Annual Report noted that "with increased capital flows and the resulting volatility in the financial markets caused by monetary conditions abroad, it is important that the authorities maintain a cautious approach in their formulation of monetary policy" (BOT 1994, 8). Again, the 1994 Annual Report (BOT

1995a, 7) noted that "high credit growth was recorded in 1994, made possible by the increased use of foreign capital by the banking system. Therefore, to ensure that domestic demand does not rise too rapidly, commercial bank credit should grow at a more moderate pace in 1995. At the same time, commercial banks and finance companies should ensure that credit is channeled to productive uses and not to luxury consumption or speculative ventures." Moreover, as the Mexican peso crisis in 1994 had illustrated, maintaining a fixed exchange-rate policy once the capital account is opened is imprudent, since the reserves of foreign exchange are finite. In fact, in their comprehensive study, Warr and Nidhiprabha (1996) warned of the dangers inherent in Thailand's program of capital market liberalization in combination with a fixed exchange rate. They explicitly warned that, if capital market liberalization was to be maintained, Thailand would require a more flexible-exchange rate system. Of course, there was a failure to respond effectively to such warnings.

The sheer magnitude of capital inflow exceeded all expectations, forcing Thailand's monetary authorities to respond quickly to too much of a good thing. Cognizant of the fact that massive inflows of short-term capital or hot money have destabilizing side-effects, such as rapid monetary expansion, an excessive rise in aggregate demand, inflationary pressures, an appreciation of the real exchange rate (which can result in the loss of export competitiveness and give rise to inflation), and a widening current account, the Thai monetary authorities introduced a number of measures aimed at discouraging such inflows and influencing the maturity structure of banks' foreign borrowing.[26] Specifically, given the limited policy options, the authorities attempted to cope with capital inflows through a combination of monetary, prudential and market-based capital control measures.

To slow credit growth, restrict short-term capital inflows and reduce the inflationary impact of the inflows, the Bank of Thailand raised the policy rate in March 1995 and extended the coverage of the credit plan to include larger finance companies and the BIBF banks. A maximum credit-to-deposit ratio was also introduced to restrict banks from extending loans requiring foreign borrowing. In August 1995 the authorities began to introduce restrictions on capital inflows. Effective from August 8, 1995 the minimum amount on foreign borrowing on the BIBF was increased from 500,000 baht to 2 million baht to shake out small borrowers. Commercial banks were required to deposit at the Bank of Thailand (with no interest) 7 per cent of their non-resident baht deposits with a maturity of under one year. Also, reporting requirements were imposed for short foreign-currency positions. This measure, aimed explicitly at increasing the cost of raising short-term deposits from abroad, led to lower rates for short-term non-resident deposits. On April 4, 1996 the measure was extended to finance companies. In a measure effective from June 23, 1996 non-resident baht accounts with less than a one-year maturity and all commercial banks, BIBF, and finance companies were required to deposit (with no interest), at the Bank of Thailand 7 per cent of their new short-term external borrowing or deposits from abroad, both in baht and in foreign currencies. This measure was aimed at influencing the maturity structure of foreign borrowing by banks to shift it from short- to longer-term maturities (BOT 1998a, 24–6). In terms of the BOT's prudential measures, supervision of financial institutions was progressively strengthened to guard against systemic risk. For example, the capital-to-risk asset ratio of commercial banks was raised from 8 per cent to 8.5 per cent in October 1996, while that of finance companies was raised from 7 per cent to 7.5 per cent in January 1997 (BOT 1998b, 17). The authorities even resorted to moral suasion by seeking cooperation from commercial banks, and licensed the BIBF to lengthen the maturity of their borrowing, especially through the BIBF.

Yet these measures were not very effective. Although they somewhat reduced the profitability of the BIBF transactions, they did not reduce the size of the capital inflows. As BIBF loans became more expansive, large corporations shifted to direct foreign borrowing. Also, as the BOT (1998) observed in hindsight, while the measures succeeded in somewhat slowing the relative share of short-term capital inflows, they could not take care of the misallocation of resources – in particular, the lending to unproductive sectors and sectors with no foreign-exchange earnings potential to service the foreign currency loans.[27] Part of the problem stemmed from the fact that, despite a widening current account deficit, the Bank of Thailand repeatedly stated its commitment to the official rate of exchange. This exchange-rate policy had two primary effects. The first was a loss in international competitiveness that stemmed from the choice of the peg. The second was heightened borrowing from abroad, which was encouraged by the implicit guarantee of an exchange-rate parity. With the exchange rate assumed to be fixed (after all, the rate had been tied for so long to the US dollar), many market participants ignored the exchange-rate risk and took advantage of the lower interest rates on offshore loans and significantly increased their borrowing from such sources. As was noted earlier, this option was greatly helped by the establishment of the BIBF – which loosened regulations on foreign borrowing by Thai banks. Assuming that the exchange-rate regime would be maintained, firms undertook large, unhedged positions. Finally, as Nidhiprabha and Warr (2000, 106) note, "these measures [BOT's response] were not quantity restrictions. They simply imposed higher costs on foreign borrowing. But these policy responses to capital inflows were too lenient and too late to stop huge inflows to the private sector. Both banks and non-bank corporations were already highly leveraged with unhedged short-term foreign liabilities."

It is important to note that the BOT, by indirectly encouraging short-term borrowing by non-bank financial institutions, greatly exacerbated the macroeconomic imbalance. First, the entry of foreign banks with the establishment of the BIBF increased competition for prime customers such as multinationals – who were attracted by the lower cost of funds on the BIBF. This increased competition squeezed the lending margins of the domestic banks, forcing them to move into more lucrative, but also more risky activities – a shift that was facilitated by the relaxation of the regulations governing the permissible activities of banks. Second, for many years before the crisis, banking licences in Thailand had been a highly profitable business. Since the issuance of new licences was tightly controlled by the BOT, Thai finance companies competed aggressively with one another to be selected. They were impelled to engage in this activity because, compared to commercial banks, finance companies had a greater incentive to lend, because to do so would send a signal to the Bank of Thailand that their credit portfolios were large enough to be awarded the much-coveted banking license. Hence, in order to project themselves as important players in the domestic financial market, many finance companies were willing to borrow large sums abroad and lend domestically at low margins – thereby taking risks they would not ordinarily take. By the end of 1996, Thai banks and finance companies had become gravely exposed to credit risk and maturity mismatches. In time, such risks would cost them dearly.

One common policy measure that a central bank can use to cope with excessive inflows of foreign capital is *sterilization*. In a successful sterilization operation, the domestic component of the monetary base (bank reserves plus currency) is reduced to offset the reserve inflow, at least temporarily. In theory, this can be achieved in several ways: by encouraging private investment overseas and by allowing foreign investors to borrow from the local market. However, the conventional form of sterilization has been through the use of open-market operations via the selling of Treasury Bills and other such instruments to reduce the domestic component of the monetary base. In practice, however, such operations can be self-defeating, as they may raise domestic interest rates and stimulate even greater capital inflows. In Thailand (and other crisis-hit Asian countries), the monetary authorities made some attempt to sterilize capital inflows as a means of limiting the growth of domestic credit. In particular, the monetary measures included the conventional form of sterilized intervention (designed to offset the effect of reserve inflows on the monetary base by open market sales of domestic securities), increases in reserve requirements (designed to limit the impact of reserve inflows on the growth of monetary aggregates by reducing the money multiplier), shifting of government deposits from commercial banks to the central bank, and an increase in the discount rate, or otherwise a greater limit on the discount window, moral suasion and credit controls. Indeed, during the period of heavy capital outflows during late 1996 to May 1997, foreign-exchange market intervention was carried out by the Bank of Thailand to defend the currency peg. The BOT intervened not only to manipulate the local exchange market, but also offshore spot and forward exchanges markets, including those in Singapore and Hong Kong.

However, lacking the depth of markets in government securities, Thailand (and other crisis-hit Asian central banks) supplemented operations in government securities by issuing their own debt instruments. In 1987, the BOT began to issue short-term BOT bonds with maturities of 6 months to one year. But, given the fact that the BOT's main goal was to sterilize the inflows effects on the domestic money supply, domestic interest rates were increased, despite the fixed exchange rate and the increased openness of the capital market. However, as has been noted, such operations typically entail costs to the central bank, owing to differentials between the cost of issuing securities and the return on foreign assets, not to mention the fact that sterilization operations tend to attract further inflows, as they tend to keep interest rates high. Indeed, in Thailand, where sterilization took place amidst a liberalized environment, there was very little to prevent capital inflows, including short-term foreign investment – which entered the country in surges in response to the increased rate of return. Thus, in raising interest rates Thailand was simply providing an impetus for further capital flows, since the latter were very responsive to interest arbitrage opportunities. Moreover (as was noted earlier), the high domestic interest rates, together with the commitment of the baht–dollar exchange rate, made it much cheaper for Thai businesses to borrow foreign loans at lower costs than they could borrow domestically. The BIBF license-holders could borrow dollars and still make a tidy profit re-lending the dollars to local borrowers at lower rates than those of baht loans. As Boskin (1998, 3) notes, "Thai bankers were borrowing at 6 per cent in dollars and lending at 12 per cent in baht ... what a moneymaking machine, so long as the value of the baht relative to the dollar stayed constant." As investor perceptions regarding Thailand strengthened during this period, capital inflows became more sensitive to the measured interest-rate differential. For example, the BOT's efforts to slow an overheated economy by raising interest rates in 1995 caused foreign borrowing to grow even more rapidly.

The high rate of capital flows was reflected in Thailand's skyrocketing external debt, which more than tripled from US$29 billion in 1990 to US$94 billion by mid-1997. In relative terms, total debt outstanding jumped from 34 per cent of GDP in 1990 to 59 per cent of GDP by mid-1997. This rapidly increasing debt not only distorted the current savings–investment gap, but also increased future debt-service obligations. Indeed, the debt-service proportion of Thailand's current account deficit grew from 37 per cent in 1990 to 50 per cent in 1996. Moreover, the bulk of the debt was private – which can negatively impact on the current account, because private debts are generally charged at higher interest rates and have shorter maturities. Also, much of the private debt was incurred by the non-bank sector, because Thai commercial banks were subject to limitations on their net foreign-exchange positions.[28] Non-bank private external debt was not only large, but also rapidly growing, from 51 per cent of external debt outstanding in 1990 to 72 per cent in mid-1997. Likewise, the *short-term* portion of the debt jumped from 22 per cent in 1990 to 50 per cent in 1995–96 – that is, the outstanding short-term Thai debt totaled US$45 billion out of the US$90 billion of total external debt in 1995–96. This put both individual borrowers and the country at risk of a liquidity shortage should creditors (mostly foreign) decide not to roll over maturing debt (Vajragupta and Vichyanond 1999, 56–7).

### Export slowdown and risky investments

There were also growing problems in the tradeables sector. Export manufacturers faced increasing bottlenecks in the availability of complementary domestic inputs, especially with respect to skilled labor and transportation facilities. This contributed to the growing problem of inflation. In both Thailand and Malaysia, the worsening transportation and communication bottlenecks added to the growing production costs, while the tightening labor markets and the resultant rise in real wages led to a decline in the countries' competitiveness in labor-intensive export industries. By the early 1990s, the era of cheap labor was over. As the supply of surplus agricultural labor ran out, the tighter labor market pushed up wages, without commensurate increases in labor productivity.[29] In Thailand, for example, "over the thirteen years from 1982 to 1994, real wages increased by 70%, but this increase was heavily concentrated in the years after 1990. Over the years 1982 to 1990 the compound average annual rate of increase was 2%, but over the following four years to 1994 the real wage increased at an average rate of over 9%" (Warr 1998, 57). This, coupled with rapid growth in demand for imported inputs in both the tradeables and non-tradeables sectors, led to a growing current account deficit.

These input-related production problems were compounded by the financial sector problems rooted in the effective pegging of the baht (and other regional currencies) to the strengthening US dollar. The 1987 Plaza Accord brought down the value of the US dollar and ushered in a new era of the appreciating yen. Between 1985 and 1988, the yen almost doubled in value *vis-à-vis* the dollar and other Asian currencies tied to the dollar. More broadly, by 1988, the yen was almost 30 per cent above its average for the 1980–85 period on an inflation-adjusted, trade-weighted basis. By the mid-1990s, the era of the strong yen was over, with the sharp appreciation of the dollar in 1995, and especially its appreciation *vis-à-vis* the yen. As the dollar rose relative to the yen, the currencies of the countries tied to the dollar (like Thailand) rose in comparison with the yen also.[30] In the case of Thailand, since the US dollar carried the greatest weight in the basket, the movement of the baht–dollar rate was negatively related to the strength of the dollar against other major currencies. The appreciation of the yen against the dollar in early 1995 caused appreciation of the baht against the dollar. In fact, the process of real appreciation that was set in motion in the early 1990s gained renewed momentum in 1995 with the depreciation of the yen relative to the US dollar – meaning that any currency pegged to the dollar would suffer a real appreciation. Although the baht had edged down by about 4 per cent against the dollar in the two years leading up to the July 2, 1997 devaluation, its real effective exchange rate (trade-weighted) had appreciated by about 15 per cent over the same period. This largely reflected its sharp appreciation of approximately 35 per cent against the yen. As a result, Asian countries that had pegged their currencies loosely to the dollar suffered a sharp slowdown in exports on the back of the weakening yen. With higher yen (and deutsche mark) weights on Thai imports than exports, the April 1995 fall in the US dollar (which accounted for the largest weighting in the baht peg) induced import prices to rise faster than export prices. As Tan (2000, 62) notes, "by 1996, the baht was about 10 per cent above its 1990 value relative to the US dollar. This made Thai exports increasingly uncompetitive in world markets." Thus, as the dollar rebounded in mid-1995, Thailand's fixed-rate system started to work inexorably against the country's exports.

Specifically, Thailand, which had seen its exports soar to the unprecedented rate of 22.2 per cent in dollar terms in 1994, followed by an even higher growth rate of 24.7 per cent in 1995, saw its export growth decelerate sharply to 1.9 per cent and 0.2 per cent in dollar and baht terms respectively in 1996 (Nidhiprabha 1999, 70). During 1997–98, Thailand's average export unit value fell by about 17 per cent – significantly more than the 11 per cent decline in world average prices of manufactures and non-fuel commodities (weighted by Thailand's exports). Prices of agricultural products fell by 34 per cent during the same two-year period, largely reflecting the decline in world commodity prices. Since Thailand has been more of an "Asian-centric" exporter, the depressed Asian markets greatly affected its export earnings (IMF 2000, 75). The appreciation of the real exchange rate not only resulted in Thai exports losing their competitiveness, but also meant that direct investments from Japan slowed down, depriving Thailand of the long-term investments that were crucial sources of innovation and productivity growth. Also, as was noted earlier, the exchange-rate policy of pegging to a basket of currencies in which the dollar was weighted heavily heldback the government from allowing the baht to depreciate against the dollar at a faster rate to stimulate exports. In fact, by preventing the nominal exchange rate from departing significantly from the central peg (in particular, by preventing the exchange rate from appreciating), the policy resulted in a fairly predictable nominal exchange rate, which reduced the foreign-exchange risk faced by investors and increased the incentives for domestic residents to incur unhedged, short-term foreign debt.[31]

Since the net inflows of capital greatly increased the supply of money in circulation, Thai financial institutions (flush with capital) engaged in an orgy of lending. According to an IMF study, total credit outstanding grew on average 22 per cent per annum in real terms between 1988 and 1995. The loan portfolio of finance companies grew at an even faster rate – on average 30 per cent in real terms per annum, as against 20 per cent for commercial banks over the same period. This is hardly surprising, since finance companies specialized in lending to Thai consumers and businesses on easy terms (with low interest rates and little money down), in some of the economy's hottest areas, such as real estate and purchases of stock on margin.[32] Under such circumstances, loan growth outpaced the growth of GDP 1.8 times on average and 2.3 times in the case of finance companies (Alba *et al.* 1999, 26). In the immediate period before the crisis, from 1995 through to the end of 1996, the growth rate of real private credit averaged above 15 per cent, or twice the rate of real GDP growth. In their competition for clients, commercial banks and finance companies extended credit at a rapid pace, averaging above 10 per cent and 20 per cent respectively on an annual basis (IMF 2000, 47). Much of the credit was extended imprudently – without proper review of the client's creditworthiness or the soundness of the proposed investments. Jeffrey Sachs (1997) notes that:

> Banks and near-banks – such as Thailand's now notorious financial trusts – became intermediaries for channeling foreign capital into the domestic economy. The trouble is that the newly liberalized banks and near-banks often operate under highly distorted incentives. Under-capitalized banks have incentives to borrow abroad and invest domestically with reckless abandon. If the lending works out, the bankers make money. If the lending fails, the depositors and creditors stand to lose money, but the bank's owners bear little risk themselves because they have little capital tied up in the bank.

The BIBFs, whose "out–in" lending was entirely foreign-currency denominated, expanded credit at the fastest pace, recording average annual growth rates of over 35 per cent (IMF 2000, 47). This outcome was quite different from the original intent of the BIBF – to establish Thailand as a regional banking center and serve as an intermediary between offshore lenders and borrowers. On the contrary, the BIBF ended up unintentionally serving as a conduit for local firms vastly to expand their loans from foreign banks. However, borrowing via BIBF considerably enlarged the short-term portion of Thailand's external debts, as most BIBF credits were on a short-term basis. Not surprisingly, short-term debt liabilities rapidly outgrew the country's foreign-exchange reserves. Worse still, corporations invested these funds in risky ventures with inflated project costs and optimistic revenue projections. In many sectors, growth in assets outstripped sales and profit growth. For example, while some of the foreign loans were invested in a wide range of manufacturing industries (for example, steel and petrochemicals), in which there was a growing world over-supply, much of this money went into the unproductive non-tradeable sector, in particular, into property construction and real estate – commercial as well as residential property. Assets in the property sector grew by 115 per cent during 1993–96 as profits declined by 69 per cent (Nabi and Shivakumar 2001, 14). Greatly compounding the problem was the fact that such investments were not generating the foreign-exchange earnings to service the foreign borrowing.[33] Rather, "greater access to funding prompted many real estate companies to enlarge their land banks, invest in speculative and unproductive purchases such as vacant land, initiate projects without seeking adequate information on market conditions and demand, and subsequently become highly engaged in projects with inferior risk-return trade off" (BOT 1998b, 8). On the demand side, the facts that interest payments on housing loans were tax-deductible up to 7,000 baht per year; that commercial banks were encouraged to extend more housing loans to middle- and low-income earners; and that the limit of foreign ownership in condominiums was raised from 25 per cent to 40 per cent fueled investments in property and real estate (BOT 1998b, 90). Inevitably, "as a result of the rapid buildup of assets, Thailand had one of the highest ratios of capital to output among the middle-income countries" (Nabi and Shivakumar 2001, 14).

Between 1986 and 1990, the construction sector expanded on average by 14.9 per cent per annum, and land prices soared 3–4 times within 7–8 years (BOT 1998b, 15). At the end of 1997, real-estate related wealth in Bangkok stood at 2.2 trillion baht, equivalent to about 45 per cent of GDP and greater than the total capitalization of the country's stock exchange of an estimated 1.1 trillion baht. In the residential sector, the number of housing units in greater Bangkok increased by some 1.25 million between 1988 to 1997 – raising the vacancy rate to around 14 per cent in 1997. At the height of the recession in 1998, the number of new vacant housing units stood at 350,000, a vacancy rate of 28 per cent (Nabi and Shivakumar 2001, 13). In the commercial sector rapid increases in office space construction (even though the price of office space had peaked in 1991), led to an increase in the vacancy rate to around 20 per cent before the crisis (IMF 2000, 5). According to one account, in the Bangkok CBD (Central Business District), completed first-grade office space "was less than 1.5 million square meters in 1991. By the end of 1997, total supply had quadrupled to 6 million square meters, with nearly 2 million of those located in the CBD. Around 900,000 square meters of office space were added to the stock each year for three consecutive years up to 1995 . . . Between 1991 and 1997, an average of 360,000 square meters of shopping area were added to the city [Bangkok] every year" (Renaud 2000, 189). Similarly, Blustein (2001, 57) notes that "the most spectacular real estate boondoggle was a $1 billion-plus development on the city's [Bangkok's] outskirts called Maung Thong Thani Estate, which was designed to house hundreds of thousands of people and included high-rise condominium buildings, townhouses, retail shops, and a sports complex. Sales were abysmal, and with weeds growing high amid the unoccupied buildings, the desperate developer – allegedly a major contributor to the ruling party – furiously lobbied for government deals to move Parliament and part of the Defense Ministry onto the property." In fact, over-expansion resulted in over-supply, creating a classic "bubble economy" – where real-estate prices continued to rise well beyond levels justified by the productivity of the assets. As Lester Thurow (1998, 22) notes, "Bangkok, a city whose per capita productivity is about one twelfth that of San Francisco, should not have land values that are much higher than those of San Francisco. But it did – as did other Southeast Asian cities. Grossly inflated property values had to come down." However, as long as the prices continued to rise existing investors were rewarded and collateral was created for new loans to finance further investment – until the inevitable bursting of the bubble. Indeed, when the investments went sour, bad loans proliferated as interest rates on debt rose sharply, while occupancy rates and rental fees fell rapidly. The worst part was that most of these loans were denominated in foreign currency (about US$49 billion at the end of 1997 – equivalent to 33 per cent of GDP), with usually no hedging against currency depreciation. The bursting of the bubble destroyed many of the companies that had undertaken real-estate construction, and others who had provided the finance.

According to one study, in spring 1996 approximately 54 per cent of the outstanding property credit originated from banks and 46 per cent from finance companies. To put it bluntly, the Thai banking and financial sector now faced the problem of both exchange-rate risk and domestic default. Specifically, the increased level of bank's foreign indebtedness relative to the lending base of the banks increased their exposure to exchange-rate risk, and the increased level of bank credit to GDP increased their exposure to domestic contraction. While weak domestic financial intermediation and poor corporate governance of Thai banks have been widely blamed for their difficulties, it was the increased exposure of the Thai banks that was primarily the reason behind their problems – something that could not have been corrected by tighter supervision alone.

## The gradual meltdown

The continually rising value of the baht created major problems. By mid-1996, Thailand's current-account deficit had reached 8.5 per cent of GDP – much of which was financed by large inflows of short-term portfolio investment and foreign loans. In fact, Thailand's current account deficit was at the same level that was responsible for the Mexican peso crisis in 1994.

Also, as was noted earlier, the export growth-rate had plummeted to virtually zero in 1996. This combination of widening current account deficit, export slowdown (while imports continued to grow), the worsening debt situation and currency appreciation caused widespread expectation that the central bank could not defend the baht much longer. As foreign investors became concerned over Thailand's ability to repay its huge foreign debt, they began to move their money out of the country. By the second quarter of 1996 the considerable appreciation of the baht against non-US currencies induced active speculation, as the non-resident baht account (NRB) became heavily used by foreigners as a means of speculative transactions. It was now a matter of time before more sustained speculative attacks would begin.

The attack came in several waves: first on May 10, 1996, when the country's ninth-largest commercial bank, the Bangkok Bank of Commerce (BBC) collapsed (despite the massive injections of liquidity by the BOT), under the weight of non-performing property loans that totaled nearly half its US$7.2 billion of assets (*Economist* 1996, 77). Though the BBC was run by a well-connected former central bank official, Krikkiat Jalichandra, it came to public light "that the central bank knew in 1993 that nearly 40 per cent of BBC's total assets consisted of nonperforming loans, many of which consisted of loans to Krikkiat's associates, other bank insiders, and influential politicians to finance speculation in real estate and corporate takeovers. Yet the central bank had refrained from taking any serious enforcement actions" (Blustein 2001, 57–8). While the collapse of the Bangkok Bank of Commerce was the result of gross mismanagement and fraud, the government's decision to bail out depositors, creditors and shareholders of the failed bank, and its reluctance to prosecute those responsible, sent a bad signal to the financial community. Compounding this, rumors in Hong Kong about an imminent baht devaluation in response to the large debt, mounting current account deficit and poor export performance only served to further fuel the attack. Foreign investors began by selling baht for dollars, causing a serious liquidity shortage in the domestic money market. Speculation against the baht took the form of direct position-taking in the forward market, which created downward pressure on the forward rate, and use of explicit baht credits, which, when converted into foreign currency, created a short position on the baht. Foreign speculators sold baht for dollars in the Hong Kong market, while many Thai banks borrowed heavily from money markets to purchase dollars, sending the interbank rate up to 25 per cent. Thus, the conversion of baht credit into foreign currency represented a capital outflow, placing downward pressure on the spot exchange rate.

To defend the baht, besides periodically denying devaluation rumors and making written commitments not to devalue the baht, the BOT also raised short-term interest rates and intervened heavily in the market, bringing billions of baht forward. In particular, the BOT took the unprecedented step of intervening in Singapore and Hong Kong by selling dollars in the forward markets, where some commercial banks were speculating on the baht/dollar exchange rate by dumping baht for dollars. On August 1, 1996 alone, the BOT spent some half a billion US dollars from its international reserves to defend the baht. Of course, *ipso facto*, this resulted in a decline in reserves and/or increase in the central bank's forward commitment. Moreover, commercial banks were advised to refrain from accommodating foreign speculators' demand for foreign exchange, and the onshore and offshore foreign-exchange markets were split, with credit restrictions imposed upon non-residents. The resultant domestic credit squeeze reduced asset prices and collateral values and increased the levels of non-performing loans. This only served to put additional pressure on the already weak financial institutions, and several more finance companies collapsed. Nevertheless, the BOT's intervention pacified the market as "market participants perceived that if the BOT were planning to devalue the baht it would not favor speculators by cheapening the cost of speculation. Confidence in the baht was restored because of the swift and massive intervention in offshore markets where daily transactions tripled the size of domestic foreign transactions" (Nidhiprabha 1998, 207).

However, this was just a lull. With large and rapidly increasing short-term debts, shrinking foreign reserves, and an exchange rate that was pegged within a narrow range of around 25 baht to the US dollar, the baht remained a prime target for currency speculators. Indeed, the second wave of attack occurred in December 1996, as more than half the 500 companies on the stock exchange reported declining earnings, and rumors of a currency devaluation spread. This prompted withdrawal of investments out of Thailand. However, quick stabilization of the baht through direct market intervention, coupled with announcement of a substantial budget cut, helped to restore foreign investor confidence – as reflected in the renewal of inflows in early January 1997. However, this was short-lived. In February 1997, one of Thailand's largest finance companies, Finance One, found itself in deep trouble.[34] Burdened with a huge debt (Finance One had borrowed about US$600 million from abroad), excess exposure to sectors sensitive to the asset-price inflation of the 1990s, and weak underlying capitalization made Finance One (and other finance companies) particularly vulnerable to the slow-down in economic activity and asset-price decline that began in mid-1996. By early 1997, "Finance companies were saddled with $4.8 billion in margin loans to stock investors, many of which couldn't be repaid" (Blustein 2001, 57). To save it from collapse, the Finance Institutions Development Fund (FIDF) was forced to inject 40 billion baht into Finance One, besides ordering it to merge with Thailand's twelfth largest commercial bank, Thai Danu Bank, to overcome the sharp liquidity crunch.[35] On March 3, 1997, Finance One was dissolved and merged into Thai Danu. The BOT also made public the names of nine finance and one *crédit foncier* company (or housing loans broker) facing similar difficulties with high exposure to property loans, and ordered these companies to raise their registered capital. All this seemed to further aggravate market instability.

However, the attacks, the most intense yet, started again in mid-February 1997, when the Somprasong Land Company failed to make a US$3.1 million interest payment on its Euro-convertible debentures owing to cash-flow constraints caused by conditions in the Thai property market.[36] The market appeared to be convinced that a depreciation of the baht was imminent. To fight off the speculative pressure and to preserve the integrity of the exchange rate system (and thereby maintain investors confidence), the BOT had to intervene heavily to keep the baht exchange rate within the EEF's band. Moreover, domestic liquidity was tightened, sending overnight interbank rates to as high as 30 per cent from the 9–15 per cent at the beginning of the year. Yet, the pressure on the baht continued unabated. Foreign exchange reserves which stood at roughly US$40 billion in the third quarter of 1996 had fallen to US$38 billion at the end of February 1997. However, the government had also incurred forward obligations amounting to over US$12 billion. This meant that the net foreign exchange reserves had fallen from US$40 billion to US$26 billion (BOT 1998a, 26–8).

With the bursting of the property bubble following the Somprasong Land Company's dramatic default, excess capacity was prominently visible in the real estate markets, especially in Bangkok. This was followed by the rapid decline of the SET index. On March 3, 1997, the Thai government, for the first time in the SET's 20-year history, suspended trading on the stock exchange for all banking and finance companies' shares. To reassure jittery investors, the Finance Minister Amnuay Viravan and the BOT governor Rerngchai Marakanond and deputy governor Chaiyawat Wibulswasdi went on national television to announce a series of measures to shore up banks and finance companies. Measures included higher reserve requirements for all financial institutions, capital mobilization for finance companies, and an increase in the liquidity of finance companies. They also permitted ten undercapitalized finance companies 60 days to increase their capital reserves.

In early April 1997, the government established the Property Loan Management Organization (PLMO) to deal with the property sector crisis by purchasing and managing property loans from financial institutions, thereby helping to ease pressure on their balance sheets. The funds for the PLMO were to be raised by issuing seven-year zero-coupon bonds guaranteed by the government.[37] However, this failed to prevent a further loss of confidence. Rather, as Arphasil (2001, 183) notes, it "translated into an increase in withdrawal of funds from other finance companies as well as smaller banks and deposit of them into larger domestic and foreign banks. This flight resulted in the build-up of excess liquidity in some institutions. Larger banks were reluctant to lend their liquidity to other financial institutions." Furthermore, the PLMO's limited funds and the fact that property loans eligible for purchase by the PLMO had to possess collateral and be able to repay the debt within 5 years made the PLMO operation limited, and as Lauridsen (1998, 148) notes, "ultimately a failure."[38] The final nail in the PLMO's coffin was the failure of the merger between Finance One and the Thai Danu Bank. As this merger, considered a "model for further mergers, collapsed in May, the strategy collapsed with it" (Lauridsen 1998, 148). Indeed, it can be argued that the government's weak response only served to increase investor anxiety. Not surprisingly, in late April and early May 1997 there was a run on deposits of finance companies. Domestically, the deposit withdrawal represented more a flight to quality, as households and businesses moved their savings out of finance companies and into the larger commercial banks. However, foreign investors now sensed that the government could not effectively deal with the property sector problems – not to mention their recognition that the exchange rate was misaligned and that a correction was overdue. It seemed that, at long last, investments and expectations that had been based on extrapolations of past perform-ance were now being based on a realistic assessments of actual demand and supply in goods and asset markets.

On May 7, 1997, Finance Minister Amnuay announced that Thailand would not be able to achieve a balanced budget for the year – as had been earlier promised. As DeRosa (2001, 93) notes, "the market took the news hard. The bank was immediately confronted with ferocious selling of the baht and their stocks." In response, the BOT decided to switch its inter-vention from spot foreign-exchange transactions to forward transactions, buying baht against dollars for value in three and six months. In hindsight, this was a fatal error, as the BOT was now exposed to the fate of its own currency. Since, the bank negotiated these forward contracts at off-market forward exchange rates (fearing that its presence in the foreign-exchange market would drive up Thai baht interest rates), speculators "thereby effect-ively received a subsidy from the bank to take short positions in the baht. Thanks to its own central bank, the baht turned into a true one-way bet for short sellers" (DeRosa 2001, 97).

During the second week of May 1997, in an all-out attack, international hedge funds, including Soros's Quantum Fund and traders at US financial institutions such as J. P. Morgan and Goldman-Sachs, took short positions in spot, forward and options markets, betting as much as US$10 billion on Thailand devaluing.[39] In return, on three different days, May 8, 13, and 14, the BOT used or committed US$6.1 billion, US$9.7 billion and US$10 billion respectively defending the baht's dollar peg – considered key to main-taining the confidence of foreign investors. However, this was to no avail. Blustein (2001, 70–71) notes that "May 14, 1997 was an unforgettable day for the top management of the Bank of Thailand . . . everyone panicked, and some even cried. On that day, the central bank threw $10 billion into the fray, using various markets, without beating back the speculators." Now having almost exhausted its reserves, the BOT desperately imposed selective capital controls (on May 15, 1997), prohibiting commercial bank lending on bahts to non-residents, and segmented the onshore and offshore foreign-exchange markets in order to make it more costly for offshore speculators to borrow the baht. More specifically, the BOT ordered all twenty-nine local and foreign banks in Thailand to refrain from and then altogether suspend (in early June 1997), transactions with non-residents that could facilitate a build-up of baht positions in the offshore market (including baht lending through swaps, outright forward transactions in baht and sales of baht against foreign currencies). Second, any purchase before maturity of baht-denominated bills of exchange and other debt instruments required payment in US dollars. Third, foreign equity investors were prohibited from repatriating funds in baht (but were free to repatriate funds in foreign currencies). Finally, non-residents were required to use the onshore exchange rate to convert baht proceeds from sales of stocks. All this meant that the baht would cease to flow outside Thailand, unless there was a genuine, trade-related reason such as payment for imports.

These measures effectively created a two-tier foreign exchange market: the onshore market, where there was normal supply of baht, and the offshore, where the baht was scarce. No doubt, these measures were clearly targeted at decoupling the onshore and offshore markets. The two-tier system attempted to deny non-residents without valid commercial or investment transactions in Thailand access to domestic credit needed to establish a net short domestic currency position, and to inflict punitive costs on speculators – while allowing non-speculative credit demand to be satisfied at normal market rates.[40] These measures reduced the volume of trading in Thailand's swap market, where foreign investors often buy and sell to hedge currency risks for investments in Thailand. It also temporarily ended speculative attacks on the baht by causing losses for speculators, as both onshore and offshore banks (in response to official pressure) segmented the two markets by refusing to provide short-term credit to speculators.[41] In particular, the banks' refusal to provide baht credit imposed a severe squeeze on offshore players who had acquired short baht positions during the speculative attacks and had to close their forward positions. As a result of the squeeze, offshore swap interest rates rose sharply relative to onshore rates. In fact, the offshore baht overnight interest rates rose to over 1,000 per cent (BOT 1998a, 25). This forced investors who had taken positions against the baht in expectation of a devaluation to unwind their forward positions at a loss. Thus, in the absence of extensive liquidation by domestic holders of baht positions, the authorities were able to withstand the pressures on the baht by relying on extensive application of the selective capital controls until early June.

However, as DeRosa (2001, 94) notes, while "the Bank of Thailand had won the battle, it was soon going to lose the war." After the initial shock about what the Bank had done faded, attention began to turn to whether the new two-tier market was stable. The major concern was the prospect of a baht devaluation. Now hedge funds were no longer the problem. Rather, it was the domestic borrowers, namely, Thai banks and corporations, that needed to acquire billions of dollars to pay their short-term debts that were falling due soon. Compounding the problem was the fact that foreign creditors (who had earlier lent willingly) were now demanding immediate repayment, besides refusing to extend further loans. By mid-June the pressures regained momentum as panicked local corporations continued to buy US dollars to hedge their foreign-exchange exposure. This resulted in a heavy loss of reserves through the EEF window. Concerns about the stability of the baht reached fever pitch on June 19 when the Finance Minister, Amnuay Viravan, resigned in a dispute over tax policy.[42] His replacement, the unknown Thanong Bidaya, who took up office on June 21, did not inspire confidence. This caused another wave of speculative activity, and the stock market suffered a large 11 per cent decline. By the end of June, Thailand's net foreign-exchange reserves stood at only US$2.8 billion – just 7 per cent of their late 1996 value (BOT 1998a).

On June 26, 1997, in an effort to stop further liquidity drain, the Bank of Thailand suspended for 30 days the operations of 16 finance companies (including Finance One) on the basis of their capital inadequacy and the need for liquidity. These 16 companies were required to submit rehabilitation plans to the Bank of Thailand by July 11. Companies that failed to submit plans, or whose plans were rejected by the BOT/Ministry of Finance, would have their licences revoked and be absorbed by Krung Thai Thanakit, a majority-government-owned finance company. Further, to reassure creditors and depositors and to avoid financial panic, the government stated that the remaining banks and finance companies were financially sound and all their credits and deposits would be guaranteed by the government. However, these measures failed to calm the markets, largely because there was increasing uncertainty over the exact extent of the guarantees, owing to inconsistencies in official statements. With inconsistencies among the various announcements unresolved, official assurances only heightened market apprehension. As rumors of an anticipated baht devaluation grew, this triggered a wave of capital outflows, as investors sought to liquidate short-term foreign debts or to speculate against the baht. The capital outflows resulted in a sharp drop in the Bank of Thailand's foreign-exchange reserves, in large part because more than US$23.4 billion out of almost US$39 billion of total international reserves was used to defend the baht. Moreover, it was disclosed that the BOT through the FIDF had extended more than 430 billion baht (or 10 per cent of GDP) to rescue debt-ridden finance companies (Lauridsen 1998, 148).

In the face of serious difficulties in rolling over short-term debt and a rapid depletion of net foreign-exchange reserves, it was only a matter of time before Thailand would be forced to float the baht. Yet "on July 1, 1997

Prime Minister Chavalit Yongchaiyudh announced that the baht would never be allowed to devalue" (Tan 2000, 66). Yet, in the face of a serious liquidity crisis, such claims could not be honored. In the early hours of July 2, 1997 "Bangkok's top bankers were awakened before dawn and summoned to a 6.30 a.m. meeting . . . the nervous group was told that the government was abandoning the baht's peg to the US dollar" (Chanda 1998, 8). When the markets eventually opened on the morning of July 2, 1997, the baht immediately depreciated by 18 per cent from Bt 24.5 to Bt 28.8 per US dollar, plunging the country into a serious recession.[43] In desperation, Prime Minister Chavalit secretly sent emissaries to Japan and China to request bilateral loans of hard currency – without success. In late July, the Thai authorities finally requested the IMF for assistance. As Phongpaichit and Baker (2001, 85) observe, "there was no significant voice raised in opposition. The IMF was tacitly welcomed as savior."

On August 14, 1997, after Thailand signed its first letter of intent with the IMF, the Thai government (now led by Chaiyawat Wibulswasdi, who was installed as BOT governor after Rerngchai resigned on July 29), and the IMF announced mutually agreed economic adjustment programs, which included tight monetary and fiscal policies and financial sector restructuring.[44] On August 20, 1997 the IMF's Executive Board approved a 3-year stand-by arrangement totaling US$17.2 billion with Thailand. Of the total, US$1.6 billion was made available immediately, and a further US$810 million was to be available after November 30, 1997 – provided that end-September performance targets were met and the first review of the program completed. The IMF also made it clear that subsequent disbursements were to be made on a quarterly basis, again subject to the attainment of performance targets and program reviews (IMF 1997a).

### The BOT: the price of irrational exuberance

Unlike earlier financial crises in the developing world, where governments over-borrowed until they were forced to seek a bailout from the IMF, or a multilateral debt rescheduling from externally-based creditors, the Thai crisis was rooted in the private sector. That is, it was based entirely on excessive private rather than public debt. Therefore, when Thai policymakers tried to assure the markets that Thailand's economic fundamentals were sound, it sounded rather hollow, because they conveniently forgot to add that the fundamentals could be considered sound only if one ignored the private-sector component of the current account. Moreover, it is now a matter of public record that as early as November 1996 the IMF warned the Thai government about the vulnerability of its large current account deficit, particularly given the stagnant export growth (Blustein 2001, 51–83). In addition, the IMF urged the Thai government to adjust its exchange-rate system by lowering the weight of the US dollar in the fixed-rate currency basket and widening the intervention bands (Cooper 1999, 19). Surely the Thai monetary authorities must have been aware of the growing economic disequilibrium. Even if they ignored the IMF's warnings, they could hardly ignore the downward pressure on the exchange market. The question that is begging to be asked is: why was the exchange rate so badly mismanaged, in the sense it did not reflect Thailand's patterns of international transactions or the relative prices of the major trading nations. For example, the weight the baht assigned to the yen was only 13 per cent compared to 80 per cent to the US dollar, despite the fact that Japan had become Thailand's principal trading partner. Moreover, why did the Thai policy-makers fail to respond quickly and decisively to these mounting financial disintermediation? Why did they chose to continue to support the dollar value of the baht by significantly drawing down central bank foreign-exchange reserves? A large part of the blame must go to the overly sanguine assessments of the Thai monetary authorities.

From the Bank of Thailand's own published reports, we can extrapolate the thinking at the BOT at the time (1998; 1998a; 1996a; 1996b; 1996c; 1995; 1992). First, why did the BOT tolerate such high current-account deficits for so long? In the inaugural Fall 1995 issue of the Bank of Thailand's *Economic Focus*, the Bank's Economic Research Department outlined what it considered to be the key factors behind the high deficit and why it believed the deficit to be sustainable both in the short and the long term. The BOT argued that with exports rising rapidly by 25.3 per cent (1995 figures), the rise in the trade deficit did not reflect a change in Thailand's international competitiveness. On the contrary, it reflected the strength of domestic demand. It also noted that *private investment* was the most important factor behind the growth in imports and the deficit, while private consumption and government imports were only secondary factors. Finally, external factors, namely, higher import prices and the appreciation of the yen and the deutsche mark during the first half of 1995 had contributed significantly to the deficit. On the basis of these findings, the BOT concluded that Thailand's current-account deficit was sustainable because the deficit reflected the strengthening of investment, rather than increases in consumption. Moreover, the BOT argued that the deficit occurred in the context of strong GDP growth and export performance, and that Thailand had sufficient international reserves with low external debt. Hence, the BOT claimed that the current-account deficit should not be allowed to mask the strong economic fundamentals of the Thai economy. Indeed, so confident was the BOT that Bandid Nijathaworn, then the deputy director of the Bank of Thailand's economic research department, dismissed Thailand's 10 billion-baht balance of payments deficit in the first quarter of 1995, when he stated that the current-account deficit would shrink rapidly as investment reached its cyclical peak and started to slow down.[45]

Of course, the BOT was cognizant of the fact that the country's fixed exchange-rate regime (designed to remove short-term uncertainty in transactions) had allowed inefficient investments to be masked. They were also aware of the fact that the increased short-term capital mobility arising from the BIBF made the maintenance of the fixed rate increasingly problematic. Thus, another question begging to be asked: since, under a pegged exchange-rate regime, the implementation of monetary policy is undermined by an implicit guarantee of currency value – why did the BOT resist the adoption of a more flexible exchange-rate policy? Such a policy would have allowed capital flows to be regulated through the market mechanism, and eliminated the moral hazard – the direct result of the fixed exchange-rate system, which provided predictability to domestic borrowers who saw no need to hedge against exchange-rate risk. There were six reasons for this: (1) There was a belief that the economy would stabilize in the medium term through export growth, and that a stable baht was indispensable for achieving this growth. (2) The BOT questioned whether a devaluation would hold for long. This was because hedge funds and other speculators would view the move as a sign of weakness – evidence that the government lacked the resolve to keep the baht from falling even further. (3) The authorities feared that a more flexible exchange-rate policy would lead to an exchange-rate appreciation, a deterioration in the current account and a weakening of the banking system, which had large unhedged foreign exchange exposure. Policy-makers were concerned that, since the corporate liabilities were so large, any adjustment in the exchange rate would cause substantial damage to balance sheets. In particular, there was concern that large losses on unhedged foreign-currency debt would result in a large number of corporate bankruptcies, resulting in massive unemployment and related social problems. By early 1997 it was also felt that tampering with the exchange-rate system under the prevailing conditions of intense speculative pressure and eroding domestic confidence would have resulted in a run on the baht and ignited an immediate currency crisis. The BOT recognized that, even with substantial foreign reserves, it would not be able to stabilize the exchange rate given the much larger unhedged foreign-currency debt of Thai corporations – who would have rushed to close their exposure on the first signs of weakening commitment of the BOT to a stable exchange rate. (4) There was a pervasive belief that devaluation would do more harm than good, because the baht was not fundamentally misaligned. (5) The Thai government had long declared that the value of the baht would remain unchanged, and gave the explicit impression that the country's external reserves would be "used as ammunition to defend the baht" (Nabi and Shivakumar 2001, 17). And (6), as Blustein (2001, 66) notes, the BOT's "strategy was to hold the line on the exchange rate and buy time in the hopes that the government could fix the country's underlying problems."

Beyond these immediate concerns, the BOT viewed the increases in the inflation rate and the current account deficit as merely "cyclical" – the result of short-term effects due to large imports of capital equipment for infrastructure and industrial investment and upgrading. While the BOT believed that the economic situation was bound to improve in 1996, it took "appropriate precautionary measures" (which were far too timid) such as the imposition of reserve requirements and other controls to reduce speculative short-term financial flows through the BIBF. Second, the BOT argued that, while the BIBF loans did lead to an observed shortening of the average maturity of Thai foreign debt, "this was partly a statistical illusion caused by the diversion of borrowing source to the participant bank, which if foreign, used revolving funds (appearing as short-term inflow in the Thai balance of payments) to finance their long-term loans to local companies" (BOT 1996b, 8–9). Third, the BOT argued that the large short-term debt posed little risk to the Thai economy, as it was backed by more than adequate foreign-exchange reserves, and also because Thailand's strong economic fundamentals ruled out the possibility of a large capital outflow. Fourth, export stagnation in the second half of 1996 was dismissed as temporary, the result of a general decline in world trade growth, and due "to the lessening competitiveness of the more labor-intensive sectors"; it was expected to recover to a growth of 7.7 per cent in 1997, on account of the resurgence of demand from trading partner countries, as well as the impact from export promotion measures (BOT 1996c, 11–12). Suffice it to note that the BOT's unduly optimistic assessments turned out to be wishful thinking. Finally, how did the BOT defended its practice of foreign-exchange swapping during the severe speculative attack on the baht in 1996 and 1997? It has argued that, since sterilization was not feasible, owing to a shortage of bond issues, capital outflows resulting from speculative activities could be partially neutralized by a swap arrangement – whereby the bank buys local currency using its foreign reserves, with the intention of selling it later. In this way the pressure on domestic liquidity and interest rates associated with capital outflows would not occur with this buy/sell swap. However, while this is true in normal foreign-exchange transactions, under abnormal and repeated speculative attacks, the bank must have large enough foreign reserves not only to sell foreign currency in the spot market, but also to inject local currency back into the market by drawing down its foreign reserves position. Indeed, the Nukul Commission is of the opinion that the BOT should not have artificially created a balanced position through swap arrangements, but should have assessed the threat to its reserves squarely and retreated when the loss of reserves became intolerable.

Beyond the BOT accounts, it is clear that when the domestic financial institutions became swamped with funds, neither Thai firms nor banks had the capability of intermediating such volumes of capital effectively. Consequently, much of the funds was channeled into risky projects and highly cyclical sectors. Thailand's experience vividly illustrates the fact that high rates of investment are not sufficient to sustain a large current-account deficit and an expansion of domestic credit. Although, (unlike what happened in Mexico), many of the funds were invested rather than consumed, the investment was often misdirected into the non-traded goods sectors, especially construction and real estate. Most importantly, few investments were directed to activities that would earn foreign exchange. Thus the shift in the destination of the capital inflow reflected the very significant real appreciation (rise in non-traded goods prices relative to those of traded goods) that occurred over the period of the boom, itself a "Dutch disease" outcome of the high levels of capital inflow.

## The politics behind the crisis

The preceding discussion has shown that, despite the mounting evidence to the contrary, the Thai monetary authorities stubbornly resisted market sentiment for several months. In the process they rapidly ran down the nation's international reserves, and precipitated, on July 2, 1997, a bigger meltdown than would otherwise have been the case – if they had accepted the inevitable reality sooner. Some analysts have argued that, even if the technocrats wanted to devalue the currency and try to resolve the problem of the growing current-account deficits, they could not because they (1) remained overly sanguine in their assessments and (2) they were caught up in the gradual erosion of technocratic influence because of growing political constraints. Phongpaichit and Baker (1998, 15) observe:

> Partly the macro-managers had tried to have the best of both worlds – the pegged exchange rate which facilitated trade, and the liberalization of finance which stimulated investment. Partly the macro-managers had come to believe the praise accorded them. They refused to heed the advice that this combination would not work. Partly they seemed dazzled by the glamorous financial world which developed in Bangkok in the early 1990s. The regulators seemed reluctant to impose the constraints which would slow it down. But partly this reluctance has a murkier side. Powerful people could make easy money because of lax control. The two heads of the economic technocracy, the finance minister and the central bank governor, came under intense political pressure. From 1995 onwards, these posts offered only temporary employment. Many good candidates were not keen to apply. Politicians and other powerful people resisted closer supervision of the finance industry, argued against unpegging the currency and undermined the tradition of fiscal discipline. Up to and beyond the IMF bailout, policies were delayed or distorted at the behest of particular interests.

There is little doubt that certain aspects of democratic politics in Thailand were a source of systemic political weakness, and greatly reduced the capacity of the government to respond effectively to the growing economic disequilibrium. The new constitution, drawn up in 1978, reintroduced democratic institutions under carefully circumscribed conditions. While the Assembly was elected, the Senate was appointed (dominated equally by senior military and civilian bureaucrats), and unelected officials (military and civilian) were allowed to hold cabinet posts. Some government ministries were literally given over as patronage to politicians, and corruption became rife. Moreover, Thailand's multi-member electoral and party systems combined to make it virtually certain that governments would consist of shaky multi-party coalitions. Large electoral districts and proportional representation created an environment where numerous parties and candidates competed for limited posts. This combined with weak party discipline made parties and governments highly sensitive to demands from influential business constituents. As Haggard and MacIntyre (1998, 336) note, "electoral rules discouraged politicians from identifying with their parties, and instead pushed them to pursue individualized campaign strategies, often featuring tactics such as vote buying . . . this created a high demand for cash, thereby rendering politicians beholden to large economic interests." Similarly, Bunbongkarn (1999, 56) notes that "the excessive use of money and an increase in vote-buying were evident in elections in the 1990s. In 1996, for example, it was estimated that around 10 billion baht (US$800 million) had been spent legally on the election, and another 30 billion baht had been spent on buying votes."

The fundamental problem lay in the fact that Thailand had moved towards democratic politics with fragmented political parties heavily dependent upon rural votes to win office. Since provincial constituencies supply over 80 per cent of seats in the lower house of parliament, to get elected in these constituencies politicians depend heavily upon the support of networks of local *chao pho* (political middle-men and businesspeople), who can get the vote out on election day. As the power of provincial leaders increased, it made them formidable competitors with the traditional elites (military, urban-based politicians and business people) for rents and other privileges. Among the main prizes in this intense competition is control of key cabinet seats and the power to allocate quotas, licenses and contracts. Thus, Laothamatas (1996) explains that "two distinct notions of democracy" characterized Thailand in the 1980s and 1990s. A rural version more oriented to concrete material benefits and an urban middle-class version offended by rampant vote-buying, corruption and the rise of violence prone bosses in the countryside. Those who were able to buy votes in the countryside were able to consolidate their control over parliament – and through parliament the cabinet. Laothamatas (1996) adds that, by the mid-1980s, even the supervisory capacity of the BOT was no longer immune from the "incompetence and corruption that had long pervaded other agencies."

One of the major consequences of this kind of politics is a lack of cohesive governance. Indeed, all Thailand's democratically elected governments prior to the crisis rested on highly factionalized multi-party coalitions. The governments were composed of internally weak and fragmented parties that allowed narrow particularistic interests to gain access to the policy process. In this environment, party leaders hastily constructed parliamentary majorities from a pool of approximately a dozen parties, and coalitions typically consisted of six or more parties. For example, elected in July 1995 after the fall of the Chuan Leekpai government, the seven-party coalition government headed by Prime Minister Banharn was viewed as a "lame-duck administration" from the very beginning. Banharn's Chart Thai Party, widely seen as the chief culprit in Thailand's complex vote-buying system, was too preoccupied with domestic issues to pay much attention to the economy. As King (1999, 207) notes, "the Banharn government ignored the economic warning signs and did little to stop Thailand's economic decline." The fact that Banharn appointed as finance minister an individual with no experience in a major financial post and as vice-ministers two individuals accused of malfeasance did not inspire much confidence in his administration. Moreover, in this environment, not only was cabinet instability a chronic problem; prime ministers were vulnerable to policy blackmail by coalition partners threatening to defect. In fact, in September 1996, Banharn's government collapsed after key coalition partners deserted him. Indeed, so deep-rooted was this problem that even the government of the former army commander, Chavalit Yongchaiyuth, failed to produce effective governance. While Chavalit's New Aspiration Party narrowly emerged as the largest party in parliament with 125 seats (following the collapse of the Banharn administration), Chavalit nevertheless needed the six political parties of the previous government to form his government. Preoccupied with his political survival, he ignored "repeated warnings from the IMF – Thailand's new leader did little to guard against the growing mountain of bad debt piling up in the financial system" (King 1999, 207). Chavalit eventually met the same fate as Banharn. Except for the government of Chatichai Choonavan (1988–91), which was ousted in a military coup, all democratically elected governments in Thailand since democratization in the mid-1980s met their demise in this manner.

While indecisiveness and bureaucratic log-rolling on the part of governments played a major role in generating market uncertainty (thus contributing to both the onset and the depth of the crisis), such benign neglect was not the only problem. Phongpaichit and Baker (1999, 202–3) argue that since most of the Thai business and financial conglomerates had become heavily involved in the domestic market – in particular, in the finance and property bubble as well as the dollar-denominated offshore loans – they steadfastly opposed any devaluation. Rather, they were content "to smother the gathering bad news by extending ineffective bailouts, first to the stock market, then to the finance companies and then to the property sector." The central bank's policy to defend the baht was politically supported by financial institutions and firms who feared the impact of currency depreciation on their highly leveraged balance sheets. Similarly, the nexus between politicians and business interests was simply too lucrative to pass by. An example illustrates this dynamic well: It was subsequently learned that the Bangkok Bank of Commerce had accumulated non-performing loans totaling some 50 per cent of its assets. Its former president, Kirkkiat Jalichandra, and the bank adviser, Rakesh Saxena had falsified the accounting, granting large loans to themselves, and to politicians and business people against little or no collateral. Roughly 7 billion baht were lent to politicians to finance mergers and acquisitions and to play the stock market (Sender 1997, 53–4). It was subsequently revealed that the BOT had injected 16 billion baht for a 32 per cent stake in the bank, and 1 trillion baht (US$25 billion) into "ailing but politically connected finance companies" to keep them afloat (Sender and Lee 1998, 15).

### The IMF-led rescue program: phase one

After squandering much of its foreign-exchange reserves, the Thai government turned to the IMF for assistance. On August 20, 1997, Thailand entered into a three-year Stand-By Arrangement with the IMF. This enabled the Thai government to obtain a rescue package worth US$17.2 billion – to be disbursed in quarterly installments over three years provided Thailand met the IMF's performance requirements. The principal objectives of the IMF-led program (developed in collaboration with the Thai government, the World Bank, the Asian Development Bank and bilateral donors) were rapidly to achieve effective management of the exchange rate by stemming the free fall of the baht, and restoration of financial market stability.

To achieve its goals, the IMF called for fiscal tightening. The primary aim of monetary policy in the immediate period was to stabilize the baht and prices through a high interest-rate policy. Specifically, the aim was to achieve an "orderly adjustment of the domestic economy to the sharp, forced reduction in the current account deficit to about 5 per cent of GDP in 1997 and 3 per cent of GDP in 1998 [as compared to the 8.2 per cent deficit in 1996]; a 1 per cent surplus in the public budget to cover restructuring costs; ensuring positive growth of 2.5 per cent in 1997 and 3.5 per cent in 1998; maintaining gross official reserves at the equivalent of 4.2 months of imports in 1997 and 4.4 months in 1998; limiting the end-period rate of inflation to 9.5 per cent in 1997 and 5 per cent in 1998; and initiating a credible and up-front restructuring of the financial sector" (IMF 1997a, 2). Further, the program also required an increase in capital requirements from 8.5 per cent to 12 per cent for all financial institutions, while the Bank of Thailand was required to suspend the infusion of liquidity to ailing financial institutions and to disclose the size of the reserves every two weeks.

To achieve these ambitious targets the managed-float exchange-rate regime adopted on July 2, 1997 was maintained. Indeed, with Thailand's foreign-exchange reserves almost completely exhausted, there was no alternative to floating the baht.[46] The balanced budget was to be achieved through a combination of public expenditure or spending cuts by an amount equal to 3 per cent of GDP and tax increases – primarily an increase in the rate of the value-added tax (similar to a national sales tax) from 7 per cent to 10 per cent – while exchange-rate stabilization was to be achieved through tight money and high interest rates. Financial sector restructuring included plans to close insolvent financial institutions, and a temporary guarantee to protect remaining financial institutions. The plan also took steps to minimize the moral hazard risks of the guarantee, while ensuring the viability of those remaining institutions through early recapitalization and more transparent regulatory and supervisory requirements. The Bank of Thailand was given authority to order a commercial bank or finance company to write down its capital below the value stipulated by law, to allocate share increases without a shareholders' meeting and to remove directors or executives and appoint replacements – subject to approval by the Minister of Finance. This authority allowed for timely intervention in inefficient financial intermediaries that experienced large losses, endangering the public interest. In addition, the Bank of Thailand Act was amended to reaffirm the government's commitment to have the Financial Institutions Development Fund (FIDF) guarantee depositors and creditors with full financial support from the government. In fact, the adoption of international standards for asset classification, loan-loss provisions, capital adequacy, bankruptcy and deposit insurance were to receive priority under the plan (IMF 1997a).

After much foot-dragging the Chavalit administration temporarily suspended the operation of a total of 58 (out of 91) debt-ridden finance companies, 16 of them on June 27, 1997 and an additional 42 on August 5, 1997 – after a comprehensive guarantee was issued on deposits and liabilities of financial institutions.[47] Blustein (2001, 77) notes that the idea of a guarantee on deposits and liabilities "triggered another battle – this one within the Fund itself, pitting the mission in Bangkok against much of the top brass at headquarters." The mission preferred having a guarantee to prevent a financial panic, while the headquarters saw a guarantee as a classic case of moral hazard, a giveaway to investors who had gambled on high-yielding deposits in shaky financial institutions. However, under the compromise, the Financial Institutions Development Fund (FIDF) was entrusted with the task of providing a guarantee of the deposits and liabilities of the financial institutions (with full financial support from the government), preventing further bank runs, and restoring market confidence. Yet the guarantee came with conditions. The holders of promissory notes were not fully bailed out, and only a general guarantee was issued to depositors and other creditors in all financial institutions. Overall, the FIDF provided nearly 400 billion baht in liquidity support to troubled financial institutions in the months preceding the suspension of 58 finance companies in June and August of 1997. Rapid and credible resolution of the position of the 58 suspended finance companies was critical to restoring confidence.

In order to create the legal and institutional framework for this resolution, the government issued six emergency decrees in October 1997. The decrees established two new institutions, the Financial Sector Restructuring Authority (FRA) and the Asset Management Corporation (AMC), to serve as the focal points for resolving the position of the suspended companies. Not unlike the approach adopted in the United States by the Resolution Trust Corporation to deal with the assets of the failed Savings and Loans Associations, FRA's task was: (1) to review the rehabilitation proposals of the 58 suspended finance companies; (2) to assist *bona fide* depositors and creditors of the suspended companies; (3) and to administer the liquidation of companies whose proposals were rejected by FRA – hopefully, by returning the non-performing assets to the marketplace at market-determined valuations and prices. FRA was given one month to assess the plans submitted and to make a recommendation to the ministry of finance on how many finance companies should be allowed to resume their operations. Thus Thailand opted for a strategy of virtually closing the non-bank financial sector, but letting banks deal with problem loans on a decentralized basis. This meant that commercial banks had to meet Bank for International Settlements (BIS) capital adequacy ratios through raising additional capital, from foreign investors among others. To facilitate this, the Thai government also increased the limit of foreign ownership from 25 per cent to 100 per cent of total equity.

The AMC was established to bid for the purchase of the impaired assets of finance companies that the FRA deemed no longer viable. In effect, the AMC became the buyer of last resort for impaired assets, as its major task was to buy the bad assets and then manage, restructure and sell them under the direction of FRA. The AMC was also entrusted with the responsibility of bidding for the lowest-quality assets as a buyer of last resort, to prevent fire sales of assets of the closed finance companies – which in turn could undermine underlying collateral values.[48] The government authorized 1 billion baht in capital for the new corporation, of which 250 million baht was approved immediately (Nabi and Shivakumar 2001, 32).

While there is general consensus that the financial restructuring was necessary, opinion remains deeply divided on the efficacy of the IMF's fiscal and monetary policies. From the IMF's perspective, high interest rates were required to stabilize the value of the currency, and budget cuts were necessary to make room in the budget for the interest costs of financial restructuring. It is difficult to quibble with the fact that, in the case of Thailand, high interest rates were probably unavoidable, because of its large current-account deficit caused by excessive private investment over saving. Indeed, macroeconomic theory teaches us that, with a current-account deficit that is fundamentally caused by an excess of a country's domestic demand over its output, the necessary prescription would have to be a restrictive monetary policy, since the imbalance is caused mainly by excessive private investment. Thus, when a currency suddenly loses half its value amidst massive capital outflows and collapsing confidence (as was the case in Thailand, Indonesia and South Korea), easing is not a prudent policy. The negative effects of high interest rates on a weak economy and a fragile financial system must be carefully weighed against the probable consequences of a large depreciation on the burden of foreign-currency indebtedness. Moreover, the appropriate extent and duration of monetary tightening is very difficult to assess. For Thailand, which entered the crisis with a current-account deficit of 8 per cent (much larger than the current-account imbalances of Indonesia and Korea), a larger fiscal effort seemed appropriate.

Yet the critics also raise some valid points. For the critics, the IMF's orthodox fiscal and monetary policies worsened the crisis (Radelet and Sachs 1998; Nidhiprabha 1999). As prerequisite conditions for the loan package, the IMF attached: (1) a tight monetary policy and correspondingly high interest rates, to stabilize the baht and rein in the inflationary pressures; and (2) a restrictive fiscal policy aimed at restoring a budget surplus. This tight monetary policy was continued for the next several months, only to be relaxed gradually between May and August 1998 in the face of a severe economic recession. Critics argue that the IMF's monetary and fiscal policies were typical of the program devised earlier for Latin American countries burdened with external imbalances associated with massive public-sector debt, hyperinflation and low rates of private savings. However, they correctly point out that the external imbalance in Thailand (as with most of its neighbors) lacked any of these features. That is, the Thai crisis arose from a build-up of short-term private debt, rather than profligate government spending and lack of monetary control, as in Latin America. This misguided policy, it is argued, only propelled the economy toward a low-level equilibrium. Tight monetary policy reduced credit for the private sector and raised interest rates, which reduced output. Tight fiscal policy reduced incomes, and therefore lowered total demand. With weak exports, the lowering of output and income trapped the economy in a new low equilibrium – which produced a massive contraction in private spending and literally choked the Thai economy. Hence, instead of restoring confidence, the resultant credit crunch paralyzed the corporate sector. Warr (1998, 59) notes:

> The IMF package added a public sector contraction, by requiring a budget surplus equivalent to 1% of GDP. Moreover, at a time when confidence in the financial sector was essential, the IMF required the problem institutions be

closed. Given the circumstances of the time, this requirement seemed to many observers to be as irresponsible as crying "Fire" in a crowded theater.

No doubt, these are valid criticisms. First, it is hard to distinguish the IMF's initial policy prescriptions for Thailand from those applied to Latin American countries in the 1980s. Second, there is some agreement that the recession in Thailand would have been less severe had the IMF not imposed such tough fiscal restraint. It is clear that the old-fashioned contractionary policy to accompany devaluation is inappropriate. And, third, since the underlying assumption of the tight fiscal stance had been that the foreign-exchange correction would stimulate external demand and get recovery going, with the benefit of hindsight it is clear that the IMF program did not correctly anticipate the region-wide recession. Nor did it anticipate the weakening of the country's terms of trade, or the collapse in domestic private consumption. It is hard to disagree with the view that instead of contraction, a fiscal expansion was needed to stimulate aggregate demand.

Yet, having noted this, it is important to recognize that only detailed empirical studies will shed further light on these complex questions, the case in point being a recent study by Dollar and Hallward-Driemeier (2000). The authors conducted a detailed survey of some 1,200 manufacturing firms in Thailand between the last quarter of 1997 and the first quarter of 1998. Asked to rank the causes of the current output decline (out of four possibilities), the most important factor cited by both exporters and non-exporters was the effect of the exchange-rate depreciation on input costs, followed by lack of domestic (or foreign) demand. The high cost of capital was ranked third, and lack of access to credit was ranked last. Finally, why did the US$17.2 billion IMF package failed to restore market confidence? Obviously, the market deemed the IMF package to be inadequate – in large part because it did not cover the risk of private capital outflow. It seems that what the IMF did was to provide Thailand with financing just enough to keep the public sector liquid and just enough for it to have a bare minimum international reserve. This obviously failed to generate market confidence. On the other hand, since the baht defense was conducted largely through forward swap transactions, Thailand's true foreign-exchange reserve position was not apparent from official figures – the IMF may have thought that the liquidity it was providing was enough.

## The IMF and the Chuan government: phase two

Despite the comprehensive and ambitious nature of the restructuring plans, the economic decline continued unabated. It seemed that neither the IMF program nor the political gridlock and bickering amongst the six-party coalition partners that made up the Chavalit administration failed to inspire market confidence. As the power struggle between Chavalit's New Aspiration Party and its main coalition partner, Chart Pattana, intensified, "economic policy-making by mid-October was in complete disarray" (Haggard 2000, 94). Not surprisingly, on October 31, the baht passed the US one dollar to 40 baht psychological threshold. In fact, the spot exchange rate was 41 baht per one US dollar, as compared to 26.5 baht during the middle of July 1997. As domestic and international pressure against the Chavalit government mounted, the besieged Chavalit on November 3 announced his resignation – ignominiously leaving office on November 6.

As Chavalit left office without dissolving the House and setting the date for new elections, both the existing government coalition and the opposition parties tried to form a new governing coalition. In fact, for several days it was not clear which group of parties would form the next government. Indeed, two competing coalitions even held separate news conferences within hours of each other suggesting that they would form the next government. Eventually, it was Chuan Leekpai's Democrat Party that formed the government. However, Chuan required the support of five other political parties to form his coalition government – which took office on November 15 with a slim majority of 208 seats in a 393-seat parliament. Despite such inauspicious beginnings, Chuan's administration, in sharp contrast to its predecessors, was able to provide a far more effective leadership in the macroeconomic arena.[49] Even before assuming office Chuan send the right signals to the IMF and the international financial markets by appointing two highly respected technocrats to head his government's economic team: Tarrin Nimmanahaeminda (a professional banker and former finance minister) as finance minister, and a former central bank governor, Supachai Panitchpakdi, as deputy prime minister and minister of commerce.[50]

On November 25, 1997, the Chuan administration sent the Thai government's second "letter of intent" (GoT 1997), signed jointly by finance minister Tarrin and BOT governor, Chaiyawat Wibulswasdi, to Michel Camdessus, managing director of the IMF. The primary objective was to signal to the market that the government was again firmly in charge and that the days of indecision were over. Although, the letter noted the "slower return of confidence" and a "much sharper decline" in private investment and consumption than originally anticipated, it nevertheless clearly stated the Thai government's full commitment to the earlier IMF conditions as specified in the first letter of intent of August 14, 1997 (GoT 1997, 1). Indeed, not only did the Chuan government pledge to follow the IMF orthodoxy very closely (tight monetary and fiscal policies and strict enforcement of high standards of financial sector governance), the second letter also noted that "the new economic team is determined to take a number of additional measures to strengthen the policy package and reinforce public confidence in the program . . . and is determined to proceed rapidly with implementation" (GoT 1997, 1).

The second letter outlined in some detail the economic plans and goals. It stated that the government planned to work towards a 1 per cent surplus in the 1997–98 budget, because "this will ensure an orderly offset to the anticipated costs of the financial sector restructuring, while also providing a clear signal of the government's intent to implement the economic program" (GoT 1997, 2). The 1 per cent surplus was to be achieved by increasing taxes, cutting the funding of state enterprises, raising utility prices, and lowering real wages in the public sector. In the area of monetary policy, the letter stated that "within the framework of our flexible exchange rate policy, monetary policy will need to play a greater role in stabilizing conditions in the foreign exchange market and containing the inflationary impact of the exchange rate depreciation . . . As part of the BOT's resolve to maintain such a tight monetary stance, interest rates will principally be set with the objective of helping to stabilize the exchange rate and restore confidence in domestic financial assets" (GoT 1997, 3). With regard to external sector policies, the letter noted that the BOT planned to maintain gross international reserves of at least US$23 billion (equivalent to about four months of imports), and "remove as quickly as possible the restrictions on purchases and sales of baht by non-residents as well as the restrictions on baht denominated borrowing by non-residents and on the sale of debt instruments and equities for baht" (GoT 1997, 3–4). In the area of financial sector restructuring the government stated its objective to "move ahead as expeditiously as possible with the restructuring of the 58 suspended finance companies," and elaborated a strategy to recapitalize and strengthen the remainder of the financial system "so that its regulatory framework can be brought fully in line with international best practices by the year 2000." In addition, the letter explicitly noted that "the BOT will have a clear mandate to carry out the necessary restructuring of the sector, including (i) the tightening of loan classification rules, (ii) timetables for the recapitalization of all undercapitalized financial institutions during 1998, (iii) streamlining of bankruptcy procedures, (iv) reaffirmation of disclosure and auditing requirements for all financial institutions, and (v) the expeditious disposal of assets of closed companies and reorganization of good and bad assets of remaining firms" (GoT 1997, 4–5). With these commitments, Thailand became a cooperative partner of the IMF, and soon, as Flatters (2000) notes, the IMF's "star pupil."

The Chuan administration began to implement these measures aggressively, despite the fact that "opposing groups came out of the woodwork to block its passage" (Bunbongkarn 1999, 63). On December 8, 1997, the Thai authorities announced that only two of the 38 rehabilitation plans submitted to the FRA had been approved; the other 36 had been rejected. Thus FRA and the ministry of finance announced the permanent closure of 56 out of the 58 finance companies (with a book value of 600 billion baht) that had failed to meet the tough new loan classification provisions.[51] Eligible claimants were given the option of exchanging their bahts for notes issued by two publicly controlled financial institutions, the Krung Thai Thanakit (KTT) and the Krung Thai Bank (KTB), under two distinct note-exchange schemes.[52] In early February 1998, with the assistance of international firms, FRA began the liquidation of finance company assets through public auction, in which the AMC participated as the bidder of last resort. The auction of assets began with automobiles, followed by bonds, securities and other collectable items. In fact, to encourage investors to participate in the auction, the FRA organized road-shows in the major world financial centers (BOT 1998, 12). In early 1998, twelve additional finance companies that were deemed insolvent were merged with a state-owned finance company into a new state-owned commercial "good bank" named Radanasin – set up to purchase and manage the good assets of the suspended finance companies (BOT 1998, 13). In mid-January 1998, the authorities nationalized four insolvent medium-sized banks (Bangkok Metropolitan Bank, First City Bank, Siam City Bank and Bangkok Bank of Commerce), in order to prepare them for sale to foreign financial institutions – despite the fact that their owners vociferously accused the government of selling Thailand to foreigners.

Finally, cognizant of the fact that even the country's banks and finance companies that had not been suspended faced significant risks, the Bank of Thailand tried to shore up confidence through strengthening prudential regulations and supervision. On March 31, 1998, in order to bring Thai practices up to international standards by the end of 2000, the Bank of Thailand made rules governing loan classification, provisioning and reporting more stringent.[53] For example, the definition of non-performing assets was changed to cover loans three or more months in arrears, instead of, as earlier, 6–12 months. Loan classification was tightened by requiring provisioning for, and prohibiting accrual of interest on, all loans more than six months overdue. Moreover, commercial banks and finance companies were required to increase provisions for sub-standard loans from 15 per cent to 20 per cent. Doubtful loans now required a 50 per cent provision, while local banks had to increase their capital by as much as 80 billion baht by the end of 1998, on top of the 129 billion baht previously added. Finance companies were required to add 42 billion baht of new capital in addition to the 20 billion already mandated. Also, banks had to set aside roughly 100 billion baht in new provisions for loan losses, and finance companies 43 billion baht, and all financial institutions were now required to submit quarterly (instead of annual) audits and credit reports to the central bank. The new rules also included guidelines for restructuring corporate debt – with special emphasis placed on financial institutions tightening their lending practices and credit analysis procedures. New prudential regulatory and accounting standards for specialized banks were quickly developed – paralleling those for commercial banks. The new standards addressed loan classification, provisioning, and interest accrual requirements.

The IMF had forecast that, if its conditions were followed, Thailand would experience a speedy V-shaped recovery (IMF 2000). However, the IMF had obviously underestimated the depth of the recession or the ferocity of the contagions spread in the region. Despite the Thai government's faithful adherence to strict monetary and fiscal discipline – as the finance minister and BOT governor noted in the third letter of intent to the IMF: "we have adhered strictly to the program ensuring that all performance criteria for December 31, 1997 related to monetary, fiscal and external policies as well as financial restructuring have been observed," the much predicted quick recovery did not materialize.[54] In fact, market confidence, instead of bouncing back, continued to erode. The baht continued its precipitous fall, hitting an all-time low of 56 to the dollar in mid-January 1998 (losing 55 per cent of its value since being floated on July 2, 1997) – despite a rapid rise in short-term interest rates.[55] Given the fact that many of the domestic debts were denominated in foreign currency, the rising interest rates and the collapsing baht savaged debtors' balance sheets and aggravated the already serious non-performing loan problems in the banking and financial system. This resulted in the banks and the remaining finance companies accumulating substantial losses. The resultant credit crunch made the cost of bank credit extremely high, while the near collapse of the baht made the cost of foreign loans simply unbearable. With the steep declines in manufacturing, exports, imports and investment (indeed, the overall deterioration of the real sector of the economy), the GDP, which started its decline in the second half of 1997, continued its downward spiral through the first half of 1998 – constantly outpacing the official projections. It was clear that Thailand was in a much deeper recession than had been anticipated in August 1997, when the IMF rescue package was put in place.

The socioeconomic distress caused by the continuing economic decline was devastating. Labor market adjustment took several forms. The number of those of working age shown as being "not in the labor force" increased by 600,000 between the February rounds of the labor-force surveys of 1997 and 1998. This was equivalent to a third of the numbers of unemployed in May 1998. There were also major reductions both in hours worked and in nominal wages. Mahmood and Aryah (2001, 246) note that "the crisis generated approximately 90,000 redundancies, raising the level of unemployment to 2.2 million as of June 1999. Real wages declined following the pre-crisis tightening of the labor market. Real wage growth, which stood at over 2 per cent per year in 1996, reversed itself. The real wage fell by more than 7 per cent in 1998 and by 1.5 per cent in 1999."[56] While the initial labor-force impacts were largely in urban areas, the effects were also felt in the countryside, through both return migration of urban workers and reduced remittances. Since Thailand does not have a well-developed formal social safety net (there is no unemployment insurance, and many social benefits such as health care are tied to employment), the vast majority of the displaced and unemployed workers were left to fend for themselves.[57] For those fortunate enough to be working, the rise in inflation in the context of a considerably weakened labor market exacted a further toll in terms of falling real wages and incomes. The combined effects of higher unemployment and inflation pushed large numbers of people into poverty. The most vulnerable in the workforce, including the country's 1.3 million foreign workers (mainly Burmese), were informed by the Labor Ministry that they would be forcibly repatriated. As Phongpaichit and Baker (2001, 93) note, "in March 1998, the ministry began rounding up Burmese and pushed over 200,000 across the border."

Not surprisingly, by the spring of 1998 public support for the Thai government's IMF program began to deteriorate. Business leaders "mounted a broad attack on the IMF program for concentrating too much on fiscal discipline, external stability, financial restructuring, while paying no attention to the real economy." Some even accused the IMF program of being "neo-colonial" and "imperialist" – designed to "decimate local firms and create fire-sale conditions for foreign purchasers." Rather, the critics proposed that "Thailand should declare a debt moratorium to give domestic firms a breathing space to recover" (Phongpaichit and Baker 2000, 46–7). In the countryside, farmers' organizations came together on a call for agricultural debt relief, and "then proposed to mount a massive demonstration in the capital if their demands were not met." Similarly, in the urban areas the hard-hit middle-classes and the growing ranks of the urban unemployed were quickly mobilized against the IMF program, widely perceived as "saving the rich at the expense of the poor" (Phongpaichit and Baker 2000, 47, 94).

It is clear that by the time the Thai government signed its fourth letter of intent to the IMF, on May 26, 1998, it was deeply concerned by the alarming contraction of the real sector of the economy, the rapid growth of non-performing loans, and the growing popular agitation against the IMF's allegedly harsh measures. The fourth letter of intent noted that "the conditions in the real economy are still deteriorating as the economic decline during the first half of 1998 is proving to be deeper than previously anticipated . . . thus the focus of policies will shift to adopting macroeconomic settings, strengthening structural policies and ensuring the adequacy of the social safety net" (GoT 1998a). It is important to reiterate that the initial IMF program in Thailand called for fiscal tightening that allowed little room for increased social expenditures. It was only the force of subsequent events – the deeper-than-anticipated recession, the rapidly mounting job losses, the accumulating indicators of widespread social distress and growing popular discontent – that forced the Thai government to shift the policy focus. Indeed, the Thai authorities increased the target *fiscal deficit* to 3 per cent of GDP in May 1998, a sharp contrast to the targets of a *fiscal surplus* of around 1 per cent of GDP when the IMF program was first agreed with

Thailand (GoT 1998a). It should be noted that this loosening of fiscal policy was not motivated solely by the need to increase social expenditures. Fiscal stimuli was also needed to moderate the unforeseen depth of the contraction in the real economy, especially since monetary policy could not be eased within the macroeconomic framework agreed with the IMF.

From June through to August 1998, while the Thai government began publicly (yet politely) to suggest that in the light of the huge negative aggregate demand shocks, the IMF's insistence on tight monetary and fiscal policies was misplaced, behind the scenes it "fought a pitched battle with the IMF over the crisis strategy." It seems that after much "hard bargaining" the Thai authorities were eventually able to persuade the IMF to "overturn its stringent macro conditions" (Phongpaichit and Baker 2000, 48). Indeed, in the summer of 1998, the strategy for economic recovery was broadened to halt the collapse of aggregate demand. This goal was to be met by relaxing contractionary fiscal policy, extending the ongoing reform of the financial sector, addressing the problems of Thai firms mired in debt, strengthening corporate governance, reforming state enterprises in preparation for privatization, and a major relaxation of the macroeconomic policy regime, especially on the revenue side.[58]

In keeping with the new policy thrust, the fiscal deficit targets were further reduced to −3.5 per cent on August 25 and −5 per cent on December 1, 1998. Monetary policy was switched from targeting the exchange rate to targeting money growth – with a view to producing sharp reductions in interest rates and increases in bank lending. Although the authorities realized that the fiscal deficit would increase, they felt that the overall goal was to assist the real sector through lower interest rates and to stimulate domestic demand. Also, lower interest rates were seen as a means of easing loan payments burdens on debtors. These new policy modifications were made explicit in the Thai government's fifth letter of intent, filed with the IMF on August 25, 1998 (GoT 1998b). The fifth letter of intent described in great detail the policies that Thailand intended to implement in the context of its request for financial support from the IMF. In addition to the reversal of monetary policies, the government announced additional initiatives intended to speed up the recapitalization of the banks, restructure corporate debts and increase bank lending. Also, the government's earlier commitments to providing liquidity support for troubled financial institutions and a comprehensive guarantee to depositors were clarified and reaffirmed. Without doubt, the most important new fiscal initiative was the allocation of funds for a "targeted social safety net," while avoiding entrenching new costly schemes that could introduce distortions into the labor market (GoT 1998b, 2). A significant part of the total social expenditure (roughly 12 billion baht or US$300 million) was allocated for employment creation through the Social Investment Program. The Social Security Fund, "as part of the broader effort to strengthen the social safety net" was also expanded (GoT 1998b, 4).

By the time the fifth letter of intent was signed, the Thai authorities were cognizant of the fact that they needed to find a way to deal quickly with the problems associated with the assets and liabilities of the closed financial institutions, and the enormous volume of bad debts in the financial system. As is stated in the fifth letter of intent, the Thai government committed itself to implementing (by the end of October 1998) some eleven basic economic laws related to bankruptcy, foreclosure, property rights, and restrictions on foreign investors, including the development of informal, voluntary processes (assisted by a variety of tax and other incentives) to encourage arbitration without having recourse to bankruptcy and foreclosure (GoT 1998b, 5–6). The eleven laws can be grouped into three categories: provisions for liberalizing the Alien Business Law "into a new and more liberal Foreign Investment Law," a bill to facilitate the privatization of state enterprises, and amendments to the bankruptcy and foreclosure laws and procedures. Without doubt, the most controversial were the bankruptcy and foreclosure laws. Specifically, although a new bankruptcy law had been passed in February 1998, subsequent legislative processes had rendered it weaker "to the point of almost complete ineffectiveness" (Flatters 2000, 265). The new laws had several objectives, including the introduction of a new bankruptcy court and correcting the imbalance of power of debtors over creditors with respect to foreclosure and in negotiating and enforcing debt-restructuring agreements. The second part of the new debt-restructuring strategy was to develop voluntary, out-of-court settlements (the so-called Bangkok approach) of reaching debt-restructuring agreements. Under BOT's supervision, a Corporate Debt Restructuring Advisory Committee (CDRAC) was set up in September 1998 to encourage major corporate debtors to come "to market-based debt workout agreements with their creditors" (GoT 1998b, 2). Chaired by the governor of the Bank of Thailand, and including representatives from the Federation of Thai Industries, the Thai Bankers Association, the Board of Trade, the Foreign Bankers Association, and the Association of Finance Companies, CDRAC's main task was to monitor progress on more than 700 high-priority cases (Nabi and Shivakumar 2001, 45). Finally, the government outlined incentives to encourage bank recapitalization and increased lending. The banks were offered (on a non-compulsory basis), the opportunity to receive government bonds that would be treated as tier 1 or tier 2 capital, and could be paid back at a later date when the banks were able to recapitalize from other sources. However, in return for the tier 1 capital, the banks needed to implement new loan-provisioning rules and match any government capital contributions with capital they raised on their own. To receive tier 2 support, banks would have to increase lending and debt-restructuring at a rate proportionate to the amount of new funding taken. That is, government put forward the option to financial institutions of increasing their second-tier capital by exchanging non-tradeable bonds with banks' newly issued debentures, equaling the losses suffered by financial institutions in their debt-restructuring.[59]

In 1999 the Thai government launched several new spending or fiscal stimulus initiatives. At the end of March, the authorities announced a number of major social spending programs funded with external loans provided by the Asian Development Bank, the IMF, the World Bank and Japan. By the time the seventh letter of intent was signed in March 1999, the 1998–99 fiscal deficit was targeted at 6 per cent of GDP, not including another 1 per cent in non-budgetary expenditures under the Miyazawa Plan to be disbursed in the final six months of the fiscal year ending in September. Overall, to create jobs and encourage reverse migration from urban to rural areas, the government (in March 1999) allocated 51 billion baht from its regular budget to provide direct and indirect employment in rural areas. Direct employment initiatives included some 68 rural job-creation projects involving public works, while indirect employment projects included vocational education. In addition, the government introduced income-support measures such as severance pay, tax and utility price-cuts, a price-support program for rice, and extension of health care and educational subsidies. For example, the value-added tax (VAT) was reduced from 10 per cent to 7 per cent for two years. Income tax was waived on the first 50,000 baht of income, as was a corporate tax of 1.5 per cent of sales levied on small-scale enterprises earning less than 1.2 million baht per year. In February 1999, to help rice farmers (affected by both the crisis and falling world paddy prices) the government introduced a price-support program for rice at a level above the prevailing market price. About 3,500 million baht was targeted to buy 250,000 tons of rice at fixed prices – albeit this rice was to be exported, in order not to affect domestic prices (Mahmood and Aryah 2001, 277).

By mid-1999, most indicators showed that the Thai economy had finally bottomed out, and that a modest recovery was beginning to take hold. Indeed, after seven consecutive quarters of contraction, the economy began to expand in the first quarter of 1999. Manufacturing has been the main engine of economic recovery, with a growth rate of around 15 per cent in 1999. Export volumes also turned positive. In contrast to the contraction of 7 per cent in 1998, exports in 1999 expanded by 6 per cent – benefiting from a cheaper baht (in real, trade-weighted terms) and strong external demand. In December 1999, the Thai government revised its GDP growth estimate for 1999 up to 3–4 per cent, mainly owing to the strong performance of manufacturing. However, the IMF-supported program also deserves some of the credit. The program had facilitated a rebuilding of Thailand's international reserves. External vulnerability had been substantially lowered with reductions in foreign debt – especially short-term – and the current-account surplus remained comfortable. Also, Thailand's balance of payments position became much stronger, and inflation under control.

## Beyond the IMF programs and future challenges

Thailand successfully completed a 34-month Stand-By Arrangement with the IMF on June 19, 2000. In fact, given Thailand's improved balance of payments position, the Thai authorities have not had to draw any funds under the arrangement since June 1999. Over the course of the arrangement, a total of US$14.1 billion (including US$3.2 billion from the IMF), was drawn from bilateral and multilateral contributors to the US$17.2 billion official financing package. Thailand made its first scheduled repayment to the IMF in November 2000.

Yet formidable challenges to sustainable economic recovery remain. For example, between August 1998 and August 1999, the Thai government launched three fiscal stimulus packages, including tax and tariff reductions, to boost domestic demand. Consequently, it ran a large deficit, which, on a cash balance basis, reached a cumulative 79.4 billion baht in the first half of fiscal year 1999/2000 (ending 30 September). The overall public-sector deficit, including interest costs of financial-sector restructuring for fiscal year 1999/2000, was around 7 per cent of GDP. Total public debt was estimated at about 2.6 trillion baht (US$67.7 billion) in 1999, equivalent to around 56 per cent of GDP (ADB 2000c, 37–38). Thus rising deficits in combination with very substantial financial-sector restructuring costs have contributed to a rapid increase in public-sector debt since the onset of the crisis.

Since Thailand's crisis has been largely a financial crisis, a full and sustainable recovery will require resolution of the problems plaguing the financial sector – namely, bank recapitalization, corporate debt restructuring, and the resolution of the non-performing loans problem. However, slow progress has been made on all these fronts, owing to economic and political constraints. The volume of non-performing loans has continued to remain high, despite significant reductions in interest rates. Indeed, the huge non-performing loans problem continues to cripple the financial sector and cause weak credit expansion. If the non-performing loans problem is not expeditiously resolved, it is possible that viable companies that survived the crisis may eventually succumb to the pervasive liquidity problems. This could cause another wave of business closures.

Although four major banks, the Bank of Asia, Nakorthorn, Thai Danu and Radhanasin, were sold in 1998–99 to ABN Amro, Standard Chartered, Development Bank of Singapore and United Overseas Bank respectively, privatization has remained slow and hesitant. Given the lack of incentives, many commercial banks have been reluctant to restructure problem loans and accept actual losses (or "haircuts"). Instead, most have opted for less painful rescheduling, such as stretching out the amortization schedule. As Flatters (2000, 270) notes, "the August 1998 banking package had the potential to force more speedy adjustment on the banks, but participation was made voluntary. Instead, most banks took advantage of beneficial new capital definitions to convert deposits into capital and avoided debt write-offs by agreeing to debt rescheduling rather than restructuring." These actions have helped solve short-run balance sheet problems, while putting off necessary adjustments to the future. Similarly, corporate debt restructuring has been quite slow, and by the end of 2002 the proportion of the debts that had been successfully restructured had been much smaller than expected. More troubling, some of the supposedly restructured debts have returned to non-performing status – in large part because restructuring is still hampered by an ineffective legal framework for bankruptcy and insolvency, poor enforcement, and the bias that remains in favor of debtors.

Moreover, politically well-connected debtors have been successful in stalling and resisting creditors' claims, and "strategic defaulting" (where those who are able to service their debt choose not to), and "outright looting" of corporate and banking assets continue to plague the system. It is important to note that Thailand has not opted for commercial bank recapitalization and corporate restructuring financed by the government because of the belief that such a program would encourage moral hazard and put an excessively high burden on taxpayers. However, it is just as important to note that the benefits of the market-led approach will only follow where there are sanctions that can compel action on voluntary resolution, and where there is a framework that allows acquisitions and mergers to proceed expeditiously on market terms. Progress has also been slow on the FRA auctions of the assets of failed banks and finance companies. Finally, although the eleven economic laws were finally passed by the Thai Senate and Parliament in late 1999 (far behind the planned implementation date of October 31, 1998), the ineffectiveness of its implementation is now widely recognized.

This failure of implementation reflects a political failure. As a coalition government, the Chuan administration from its very inception was intensely pressured by competing, yet powerful vested interests. While it was able to force through some unpopular measures, the government's slim parliamentary majority made it difficult always to overcome the power of the entrenched vested interests. This was reflected in the weakness of its initial new bankruptcy law, difficulties in passing the eleven new economic laws, and its inability to make headway with financial sector restructuring and recapitalization. The government's inability to turn the economy around quickly, and the widely held perception that it was bailing out rich bankers by taking over bad debt, not to mention a number of embarrassing scandals involving senior ministers (especially Tarrin), further eroded the Chuan administration's popular support and legitimacy. In October 1998, the government was forced to admit another large and influential party into the ruling coalition. While this gave it a safer parliamentary majority, it also meant that the government now had to make concessions to an even larger array of vested interests. Although the Chuan government survived no-confidence votes in February and December 1999, it was increasingly viewed as a spent force, and a captive of big financial institutions and foreign investors.

More than anything else, it was this popular angst that led to the routing of the Chuan Leekpai coalition government in the January 6, 2001 general elections. In a landslide electoral victory, the telecommunications tycoon Thaksin Shinawatra's Thai Rak Thai (Thai love Thai) Party won 248 seats, while Chuan's Democrat Party won only 128 seats in the 500-seat House of Representatives.[60] The Thai Rak Thai contested the elections on a five-point program. These included: (1) grants of one million baht to each of Thailand's 70,000 administrative villages to promote economic diversification; (2) People's Bank extending loans of up to 15,000 baht collateral-free to farmers; (3) 30-baht visits to clinics and hospitals; (4) a three-year moratorium on farm debts for farmers unable to repay loans owing to the government-owned Bank for Agriculture and Agricultural Cooperatives; and (5) the creation of a national asset management company to assist commercial banks with their non-performing loans problem – an idea that the Chuan government had strongly resisted.

In June 2001, the Thai Asset Management Corporation (TAMC) was established to help alleviate the weaknesses in the bank and corporate sectors. More specifically, the TAMC has been designed to consolidate the management of distressed assets in the public sector and provide an impetus to the restructuring of large multi-creditor corporate loans. TAMC is expected to purchase up to one-half of the financial sector's distressed assets – of which the large majority are expected to come from state-owned financial institutions. Overall, the TAMC goal is to acquire about half the financial system's non-performing loans, including almost all (1.1 trillion baht) of state banks' non-performing loans and about one-quarter (250 billion baht) of the private banks' non-performing loans. As of mid-2002, TAMC achievements have been modest. So far, the TAMC has been successful only in acquiring the non-performing loans of state-owned banks, although the non-performing loans of private banks account for the largest stock of such loans. In effect, the purchase of the non-performing loans of state-owned banks is a transfer from one government agency to another, and does little to change the lending behavior of the banks concerned. The lack of success with private banks is mainly due to the fact that the TAMC's offer price is generally below what is acceptable to private banks. Suffice it to note that resolving Thailand's notorious non-performing loans problem will depend as much on the fortunes of the country's real economy as on the success of Thaksin's TAMC.

## Notes

1 Excerpts from the address by His Honor, Mr Chuan Leekpai, Prime Minister of Thailand, to the Council on Foreign Relations and Asia Society on March 11, 1998, New York. The full address is accessible via the internet: www.foreignrelations.org/studies/pubs.html.
2 Haggard and MacIntyre (1998) also highlight how the lack of political leadership and chronic political instability contributed to the Thai crisis.
3 Since the late 1950s, when Dr Puey Ungphakorn ran the central bank with a spirit of fierce integrity, the institution had been highly regarded for its competence and independence.
4 Warr (1998, 51) notes that "Thailand has a long and proud history of stable monetary policy and low inflation." The operations of the BOT have been seen as an important contribution to that record.
5 See the works of Haggard and MacIntyre (1998); Lauridsen (1998) and Phongpaichit and Baker (1998; 1999).
6 The Nukul Commission spend three months interviewing top central bankers and finance ministry officials, and pored over boxes of documents and memos in an effort to reconstruct the events leading up to the collapse of the baht. The commission was instructed to examine three crucial issues: May 1997's failed defense of the baht; the decision to lend massive financial assistance to ailing finance companies and banks by the Financial Institutions Development Fund; and the failed examination and supervision of the Bangkok Bank of Commerce. For details, see Prachuabmoh (1998).
7 The term "irrational exuberance" is owed to the US Fed chairman, Alan Greenspan.
8 The term "fifth tiger" is from Muscat (1994).
9 Krugman (1994), in a provocative article, argued that Asia's economic growth, impressive as it was, could be explained by basic economic factors such as a high savings rate, investment in education and job-creation. In other words, it was growth in output – the result of working harder not smarter – or what he calls "perspiration rather than inspiration." However, Krugman's model predicted "diminishing returns" or a gradual loss of economic momentum, not a sudden crash.
10 Christensen *et al.* (1997, 356) note that "even firms that were not promoted by BOI could claim similar tax refunds on their export activities . . . exporters were entitled to receive rebates on customs duties, business taxes, municipal taxes, excise taxes and other taxes previously collected on particular inputs."
11 As Christensen *et al.* (1997, 357) note, "typically, an eligible entrepreneur wishing to obtain a cheap loan can issue a promissory note to be discounted by his bank and rediscounted by the central bank, both at below-market rates."
12 As will be discussed later, as the US dollar appreciated, the baht got overvalued, exposing it to a potential currency attack. The high domestic interest rates helped to control the overgrowth of domestic credit, but the credit expansion in the external sector was inevitable. Of course, the main blow to Thailand's economy was the emergence of China as its main competitor in the export sector in the 1990s. As a result, Thailand's exports in 1996 recorded a 0 per cent growth rate, while the volume of foreign debt increased sharply.

13  See, for example, Lall (1990, 45–50). Tan (2000a, 166–67) also notes that "Thailand's secondary school enrolment ratio is very low (only 37 per cent in 1993) . . . in recent years rapid economic growth has led to acute shortages of skilled labor in Thailand. In 1991, there were about 3,800 engineers in Thailand, while the demand for engineers was about 6,200."

14  The dollar–baht rate, though fairly constant, was not rigid. Rather, it depended on a special formula that included a small weighting for the value of the yen, the mark and a few other currencies.

15  Taiwanese garment firms invested in Thailand, because, in part, Thailand had not used up its quotas under the MFA. See the quotations cited in Siamwalla, Vichyanond and Vajragupta (1999, 6).

16  Thailand's contribution to the production of such medium-tech products was largely assembly work. The design, complex manufacturing processes and international marketing were located elsewhere. Hence, unlike South Korea, Taiwan or Singapore, Thailand's limited technological capability meant that it lacked the "inspiration" so critical for industrial upgrading.

17  Exchange-rate policy since 1984 has been officially described as a "managed float." However, after the devaluation, the baht stabilized at around Bt 25 per dollar. Since 1984, the Exchange Equalization Fund (EEF) served as a mechanism through which the basket-peg exchange rate policy was implemented. The EEF daily announced the mid-rate for US$/Thai baht, and stood ready from 8.30 to 12.00 a.m. to buy and sell US dollars in any amount with banks at 0.02 from the mid-rate.

18  Under the first three-year financial reform plan, the Bank of Thailand fully liberalized the interest-rate structure, thereby enabling the domestic financial system to adjust interest-rate movements on the basis of supply and demand conditions. Ceilings on commercial bank deposit rates were removed during 1989–91. In June 1992, ceilings on finance and *crédit foncier* companies' deposits and lending rates and on commercial banks' lending rates were removed. Similarly, several foreign-exchange controls were relaxed. For example, residents could now open foreign-currency accounts in Thailand (Alba *et al.* 1999, 18).

19  Until 1990 Thai citizens were not permitted to hold foreign-exchange deposits or to purchase foreign currencies for investment overseas. Thus they were unable to take much advantage of differentials between domestic and foreign rates of interest. For details, see Wibulswasdi (1995).

20  The regulatory authority of the SEC covers all aspects of the capital market, including, (1) issuance of securities by means of public offering and private placement; (2) securities trading, both in the Stock Exchange of Thailand and in the over-the-counter market; (3) securities business, including securities companies and mutual fund management companies; and (4) information disclosure and prevention of unfair trading practices.

21  High domestic interest rates were the result of the Bank of Thailand's pursuing a tight monetary policy to keep inflation in check.

22  M1 is the measure of the US money stock that consists of currency held by the public, travelers' checks, demand deposits and other check-able deposits, including NOW (negotiable order of withdrawal) and ATS (automatic transfer service) account balances and share draft account balances at credit unions. M2 is the measure of the US money stock that consists of M1, certain overnight

repurchase agreements and certain overnight Eurodollars, savings deposits (including money-market deposit accounts), time deposits in amounts of less than US$100,000 and balances in money-market mutual funds (other than those restricted to institutional investors).

23  M3 is the measure of the US money stock that consists of M2, time deposits of US$100,000 or more at all depository institutions, term repurchase agreements in amounts of US$100,000 or more, certain-term Eurodollars, and balances in money-market mutual funds restricted to institutional investors.

24  The 7–8 per cent differentials were the result of weak competition in financial markets and a government policy of maintaining high domestic interest rates in order to control inflation and rising current-account deficits. The relatively high domestic interest rates, together with fixed foreign-exchange rates, attracted short-term foreign funds, especially in the form of non-resident baht accounts.

25  Thailand's organized financial markets are made up of eight main financial institutions: commercial banks; finance, securities and credit companies; specialized banks; development finance corporations; the stock exchange; insurance companies; saving cooperatives; and mortgage institutions. The commercial banks make up the largest component in terms of total assets, credit extended and savings mobilized. In 1990 they accounted for 71 per cent of total financial assets in the country. The second largest are the finance companies, which began operation in 1969 (Warr and Nidhiprabha 1996, 39).

26  The theoretical distinction between short-term and long-term capital flows is usually intended to differentiate between flows that are easily reversible and sensitive to fluctuations in expected risk-adjusted international yield differentials (flows that are sometimes referred to as speculative or hot money), and flows that are not easily reversible and that are determined more by longer-term fundamentals.

27  The BOT (1998b, 16) notes that while "for the year 1996 as a whole, monetary base growth slowed to 12 per cent compared with 22.6 per cent in 1995, indicating an adjustment in the desirable direction, the stock of private external debt had already accumulated to US$73.3 billion by end-1996, more than half of which was accounted for by 27 foreign banks, BIBFs and 15 Thai BIBFs."

28  Commercial banks were permitted to hold net foreign assets up to 25 per cent of their capital funds, while the maximum percentage of net foreign liabilities was raised to 20 per cent.

29  Why did wage increases outstrip productivity increases in Thailand? According to Warr (1998), in the 1980s agriculture had already experienced low labor productivity, and the labor surplus that could be transferred to manufacturing was. This raised average productivity without a proportional increase in the wage rate. As the supply of surplus agricultural labor ran out in the early 1990s, the tighter labor market pushed up wages. In addition, labor productivity was constrained by a relative lack of skilled workers in Thailand. In 1995, Thailand had the second-lowest secondary school enrollment ratios in the region (only Indonesia's were lower), and an almost total absence of vocational education and R&D. For details, see Mahmood and Aryah (2001).

30  After hitting a historical high of 80 yen to the dollar in June 1995, the yen experienced a downward trend, falling to 127 yen to the dollar in April 1997 – or just before the Asian crisis broke. The yen's sharp depreciation led to a marked

deterioration in East and Southeast Asia's export performance and current-account imbalances in 1996, paving the way for the currency crisis.

31  In hindsight, it can be said that if the baht exchange rate had been determined in such a way as to reflect Thai inflation relative to US and Japanese inflation, then the depreciation of the yen against the US dollar might not have caused the deep problems it did for Thai exports, and the current-account deficits might have been smaller than they were.

32  The finance companies raised huge sums of money by selling interest-bearing "promissory notes" to the public, besides borrowing large amounts from local banks and foreign investors – much of it in the form of short-term loans.

33  One measure of return on capital investment is the incremental capital output ratio (ICOR), which compares the increases in investment relative to the increases in GDP. A rising ratio implies that investment is becoming less productive, or of lower quality. The ICOR rose steadily in Thailand from 2.8 in 1988 to almost 5.0 in 1991, to 6.2 in 1996 (Alba *et al.* 1999, 27).

34  Founded in the mid-1980s, the assets of Finance One quickly grew to US$4 billion by the mid-1990s (Blustein 2001, 56).

35  The FIDF was established in 1985. It was set up as a separate juridical entity (but with its operation housed in the Bank of Thailand) to ensure proper co-ordination in policy implementation, especially during a financial crisis.

36  Somprasong was the first Thai Company to miss payments on its foreign debt. Why did such a premier company collapse so suddenly? In large part because property loans only appear "safe" since the values of the loan collateral keep rising. However, these property prices are rising only because of the reckless lending itself, creating an "asset bubble." When the bubble bursts, the loans cannot be repaid from selling the collateral, $C$, which already plummeting in value.

37  The operating fund of the PLMO came from three sources: an initial capital of 1 billion baht allocated from the government budget; contributions from the member financial institutions of 1 million baht each; and the issuance of PLMO bonds worth 1 billion baht and guaranteed by the government (BOT 1998, 10).

38  In the early months of its operation, the PLMO purchased three projects worth 500 million baht from three financial institutions (BOT 1998, 10).

39  Of course, it would have been practically impossible for the short-sellers to accumulate such an enormous short position in the baht had it not been for the sales that the Bank of Thailand made. Reminiscent of the "blunder" made by the Central Bank of Mexico in issuing the dollar-linked *tesobono* bonds, the Thai Bank's forward contracts constituted a financial bomb that the bank itself had planted underneath the state treasury (DeRosa 2001, 97).

40  The controls exempted genuine underlying business related to current international transactions, foreign direct investment flows and various portfolio investments. Banks were required, however, to maintain documentary evidence supporting such transactions for audit and inspection.

41  According to Blustein (2001, 71), Thailand's "move inflicted acute pain on the hedge funds, to the tune of $400 million to $500 million in losses." Thus DeRosa (2001, 94) cites Soros Quantum Fund portfolio manager Stanley Druckenmiller, who states, "they [the Bank of Thailand] kicked our butts and they've taken a lot of profit we might have had. They did a masterful job of squeezing us out."

42 Lauridsen (1998) mistakenly notes that Amnuay resigned after failing to persuade the cabinet to introduce a managed-float foreign-exchange system. The fact was that he was a vocal supporter of the fixed exchange rate.

43 On July 2, 1997, the baht depreciated by 18 per cent. By the end of July, the baht had fallen by 25 per cent (relative to January 1997); in August, the baht had dropped to 38 baht to the US dollar (a fall of 34 per cent); and by the end of September was 42 per cent below its 1997 start level. From July 2, 1997 to its most depreciated rate in January 1998, the baht went from 25 baht to 54 baht per US dollar. That is, over the course of the following six months, the baht depreciated by almost 100 per cent against the US dollar.

44 The fact that Wibulswasdi had to negotiate with the IMF's Stanley Fischer (Wibulswasdi's professor at MIT) raised questions as to whether the Thai authorities had to submit meekly to all the IMF's demands (Phongpaichit and Baker 2000, 37–8). Indeed, "the initial negotiations with the IMF in August 1997 were cloaked in secrecy, and the first letter of intent was never published in full . . . the Thai ministers and officials involved gave the impression that they simply acceded to all IMF demands" (Phongpaichit and Baker 2001, 85).

45 "Thailand," in *The Far Eastern Economic Review: Asia 1996 Yearbook*, pp. 217–18.

46 It is important to keep in mind that throughout the first half of 1997 the IMF urged a continuation of a pegged exchange rate – but with a widened band and less weight given to the American dollar. The big fear was that a floating rate could easily swing out of control. However, once it became known that Thailand's foreign-exchange reserves were almost gone, there was no choice but to float.

47 There was delay in implementation because one of the coalition partners in the Chavalit administration, the Chart Pattana, some of whose senior MPs had large interests in the financial sector, including some of the suspended finance companies, tried to derail the restructuring plan.

48 The AMC began with a total funding of 1 billion baht as a buyer of last resort, to focus on the lowest-quality assets in the liquidation process organized by the FRA.

49 What made the coalition administration of Chuan Leekpai more capable in dealing with the growing financial turmoil? There are several interrelated explanations. First, the likeable and urbane Chuan's reputation as a honest man and a consensus-builder served him well. Second, Chuan's Democrat Party, as the oldest and most institutionalized political party in the country, was not only free of the more egregious corruption, but also had a track record of championing prudent macroeconomic policies. Third, although in a coalition arrangement, "the Democrat Party was the largest and he [Chuan] was able to insist that it occupy all of the top economic positions as a precondition for forming government" (Haggard 2000, 94). Finally, there was popular expectation that the new government cooperate and move with dispatch to deal with the growing economic turmoil.

50 Phongpaichit and Baker (2000, 45) note that "Tarrin Nimmanhaeminda had been Thailand's leading professional banker . . . [and] was an open advocate of financial liberalization, and quickly established the personal confidence of the IMF, Washington, and the financial markets."

51 The new loan classification was tightened by lowering the period after which a loan is non-performing from 12 to 6 months and keeping a high capital-to-risk assets ratio of 12–15 per cent (compared to the international norm of 8.5 per cent) in order to bring the sector gradually into line with international standards by 2000. The two finance companies that were re-opened were Kiatnakin Finance and Securities Public Company and Bangkok Investment Public Company Limited. The 56 of the 58 companies that were closed down were required to sell their assets by the end of 1998.

52 When the 16 finance companies were suspended on June 27, 1997, the government announced that depositors' claims on the companies would receive priority, but that creditors' claims would not. However, when 42 more finance companies were suspended on August 5, 1997, both creditors and depositors received priority. Creditors of the first 16 suspended finance companies that did not have the option of exchanging their claims had to modify their claims under a shareholder rehabilitation program or try to collect from the proceeds of the FRA's liquidation of assets. And finally, although the KTT and the KTB were in charge of administering the note-exchange programs, the FIDF was made responsible for servicing payments of interests and principal on the notes.

53 Although, the rules were announced on 31 March 1998, they were effective as of the end of 1997.

54 The third letter of intent was signed on February 24, 1998. For details, see GoT 1998.

55 The overnight central bank repurchase rate reached 22 per cent (Nabi and Shivakumar 2001, 29).

56 Flatters (2000, 264) also notes that "significant decreases in wages and hours worked are widely acknowledged. Wage reductions of 20 to 30 per cent have been common in many sectors."

57 Tan (2000, 113) notes that "poor farmers in the drought stricken villages in the country's northeast were venturing into minefields on the Thai–Cambodian border in search of an edible root called *kloy*. Many Thais were resorting to selling their organs illegally in order to survive."

58 As Flatters (2000, 265), notes, "the relaxed fiscal targets, however, were more in the nature of a passive recognition of the devastating effects of the crisis on revenues than an active attempt to provide a fiscal stimulus."

59 It turned out that few banks resorted to the capital enlargement opportunities offered by the government, in particular, the tier 1 option. It seems that banks have been reluctant to write down their capital in return for public money and accept the resultant dilution of ownership. Rather, banks choose to raise capital through the issuance of preferred stocks linked with subordinated debentures – or the so-called SLIPS (Stapled Limited Preferred Shares) and CAPS (Capital Augmented Preferred Shares). Although these new instruments are appealing in the presence of low deposit interest rates, they still have risks, as they receive no government guarantee, and returns are mostly performance-based.

60 In coalition with Yongchaiyut's New Aspiration Party, and the Chat Thai Party of Banhan Sinlapa-acha, Thaksin controlled over 300 seats. The July 2001 merger with the small Seritham Party added 14 members to parliament, increasing the Thai Rak Thai seats in the house to 263.

# 3

# Indonesia:
# crisis, reform and recovery

In Indonesia, state-owned banking gave way to a system where anyone with $1 million or so could open a bank (Little 1997, 10).

In mid-1998, a World Bank study (1998) grimly noted that "Indonesia is in deep economic crisis. A country that achieved decades of rapid growth, stability, and poverty reduction is now near economic collapse . . . no country in recent history, let alone one the size of Indonesia, has ever suffered such a dramatic reversal of fortune." There is bitter irony in Indonesia's fall from grace. Long hailed as a model of successful economic development, it was widely expected to escape the fate of Thailand.[1] Between June and August 1997, as Thailand's economy unraveled and the virulent Asian flu sent shock waves through the region, the Indonesian economy remained relatively stable – seemingly a veritable rock in the stormy sea. Even the World Bank (1997) remained upbeat about the short-term outlook, believing that a modest widening of the intervention band (from 8 per cent to 12 per cent) within which the rupiah was allowed to be traded would be sufficient to ward off contagion. The Indonesian government, which received much praise for its swift and decisive response to the crisis, went to great lengths to assure jittery investors "that Indonesia was not Thailand." Then the unthinkable happened. Indonesia suddenly succumbed to the contagion, and measured by the magnitude of currency depreciation and contraction of economic activity, it emerged as the most serious casualty of Asia's financial crisis. In fact, with an economic contraction of 15 per cent in output in 1998, Indonesia experienced the most severe economic collapse recorded for any country in a single year since the Great Depression of the 1930s.

What happened? Why did Indonesia (and the other high-performing Asian economies) collapse like hollow dominoes? In the numerous post-mortems that have followed, analysts have identified a number of related factors behind the region's dramatic reversal of fortune. In the case of Indonesia,

123

the variable that soon acquired particular salience was "crony capitalism." Initially popularized by *The Economist* (1998), the term quickly took on a life of its own. Soon thereafter, Paul Krugman would argue that crony capitalism lay at the root of Indonesia's, indeed, East Asia's, financial woes. Krugman's emphasis on crony capitalism, while not without merit, is too simplistic. After all *korupsi, kolusi dan nepotisme* (corruption, collusion and nepotism), has long been pervasive in Indonesia. It was hardly an obstacle when Indonesia notched up impressive economic growth-rates for some three decades prior to the crisis. Back then, crony capitalism was politely referred to as the "government–private sector nexus" and viewed as a unique feature of the East Asian "developmental states" and even a necessary prerequisite for development. Rather, this chapter argues that a more nuanced understanding of Indonesia's economic crisis can be gained by differentiating between the sources of "vulnerability" and the "precipitating" factors. A careful review of the events leading to the crisis shows that both these factors converged during the critical period between late August 1997 and March 1998 – and practically everything that could go wrong did over these months. The greatest source of vulnerability, indeed, the fundamental weakness lay in Indonesia's over-guaranteed but under-capitalized and under-regulated banking sector. The precipitating factors were the contagion, but also, more importantly, poor macroeconomic management by the Suharto regime; and to a lesser extent the International Monetary Fund exacerbated the crisis.

## The background

The fact that nobody saw Indonesia's impending collapse is hardly surprising. Hal Hill (1999, 8) notes that before the crisis "almost every technical economic indicator looked safe." Likewise, Furman and Stiglitz (1998) found that the Indonesian crisis was the least predictable out of a sample of 34 potentially troubled economies. Indeed, for a country that was dismissed during the Sukarno era (1949–65) as a "chronic dropout" and one that "must surely be accounted the number one failure among the major underdeveloped countries," Indonesia's economic development in the post-Sukarno era was nothing short of miraculous.[2] In the first half of the 1960s, foreign-exchange reserves shrank to zero (in 1965), inflation skyrocketed to over 600 per cent annually, government deficit rose to some 3,000 per cent of revenues, and per capita income fell by 15 per cent between 1958 and 1965 (Bhattacharya and Pangestu 1997, 390–3; Prawiro 1998, 1–18). In sharp contrast economic growth averaged 7 per cent between 1970 and 1989 and 8 per cent between 1990 and 1996 (Booth 1999, 110–12). This growth occurred alongside substantial industrialization and structural change, as agriculture's share of GDP declined from 55 per cent in 1965 to 19.4 per cent in 1990, while industrial output expanded from 13 per cent to 42 per cent – with a corresponding rise in the share of manufactures in GDP from 8 per cent to 20 per cent by 1990 (Jomo 1997, 133; Booth 1999, 113). By 1993, manufactured exports reached US$21 billion and accounted for 53 per cent of total exports (World Bank 1996, 216). It is important to note that, unlike what happened in many other developing countries, Indonesia's proportional shift from agriculture to industry did not come at the expense of agriculture. On the contrary, the first five-year plan (or Repelita 1) introduced in 1969 emphasized agricultural and rural infrastructural development. Not surprisingly, agriculture accounted for almost 30 per cent of the rapid economic growth achieved from 1967 to 1973. While Indonesia was a major beneficiary of the oil and commodity boom of 1973–81, unlike many other oil exporters it used the earnings prudently – avoiding the familiar "Dutch disease" problem (or how to protect the competitiveness of the non-oil economy from the adverse consequences of oil windfalls) by wisely investing in manufacturing and agricultural production as well as in improving social services. As Booth (1999, 114) notes, after 1973, "revenues from oil company taxes were used to increase agricultural productivity." New high-yielding and pest-resistant varieties of rice were developed and distributed. These efforts contributed to a burst of growth in rice production between 1979 and 1985, when total output of the crop increased by 49 per cent.

By the mid-1990s, manufacturing had been the leading engine of growth in Indonesia for more than a decade, contributing roughly one-third of the increase in GDP from 1983 to 1995. However, this rapid expansion of manufacturing was not simply the result of growth of industries based on processing petroleum and natural gas (in 1995 these two activities accounted for less than one-tenth of total manufacturing output); the other nine-tenths comprised a diverse range of manufacturing industries. Some of these, such as motor vehicles, were oriented largely toward the domestic market, while wood products, garments, textiles, footwear and electronics were mainly sold abroad. As a result, by the late 1980s the economy had become more trade-dependent, with total trade flows as a percentage of GDP rising sharply from 14 per cent in 1965 to 54.7 per cent in 1990. These developments increased the capacity of the economy to mobilize savings, as reflected in the rise of national savings as a percentage of GDP from 7.9 per cent in 1965 to 26.3 per cent in 1990 (Jomo 1997, 133).

Equally impressively, the quality of life for the average Indonesian improved greatly, as per capita income rose from US$75 in 1966 to US$1,200 in 1996. These gains were spread fairly equitably. For example, between 1976 and 1990 income per person in the poorest quintile of Indonesia's population grew by 5.8 per cent per year, whereas the average income of the entire population grew by 4.9 per cent per year. To put this success in some comparative context: in 1967 per capita income in Indonesia was less than one-half that of India, Nigeria or Bangladesh. By mid-1997, it was five times that of Bangladesh, four times that of Nigeria and three and a half times that of India (Kenward 1999a, 73). With such growth, the proportion of population living below the official poverty line declined from 64 per cent to an estimated 11 per cent between 1970 and 1996 – one of the largest reductions in poverty recorded anywhere in the world during the period.[3] Other socioeconomic indicators bear out this success. For example, consumption of foodstuffs such as rice, meat and dairy products rose continually since the late 1960s. Between 1968 and 1995, daily protein intake per Indonesian improved by more than 60 per cent – from 43.3 to 70.0 grams (Booth 1999, 129). Infant mortality declined from 145 per 1,000 live births in 1970 to 53 per 1,000 in 1995, life expectancy rose from 46 to 63 years during the same period, and the country achieved universal primary education in 1995. While Java, in particular greater Jakarta, was the main beneficiary, the benefits of economic growth extended to all Indonesia's twenty-seven culturally diverse and far-flung provinces (World Bank 1998, 75). Mills (1995, 7) sums up Indonesia's achievements in these words:

> Indonesia's growth rate over the past 25 years has transformed a desperately poor society in which malnutrition, illiteracy and infant mortality were widespread into one with a large middle class, one in which nearly all children are educated and in which infant mortality and malnutrition have decreased dramatically. The benefits of such relatively rapid growth are not shared equally in any society, but all major groups benefitted greatly: farmers, factory workers, industrialists, small business owners, government employees and the urban poor.

One of the repeated boasts of Suharto New Order Government (1965–98) was its defeat of the rampant hyperinflation of the Sukarno era, and its ability to keep budget deficits low and in balance.[4] Indeed, prudent macroeconomic management kept the budget broadly balanced for an unprecedented 30 years – or the entire length of the Suharto era. Immediately on assuming office, the Suharto regime eliminated the fiscal deficit through drastic expenditure cuts and passed a "balanced budget" law in 1967 prohibiting domestic financing of the budget in the form of either debt or money creation. Again, effective macroeconomic management helped Indonesia steer through the difficulties of the steep oil price increases and declines in the 1970s and 1980s, and kept the macro-economy largely in balance right up to the onset of the crisis in mid-1997. As was noted earlier, the government essentially proscribed domestic financing for the budget throughout – a strategy that kept both expenditures and monetary growth under relative control. Moreover, the government also adopted a stringent monetary program to bring down inflationary pressures. By 1969, inflation had been reduced to less than 20 per cent and external accounts were brought into balance (Bhattacharya and Pangestu 1997, 394). Since the mid-1980s, inflation has been kept within single digits, and on the eve of the crisis was about

6 per cent (McLeod 1999, 209). Finally, the exchange-rate was adjusted to realistic levels through large devaluations, while the administered system of foreign-exchange allocation was gradually replaced by a market mechanism. Following the unification of the exchange rate in 1970 and a further devaluation in 1997, the capital account was fully liberalized. In 1967, Indonesia rejoined the World Bank and the IMF, which enabled it to receive substantial foreign assistance for its adjustment program and work out arrangements to reschedule its foreign debt.

In contrast with those of Thailand and Malaysia, Indonesia's current account deficit in the 1990s averaged only 2.6 per cent of GDP. In fact, not once in any year between 1990 and 1996 did its annual current-account deficits ever exceed the average over the period 1983–89. The 1996 current account deficit of 3.5 per cent was comparable to those of previous years, and less than half the level in Thailand. Thus, the deficit on the current account of the balance of payments looked healthy and manageable. Also, unlike the case in Thailand, there was no serious exchange-rate misalignment, as Indonesia's exchange-rate policy was gradually relaxed (via widening of the intervention band) by Bank Indonesia, the country's central bank. Two large devaluations of the rupiah in 1983 and 1986, and the ensuing policy of allowing it to float (within a band) downward relative to the US dollar led the exchange rate to decline steeply over time in real terms. Because of this policy, which lasted until the rate was freed in August 1997, Indonesian exports could be competitively priced in dollar terms on world markets. This policy enabled Indonesia to compete successfully with producers of labor-intensive manufactures in the region, including China.[5] Finally, Bank Indonesia had substantially increased its stocks of international reserves. Indeed, international reserves, both in absolute terms and in months of merchandise imports, were comfortable and rising just prior to the crisis. The external debt to GDP ratio was gradually declining, and was appreciably lower than during the difficult adjustment period of the mid-1980s. And, with the exception of 1990, Indonesia had an excess of private savings over investment in the period 1990–96. The budget surplus averaged over 1 per cent in the four years prior to the crisis, and credit growth was modest. In short, the traditional economic indicators looked sound.

## Sources of vulnerability

With such an enviable record of development and seemingly sound economic fundamentals, what went wrong? The roots of the crisis can be traced back to the mid-1980s, when Indonesia embarked on an ambitious economic reform program. The reforms were designed to diversify the economy in order to reduce its dependence on the oil sector, encourage the development of a competitive non-oil export-oriented industrial base that would absorb the rapidly growing labor force, and expand the role of the private sector, including foreign capital. Key elements of the reform measures between 1985 and 1996 included: (a) gradual liberalization of direct investment inflows to promote non-oil exports and economic diversification; (b) maintenance of a competitive exchange rate; (c) trade liberalization and tariff reform; (d) improvements in monetary management; (e) financial sector reform through liberalization of external inflows; and (f) the promotion of competition in the banking sector. For example, in October 1988 deregulation removed most of the entry barriers. New banks, whether joint ventures or domestic, could now be set up with capital requirements of Rp. 50 billion and Rp. 10 billion respectively. Regulations on opening new branches were substantially relaxed and reserve requirements were drastically reduced (Bhattacharya and Pangestu 1997, 417). In addition to all this there was an objective of encouraging the growth of the capital market by extending the role of the market in raising funds for investments and lengthening the maturity of money-market instruments. Further, in 1989 the authorities liberalized portfolio capital inflows by eliminating quantitative limits on banks borrowing from non-residents. Foreigners were allowed to own up to 49 per cent of the shares issued by listed domestic companies (except banks), while domestic companies were allowed to raise funds by selling securities in local and international stock and bond markets. In 1990, restrictions on direct investment inflows were further relaxed, and foreign direct investors were allowed to sell foreign exchange directly to commercial banks instead of through the central bank, and to purchase securities on the stock market and on the over-the-counter bourse. However, as the following sections will illustrate, such rapid liberalization without putting the necessary prudential regulations in place, combined with haphazard implementation of the reform measures, made Indonesia highly vulnerable to economic shocks.

Indonesia's seemingly endless growth potential and its adoption of market-friendly economic policies attracted foreign investors. Moreover, "commercial banks bustled to get more overseas funds. Their activities resulted in an increase in liabilities from Rp. 11 trillion in March 1989, to Rp. 17.5 trillion in March 1990, and to Rp. 31.6 trillion in March 1991" (Rosul 1998, 246). In fact, capital inflows increased almost two and one-half times from 1990–94, reaching US$14.7 billion (Nasution 1999, 76). Overall, between 1990 and 1996, Indonesia experienced a surge in capital inflows averaging about 4 per cent of GDP. Although not as large as the inflows received by Thailand (10 per cent of GDP) and Malaysia (9 per cent of GDP), cumulatively it still represented a large volume of capital for the economy to absorb effectively. Indeed, by mid-1997, Indonesia's total debt outstanding to foreign commercial banks amounted to US$59 billion. What made Indonesia particularly vulnerable was the maturity structure of the foreign borrowing. According to the Indonesian government's own figures, by the end of June 1997, out of the US$140 billion (about 60 per cent of GDP) in external debt, approximately US$33 billion was short-term debt with maturities due within one year (IMF 1997a). In addition to this amount, Indonesian firms also took out large lines of short-term credit in foreign currencies both directly from foreign lenders and from Indonesian banks – greatly adding to their foreign currency exposure. By contrast, foreign exchange reserves in mid-1997 stood at about US$20 billion. In other words, short-term debts owed to foreign commercial banks were about 1.75 times the size of Indonesia's total foreign exchange reserves (Radelet 1999, 3).

The massive inflow of short-term capital was no accident. Indonesia's exchange-rate system made short-term debt particularly attractive. From the mid-1980s until August 14, 1997, the Indonesian government maintained an intervention band system (the so-called "crawling peg regime") under which the government pledged to intervene in the markets through means such as foreign-exchange purchases and interest-rate adjustments if the rupiah depreciated or appreciated against the US dollar beyond a set percentage. The authorities typically targeted the nominal depreciation of the rupiah against the dollar at between 3 per cent and 5 per cent per annum. There was little variation in this, as Bank Indonesia intervened in the foreign-exchange market by buying and selling the rupiah in an intervention band around the central rate. The reasoning behind such an activist policy was to stabilize the real exchange rate, thereby discouraging speculative capital inflows and giving monetary authorities greater flexibility to control monetary aggregates. However, the predictability of the exchange rate made short-term dollar loans seem less risky, and therefore much more attractive. For example, an Indonesian bank borrowing in US dollars could simply compare the cost of purchasing a hedging instrument with the maximum depreciation of the rupiah against the US dollar permitted under the intervention band during the term of the loan. Thus, hedging the currency exposure would only be economically justified when the cost of the hedging instrument was less than the maximum potential depreciation of the rupiah under the intervention band system. Because short-term funding on an unhedged basis was so attractive, and because of the fact that borrowers were led to believe that the expected losses from currency depreciation would be less than the cost of hedging foreign borrowings, the greater part of the banking sector's foreign borrowing remained unhedged. As Radelet (1999, 3–4) notes, "this predictability [of the exchange rate] also undercut the incentives for firms to hedge against their exposure to exchange rate movements. According to one estimate, hedging [against the risk of exchange rate movements] would have added about 6 percentage points to the cost of borrowing. Very few firms covered their exposure." Thus, Indonesian banks were faced with an unhedged funding mismatch between borrowing short-term offshore in foreign currency and lending long-term in rupiah. This mispricing of foreign credits, combined with the increased supply of funds in the global financial markets, contributed to very large capital inflows and created vulnerability for firms with substantial foreign-exchange exposure.

In addition, domestic firms and corporations found short-term foreign-currency loans appealing, since they carried relatively lower interest rates. In fact, firms assumed that they would be able to roll over their loans easily when they fell due – after all, this is what they had done for several years before the crisis. Foreign lenders also complied, often not undertaking adequate appraisal of their investments. Radelet (1999) aptly notes that Indonesia's vulnerability was all the greater because its largest creditors were Japanese banks, which provided about 40 per cent of the total credit from foreign banks. The underlying weaknesses of Japanese banks made them more likely to try to pull their loans quickly once the crisis began. Indeed, this is precisely what happened. In mid-August 1997, as Thailand reached agreement with the IMF on its first program, Japanese banks agreed to keep US$19 billion in trade and other credit facilities open for certain Thai commercial bank borrowers. Not wanting to be caught again in similar situations in other countries in the region, the Japanese banks began to withdraw their credits from Indonesia, Malaysia, Korea and other countries – helping to spread the crisis further.

Indonesia's crawling peg regime unintentionally contributed to another problem: a modestly overvalued exchange rate and slowing export growth. This trend sharply increased after the 1987 Plaza Accord, which brought down the value of the US dollar and ushered in a new era of the appreciating yen. Between 1985 and 1988 the yen almost doubled in value *vis-à-vis* the dollar and other Asian currencies tied to the dollar. More broadly, by 1988 the yen was almost 30 per cent above its average for the 1980–85 period on an inflation-adjusted, trade-weighted basis (Ito and Iwaisako 1996). By the mid-1990s, the era of the strong yen was over, as was indicated by the sharp appreciation of the dollar in 1995, and especially its appreciation *vis-à-vis* the yen. As the dollar rose relative to the yen, the currencies of the countries tied to the dollar (like Indonesia) rose in comparison with the yen also.[6] Radelet (1999, 4) notes that between 1990 and mid-1997 the rupiah appreciated approximately 22 per cent in real terms, while growth in Indonesian non-oil exports slowed from an annual average of 26 per cent in 1991–92 to 14 per cent between 1993 and 1995 to just 10 per cent in 1996–97. This modest overvaluation and export slowdown, although smaller than in the other crisis-affected countries, clearly pointed toward the need for some moderate adjustments to re-establish the international competitiveness of Indonesian firms. Moreover, although the Indonesian monetary authority maintained a more flexible foreign-exchange policy by adjusting its currency according to its current-account deficit levels, this was not enough to correct the productivity gap between Indonesia and its competitors in the region. Indonesia's real effective exchange rates appreciated despite the nominal depreciation, and its export markets, dependent upon imported raw materials and cheap labor, were eroded by the competition from China and Vietnam in the early 1990s.

Vulnerability also came from the way the capital inflows were utilized. The massive capital inflows soon created problems of absorption. While capital was invested in productive investments such as infrastructure development, electricity generation and heavy industries such as petrochemicals and automobile assembly, a significant portion also found its way into the non-tradeable sector and, in particular, real estate. As Dominique Fischer (2000, 225) notes, "from an almost non-existent stock in 1987, modern office space grew to 2.8 million square meters, shopping centers reached 1.2 million square meters and the stock of luxury condominiums was estimated at 15,000 units." Such aggressive development only fueled speculative overbuilding, particularly in Jabotabek, or the greater Jakarta area.[7] Why real estate? The surge in private capital inflows relative to the size of the equity market quickly drove equity prices up. Investments in real estate, especially, housing, hotels and tourist resorts, amusement parks, golf courses and shopping malls, looked promising. Foreign lenders able to easily purchase stock, commercial paper and real estate were only too eager to finance these projects – not only because they seemed to be good investments, but also because, with many of these projects controlled either directly or indirectly by Suharto's family and their cronies, they assumed that the projects carried an implicit guarantee from the Indonesian government (Sender 1994; 1997).

Perhaps Indonesia's greatest vulnerability lay in its weak financial system, especially its dangerously undercapitalized and poorly supervised banks. What explains this weakness, and why was it allowed to persist? A brief background is necessary. First, while the central bank, Bank Indonesia, was responsible for supervising the country's banking system, it nevertheless reported directly to the president during the Suharto era. This left the entire banking system open to both indirect and direct political interference. It is widely agreed that on numerous occasions prudential rules were violated by the well-connected without fear of any punishment from the central bank. In fact, during the latter part of the Suharto era, banks not only lent amounts well in excess of legal lending limits, but politically-driven lending to well-connected borrowers and projects took place without regard to the underlying economic viability of the borrowers or the projects. Thus, although Indonesia had, on paper, a modern and fairly comprehensive set of banking regulations, the rules were hardly enforced. Such irregularities only raised the moral hazard stakes.

Second, while reform of the Indonesian banking system was initiated in 1983 with the abolition of Bank Indonesia's control over interest rates on deposits and loans,[8] it was in October 1988 that Bank Indonesia enacted a package of major banking reforms known as the "October 1988 Package" or PAKTO 88 – which according to former Bank Indonesia Governor,

J. Soedradjad Djiwandono (1998, 7–8), "fundamentally changed the face of banking in Indonesia."[9] Since the government saw banks as the key financial intermediaries in mobilizing funds, the main aim of PAKTO 88 was to encourage competition in the banking sector by lowering the barrier to entry, including the liberalization of the requirements for the establishment of new private domestic banks and joint-venture banks. To this effect, PAKTO 88 ended segmentation of the financial market and improved market competition. Also, PAKTO relaxed the restrictions on the establishment of private and foreign-owned banks, as well as the restrictions on existing banks opening new branches – this included the granting of permission to state-owned firms to deposit 50 per cent of their short-term funds with private banks, instead of only with state-owned banks. In addition, for the first time, foreign banks were permitted to set up branches outside Jakarta in any of the nation's six major cities, provided that 50 per cent of their loan portfolio went to export-oriented businesses. Foreign partners could also hold up to 85 per cent of the value of the new banks, which had to have minimum paid-up capital of US$30 million (Djiwandono 1998, 8; Prawiro 1998, 242).

Moreover, PAKTO permitted extremely low capitalization, setting the minimum paid-in capital requirement for newly established banks at the rupiah equivalent of US$5 million. It also allowed more foreign ownership of domestic assets and abolished the limits on inflow of foreign direct investment and foreign ownership of equities issued in domestic stock markets. Further, bank reserve requirements were sharply cut from 15 per cent to 2 per cent of third-party funds (defined as all demand, savings, and time deposits, plus certificates of deposit from unrelated parties). Deregulation in 1989 eliminated the need for Bank Indonesia's approval for medium- and long-term loans and removed ceilings on offshore loans (Montgomery 1997, 11–12; Djiwandono 1998, 8–10). In addition, the government moved to deregulate equity, bond, insurance and related financial activities. Not surprisingly, two months after PAKTO 88 there were 111 commercial banks and 1,957 bank offices. By the end of 1992, the numbers had jumped to 208 and 5,495 respectively. By the end of 1996, commercial banks dominated the financial system in Indonesia. Most of the new entrants were small or joint-venture banks, which fragmented the sector and intensified the competition for funds. In 1996, out of a total of 238 commercial banks, there were 7 state-owned banks, 27 regional government banks, 160 private banks, 34 joint-venture banks, and 10 foreign banks. In addition, there were approximately 9,200 rural banks called *bank perkreditan rakyat* (BPR), and one Islamic bank (Bank Muamalat). Non-bank financial institutions included 252 finance companies, 163 insurance companies, about 300 pension and provident funds, and 39 mutual fund companies. Total assets of the system were equivalent to about 90 per cent of GDP. Commercial banks held 84 per cent of total assets, while rural banks held about 2 per cent.

The remaining assets were held by finance companies (7 per cent of total assets), insurance companies (5 per cent), and other non-bank financial institutions (2 per cent).[10] As Pincus and Ramli (1998, 725) note, "by the early 1990s, Indonesia possessed one of the most liberal banking systems in the world."

While these reforms succeeded in transforming a closed banking sector dominated by a small number of state-owned banks into a more diverse and competitive system, and brought benefits to the economy, such as more efficient credit allocation and financial intermediation (not to mention, providing Indonesians with many more options for financial services), banking deregulation also posed challenges that the authorities failed to meet. First, in 1983–88, the seven state banks' share of total out-standing bank credit hovered around 65 per cent, but after three years of liberalization their share had dropped to 56 per cent in 1991 and to 40 per cent by the end of 1997 (Chou 1999, 37). State banks have historically played an important role in the allocation of subsidized credit (at preferential interest rates), known as "liquidity credit," to priority sectors assigned by Bank Indonesia. This credit-allocation system, often subject to political abuse, greatly curtailed the state banks' ability to compete with private banks. Liquidity credits and access to Bank Indonesia re-discounting facilities were extended to sugar estates and refineries, rubber and palm-oil plantations, and construction contractors among others. As will be discussed, such practices dragged the entire state sector into the red by 1994. Second, the problem of moral hazard occasioned by explicit or implicit government guarantees induced reckless lending, especially to the well-connected. Indeed, there was a strong presumption in the financial and business community that neither investors nor lenders would ever bear the full cost of any corporate or bank failure. This belief was fostered by the close links between powerful business groups, who also often controlled financial institutions, and the government. Investors and bankers were led to assume that the government would eventually bail them out if they got into trouble, even in the absence of explicit government guarantees. As Krugman (1998) observes, when government actions suggest that there is an explicit guar-antee against either bank or corporate failure, such implicit guarantees can trigger asset price inflation and make the financial system vulnerable to collapse. And, third, the failure to develop simultaneously the necessary prudential supervisory, regulatory and legal framework (and enforce what regulation did exist) made Indonesia highly susceptible to a system-wide banking crisis.

For example, the financial reforms resulted in a rapid expansion of bank credit – a variable widely regarded in financial markets as an indicator of financial vulnerability, since high credit: GDP ratios weaken the capacity of central banks to push up interest rates in defense of the currency during a crisis. Outstanding bank credit increased by an average of 24.3 per cent per year from 1992 to 1996. Part of the credit expansion was financed by foreign borrowing, and when restrictions on lending were lifted, banks began to expand credit to property and real estate, including ambitious and costly infrastructure projects. Bank Indonesia's own figures show that bank lending to the property and real estate sector increased by roughly 40 per cent from 1995 to 1996 (Djiwandono 1999; 1999a). While the competitive, if not speculative, market environment (not to mention the easy availability of bank credit), increased the pressure on banks to lend without careful risk-assessment, Nasution (1999, 80), notes that "Indonesia's prudential rules and regulations were poorly implemented and largely unenforced . . . bank credit officers who were reared in the pre-reform environment may have lacked the expertise to evaluate new sources of credit and market risk." Furthermore, the comparatively poorly compensated officials at the state-owned banks, who viewed their job security and career advancement as being essentially dependent on their ability to satisfy powerful individuals and the well-connected, hardly bothered to assess the creditworthiness of the borrowers. Not surprisingly, in the case of the state-owned banks, risky lending practices were often the result of both explicit and implicit pressure exerted by members of the Suharto family, their cronies and other high-ranking military and government officials to make loans to favored borrowers. Indeed, the practice of making loans based on political pressure became known as "memo lending," because such loans were extended on the basis of a "memo" sent by the powerful and well-connected. Soon memo lending and other illegal practices led to high levels of non-performing loans at the state-owned banks.

The case of a government-owned development bank, Bank Pembangunan Indonesia (also known by its acronym as Bank Bapindo), is illustrative. In 1994, Bank Bapindo lent some US$436 million to the Golden Key group, at that time a little-known Indonesian *konglomerat* (conglomerate) owned by a colorful businessman, Eddy Tansil, with close links with senior military and government officials. The loan was never repaid, and a later government investigation alleged that the loan had been extended on the basis of fraudulent documentation and with the complicity of key Bapindo executives and government officials, including the former minister of finance, Johannes Sumarlin – who at the time was also a member of Bapindo's board of commissioners (Habir 1999). Regulators and central bank supervisors were also involved in fraud and collusion. However, instead of closing down or restructuring the bank, the government allowed the bank to continue to operate. Also, only bank officers (but not the managers) were punished for corruption. Similarly, in the case of commercial paper issued by PT Bank Pacific, PT Bank Arta Prima and PT Bank Perniagaan, only four supervisors of Bank Indonesia were arrested in early August 1997 for allegedly taking bribes during inspections between 1993 and 1996. Nasution (1999, 83) supplies the macro dimension of the problem:

Despite average annual economic growth of over 6 per cent since 1990, the volume of problem loans held by Indonesia's banks remained considerable. In 1995, 8.8 per cent of total bank credit outstanding was classified as sub-standard, doubtful, or bad debt. As of November 1996, the bad debt of the banking system amounted to Rp. [rupiah] 10.4 trillion (equivalent to about 2 per cent of GDP or around 10 per cent of total loans). Of this amount, state-owned banks held Rp. 7.1 trillion (68 per cent).

Thus the rapid growth of the private banks was achieved at the expense of sector soundness. That is, in the case of the private banks, risky lending practices usually involved banks making loans to affiliated companies – which also included affiliated property companies. Specifically, since liberalization increased the attraction of the financial sector to commercial and industrial concerns, many of Indonesia's large business conglomerates opened one or more private banks. Most of these banks were not managed on an independent basis, but as funding sources for the affiliated businesses – extending loans to suit the funding needs of the businesses and on terms dictated by the affiliated businesses' senior office-holders, rather than on the basis of diligent risk-assessment of the companies' creditworthiness. While there were rules regarding the aggregate amount that a bank could lend to its affiliated companies, there were no clear provisions to enforce the rules. Not only were the staff and resources of the central bank insufficient to allow for adequate inspections of the banks under its supervision; indirect or intra-group lending could in any case easily be concealed. Thus, loans to affiliated companies were among the riskiest loans held by the private banks.

The case of Bank Summa is illustrative. This bank was one of the first private banks established after the enactment by Bank Indonesia of the 1988 banking reforms. Prior to its collapse, Bank Summa was one of the ten largest banks in Indonesia. It was owned by the influential Soeryadjaya family, who also had major controlling interest in Astra International, one of Indonesia's largest conglomerates. In the second half of 1990, Bank Summa began to face serious financial problems, mostly as a result of the deteriorating quality of its large portfolio of loans. Many of the "bad" loans were in the real estate sector, and 70 per cent of these loans had been extended to related parties, exceeding the legal limit by far (Enoch *et al.* 2001, 23). For two years, Bank Indonesia relied on its traditional approach of holding talks with the shareholders and trying to persuade them to solve the bank's problems while continuing to provide liquidity support – which by the end amounted to 25 per cent of the bank's total liabilities (Enoch *et al.* 2001, 24). In June 1992, a memorandum of understanding formalized the owners' commitment to repay the non-performing connected loans and recapitalize the bank. However, the owners failed to meet their commitment. Faced with a fast-growing liquidity need, Bank Indonesia decided in November 1993 not to grant any additional liquidity support, and revoked Bank Summa's license. In December 1992, Bank Summa collapsed. At the time of Bank

Summa's liquidation, it was estimated that more than 70 per cent of its loan portfolio was non-performing and that a high percentage of these loans had been made to its affiliated companies. In total, Bank Summa had amassed more than US$750 million (0.6 per cent of GDP) in non-performing loans (Enoch *et al.* 2001, 23). Nasution (1999, 85–6) notes:

> Indonesia's weak market infrastructure, malfeasance and malversation together have allowed the emergence of so-called "swindle" banks. The typical swindle bank makes loans to non-bank companies owned by its principal owner(s) to finance questionable investment projects, usually at inflated prices. Liabilities of such banks are mainly deposits owned by the general public, liquidity credit from Bank Indonesia, unsecured commercial paper sold to the general public (including foreigners), and equity shares owned by Bank Indonesia and other state-related institutions . . . Such banks typically have negative net worth.

By the early 1990s, Bank Indonesia was quite aware that the country's banks, given their high level of exposure to property companies, faced a potentially disastrous problem. As is well known, investments in property and real estate are long-term and highly risky, because they are very sensitive to future growth expectations. In contrast, the liabilities of the banks were mostly short-term and denominated in US dollars, Japanese yen and other foreign currencies. Also, in many cases, banks had taken no collateral, and those that had taken collateral took a pledge over property as collateral for loans. In any case, they could hardly collect, because a fall in real estate prices would mean that by the time of default the property used to secure a loan would be worth only a small fraction of the outstanding principal amount loaned. Moreover, as was noted earlier, short-term borrowing from abroad was a relatively inexpensive source of funds provided that the banks did not incur additional costs purchasing hedging instruments to protect themselves from any depreciation of the rupiah against the currency they had borrowed. Unhedged foreign-currency borrowing posed an obvious risk to a bank, in that any depreciation of the rupiah during the term of the loan would mean that the amount in rupiahs needed to repay the loan on maturity would be far greater than the amount the borrower received upon drawing the loan. In short, Indonesian banks were faced with an unhedged funding mismatch between borrowing short-term from abroad in foreign currency and lending long-term in rupiah. All these asymmetries of the banks' balance sheets added greatly to their overall riskness.

In an effort to address these problems, the Indonesian government enacted the Banking Law (known as Banking Act No. 7) in 1992. The Banking Law allowed sanctions to be imposed on bank owners, managers, and commissioners for violations of laws and regulations related to bank management. Also, the law contained provisions designed to restrict the aggregate amount that a bank could lend to affiliated companies to 20 per cent of the bank's capital, and converted some state banks to limited liability companies and permitted them to lend only to non-priority sectors. In October 1992, as part of the project to limit the number of banks, the capital required to set up a domestic bank was increased fivefold. In 1995, reserve requirements were raised from 2 per cent to 3 per cent effective February 1996. In addition, the minimum capital required for banks with foreign-exchange licenses was tripled, and the capital adequacy ratio for these banks was raised from 8 per cent to 12 per cent – with both these measures to be phased in over a five-year period ending in 2001. Bank Indonesia also developed a supervisory system patterned on the United States CAMEL system (Capital, Asset Quality, Management, Earnings, Liquidity), including annual on-site examinations of banks. Moreover, the system stipulated necessary qualifications of bank owners and managers, a schedule to meet the Bank for International Settlements (BIS) capital adequacy requirement (CAR) of 8 per cent on risk-weighted assets, stricter information and reporting requirements, and tougher limits on lending within a corporate group or to one individual. In fact, by the end of 1996 prudential practices in Indonesia's banking sector were largely in line with those recommended by the Basle Committee, and comparable to those adopted in the United States and the European Union.

However, the Indonesian government's efforts to improve and promote best practice came when the sector was already deeply troubled by high levels of non-performing loans. Moreover, the enforcement of these measures was generally quite lax, and violations rampant. Bank Indonesia's own report acknowledged that as of March 1997 a significant number of banks remained undercapitalized and not in compliance with the prudential rules. While these figures very probably understate the extent of non-compliance, according to Bank Indonesia 15 banks did not meet the required 8 per cent capital adequacy ratio in April 1996, while 41 banks did not comply with the legal lending limit, and 12 licensed foreign-exchange banks did not meet the rules on net open foreign-exchange exposure (Montgomery 1997, 13). Also, many of the banks continued to maintain their high level of exposure to the property and real estate sector. During 1996, even as the glut in the property market became apparent and real estate prices began to nosedive, Indonesian banks continued to lend to property companies. In 1997, despite large-scale losses reported by the property industry, bank lending to the property sector totaled about 19.4 trillion rupiah, a 21 per cent increase from 1996 (Hammond 1997). In July 1997, Bank Indonesia issued a decree that was intended to restrict bank credit to real estate developers severely; but it was too little too late. Undercapitalized and, in large measure, burdened with poorly diversified and badly performing loan portfolios, Indonesia's over-guaranteed but under-regulated banking system lay exposed and highly vulnerable to economic shocks.

Finally, lurking menacingly beneath were the political vulnerabilities. Specifically, as Indonesia's patrimonial-authoritarian regime succumbed to favoritism and cronyism, this began to take its toll on economic activity. Specifically, in the late 1980s and early 1990s, Suharto's children and the regime's close allies rapidly expanded their business activities. Soon Suharto's children and cronies were involved in almost every economic activity in the country – first in natural resource-based ventures, then in manufacturing, and later in a range of services, from construction to the operation of toll roads, telecommunications and financial services.[11] Richburg (1998, A40) lucidly describes the nature of "Suharto Incorporated."

> The Suharto children are all reputed to have become multi-millionaires by trading on their direct line to the presidential palace, which involved everything from clove cigarettes to toll roads, from petrochemical plants to automobile manufacturing. So pervasive is the first family's reach into the Indonesian economy that a long-running joke here is that the corruption begins as soon as you arrive at Jakarta's international airport: You can buy a pack of cigarettes, hop in a taxi, take a toll road to the city and check into a hotel, putting money into a Suharto family member's pocket with each step.

Indeed, as Blustein (2001, 91) notes, "by the 1990s, the Suharto family's avarice was so pervasive that almost any foreign firm investing in, say, a power plant or phone system or petrochemical factory had to hand over lucrative partnership rights to one presidential relative or another to grease the project's way through the country's bureaucracy." Yet, as was noted earlier, while corruption and cronyism were hardly new in Indonesia, what differentiated the late 1980s and 1990s was Suharto's unwillingness to make prudent economic decisions when his children's and cronies' business interests were at stake. Indonesia's "national car" policy is illustrative. In February 1996, Suharto announced a national car policy designed to provide competition in the automotive industry, especially to the monopoly held by the Astra Group, led by an ethnic-Chinese Indonesian entrepreneur, William Soeryadjaya, and its Japanese partners, Toyota, Daihatsu and Isuzu. The program gave a three-year exemption from import duties and luxury taxes to those Indonesian companies that manufactured cars locally using an Indonesian brand-name and local parts. The conditions attached to these exemptions were demanding. They required companies to attain a local content of 20 per cent after the first year, 40 per cent after the second year, and 60 per cent after the third year. However, as Hale (2001, 631) notes, "it was what happened next, however, that really stunned the domestic business community and international observers." On February 27, 1996, the national car policy promulgated in the Presidential Instruction No. 2/1996 gave a "pioneer" status to PT Timor Putra Nasional (TPN) – jointly owned by Suharto's youngest son, Hutomo ("Tommy") Mandala Putra and the KIA Motor Corporation of South Korea. This special status gave TPN a one-year exemption on tariffs and taxes, despite the fact that the company did not even make cars. Moreover, this exclusive status exempted the company from paying the 65 per cent maximum import duties for car spare parts, and the 35 per cent maximum import duty and luxury goods sale tax that make up over 60 per cent of the cost of car production in Indonesia. Also, as Hale (2001, 632) notes, "adding insult to injury, in June 1996 President Suharto issued the presidential decree that allowed the national car to be assembled in Korea for the first year of operation." In effect, TPN was given permission to import CBU Kia sedans from South Korea and sell them under the Timor brand-name for one year. Furthermore, TPN could sell these cars at a duty-free price that significantly undercut those of its competitors; to boost the sale of the car, the public sector was required to purchase it."[12] Finally, fully backed by the Indonesian government, Bank Indonesia, and a consortium of 4 state-owned banks and 12 private domestic banks, the company received an initial US$960 million for its production and assembly facility. Despite these advantages, "the inability of Tommy's newborn firm to organize itself quickly or well enough to assemble Kia's components in Indonesia had led Suharto to indulge his son: For one year, Tommy could bring up to 45,000 finished Timors into the country from South Korea for sale free of the stiff tariffs and luxury tax that other such imports would still have to face" (Borsuk 1999, 149). As King (2000, 617) notes, "this cronyism was so brazen . . . as to anger even the regime's staunchest supporters." Indeed, in July 1997, with Thailand already in the early stages of the crisis, "Indonesia's biggest state and private banks were arm-twisted by the government to supply US$650 million to Tommy to build a Timor factory east of Jakarta" (Borsuk 1999, 149).

Likewise, against the advice of respected economists, Suharto continued to support the lucrative monopolies his children and cronies enjoyed over the soybean and cloves industries. Specifically, since the mid-1980s, PT Sarpindo Soybean Industri – owned jointly by two of Suharto's children and his wealthiest and oldest friends, Liem Sioe Liong of the Salim Group and the plywood magnate, Mohamad ("Bob") Hasan – had been the sole processor of soybeans into bean curd (a major source of protein for Indonesians), and the sole producer of soymeal, an important ingredient in animal feed. Moreover, while only the state food distribution agency (Badan Urusan Logistik or BULOG), was allowed to import soybeans to meet the growing demand, it had to use Sarpindo's crushing facility for processing soybeans. As Borsuk (1999, 150) notes, "Bulog paid a fee substantially higher than the world price for crushing soybeans. Sarpindo got a further bonus in the form of the soybean oil that crushing yielded, which Sarpindo was allowed to keep and sell at a handsome profit." Besides this, Liem controlled Indofood, the world's largest instant-noodle maker and Bogasari Flour Mills, the world's largest flour-milling operation, which held effective monopolies in the Indonesian market thanks to government contracts, special import licenses and subsidies. Cloves, on the other hand, are the key ingredient used in the manufacture of Indonesia's distinctive spice-flavored cigarettes known as *kretek*. In order to corner this lucrative market for his son Tommy, Suharto designated cloves an "essential commodity," to be regulated by the state. This decision was followed in early 1991 by the creation of the Clove Support and Marketing Agency (*Badan Penyangga dan Pemasaran Cengkeh* or BPPC), with Tommy as chairman. As Borsuk (1999, 152) notes, "to keep the monopoly going, Suharto ordered the central bank to give more than $350 million in subsidized credit to the BPPC. Thus did Tommy's scheme make losers of the farmers, the firms, the government, and the smoking and non-smoking public. The only winners were Tommy himself and the BPPC."

### The trigger and the fallout

All the growing vulnerabilities now needed was a trigger. The trigger was the contagion from Thailand. On July 2, 1997, when the Bank of Thailand abandoned the baht's peg to its traditional basket, the baht immediately depreciated sharply against the US dollar. Pressure then quickly intensified against the Philippine peso and the Malaysian ringgit – each of which received only limited support from their central banks. On July 8, the rupiah came under pressure. Although Indonesia had stronger macroeconomic fundamentals than Thailand (as these pertained to exports and the fiscal balance), and only a modest current account deficit, the rupiah was, nevertheless, vulnerable for two principal reasons. First, the huge foreign-debt burden of the private Indonesian corporations (much of it short-term and not hedged against exchange-rate changes), and second, the fundamental weakness of the financial and banking sector raised doubts about the government's ability to defend the currency peg.

The Indonesian government's initial reaction to speculation against the rupiah was decisive. Unlike Thailand, rather than defending its currency and squandering a large portion of its reserves, Bank Indonesia, on July 11 widened the trading band for the rupiah from Rp. 192 (8 per cent of the central rate) to Rp. 304 (12 per cent of the central rate), in a pre-emptive move designed to deter speculation. It also limited non-resident transactions in the forward market and introduced an array of tight monetary policy along with administrative measures to limit the external borrowings of commercial banks.[13] Indeed, Indonesia was widely praised for its strategy of "deft macroeconomic management" (Blustein 2001, 97). Yet it was too early to celebrate. Despite the vigorous defense the rupiah continued to slide. As the then Governor of Bank Indonesia, J. Soedradjad Djiwandono (1999a, 145) noted, "the market reaction to the central bank (Bank Indonesia) move was contrary to experience." Every time the Bank Indonesia intervention band had been widened previously (five times from 1994 to 1997), an appreciation of the rupiah followed. This time, the rupiah rapidly depreciated instead. This was in large part because foreign creditors began to reduce their exposure to Indonesia, and large domestic conglomerates, fearful that they would not be able to repay their foreign debts if the rupiah fell significantly, rushed to hedge these debts by buying US dollars. In fact, as unhedged domestic borrowers jumped into the market to try to cover their positions, this pushed the rupiah even further downward. By July 21 the rupiah fell by 7 per cent, in effect sharply depreciating to near the bottom of the new band. This only made domestic capital flee to safer havens offshore. In response, on July 23, Bank Indonesia raised interest rates from 12 per cent to 13 per cent, and intervened heavily in support of the rupiah. But this was to no avail, as the panic selling of rupiah and assets denominated in rupiah continued. When the rupiah depreciated by 13 per cent (from 2,400 per US dollar in July to 2,700 on the August 13), it was the last straw.

On August 14, the Indonesian authorities, reluctant to squander more foreign reserves, allowed the rupiah to float.[14] Immediately the rupiah depreciated sharply against the US dollar and other currencies in which the Indonesian banks had borrowed. As the currency depreciated, the rupiah-denominated value of the interest and amortization of foreign debts surged, causing a serious balance-sheet problem in both the corporate and banking sectors. In particular, because of the depreciation, the amounts of rupiah that Indonesian banks earned on their long-term loans to the property sector and other industries were no longer sufficient to service their short-term foreign borrowing. Moreover, the banks could no longer attract new funds from abroad that could be used to repay the short-term borrowing coming close to maturation. In response, the Indonesian government raised short-term rupiah interest rates in order to attract rupiah deposits and stabilize the currency. For example, on August 11, 1997, the overnight Jakarta inter-bank rupiah rate (or JIBOR) was 15.8 per cent. A week later, on August 18, the overnight JIBOR was 51.4 per cent, and by August 22, the overnight JIBOR was 87.7 per cent. However this failed to bring much reprieve, as the rupiah continued to weaken. The Ministry of Finance responded by cutting government spending by rescheduling projects worth about US$16 billion and limiting routine expenditures on non-priority items (Pincus and Ramli 1998, 725). It also further tightened liquidity by instructing the public sector (including state-owned enterprises) to shift their deposits from (mainly state-owned) commercial banks to Bank Indonesia. However, this also proved ineffective, as the rupiah continued to slide – gaining renewed momentum downward on August 21. In desperation, on 29 August, Bank Indonesia issued a new rule limiting the forward sale of dollars to non-residents to US$5 million in order to reduce currency speculation.

It is not clear if the Indonesian authorities were in consultation with the IMF regarding the tight money policy. Bank Indonesia argued that the tight money policy was necessary to keep inflation under control and to stem the tide of large shifts into dollar holdings by residents. This is similar to the long-held IMF position that stresses the importance of high interest rates in keeping domestic currency holdings attractive, even if this complicates the situation of weak banks. In hindsight, an "overshoot" in the interest rate rise, through the tightening of liquidity by the Indonesian authorities, was very much responsible for the severe financial crisis that ensued. More than anything else, the tight money immediately exposed Indonesia's weak financial and banking systems. Bank runs emerged as early as the second half of August 1999, when the process of "flight to safety" began. Faced with the prospect of widespread bank failures, Bank Indonesia had to scramble quickly to supply banks facing liquidity problems with funds, and by the end of August 1997 had put up some US$500 million for the troubled banks (Soesastro and Basri 1998, 9).

The injection of new liquidity and the lowering of short-term interest rates (the JIBOR rate fell to 40 per cent in the first week of September) did provide temporary reprieve.[15] On September 23, the finance minister Mar'ie Muhammad unveiled a comprehensive policy program to deal with the crisis (Muhammad 1997). The program included: (a) stabilization of the rupiah at a new equilibrium level; (b) strengthening of fiscal policies and fiscal consolidation; (c) reduction of the current account deficit; (d) strengthening of the banking sector; and (e) strengthening of the private corporate sector. To achieve these objectives, the government made a pledge further to "loosen liquidity gradually and in accordance with the situation through fiscal and monetary instruments." Furthermore, the government made a commitment to reduce interest rates and to cancel or postpone over 200 public sector-related development projects that would save the government some US$37 billion. These included the postponement of costly mega-projects such as the construction of the Jakarta Tower, of the bridge between Sumatra and the Malaysian peninsula, and of the Menara Jakarta bridge. With regard to the banking sector, the government announced its intention to merge state banks and liquidate the insolvent ones. Also, it made a commitment to follow up quickly on the plan to encourage weak private banks to explore the possibility of mergers. Finally, in a dramatic move, the 49 per cent foreign ownership limit on Indonesian stocks was scrapped in order to increase foreign investment in the stock market.

These announcements succeeded in bringing a measure of calm to the markets. As the rupiah stabilized around Rp. 3,000 per US dollar some thought that the worst was over. However, it was only a temporary reprieve – the calm before the storm. Part of the dilemma was that Indonesia was facing a confidence problem, and despite all the concerted effort, the government failed to restore confidence. However, a bigger problem was that, ambitious as the finance ministry's program was, it did not go far enough. For example, rather than postponing or dismantling inefficient and profligate monopolies, such as the Suharto protégé, Bacharuddin Jusuf Habibie's, pet project, the state-owned aircraft manufacturer Industri Pesawat Terbang Nusantara (IPTN), or the national car project owned largely by Suharto's youngest son, the government reaffirmed its commitment to continue to support these projects. Equally blatant was the government's approval of the 1,350 megawatt Tanjung Jati C power plant (in which Suharto's daughter, Tutut, had a major stake), when the Java–Bali power grid was facing up to 70 per cent over-capacity (Tan 2000, 172; also Eklof 1999, 101). As regional currencies and stock markets continued to plummet, and amidst reports that Indonesian banks and private companies were having great difficulty in meeting their external debt-service obligations, the pressure on the rupiah re-intensified. By early October the rupiah had fallen by more than 40 per cent since July (the fastest depreciation among the crisis countries), while the Jakarta Stock Market Index dropped by 44 per cent (Soesastro and Basri 1998, 10). On October 6, the Indonesian government sold another US$650 million in the foreign-exchange market to stabilize the external value of the rupiah (Nasution 1999, 88). Again, this was to no avail. On October 8, when the exchange rate passed 3,800 rupiah to the US dollar, Indonesia turned to the IMF for "consultation and technical assistance."[16]

On October 31 (after some three weeks of discussions), the Indonesian government negotiated a financial bailout package totaling some US$43 billion in international assistance with the IMF and bilateral donors. The package consisted of US$23 billion of the so-called "first line of funds" negotiated with the IMF and a "second line of funds" negotiated with bilateral donors. These included Japan (US$5 billion), Singapore (US$5 billion), United States ($3 billion), Malaysia (US$1 billion), Australia (US$1 billion), Brunei (US$1.2 billion) and China and Hong Kong SAR.[17] Of the US$10 billion from the IMF, US$3 billion was to be disbursed immediately, and a further US$3 billion was to be made available after March 15, 1998, provided the Indonesian government met the program's economic targets. The rest of the money was to be disbursed on a quarterly basis, provided the targets continued to be met (IMF 1997c). The entire agreement was to be implemented over a three-year period and carefully monitored jointly by the Indonesian government and the IMF, including experts from the World Bank and the Asian Development Bank.

The mood was one of cautious optimism after the signing of the October 31 agreement. It was widely believed that the agreement would restore investor confidence and arrest the rupiah's continuing plunge. The IMF Managing Director, Michel Camdessus, summed up the prevailing mood when he noted that "these measures should restore confidence in the Indonesian economy and contribute to the stabilization of regional financial markets" (IMF 1997b, 3). Indeed, initially the program received positive response from the market, resulting in the rupiah strengthening from Rp. 3,700 to Rp. 3,200 per dollar. However, it was too early to celebrate. The economic program the Indonesian government had committed to in its "letter of intent" to the IMF (which now became part of the agreement) was quite extensive, given the IMF's objectives of restoring market confidence via restricting aggregate demand by raising interest rates and cutting the budget, and improving the real sector's efficiency by eliminating monopolies.[18] Thus the program included, among other things (a) trade policy reform, in particular, trade deregulation for various commodities via the elimination of the monopoly of BULOG (Badan Urusan Logistik – Food Distribution Agency) on the import of wheat, wheat flour, soybeans and garlic, effective January 1, 1998; (b) a gradual reduction of import tariffs on chemical products, iron and steel, and fisheries products; (c) industrial policy reforms such as the elimination of the local content program for automobiles by 2000 and the implementation of the WTO decision on the National Car project by 2000;[19] and (d) macroeconomic policy targets for economic growth, the inflation rate, the current account deficit and fiscal balance, as well as economic reform measures covering investment and financial institutions (IMF 1997e). At the core of this last was the program to reform the banking industry.

Specifically, on the basis of data made available by Bank Indonesia on the financial condition of 92 of the 238 banks, representing 85 per cent of the assets of the banking system, the IMF and the Indonesian government agreed on a comprehensive bank resolution package consisting of:

1   intensified supervision, including frequent and detailed reviews, in addition to daily monitoring of key elements like liquidity and foreign exchange exposure for six of the country's largest private banks (market share: 18 per cent) in which some critical weaknesses had been identified;
2   rehabilitation plans for seven small private banks;
3   conservatorship for three small, severely under-capitalized private banks, and for six insolvent regional development banks (market share 0.4 per cent);
4   transfer of the performing assets for two insolvent state-owned banks (market share: 9.6 per cent) to a third state-owned bank; merger of the two insolvent banks and transformation of the resulting entity into an asset-recovery agency;
5   definition and implementation of rehabilitation plans for 10 insolvent private banks (market share: 3 per cent) that had benefited from a Bank Indonesia-sponsored and legally binding rescue package prior to the crisis, accelerating their return to solvency; and
6   closure of 16 small and deeply insolvent private banks (market share: 2.5 per cent), with protection limited to small depositors, or those with deposits of up to 20 million rupiah (around US$6,000). Indeed, the IMF press release stated that the Indonesian authorities "are determined that only a small portion of the costs of the restructuring will be met from the public purse. The government will compensate small depositors only, and not private shareholders and creditors. The government will not guarantee any liabilities of private non-financial companies, domestic or foreign" (IMF 1997e, 2).

In total, the agreement included 50 banks, representing 34.3 per cent of the banking system. However, on November 1, 1997 (less than 24 hours after reaching the agreement with the IMF), the Indonesian government abruptly suspended the operating licenses of 16 banks – in effect, closing them down.[20] Among the closed banks, two were partly owned by Suharto's son and half-brother. Although the government hoped that its decisive action would be interpreted by the public as showing that the authorities were finally serious about reforming the banking sector, the outcome was quite the opposite. In short, the action proved to be disastrous.[21] As Soesastro and Basri (1998, 19) note, "the closure of 16 commercial banks created panic in the country, leading to large withdrawals by depositors even from banks that were generally believed to be healthy." Suddenly, confidence in domestic private banks was shattered.[22] As a result there was further "flight to quality," as depositors sought to move their funds out of the private banks that were believed to be in trouble into the state banks, which were widely thought to be more secure. Literally overnight, many banks lost their deposit base, besides finding that trade and other financial lines from their bank business abroad were terminated. Letters of credit issued by many Indonesian banks were no longer accepted overseas (Djiwandono 1999a, 148). It seemed that market confidence had been completely lost. *Why did the closure of just 16 small and insolvent banks with only 2.5 per cent of the total banking assets generate such a panic?*

According to Sachs (1997), the reason was the IMF's "misguided policies." He claims that the closure of the banks was not necessary. By hastily closing banks in an environment where no deposit insurance was in place, the IMF generated panic that quickly became a full-blown financial crisis. Indeed, the closures exacerbated the ongoing liquidity squeeze in financial markets, making it much more difficult for all banks to continue their normal lending operations. Yet it is also important to recognize that Sachs is only partly correct, and the IMF only partly to blame for Indonesia's financial crisis.

While there is little question that pressure from the IMF forced the Indonesian government to take its first significant step toward restructuring the banking sector (by liquidating 16 of the weakest private banks), the problem was not the closure of these weak banks *per se*, but the manner in which this was brought about.[23] First, while the agreement mentioned 50 banks, only 16 were closed – and these 16 were clearly insolvent on the basis of data provided by the banks to Bank Indonesia. Since the remaining 34 banks were not identified, the move created uncertainty among the general public regarding the fate of all other banks. After all, not only was the public generally aware that some well-connected banks were not listed, but the IMF's initial program failed to make provisions for a deposit insurance.[24] Suffice it to note that under such uncertainty even rumors about a bank's solvency could spark a bank run. Second, the abrupt closure of banks in the midst of very volatile capital withdrawals and without a comprehensive and well-thought-out financial restructuring plan in place only added to the panic. Third, there was no strategy in place for dealing with the liabilities and assets (both good and bad) of either the closed banks or those that remained open. This lack of disclosure regarding the health of remaining banks further fueled depositor concerns about the overall health of the banking sector. Indeed, as it turned out, the depositors' initial concern soon ballooned and initiated a full-scale run on the banking system. As Azis (1999, 81) notes, "even with 15 to 20 per cent higher interest rates in the remaining local banks, most depositors went in a panic to the foreign banks operating in Jakarta." This dramatic move therefore only served further to undermine the banking system as a whole.

Fourth, among the 16 banks listed for closure were Bank Andromeda (of which 25 per cent was owned by one of Suharto's sons, Bambang Trihatmodjo), Bank Jakarta (partly owned by Suharto's half-brother, Probosutejo), and Bank Industri (owned by Suharto's daughter, Siti Hedijanti Herijadi and Hashim Djojohadikusumo, her brother-in-law. These banks included the smallest and weakest banks in the country – with less than 2.5 per cent of Indonesia's total banking assets. Their plans for closure failed to generate public confidence – despite the fact that the government announced it would protect small depositors by guaranteeing all deposits up to 20 million rupiah. But on the contrary, the public, including foreign investors, cognizant of the fact that these 16 closures would hardly have a significant impact on the health of the banking system as a whole, braced themselves for more bank closures. More importantly, the deposit guarantee proved woefully insufficient to generate confidence. Domestic investors transferred deposits from private banks to state banks, in a flight from quality to safety. Many also transferred funds to foreign banks, or exchanged rupiah for dollars and repatriated their funds. Blustein (2001, 107) sharply observes the unfolding of the panic:

> toward the end of the first week of November, the reaction to the bank closures took an ominous turn. Anonymous lists of "good banks" and "bad banks" began circulating around Jakarta . . . Before long, a full-fledged run on privately owned banks was under way. Bearing bags and boxes to hold cash, crowds thronged to withdraw their deposits from branches of the giant Bank Central Asia, owned by Suharto's pal Liem Sioe Liong, in the second week of November. Many depositors rushed their money from private banks to state-owned banks, figuring the state-owned ones, whatever their problems, were at least backed by the government; others showed up with bags of rupiah to deposit at the Jakarta branches of Citibank and other foreign institutions.

Fifth, the situation was made worse when Bambang Trihatmodjo (on November 5) filed a lawsuit against the Governor of Bank Indonesia and the Minister of Finance over the closure of his Bank Andromeda.[25] The fact that Bank Andromeda was back in operation in no time – under the

146

name of Bank Alfa (but using the same building and employees and a new foreign exchange license issued by Bank Indonesia), and that several of the earlier-canceled "development" projects of Suharto's family and cronies were soon suddenly back in operation, convinced many that Suharto was intent on protecting his family's business and commercial interests at all costs, and that the regime was not serious about implementing the agreed reforms.[26] This perception was only confirmed when large deposit withdrawals from private banks prompted the central bank to issue emergency credits in ever-increasing amounts to ensure that these banks did not go under. Some of these huge lines of credit were channeled to banks owned by the well-connected. Thus, rather than instilling fresh confidence in the banking system, these developments caused further panic withdrawals of deposits from most private banks.

What is then the final verdict on the initial IMF policies? First, the sudden bank closures of November 1, which precipitated the general loss of confidence in the banking system, were conducted under IMF direction. There is also no doubt that the IMF gravely mis-diagnosed the problem by perceiving the crisis as a limited banking problem affecting only a small number of banks. More broadly, the IMF's prescription of a fiscal surplus was seemingly based on the premises of a profligate public sector and high inflation – neither of which was accurate. Nor did the demand for tighter fiscal and monetary policy when budgets were broadly in balance, and when the economy was already beginning to contract, make sense. Hill (1999, 52–3), aptly blames the IMF's "scatter-gun" approach, which "overloaded the reform agenda, forcing bureaucratically stretched governments to quickly tackle a vast array of highly complex and sensitive policy issues" and when it "attempted to resolve banking sector distress too quickly, aggravated the general loss of confidence." The IMF should have known that reforms requiring fundamental legal and institutional change take months, if not years, to implement effectively.

From late November onwards, things began to go seriously wrong. For a start, the extent of the private sector foreign debt was revealed to be much larger than most analysts had realized.[27] The vast majority of the Indonesian firms and financial institutions previously thought sound had a large debt burden in foreign currencies that they could not service from their rupiah earnings at the prevailing unfavorable exchange rate. Specifically, they had failed to take the prudent step of hedging themselves against a drop in the rupiah by purchasing contracts in the currency markets ensuring that they would be able to obtain dollars at a reasonable rate.[28] These entities were now effectively bankrupt. Furthermore, as the international financial markets lost confidence in Indonesian banks they refused to roll over short-term debt and accept letters of credit. Also, the government decision to limit access to foreign borrowings and to shift public sector deposits from (mainly state-owned) commercial banks to the central bank squeezed liquidity. With banks suddenly illiquid, default by corporate borrowers increased. In this capricious and unpredictable environment, bank deposit runs multiplied amid rumors that a new wave of bank closures was under preparation. By mid-December, 154 banks, representing half of the total assets of the system, had faced, to varying degrees, some erosion of their deposit base (Enoch *et al.* 2001, 31). Also, during December 1997, Bank Indonesia's liquidity support (in the form of *Bantuan Likuiditas Bank Indonesia* or BLBI) increased from 13 trillion rupiah to 31 trillion rupiah, equivalent to 5–7 per cent of GDP (Lindgren *et al.* 1999). In so far as the liquidity support, paid in rupiah, was needed by banks to meet reductions in dollar deposits, in effect it served to fuel capital flight and, thus, the continuing depreciation of the exchange rate.[29] In contrast to the situations in other crisis-hit countries, in Indonesia efforts at sterilization were not successful, reflecting a loss of monetary control by Bank Indonesia. By late December, the rupiah was fluctuating in a wide range around Rp. 5,000 to 6,000 per US dollar.

### The banking crisis becomes systemic

On January 6, 1998, President Suharto presented to the Parliament a draft budget for the fiscal year 1998/99.[30] The proposed budget totaled Rp. 133 trillion, a 32.1 per cent increase as compared to the preceding year's budget of Rp. 101 trillion. The draft budget was based on the "balanced budget" principle (which limits the size of budget deficit to the level that can be financed by foreign aid and loans), and calculated on the basis of certain assumptions about future conditions, such as a particular exchange rate (Rp. 4000 per US$1), an annual economic rate of growth of 4 per cent, and an inflation rate of 9 per cent. The budget also failed to produce the surplus of 1 per cent as stipulated in the IMF agreement. In fact, the expansionary budget was in direct contravention of IMF requirements for a 1 per cent budget surplus.[31] Almost immediately, the markets reacted negatively to the "unrealistic" expansionary budget.

As questions about Suharto's commitment to implementing the program once again came to the forefront, the rupiah headed into a free fall.[32] From Rp. 5,450 per US$1 on January 1, it dropped to 6,000 per dollar on January 2 – which put the value of the rupiah 60 per cent below its level of the preceding summer. Then came the infamous "black Thursday" on January 8, when the rupiah fell below the "psychological threshold" of Rp. 10,000 to US$1 – leading to panic food buying and social unrest.[33] In desperation, Suharto hinted at the possibility of issuing Indonesian dollar banknotes that could replace real dollars and be put in a special dollar deposit with high interest rates. The president's daughter, Siti Hardijanti Rukmana (Tutut), promoted *Gerakan Cinta Rupiah* or *"Getar"* (the "we love the rupiah movement"), to encourage citizens to change their cash dollar holdings into rupiah.

Their desperation was cruelly displayed when Tutut and Suharto coordinated the campaign with a racially-tinged attack on the prominent *non-pribumi* (Chinese-Indonesian) businessman, Sofyan Wanandi, after he refused to go along with the campaign.[34] In the end the initiative was to no avail. The value of the rupiah continued to slide, reaching Rp. 10,200 to US$1 on 11 January 1998. Compounding the growing disarray was the sudden collapse (on January 13, 1998) of Peregrine Investment Holdings – Asia's largest home-grown investment bank outside Japan. The immediate cause of the Hong Kong-based Peregrine's insolvency was its exposure to over US$400 million in Indonesian corporate debt. However, Peregrine's largest exposure was its underwriting a loan of US$236 million (which amounted to about one-third of its equity) to PT Steady Safe, a local taxi company in Jakarta.[35] It seemed that the bottom had fallen out of the Indonesian economy. Fearing that worse was yet to come, ordinary Indonesians went on a rampage of panic buying of every available food commodity as rumors grew that a ban on food imports and large-scale rationing might be imposed at any time to save the country's rapidly falling currency. Under these circumstances, and subjected to growing pressure from "an array of heads of state – from Washington, Tokyo and Canberra," including the "US president urging Suharto to work with Michel Camdessus, who was due to arrive in Jakarta the following week," the Indonesian government had little choice but to concede to the IMF (Azis 1999, 85; Blustein 2001, 208).

On January 15, 1998 in a nationally televised official ceremony witnessed by the IMF managing director Michel Camdessus (who stood imperiously over the president), Suharto signed the second "Letter of Intent" with the IMF, politely acceding to all the IMF's demands.[36] Labeled a "much strengthened program" by Camdessus, it was clear that the IMF's second reform program was able to exact a far greater range of reform commitments from Suharto. Specifically, as stated in the letter of intent, the Indonesian government pledged to implement a 50-point "Memorandum of Economic and Financial Policies" agreed with the IMF (1998a, 1998b). The program included provisions such as, on fiscal policy, calling for the revision of the draft budget for fiscal 1998/99. However, it should be noted that the IMF recognized that, with the sharp depreciation of the rupiah and the deterioration in the economy, it was no longer feasible to aim at a surplus of 1 per cent of GDP – it relaxed its monetary policy stance by settling for a deficit, at 1 per cent of GDP. This was to be achieved via expenditure reduction, namely, the elimination of fuel and electricity subsidies. Non-budget expenditures such as the investment fund and the reforestation fund were to be incorporated into the central government budget. Regarding public sector projects, the program called for "canceling immediately the 12 infrastructure projects that were recently postponed or placed under review. Moreover, budgetary and extra-budgetary support and credit privileges granted to IPTN's airplane projects will be discontinued, effective immediately. In addition, all special tax, customs, and credit privileges for the National Car project will be revoked, effective immediately." The program also made it clear that Bank Indonesia should continue to adopt a tight monetary policy, and must be "given full autonomy to conduct monetary policy, and start immediately to unilaterally decide interest rates on its SBI [central bank] certificates."[37] In order to improve domestic competition, the program required cartel-like marketing arrangements, including those of the Indonesian Plywood Association (APKINDO) monopoly over plywood exports and the existing monopolies over the import and distribution of sugar, wheat flour, cement, paper and steel to be eliminated by February 1. The Clove Marketing Board was to be eliminated by June 1998. This meant that "from February 1, 1998 BULOG's monopoly will be limited solely to rice." On investment and foreign trade, the program called for the elimination of restrictions on foreign investment in palm oil and wholesale and retail trade, and of content regulations and export taxes on a wide range of products, including leather, cork, ores, logs, sawn lumber, rattan and minerals. Finally, it called for the deregulation and privatization of selected state-owned enterprises and strategic industries.

Despite the seemingly comprehensive nature of the reform package, it failed to restore market confidence. On the contrary, the rupiah fell 6.5 per cent against the US dollar the very day the second letter of intent was signed, and by another 5.4 per cent the following day. According to the IMF the problem was that currency traders and investors were skeptical that the wide-ranging measures would be implemented by Suharto. The widely held (and generally correct) perception was that the wily Suharto had signed up to the program only reluctantly, and that he did not intend to follow through with a program that would hurt the business interests and the vast financial empire controlled by his children (estimated to be worth around US$30 billion),[38] and the interests of his close associates (Eklof 1999, 126–7). In fact, even before the IMF team had left Jakarta, one could sense the growing rift between the IMF and the Suharto regime. Suharto began sending mixed signals regarding his commitment to the program. According to Soesastro (2000, 132), "confidence was further weakened because the government, the President in particular, did not show any will to implement the agreement with the IMF in good faith." Similarly, Winters (2000, 46) notes that "Suharto quietly reneged on most of what he had agreed to in public."[39] Indeed, in an act of open defiance, Suharto made it public that he wanted his long-time friend and the big-spending Technology Minister, B. J. Habibie, as his vice-presidential candidate (and presumed successor) in the upcoming March polls – in spite of the well-known antipathy towards Habibie within the IMF and the international financial community.[40]

Yet the IMF's policies must share part of the blame. Specifically, the wide-ranging character of the Fund's policy, and in particular, its zealous aim of including as many structural reform measures as possible in its programs, did little to shore up market confidence. Radelet (1999) aptly notes that the new IMF program, which eased up slightly on fiscal policy and on the capital adequacy ratio required for banks, but otherwise kept the same basic strategy as the first policy, was misguided. That is, since excess demand was not at the root of Indonesia's problems, and the capital withdrawals well under way meant that the economy was already contracting significantly, the initial fiscal tightening simply added to the contraction, further under-mining investor confidence and fueling capital flight.[41] Also, the structural reforms envisaged in the program, while necessary over the long term, did not provide any concrete solutions to the immediate problems of the bank-ing and currency crisis. Indeed, the most often-cited complaint about the IMF program was that it lacked a clear plan for dealing with the primary source of worry about the rupiah – the increasingly crippling foreign debt of Indonesian companies.[42] Furthermore, the program did not articulate a clear strategy to resolve the banking sector problems (i.e. it did not contain concrete bank rehabilitation and restructuring measures that could restore confidence in the banking system), nor did it provide a plan to deal with Indonesia's mushrooming short-term foreign debt. The market's lack of confidence was reflected in the continued downhill slide of the rupiah. Less than a week after the signing ceremony between the IMF and Suharto, the rupiah fell to an unprecedented all-time low of Rp. 17,000 to the US dollar on January 22. Also, left unattended, the banking sector problems turned into a full-fledged systemic crisis, with liquidity support from Bank Indonesia exceeding over 60 trillion rupiah (about 6 per cent of 1998 GDP), with the risk of hyperinflation and complete financial sector meltdown looming menacingly on the horizon.

Finally, on January 27, 1998, with their backs against the wall, both the IMF and the Indonesian government took steps to deal with the banking sector problems. Finance Minister Mar'ie Muhammad announced a three-point emergency plan. *First*, in response to depositor panic and the refusal of international banks to accept letters of credit issued by Indonesian banks, Bank Indonesia announced a blanket guarantee of the rupiah and foreign currency denominated debts of all domestically incorporated banks for two years – effectively assuming banking sector risk. The guarantee extended to deposits and most types of creditor claims, excluding subordinated debt.[43] The blanket guarantee on deposits (confirming Bank Indonesia's determina-tion to exercise its last-resort function even if this exacted a heavy toll), was designed to stem bank runs and thereby stabilize the banking system. The IMF, which had been resisting a government guarantee on bank deposits since late 1997 (because of concerns regarding moral hazard), relented, since the bank runs were so devastating. In addition, Bank Indonesia placed restrictions on credit growth and announced it would set weekly ceilings on the maximum interest rates that banks could pay on deposits.

*Second*, a new regulatory public body for the banking industry, the Indonesian Bank Restructuring Agency (IBRA) was established under a presidential decree for a period of five years, under the auspices of the Ministry of Finance.[44] Established as an "independent agency, reporting to the Ministry of Finance" (but with advisors from the New York-based investment banks Lehman Brothers and JP Morgan), IBRA's task was to take over and rehabilitate weak banks and administer the government's guarantee program for bank debts. IBRA was also empowered to establish a separate asset-management entity called the Asset Management Unit (AMU) to take over non-performing assets from banks that were either to be liquidated or merged into stronger institutions. The loan-recovery plans were to involve a variety of methods, including collection, loan workouts and packaging of the loans for sale to third parties. The rationale for transferring these assets to the AMU was that, by disposing of the burden of problem loans on management and financial resources, the surviving banks would be in a better position to provide new credit to the market, besides becoming more attractive propositions to new investors. Furthermore, not only was the Banking Law amended to give the AMU the power needed to deal with problem banks, but all banks were required to have their loan portfolios reviewed by internationally recognized audit firms by the end of 1998. Also, IBRA was given the responsibility for collecting from the majority shareholders of the private banks the amounts that their banks owed Bank Indonesia in connection with the liquidity support that they had received. *Third*, a framework for handling corporate restructuring was proposed: in particular, the plan recommended a temporary voluntary suspension of corporate external debt payment. However, the government made it clear that there would be no use of public financing, guarantee or subsidy to bail out the debt and reimburse unguaranteed creditors looking for financial redress.

However, IBRA was hardly an autonomous agency. In fact, the agency not only "had to operate subject to intense political oversight, its effectiveness was compromised by a weak legal and regulatory framework and its need to obtain political authority, even for technical operations" (Enoch *et al.* 2001, 15). Nevertheless, the fact that IBRA's restructuring agenda looked feasible raised hopes that finally something substantive was being done to deal with the country's banking problems. On the basis of its review of the banks' financial position, IBRA divided banks that had received substantial liquidity support from Bank Indonesia (i.e. more than 500 per cent of their total equity) into categories A and B. Category A banks included those that had received liquidity support equal to or in excess of 75 per cent of their total assets, and Category B banks were those that had received less than 75 per cent, but in sums still equal to or in excess of two trillion rupiah. Category A banks were to be liquidated, whereas Category B banks were to have the rights of their shareholders suspended and their existing managers replaced by IBRA – which would assume full management control.[45] IBRA also made it explicit that the former majority shareholders of the suspended banks should pay the government two separate amounts: first, the outstanding negative balance that their bank had accumulated with Bank Indonesia, and second, the amount by which their bank's intra-group lending exceeded the affiliated lending limits before September 21, 1998 (Witcher and Solomon 1998). The announcement of this new and ambitious plan was able to slow bank runs and restore a modicum of financial stability. On January 28, the exchange rate recovered to Rp. 12,500 per US dollar, and appreciated further in the subsequent days to rally at Rp. 9,950 per US dollar on February 16. IBRA's early actions resulted in the closure of a large number of banks that had severely negative net worth and no significant value or franchise importance to the system. Specifically, by 14 February, 54 distressed banks (consisting of 4 state banks, 39 private national banks and 11 regional development banks, comprising 36.7 per cent of the banking sector), that had borrowed heavily from Bank Indonesia were brought under the auspices of the IBRA. The four state-owned banks (Bapindo, Bank Bumi Daya, Bank Dagang Negara or BDNI and Bank Exim), accounted for 24.7 per cent of the liabilities of the banking sector (Lindgren *et al.* 1999, 59).

However, just when the government's plan seem to be working – making believers of some of the cynics – interference by Suharto and his cronies once again undermined the efforts (Sadli 1999). Enoch and his co-authors (2001, 14) note that "the restructuring process created a permanent tension between its [IBRA's] officials and the wider political forces whose interests were likely to be threatened. As the extent of the necessary restructuring became apparent, these tensions increased." First, Suharto refused to publicize the operations of IBRA. As a result, IBRA officials had to work over the following weeks against a public perception that IBRA was a "paper tiger" and still not operational (Enoch *et al.* 2001, 33). As the IMF study reports, "the initial workings of IBRA were not apparent to the public, there was confusion as to the authorities' intentions, and the momentum generated by the January 27 announcement was largely lost" (Lindgren *et al.* 1999, 59). More damaging, on February 17, Suharto abruptly fired one of the few reformers in his regime, the highly respected Governor of Bank Indonesia, Sudradjad Djiwandono, less than two weeks before the official end of his tenure.[46] It was reported that Suharto fired Djiwandono after the governor "had argued that Suharto was about to subvert an economic recovery plan he reluctantly signed just last month with the IMF" (Sanger 1998). In late February, Suharto dismissed the head of IBRA, the highly regarded senior finance ministry official, Dr Bambang Subianto, after only a month in the job, "reportedly for being too diligent in pursuing his responsibilities" (Enoch *et al.* 2001, 15). To make matters worse, Suharto started making increasingly hostile remarks about the IMF, culminating in a reported statement to a largely Muslim audience that the IMF package could not be implemented because it violated Article 33 of the Indonesian constitution.[47] If Suharto's obscurantism and well-worn pattern of *double-entendres* and half-measures frustrated the IMF and the donor countries, his plan (which according to Soesastro (2000, 133) was conceived "clearly on the advice of his children"), to create a fixed exchange-rate system for the volatile rupiah through a currency board in direct opposition to the IMF, the United States, the European Community, Japan and other donor governments, was more than could be tolerated.

While rumors that Indonesia might adopt a currency board had been around for weeks, by mid-February Jakarta began to send implicit messages that it would unilaterally establish a currency board, unless the Fund came up with a better alternative for strengthening the rupiah. On February 11, the minister of finance announced that the government was preparing steps towards setting up a currency board system – by the end of February at the latest. Following the appointment on February 17 of the US trained economist, Sjahril Sabirin, as the new Bank Indonesia Governor, and the strong currency-board advocate and Johns Hopkins University economist Steven Hanke (who was named advisor to President Suharto's economic council), the Indonesian government embarked on a media blitz to make its case for a currency board regime. The government now claimed that, unlike an ordinary exchange-rate peg, the predictability and rule-based nature of a currency board would impose strict discipline on the government – preventing it, for example, from abusing the central bank's printing presses to fund large deficits. Using the example of the Hong Kong dollar (which had been officially fixed at HK$7.80 per American dollar since the board was introduced in 1983, and had weathered the crisis reasonably well), supporters argued that since the currency board holds extremely low-risk interest-bearing bonds and other assets denominated in the anchor currency, it not only encourages arbitrage, but also offers an effective barrier against speculative attacks and rapid currency appreciations. Moreover, they claimed that currency boards provide stability to the banking and financial system by maintaining market-adjusted interest rates and prudentially controlling destabilizing international capital flows.

Indeed, at first glance, Indonesia seemed to be a strong candidate for a currency-board arrangement. Such an arrangement would replace the existing regime that permitted Bank Indonesia wide operational discretion with a rules-based system. No doubt, under a currency-board system, a number of controversial operations (in particular, the provision of liquidity to the banks), would be severely curtailed or prohibited. After all, several countries, most notably Argentina and Bulgaria, had recently introduced successful currency-board systems to deal with problems similar to those that Indonesia was facing. While the IMF in principle is not opposed to emerging economies' establishing currency boards, it strongly opposed the Indonesian plan (threatening to withhold funding) because it felt that a currency board was a "quick-fix and ultimately unsustainable solution for

Indonesia."[48] Rather, the IMF argued that it was important for Indonesia to implement the agreed-upon reforms before establishing a currency board. This meant that, although the IMF supported the objective of achieving an appreciation of the exchange rate, it argued that this had to be achieved by a comprehensive macroeconomic and financial program. This was based on sound economic reasoning: a currency-board arrangement can only work effectively if the banking system has the capacity to tolerate significant movements in domestic interest rates. Without this capacity, the currency-board arrangement will induce a conversion of deposits into foreign exchange, further shrink the monetary base and greatly increase interest rates. Since a currency board must hold reserves of foreign exchange (or gold or some other liquid asset) equal at the fixed rate of exchange to at least 100 per cent of the domestic currency issued, the IMF appropriately concluded that Indonesia's US$12 billion in disclosed foreign-exchange reserves (as of March 20, 1998), and a foreign debt of $130 billion were simply inadequate to back the estimated 24 trillion rupiah in circulation – for a board system would drain the reserves in a few weeks, if not days (Tesoro 1998b).

Moreover, the IMF had good reason to suspect that the Suharto regime would dip into the loans to support the currency board – after all, it was already injecting massive doses of liquidity to bail out the country's weak banking system. The IMF correctly found the Hong Kong example to be spurious. As was noted in the introductory chapter, in Hong Kong, the Exchange Fund is committed to 100 per cent foreign-currency backing for Hong Kong dollar bank notes, and the Hong Kong Monetary Authority (HKMA) has an explicit mandate to act as an official lender of last resort, and has been involved in open-market operations since 1990. Also, Hong Kong (unlike Indonesia) has formidable foreign reserves, totaling over US$85 billion (in 1997–98), to cover the currency in circulation plus demand deposits. This gives the HKMA tremendous autonomy to raise short-term interest rates to make it expensive for speculators to obtain Hong Kong dollar credit. Unlike Indonesia's banks, Hong Kong's well regulated and capitalized banks, with very low levels of non-performing loans, could cope with the increases in short-term interest rates that might be needed to defend the currency board. In addition, with justifiable reason, the Fund remained highly suspicious of the "Suharto plan" under which the rupiah's rate would be 5,000 to the dollar, or about twice as strong as the then current rate. That is, with the rupiah trading at around 8,000 rupiah to the US dollar at the time of the announcement, the proposal involved an appreciation of around 40 per cent – essentially by administrative fiat. Needless to say, such a move would hardly be credible to the markets. Finally, since a currency board is committed to exchanging on demand and without any limit, foreign currency and local currency, and in some cases must also exchange bank reserves at a pre-announced exchange rate, the IMF felt that the currency board was a ploy to allow Suharto's children and cronies to retrench their discretionary and egregious rent-seeking structures and quickly change their substantial rupiah holdings into dollars at an artificially high rate and then move those funds into offshore accounts.[49] It should be noted that, if capital outflows are sufficiently large, a currency board could collapse because of a shortage of foreign assets. In Indonesia, where the government in 1997–98 could not even provide complete cover for the domestic currency, the currency board would simply wipe out its remaining foreign-currency reserves before the entire domestic currency stock had been converted. In fact, some estimates indicated that if sustained capital flight did emerge after the pegging of the rupiah at 5,000 to the US dollar, the country would have reserves to defend the peg for less than one week (Enoch *et al.* 2001, 86).

### The end of the New Order[50] to *Orde Reformasi*

In the ensuing weeks, as the embattled Suharto vacillated and stalled, the economic downturn deepened and the Indonesian economy was brought to the brink of total collapse. Liquidity support to the banking sector continued to increase, in large part to meet continuing deposit withdrawals. This only further eroded the public confidence in the banking reforms under way. As tensions between Suharto and the IMF intensified, the White House dispatched (on March 3, 1998) the former US vice-president, Walter Mondale, to Indonesia to act as an intermediary between Suharto and the Fund. Yet this was to no avail (Blustein 2001, 230–2). Finally, the IMF's managing director carried out what he had threatened in a leaked letter in mid-February. On 6 March, the IMF announced the suspension of the second installment of Indonesia's bailout package (the second US$3 billion tranche), pending Suharto's choice of a new cabinet (C. Johnson 1998, 27–8). Suharto responded on March 10. The People's Consultative Assembly chose, by acclamation, Suharto as president and B. J. Habibie as vice-president.[51] With the 77-year-old Suharto now set to serve an unprecedented seventh five-year term as president (ending in the year 2003), all hopes for an early resolution of the stalemate with the IMF were dashed. Indeed, in an open act of defiance to the IMF and bilateral donors (especially the United States), Suharto refused to appoint reformers to key cabinet positions. In fact, ministers who were seen to be sympathetic to the IMF reform program, such as the finance minister Mar'ie Muhammad, were dropped from the cabinet. Instead, Suharto choose to appoint a "crony cabinet" – chosen from a close circle of loyalists, including his eldest daughter, Tutut, and his long-time business crony and golf partner, Bob Hasan. Hasan was given the key trade and industry portfolio. Also, a close family and business associate, Fuad Bawazier, was given charge of the all-important finance portfolio, and a long-time crony, Tanri Abeng, the state enterprises portfolio.[52] Several new ministers, including Hartono, minister of home affairs, and the labor minister, Theo Sambuaga, were also appointed for their personal loyalty to Suharto and his children, not their competence. It seemed that the old corrupt establishment was trying to re-entrench itself for the long haul – despite increasing demands (both domestic and international) for reform.

With rising unemployment and skyrocketing prices of basic commodities (in large measure the result of reductions in government subsidies), thousands of Indonesians took to the street demanding Suharto's ouster. Concerned about the potential chaos in the world's fourth most populous nation, and still unwilling to give up on Suharto, President Clinton and the US Treasury encouraged the IMF to continue talking with Suharto.[53] The third round of negotiations between the IMF and the Indonesian government began on March 17, amidst reports of widespread looting and rioting in several major cities and towns throughout the country. These developments seemed to convince the IMF of the need to adopt a more flexible approach in its negotiations, and in particular, it was persuaded into allowing BULOG to continue to retain the subsidies on basic commodities. For his part, Suharto quietly dropped the currency board idea by announcing that his government would "study" other alternatives. Thus it was in this context, in spite of the lingering hostility and mistrust, that the IMF and the Indonesian government reached their third agreement on April 9, 1998 (IMF 1998c). The new agreement reiterated the points agreed in the earlier ones, and added some more. Altogether, the "bullet-points" now totaled 117 specific requirements, including more specific targets and a timetable for implementation. On its part, the IMF announced that it would release its US$3 billion tranche to Indonesia – albeit, in portions of US$1 billion per month, rather than in its customary single total disbursement.

However, even before the ink was dry on the agreement, Suharto implicitly dismissed what he had just signed, calling instead for an undefined "IMF plus" program. The financial markets, however, having witnessed the drama before, failed to react to the agreement. Yet, the same could not be said of the rapidly growing popular opposition to Suharto's rule. Following weeks of largely peaceful student demonstrations at dozens of universities across the country, events soon turned violent after a harsh crackdown by the security forces. The situation turned decidedly worse on May 4. On this day, as the IMF released its first US$1 billion monthly tranche, the Suharto government abruptly announced sharp increases in fuel prices, including a hefty 71 per cent for gasoline and 25 per cent for kerosene.[54] Claiming wrongly that the price increases were mandated by the IMF, the Suharto regime hoped that the popular anger would be directed at the IMF. However, this gamble backfired. Instead, the call for Suharto's resignation grew louder following the government's ill-advised decision. In desperation, regime supporters, led by the Minister of the Interior Syarwan Hamid, blamed the price rise on *non-pribumi* ethnic Chinese (whom he called "rats disloyal to Indonesia"), as a result of their hoarding goods, thereby causing the sharp price hikes.[55]

Between May 12 and May 17, the pent-up frustrations and racial tensions exploded. On May 12, some 20,000 students at Gajah Mada University in Yogyakarta protested, calling for Suharto's resignation, and at Trisakti University in Jakarta, six student protesters were killed by soldiers. On May 13 a nationwide student protest quickly erupted in violence. Widespread violent rioting occurred simultaneously in many cities and towns through-out the country, and most tragically in Jakarta, where over a thousand people (mostly ethnic Chinese) were killed by mobs, reportedly organized and led by rogue elements of the Indonesian armed forces.[56] In Jakarta alone some "5,000 buildings were damaged or burned and close to 2,000 vehicles were torched" (Azis 1999, 86). Suharto's son-in-law, General Prabowo Subianto, head of the powerful *kostrad* (strategic military com-mand based in Jakarta), tried to exploit the situation further with threats and claims that the military was fully behind Suharto (Emmerson 1999, 306–9). In this uncertain and chaotic environment expatriates, businesses and capital fled Indonesia – including the IMF and World Bank staffers based in Jakarta, who joined the exodus. On May 18 several thousand students occupied the parliament grounds demanding an immediate special session of the People's Consultative Assembly and Suharto's resignation. The students were joined by prominent opposition political leaders such as Dr Amien Rais and Professor Emil Salim – who openly supported the students' demand for *reformasi total*, or total reform. By 3.30 in the after-noon, the Speaker of the House, Harmoko, flanked by two deputy speakers, announced that the parliamentary leaders were calling on Suharto to *lengser keprabon* (or step down) immediately for the sake of national unity (Anwar 1999, 34). However, hope faded as, later in the evening, General Wiranto, the head of the armed forces, announced that Harmoko had spoken as an individual and that his call for Suharto's resignation had no legal authority.

Indeed, soon afterwards Suharto announced that he would not step down immediately. Instead, he promised to revise the political laws through a reform committee, the members of which would include representatives of the student protesters. In addition, Suharto announced that the cabinet would be reshuffled immediately, and the central task of the new *kabinet reformasi* (reform cabinet) would be to deal with the growing economic and political crisis. Finally, Suharto promised that new elections would be held as soon as possible. However, all this was too little too late. By May 20 (Indonesia's National Day of Awakening), the number of students occupy-ing the parliament grounds had swelled to over 30,000. On the morning of May 21 the Speaker of the parliament announced that all factions of parlia-ment (including the military) were agreed that Suharto should resign imme-diately or face impeachment proceedings. Without the military's backing, Suharto's New Order was fundamentally and irrevocably damaged. Under intense domestic and international pressure, and in the face of mass demon-strations, Suharto abruptly resigned on May 21, 1998, after thirty-two years as president.[57] It marked the beginning of the end of the "New Order" regime.

In accordance with the constitution, vice-president B. J. Habibie was sworn in as "interim president" to serve out the remainder of Suharto's five-year term. Habibie inherited a nation in crisis. Lacking popular support and legitimacy, the new government seemed initially paralyzed.[58] The wanton destruction of property and infrastructure began to take its toll, severely disrupting economic activity. The service sector, including financial and business services, trade, hotels and restaurants, suffered huge losses. Equally savaged was the critical export sector. Indeed, some foreign buyers temporarily stopped placing orders for Indonesian exports. Moreover, both during and in the immediate aftermath of the riots, there were massive runs on all banks, in particular, Bank Central Asia (owned by two of Suharto's children and his crony Liem Sioe Liong), the nation's largest private bank, accounting for 12 per cent of the total banking sector liabilities. Bank Indonesia, in conjunction with two of the state banks, supplied over 30 trillion rupiah in cash to Bank Central Asia over the week following May 16 as deposits were withdrawn. Finally, on May 29, Bank Central Asia was brought under the auspices of IBRA, and the owners' rights were suspended. In this climate of chaos and uncertainty, the rupiah fell to below 12,000 to the dollar by the end of May, and continued to nosedive, reaching Rp. 16,500 against the dollar on June 17 – a cumulative depreciation of 85 per cent since June 1997.

In the face of growing social unrest and international pressure, President Habibie, in a surprise *volte-face*, accepted the charge that the New Order regime was undemocratic. He now promised rapid implementation of the long-awaited *keterbukaan* (political openness) and the establishment of *Orde Reformasi* (Reformation Order). To show his commitment, the Habibie government immediately freed the press from the draconian constraints that had been in force under Suharto, and in a dramatic move dismissed Prabowo (Suharto's son-in-law) from the Indonesian armed forces (Mietzner 1999, 88–9). Moreover, the Habibie administration revoked the law that limited the number of political parties to two, released political prisoners and voiced support for legal reforms – in particular, the protection of human rights (Anwar 1999, 39–43). Habibie also announced that fresh parliamentary elections (to be preceded by the rewriting of New Order election and political party laws) would be held in June 1999, followed by a significant decentralization of political and economic power away from Jakarta (to be discussed later). In the economic realm, recognizing the severity of the crisis, the government began to take steps to repair the distribution system to ensure adequate supplies of food and other necessities to all parts of the country. Although Habibie's Minister for Co-operatives, Adi Sasono, espoused the populist *Ekonomi Rakyat* (or an economy based on government assisted cooperatives), in practice "President Habibie and most of the new cabinet showed a greatly increased commitment to implementing the IMF program. Specifically, immediate pressure was off Bank Indonesia to do anything more than restore financial stability. There was significant easing of political pressures to bail out banks, and no apparent pressure on BI to reduce interest rates prematurely again" (Kenward 1999, 124). Moreover, Habibie affirmed that Coordinating Minister for the Economy, Ginandjar Kartasasmita, the official most trusted by the IMF in the last days of Suharto's presidency, would remain in office – despite a long history of political, policy and personal conflict between Habibie and Ginandjar. Perhaps what pleased the IMF (not to mention a section of the Indonesian business community) most was Habibie's announcement that the University of Indonesia economics professor Widjojo Nitisastro would have an enhanced advisory role in the government.[59] On June 24, the IMF and the Indonesian government signed the "Second Supplementary Memorandum of Economic and Financial Policies" (IMF 1998d) – a revised version of the economic program signed on April 10, 1998 (IMF 1998c). The new memorandum bleakly noted that "with the disruptions to economic activity and damage to business confidence in recent weeks, it is now expected that real GDP will decline by more than 10 per cent in 1998" (1998d).

Bad as this news was, there was more to come. Compounded by the severe drought brought on by the effects of El Niño, food crop production declined by as much as 8 per cent per capita in 1997–98, resulting in the first large-scale rice imports in over a decade. Overall, the economy contracted by some 13.2 per cent in 1998 (one of the most abrupt one-year slides recorded anywhere in the world in recent economic history), and nominal per capita incomes declined by 65 per cent between 1997 and 1998, from US$1,079 to US$380 (Tan 2000, 118). Literally overnight, hundreds of firms became insolvent and thousands became unemployed. Compounding the problem was inflation. The price of basic commodities such as rice and fuel skyrocketed as inflation jumped to 58.5 per cent. In many parts of Indonesia, the price of rice rose from 800 Rp. per kg to 2,000 Rp. per kg between 1997 and 1998. However, in drought-stricken West Java and East Kalimantan the price of rice rose from 1,000 Rp. per kg in 1998 to more than 5,000 Rp. per kg by the middle of that year. As a result, tens of thousands of Indonesians, many of whom had lived just above the poverty line, were once again reduced to destitution.[60] To deal with the rising social discontent, the Habibie government in consultation with the IMF introduced policies to ease the burden on the poor. Most importantly, in July 1998, the government introduced a special market operations program (OPK), under which BULOG was allowed to sell rice to 7.5 million low-income families at a subsidized price of Rp. 1,000 per kilogram. Each family was entitled to receive ten kilograms of rice per month.[61]

In late June 1998, audit results of banks (taken over by IBRA), conducted by international accounting firms during the spring and summer of

1998, were leaked to the press. The results were devastating. The large extent of delinquent loans, together with the high level of connected lending, illustrated the degree to which the banks had been used as vehicles for directed lending to non-productive ventures. Overall, the level of non-performing loans ranged from 55 per cent to more than 90 per cent of the banks' portfolios (Enoch 2000, 16). While for most of these banks the loans portfolios were dominated by memo-lending, banks also incurred huge losses as a result of the need to make substantial provisions against problem loans even as earnings capacity was eroded as recording of interest income on non-performing loans changed from an accrual to a cash basis. The huge losses wiped out the capital bases of much of the banking sector, leaving it deeply insolvent. By early August, the results of the portfolio reviews for a group of 16 large banks, all of them non-IBRA (except for Bank Central Asia) became available. The results showed that the financial condition of these banks was also very weak. Given that many of these banks would have been expected to be among the strongest in the country, these reviews confirmed the deep insolvency of the banking system as a whole. The immediate consequence was shock that the state of the banks was so bad; but beyond that, the leak put an end to denial of the seriousness of the banking problems and forced the Indonesian authorities to recognize that the implementation of banking reforms was of the utmost urgency.

### Financial sector reforms: achievements and challenges

Some important steps have been taken to improve supervision of the financial sector. Effective May 1999, a new central bank law significantly enhanced the powers and authority of the nation's central bank, including making it more accountable through requiring periodic presentations by the bank governor to parliament. The new law clearly stipulates that Bank Indonesia has one central objective: to achieve and maintain the stability of the value of the rupiah. To achieve this goal, the law enhanced the Bank's independence as a state institution outside the administration of the executive branch. This meant that the central bank is no longer to report directly to the president, but to the House of Representatives – and that neither of these institutions have the powers to remove the bank governor or members of the board unless they are found guilty of criminal acts. Despite this, it will take time to improve the supervisory skills at the central bank. That is, although the central bank has developed a "master plan" to enhance supervision, and the IMF has agreed to assist the bank with the implementation of reforms necessary to bring skills on a par with international standards, implementation will take time.

The massive insolvency of the Indonesian banking system called for a major restructuring of the entire sector. In September 1998, with the IMF's full support, Bank Indonesia outlined an ambitious multi-billion-dollar bank recapitalization plan, and in October the Indonesian parliament passed amendments to the banking law that modified previous requirements regarding bank secrecy and ended restrictions on foreign ownership of banks.[62] These amendments also strengthened the legal powers of IBRA and AMU, enabling them to operate more effectively – for instance, to be able to transfer assets and to foreclose against a non-performing debtor. To show that it was serious about implementing the plans, the government announced (in mid-September), that IBRA would work expeditiously to reduce the total number of small, poorly capitalized banks in the country by promoting bank mergers. True to its word, IBRA carried out the formal merger of 4 large state-owned banks (Bank Dagang Negara, Bank Ekspor-Impor (or EXIM Bank), Bank Bumi Daya, and Bapindo) and the corporate business of a fifth state bank (Bank Rakyat Indonesia) into a new institution, Bank Mandiri – which was established on September 30 as the holder of 100 per cent of the shares of the component banks.[63] The large capital injection into Bank Mandiri was to make it a financially strong institution capable of being a leading bank in the restructured Indonesian banking system. By the end of 2001, the restructuring program had left the country with 5 state banks and 26 regional development banks, while 160 private banks were consolidated into 85. The restructured state and private banks account for about 90 per cent of the total commercial banking assets of the country.

Moreover, as part of Indonesia's commitments to the IMF (as expressed in various letters of intent), the government took steps to review and strengthen the prudential and regulatory framework of the banking system. The top priority was to raise the quality of the country's banking supervision to be move closely in line with international standards. Specifically, three new regulations in the area of loan classification, provisioning and debt-restructuring operations came into effect in late December 1998. In the area of liquidity management, effective early 1999, banks are required to submit a liquidity report twice monthly for their global consolidated operations. Among other things, the report must contain both a foreign-currency liquidity profile and a rupiah and foreign-currency profile. In addition, banks are now required to publish unaudited quarterly financial statements within two months of quarter's end and audited financial statements within four months of the end of the reporting year (December 31). Also, since the over-concentration of lending to individual debtors or group of debtors was a major problem, the legal lending limit amounts have been significantly tightened.[64] No doubt, the frequency and completeness of financial disclosure by banks will greatly assist regulators, as well as the general public, to make a more accurate assessment of a bank's financial condition and overall performance. In the area of capital adequacy requirements, banks were given until December 31, 2000, to comply with a minimum capital adequacy requirement of 8 per cent. In January 2002, the government began finally to crack down – issuing notices to banks that failed to meet the standard that their assets would be transferred to IBRA for resolution if they failed to meet the requirements in the new specified time. Similarly, banks are now required to maintain their net open position in foreign currency at less than 20 per cent of their capital. This is to be reported to the central bank on a weekly basis for the consolidated domestic operations and consolidated domestic and foreign operations. New commercial banks must have a minimum paid-up capital of 3 trillion rupiah, while new rural banks are required to have between 500 million and 2 billion rupiah, depending on where they are located.

The more difficult challenge lies in the area of bank recapitalization. Keeping in mind that non-performing loans are estimated at 60–85 per cent of all loans, and bank recapitalization costs are estimated at a staggering Rp. 643 trillion (about US$89 billion), or 60 per cent of GDP, it will probably take several years to restore the financial sector to health (Lindgren *et al.* 1999, 65). The recapitalization is being financed by domestic bond issues, pushing up domestic public debt to unprecedented levels.[65] The first significant step towards recapitalization of private banks began in early 1999 – after the government completed (in December 1998), an audit to separate the banks into sound banks, salvageable banks and bad banks. Specifically, the audit carried out by independent auditors of all state banks, nationalized banks, regional banks and private banks, ranked banks into three categories according to their capital adequacy ratio (CAR).

Under the new ranking system, owners of banks in category C (those with a capital adequacy ratio of less than negative 25 per cent) were given an opportunity to inject sufficient equity to push them into a higher category, and thus make them eligible for recapitalization, or face liquidation. In March 1999, the government announced that 38 banks, all deeply insolvent and with no hope of recovering, were to be closed and "their owners will be required to repay their connected [i.e. memo] lending" (Government of Indonesia (GoI) 1999). Indeed, the government announced a list of the 200 largest defaulting borrowers and began the process of actively collecting from the 20 largest defaulters – in recognition of the fact that many owners "generally have substantial outside assets, even after the failure of their banks" (Enoch *et al.* 2001, 19). Banks with a ratio of negative 25 per cent to less than 4 per cent were assigned the status of Category B. These banks would be eligible to participate in the recapitalization program provided that their owners inject 20 per cent of the new capital required to attain a CAR of 4 per cent. In all, 9 Category B banks were deemed eligible for recapitalization, while 7 category B banks were taken over by IBRA. The seven banks were in serious financial difficulty, although it was stated that, owing to their extensive branch networks, they would be taken over (and not closed) to minimize disruption to the payments system. Former owners of these institutions were blocked from further roles in the management of banks. The intention was to restructure these banks, improve their financial performance, reduce their burden on the budget and prepare them for privatization. The 74 category A banks (those with a capital adequacy ratio of 4 per cent or higher) were allowed to continue business after being subjected to "fit and proper" tests (GoI 1999).

In view of the fact that Indonesian taxpayers were providing the funds (since there was very little useable collateral in the banks), recapitalization was contingent upon two criteria being met. First, all banks were required to submit business plans that showed their viability over a three-year period, and their managements were required to pass tests ensuring that they were technically competent to run a bank. And second, since many of the banks eligible for recapitalization were owned by some of the country's major conglomerates, recapitalization required the existing shareholders to provide at least 20 per cent (in cash) of the total funds necessary to restore the bank's capital adequacy ratio to 4 per cent before IBRA would put in any funds. That is, for every one rupiah of new capital that the owners of the bank injected into the bank, the government agreed to add 4 rupiah – meaning that the government agreed to take on 80 per cent of the cost of bank recapitalization. However, the bank owners have the option of repurchasing the government's shares within three years, and the right of first refusal to buy the shares for three to five years. In addition, the government agreed to allow these banks to swap some of their non-performing loans for government bonds. Under the plan, banks are allowed to continue to try to collect the bad loans, and if successful may use the proceeds to buy back part of the government's capital share.

Not surprisingly, since the government provided the recapitalization funds on very generous terms, the proposal has been attractive to many banks. By the end of 2000, the Indonesian banking sector has been significantly consolidated. Since mid-1997, the number of private domestic banks has been nearly halved through closures or state takeovers. By the end of 1999, banks under state control held about 70 per cent of liabilities, compared to 40 per cent before the crisis (Lindgren *et al.* 1999, 65). In sum, it remains to be seen whether recapitalization will bring some rationality to the banking sector. It should be noted that the recapitalization plan provides little incentive for the banks either to restructure debts owed by corporations or to make new loans. In this regard, Indonesia's recapitalization plan differs from Thailand's – which ties some of the government's capital injections to the amount of corporate debt the bank writes down and the amount of new lending it undertakes.

By mid-1999, the public contribution to financial sector restructuring has been equal to 51 per cent of GDP. The largest share of this has been used to recapitalize banks and provide liquidity support. As was noted earlier, IBRA is financed by a mix of medium- and long-term government-guaranteed bonds, some inflation-indexed, others not. These bonds pay high rates of interest, averaging 14 per cent annually. IBRA has exchanged these bonds for the worst non-performing loans in the banking system (the so-called "Category 5" loans). In the process, IBRA has acquired billions of dollars-worth of assets – measured at face value, not market value.[66] First, the question of how best to manage, and ultimately to dispose of these mounting assets remains a major challenge for the regulators. Although the devaluation of the rupiah has made Indonesian assets relatively inexpensive for investors holding strong currencies such as the US dollar, the problems of determining the fair market value of non-performing assets has prevented expeditious sales of assets to foreign investors. Moreover, the potential international market for Indonesian assets has been limited by the fact that foreign fund managers and other institutional investors are generally restricted from purchasing assets that do not have a so-called "investment grade" credit rating from an internationally recognized credit-rating agency. In Indonesia, such assets are far and few between.

Second, although IBRA has been given substantial extrajudicial powers to deal with recalcitrant debtors (it has used threat of criminal prosecution to compel the owners of the suspended and nationalized banks to make the required payments, besides being empowered by the Indonesian government to seize the personal assets of bank owners who fail to make their payments), this has hardly improved IBRA's performance. An ineffective bankruptcy system and political interference and corruption remain major impediments. For example, the implementation of the program came to an abrupt halt in August 1999 with the outbreak of the Bank Bali scandal. The scandal allegedly implicated senior officials at Bank Indonesia, the Ministry of Finance and IBRA. With the apparent cooperation of these officials, US$80 million was paid by a Habibie-connected company to a private bank (Bank Bali) to recover claims that were in fact already guaranteed by the government, and allegedly to bolster Golkar's election war-chest for the June 1999 ballot. IBRA's chairman pointed to aides in Habibie's Golkar party (and indirectly to the president himself) as behind the scandal. The incident vividly illustrated the fact that, if not corrupt itself, IBRA was unable to prevent abuses. The scandal led to the suspension of the IMF funds in September 1999. In fact, since the Habibie government failed to deal with the scandal, the parliament took on the task of investigating the case. However, when the parliament failed to make any progress, the IMF forced the government to invite an international auditor, Price-Waterhouse-Coopers, to undertake the audit and to make the results public. When the audit was completed, the government refused to publicize the full report. This, in turn, prompted the IMF to postpone the disbursement of funds. The IMF resumed its review and support only after the Habibie government was out of office.

Not surprisingly, the pace of asset disposal and loan recovery by IBRA is quite poor. As of May 2002, IBRA had acquired (at face value) a total of Rp. 360 trillion in non-performing loans (about 21 per cent of GDP in 2001) from troubled financial institutions. However, its asset-recovery rate is only about 10 per cent or less, and, by mid-2002, IBRA had disposed of only 12 per cent of its non-performing assets (ADB 2002, 28). At the heart of the problem is the low quality of the assets of many Indonesian banks. This is reflected in the non-performing loan level – which was 15.8 per cent in July 2001, down slightly from the December 2000 rate of 18.8 per cent. In an attempt to speed up asset-disposal, IBRA launched (in June 2002) its largest-ever asset-sale program of bank loan assets worth Rp. 150 trillion (US$17 billion). The sale, which is open for local and international investors, involves 2,500 credit portfolios consisting of restructured and non-restructured loans (ADB 2002, 28). In the light of its burdens, IBRA's goal of returning all assets under its management to the private sector by its sunset date of February 2004 remains highly optimistic.

Clearly, the level of non-performing loans in the Indonesian banking system is simply unprecedented. Since coming into operation, the AMU has taken over loans from a variety of institutions: closed banks, banks taken over, state-owned banks, and banks participating in the recapitalization schemes. However, not all these loans have been transferred. Moreover, given its limited resources, IBRA has been unable to administer all these loans on its own. In fact, bad loans of less than 5 billion rupiah are handled by the individual banks, bad loans valued at between 5 billion and 35 billion rupiah are subcontracted back to the individual banks (implementation remains under the supervision of the AMU), and bad loans in excess of 25 billion rupiah are handled directly by the AMU. In addition to loans, some non-core assets, including automobiles and office equipment, have been transferred to the AMU. According to the Indonesian government, the total amount of problem debt transferred to the AMU as of January 2000 was approximately 250 trillion rupiah (Root *et al.* 2000, 192–3).

By year-end 1997 domestic private corporations had borrowed US$53.6 billion from foreign banks, which left the corporate sector (as well as Indonesian banks exposed to these corporates) highly vulnerable to sudden depreciation. By late 1998, of the estimated US$118 billion corporate debt, nearly 60 per cent was owed to foreign creditors and about half the remaining 40 per cent was denominated in foreign currency. This, in effect, rendered the Indonesian corporate sector systematically vulnerable to large-scale depreciation of the rupiah. Indeed, in the early stages of the crisis, the extreme currency volatility and high interest rates saw many debtors stop payments on their debt, while the widespread rupiah depreciation that took place during the height of the crisis drove almost half of Indonesian corporations into insolvency and caused many more corporations difficulties in meeting their debt-servicing obligations. Of course, as Root and his co-authors (2000, 202) note, "this was compounded by the inconclusive steps taken by the Indonesian authorities in the early stages of the crisis to restore confidence in the banking system. Many debtors were simply unwilling to negotiate debt payments with institutions that faced possible closure." It should also be noted that given the ongoing political instability at the time, many debtors were unwilling to enter into negotiations. In this climate, if some hoped that the problem would go away, others used stalling tactics in anticipation of improvements in the exchange rate.

Under IMF's oversight, the Indonesian government has also taken steps to deal with the massive debt problem. In June 1998, the government reached agreement (the Frankfurt agreement) with a group of private creditors on restructuring three categories of debt. In regard to *trade credits*, the agreement stipulated that Indonesian commercial banks would repay all trade credits that were in arrears, and in return, foreign banks would maintain trade credits at the April 1998 level. Bank Indonesia agreed to guarantee new trade credits. In regard to *inter-bank debt*, foreign banks would exchange new loans of maturities of between one and four years for obligations owed by Indonesian commercial banks maturing by March 31, 1999. Again, the new loans are guaranteed by Bank Indonesia. The government's strategy for *corporate debt* restructuring has included three elements: first, the establishment of the Indonesian Debt Restructuring Agency (INDRA) to provide foreign-exchange cover for Indonesian corporations with foreign currency-denominated debt once they have reached debt-restructuring agreements. The INDRA plan was voluntary, and under it private sector offshore debt would be restructured so that it could be repaid over an eight-year period, the first three years of which were a grace period during which only interest was payable. The Indonesian government effectively facilitated the debt repayment by offering debtors a subsidized exchange rate so that they could service their loans. In other words, if both parties (the debtors and creditors) agreed, the plan saw debtors paying INDRA in rupiah and INDRA paying creditors in foreign currencies. In this way INDRA is designed to provide protection for the debtors against the risk of further real depreciation of the rupiah, and to give assurance of foreign-exchange availability for debt repayments.[67]

While the first two initiatives have been relatively successful, INDRA has not been successful, and corporate debt restructuring has been extremely slow. There are several reasons for this. First, even with the exchange-rate guarantee, current exchange rates are simply too unfavorable for most corporations to repay debts. After all, the plan provides little actual cash relief for debtors, since they must still make regular rupiah payments to INDRA. Second, many creditors (especially Japanese banks) have been quite unwilling to write down the value of the loans substantially. It is now recognized that for plans like INDRA to work it is essential to improve implementation of the bankruptcy law. Specifically, voluntary mechanisms for restructuring corporate debt will have greater appeal if creditors have reasonable expectations of being able to enforce their claims against debtors speedily through legal means, should voluntary methods fail.

The failure of the INDRA plan led the Indonesian government to introduce its second and third initiatives on corporate debt restructuring, the Jakarta Initiative and the Jakarta Initiative Task Force (JITF) in September 1998, to facilitate voluntary negotiations between debtors and creditors for corporate restructuring and to provide a regulatory "one-stop shop" for administrative procedures pertaining to debt resolution. Unlike the earlier Frankfurt Agreement of June 1998 (which dealt entirely with private foreign debt), the Jakarta Initiative introduced a set of principles based on the London Approach to guide voluntary out-of-court corporate restructuring.[68] The JITF was intended to facilitate negotiations between debtors and creditors (particularly, foreign lenders), and to obtain necessary regulatory approvals for deals. As of the end of May 2002, JITF had received a total of 130 registered cases, with a debt value amounting to US$30.3 billion, and completed the mediation of 71 cases, with a debt value of US$15.4 billion. Although debt-restructuring under JITF has been more successful than under IBRA, there are concerns over the quality of debt-restructuring by JITF, as debt-rescheduling still remains the predominant method of restructuring. Also, the initiative has done little to address the fundamental problem of making progress on burden-sharing between the creditors and debtors. In fact, poor enforcement of laws to protect creditors has given debtors little incentive to agree to restructuring deals likely to result in debt-to-equity conversions and substantial dilution of their shareholdings.

Under IMF oversight, in August 2000, the Indonesian government passed the Company Bankruptcy and Debt Restructuring and/or Rehabilitation Act, modeled on US Chapter 11, to facilitate reorganization of illiquid, but financially viable companies. The new bankruptcy system also introduced a special commercial court (to deal with the administration of the bankruptcy law) in order to provide a credible threat. The new bankruptcy law ensures that all creditors have equal rights to the assets recovered as the result of a bankruptcy proceeding. Moreover, it seeks to give creditors increased power to force debtors to restructure and pay off their debts, including giving creditors greater ability to liquidate the assets of the debtor in the event the debtor refuses to pay. The effectiveness of the bankruptcy law remains to be seen.

## Democracy and reforms

On June 7, 1999 Indonesia held a democratic election for the first time since 1955. Forty-eight political parties competed, with 21 winning at least one of the 462 contested seats in the 500-member national Dewan Perwakilan Rakyat or parliament (the additional 38 seats are made up of appointed armed forces delegates). Simultaneous elections were held for legislatures in 26 provinces and more than 300 districts and municipalities. Over 90 per cent of registered voters turned out for the three-level elections.[69] At the national level, the PDI-P (Partai Demokrasi Indonesia-Perjuangan), a secular nationalist party, received the highest share of the popular votes winning 34 per cent of the vote and 153 seats in parliament, Golkar (Golongan Karya) won 22 per cent, of the vote and 120 seats, the PKB (Partai Kebangkitan Bangsa) won 12 per cent of the votes and 51 seats, PPP (Partai Persatuan Pembangunan) won 10 per cent of the votes and 58 seats and PAN (Partai Amanat Nasional) won 7 per cent of the votes and 34 seats.[70] On October 20, 1999, the 700-member Majelis Permusyawaratan Rakyat (People's Consultative Assembly) met to elect a new president and vice-president to govern the world's fourth most populous nation for the next five years.[71] Given that Habibie's Golkar party performed poorly in the election, not to mention that he was badly tainted by the Bank Bali scandal, Habibie resigned his candidacy for president before the October 20 vote. This left the assembly to choose between the enigmatic Abdurrahman Wahid, the leader of Indonesia's largest Islamic group (the 40-million strong Nahdlatul Ulama), and Megawati Sukarnoputri, daughter of Indonesia's first president. Despite her party's having gained a higher share of the popular vote in June than any other group, Megawati lost the contest for the presidency. The Muslim parties and Golkar cooperated to elect the long-time democratic activist and PKB leader, Abdurrahman Wahid (also fondly known as Gus Dur), as president. Wahid received 373 votes, as against PDI-P's Megawati Sukarnoputri with 313. Megawati's supporters mounted large protests in Jakarta and elsewhere in Indonesia, and on October 21 Megawati was elected with an overwhelming majority as vice-president. She was constitutionally poised to succeed the sickly Gus Dur (who had already suffered two strokes) if he did not finish his five-year term.

The Wahid government inherited an economy that was slowly on the mend. Indeed, as Emil Salim (2001, 211) notes, "the Habibie administration made substantial gains in economics." In 1999 the rate of economic growth was 2 per cent, and in 2000 around 4 per cent – signaling that the worst of the contraction may be over. Similarly, inflation, which stood at 77 per cent in 1998, dropped to around 2 per cent by December 1999, and the new floating exchange rate seems to be functioning well, stabilizing at around Rp. 7,000–7,500 to the US dollar. However, Indonesia has not experienced the "V-shaped recovery" evident in the other Asian crisis economies. In spite of the sharp real depreciation of the rupiah and the recovery of oil prices, export performance has been disappointing. It seems that foreign investors and the Sino-Indonesian business community are still holding back, pending clear signals regarding political stability and security.

After his first 100 days, President Wahid began 2000 amidst popular goodwill. He committed his government to the rapid implementation of the economic reform measures, and immediately after the October elections signed a new letter of intent with the IMF. However, policy-making and implementation in a deeply fragmented parliament with its competing parties and factions has not been easy. Moreover, President Wahid's well-intentioned decision to form a "national unity cabinet" created its own problems. In the economic arena, it was reflected in the fragmentation of economic decision-making authority within the cabinet between a number of competing ministers and their outside advisors. This delayed the implementation of reforms, in particular, corporate debt restructuring – culminating in the embarrassing suspension of US$400 million in IMF support in late March 2000.[72] However, the IMF action seemed to act as a wake-up call, as since then the Wahid administration has made concerted efforts to implement economic reforms, including addressing the problem of corruption and the Suharto family wealth.

To compensate for the problems associated with the Bank Bali scandal and to renew its commitment to reforms, the Wahid government gave IBRA extraordinary powers (the so-called PP17 powers) effective from October 1999 to seize the assets of uncooperative debtors. IBRA used its PP17 powers for the first time in December 1999, seizing two properties, including fourteen hectares of land in Jakarta from a firm owned by a Suharto family member. Similarly, in an effort to energize the JITF, the government has approved time-limited procedures for JITF mediation of its cases and agreed that the JITF may refer cases of uncooperative debtors to the government's Financial Sector Policy Committee for action by the attorney general's office in the Bankruptcy Court. Also, the government has made concerted efforts to address the negative perceptions about governance in judicial processes. There is a realization that delays in corporate debt restructuring will impede economic recovery. Likewise, while Indonesia undoubtedly faces daunting challenges to reforming its banking and financial sector, the realization that a weak banking sector made Indonesia particularly vulnerable, and deepened the depth and duration of the crisis, is a strong incentive to move forward with the reforms.

For some five decades, Indonesia has been a multi-tiered unitary state, with provinces as the second tier below the center, and the local (district) governments as the third tier, with the village serving as the fourth tier. The centralization of authority in Jakarta was long justified as a way of maintaining national unity in a multi-ethnic society, spread across some 14,000 islands and 2 million square kilometers. With the collapse of the Suharto regime, power quickly began to shift away from the center to the provinces and districts. Cognizant of this reality, the Habibie government passed in May 1999 two laws (which came into effect on January 1, 2000), designed to change intergovernmental political and fiscal relations in Indonesia dramatically. The two laws – Law No. 22/1999 on Regional Government (UU PD) and Law No. 25/1999 on the Fiscal Balance between the Central Government and the Regions (UU PKPD) – significantly devolved power to the local districts, rather than to provincial governments. First,

Law No. 22/1999 eliminates the hierarchical relationship between the provincial and the district governments. The district governments, both the *kota* (municipality) and *kabupaten* (district), are now fully autonomous, and need no longer report to the governor of the province. Instead, the district heads will be responsible to the locally elected assembly, the Dewan Perwakilan Rakyat Daerah. In contrast, the provinces will retain a hierarchical relationship with the central government. Second, Law No. 25/1999 fundamentally alters the transfers received by local governments from the central government. Most importantly, the law introduces revenue-sharing for provincial and district governments, assigning each level of government its share of revenues from taxes on land and buildings, forestry, mining, fisheries, oil and gas. Of course, this means that provinces rich in oil and natural gas, such as Riau and East Kalimantan, have the potential to benefit. While it is hoped that such unprecedented decentralization will empower local communities, make government more accountable (and thereby reduce corruption), and promote more sustainable and equitable patterns of economic development, only time will tell if devolution fulfills its ostensible goals.

By mid-2000, President Abdurrahman Wahid had squandered his political capital. In August 2000 he was censured by parliament, and only survived in office by apologizing. In February 2001 he once again received a parliamentary censure – which was supported by 86 per cent of legislators in the House of Representatives (DPR). Supposedly at issue was his implication in two financial scandals and his alleged refusal to acknowledge the DPR as his constitutional equal. Tainted with corruption and politically isolated, Wahid functioned as a lame-duck president until his removal from office by the MPR on July 23, 2001. The performance of Wahid's successor, Megawati Sukarnoputri, has been much better. In sharp contrast to Wahid, the Megawati administration improved relations with the IMF and introduced modest reform measures. Nevertheless, corruption remains rife, the implementation of economic reforms haphazard, and the ill-planned implementation of decentralization laws continues to erode central authority. Clearly, the legacy of the 1997–98 economic crisis is so devastating that successive governments will continue to grapple with Indonesia's formidable economic problems.

## Notes

1   Furman and Stiglitz (1998) find that Indonesia's crisis was the least predictable within a sample of 34 troubled countries.
2   Quoted in Higgins (1968, 678).
3   Critics have argued that the official Indonesian data on the poverty line – the average consumption by household members below which a given household is

classified as poor – were originally set too low, resulting in a low estimate of the incidence of poverty and possibly an overestimation of the reduction in poverty over time. While Indonesia's poverty line has indeed been rather low compared to those of other Asian countries, "all things considered, and whatever its exact dimensions, a prolonged and broad-based improvement in living standards under the New Order did take place" (Booth 1999, 129).

4 Hollinger (1996, 20) writes that "in the early years of the Soeharto administration a new foundation for fiscal policy was put into place: the so-called 'balanced budget principle' which was enacted into law. This still remains today as the guiding rule on the budget and is embodied in each year's annual budget law as passed by parliament. 'Balanced' has a specific meaning in the Indonesian policy context. The requirement is that the total of government expenditures, including both the 'routine' expenditures and the 'development' expenditures into which the Indonesian budget is divided, cannot exceed the total of tax revenues collected domestically plus official foreign aid."

5 As was noted earlier, the steep appreciation of the currencies of Japan, South Korea and Taiwan after 1985 led producers of exports in these countries to relocate their labor-intensive manufacturing processes to other parts of Asia where wage costs were lower. Indonesia, along with Thailand and Malaysia, benefited from the resulting flow of foreign investment from East Asia – much of it in export manufacturing.

6 After hitting a historic high of 80 yen to the dollar in June 1995, the yen experienced a downward trend, falling to 127 yen to the dollar in April 1997 – or just before the Asian crisis broke. The yen's sharp depreciation led to a marked deterioration in East and Southeast Asia's export performance and current-account imbalances in 1996, paving the way for the currency crisis.

7 Jabotabek, or the greater Jakarta metropolitan region, comprising Jakarta–Bogor–Tangerang–Bekasi.

8 Other measures included (a) the removal of credit ceilings for all banks, and (b) the elimination of taxes on interest, dividends and royalties on foreign-currency deposits in all state banks (Prawiro 1998, 226–7).

9 The 1983 reforms were enacted at a time when Indonesia's earnings from oil (its principal export commodity) were declining. In the two-year period 1982–83, Indonesia's export earnings from oil fell by 24 per cent. The Indonesian government recognized that a more efficient and well-developed banking system would help foster the creation of a more diversified national economy. For details, see Bennett (1995).

10 See Lindgren *et al.* (1999, 13).

11 For example, Suharto's eldest daughter, Siti Hardiyanti Rukmana, held interests in telecommunications, agribusiness, toll road construction and shipbuilding. The president's son, Bambang Trihatmojo, controlled the large Bimantara group, which was active in telecommunications, real estate, agribusiness, food retailing, construction and electronics. In fact the Bimantara Group was granted special concessions for overseas distribution of the state petroleum company's products, and high tariffs to protect a US$2.2 billion plastics plant built jointly with German and Japanese multinationals. Suharto's youngest son, Tommy, had similar interests, including petrochemicals and automobiles. Likewise, Suharto's other children, Sigit Harjoyudanto, Siti Hediati, Siti Hutami Endang Adiningsih,

and his grandson, Ari Harjo Wibowo, and Suharto's half-brother, Probosutejo, controlled large business conglomerates. It is not known exactly how far Suharto's own business interests extended. He and his wife, Tien (before her death in April 1996), controlled several non-profit foundations or *yayasan*, which were not required to disclose their economic holdings and activities. For details, see Eklof (1999).

12  Hale (2001, 632) notes that, "for example, a similar type of car such as the Toyota Corolla would be subjected to an import duty of 50%, a luxury tax of 35%, an import surcharge of 2.5%, and a value-added tax of 10%. The Timor car, on the other hand, was exempt from all but the 10% value-added tax. The Corolla thus sold for around 70 million rupiah, or $30,000 at pre-crisis exchange rates, whereas the Timor sold for about half that price. In fact, at a market price of 35.75 million rupiah the Timor was considerably cheaper than other similar import models such as those from Opel (GM) and Peugeot as well."

13  Bank Indonesia's Monetary Management Director, Dr C. Harinowo, explained that "the benefit [of widening the rupiah band] is providing us more autonomy to managing monetary policy. We do not need to be concerned with the exchange rate, which affects monetary aggregates. It gives us a bigger cushion if there are any speculative attacks. It provides us with an experience of a floating-rate regime, but within a narrow confinement" (Henderson 1998, 127).

14  Soesastro and Basri (1998, 7) note that between 20 July and 13 August Bank Indonesia's interventions in the market had depleted the reserves by over US$1.5 billion.

15  This measure, of course, reduced the costs incurred by banks borrowing in the interbank market.

16  The finance minister Mar'ie Muhammad made it clear that the government was only seeking the IMF's technical assistance, and would explore the possibility of financial support only as a precaution. Indeed, on October 8, the IMF was invited for consultation only, and no explicit request for a loan was made (Soesastro and Basri 1998, 10; also Hill 1999, 15).

17  While the technical details of the bilateral assistance were worked out between Indonesia and the individual countries, the United States made it clear that its loans could only be drawn upon if Indonesia followed the agreement with the IMF. It should also be noted that US$5 billion out of the total IMF package included Indonesia's own assets.

18  The "letter of intent" released by the Indonesian government on October 31, 1997 described the policies that Indonesia intended to implement in the context of its request for financial support from the IMF. For details, see (IMF 1997e).

19  Borsuk (1999, 149) notes that "the blatant dispensation given by Suharto to his son made a farce of the 'national car' policy and strengthened the case being made in Tokyo and elsewhere that it broke WTO rules." In March 1998, the WTO verdict argued that the Timor's tax advantages violated international trade rules.

20  According to the finance minister Mar'ie Muhammad, the banks were "insolvent to the point of endangering business continuity and disturbing the whole banking system" (Eklof 1999, 107). The liquidated banks were: Bank Harapan Sentosa; Sejahtera Bank Umum; Bank Andromeda; Bank Pacific; Bank Guna Internasional; Bank Astria Raya; Bank Dwipa Semesta; Bank Jakarta; Bank Industri; Bank Citrahasta Dhanamanunggal; South East Asia Bank; Bank

Mataram Dhanarta; Bank Pinaesaan; Bank Anrico; Bank Umum Majapahit Jaya; and Bank Kosagraha Semesta.

21 On the other hand, as Blustein (2001, 106) notes, "many foreign analysts praised the bank closures in particular as a sign that Indonesia was being forced to change its ways."

22 Likewise, Djiwandono (1999a, 148) notes that "the domestic reaction to the closure of the banks was the reverse of what was expected. It was ironic that a step designed to restore confidence to the banking sector resulted in the collapse of confidence and plunged the banking sector into chaos."

23 Indeed, the IMF saw the forced liquidation of the 16 banks as a sufficiently important step towards reforming the banking system. Thus, on November 5, 1997, the Fund approved the three-year Stand-By Arrangement (totaling US$10 billion) – and released the first installment of the promised aid package.

24 In all fairness it should be mentioned that a blanket deposit guarantee was not introduced because of the moral hazard effect. It was believed that the 16 banks being closed were very small, and hence, that there was no need for such a guarantee.

25 Eklof (1999, 108) writes that "Bambang filed a lawsuit against Mar'ie Muhammad, claiming that the minister had closed the banks in order to discredit his family and, indirectly, to topple his father."

26 Eisuke Sakakibara, the Japanese vice-finance minister, gives a first-hand account of his dealings with Suharto. He states, "He [Suharto] flatly stated that he would agree with the IMF plan, but had no intention of observing the conditions. . . . The president, his family and cronies began to realize that the structural reform plan initiated by the IMF and technocrats might shake the foundations of the Suharto administration" (DeRosa 2001, 102).

27 While no authoritative figures existed on the size of the debt, it was widely believed to be substantial. Estimates ranges from US$35 to US$70 billion – much higher than Indonesia's official foreign reserves.

28 Blustein (2001, 99–100) observes, "nobody – not Bank Indonesia, not the IMF, not the World Bank – seemed to have the faintest idea about what had suddenly become a hugely troubling question: How many dollars would Corporate Indonesia have to obtain in the next few months to pay its foreign creditors what it had borrowed?" Equally troubling was the realization that "the demand for US$ to cover unhedged borrowings has been far greater than first thought by Bank Indonesia, or by private sector analysts."

29 Moreover, these credits added substantially to the money supply and helped to fuel inflation in early 1998.

30 The budget would take effect from April 1, 1998.

31 Why did Suharto choose to defy the IMF? There seem to be two considerations. There was concern, first, that a contractionary budget would force many Indonesian companies, including those owned by his family members and cronies, into bankruptcy, and second, that the elimination of food and fuel subsidies would ignite civil disorder.

32 A report in the *Washington Post* (January 8, 1998), mentioned that both the IMF and the United States Treasury were unhappy with Suharto's budget, and questioned his commitment to implementing the agreed IMF program (Radelet 1999, 11).

33 According to Azis (1999, 85), "pandemonium set in when on 8 and 9 January, people went on a buying spree to hoard foodstuffs."

34 The ethnic Chinese have long been easy targets. While they make up 3 per cent to 4 per cent of the population, they are rumored to control 70 per cent to 80 per cent of the economy (Azis 1999). However, others have questioned this figure, arguing that the Indonesian Chinese control far less (Wanandi 1999). For details on how Suharto and his son-in-law tried to promote the anti-Chinese campaign, see Mietzner (1999) and Eklof (1999).

35 Peregrine made its loan to Steady Safe as part of a deal whereby Peregrine was the underwriter for the bonds that Steady Safe was issuing to refinance its short-term debt and a US$118 million loan from Hong Kong Bank. Peregrine was to square its position once the bonds were sold. Unfortunately for Peregrine, investor interest in bonds evaporated when the financial crisis broke, and it was unable to square its position. A debt–equity swap was not feasible because the crisis in the Indonesian economy following the massive depreciation of the rupiah had drastically reduced the market value of Steady Safe to only US$4.7 million (Sender and Granitsas 1998). It is useful to note that, prior to the outbreak of the crisis, Steady Safe had used US$145 million to buy 14 per cent of a toll-road building company owned by Suharto's eldest daughter, Tutut. She was then named to the Steady Safe board. Yet the main earnings of Steady Safe came from its Jakarta taxi franchise. Steady Safe had no dollar revenues, and its annual income was equivalent to only US$9 million. Its high price–earnings ratio before the crisis was due to the as yet unrealized promises of the toll-road company, which were contingent on its close relationship with Suharto's daughter.

36 Much was made of this event by the media. As Bresnan (1999, 93) notes, "as Suharto affixed his signature, IMF managing director Michel Camdessus stood over him, arms folded across his chest, looking every inch the school-master he was playing in the drama. The photograph of this scene became a symbol of the charged issue at the heart of the negotiations – whether the IMF, and through it the United States, had the right to dictate terms to the Indonesian government in return for help in restoring confidence in its economy."

37 SBIs, or "Sertifikat Bank Indonesia" are issued every Wednesday with a one-month duration, but from October 1998 Bank Indonesia also began to issue three-month SBIs.

38 See Shenon 1998.

39 Similarly, Enoch *et al.* (2001, 13) note that "there was evidence that the [Indonesian] authorities had limited commitment to the program they had agreed with the IMF, and had made numerous policy reversals."

40 It was well known that Habibie, who had major financial stake in almost every business activity in Indonesia, epitomized the unscrupulous crony capitalism and the perverse business subculture. Habibie's government-funded aircraft project was among those targeted by the Fund. It was no secret that the IMF and the United States did not want him to be vice-president. For details, see Bresnan 1999, 92–4.

41 Of course, several months later the IMF recognized this fatal mistake and eased up on its fiscal targets in Indonesia (as it did in Korea and Thailand); but the damage had been done.

42  Blustein (2001, 216) observes, "the obvious question is why the IMF sidestepped the matter in the January 15 program. Part of the answer is that the Fund, for all its expertise in macroeconomic policy, has few specialists in corporate finance."

43  The guarantee was due to expire on January 31, 2000. At that time it would be replaced by a deposit insurance scheme. The guarantee was retroactively applied to the 16 closed banks. The guarantee initially excluded debts of bank owners, connected lending and subordinated debts. However, under enormous pressure from large depositors in the banks that had been closed in November 1997 (which included a number of powerful foundations), the finance minister announced in February 1998 that the guarantee would also be applied retrospectively to those banks.

44  Prior to the creation of IBRA, Bank Indonesia was the primary supervisory body for the banking industry. IBRA is known in Bahasa Indonesia as Badan Penyehatan Perbanken Nasional (BPPN). IBRA initially operated out of the premises lent by the central bank. Later in 1998, it took over the headquarters of a bank it had closed. Most IBRA staff initially were seconded and paid by their seconding institutions.

45  For details, see Republic of Indonesia Presidential Decree No. 27/1998, January 26, 1998, www.indoexchange.com/babong/general/bppn/who/tengah.html.

46  Kenward (1999, 122) notes that "by mid-April [1998], all senior management at the central bank had been changed. Among the new Managing Directors, barely half had experience in a central bank."

47  For details regarding Suharto's remarks, see *The Singapore Straits Times*, March 9, 1998.

48  In mid-February 1998, a leaked letter from the IMF's managing director threatened the withdrawal of financial support if a currency board was established (C. Johnson 1998, 27–8). However, Blustein (2001, 225) explicitly notes that "on February 11, Camdessus sent Suharto a private letter warning him against proceeding with Hanke's plan. The second $3 billion tranche of the Fund's $10 billion, three-year loan for Indonesia was scheduled for consideration by the Executive Board in mid-March, and Camdessus's letter left little doubt that a currency board would cause the Fund to cut off money to Jakarta."

49  DeRosa (2001, 104) notes "the rupiah was trading well above 10,000 at the time. Market participants and pundits quickly concluded that the Suharto family was planning to loot the central bank's reserves by converting rupiahs for dollars at a massively preferential rate of exchange, meaning that they would have first dibs on the central bank's dwindling foreign reserves."

50  The name "New Order" was originally meant to distinguish the Suharto regime from its immediate predecessor, the "Old Order" of President Sukarno.

51  On August 18, 1945, the Republic of Indonesia promulgated its first constitution. According to this charter, in effect from 1945 through to 1949 and reinstated in 1959, the People's Consultative Assembly (PCA) or the Majelis Permusyawaratan Rakyat (MPR) is the country's highest governing body. The MPR met quinquennially, within a few months after a parliamentary election, to elect the president and vice-president and establish the broad outlines of state policy for the next five-year term. The president holds a mandate from the assembly to carry out the program. Below the assembly is the parliament or DPR (Dewan Perwakilan Rakyat), which meets annually. Parliament is responsible for

legislation and must approve the budget submitted to it each year by the government. The number of seats in the assembly was set at twice that of parliament. In 1997, the DPR consisted of 500 members – 400 of these were elected and the remaining 100 were military appointees. The so-called super-parliament, the People's Consultative Assembly, consisted of all members of the DPR, plus an additional 500 appointees appointed by Suharto. Thus, in practice, Suharto controlled the appointment of 60 per cent of the delegates in the assembly which elected him. Every fifth year between 1973 and 1998, the MPR unanimously re-elected Suharto to the presidency. Similarly, official control of the party system was pervasive. Only three entities were permitted to contest elections: the state party called Functional Groups (Golongan Karya or Golkar), the Development Unity Party (Partai Persatuan Pembangunan or PPP), and the Indonesian Democracy Party (Partai Demokrasi Indonesia or PDI).

52 Bawazier was also a strong proponent of the currency-board system.

53 For details, see Blustein 2001, 230–3.

54 The fuel price increase (although not its precise timing) was one of the IMF conditions. Although the IMF defended the Indonesian government's decision to raise the prices, it is not clear if the IMF wanted the measure to be implemented incrementally or all at once, albeit the April agreement allowed for the gradual phasing out of the subsidies. In any case, the Suharto government imprudently implemented the measure all at once – with severe consequences for the vast majority of Indonesians.

55 Newspaper reports quote Syarwan as regularly referring to Chinese-Indonesians as "rats." Eklof (1999, 136) notes that "Lieutenant-General Syarwan Hamid, spoke about the need to eradicate rats in Indonesia's economy, saying: these rats took away the fruits of our national development and work for their own self interest. Don't think that the people do not know who these rats are. It's time to eliminate these rats." For details on how Suharto and his cronies targeted the Indonesian-Chinese community, see Eklof (1999, 134–43).

56 Leo Suryadinata (2001, 506) notes that "starting on May 13, Jakarta saw two days of large-scale unrest directed against the city's ethnic Chinese population. Their shops were ransacked, looted, and burned down; many were attacked; and numerous ethnic Chinese women were tortured, raped and killed."

57 Anwar (1999, 34) notes that Suharto's "abrupt decision came about because he could not find anyone to join his new reform cabinet."

58 It should be noted that some argued that since Suharto and Habibie were elected together as president and vice-president, both should resign. The question of legitimacy thus dogged Habibie's presidency. For details, see Anwar 1999.

59 Professor Widjojo Nitisastro is considered the chief architect of the New Order development policy. He served as Suharto's chief economic advisor from the mid-1960s to the early 1980s. In later years he was frequently called upon to rescue the economy from the depredations inflicted on it by Suharto's children, and by big spenders such as Habibie and Ginandjar. Widjojo's commitment to market-oriented macroeconomic policies reassured both the IMF and sections of the Indonesian business community.

60 For details on the various estimates of poverty, see Booth 1999a.

61 While the program did provide immediate relief to many of the hardest hit, it had little impact on the large number of urban poor who have no official

resident status. In October 1998, the government announced that the OPK program would be extended to 17 million families, with each family entitled to receive 20 kilograms of rice per month. In addition, a supplementary food program for children and expectant and lactating mothers was initiated in late October 1998.

62  Under the recapitalization plan, for every rupiah of fresh capital injected into banks that qualified for recapitalization, the government would put up Rp. 4. In return for its injections of capital (which were to be refunded by bond issue) the government would receive equity stakes in the banks. Bank owners would then have three years to redeem part of or the entire government stake.

63  Following the legal merger in July 1999, the government began plans to privatize Bank Mandiri and the three remaining state-owned banks.

64  The legal lending limit for an individual non-connected debtor or group of debtors is 30 per cent of capital until December 31, 2001; 25 per cent of capital during the year 2002; and 20 per cent of capital as of January 1, 2003. The legal lending limit for connected parties (both individual debtors and groups of debtors) may not exceed 10 per cent of capital, and the legal lending limit for the total of connected parties may not exceed 10 per cent of capital (Root *et al.* 2000, 197).

65  The recapitalization scheme involves an exchange of government bonds for outstanding shares between the government and the recapitalized bank – and thus requires no cash up-front. The only initial cost is fiscal, with the interest cost of bonds estimated at Rp. 38 trillion in the FY 1999/2000 budget. The fiscal costs are to be financed by the proceeds of privatization and assets of IBRA. These assets include non-performing loans and capital assets transferred to IBRA by the banking system.

66  According to Hufbauer (1999), as of August 1999 IBRA had acquired some Rp. 500 trillion (US$85 billion) of assets, measured at face value, not market value. According to an IMF study (see Enoch *et al.* 2001, 39), by late 1999 IBRA had assumed responsibility for assets with a face value of 441 trillion rupiah (36 per cent of GDP). It had 174,878 debtors, out of whom those owing over Rp. 50 billion represented 68 per cent of the value of the debt, but less than 1 per cent of the total number of debtors.

67  However, INDRA does not provide commercial risk protection if debtors do not make payments in rupiah.

68  The London Approach, formulated by the Bank of England in the 1970s and developed further in the 1990s, consists of a set of non-binding principles to guide debt-restructuring processes. It has three objectives: to minimize losses to creditors and other parties; to avoid unnecessary liquidations of fundamentally viable debtors; and to ensure continued financial support to viable debtors.

69  Liddle (2000). East Timor at that time was still the 27th province, but did not participate in the elections.

70  Two other parties with significant support were PBB (Partai Bulan Bintang) and PK (Partai Keadilan), which won 2 per cent and 13 seats and 1 per cent and 6 seats, respectively (Liddle 2000, 33).

71  The 500-member DPR plus 200 appointed representatives from various social groups and Indonesia's 27 provinces (five delegates for each of the 27 provinces, giving a total of 135) constitute the 700-member MPR – which selects the

country's president and vice-president, sets out guidelines for administration policy, and is responsible for holding the administration accountable for its activities at the end of every presidential term. With the departure of East Timor, the number of regional representatives dropped by five, for a final total Assembly membership of 695.

72 The IMF delayed its disbursement because it found that Indonesia had made almost no progress on the promises it made in January 2000.

# 4

# Korea:
# crisis, reform and recovery

We don't know whether we would go bankrupt tomorrow or the day after
tomorrow. I can't sleep since I was briefed. I am totally flabbergasted . . . This
is the bottom. It's a matter of one month, no, even one day. I just can't
understand how the situation came to this (President-elect Kim Dae-Jung,
December 23, 1997).[1]

In the 1950s, Korea was among the poorest countries in the world, with a
per capita income of under US$100. In per capita terms, this placed the
country below Haiti, Ethiopia, Peru, Honduras and India, among others.
Ravaged by a brutal war between 1950 and 1953, a divided Korea was
predicted to remain a "basket-case" for the foreseeable future. However,
South Korea (hereafter Korea), defied the dire predictions – becoming in
less than a generation the quintessential developmental success story, and a
model for other developing countries to emulate. With the exception of a
relatively short-lived recession in 1979–80, Korea enjoyed continuous economic growth between 1960 and 1997. With a well-educated population
of 42 million in 1996, and an economy expanding at an annual rate of over
8 per cent, Korea's per capita income had grown to US$10,973 by mid-
1997.[2] This earned the country its coveted membership of the exclusive
OECD (Organization for Economic Cooperation and Development) group
of nations.[3] Already the world's eleventh largest economy in 1996, Korea's
publicly stated ambition was to outperform Japan technologically in the
new millennium. Indeed, the "miracle on the Han" seemed to know no
bounds. As the world's top producer of the dynamic random access memory
(D-RAM) computer chips, the second largest shipbuilder, the third largest
producer of semiconductors, the fourth largest electronics manufacturer, the
fifth largest automobile maker, the sixth largest steel producer, and the
seventh largest textile producer, Korea's aspiration was hardly an empty
threat.[4]

When the financial crisis unexpectedly hit Southeast Asia following the devaluation of the Thai baht on July 2, 1997, it was widely believed that the contagion would not spread to Korea. Not only was the Korean economy the second largest in East Asia, with a gross domestic product of 376 trillion won (or US$454 billion); all the key macroeconomic fundamentals looked sound (Ariff and Khalid 2000, 63). First, since the early 1990s, the Korean economy had grown at an impressive rate. Though not as high as the double-digit growth rate of the late 1980s, the growth rate still exceeded 8 per cent in 1995, and 6 per cent during the first three quarters just prior to the crisis. Second, inflation was not only under control – since 1993 it had remained relatively low, fluctuating between 4 per cent and 5 per cent. Price stability and expectations of low inflation also led to a gradual decline in nominal interest rates.[5] Third, the real exchange rate was not significantly overvalued. In fact, in the three years prior to the crisis, the real exchange rate was essentially flat. Fourth, the gross domestic savings remained high, exceeding 30 per cent in 1995–96. Fifth, the fiscal deficit, which was about 2.5 per cent of GDP in the early 1980s, was turned into a surplus in 1993 – a position it maintained on the eve of the crisis. Sixth, the government budget was close to being in balance, and between 1990 and 1995, Korea's current account deficit averaged 1.9 per cent of GDP. It increased significantly in 1996 to US$24 billion (4.9 per cent of GDP), because the Korean monetary authority decided to adhere to a strong won policy, despite market pressures for devaluation, because they were concerned about price stability. However, as the Japanese yen became strong again by early 1997, the current account deficit fell to 2.5 per cent of GDP, and by mid-1997 to US$8.2 billion, or 1.9 per cent of GDP.[6] Thus, on the eve of the crisis, Korea's external position was fairly sustainable. After all, its current-account deficits were used to finance investment rather than consumption. Seventh, although Korea's foreign debt had grown significantly in the 1990s, it was not unsustainable. That is, the Korean debt/GNP ratio in 1996 was still only 22 per cent – well under the critical level of 48 per cent specified by the World Bank.[7] Moreover, the debt-service ratio of Korea was low, at only 5.8 per cent (Chang 1998). Finally, unlike the other crisis-hit economies, Korea was blessed with a 99 per cent literacy rate (Ariff and Khalid 2000, 62). From a macroeconomic perspective, the Korean economy seemed well managed and sound.

In November 1997, when Thailand, Indonesia, Malaysia and the Philippines were in the throes of a deepening financial turmoil, the headlines in the Korean media consisted mainly of stories dealing with the upcoming presidential election. Thus, on November 19, when President Kim Young Sam announced his decision to fire several key economic policy-makers on the grounds of gross economic mismanagement, most Koreans were surprised at the news. However, two days later, on the morning of November 21, the Korean public, and also many outside observers, were shocked to learn that the Korean government had formally requested the IMF (International Monetary Fund) for emergency standby loans because Korea's own foreign reserve level was very low (at US$7.3 billion) and most foreign financial institutions were unwilling to roll over their short-term loans to Korea.[8]

On December 3, 1997, in order to calm the financial markets, the IMF and the Korean government announced that they had agreed to a loan package totaling an unprecedented US$57 billion to assist Korea overcome a mounting foreign-exchange problem and stop the rapid deterioration of the nation's credit standing. Of this, US$21 billion would came from the IMF, US$10 billion from the World Bank, US$4 billion from the Asian Development Bank, and the remainder from bilateral sources, including US$10 billion from Japan and US$5 billion from the United States. Owing to Korea's desperate situation, the IMF's part of the package was to be released quickly under the Fund's accelerated emergency financing mechanism.[9] However, the Korean government had to accept virtually all the IMF's conditions. On December 4, the IMF released US$5.56 billion to the Korean government. An additional US$3.58 billion was to be made available following the first review on December 18, and an additional US$2 billion on January 8, 1998 following the second review. The sheer magnitude of the bailout package and the acceptance of the IMF's many conditions led most Koreans to the same conclusion as their President, that "we have lost our economic sovereignty." The Korean media designated December 3 as the "second day of national disgrace" (*che iui kukchiil*), and President Kim Young Sam in a televised address warned his fellow-citizens to prepare for an indefinite period of humiliating "bone-carving pain."[10]

### What went wrong? Competing explanations

Why did an economy with such seemingly sound fundamentals succumb so quickly to the economic shock? Two general interpretations have informed the discussion. According to the "fundamentalist" view, the Asian crisis was caused by poor economic fundamentals and policy inconsistencies. Proponents of this view argue that apparently sound macroeconomic indicators masked systemic structural problems. For example, Korea, like many other Asian economies, provided implicit guarantees to the banking system. This meant that banks were often engaged in lending practices that favored financially connected (and not always unqualified) borrowers – in particular, the *chaebols* or big family-controlled conglomerates. These implicit guarantees led banks to lend recklessly. This, in conjunction with poor corporate governance, created a stock of non-performing loans, thereby risking bank collapses (Corsetti, Pesenti and Roubini 1998). *The Economist* (1997, November 15, 33) is more blunt: "Most of the financial mess is of Asia's own making, and nowhere is this clearer than in South Korea. For years, the government has treated the banks as tools of state industrial policy, ordering them to make loans to un-creditworthy companies and industries."

By contrast, the "panic" interpretation views the "asymmetric information and self-fulfilling pessimism of international lenders" as the root cause of the crisis (Hahm and Mishkin 2000). Highlighting the fact that between October and December 1997 capital outflows from Korea amounted to about US$9.8 billion, the more sophisticated version of this argument interprets the crisis as a classic liquidity crisis – where Korean banks had insufficient reserves and insufficient access to funds, and where investors, suddenly seized with panic, refused to roll over short-term debt, besides demanding immediate payment (Radelet and Sachs 1998).

From the perspective of actual experience, analytical distinctions between the "fundamentalist" and the "panic" perspectives are less sharp than they are made in the literature. Indeed, it is impossible to point to any emerging market economy that experienced a financial crisis, but did not have significant fundamental weaknesses that called into question the sustainability of its policies. Indeed, in the case of Korea, as the currency crisis began to unfold it became clear that the Korean economy possessed a number of serious structural weaknesses, most notably weak financial sectors and over-indebted corporate sectors. Yet, it is also impossible to ignore the fact that "reputational externalities" were almost certainly at work.[11] That is, a crisis in one country affected investors' expectations and perceptions about common structural conditions and vulnerabilities in other countries. Yet, even while acknowledging the impact of structural problems in the Korean financial and corporate sectors, it is hard to avoid the judgement that Korea's punishment was disproportionate to the crime – because there is no doubt that panic withdrawal of capital and poor policy responses greatly exacerbated the crisis.

This chapter, while building on the insights of the "fundamentalist" and "panic" interpretations, provides a third perspective. It argues that Korea's financial crisis had both long-term and short-term causes. Weaknesses in both the financial and corporate sectors, especially inefficient management and imprudent lending among financial institutions, coupled with over-investment and low profitability in the corporate sector, made them vulnerable to external turbulence. In fact, it will be argued that poor corporate governance was a major destabilizing factor for the Korean economy. Because the *chaebols* (a conglomerate group of firms, linked by indirect cross-shareholdings), were highly interdependent financially through cross-shareholdings and cross-loan guarantees, the financial trouble of one *chaebol* could easily lead to a disaster for the whole group, including the banking system.[12] Indeed, six of the thirty largest *chaebols* (Hanbo, Sammi, Jinro, Kia, Haitai and New Core) had already filed for court protection in bankruptcy proceedings in early 1997 – several months before the collapse of the

won. Compounding this was poorly sequenced capital account liberalization – or liberalization that was not accompanied by prudential supervision
of the financial system and concurrent measures to discourage excessive
capital inflow. These oversights only increased the economy's vulnerability
to financial panic and economic collapse. Despite a relatively low overall
external debt level and a moderate and sustainable current-account deficit,
Korea had high short-term debt relative to its international reserves – which
made it vulnerable to a balance-of-payments crisis. The sharp deterioration
in terms of trade in 1996, the bankruptcy of a number of important *chaebols*,
and a change in international market sentiment following the collapse of the
Thai baht in mid-1997 were the proximate causes.

Specifically, starting in the early 1990s, the Korean government embarked
on an ambitious drive towards globalization, or *segyehwa*. To this effect,
the government began to relax its control over the financial sector, especially
its restrictions on foreign borrowing. As a result, the number of financial
institutions engaged in foreign-currency-denominated activities increased
sharply. This process was greatly accelerated (partly in order to meet OECD
requirements) under the first civilian government in thirty years – the Kim
Young Sam administration, which came to power on February 23, 1993. As
Samuel Kim (2000, 2) notes, "indeed, no state in the post-Cold War cast its
lot with globalization as decisively or as publicly as Korea did under the
Kim Young Sam administration, which viewed it as the most expedient way
for Korea to become a world-class, advanced country. *Segyehwa* has been
touted as no longer a matter of choice but one of necessity – globalize or
perish."[13]

Thus, during the Kim Young Sam administration (February 1993–
February 1998), controls on short-term external borrowings by banks were
greatly eased, while the government maintained quantity restrictions on
medium- and long-term foreign borrowing as a means of capital flow management. In fact, in what became known as *window guidance*, the authorities
drove the banks to rely heavily on short-term financing by limiting the
amounts that it was permissible to borrow on a medium- and long-term
basis from international sources. That is, the Korean government provided
financial institutions with real incentives to borrow for the short term by
making it mandatory for them to notify authorities of long-term foreign
debts, whereas short-term loans, regarded as trade-related financing, were
hardly regulated. Similarly, for non-financial borrowers, it was the short-
term trade and other credits that were liberalized, while long-term suppliers'
credit and foreign access to bond markets remained restricted. Moreover,
the authorities retained *de facto* control of many bank interest rates and
corporate bond yields, while completely deregulating interest rates for short-
term securities such as commercial paper. Finally, the government allowed
the entry of many new merchant banking companies during 1994–96. From
1994 to 1996, a total of 24 finance companies were made into merchant

banking corporations, which meant a corresponding increase in the number of participants in international financial markets, because merchant banks were allowed to engage in foreign-exchange transactions, while finance companies were not. During the same period, Korean banks opened 28 foreign branches, which gave them greater access to foreign funds. These banks borrowed heavily in the short term, but invested in long-term assets. These policies would ultimately have dire consequences. For example, the shortening of the maturity of the financial liabilities of Korean corporate borrowers and of the foreign liabilities of Korean banks and non-bank financial intermediaries made the economy extremely vulnerable to external shocks. Moreover, the increasing mismatch in maturity between foreign liabilities and assets in merchant banks, including the fact that these financial institutions were not properly monitored or supervised, made the economy vulnerable to a foreign-exchange crisis.

The following sections will show that because of the eased control on short-term external borrowing, Korea's big businesses, in particular the *chaebols*, undertook an aggressive investment drive. This investment drive was financed mainly by large increases in borrowing from domestic banks, in particular merchant banks. As a result the number of merchant banks and the volume of their foreign-currency business expanded rapidly. These changes in the institutional framework contributed greatly to the rapid growth in foreign-currency borrowing. Moreover, financial liberalization and tight monetary policy (which kept domestic interest rates above world interest rates) only encouraged commercial and merchant banks to rely heavily on cheaper foreign credit – perceived to be cheaper because of the pegged exchange rate. As Sylvia Maxfield (2000, 99) aptly notes, "after the financial market was deregulated, newly licensed Korean merchant banks and *chaebols* began to borrow internationally with all the self-restraint of children let loose in a candy store."

However, the excessive investments in capacity expansion during the boom years of the early 1990s soon caught up with the *chaebols*. The high leverage ratios of the *chaebols* and their low profitability made them extremely vulnerable to any shock to their cash flow. In turn, the health of the banking system was highly dependent on the viability of the *chaebols*, as the banks were exposed to the *chaebols*, both directly through loans and discounts, and indirectly through the guarantee of corporate bonds and commercial paper. Financial liberalization also played a major role in producing the deterioration in financial sector balance-sheets. Specifically, while regulations on financial institutions were being relaxed in order to enable them to engage in a wider set of activities, an implicit government safety-net for financial institutions along with weak prudential supervision led to excessive risk-taking. Inevitably, the result was growing bad loan problems and deterioration of financial institutions' balance-sheets. It is now recognized that the source of moral hazard that helped produce a deterioration in both financial and non-financial balance-sheets was the tradition of the government's coming to the rescue of troubled corporations and financial institutions, not to mention government involvement in the credit market, which created the impression that the *chaebols* were simply "too big to fail." These conglomerates had huge leverage, and lending to them increased in the 1990s despite the weakness of their profitability. Banks and other financial institutions kept lending because they expected that the government would not allow the *chaebols* to go bankrupt – thus in effect guaranteeing their loans. Moral hazard was a bigger problem for the non-bank financial institutions, many of which were owned by the *chaebols*. Since these institutions were largely independent of the government, supervisory standards and monitoring of prudential regulations were extremely lax. They soon developed major maturity mismatch problems.

When the domestic recession and a disruption in the terms of trade aggravated the cash-flow problems of highly indebted firms, corporate insolvency became widespread. During 1996–97, several highly leveraged *chaebols* failed and went into bankruptcy. The slowing domestic demand coupled with a deteriorating movement in Korea's terms of trade could not support an economy burdened with an excessive build-up in capacity. The resulting bankruptcies of a number of major companies, in addition to increasing failures of medium and small businesses, resulted in a deterioration in the balance-sheets of Korea's financial institutions – resulting in a rapid decline in their international creditworthiness. As the structural weaknesses and the government's inability to cope with them became exposed following the string of large corporate defaults in early 1997, foreign investors began to take a fresh look at Korea. Arguably, the deepening crisis in Southeast Asia was the last straw. The collapse of the Thai baht in July 1997 increased the concerns of foreign creditors about the strength of Korea's corporate sector and the soundness of its financial system, despite the Korean government's repeated attempts to calm foreign creditors. The Hong Kong stock market turmoil in late October 1997 triggered a sudden loss of market confidence. The capital inflows that had helped to finance Korea's rapid economic growth were sharply reversed. Jittery foreign investors, many reeling from losses in other East and Southeast Asian economies, decided to lower their exposure to Korea and pulled their funds *en masse*, contributing to the severity and duration of the crisis.

Korea's economic crisis erupted as a speculative attack on the won in a context of very low foreign-exchange reserves. Because the government had allowed foreign finance to enter through the banking system while continuing to limit inward FDI and foreign purchases of Korean securities, it ended up with liabilities that were owed to foreigners and denominated in foreign currency. Under these circumstances, the capacity of the government and the central bank to lend in the last resort was limited by the stock of international reserves. By the end of 1996, short-term external liabilities as a share of foreign-exchange reserves had risen to some 300 per cent (Balino and Ubide 1999). Thus the Korean crisis was not a *current account*, but a *capital account* crisis. Conventional current-account crises are caused by the deterioration of domestic macroeconomic fundamentals, manifested as price inflation, fiscal deficits and low rates of saving. A capital account crisis is characterized by massive international capital inflows, usually large enough to surpass the underlying current-account deficit and composed mainly of short-term borrowings denominated in foreign currencies. This leads to currency and maturity mismatches, which adversely affect the balance-sheets of domestic financial institutions. There is thus a dual financial crisis – a currency crisis due to currency mismatch that leads to international liquidity problems, and a domestic banking crisis resulting in credit contraction. Moreover, currency depreciation further adversely affects the balance-sheets of corporations by inflating the value of liabilities in domestic currency terms, thereby precipitating a currency and banking crisis. The Korean crisis also illustrates the fact that, although the alliance between the government, the *chaebols* and the banks had been in place since the 1960s, it was no longer compatible with Korea's integration into the global financial market. In sum, the Korean crisis reflected a fundamental structural misallocation of resources to which investors suddenly awoke when financial turmoil engulfed Asia. The withdrawal of funds from Korean banks and the ensuing crisis were simply triggers for a long-overdue process of industrial and financial restructuring.

## The rise of the *chaebols*

Most accounts of Korean economic development depict the 1960s as the pivotal decade (Amsden 1989; E-M. Kim 1997). As the key protagonist of the era, General Park Chung Hee himself, noted, "in the 1960s Korea changed from a pre-modern, underdeveloped society to a modern, productive, constantly growing society."[14] Indeed, following the successful coup on May 16, 1961, the military government of General Park Chung Hee embarked on an ambitious plan for national economic development through the strategy of *suchul ipguk*, or "nation-building through exports" (Kim and Leipziger 1997, 155). This meant that in practice the government's "external economic policies were marked by mercantilistic trade that encouraged exports and suppressed imports" (Dobson 1998, 162). But, first, as a prerequisite, "Park proposed two important strategies: (1) restructuring the government to become a comprehensive developmental state, and (2) elimination of corruption in the political and economic systems" (E-M. Kim 1997, 100). After ruling the country for two and a half years as coup leader, Park was elected president. This served to increase further the institutional coherence and capacity of the state. Park "quickly converted the 'corrupt soft' state he had inherited into a 'developmental hard' state . . . He then proceeded to execute an industrial policy, using a large battery of targeted and un-targeted interventions to implement his detailed vision of the public interest" (Adelman and Yeldan 2000, 97). Among the first items on the new regime's agenda was purging the bureaucracy of sloth and corruption. Lie (1998, 53) states that, to extirpate corruption, the Park regime fired nearly one-sixth of South Korea's 240,000 civil servants, besides arresting leading businessmen on charges of illicit profiteering. Similarly, Campos and Root (1996, 166) note that:

> Under Park the link between leadership and bureaucratic accountability was cemented. Park granted the economic bureaucracy wide-ranging authority while guarding against its capture by the private sector. Viewing bureaucratic competency as essential to economic performance, Park introduced features modeled upon the Japanese bureaucracy, such as competition in the recruitment and promotion of personnel and control over foreign exchange. He exercised a strong and direct role over the promotion and firing of bureaucrats. His close surveillance of the bureaucracy allegedly included allowing the Korean Central Intelligence Agency to monitor bureaucrats.

Moreover, just two months after the coup, a new "super-ministry," the Economic Planning Board (EPB), was created to serve as an apex body for economic policy and planning. The EPB enjoyed a broad mandate and was granted extensive administrative powers to supervise and coordinate the work of other ministries that had any bearing on the economy. For example, planning was taken over from the Ministry of Reconstruction, budget preparation and coordination was shifted from the Ministry of Finance, and the collection and analysis of statistics was removed from the Ministry of Internal Affairs. In July 1962, the EPB was given the power to extend government guarantees to loans and to audit and oversee the activities of the borrowing firms. Finally, the EPB was given the power to select those capital goods imports and importers that qualified for government-aided deferred payment privileges. These powers gave the EPB a strong say with regard to the economy. As Cumings (1984, 29) notes, "The EPB. . . . took over from a previous ministry the entire budgeting functions: it decides which industries and firms to promote, which to phase out; it closely supervises both the development and the implementation of planning, along with an official trade promotion agency . . . it surveys the world for needed markets, capital and technology." In effect, throughout the 1960s and 1970s, the EPB "remained as the most prestigious ministry within the government bureaucracy" (E-M. Kim 1997, 102). The EPB articulated the nation's developmental blueprint in the first five-year plan (1962–66), and the six other five-year plans up to 1994 – when the EPB was formally disbanded.

The EPB gave the Korean state a commanding role in the economy. In late 1961, the Park administration nationalized most of Korea's commercial banks by repossessing the shares held by large stockholders.[15] Thus, as

Park and Kim (1994, 215) note, "it is not an exaggeration to say that the commercial banks were little more than government agencies delegated the task of mobilizing savings and allocating them according to directives and guidelines issued by the government." Further, in May 1962 the government amended the Bank of Korea Act, thereby bringing Korea's central bank, the Bank of Korea (BOK), under the direct control of the Ministry of Finance (MOF). This meant that the BOK functioned as the executor of government policies. Its role was to assist the policy-makers to bring about desired levels of economic activities through interventionist policies. Thus, the BOK provided financing for strategic sectors at preferential lending rates through direct loans programs and re-discounting of bills presented by commercial banks. In fact, the central bank was not independent of the government until it was restructured in 1997–98 following the IMF intervention. In addition, the government assumed the power to appoint the heads of all commercial banks. A government-directed credit-rationing program obliged commercial banks to extend so-called "policy loans" to strategic industries.[16] These measures more clearly signaled that it was the government, not the central bank, that was ultimately responsible for monetary and financial policy. Indeed, the government's new powers enabled it to influence the sectoral allocation of credit, both directly through the appointment of bank management and credit controls, and indirectly through various regulations and incentives.[17] The government also established several special-purpose banks such as the Korea Development Bank (1961), Kukmin Bank (1963), and the Foreign Exchange Bank (1967), the Small and Medium Industry Bank, the Korean Reconstruction Bank, and the Central Federation of Agricultural Cooperatives to administer generous subsidized loans called "policy loans" on behalf of the government to favored industries.[18] "Policy loans" were distributed to beneficiaries through direct deposit, preferential "rediscounting" for lending to priority sectors at the central bank, credit floors and credit ceilings. Interest rates on loans varied considerably across categories of borrowers, even among preferential credit recipients. These mechanisms not only allowed the Korean state to allocate scarce monetary resources directly to preferred industries, but the monopoly the government exercised over financial institutions gave it important leverage to direct the private sector. In addition, interest rates were administered and competition in the banking system was limited. It is no exaggeration to say that the banks in Korea were hardly market-based, but an arm of the government for allocating financial resources. Because access to funds was crucial to corporate growth, the fact that private enterprises, and in particular the *chaebols*, had to rely on government-backed financing, only served to enhance the state's control over the private sector.

This quintessentially cozy "synergistic" and cooperative relationship between the Korean state and the private sector have led some to dub it "the Korean development model" (Amsden 1989; Kim and Leipziger 1997;

Wade 1990). This model, which essentially refers to a strategy of government-led outward oriented economic development through the promotion of industries using government directed or government influenced subsidized credit allocations as its main means, can be divided into roughly four phases. According to B. Lee (1998), these include (1) export-oriented industrialization via labor-intensive manufactures from 1961 to 1972, (2) export-oriented industrialization via heavy and chemical industries (HCI) from 1973 to 1981, (3) industrial adjustment from 1982 to 1987, and (4) economic liberalization from 1988 to the present.

In the first phase, the Park regime favored light industries as the main beneficiaries of government support – with manufacturing industries that produced for export markets receiving special treatment. Specifically, cognizant of the fact that Korea lacked a large domestic market and natural resources, the state promoted labor-intensive manufactured goods for export by providing preferential financing to export manufacturers, including unrestricted access to tariff-free import of raw materials and intermediate products used for the production of exports. Moreover, the Korea Trade Promotion Corporation (KOTRA) was established in 1962 to help exporters create overseas marketing networks by providing administrative services and serving as a conduit for information between Korean producers, traders and foreign buyers.[19] During the second five-year plan (1967–71), Korea's economic policy became even more interventionist as the government made a big push towards the promotion of heavy and chemical industries. The HCI strategy placed special emphasis on seven "strategic" industries: machinery, shipbuilding, textiles, consumer electronics, petrochemicals, iron and steel and non-ferrous metals. These strategic industries were subject to industrial targeting – for example, the promotion of basic industries such as steel and petrochemicals was required for developing the defense industry and ensuring a more stable supply of these key materials. The selection of electronic and shipbuilding industries was motivated by another strategic consideration, namely, that these relatively labor-intensive industries could gain competitiveness within a short period.

However, in the early 1970s, as the new climate of protectionism spread, along with the worldwide stagflation caused by the first oil crisis, it reduced the demand for Korean exports. Moreover, Korea's labor-intensive light industries were losing their competitiveness as a result of rapid wage increases and fierce competition from other developing countries. It soon became clear to policy-makers that Korea needed to move to higher value-added manufacturing to avoid becoming uncompetitive with the new entrants in the consumer light manufacturing industries. These changing circumstances led the Korean government to introduce *Yushin* (or "revitalizing reforms") – and thereby greatly to accelerate the HCI strategy under the third five-year plan (1972–76).[20] Indeed, the urgency seemed so great that, in order to expedite HCI expansion, the government did not even put HCI projects for bids. Rather, strategically placed large enterprises and conglomerates (*chaebols*) – including those already involved in heavy industry and some in light manufactures – were assigned to carry out each project in the steel, petrochemical, shipbuilding, machinery and electronics industries. Fields (1995, 97) argues that even the largest *chaebols* "were reluctant to assume the risks entailed in these projects, and participated only when the state provided a combination of guarantees, equity participation and increasingly distorted incentives in the form of tax concessions and preferential low-interest credit." Over the course of the third plan, almost 60 per cent of the total bank loans and more than 75 per cent of total manufacturing invest-ment went to these sectors (H. Smith 2000, 60). The main tool of promotion was preferential access to bank credit. As Wontack Hong (1998, 146) notes, "the success of Korea's export-oriented growth owes very much to the late President Park's effort to establish an automatic loan allocation system for exporters . . . Under Park's regime (1961–1979), any entrepreneur could auto-matically attain access to short-term bank credits at subsidized interest rates without collateral by undertaking export-related activities . . . The effici-ency of credit rationing was maintained by the efficiency of Korea's export sector." Overall, the state support for the HCI drive was massive, as the Korean Development Bank provided long-term loans, underwrote corporate bonds and stocks and guaranteed foreign loans. In addition to preferential access to subsidized credit (the so-called "policy loans"), the *chaebols* were granted favored access to import licenses, tax exemptions and tariff rebates, monopoly or oligopoly market positions, protection and restrictions on competing foreign investment, fiscal incentives, and guaranteed sales through government procurement.[21]

However, the *chaebols* had to perform – after all, the state had the abil-ity to reward export success and penalize poor performance. The *chaebols* knew that they were only to receive subsidized credit and other benefits as long as they were successful in exporting their products. Indeed, firms seeking credit and licenses had to meet Park's basic criterion: "How much have you exported for me lately?"[22] Export performance was used to allo-cate preferential credit and to determine who would get valuable licenses from the government to produce promoted products. The determined HCI drive proved highly successful, producing several spectacular successes in the development of automotive, shipbuilding and semi-conductor indus-tries. Not surprisingly, exports as a proportion of GNP rose from 7.4 per cent in 1967 to 27.2 per cent in 1997 and 36.7 per cent in 1987 (Kim and Leipziger 1997, 158). However, the export orientation also strengthened the *chaebols*. Thus, if in 1973 the top fifty *chaebols* accounted for 32 per cent of GDP, by 1980 the *chaebols* dominated the economy, accounting for 49 per cent of GDP, 24 per cent of total sales, 18 per cent of manufacturing employment, and over half of Korea's total exports.[23] As Woo-Cumings (1999, 120) notes:

The Korean *chaebol* grew as fast as they did because of the steady and massive provision of investment capital from the banks. Almost all of the *chaebol* groups began when Korea was in the phase of export-led, light industrial production. Lucky made toothpaste, Goldstar made radios, Samsung made clothes, and Hyundai began with U.S. military contracts during the Korean war. . . . Daewoo was founded only in 1967. They acquired their typical large and diversified structure even more recently, during the Third Five-Year Plan in the early 1970s, which developed heavy industries: steel, chemicals, machine tools, automobiles, shipbuilding, and power generation. By the 1980s, electronics had also become a huge part of the *chaebol* repertoire. The expansion of these firms was stupendous: between 1970 and 1975, the three fastest-growing *chaebol* (Hyundai, Daewoo and Ssangyong) grew at annual rates of 33 per cent, 35 per cent and 34 per cent, respectively.

Nevertheless, the Korean government's ambitious expansionist policies had some unintended consequences. First, by the late 1970s there was the problem of growing industrial concentration and sectoral imbalance in favor of the *chaebols*. H. Smith (2000, 60–1) notes that "by 1977, 93 per cent of all commodities were produced under monopoly, duopoly or oligopoly conditions in which the top three producers accounted for more than 60 per cent of market share. Between 1973 and 1982, the share of manufacturing output of the twenty largest groups increased from 7 per cent to 29 per cent." Small and medium-sized industries – the very backbone of Korea's successful export of labor-intensive manufactures – faced a credit squeeze, as more and more of the resources were channeled to the *chaebols*, and the large enterprises that "grew and became *chaebol* during the 1970s" (E-M. Kim 1997, 152). Second, the cross-subsidization of *chaebol* subsidiaries compounded the difficulty of identifying whether capital was being used profitably. In fact, the complex pattern of cross-subsidization within the *chaebols* enabled unprofitable companies to survive. Soon the *chaebols* became a serious threat to fair competition between affiliates of the *chaebols* and non-affiliates, including small and medium-sized businesses. As Kang (2000, 89) notes, "the *chaebol* presented formidable entry barriers that discouraged competition from newcomers. In short, behaving in an oligopolistic manner, they skewed the economy to favor their own interests and impeded free competition."

Third, the years of a politicized policy environment and the resultant easy availability of cheap credit via the "policy loans" created problems. In particular, the socialization of bankruptcy risk that accompanied the plan, combined with the low interest-rate ceilings, made the cost of debt financing very cheap for firms in targeted sectors – encouraging firms to take on excessively high levels of debt and to increase market share rather than profitability and shareholder value. In addition, not only was there much waste, but the *chaebols* also made excessive and redundant investments in heavy and chemical industries. Cho and Kim (1995) aptly observe that the use of directed credit by the Korean government over an extended period of time proved to be fundamentally damaging. Most notably, in an oligopolistic market environment, the implicit co-insurance of bank lending by the government induced banks to lend and encouraged firms to invest in risky projects. Commercial banks in Korea functioned almost like development banks, and ended up being saddled with huge non-performing loans equal to almost 20 per cent of GDP. Problems faced by banks were mirrored in deteriorating industrial performance – an important cause of the economic downturn of 1979–80.

Fourth, in their rush to expand and diversify their activities, the *chaebols* took excessive risks, and as a result the financial structures of some of the largest *chaebols* became increasingly fragile owing to the heavy debt contracted through the state-owned banking system. Mathews (2001, 159) notes that "across the board, Korea's top 30 *chaebol* were leveraged to the extent of debt exceeding shareholders' equity by nearly 4 times (actually, a ratio of 3.87) – compared with the situation in other countries, such as Taiwan (0.85), Japan (2.0) and the US (1.6)." However, as we noted, the growing debt burdens did not seem to concern the *chaebols*, as they remained confident in the knowledge that the state would bail them out if they got into difficulty.

Fifth, as economic power accumulated in the hands of the *chaebols*, they gained greater influence over how preferential credit was to be allocated. By the 1970s, selective credit policy was highly politicized, and it was no longer possible to specify whether the *chaebols* or the government actually controlled Korea's credit-allocation policy. Furthermore, the growing diversification in *chaebols'* businesses, especially in non-bank financial services, gave the *chaebols* a degree of autonomy from the state. That is, the considerable economic and political weight of the *chaebols* made it extremely difficult for the government and the banks to impose fiscal discipline or to disengage completely from supporting the *chaebols*. Indeed, "the lack of transparency in privately owned companies, facilitated by *chaebols'* control of non-bank financial institutions, stymied government efforts to restrict cross-subsidization. And banks, which had high volumes of loans to individual *chaebol*, had powerful incentives to continue lending rather than to force companies into liquidation" (Noble and Ravenhill 2000, 86–7). The nation's economy had become so dependent on the *chaebols* that their collapse could pull down the entire economy. Thus a "too big to fail syndrome" developed, "with governments concerned about the effects on employment, economic stability and the financial system should one of the larger corporate groupings or commercial banks be permitted to go bankrupt" (Noble and Ravenhill 2000, 87).

Finally, not only had the *chaebols* become economically "too big to fail," but it was well known that a clientelistic relationship had developed between the government and the *chaebols* – whereby big business routinely paid the so-called "political taxes" that financed the ruling party in return for favorable treatment on a range of discretionary policies from credit allocation to taxation (Haggard and Moon 1990, 227). Thus the politicization of credit policies also meant that recipients of preferential credit made *jun jo-seh* or contributions to political parties or individual politicians as a sign of appreciation. As will be discussed, by the early 1980s several corruption scandals involving high-ranking politicians and *chaebols* had been made public.

As was noted earlier, between 1979 and 1980, the Korean economy faced significant external and domestic shocks. Economic growth-rates that had averaged almost 10 per cent a year between 1962 and 1978 fell to just over 2 per cent between 1979 and 1981. Inflation rose to 26 per cent from an annual average of 16 per cent between 1962 and 1978. Exports fell from a 27 per cent average annual rate of real growth between 1962 and 1978 to 7.5 per cent between 1979 and 1982. The current-account deficit widened from US$1.1 billion in 1978 to US$4.4 billion in 1981.[24] Compounding the situation was the second oil shock, which worsened Korea's terms of trade and balance of payments, while rising interest rates increased the country's debt-service burden. Faced with mounting challenges, the EPB hurriedly devised an economic stabilization plan. However, before the plan could be implemented, President Park was assassinated on October 26, 1979. Following a period of increasing uncertainty, the military seized power in May 1980 under the leadership of Chun Doo-Hwan. The economic subcommittee of the interim National Security Council was now to dictate the economic policy of the Fifth Republic – inaugurated by the passage of the September 1980 constitution.

The Chun regime introduced financial liberalization as part of its overall structural adjustment program. In its effort to channel curb market funds into formal financial institutions and mobilize savings, interest rates were partially liberalized.[25] Notable developments in capital markets during the period include the establishment of an over-the-counter stock market in 1987, providing a market for small and medium companies and venture businesses not eligible for listing on the Korea Stock Exchange. The Securities and Exchange Act was further amended in 1987, strengthening regulations against insider trading and for the disclosure of information. Various measures for opening capital markets were also taken, including allowing foreign securities companies to operate, and the domestic stock market was partially opened to foreign investors. In addition, the government sold off the government-held shares in commercial banks and imposed an 8 per cent limit on the number of shares of a bank that an individual or *chaebol* could own. The introduction of the Fair Trade Act of 1980 included the prohibition of cartel practices and cross-investment among affiliated companies, a ceiling on credit to the larger *chaebols*, and restrictions on their vertical and horizontal integration. The Korean government also directed the thirty largest *chaebols* to restructure their businesses around fewer core sectors. Further, the government removed a number of entry restrictions, thereby making possible the establishment of foreign joint-venture banks, non-bank financial institutions (NBFI), insurance companies, regional banks and security companies. Starting in the mid-1980s, commercial banks were privatized and given the right to set interest rates on regular deposits and loans. Finally, banks were allowed to underwrite privately placed corporate bonds and issue CDs (certificates of deposit), which were not subject to legal reserve requirements.

However, these measures hardly had any negative impact on the *chaebols*. There are several reasons for this. First, high-ranking politicians, including President Chun, were dependent on the *chaebols* for funds. In fact, Chun had built up a huge slush fund totaling some US$1.8 billion by demanding contributions from *chaebols*, threatening to cut off credit to firms that did not comply (Oberdorfer 1997, 376). Second, and more importantly, Heather Smith (2000, 62) notes that "a significant gap existed between policy pronouncements and implementation, as the *chaebol* continued to grow." Likewise, Byung-Sun Choi (1993, 42) notes that, "big business saw financial liberalization as a means of limiting the government's intervention in economic decision making . . . businesspeople abhorred the situation in which their fate was at the disposal of government policymakers' fickle political judgements. In addition, to meet its rapidly increasing capital needs more flexibly, big business felt a need to own and control financial institutions." Indeed, the change in corporate financing only further increased the autonomy of the *chaebols* from the Korean state, as they became less dependent on the government-controlled commercial banks for financing. Third, the privatization of commercial banks only enabled the large *chaebols* to acquire controlling shares in these banks indirectly through the holding of shares by the non-bank financial intermediaries under their control, while the large state-owned banks such as the Korea Development Bank (KDB) and the Korea Export–Import Bank (KEXIM) continued to remain important sources of financing for the *chaebols*. Fourth, the *chaebols* as owners of NBFIs (in 1998 the top 30 *chaebols* owned 12 security companies out of a total of 25; 18 insurance companies out of a total of 35; and 18 investment trust companies out of a total of 38), had easy access to funds from the NBFIs. The NBFIs' share in total deposits increased from less than 30 per cent in 1980 to more than 60 per cent by the early 1990s. Their share of NBFI loans and direct financing increased from 38.1 per cent in 1980 to 67.5 per cent in 1988 and to 69.3 per cent in 1990. Moreover, foreign bank loans to large firms decreased significantly in the 1980s, as the *chaebols* began to raise funds directly from the foreign bond markets.[26]

By the early 1980s, the formidable presence of the *chaebols* in the Korean economy could not be denied. According to Oh (1999, 211), the *chaebols* had evolved from being "servants of the state" to "partners" as they gained control of the financial system. For Eun-Mee Kim (1997), the dramatic rise of the *chaebols* led to a simultaneous "decline of Korea's developmental state." Thus, although the semi-authoritarian regimes of Chun Doo Hwan (1980–88) and Roh Tae Woo (February 1988–February 1993) attempted to restructure *chaebol*–state relations, both regimes' efforts were structurally constrained by the former's very considerable weight in overall economic activity.[27] For example, the Chun regime devised the Credit Administrative System for Big Business, requiring the *chaebols* to sell off certain subsidiaries and to liquidate "unproductive" real-estate investments that were unrelated to their main line of business. The measure was specifically directed at 26 groups that held a total of 631 subsidiaries. Further availability of credit was made contingent on compliance. Similarly, the enactment of the Anti-Monopoly Regulation and Fair Trade Law in April 1981 (to be enforced by the newly created Korean Fair Trade Commission, KFTC) was designed to reduce the dominant position of the *chaebols* in the domestic market, besides improving their performance. Although the state was somewhat successful in reducing the subsidies to the *chaebols* in the Chun regime's initial years, overall the regime (and its successors) failed to tame the *chaebols*. As Yoo and Moon (1999, 269) note, the anti-monopoly "law in itself contained numerous exemptions to ensure that competition would remain subordinate to industrial policy goals." Until 1994 there were few actions in number that were taken against the *chaebol* by the KFTC, and those that were initiated seemed to be based more on political than economic considerations. In essence, the Korean state quickly relented and acceded to the demands and imperatives of the private sector. As Kang (2000, 91) notes:

> Even under the semi-authoritarian governments of Chun Doo Hwan and Roh Tae Woo, the balance of power between the state and the *chaebol* was slipping in favor of the latter. When Chun and Roh attempted, each in his own way, to check the abuses of the *chaebol* in response to public resentment, they found it difficult to do. For instance, when Roh launched an anti-big business campaign, Koo Ja-kyung, chairman of the Lucky-Goldstar Group and of the Federation of Korean Industries (FKI), "warned politicians – both ruling and opposition – of potential retaliation through the discretionary use of political contribution" and "declared that the FKI would henceforth provide donations only to politicians willing to support and protect business freedom." Eventually, Roh had to abandon the anti-*chaebol* campaign.

Indeed, the number of subsidiaries under each *chaebol* had increased dramatically since 1970. Pyo (2000, 18) notes that "the Kia Group expanded its car production capacity drastically and, at the same time, pursued both unchecked vertical integration (Kia Special Metals Co.) and unconventional horizontal diversification into construction and financing business . . . the Hyundai group announced its intention to enter steel manufacturing, which had been monopolized by the Pohang Steel Co." Overall, the top 30 *chaebol* had on average 4.2 subsidiaries in 1970, 17.8 in 1989 and 26.8 at the end of 1997 (Beck 1998, 1022). The ten largest *chaebols* continued to grow rapidly during the 1980s. Kia, for example, grew by 30.5 per cent average annual growth rate, followed by Samsung with a 25 per cent growth rate. Oh (1999, 65) notes that "ten of twenty-seven private concerns in developing countries that made the Fortune 500 list in 1982, for instance, were Korean *chaebols*." Also, by 1987, sales from the five largest *chaebols* comprised 75.2 per cent of manufacturing GDP (E-M. Kim 1997, 183–4). It was clear that by the mid-1980s, the ubiquitous *chaebols* had come to occupy an extremely powerful position in the economy, and their demands were proving difficult to ignore. Powerful family patriarchs were able to dominate their *chaebols* with little or no oversight on the part of board of directors, minority shareholders, or even outside auditors (S-N. Choi 1996). By the early 1990s, the level of economic concentration had deepened substantially, and the *chaebols* enjoyed an even more protected monopolistic position in the domestic market. In 1991, the top five *chaebols* had revenues of US$116 billion, equivalent to just under half Korea's 1991 GNP, while the combined revenue of the top ten conglomerates equaled three-quarters of the country's GNP (Fields 1995, 35; E. C. S. Kang 2000, 89). Not surprisingly, Korea's media soon cynically began to refer to their nation as the "*chaebol* Republic" (E-M. Kim 1997, 167).

### Democracy and the *chaebols*

The Korean form of democratization most closely follows what Samuel Huntington has called "transplacement" – where the sitting government makes a concession and opposition groups accept the compromise in order to avoid political gridlock or civil disorder. This type of democratic transition is different from "replacement," under which "democratization results from the opposition gaining strength and the government losing strength until the government collapses or is overthrown" (Huntington 1991, 142). In Korea, after weeks of massive demonstrations demanding democratization and reform, the autocratic Chun regime agreed to allow a direct, popular election to choose Chun's successor. However, wishing to have a say in the future government, Chun invited some thirty top lieutenants of the ruling Democratic Justice Party (DJP) to the presidential mansion on June 2, 1987 and revealed his decision to anoint Roh Tae-Woo his successor, to be elected by the electoral college that Chun controlled. Roh Tae-Woo took a dramatic step towards democratization with his June 29, 1987 declaration of an eight-point program – accepting the opposition Reunification Democratic Party's key demands. Roh's declaration called for direct presidential elections, amendment of the constitution (to be approved by national referendum), freedom of the press, freedom for political prisoners and restoration of their civil rights, local autonomy, guaranteed protection of all "sound" political parties and an end to corruption. The December 1987 presidential elections were acknowledged (despite some irregularities) to be free and democratic, with voter turnout in excess of 89 per cent (Oh 1999). The opposition had a chance to defeat Roh, but because of divisions among themselves, the "three Kims" (Kim Dae-Jung, Kim Young-Sam and Kim Jong-Pil) were unable to agree on a unified opposition ticket, splitting the vote and allowing Roh to win the election. Roh's inauguration on February 25, 1988 marked the first peaceful transfer of presidential power in Korea since 1948, and the voters directly elected the president for the first time in sixteen years.

While Roh Tae-Woo won the presidency, he only obtained 36.6 per cent of the total vote, because (as noted above) the opposition failed to agree on a unified candidacy and ran two candidates. Kim Young Sam garnered 28.1 per cent and Kim Dae-Jung 27.1 per cent. During the general election for the National Assembly held in April 1988, the ruling DJP failed to win a working majority, raising the specter of political gridlock. However, in February 1990, in an unprecedented merger of three parties, Kim Young Sam's Reunification Democratic Party and Kim Jong-Pil's New Republican Party joined the DJP to form a new party, the Democratic Liberal Party (DLP) – giving the DLP a comfortable majority in the National Assembly.[28] More importantly, the merger gave Roh Tae-Woo's regime political legitimacy. The Roh interregnum made some important changes in the political life of the nation. First, the constitution of the Sixth Republic was made more democratic. Second, the role of the National Assembly was strengthened. Third, the judicial system was made more independent of executive control; and finally the presidency was limited to a single five-year term. However, despite this new-found autonomy, and despite the fact that president Roh tried to initiate a number of measures to reform the *chaebols*, the Roh regime (1988–93) was ultimately unsuccessful in its efforts.

Kim Young-Sam became the DLP's presidential nominee, and he won the December 1992 presidential election by securing 42 per cent of the vote over the 34 per cent received by Kim Dae-Jung of the Democratic Party. When Kim Young-Sam took the presidential oath for a single five-year term on February 25, 1993, this marked an important political milestone for Korea, as Kim was the first civilian to be democratically elected in thirty-two years. No doubt, the Kim regime (February 1993 to February 1998), was in a far stronger position than that of his immediate predecessor to implement political and economic reforms.[29] Indeed, in the political arena, the Kim government introduced a number of measures to eradicate further authoritarian legacies of the past. For example, the government tried to reduce the military's involvement in politics by reshuffling key military leaders and purging those generals associated with the past military-backed governments. Further, the Kim regime tried to de-politicize the nation's intelligence agencies, including banning the much disliked Agency for National Security Planning and Defense Security Command from political activities, besides reducing their investigative authority. Kim also ordered public investigations into corruption in the military and civilian bureaucracies – which led to the dismissal of scores of politicians, senior bureaucrats, prosecutors and judges guilty of improprieties. In keeping with his promise of clean politics, Kim declared that he would not accept any political contribution, and voluntarily made public his family's financial assets. The regime also revised the Public Officials Ethics Act in the National Assembly, thereby requiring all high public officials to disclose their assets for public scrutiny. Finally, in August 1993, under a presidential decree, Kim passed the Real Name Financial Transaction System (which outlawed the practice of holding bank accounts under assumed names) and the Real Name Real Estate Ownership System, designed to prevent property monopoly and block the illegal flow of political donations.

Important as these measures were, the new democratic government (like its authoritarian predecessors) failed to break the complex relations between power and money in Korean politics, let alone to tame the *chaebols*. As Noble and Ravenhill (2000, 100) note, "governments in the democratic era before the 1997 crisis were no more successful than their predecessors in constraining the *chaebol*." On the contrary, democratization further strengthened the political power of big business in Korea. Why was this the case? Two complementary explanations have been advanced. First, some lay the blame on "Korea's democratic deficit" – in particular, the growing "role of business money in electoral politics" (Kong 2000, 374). Likewise, Heo and Kim (2000, 493–4) argue that "South Korea was in the middle of a transition from the government-led economy to a more market-oriented one, and from a government based on dictatorship to a more democratic system. During this transition, both the government and the business sector needed time to implement structural changes. When the financial crisis hit the Korean economy, the relevant institutional mechanisms to deal with such a crisis were not yet in place. Neither the government nor the market economy were sufficiently institutionalized to cope with the sudden shock to the foreign-exchange market that produced the severe economic downfall." In a similar vein, some stress the pervasive "political gridlock" – the direct result of the "immaturity of Korean democracy" (Mo 2001). Specifically Jongryn Mo and Chung-In Moon (1999, 173–4) note:

> In many ways, however, Korean democracy is still maturing. In the context of the economic crisis, it was particularly costly that the formal and informal rules required for or compatible with the effective functioning of democracy were not fully developed, especially such behavioral requisites as tolerance, willingness to negotiate and compromise, and respect for the rule of law. The immaturity of Korean democracy has produced many negative effects . . . But the greatest damage to the Korean economy came from ten years of policy gridlock under an immature Korean democracy. The Korean government under democracy made numerous attempts to reform the very features of the economic system that caused the economic crisis, such as rigid labor markets, business practices of *chaebol*, and the backward banking and financial sector.

But in almost every case, reform debate continued without a lasting resolution, which resulted in increased uncertainty and confusion. The government's handling of the crisis has also been hampered by its inability to resolve policy conflicts.

And second, it has been argued that since Korean national elections are very expensive, and the political parties have no independent sources of funding, the Federation of Korean Industries (FKI), the *chaebols'* principal lobby group, has been the largest source of political funding in Korea since its establishment in 1961. As Kong (2000, 376) notes, "democracy transformed the government–*chaebol* relationship in the latter's favor. Given the cost of fighting elections . . . aspiring politicians of all colors needed to attract business support. It was therefore advantageous for politicians to cultivate smooth relations with big business and seek its financial support . . . Having grown in economic power through three decades of state nurture, the *chaebol* had become more resilient to state sanctions." In fact, under the democratic regime, the pervasive "government–business nexus" (*jeong-kyeong yuchak*) not only became rife with patronage and corruption, but was fundamentally transformed. Kong (2000, 376) adds that "by the late 1980s, government–business relations had developed beyond the mutual exchange of favors by interdependent parties. Relationships had become more personalized as families of business leaders and senior government officials became closely interconnected through the marriage of their children."

Not surprisingly, as Chang, Park and Yoo (1998, 741) note, under the Kim government, "for the first time in post-1960s Korean history, we heard the names of particular *chaebols*, such as Samsung, talked about as being close to the regime." Certainly, *chaebols* as a group enjoyed preferential treatment under previous regimes – but they were all treated equally, with no one particular *chaebol* enjoying an advantage over the others. However, under the Kim government there was a fundamental change in state–business relations – "which meant the major manufacturing sectors became less insulated from the corrupt political exchanges than they had been previously" (Chang, Park and Yoo 1998, 741). For example, close associates of President Kim, including his son Kim Hyun Chul and the former Construction Minister Kim Woo Suk, were accused (and eventually convicted) of money-laundering, influence-peddling and accepting bribes from the steel manufacturer, Hanbo (then the eleventh largest *chaebol*). Despite having a poor record in manufacturing and a low ratio of self-owned capital (about 300 billion won), Hanbo Steel was able to borrow 5 trillion won for investment in a steel plant – through political connections. Also, through connections, Hanbo Steel instead of Hyundai was granted the license to enter the steel industry. To make its bid successful, Hanbo had its loans rolled over, despite experiencing acute financial problems. Similarly, the government's decision to grant Samsung a permit to build an automobile factory was largely "political." Yeon-ho Lee (2000, 121) notes that "economic elucidation can account for only a part of its hidden motivations. A crucial motivation lay in the owner-chairman's ambition to become the largest *chaebol* owner in Korea." Chang, Park and Yoo (1998, 740–1) state more bluntly:

> The Kim government also licensed Samsung to enter the already overcrowded car industry in 1993. What is fascinating about this entry is that it destabilized the industry before it produced a single car – Samsung's cars did not come on the market until 1998. Relatively lacking in strength in machine-related industries and having deliberately located the factory in the president's hometown, Pusan, despite the fact that the (reclaimed) site needed massive fortification, Samsung's venture looked questionable from the beginning.

Thus, although the Kim Young Sam government "promised a new revitalized economy as one of the regime's primary goals, including reforming the *chaebols* complex system of cross-shareholdings, its economic measures ostensibly served the interests of the *chaebols*" (Oh 1999, 136). For example, in March 1993, a month after his inauguration, the Kim Young Sam government abolished the practice of five-year planning (which had provided an overarching policy coordination framework since its inception in 1962), in favor of a 100-day new economic development plan. Such measures, while impressive on paper, made for hasty and uncoordinated policy formulation. In the end, besides reducing public utility fees such as charges for water and electricity and lower prices on twenty basic consumer items such as rice, beef, sugar and milk, the government's new plan "accelerated the kinds of deregulation demanded by the *chaebol* without promoting real competition and efficiency" (Kang 2000, 92). Specifically, Kims "new economy" plan outlined an immediate deregulation of the Korean economy, including liberalization of capital market and securities businesses to align Korea with the growing "globalization trends" (Oh 1999, 137). By early 1994, the impetus for *chaebol* reform began to wane because of concern that restrictions on the activities of the *chaebol* could impact adversely on growth and employment – given the *chaebols'* large presence in the domestic economy. As the following sections illustrate, the hastily implemented liberalization plan, biased towards short-term borrowing, and without effective prudential regulation and supervision in place, was hardly designed to rein in the *chaebols*. Indeed, these "mostly half-baked measures, often not backed up by improvements in the supervisory and disclosure framework would have a profoundly negative impact on the economy" (Claessens, Ghosh and Scott 1999, 83). In short, they made Korea vulnerable to the financial firestorm that eventually swept East Asia in 1997.

### Liberalization without regulation

The Korean financial system comprises three main types of institutions: (a) commercial banks, (b) the specialized and development banks, and

(c) non-bank financial institutions (NBFIs).[30] In addition, there also exists an informal and unregulated financial market known as the "curb market."[31] The commercial banks account for over half the assets of the financial system. They are owned by small shareholders (prior to the crisis, no shareholder could own more than 4 per cent of a nationwide commercial bank or more than 15 per cent of a regional bank), and engage in both traditional short-term banking operations and long-term financing of the corporate sector, including leasing. The commercial banks consist of 16 nationwide banks, 10 regional banks, and numerous (52 as of September 1997) foreign banks. Commercial banking is highly concentrated, with the top eight banks accounting for about two-thirds of commercial bank assets (Balino and Ubide 1999, 7–9). The specialized and development banks (which are partly or wholly owned by government) were established in the 1950s and 1960s to provide funds to specific strategic sectors. They account for roughly 17 per cent of financial system assets.[32]

In an effort to bring the unregulated money markets under control, the MOF enacted the Short-Term Financing Business Act in 1972. The Act was designed to encourage the establishment of a variety of non-bank financial intermediaries, including investment and finance companies, mutual savings firms, and general finance companies. Permitted to offer higher deposit interest rates, these NBFIs expanded their market share rapidly.[33] As institutional investors and underwriters, they also played an important role in the stock market. Not surprisingly, many *chaebols* came to acquire controlling shares of NBFIs by the late 1970s. The non-bank financial institutions comprised 30 per cent of financial system assets at the end of 1997. They consisted of three types of institutions: investment institutions; savings institutions; and insurance companies. Of these, investment institutions, which consist of merchant banks, investment trust companies and securities companies, are the largest in terms of assets, followed by savings institutions. As Balino and Ubide (1999, 10) note, "NBFIs have been directly or indirectly owned mainly by *chaebols* and other large shareholders. They are used to finance activities within the *chaebol* group and have become an increasingly significant source for intermediating *chaebol* notes and other paper. For example, most of the 30 merchant banks in operation in mid-1997 were owned by the *chaebols*, while the securities companies acted as their underwriters and brokers.

Prior to the post-1993 liberalization, the Korean government controlled all the internal and especially cross-border financial flows very tightly. Although there were a series of financial liberalization measures introduced in the 1980s, these were limited in scope. For example, the fact that no shareholder was permitted to own more than 4 per cent of a bank's equity resulted in fragmented ownership. In practice, this meant that the managements of banks were not accountable to anyone, except to the government. Also, up until the 1990s, decisions regarding credit allocations that commercial banks could make were dominated by the government's policy of favoring investment loans to large corporations engaged in export activities. Foreign-exchange transfers were heavily regulated – Korean nationals were not allowed to borrow freely on the international market and the ability of foreign residents to buy, own and sell domestic assets was limited. However, from the early 1990s, the Korean government began to relax its control over the financial sector and "under the Kim Young Sam government the liberalization process was greatly accelerated (H-J. Chang 1998, 1557). The Kim government's ambitious liberalization agenda was outlined in its *Blueprint for Financial Liberalization and Market Opening* (July 1993) and *Foreign Exchange Reform Plan* (December 1994). Figure 4.1 briefly outlines some of the major financial liberalization measures in Korea during the 1990s.

As Figure 4.1 shows, the liberalization program was wide-ranging in its scope. By mid-1997, many restrictions on the financial markets and foreign-exchange transactions were relaxed or abolished. By July 1997, most interest rates had been liberalized, while entry barriers to the banking and non-banking sector had been significantly relaxed. Restrictions on foreign capital flows were substantially removed. Furthermore, to expedite liberalization, the government merged the Economic Planning Board (EPB) and the Ministry of Finance (MOF) into the Ministry of Finance and Economy (MOFE). However, this only made policy coherence and accountability very difficult.[34] Similarly, the Foreign Exchange Reform Plan of 1995, in liberalizing interest rates (and reducing the government's monitoring role), only allowed for faster portfolio than direct investment inflows – thereby making the country more vulnerable to mass international capital movements.

Why did the Korean government pursue such far-reaching (and poorly sequenced) liberalization measures? There are several interrelated explanations. According to Ilpyong Kim and Uk Heon Hong (2000, 70–71), the Kim Young-Sam administration, determined to create "a New Korea" (*sin Hankuk ch'angjo*) and enamored with *segyehwa* (or globalization) "believed that only a full-blown market economy could build an economy competitive at the world level." Administrators therefore worked to increase the role of the private sector, to loosen the concentration of the *chaebols*, and to deregulate further the financial markets. Also, Chang, Park and Yoo (1998, 740) compellingly note that, by the early 1990s, the increased credit ratings of Korean corporations and banks in the international financial markets meant that the private sector began to regard government involvement in their foreign-exchange transactions as a burden – and the "*chaebols* now hankered for greater freedom in their investment decision-making." Similarly, Lee (2000, 10) notes that "the 1990s saw an increasing demand from *chaebols* for deregulation such as lifting the ceiling on their ownership of bank shares, financial opening for greater freedom in foreign borrowing, raising the aggregate credit ceiling, and so on." Furthermore, the decision by the Kim government to apply for Korea's membership in the OECD meant that Korea had to liberalize substantially the country's financial

**Figure 4.1**  *Major financial liberalization measures in Korea*

1   *Interest rates deregulation* (in four stages: 1991 to July 1997)
    • by 1997, all lending and borrowing rates, except demand deposit rates, were liberalized

2   *More managerial autonomy for the banks and lower entry barriers to financial activities*
    • freedom for banks to increase capital, to establish branches and to determine dividend payments (1994)
    • enlargement of business scope for financial institutions (1993), which included (a) continuous expansion of the securities business of deposit money banks (1990, 1993, 1994, 1995), (b) freedom for banks and life insurance companies to sell government and public bonds over-the-counter (1995) and (c) permission for securities companies to handle foreign exchange business (1995)
    • abolition of the limits on maximum maturities for loans and deposits of banks (1996)

3   *Foreign exchange liberalization*
    • introduction of "free won" accounts for non-residents (1993)
    • allowance of partial won settlements for the export or import of visible items (1993)
    • Foreign Exchange Reform Plan (1994), which included a detailed schedule for the reform of the foreign-exchange market structure
    • a very significant relaxation of the Foreign Exchange Concentration System (1995)

4   *Capital market opening*
    • foreign investors are allowed to invest directly in Korean stock markets with ownership ceilings (1992)
    • foreigners are allowed to purchase government and public bonds issued at international interest rates (1994), equity-linked bonds issued by small and medium-sized firms (1994), non-guaranteed long-term bonds issued by small and medium-sized firms (January 1997), and non-guaranteed convertible bonds issued by large companies (January 1997)
    • residents are allowed to invest in overseas securities via beneficiary certificates (1993)
    • abolition of the ceiling on the domestic institutional investors' overseas portfolio investment (1995)
    • foreign commercial loans are allowed without government approval in so far as they meet the guideline established in May 1995
    • private companies engaged in major infrastructure projects are allowed to borrow overseas to pay for domestic construction cost (January 1997)
    • liberalization of borrowings related to foreign direct investments (January 1997)

5   *Policy loans and credit control*
    • simplifying and slimming down the controls on the share of a bank's loans to major conglomerates in its total loans

*Source*: Chang, Park and Yoo (1998, 737).

markets, in particular, both the current and the capital accounts.[35] Beyond these domestic structural explanations are the external factors, in particular, the continued pressure from the US government for Korea to deregulate and open her financial markets. Yet, whatever the explanation, there is general consensus that the liberalization program was accompanied by extremely lax supervision and prudential regulation.

For example, a history of government involvement in bank lending decisions had hampered the development of a commercially-oriented and sound banking system, besides creating moral hazard. Within banks, lending decisions tended to be highly centralized, and the internal risk-control structures as well as credit analysis skills and procedures did not mature fully. As a result, credit decisions tended to rely on collateral and inter-company guarantees, as well as informal government guidance, rather than projected cash flows. Loan review processes and management information systems were rudimentary. Thus Balino and Ubide (1999, 16) succinctly note that "although government involvement in bank lending decisions was gradually withdrawn, banks developed few skills in credit analysis or risk management. Lending decisions were still largely based on the availability of collateral rather than on an assessment of risk or future repayment capacity. Because of their large exposures and inadequate capitalization, banks were generally in a weak position relative to their *chaebol* clients. Reflecting the history of directed lending, banks did not insist on, or receive, full financial information from *chaebols*." In addition, basic accounting, auditing and disclosure practices were significantly below international best practice. Commercial banks were under the direct authority of the Monetary Board (the governing body of the Bank of Korea) and the Office of Banking Supervision (OBS). However, specialized banks and NBFIs were under the authority of the Ministry of Finance and Economy (MOFE). This lack of a unified system of supervision and regulation comprising both bank and non-bank financial institutions created conditions for regulatory arbitrage and the development of risky practices.

Similarly, the standards for loan classification and provisioning were significantly laxer in Korea than in the other OECD countries. Non-performing loans were defined as loans that had been in arrears for six months or more, compared to a standard definition of three months or more. Bad loans were defined as the portion of non-performing loans not covered by collateral. The classification system was based on the loans's servicing record and the availability of collateral without regard to the borrower's future capacity to repay. Banks also lacked good internal liquidity-management controls, and regulations were not sufficiently stringent, especially in regard to foreign exchange. In order to ensure the liquidity of banks, the OBS required that long-term loans (defined as those with a maturity between one and ten years) should be financed with funds with maturities of at least a year. However, banks were not expected to invest an amount equivalent to more than 100 per cent of their equity capital in securities with maturities over three years. Moreover, all these calculations included only domestic liquidity positions, not taking into account positions of overseas branches and offshore funds – which accounted for more than 60 per cent of domestic financial institutions' short-term external liabilities in 1996. Yet, despite the growing maturity mismatches in banks' balance sheets that resulted from the capital account liberalization, no special consideration was given to the prudential regulation of liquidity-management in foreign exchange (Chopra *et al.* 2001). Finally, Korean banks were subject to considerable restrictions on product innovation, while controls on interest rates limited price competition. Labor laws made it difficult to reduce excess personnel. With little control over their credit policy or costs, and with relatively little concern about insolvency, the banks were usually more concerned with achieving profits through asset growth than in maintaining asset quality.

Another consequence of the deregulation was the rapid growth of merchant banks. As was noted earlier, many of these newly established merchant banks were previously (in the 1970s and 1980s) small-scale investment finance companies created to reduce the importance of the informal curb markets. However, with deregulation they simply changed their names and became merchant banks. In 1994, nine such merchant banks were established, and by 1996, sixteen more were added to the group. At the end of 1996, there were 30 merchant banks in the country. Merchant banks as wholesale financial institutions engaged aggressively in underwriting, leasing and short-term lending. Soon they began to cut into the profitability of the banking sector. The merchant banks (which were the dominant lenders in the issuance and discounting of commercial paper) funded themselves by issuing notes and short-term bonds to overseas investors, by inter-bank deposits and by borrowing in foreign markets. As was also noted earlier, most of these newly established merchant banks were either owned or controlled by the *chaebols*. Similarly, the significant relaxation of restrictions on *chaebol* ownership of other non-bank financial institutions such as life insurance companies and investment-trust companies enabled the *chaebols* to further expand and concentrate their financial operations.[36] Indeed, there were no effective laws to prevent excess concentration of lending. Korea did not have laws to restrict lending to multiple borrowers belonging to the same group. That is, different firms that belonged to the same *chaebol* family were treated independently. The result was heavy concentration of lending. Finally, although the merchant banks often competed directly with commercial banks, they were subject to different regulatory regimes. In fact, the merchant banks faced far fewer regulatory restraints than the commercial banks, and therefore quickly developed some distinct vulnerabilities. For example, owing to the relatively lax regulatory regime, merchant banks assumed much higher interest rate and currency risk than the commercial banks. Their lending concentration inside affiliated groups was greater, and merchant banks usually lent without collateral – and thus had less protection in case of default.

Compounding this problem was the maintenance of tight monetary policy and a regulatory framework that was explicitly biased towards short-term borrowing. That is, short-term loans regarded as trade-related financing were hardly regulated, whereas long-term borrowing was subject to much stricter restrictions, requiring one to provide detailed information, besides obtaining permission from the MOFE.[37] Also, since the government expected that the credit rating on bank loans of Korean companies would improve in the international financial market, it further induced financial institutions to transform long-term external debts into short-term debts (MOFE 1998). However, other "borrowers seem to have taken a 'wait and see' approach by continuously rolling over short-term loans rather than taking out long-term ones, an approach supported by the international lenders who were perfectly willing to roll over Korean loans until the eve of the crisis" (Chang, Park and Yoo 1998, 739). Overall, the bias towards short-term foreign borrowing only encouraged the development of large maturity mismatches in the banks' balance sheets.

Moreover, financial liberalization and tight monetary policy (which kept domestic interest rates above world interest rates) only encouraged commercial and merchant banks to rely heavily on cheaper foreign credit. Korean banks borrowed on the overseas interbank market, taking advantage of lower interest rates and passing the funds on to their domestic customers. This strategy was fraught with problems, since it meant that Korea was borrowing short-term money abroad (money that had to be repaid in hard currency) and lending it long-term to their *chaebol* and other customers. Secondly, foreign credit was perceived to be cheaper because of the pegged exchange rate. No doubt, a pegged exchange rate in normal circumstances would eliminate the foreign-exchange risk associated with foreign loans for domestic borrowers. However, Korea's exchange-rate policies contributed to reckless foreign borrowing. Prior to the crisis, the Korean won was effectively tied to the US dollar, with very little or predictable variation. Specifically, in March 1990, Korea adopted an approach to exchange-rate management known as the Market Average Exchange Rate System (MAR). Under this system, the daily won/dollar rate was allowed to fluctuate each day within a band centered around the preceding day's weighted average spot rate. The band width was initially set at plus or minus 0.2 per cent. Between 1990 and 1996, the exchange rate was tightly managed – with the won depreciating fairly steadily by an annual average rate of 2 per cent.[38] The daily fluctuation band was gradually widened in the period before the crisis, reaching plus or minus 2.25 per cent in 1996. In maintaining such a tight exchange rate, the Bank of Korea, in effect, absorbed the exchange-rate risks on behalf of market participants. With little variation of exchange rates and high domestic interest rates, it is not surprising that *chaebols* and financial institutions increased their offshore borrowing, especially with short-term maturity loans. Moreover, although the exchange rate was not fixed, its undervaluation in a managed float system and relatively high interest rates at home had substantially increased the attraction of foreign borrowing. Yen-denominated loans became especially attractive in the couple of years before the crisis, because the continuing decline in the value of the yen against the US dollar lowered the real cost of yen loans to domestic borrowers.

The resultant wave of excessive short-term foreign borrowing was intensified by ineffective policy response and poor prudential supervision. Specifically, the mounting balance of payments surplus due to the increasing exports and the inflow of capital forced the monetary authority to engage in a massive sterilization operation by issuing Monetary Stabilization Bonds (MSBs) on a large scale, leading to a circle of higher interest rates and larger inflows of foreign capital. Second, lax regulation of banks, in particular, merchant banks (for example, there were no asset classification, capital or provisioning rules for merchant banks) and the regulatory distortions that favored short-term borrowing contributed heavily to the accumulation of short-term foreign debt, increasing the banks' vulnerability to maturity mismatch. As Chang, Park and Yoo (1998, 738) note, "leading this rapid build-up of short-term foreign debt were the inexperienced merchant banks." For example, in a period of almost three years, merchant banks managed to acquire US$20 billion in foreign debt – 64 per cent of which was short-term debt, while 85 per cent of their lendings were long-term. Overall, foreign debt jumped from US$44 billion in 1993 to US$120 billion in September 1997 (a 33.6 per cent per annum increase between 1994 and 1996), while the share of short-term debt (or debt with less than a year's maturity) in total debt rose from an already high 43.7 per cent in 1993 to 58.3 per cent at the end of 1996 (Chang, Park and Yoo 1998, 738–9). However, these figures underestimate the actual size of the debt, since they do not include offshore borrowing of domestic enterprises and Korean banks and their overseas branches and subsidiaries. By the mid-1990s, low profits and soft lending combined to make the *chaebols* highly leveraged in terms of their debt/ equity ratios. As Table 4.1 shows, at the end of 1997, the top 30 *chaebols* had an unprecedented debt/equity ratio average of 519 per cent – which was more than twice the international banking norm of 200 per cent.

### Economic vulnerabilities: the road to the crisis

High as the foreign debt figure was, it was not necessarily at an unsustainable level. As was noted earlier, in 1996, Korea's debt/GNP ratio stood at 22 per cent, far below the World Bank's definition of "less indebted," at 48 per cent. Similarly, Korea's debt-service ratio of 5.8 per cent was well below the critical 18 per cent specified by the World Bank. Also, the current account,

**Table 4.1**  *Debt/equity ratio of the top 20* chaebols

| Rank | Company | Debt/equity ratio (%) | |
|------|---------|------|------|
| | | *1996* | *1997* |
| 1 | Hyundai | 376 | 579 |
| 2 | Samsung | 206 | 371 |
| 3 | Daewoo | 337 | 472 |
| 4 | LG | 313 | 506 |
| 5 | Sunkyong | 320 | 468 |
| 6 | Hanjin | 619 | 908 |
| 7 | Ssangyong | 297 | 400 |
| 8 | Hanwha | 619 | 1,215 |
| 9 | Kumho | 465 | 944 |
| 10 | Dong-Ah | 320 | 360 |
| 11 | Lotte | 179 | 216 |
| 12 | Halla | 2,930 | N/A |
| 13 | Daelim | 344 | 514 |
| 14 | Doosan | 625 | 590 |
| 15 | Hansol | 290 | 400 |
| 16 | Hyosung | 315 | 465 |
| 17 | Kohap | 472 | 472 |
| 18 | Kolon | 350 | 434 |
| 19 | Dongkuk Steel | 323 | 324 |
| 20 | Dongbu | 338 | 338 |
| Top 30 *chaebols* | | 387 | 519 |

*Source*: Beck (1998, 1023).

which had recorded a deficit of US$23.7 billion (4.9 per cent of GDP) in 1996, had decreased to US$8.8 billion by April 1997. It is important to note that (unlike what happened in Mexico), the current-account deficit was used to finance investment rather than consumption, and it was thought that the trend of increasing deficits would be reversed quickly as soon as the falling international prices of major export items such as semiconductors, steel and petrochemical products rebounded. Moreover, private corporate sector profligacy was not as widespread in Korea as it was in Indonesia or Thailand, nor was Korea highly exposed to real-estate and property inflation.[39] In fact, much of the foreign borrowing went into the tradeable sector, and not to fuel speculative asset bubbles in the non-tradeable sector. Land prices, which had risen at a rapid pace in the second half of the 1980s, were basically stable in the 1990s. Instead, foreign borrowing primarily financed an expansion of industrial capacity. That is, the *chaebols* were investing in export industries with stable returns, and in which they were particularly well represented – namely petrochemicals, petroleum refining, iron and steel, automobiles, electrical equipment, electronics and communications and shipbuilding. Yet, these only reflected part of the economic picture. Looming alongside were growing economic vulnerabilities, which the history of impressive macro-economic performance had served to cover up.

Specifically, the heavy indebtedness of the *chaebols* (and their subsequent insolvency) are to be found in the investment boom of the early to mid-1990s. During 1994–96, facility investment in manufacturing rose by 38.5 per cent per year. However, the investment boom was not uniform across sectors, but concentrated in manufacturing. Within manufacturing, the bulk of the investments (65.7 per cent) went to expand existing production lines, while a relatively small amount was allocated to corporate restructuring (15.5 per cent). Moreover, investments in heavy and chemical industries grew at an annual rate of 43.1 per cent, while the rate of growth for light industries was only 15 per cent (OECD 1998a). Also, investments by large firms grew 45.7 per cent, while small and medium-size enterprises increased their investments by 17.7 per cent. In sum, the boom was dominated by the large *chaebols* investing in heavy industries such as steel, automobiles, petrochemicals and electronics. However, this boom soon resulted in gross over-investment. Blustein (2001, 121–2), for example, vividly illustrates the fact that "from 1994 to 1996, spending on new plants and equipment rose by nearly 40 per cent a year . . . these expansion programs reeked not only of excessive ambition but even megalomania. The Ssangyong Group, whose chairman, M. P. Kim, was a car buff . . . invested $4 billion to enter the Korean automobile market, where three giants (Hyundai, Daewoo and Kia) already dominated. Samsung, whose chairman also cherished a personal car collection, insisted on following its rivals into the crowded automotive industry as well – and reportedly got permission from the administration of President Kim Young Sam by locating its plant in Pusan, Kim's home base."

Thus, in an environment marked by zealous expansion and the near-complete absence of investment coordination, it was only a matter of time before investments would lead to overcapacity and declining profitability. Indeed, the profit rates (return on assets) in the manufacturing sector had fallen continuously from over 4 per cent in 1988 to 0.9 per cent in 1996. The decline of rates of return to capital during this period was caused at least partly by excessive and misallocated investment. In addition, using firm-level data in eight major industries, Bailey and Zitzewitz (1998) have shown that much of the rapid growth in the Korean economy could be accounted for by input growth rather than by productivity increase, and that the returns to capital (or profit rates) of Korean firms were lower than those of American and Japanese firms. They find that many *chaebols* recorded little or no profit even as their sales were expanding at a rate of 30 per cent per year in 1996.[40] Similarly, studies by Borensztein and Lee (1999) and Choi, Jen and

Shin (2000) have found that many *chaebols* recorded little or no profit in 1996. Corsetti, Pesenti and Roubini (1998, 6), note that in 1996, 20 of the largest 30 *chaebols* showed a rate of return below the cost of capital.[41] Hence, by 1996, Korea's corporate sector was characterized by low levels of profitability and high levels of debt – reflecting the tendency of the *chaebols* to diversify into capital-intensive industries using short-term bank loans. Hong and Lee (2000, 209), citing World Bank figures, note that "by 1996 the average debt-equity ratio of firms was over 300 per cent and it reached 620 per cent for a median firm. The ratio exceeded 500 per cent for the 30 largest *chaebols* and reached even 3,000 per cent for some *chaebols*." Banks, on the other hand, carried substantial non-performing loans and inadequate capital–asset ratios. Borensztein and Lee (1999, 7) aptly note that Korea's economic performance in recent years "is one of economic growth sustained by higher and higher levels of investment even in the face of declining productivity of capital and almost vanishing corporate profitability."

The aggressive borrowing, especially of short-term foreign loans, had dire consequences. While there is nothing intrinsically wrong in borrowing from abroad to finance rapid industrialization, it is necessary to apply risk-management to those foreign loans. First, in Korea, banks were exposed to large maturity mismatches in their foreign-currency operations because they relied on foreign-currency-denominated short-term borrowing to fund long-term domestic-currency-denominated loans. Hahm and Mishkin (2000, 29) note that "gross external liabilities had been growing at rates exceeding 30 per cent from 1994 to 1996. . . . the amount of external liabilities relative to GDP was also rising rapidly over the same period, rising from the 20 per cent level prior to 1994 to above 30 per cent by 1996 and 1997." It is estimated that, prior to the crisis, corporate debt totaled some US$75 billion, and the ratio of short-term external debt to total external debt was over 50 per cent (Lee and Orr 1999, 97). Moreover, there was a sharp mismatch between the short-term debts and official foreign reserves. In fact, the ratio of short-term external debt to official foreign reserves increased continuously in the 1990s (from 34 per cent in 1992 to 63 per cent by the end of 1996), reaching an unprecedented high of 252 per cent in 1997 (H. Smith 1998, 67). By June 1997, Korea's short-term debt was more than three times the size of its reserves, a higher ratio than for any other country in the region. As Dongchul Cho (1998, 105–6) notes, "at the end of November 1997, [Korea's] short-term debt comprised almost 60 per cent of the approximately $110 billion total foreign debt." It was asserted that Korea was protected from "hot money" because liquid asset markets were not open to foreigners; but once the country's credibility was lost, short-term debt became virtually hot money.

Second, much of the foreign loans (which were short-term debts denominated in foreign currencies) was without an appropriate hedge. Third, the continued government support of industrialization through foreign debt was not accompanied by any improvement in the transparency of accounting standards in the leveraged *chaebols*. In fact, prudential regulation and supervision simply failed to keep up with the increasing concentration of risk in the domestic financial system. Not only were the banks lax in examining the large-scale investment project loans for which bank credits were requested by *chaebols*, but formal feasibility studies and risk analysis were also lacking. More often than not, bank managers decided on credit extension according to the size of borrowing firms, swayed by the charms of the "too big to fail" argument. That is, because *chaebols* were considered to be "too big to fail" financial institutions believed that the government would protect them from any harm. Further, the banks did not bother to check into possible misuse of loans by borrowers in the form of financial contributions to politicians and political parties, while foreign investors provided funds to domestic financial institutions without due vigilance, since they were perceived as having implicit government guarantees. In fact, this reflected a long-established tacit understanding among Korean banks that if their *chaebol* clients got into trouble, the government would step in to protect everyone against a major loss.

Reflecting this lack of consolidated supervision, the increasingly risky activities of the merchant banks and other non-bank financial institutions, as well as the overseas subsidiaries and foreign branches of domestic financial institutions, were largely overlooked. The ill-experienced managers in merchant banks and financial companies were prone to allowing high-risk exposure owing to their inability at managing short-term foreign capital. Without effective supervisory regulations, the merchant banks engaged in increasingly risky business – for example, investing in high-yield foreign junk bonds with funds borrowed cheaply using Korea's high credit rating in international financial markets. Thus they exposed themselves to significant interest-rate, currency and credit risks. Indeed, when foreign lenders started to recall loans in late 1997, these assets turned out to be illiquid. Finally, the liberalization of foreign-exchange transactions on the current account allowed exporters to avoid depositing their foreign-exchange revenues with the Central Bank. As a result, foreign-exchange deposits in the commercial banks declined sharply – the build-up of short-term foreign debt far exceeding Korea's foreign-exchange reserves.

The economic boom began to slow down by the mid-1990s. Industrial output growth slowed down from an annual growth rate of 14 per cent in 1995 to 10 per cent in 1996. Growth in manufacturing sales declined from 20 per cent in 1995 to 10 per cent in 1996. More troubling, Korea's export engine slowed down significantly owing to its deteriorating international competitiveness, and to the currency devaluation by China and Japan – Korea's major competitors in the export market. In addition, with wage increases rapidly outstripping productivity increases, Korea simply could not effectively compete against Japan for high-valued products, and against

China for low-value goods.[42] As the world export demand receded, the *chaebols* suffered heavy losses. In particular, the slowdown in international trade in semiconductors (especially the memory chips market), office automation equipment, and consumer electronics, which began to slow down imperceptibly in 1995, but reached crisis proportions by mid-1996, severely hurt the Korean economy, which had invested heavily in it.[43] In fact, the terms of trade deteriorated by approximately 20 per cent in 1996 – the largest external shock since the first oil shock of 1974. However, as Noble and Ravenhill (2000, 90) note: "Korean companies ignored the softening demand for 4 MB and 16 MB chips in the mid-1990s and continued to expand production capacity." The 16-megabit memory chip, which accounted for approximately 20 per cent of Korean exports, saw its price tumble from a high of more than US$50 to under US$7 by mid-1997 owing to a worldwide glut, declining demand, and the entrance of new competitors (in particular, Taiwan and Singapore) in the marketplace.[44] By mid-1996, the unit price of semiconductors had fallen by more than 70 per cent, which alone was estimated to have decreased the value of Korean exports by more than US$10 billion, or over 2 per cent of GDP, severely affecting the top three semiconductor companies: Samsung Electronics, Hyundai Electronics and LG Semiconductors. In addition, international prices of many of Korea's other export items, such as steel and chemical products, fell in 1996. As a result, the terms of trade deteriorated by more than 20 per cent in 1996. Since the *chaebols* financed the construction and expansion of costly multibillion-dollar chip-fabrication factories known as "fabs" with massive doses of short-term dollar-denominated loans, they now faced an impending financial disaster as the huge losses in this critical sector mounted. Compounding the problem was the weakening profitability associated with cyclical downturns in sectors such as autos, shipbuilding, and the labor-intensive textiles and steel.[45] All this not only resulted in deteriorating terms of trade (during 1996–97, Korea's terms of trade deteriorated by more than 20 per cent cumulatively), but also severely constrained the *chaebols'* ability to cross-subsidize their investments.

As the new year began in 1997, foreign investors began to take a closer look at Korea – not only because of the unexpectedly sharp economic slowdown, but also because Korea's current-account deficit of 5 per cent in 1996 (the largest in five years) raised concerns. Then, on 23 January, the 14th largest *chaebol*, Hanbo Steel and Construction, declared bankruptcy, with a total estimated debt of US$6 billion spread across 61 banks and non-bank financial institutions. Other affiliates of the Hanbo group, which had been forced to act as guarantors of Hanbo Steel's debts, also collapsed, effectively bringing down the entire group. On February 19, Moody's lowered the long-term ratings of three Korean banks (Korea Exchange Bank, Korea First Bank and Cho Hung Bank), all of which had substantial exposure to the Hanbo Group.[46] However, this was just the beginning. Hanbo's collapse was followed by four more large *chaebol*: Sammi Steel on March 19 (with a 2.3 trillion won debt, 33 times its capital base), Korea's largest distillery, the Jinro Group (with a 3 trillion won debt)[47] on April 21, the retail chain Dainong in May and the 6th largest *chaebol*, Ssangyoung, in June. Each went into bankruptcy, dragged down by excessive investment, declining profits and a substantial debt burden. As noted earlier, because of the cross-guarantee of debts among the affiliated firms of a *chaebol* group, the bankruptcy of one affiliate firm led to the bankruptcy of other affiliated firms. Moreover, these large corporate insolvencies inevitably undermined the health of the financial institutions with large exposure to these conglomerates.

By mid-1997, it became clear to investors that Korea's corporate sector difficulties would have significant repercussions on the financial sector. The growing economic turmoil in the region, especially the collapse of the Thai baht on July 2, 1997, and the subsequent contagion to other regional currencies pegged against the US dollar, brought Korea's growing financial and corporate sector problems into sharper focus. When, on July 15, Kia Motors, Korea's third-largest car-maker and eighth-largest *chaebol*, asked for emergency loans to avoid bankruptcy, the credit agencies immediately began downgrading ratings for several major Korean banks, as they estimated that the fiscal bailout for the banking system would cost as much as 20 per cent of GDP (D. Park and Rhee 1998, 170). In the face of the growing crisis, the Kim Young Sam government remained indecisive – if not paralyzed.[48] Although the Bank of Korea had alerted President Kim to the danger of a foreign-exchange crisis as early as July 1997, "the Ministry of Finance and Economy (MOFE) and the presidential economic secretary downplayed it by emphasizing the 'healthy fundamentals' of the macroeconomy. Kim's aides thought they could put off the IMF bailout until Kim's tenure was over. His poor monitoring and mismanagement aggravated the crisis by mis-timing effective intervention."[49] Thus an indecisive and discredited president (as a result of the Hanbo scandal), coupled with a divided ruling party, pervasive intra-bureaucratic fragmentation, and an opposition resistant to reform legislation, produced political gridlock and policy incoherence.[50]

Finally, after weeks of sending mixed signals, the government began to take action. In early August, the government announced a set of measures aimed at increasing confidence in the Korean financial market. First, official support was provided by the Bank of Korea in the form of special loans and a capital injection in exchange for government bonds to Korea First Bank. However, the government's response of guaranteeing the foreign liabilities of financial institutions only called into question the Bank of Korea's ability to act as the lender of last resort. In addition, a special funding facility was created to assist 21 merchant banks (out of the 30) whose exposure to bankrupt companies exceeded 50 per cent of their equity. Second, the government announced guarantees covering the foreign liabilities of Korean financial institutions, including both commercial and merchant banks. And, third, for the disposal of non-performing assets at financial institutions, an Act on the Efficient Disposal of Non-performing Assets of Financial Institutions and for the establishment of the Korea Asset Management Corporation (KAMCO) was passed in November 1997. Under this Act, the Non-performing Loans Management Fund was set up under the umbrella of KAMCO in order to help financial institutions dispose of their non-performing assets at the earliest date possible.[51] In exchange, banks would receive KAMCO bonds, which they could liquidate at any time.

It is now clear that the markets perceived these measures as insufficient. On October 24, 1997, Standard and Poor downgraded Korea's sovereign status, citing corporate and financial problems and the government's weak response. This struck a major blow to market confidence, making it difficult for Korea's private sector to obtain foreign-currency funds. Indeed, by October 1997, the balance-sheets of Korean financial institutions had deteriorated severely. The share of non-performing loans in total assets of commercial banks had increased by about 70 per cent between December 1996 and September 1997 – and amounted to about 80 per cent of banks' capital. As a result, the net worth of many financial institutions fell perilously low, and a significant shortfall in capital adequacy emerged. Of the 26 commercial banks, 14 had capital adequacy ratios below 8 per cent, of which two were deemed to be technically insolvent. In addition, 28 of the 30 merchant banks had capital adequacy ratios below 8 per cent and 12 were deemed technically insolvent (Balino and Ubide 1999, 30). Daekeun Park and Rhee (1998, 171) point out that the Korean government "made a critical mistake when it decided to bail out the near-bankrupt Kia group on October 22, 1997." Immediately after the Kia decision, foreign banks refused to roll over loans, forcing Korean banks and corporations to buy dollars in the foreign-exchange market to service their obligations – adding to the pressures on the exchange rate. Indeed, "this was the moment that Korea's private banking crisis officially turned into a sovereign one." Standard and Poor harshly criticized the Korean government's decision to bail out Kia, stating that "the bailout might alleviate short-term pressures but the long run economic consequences are unambiguously negative" (D. Park and Rhee 1998, 171). Cha (2001, 43) more bluntly notes: "the government's decision to 'nationalize' Kia was interpreted by international capital markets as a signal that the Korean government had neither the will nor the courage to correct the economy's structural problems. Foreign investors lost their confidence completely." In this environment, capital flight picked up speed as foreign investors began to pull out of Korea and domestic residents shifted funds to foreign-currency deposits. The once-solid Korean bonds tumbled to junk levels as investors became nervous that the world's eleventh largest economy was heading for a Mexican-style crisis.

By late October 1997, it was clear that not only were the foreign banks reluctant to roll over short-term loans, but the massive outflow of capital continued unabated.[52] The Bank of Korea tried to intervene in the exchange market with its foreign reserves in order to restore confidence. This meant that now a part of the current-account deficit had to be financed from central bank reserves – and soon the central bank reserves began to fall rapidly, as private capital inflows virtually vanished. Even before the collapse of Yamaichi Securities (Japan's fourth-largest securities company), and the bankruptcy of Japan's Takushoku Bank on November 15, Japanese banks began to call in their loans from Korea, thereby precipitating a liquidity crunch for the Korean banks.[53] As Yanagita (2000, 21–22) notes, "already facing their own crisis as the economy bubble burst in the early 1990s, Japanese banks began to collect maturing debts in the region. Once the Japanese banks, which were most familiar with the Korean economic situation as the largest Korean creditors, started to collect matured short-term debts, other countries' banks followed suit in short order, abruptly prompting the liquidity squeeze on the Korean foreign exchange. As a result, US$34.2 billion in private capital flowed out of Korea in a few short months, including US$9.2 billion collected by international banks and US$25 billion of short-term capital." As the merchant banks' weakest borrowers began going bankrupt, foreign and Korean commercial banks further curtailed their lending. To stay afloat, the merchant banks were forced to call in loans – causing more bankruptcies. They bought up dollars or yen with won to pay their foreign-currency debts, and these won sales contributed to the drastic decline in the won's value. The won dropped sharply from 915 won per dollar on October 21, 1997 to 965 won per dollar on October 31, 1997.

A sharp export slowdown and a growing current-account deficit in 1996 led many to suspect the possibility of an overvalued exchange rate. In spite of the perception that the won had been overvalued since the second quarter of 1996, when the price of semiconductors collapsed, the Bank of Korea nevertheless actively intervened in the foreign-exchange market to uphold the value of the won. However, this intervention contributed to the rapid depletion of foreign reserves. For example, the government sold off more than US$7 billion in official foreign reserves between June 1996 and the end of March 1997, reducing reserves from US$37 billion to US$29 billion. Why did the Korean government try to uphold the value of the won despite a growing current-account deficit? In large part because the authorities expected the current-account balance to improve soon, and worried that a devaluation would trigger inflation and increase the debt-service burden of the private sector. After October, domestic financial institutions found it extremely difficult to roll over their loans. As a result, Korean banks and corporations had to buy dollars in the domestic exchange market to service their external obligations. This situation also meant that the central bank had to supply foreign exchange to banks in the form of deposits at overseas branches.[54] However, the supply of foreign exchange declined sharply with the expectation of a won depreciation. In this fast-deteriorating environment, the Korean authorities made another fatal mistake by wasting a substantial part of the country's foreign reserves in this futile foreign-exchange market intervention. That is, instead of letting the won float, the Korean government tried to defend it by spending approximately US$15.1 billion in October and November 1997.

Korea's liquid foreign reserve, which was US$22.4 billion in early October, dropped to a paltry US$7.3 billion by mid-November. According to an IMF study, Korea's usable foreign exchange reserves fell dramatically in November, at a rate of US$1 billion to US$2 billion daily, bottoming out at around US$5 billion by the end of the month.[55] Although the central bank of Korea tried to calm the financial markets by announcing that its reserves were around US$30 billion, the strategy backfired. Specifically, as Daesik Kim and Park (2000, 89) note, "confidence was eroded further when it became apparent that monetary authorities had lied about foreign exchange reserve levels. The government insisted that the Bank of Korea held about US$30 billion in reserves in November. However, simple calculations revealed that this claim could not be true, and only about US$15 billion remained." Similarly, Daekeun Park and Rhee (1998, 172) observe that "the market ridiculed the government's denial attitude." Likewise Dongchul Cho (1998, 105) adds that "given the public knowledge of the heavy government intervention in the exchange market, this statement did not make sense at all." This incident decisively destroyed the credibility of the Korean government, and foreign investors began to distrust even official statistics unless they were endorsed by the IMF. Foreign investors estimated that the actual reserves were as low as US$15 billion – which totaled about five weeks' worth of imports and only a fifth of Korea's short-term debt. With the markets cognizant of the fact that the announced reserves did not include dollars borrowed through forward market intervention (contracted by offshore entities), and recalling that Thailand had committed as much as two-thirds of its reserves in this way, the Korean government's lack of candor cost it its credibility, besides fueling rumors among international financial investors regarding the actual amount of Korea's usable foreign-exchange reserves. By the end of October 1997, 6 out of the top 30 *chaebols* had filed for court protection or court-ordered receivership, and a seventh went into bankruptcy in December. These large bankruptcies, together with rising bankruptcies among small and medium-sized enterprises significantly damaged the asset position of financial institutions (MOFE 1998).

By early November, Korea was confronted with a "twin crisis" – a banking and currency crisis. Specifically, the wave of corporate bankruptcies and rising non-performing loans created doubts about the overall health of the financial system and drove foreign banks to withdraw their credit lines to Korea. In turn, this drying up of foreign credit lines made it extremely difficult for Korean banks to roll over their large volume of short-term external debt – creating the potential for a currency crisis and contributing to capital flight and further decline in the value of the won. In response, the Korean authorities widened the won's daily fluctuation band to plus or minus 10 per cent. However, on November 16 Korea finally abandoned its defense of the battered won and allowed the exchange rate to float freely. This sent the currency crashing through the psychological 1,000/dollar level, with shock waves hitting the baht, the rupiah, the ringgit and other regional currencies, which fell even further relative to the dollar. On November 18, the affable reform-oriented deputy prime minister and minister of finance and economy, Kang Kyung Shik, announced Korea's intention to seek IMF support. However, Kang's "economic recovery plan" was voted down by the National Assembly. On November 19, Kang took responsibility for the crisis, and was abruptly dismissed from both his official positions. The newly appointed finance and economy minister, Lim Chang-Yuel, downplayed the gravity of the situation, referring to Korea's problems as a "temporary funding shortage" and the "idea of IMF aid" as "unthinkable."[56] Lim immediately pressed the United States and Japan for assistance, asserting bluntly that "it is in their national interests to help . . . if the Korean currency depreciates beyond its value, it will seriously affect the Japanese economy" (Blustein 2001, 131). Moreover, he announced that the government would form an emergency economic presidential advisory committee to solve the nation's financial problems. In the late evening of November 19, Lim unveiled an emergency financial bailout package. However, seen as "too little to late," these last-minute attempts failed to restore market confidence. On November 20 the won fell by another 10 per cent to 1,139 won per dollar. With some US$158 billion in external debt (US$90 billion of which was in short-term debts with maturity of less than one year, mostly held by the *chaebols*), the country now teetered on the brink of defaulting on its debt repayments. Following marathon all-night negotiations with the IMF team led by the Fund's number two man, Stanley Fischer, the weary and somber-looking finance minister, in a nationally televised press conference (on November 21) reluctantly announced that Korea would seek emergency financial assistance from the IMF.

However, with Korea's presidential elections due to be held later in December 1997, the IMF made it clear that its support would be contingent upon all presidential candidates' approving (in writing) the terms of the IMF agreement. This was done because two of the leading candidates, the populist Kim Dae-Jung and Rhee In Je, had made it public that if they were elected they would renegotiate the terms of the IMF rescue package if the level of unemployment and corporate bankruptcies turned out to be too high. In this climate of uncertainty the won dropped to 1,800 won to the US dollar in late November. Finally, President Kim Young Sam had to seek written commitments from all the major contenders they would uphold the

IMF agreement if elected. After some ten days of tense negotiations, on the late evening of December 3, 1997, it was announced that the IMF and the South Korean government had finally reached an agreement. On December 4 Michel Camdessus, Managing Director of the IMF, and finance minister Lim signed a three-year standby arrangement under which the IMF agreed to provide a record-breaking US$57 billion rescue package to South Korea. The US$21 billion IMF portion was the largest the Fund had ever lent to a single country, and it was more than six times the amount Korea would normally be allowed to borrow (IMF 1997d). About US$10 billion was lent by the World Bank and US$4 billion came from the Asian Development Bank. The remaining US$22 billion was to be provided on a bilateral basis from governments of the G-7 countries. This portion was earmarked as the "second line of defense funds" – to be provided only if the multilateral loans proved insufficient. Under the agreement, Seoul would receive the first payment of US$5.6 billion immediately, and the second tranche after December 17, following review of Korea's adherence to the comprehensive economic reform program underpinning the loan.[57] After signing the agreement, President Kim Young Sam publicly conceded that "we have lost our economic sovereignty" and apologized for "capitulation to IMF trusteeship." Nevertheless, he stated with unusual candor that his government would honor the stringent IMF conditionality, and pleaded with the nation to endure "humiliating and bone-carving pain."

The December 3 program was based on the expectation that a large financing package, comprehensive structural reform measures, and firm monetary and fiscal policies would be sufficient to restore market confidence. In the first couple of days after the signing of the agreement, the won began to stabilize. The IMF claimed that its program was now starting to work (Blustein 2001, 180–81). However, beginning on December 8 and continuing for the next five days, the won plummeted by the 10 per cent limit each day, ending at 1,712 per dollar on December 12. On December 23 it reached 1,962 won per dollar, while usable reserves had fallen to US$4 billion. The proximate causes for this loss of confidence were several. First, Kim Dae-Jung's announcement on December 6 that if elected he would renegotiate the agreement (despite having signed a pledge to support it) unsettled the markets. Moreover, the fact that his campaign took out ads in major newspapers attacking the deal only worsened matters. Second, the government's decision (on December 9) that it would invest US$1 billion in two large ailing commercial banks, rather than shutting them down as the agreement had stipulated, served to convince the markets that Korea was not serious about implementing the program. Third, when *Chosun Ilbo*, a leading Korean daily, published a leaked version of the December 3 IMF staff report, showing that Korea's foreign debt falling due over the coming year (1998) was over US$116 billion, instead of the officially reported US$65 billion, market confidence was shattered (Blustein 2001, 180–83). It now began to sink in that, large as the IMF bailout was, it did not provide Korea with sufficient hard currency to deal with its debt or to meet its short-term financial obligations.

As panic set in, foreign banks refused to roll over short-term loans to Korean borrowers. Korea's central bank became besieged as it "scrambled to respond to the flood of requests for hard currency that were coming in from Korean commercial bank branches around the world" (Blustein 2001, 183). In this difficult environment, the once unthinkable – allowing Korea to default – was now being contemplated by the IMF and the US Treasury. Yet, recognizing that the potential consequences of default were simply too great to risk, the IMF made one final attempt to rescue Korea. The first order of business was to get Kim Dae-Jung on board. As Blustein (2001, 190–98) documents, this proved much easier than expected. Elected president of Korea on December 18, 1997, Kim Dae-Jung dramatically reversed his policy stance.[58] On accepting his electoral victory in an address to the nation on December 19, 1997, Kim Dae-Jung delivered a ringing endorsement of economic reforms and promised to implement the conditions attached to the IMF program expeditiously. The president-elect noted: "I shall state once more with utmost clarity and emphasis, we shall cooperate with the IMF fully and completely. We shall also faithfully abide by the agreement between the IMF and the present government of this Republic. For that, we shall try our best to legislate the necessary laws in the National Assembly" (Sohn and Yang 1998, 206).

The second IMF plan (coupled with the moral suasion of the United States Treasury, the US Federal Reserve's Alan Greenspan and G-7 governments) was to get Japanese, European and American banks to agree to roll over their maturing short-term loans (with the intent of converting them subsequently into long-term bonds) until March 1998. Again, as Blustein (2001, 190–200) documents, this proved easier than expected. The roll-over, or the "bail-in," as it was called, gave the Korean government the much-needed breathing space to negotiate a more comprehensive restructuring package – albeit it should be noted that the rolled-over debt was owed by domestic private entities to foreign private entities. The Korean government took a central role in the debt negotiations, including providing financial guarantees for the rescheduled loans, because it placed a priority on preserving the access of domestic banks to international credit – even at the risk of fostering moral hazard. On January 16, 1998, the Korean government and the foreign banks reached agreement on the rescheduling of some US$24 billion in short-term debt owed by Korean companies. The debts were converted into new obligations with a maturity of one to three years, backed by government guarantees. To secure foreign-currency liquidity, the government also floated a total of US$4.1 billion worth of foreign-currency-denominated Foreign Exchange Stabilization Fund guaranteed bonds in April 1998.[59] Although the agreement was criticized by some for being too favorable to foreign lenders, it nevertheless, enabled the country to avoid defaulting on the repayment of its short-term foreign debts. In return, the IMF agreed to speed disbursement of US$2 billion on December 30 – well ahead of schedule. The World Bank and the Asian Development Bank also agreed to disburse a combine US$5 billion ahead of schedule. On their part, the Korean authorities agreed to accelerate many of their promised reforms, as well as undertake new ones.

## Under the "IMF Shidae" (Era)

The financial crisis had a devastating impact on the Korean economy, causing Korea's worst recession in the post-war period. As has been noted earlier, real GDP growth fell from levels that had been running in the positive 7–12 per cent range before the crisis to a negative 5.8 per cent in 1998. The won had lost 60 per cent of its value against the dollar, and the Korean stock market dropped 50 per cent in 1997. Worse still, per capita income declined from US$10,543 in 1996 to US$9,511 in 1997. More than 17,000 companies (mostly SMEs, or small and medium enterprises) went bankrupt, including eight conglomerates.[60] SMEs were hit particularly hard. Since more than half the SMEs had subcontracting relationships with the larger *chaebols*, their access to credit contracted sharply as banks (the primary source of external finance for SMEs) refused to transact with SMEs without established credit records or collateral. During the first half of 1998, the losses of Korean listed companies reached new historical heights (about 14 trillion won in the first half of 1998), and unemployment rose from pre-crisis levels of 2 per cent to 6 per cent in 1998 and to 8.7 per cent in March 1999 – the highest in thirty years.[61] Real wages also saw a substantial decline of 20.7 per cent during the same period (World Bank 1999, 34). In the midst of all this, a leaked confidential IMF document further spooked the market by revealing that Korea's short-term debt was nearly twice as large as had been previously declared by the government. It was estimated to be more than US$100 billion once offshore borrowing by Korean banks, enterprises, and their overseas branches and subsidiaries were accounted for (World Bank 1999).

It should be noted that, even before the ink was dry on the agreement the Korean government had reached with the IMF, criticism of the program had begun to mount. As Daekeun Park and Rhee (1998, 173) note, "the public's reaction to the IMF arrangement was unreasonably negative. Local news media portrayed the IMF not as a counterpart for cooperation but as an invading army. Many believed that Korea had lost its economic sovereignty as it was now under a neo-colonial 'IMF *shidae*.'" However, to halt the spiraling economic decline and jump-start the faltering economy, the Kim Dae-Jung administration (which took office in February 1998) committed itself to the IMF's program of macroeconomic adjustment and structural reform. In fact, in its February 7, 1998 "Letter of Intent" to the IMF, the Kim Dae-Jung government did more than accept the "steadfast implementation of the very tight monetary and fiscal policy stance proposed by the IMF" (IMF 1998e). The government also closely worked with the IMF and the World Bank to devise a wide-ranging and politically challenging structural adjustment program designed to address outstanding problems in the financial and corporate sectors.[62]

Although the IMF-sponsored program underwent several revisions, it consisted of three basic elements: macroeconomic stabilization, financial and corporate sector reforms, including comprehensive dismantling of the old financial system, and further measures related to trade liberalization, capital account liberalization and labor market reform. This reflected the IMF's view that the crisis originated from structural weaknesses in the Korean economy, especially from its financial system (IMF 1997d). However, the IMF believed that the immediate challenge was to achieve macroeconomic stability and restore confidence in the currency. To achieve this the IMF program required that: (1) money supply be squeezed, or at least be limited to a rate consistent with containing inflation at 5 per cent or less; (2) the government maintain a balanced budget by reducing its spending level to match its tax revenue – which was expected to decline; (3) the exchange rate be determined by market forces; (4) interest rates be allowed to rise to the highest possible level to stem capital outflows and discourage speculation (On December 1, 1997, the statutory ceiling on interest rates was raised to 12.3 per cent. However, it was increased to 20.7 per cent on December 3, and to 30.1 per cent on December 23. The high interest-rate policy continued throughout the first two quarters of 1998.); (5) the government work hard to accumulate foreign exchange; and (6) a tight fiscal stance be maintained for 1998 to alleviate the burden on monetary policy and to provide for the interest costs of restructuring the financial sector.

In the area of financial sector reforms, the program was designed to: (1) restructure and recapitalize the banking system to address the problem of the stock of bad loans and the weak capital base This meant decisively dealing with problem institutions and problem loans by closing down the former and by selling off the latter, and substantially improving the health of the remaining financial institutions by injecting additional capital. Indeed, at the outset of the program, in order to maintain public confidence, the government guaranteed all deposits of financial institutions until the year 2000 and suspended the operation of fourteen insolvent merchant banks. In addition, two commercial banks were placed under supervision, while all remaining financial institutions were required to submit plans for capital restorations needed to meet the Basle standards; and (2) strengthen the disclosure rules, enforcing transparency requirements and establishing a prudential regulatory framework in order to prevent the recurrence of similar problems.

On December 29, 1997, the Korean National Assembly passed a package of thirteen financial reform bills designed to facilitate financial restructuring, improve prudential regulation and speed up capital market liberalization. Specifically, the new Bank of Korea Act provided for the independence of the central bank, the Bank of Korea. Taking effect immediately, the Act placed the Monetary Board, the supreme policy-making body of the Bank of Korea, under the direct authority of the Governor of the Bank instead of the Minister of Finance and Economy. The aim was to consolidate the Bank of Korea as the principal instrument of the country's monetary policy, in charge of setting prime interest rates. The responsibility of the central bank was also narrowed to maintenance of price stability, whereas earlier it had also been responsible for the maintenance of exchange-rate stability and regulation of the financial system. The Ministry of Finance and Economy (MOFE) was to retain the authority over macroeconomic and broad financial policy and license the establishment of financial institutions. Indeed, such a restructuring was seen to be critical to breaking the nexus between monetary policy and supervision of financial institutions – which was one of the factors allowing situations like the Hanbo scandal to persist for so long.[63]

The reform bills further consolidated all financial sector supervision (for banks, non-bank financial institutions, insurance and securities markets) in a single and independent (albeit interim) Financial Supervisory Commission (FSC) established in April 1998.[64] The FSC, separate from the government, was established to function as a neutral and independent supervisory and policy-making body, besides playing a central role in financial restructuring (World Bank 1999). The FSC's immediate priority was to ensure capital adequacy guidelines were met and risk management and accounting standards improved. To perform its duties effectively, the FSC was given considerable powers to impose civil and criminal liabilities on directors of financial institutions, including the powers to impose sanctions on external auditors and examiners of supervisory authorities for neglect of duties. Also, under the FSC supervision, a sub-committee called the Securities and Futures Commission (SFC) was created to provide for the orderly functioning of the financial market. The reform bills also strengthened the deposit insurance system. In April 1998, the FSC merged all deposit insurance protection agencies into a newly established body: the Korea Deposit Insurance Corporation (KDIC).[65] The KDIC not only authorized funds for capital injection and deposit loss coverage for ailing financial institutions, but also required the submission of rehabilitation plans by 12 commercial banks that did not meet the 8 per cent capital adequacy ratios. Mathews (2001, 164) notes that the FSC "revealed that it had teeth when in July 1998, only three months after its establishment, it ordered the closure of five non-viable commercial banks, and gave seven further banks 'conditional approvals' requiring them to undergo substantial restructuring, including replacement of senior management."

Corporate sector reforms were explicitly designed to reform the *chaebols* by (1) reducing their high debt/equity ratios, (2) ending intra-group debt guarantees, (3) requiring *chaebols* to divest themselves of non-profitable activities, and (4) requiring transparency of balance-sheets through the enforcement of independent external audits, full disclosure and consolidated statements for all conglomerates, including the publication and dissemination of key economic and financial data – giving them until 2000 to comply. In the area of economic liberalization, the IMF urged Korea to open up the economy rapidly and completely – with open trade in commodities, services, intellectual property rights and foreign exchange. In fact, under the arrangement trade was to be liberalized by setting a timetable in line with World Trade Organization commitments to eliminate trade-related subsidies. Capital flows were to be completely opened and the capital account transactions substantially liberalized. Specifically, the capital account was to be liberalized by opening up the Korean money, bond and equity markets to capital inflows and liberalizing foreign direct investment. Labor-market reform, including wage-cuts and flexible layoffs, was also required to facilitate the redeployment of labor.

However, the IMF-mandated program, in simultaneously pursuing structural reform and foreign-exchange market stabilization, posed a fundamental dilemma. Specifically, in order to stabilize the foreign-exchange market in the short run, contractionary fiscal and monetary policies were needed. On the other hand, expansionary policies were required to alleviate the pains from the credit crunch that inevitably accompanied structural reform. As it turned out, although the IMF program helped to restore some measure of international investor confidence, it also produced severe negative economic shocks. In particular, the very tight macroeconomic policies (designed to restore stability in the financial and exchange markets), contributed to the substantial contraction of bank credit and extreme stress in the corporate sector. Further, devaluation and high interest rates produced recession and inflation. Consumer prices rose from an annual rate of 4.5 per cent in 1997 to roughly 20 per cent during the first two months of 1998; unemployment increased sharply from 0.5 million to 1.3 million; and the exchange rate, which had dropped to near 2,000 won per US dollar on December 24, 1997, improved only modestly, fluctuating around 1,600 to 1,700 won per dollar in mid-January 1998. Moreover, as banks became reluctant to provide new loans to firms in order to meet their Basle requirements, the number of bankrupt firms jumped from one thousand per month in September 1997 to three thousand per month by December 1997 – taking an indiscriminate toll on both weak and healthy firms alike (Suh 1998, 5). In turn, company bankruptcies led to the insolvency of financial institutions and scared off foreign investors, decreasing the inflow of foreign capital.

Even as the IMF program was being implemented, Jeffrey Sachs (1997a) pointed out (and in hindsight, correctly) that, in the case of Korea, there was no need for such excessively tight monetary and fiscal policy, since Korea's macroeconomic policy was sound, with "the budget in balance, inflation is low, the savings rate is high, and the economy is poised for export growth." According to Sachs, the IMF gravely misjudged the Korean crisis by equating it with the Mexican peso crisis. However, while Korea and Mexico suffered from the same liquidity crisis, the causes of the crisis were not the same. In the case of Mexico, it was profligate spending and consumption, while in Korea it was highly leveraged investment burdened with short-term debts. By applying the same prescriptions as it did during the peso crisis, the IMF severely aggravated the Korean crisis. Because of this miscalculation, the sharp increases in interest rates failed to stabilize the exchange rate – which quickly depreciated far below the targets set in the IMF program. In agreement with Sachs, Kihwan Kim (2000, 204), also adds that the IMF's decision to release its funds in small increments was shortsighted "as foreign banks judged these amounts to be altogether inadequate, particularly for Korea's need to meet its short-term obligations." No wonder, then, the foreign banks "accelerated the withdrawals of their funds from Korea, thus pushing the country to the verge of a sovereign default in less than 10 days after the initial agreement was signed" (Kihwan Kim 2000, 204). Both Sachs and Kihwan Kim note that the IMF's excessively high interest-rate policy had disastrous consequences (also see Yoo and Moon 1999; In-June Kim and Rhee 1998). The high interest rates were recommended on the rationale that they would serve to bring in foreign capital and discourage the outflow of funds – thereby stabilizing the exchange rate. However, coupled with the sharp devaluation of the won, the immediate effect of the high interest-rate policy was to increase the debt burden carried by Korean businesses. Given the fact that Korean companies were highly leveraged, the high interest rates drove an usually large number of firms into bankruptcy. Kihwan Kim (2000, 205) points out that the IMF's demand that Korean financial institutions meet their BIS capital adequacy ratio in a very short period of time "resulted in a credit crunch of unprecedented proportions. As all banks and financial institutions were preoccupied with the need to improve their BIS ratios, they not only ceased to make new loans but hurriedly recalled their outstanding loans as well. This, more than anything else, was responsible for the sharp contraction of economic activities during the first three quarters of 1998."

Martin Feldstein (1998, 26–7) also severely criticized the IMF program, arguing that the traditional prescription of budget-deficit reduction and a tighter monetary policy (which together depress growth and raise unemployment) was inappropriate for Korea given the country's balanced budget and a national savings rate that was already one of the highest in the world. He aptly states that Korea was "a case of temporary illiquidity rather than fundamental insolvency . . . what Korea needed was coordinated action by creditor banks to restructure its short-term debts, lengthening their maturity and providing additional temporary credits to help meet the interest obligations . . . Although many of the structural reforms that the IMF included in its early-December program for Korea would probably improve the long-term performance of the Korean economy, they are not needed for Korea to gain access to capital markets." Rather, the IMF's primary task should have been to persuade foreign creditors to continue to lend by rolling over existing loans as they came due. Given the fact that Korea had the advantage of a relatively strong economy, this arguably would not have been very difficult. By highlighting the fact that Korea's lack of adequate foreign-exchange reserves was a temporary shortage, not permanent insolvency, the IMF might have been able to persuade creditors to exercise forbearance.

As was noted earlier, the IMF was able to get the creditors to roll over Korea's debt until March of 1998, including getting banks to reschedule US$21.8 billion of short-term debt into one- to three-year loans. As a result, the share of short-term debt dropped to 30 per cent of the total external debt, and, by the end of March, the level of usable foreign reserves had increased to US$24 billion (Lee and Orr 1999, 100). Moreover, from the IMF's perspective tight monetary policy was needed to restore investor confidence, and high interest rates were necessary (particularly at the outset) to stabilize the exchange rates and restructure the corporate sector. That is, the IMF reasoned that high interest rates were necessary to reduce the excessive financing that was the main culprit for excessive investment by the *chaebols*, and to improve the current-account balance by reducing investment and increasing savings. Indeed, considering the need at the time to stabilize the foreign-exchange market and strengthen the weak won through the introduction of foreign capital and a general improvement in the current-account balance, there seemed little choice other than to follow a high interest-rate policy. Arguably, the high interest rates that the Korean authorities were forced to maintain to encourage the markets to take up the sovereign-guaranteed bonds helped avoid default. Morever, they also facilitated the stabilization of the foreign-exchange market and the rapid restoration of the country's creditworthiness.[66] Regarding monetary policy, the IMF arrangement did achieve its basic objective in curbing the depreciation–inflation spiral.

However, in retrospect, there is little doubt that the IMF's program was too contractionary in the short run, thereby making it very costly to implement structural reform. The IMF, in pursuing tight monetary policies, while simultaneously requesting Korean banks to observe, within a short period of time, the capital adequacy ratio set by the BIS, unleashed problems. Fearful of the penalty they would receive if they could not meet the ratio, banks rushed to withdraw loans from companies, thereby deepening the credit crunch and pushing interest rates up even further. This drove many, including profitable, but highly leveraged, firms into bankruptcy.

Indeed, the increase in the cost of credit raised the firms' debt-service burden so severely that many firms, including some that would have been financially viable under normal circumstances, were driven into bankruptcy.[67] The most severely affected were the medium and small firms. The credit squeeze and excess capacity in industry negatively hit medium and small establishments, as most were heavily dependent on the *chaebols* for business. With the economy rapidly contracting as their big business customers cut back on production and investment, these establishments faced plummeting sales and bankruptcies. As Kwan Kim (2001, 40) notes, "during the first five months of 1998 all but 18 of the 5,239 bankrupted corporations were small firms with fewer than 300 employees. In Korea, small firms employ three times the work force of large companies."

The economic contraction and resultant bankruptcies, in turn, lowered the capital base of banks owing to the losses – which only speeded up foreign banks' collection of loans from the Korean banks, since they became fearful of the growing insolvency of the Korean banks.[68] Moreover, the decision to permit the exchange rate to continue to float, rather than readjusting the pegs to rates deemed defensible, only opened the door to continued market depreciation. No wonder the high interest rates failed to attract foreign capital, as the credit risk involved in the payment of principal was too high, not to mention the fact that it diminished investors' confidence in the economy, as they were concerned that the excessively high rates could push Korea's corporate sector into insolvency. Finally, the high interest-rates policy negatively affected exports – the locomotive of the Korean economy. Kwan Kim (2001, 38) notes that "exports fell over the first seven months under the IMF regime, a decline by 13.9 per cent to $10.1 billion in July 1998 for the third consecutive month. Shipments dipped 3.5 per cent in May and 6.6 per cent in June of the same year." The Korean case vividly highlighted the fact that the gap between domestic and international interest rates is not in itself a sufficient condition for stabilization of the exchange rate through interest arbitrage. Finally, as Sachs has noted, in Korea the budget was balanced, with a slight surplus. Therefore, the IMF prescription of budget cuts (which is the standard way to deal with irresponsible governments running large deficits in their current accounts) was not only inappropriate for Korea, but it also aggravated the crisis. Given this, it is difficult not to agree with the critics that the IMF's fiscal austerity program for Korea was fatally misguided.

Alarmed by the sharp continuous downturn of the economy, the IMF began to rethink its program. It can be argued that the IMF even recognized its mistakes. Hubert Neiss (1998, 22), Director of the IMF's Asia and Pacific Department, argues that the Fund's major macroeconomic projections proved incorrect in the case of Korea because "important decisions in several complex and painful areas had to be made almost overnight and without full information." In any case, the IMF began to soften the stringency of its program. Beginning with the second quarterly review of the standby arrangement, on February 17, 1998, monetary policy was eased. The fiscal target for 1998 was lowered from a surplus of 0.2 per cent of GDP in the original program (including bank restructuring costs) to a deficit of 0.8 per cent of GDP. Although monetary policy was expected to remain tight as long as the exchange-market situation remained fragile, the program, nevertheless, allowed for a gradual decrease in the interest rate and a slight increase in the growth of reserve money. As the won stabilized to the level of 1,350–1,400 won per dollar by the end of April 1998, this enabled the Korean government to lower interest rates below the 20 per cent level – after consultation with the IMF. The program was also broadened to include measures to strengthen the *sahoe anjonmang* ("social safety net") by expanding the unemployment insurance system and increasing labor-market flexibility through public works and other programs, including vocational training, job placement and social protection for the unemployed. As Kang and his co-authors note (2001, 108–9), "to implement these unemployment policy measures, the government spent almost 10 trillion won in 1998 . . . and total labor market-related expenditures expanded to 2.2 per cent of GDP in 1998." In the third quarterly review on the standby arrangement on May 28, 1998, the conditionality of the macroeconomic policies was adjusted in order to counter the recession and to strengthen the structural reform agenda. There was agreement on easing the restrictive monetary and fiscal policy by increasing the target for the budget deficit to 4.0 per cent of GDP. In effect, the high interest-rate policy was terminated, and the real interest rate was left to find its own level. In the fourth review signed on July 28, 1998, the Korean government and the IMF agreed to ease fiscal policy further. In September 1998, in a bold move, the Korean government lowered interest rates, extended more credits to small and medium-sized enterprises, and widened the fiscal deficit to revive the economy – despite criticisms from the IMF that a premature stimulus of the economy might undermine the restructuring process. In the fifth program review, signed on November 18, 1998, the deficit target was further increased to 5 per cent of GDP.

### Economic reforms under Kim Dae-Jung

As has been noted earlier, Korea's three-year standby agreement with the IMF, approved on December 4, 1997, was for a total of US$21 billion, or 950 per cent of Korea's IMF quota. Korea made ten drawings, totaling US$19.5 billion, under the arrangement. The last drawing was made in May 1999, and Korea was eligible to make six further drawings totaling US$1.5 billion. On August 23, 2000, the IMF completed the seventh and eighth reviews under the standby credit for Korea. The IMF's executive board announced that, given the economic recovery, Korea did not intend to draw the funds still available to it (IMF 2000e). In keeping with its intent, Korea's three-year standby arrangement with the IMF expired on December 4, 2000.[69] By then Korea's macroeconomic fundamentals had improved considerably, especially the current-account balances.

The sharp turnaround in current-account balances contributed towards a rapid accumulation of foreign-exchange reserves (from US$20.4 billion in December 1997 to US$52.3 billion on December 15, 1998, and US$65 billion in July 1999), thereby making the Korean economy more resilient to external shocks. Also, by August 1999, the won had appreciated nearly 30 per cent against the US dollar (in nominal terms) since bottoming out in January 1998. Just as impressive, the ratio of short-term debt dropped to 20 per cent of the total debt from more than 40 per cent in 1997, and the won–dollar exchange rate significantly declined from a high of 1,962 won on December 23, 1997 to around 1,200 for most of 1999. By March 1999, interest rates had dropped significantly from above 20 per cent to single-digit rates, and in the first quarter of 1999, total FDI was about US$2 billion – a 250 per cent increase over the first quarter of 1998. By mid-1999, unemployment had been reduced to 8 per cent (still high by Korean standards) and inflation contained. Finally, a wide range of structural reforms have made Korea's economy more competitive and open. Significant progress has been made in stabilizing the financial system, addressing corporate distress, strengthening the institutional framework for corporate governance and financial sector supervision, liberalizing foreign investment, and improving transparency. Korea's V-shaped recovery and reform achievements surpass those in other crisis-affected economies.

Korea's impressive achievements are the result of a combination of factors, including the early resolution of creditor panic, the export-oriented industrial structure, the favorable external economic environment, the expeditious implementation of the IMF-mandated structural reforms – in particular, the implementation of a wide range of structural reforms that addressed the weaknesses that contributed to the crisis, the Korean government's expansionary macroeconomic policies, and Kim Dae-Jung's personal commitment to democracy and economic reform.

Yet Korea's achievements have been seen by some as a vindication of the IMF policies (Chopra *et al.* 2001). No doubt, the Kim Dae-Jung government did more than accept the very tight monetary and fiscal policy measures requested by the IMF to defend the exchange rate. The Kim administration also collaborated with the IMF and the World Bank to devise a wide-ranging and politically difficult structural adjustment program to address the outstanding problems in the financial and corporate sectors and labor markets. Yet such claims only tell part of the story. What is not well known is that Kim Dae-Jung, along with senior government policy-makers, was actively involved in all the eight formal meetings Korean officials held with the IMF during 1998 to review the progress of the programs. They were hardly passive participants, but were actively involved in questioning and shaping the content of the programs. Furthermore, once the policies were agreed to, Kim Dae-Jung took an active interest to see to their effective implementation. Suffice it to note, if policies are to be effectively implemented, this requires commitment from the political leadership. Kim Dae-Jung's unequivocal anti-*chaebol* world-view and strong belief that "the economic crisis in South Korea was due to the collusive relationship between the government and business, the state-controlled financial sector, and the octopus-like overexpansion of the big business conglomerates" explains the zeal and determination with which his administration has attempted to reform the Korean economy.[70] Moreover, the fact that Kim Dae-Jung brought to his administration a number of key advisors with strong anti-establishment views greatly strengthened his capacity to move ahead with difficult reform measures.

The Kim Dae-Jung administration's achievements are all the more impressive in light of the fact that the conditions surrounding Kim Dae-Jung's electoral victory did not appear particularly auspicious for effective crisis management or for the formulation and implementation of reformist macroeconomic policies. Kim Dae-Jung ran as an unsuccessful presidential candidate three times, in 1971, 1987 and 1992, before he finally won the office of president on December 18, 1997. However, the margin of his victory was paper-thin. With 80.7 per cent of all qualified voters participating, Kim Dae-Jung received 40.3 per cent, Lee Hoi Chang 38.7 per cent, Rhee In-Je 19.2 per cent, and the labor leader Kwon Young-Gil 1.2 per cent of the votes. Thus, Kim Dae-Jung's victory over Lee Hoi Chang was only about 391,000 votes out of the over 26 million votes cast (Oh 1999, 231). Moreover, Kim Dae-Jung's party, the National Conference for New Politics (NCNP), remained essentially a minor party in the National Assembly, with only 78 of the institution's 299 seats. On the other hand, Lee Hoi Chang's Grand National Party (GNP) controlled a comfortable majority in the parliament, with 161 seats. However, Kim's victory was possible because of a split within the ruling party and an unlikely alliance between Kim Dae-Jung's NCNP and the conservative Kim Jong Pil and his United Liberal Democrats (ULD).[71] However, the ULD delegation held only 42 seats, "and so to further buttress the coalition's parliamentary standing the Kim government also engaged in efforts to get members of the GNP to defect" (Hong Nack Kim 2000, 895). Such actions, coupled with the NCNP's marriage of convenience, raised the possibility of intra-coalitional conflict and gridlock. Indeed, from his first day in office, Kim Dae-Jung's ruling coalition faced a divided government, with the former ruling Grand National Party (GNP) holding a legislative majority. It was only in September 1998 that the ruling coalition secured a majority in the National Assembly "by enticing a large number of opposition lawmakers to defect" (Hong Nack Kim 2000, 895).

Given these formidable challenges, what explains why the Kim Dae-Jung administration was relatively successful in implementing measures to reform the Korean economy and the *chaebols*, where his predecessors had failed? No doubt, while economic crises coupled with externally-driven pressures (such as the IMF mandates) provide opportunities to implement major reforms, in the case of Korea, there is consensus that Kim Dae-Jung skillfully used every opportunity to pursue reforms. As Haggard (2000, 101) notes, "Kim Dae-Jung was able to make substantial progress on his program by exploiting the crisis and his political assets wisely at the outset of his administration."[72] For a start, as the perennial political outsider Kim Dae-Jung had little problem in portraying himself as a man of the common people, who was above the fray of partisan politics, and who represented the aspirations and interests of the working people against the sectarianism and self-interested machinations of traditional politicians. In fact, of the key party leaders, only Kim Dae-Jung could completely distance himself from the discredited Kim Young-Sam, and indeed, from earlier governments. This he did with great deftness. Second, Kim Dae-Jung's international reputation as a champion of human rights and democracy served him well. As Bridges (2001, 41) notes, Kim Dae-Jung's warm relations with world leaders, including President Clinton, the Japanese prime minister Hashimoto Ryutaro and the financier George Soros "worked wonders in transforming international perceptions of Kim Dae-Jung in a favorable direction."

Perhaps more importantly, Kim Dae-Jung's robust in-charge approach and decisive actions during the interim period between his election (December 18, 1997) and inauguration (February 25, 1998), inspired confidence and greatly diminished the perception that there was a power vacuum at the center during the transition period. For example, just two days after the election, Kim Young Sam and Kim Dae-Jung met and formed a joint 12-member Emergency Economic Committee (ECC). Haggard (2000, 101) notes that "For the two months before the inauguration, this body made up of six members from the outgoing and incoming governments but effectively under the president-elect's control, served as the de facto economic cabinet." Kim's coalition (NCNP and ULD) and the majority GNP also agreed to convene a special session of the National Assembly to deal with a series of reform bills required under both the original IMF program and its December 24 revision. Not only did these institutional arrangements provide effective leadership during the immediate crisis period, but Kim Dae-Jung also used this transition period to push through important financial reform legislation that had been stalled under the previous government.

Moreover, the president-elect cooperated with the outgoing government and ruling party to get legislative backing for several important reform measures. In particular, the delegation of substantial powers to the newly-created Financial Supervisory Commission (FSC) greatly enhanced the government's powers. The FSC, in exercising *de facto* control over the entire banking system, including control over the allocation of credit, provided the government with substantial leverage over the *chaebols*. Finally, unlike his immediate predecessor, Kim Dae-Jung turned out to be decisive, and with a clear grasp of the causes of the crisis. His apt observation that "past government failures" and the "collusive links between companies and politicians" lay at the heart of Korea's crisis resonated with the Korean public (Dae-Jung 1998, 280). Fully cognizant of this, Kim Dae-Jung shrewdly exploited the intense unpopularity of the *chaebol* management and the *chaebols'* financial weakness to formulate and implement an ambitious agenda of corporate restructuring. In fact, well before his inauguration, Kim Dae-Jung reached an agreement with *chaebol* leaders regarding plans to restructure and reform their companies. He outlined an ambitious program to achieve his desired goals. As Mathews (2001, 166) notes, Kim Dae-Jung "showed that he meant business by calling a meeting of the country's top five business leaders – the heads of the leading *chaebol* – in January 1998, only three weeks after his election and six weeks before his inauguration, to secure their agreement to a binding five-point undertaking." The agreement committed the *chaebols* to: (1) producing consolidated balance sheets, prepared according to international accounting standards, (2) terminating the cross-divisional payment guarantee system for raising loans, (3) requiring affiliates to perform profitably, and merging or divesting those that are not profitable, (4) promoting partnerships between the *chaebol* and small and medium-sized enterprises, (5) committing the *chaebol* leaders to place their personal wealth into their companies to improve their equity base.[73] Thus, Tan (2000, 197) notes that "much of the improvement in South Korea's economic performance was due to the dogged determination of President Kim Dae-Jung to force economic reforms on the *chaebols* and the country's ailing banks."

Bridges (2001, 73–81), has noted that Kim Dae-Jung used both the "carrot" and the "stick" strategies to reform the *chaebols*. Immediately following inauguration, the Kim Dae-Jung government pushed for revision of the Outside Auditor Law to facilitate the adoption of consolidated financial statements and to require that all firms establish an "outside auditor selection committee" and report combined financial statements in accordance with international standards, beginning in 1999 (Sunhyuk Kim 2000, 167). Furthermore, since cross-guarantees allowed loss-making affiliates and subsidiaries with *chaebol* groups to continue to borrow from banks and drain financial resources from healthier firms, on April 1, 1998 the government (1) prohibited any new intra-*chaebol* mutual payment guarantees and ordered the phasing-out of the existing guarantees by March 2000, and (2) directed banks to negotiate financial restructuring agreements with *chaebol* groups to reduce any outstanding debts, including closing insolvent firms. No doubt, the government's commitment to introduce internationally accepted accounting practices, including independent external audits, full disclosure, and submission of consolidated statements by conglomerates, will help to improve the transparency of corporate balance-sheets.

Despite the various attempts by *chaebols* to undermine, if not sabotage, the reform efforts, the administration's steadfast commitment to reform did not falter. On the contrary, the government, both symbolically and literally also played hard-ball by "using the stick." For example, since the restructuring of the top 5 *chaebols* was viewed as too complex for either the courts or the banks by themselves, the government required them to restructure "on their own" through "voluntary capital structure improvement plans" (CSIPs) that were agreed by the banks, the government and the *chaebols*. However, by September 1998 – after several rounds of delays by the top 5 *chaebols* in submitting their revised CSIPs – the government issued an ultimatum. Failure to move on their restructuring plans would result in credit sanctions. Moreover, the government began to "increase pressure on the top 5 *chaebols* to engage in what became known as the 'big deals' – or the idea that the *chaebol* should reduce their level of horizontal diversification and concentrate on their 'core businesses'" (World Bank 1999, 103). Under this program, the five largest *chaebols* agreed to swap major lines of business among themselves to consolidate excessive and duplicative investments while simultaneously achieving greater economies of scale and "industrial rationalization."[74] As Meredith Woo-Cumings (2001, 367–8) observes, "the democratic government of Kim Dae Jung did not shy away from using strong-arm tactics to bring about the desired results. When LG Group decided to pull out in the midst of merger negotiations, objecting to Hyundai taking the controlling share, the Financial Supervisory Commission immediately called in LG Group's creditors to discuss punitive measures, including immediate suspension of credit and recall of existing loans. On top of that, the government threatened to conduct a tax probe."

In the end, LG Group agreed to the merger, relinquishing management control and selling its semiconductor business to Hyundai. Similarly, Samsung was encouraged to sell its automotive operations to Daewoo. Other "big deals" included the sale of Hyundai and Samsung power-generation businesses and Samsung's ship-engine operations to Korea Heavy Industries, the acquisition of Hanwha's oil-refining operations by Hyundai, the merger of Samsung, Daewoo and Hyundai's aerospace operations, and the merger of Samsung General Chemicals and Hyundai petrochemicals. Some of these deals were accomplished at the cost of some of the *chaebols'* (in particular, Hyundai and Daewoo) taking on substantial additional debt to finance the acquisition. While there have been improvements in the area of transparency, and debt-reduction and the cross-debt guarantees among *chaebol* affiliates in unrelated industries have been reduced, it remains to be seen if the "big deal" concept reduces the surplus capacity or improves competitiveness. Negotiations have been plagued by sharp differences over the valuation of assets, problems about how the different operations can be effectively integrated, and uncertainty over the final corporate form the new entities would take. Also, the proposed swaps will require huge public funds to enable creditor banks to swap debt for equity, and therefore have the potential of "giving the *chaebols* back door access to public funds to reduce their large debts" (Tan 2000, 195). Despite these challenges, the government has been modestly successful in getting the *chaebols* to change their owner-ship structure by separating ownership from management. Furthermore, there has been reform in *chaebol* corporate governance through consolid-ated financial statements, independent external audits and reduction of intra-group mutual payment guarantees. *Chaebols* have also streamlined their operations by reducing their excessive leverage and consolidating their many operations in a few core competencies. Some have also reduced their debt burden and increased their profitability.

In December 1998, the top 5 *chaebols* finally submitted their revised CSIPs. These were approved by the government and the lead banks in January 1999. The top 5 *chaebols* agreed to: (1) reduce the debt-to-equity ratio to 200 per cent by the end of 2000; (2) be subject to sanctions if they failed to meet the deadline; (3) reduce the number of subsidiaries and affiliates and remove existing cross-guarantees between subsidiaries engaged in different lines of business; and (4) raise new equity and sell off affiliates. While the implementation of these measures is to be spread over the next several years, the government, to its credit, has been aggressively following up on them. By the end of 1998, the top 5 *chaebols* reduced their combined debt-to-equity ratio to 386 per cent, down from 470 per cent at the end of 1997. Overall, the CSIP implementation review (released in the first quarterly review for January–March 1999) reported that while the top 5 made satis-factory progress in reducing cross-debt guarantees and improving corporate governance standards, they were still lagging behind in meeting their pledges on asset sales, divestitures, foreign capital inducement and debt reduction. The review also noted that while LG and SK (formerly Sunkyung) made important progress in improving their capital structure and debt–equity ratios via asset sales and strategic alliances with foreign investors, Daewoo (Korea's second largest *chaebol*) and Hyundai had not. Rather, Hyundai increased its debt to 79 trillion won (US$66 billion)[75] in 1998, and its debt/equity ratio at the end of 1998 rose to 769 per cent – excluding asset revalua-tions (World Bank 1999, 106).

At the end of 1998, the Daewoo group had 37 affiliates and 253 overseas units. Among the affiliates, Daewoo Corporation, Daewoo Heavy Industry, Daewoo Motor and Daewoo Electronics accounted for 82 per cent of the group's total assets. The 37 affiliates employed over 96,000 people. How-ever, Daewoo imprudently assumed some 17 trillion won in additional debt in 1998. Thus, Daewoo's debt-to-equity ratio increased sharply from 474 per cent at the end of 1997 to 527 per cent at the end of 1998 and to 588 per cent at the end of June 1999. By July 1999 it became clear that Daewoo could no longer continue to roll over its considerable short-term debt burden. Clearly, the prolonged and ultimately unsuccessful negotiations with both foreign and domestic groups regarding restructuring led Daewoo to near bankruptcy in mid-1999.[76] Compounding this, Daewoo's failure to address core problems, including acquiring debt-laden Ssangyong, further increased its debt to equity ratio. No doubt, Daewoo presented the government with the substantial dilemma of being "too big to fail." Fearing that systemic risk from a Daewoo bankruptcy could undermine financial stability, the government urged creditors to roll over Daewoo's short-term debt. However, the urging proved insufficient. Finally, under growing pressure to save Daewoo, the government stepped in to work with creditors to prepare an emergency financing package (worth US$14 billion) predicated on a substantial re-structuring plan. As part of the package, Daewoo was required to adopt an accelerated restructuring program, including asset sales, raising of more equity, debt-for-equity swaps and a break-up of the *chaebol* into several independent corporate entities. Daewoo was also required to put up new collateral of 10 trillion won, including 1.3 trillion won of Daewoo Chairman Kim Woo-Chung's personal shareholdings – which creditors would be free to sell if Daewoo failed to live up to its commitments under the agreed restructuring and financing plan. In spite of all this assistance, Daewoo could not be saved. With roughly US$80 billion in debt, Daewoo went bust in late 1999 – resulting in the largest corporate bankruptcy in South Korea's history. No doubt, the decision by the Kim Dae-Jung government to let Daewoo fail emphatically demonstrated that the government was prepared to make difficult decisions and that no *chaebol* now was "too big to fail." The ability of creditors to force a number of large *chaebol* into receivership and to take control of Daewoo should help deter imprudent corporate investments in the future.

Arguably, with the Daewoo mess on his mind, President Kim made a forceful address to the nation on the 54th anniversary of National Libera-tion on 15 August 1999. He stated that "without restructuring the corpor-ate giants, the *chaebol*, the most problematic element in our economy, the economic reforms cannot be completed . . . I am determined to go down in Korea's history as a President who first accomplished corporate reforms" (Kim Dae-Jung, 1999, 533). Soon after, a second agreement was reached between the top five *chaebols*, the government and the creditor banks. Under the terms, the *chaebols* agreed to a series of potentially far-reaching reforms, including increased transparency, greater accountability and inde-pendent subsidiaries with professional managers in control. The agreement also poses a real threat to founding family control of the *chaebols* by requir-ing enforcement on inheritance tax, among other things.

As for the sixth to the sixty-fourth *chaebols* (or the so-called 6–64 *chaebols*), restructuring has been carried forward through the "voluntary workout program." These workouts have been nominally organized around the so-called London rules, a voluntary extra-judicial process under which banks reschedule debt obligations in return for restructuring plans that include asset sales, closure of business lines, and other operational and organizational restructuring measures. To address the debt overhang problem of the most troubled *chaebols*, a Corporate Restructuring Agreement (CRA) was signed in June 1998 by some 200 Korean banks and non-bank financial institutions which committed them to follow agreed workout procedures. These procedures included the appointment of eight lead banks to negotiate the workouts with the major corporate groups, and the establishment of an arbitration and quality-control body in the form of the Corporate Restructuring Co-ordination Committee (CRCC). The CRCC, besides helping resolve disputes among creditors or between creditors and debtors, also has the authority to act as an arbitration committee in the case that the banks cannot agree on a workout strategy among themselves, or when the lead bank and the debtor fail to come to an agreement. The FSC monitors the workouts agreed under the CRA to ensure consistency with the guidelines issued for the workouts. If a CRA signatory fails to comply with an approved workout agreement or a CRCC arbitration decision, the CRCC can impose penalties. Between June 1998 and mid-1999, some 90 companies had applied to the formal workout program within the CRCC (Lieberman 1999). Despite these accomplishments, a large number of companies are still in deep distress, and several are close to insolvency. Much of the corporate sector remains highly leveraged by international standards and continues to suffer from low profitability.

Unlike what happened in Indonesia or Thailand, bank closures in Korea did not result in a massive flight of depositors. In January 1997, the authorities introduced a deposit insurance scheme funded by low-premium contributions from banks. The scheme provided for full coverage of all deposits not exceeding 20 million won per individual depositor. In mid-November 1997, the government announced that it would guarantee all deposits of financial institutions until the end of 2000. The blanket deposit guarantee succeeded in reassuring depositors – despite the delays in repaying depositors at the start of the process. Nevertheless, since one of the main sources of corporate failure in Korea was the weak financial system, financial institutions have assumed a leading role in corporate restructuring.

In early 1998 the Kim Dae-Jung administration amended the bankruptcy laws simplifying legal proceedings for corporate rehabilitation and bankruptcy filing, streamlining provisions for non-viable firms to exit markets, and improving credit bank representation during resolution. In the first round of financial sector restructuring, the government committed 64 trillion won (roughly US$53 billion) in April 1998 to recapitalize financial institutions, pay deposit and credit claims of bankrupt institutions, and reduce the level of non-performing loans. When most of this fund had been exhausted by the end of 1999, the government's commitments for financial sector restructuring had reached 74 trillion won. In early December 2000, an additional 40 trillion won (US$33 billion) of public funds was approved to complete the second round of financial sector restructuring (IMF 2000f). Second, in December 1997, following portfolio reviews of merchant banks and their rehabilitation programs, the government closed 14 merchant banks and required the other 16 to follow a timetable to achieve capital adequacy ratios of at least 6 per cent by the end of June 1998 and 8 per cent by the end of June 1999. Of the 26 commercial banks, two institutions (Korea First Bank and Seoul First), accounting for 40 per cent of commercial bank assets, were quickly sold off. In January 1998, in a dramatic show of its commitment, the Kim government nationalized Korea First and Seoul and sold them to foreign investors. The 12 banks that failed to meet the capital requirements were either merged into healthier banks or recapitalized with government fiscal support (World Bank 1999, 17). In May 1998, it was agreed that the restructuring of non-bank financial institutions (NBFIs) such as securities houses, investment trust companies, leasing companies and insurance companies were to be carried out under the responsibility of the major shareholders. However, if the institution's liabilities exceeded its assets, the institution is to be ordered to reinstate its financial strength through measures such as recapitalization or merger. However, if it still fails to meet the minimum capital adequacy requirements, then the Financial Supervisory Commission (FSC) – which succeeded the bank supervisory function from the Bank of Korea – could decide to suspend its operation and transfer assets and liabilities to another institution. The FSC can do this, since it has operational autonomy and can license and de-license financial institutions.

In May 1998, a group of creditor banks established a formal review committee to assess the viability of 313 client firms with weak capital structure. The committee have agreed no longer to extend credit to insolvent firms, and to prevent bailouts from affiliated companies. Further, in June 1998, 5 out of the 33 commercial banks deemed non-viable were allowed to be acquired by 5 stronger banks, while 7 undercapitalized banks were required either to merge with healthy banks or to arrange mergers among the undercapitalized banks with government assistance. The FSC ordered the five non-viable banks to undergo a "transfer of businesses" under a purchase and assumption (P&A) arrangement. That is, the government offered incentives for acquiring banks. Under the P&A arrangement, a closed bank could transfer only performing assets to an acquiring bank, and non-performing loans to the newly established KAMCO or the Korea Asset Management Corporation (to be discussed later). However, if the failed bank's total liabilities exceeded total performing assets, the Korea Deposit Insurance Corporation (KDIC) would pay the difference. In addition, the acquiring bank would be allowed to exercise a put-back option that permitted the bank to resell to KAMCO the non-performing loans that occurred within six months of the P&A transaction. By the end of 1998, the

Kim Dae-Jung administration had committed almost US$50 billion in additional public funds to bank recapitalization, deposit protection and the purchase of non-performing assets. As most merchant banking corporations were forced to exit the market, their number plunged to just four at the end of June 2001 from 30 at the end of 1997. Also, seven securities companies, seven investment trust management companies, 11 insurance companies, and 118 mutual savings and finance companies were also liquidated or merged during the same period.

While these measures have brought a modicum of stability to the financial markets, the banking system remains fragile. Many financial institutions are still effectively owned by the government – which is desperately trying to consolidate weak banks under a financial holding company or to merge them with healthier institutions. Further, Korea's financial system remains vulnerable, as an estimated 20 per cent of bank loans are non-performing. As Noland (2001, 2) notes, "on a scale of A to E, with A indicating a system of exceptional financial strength and E indicating a system with very weak intrinsic financial strength and in which many banks will likely require outside support such as from the government, at the end of 2000 the ratings agency Moody's assigned the South Korean banking system an E+, worse than Mexico's and on the same level as China's. Over the long term, since much of the banks' portfolios are tied up in credits to large *chaebols*, viable and profitable companies are critical for the banks' full recovery".

Nevertheless, the Korean government's financial sector restructuring efforts have strengthened banking supervision and regulation and created an environment where market discipline plays an increasingly important role. Notable progress has been made in raising banks' capital ratios – which in a number of cases now exceed the minimum standards recommended by the Bank of International Settlements. Korea is now close to meeting international best practice. In addition, measures have been adopted to strengthen prudential regulations in the areas of loan classification and provisioning, foreign-exchange liquidity, large exposures and connected lending. Recognizing that foreign ownership and management of banks can play an important role in recapitalizing banks, increasing competition in financial markets and improving the overall management of banks, the government approved (in December 1997), full foreign ownership of merchant banks, besides allowing non-resident purchases of equity in banks and other financial institutions.

To deal with the non-performing loans problems, and in particular to minimize the impact on creditors (i.e. companies that borrowed from these banks), the government established a "bridge merchant bank," Hanareum Banking Corporation (HMBC) in December 1997 to assume all deposits and selected liabilities and to accept in payment the "good" financial assets of the suspended merchant banks. The HMBC was only temporarily to assume some of the debt held by the suspended banks, until they could be liquidated, merged or sold. Moreover, the Korean government did not directly commit resources to recapitalize merchant banks in view of their small size and the fact that many are owned by *chaebols*. Rather, any assets and liabilities remaining after the transfer to HMBC were sent for bankruptcy.

To deal specifically with the problem of increasing non-performing loans, the government established a special institution in November 1997, the Korea Asset Management Corporation (KAMCO), modeled after the Resolution Trust Corporation in the United States. Like the Resolution Trust Corporation during the US savings and loans crisis, KAMCO is designed to deal with the resolution of bad loans of commercial banks and merchant banking corporations. Specifically, KAMCO operates by purchasing non-performing assets from banks and merchant-banking corporations. KAMCO buys bad loans according to a rough estimate of the discount price – which varies from 30 per cent for loans with collateral to 80 per cent for those without. After a through assessment of the market value of the loans, KAMCO settles with the bank to account for the differences between the initial purchasing price and the new assessment price, if any. Also, KAMCO is empowered to purchase impaired assets (such as collateralized non-performing loans) from all financial institutions covered by the deposit guarantee and sell them off to domestic and foreign bidders. By December 12, 1997, the funds initially available to KAMCO amounted to 20 trillion won, with 3 trillion won provided by the Bank of Korea and other financial institutions, and the reminder obtained by bond-issuance. In order to enhance transparency, KAMCO is required to audit and publish its accounts on a semi-annual basis.

By June 1999 KAMCO had purchased non-performing loans with a face value of 46 trillion won for 20.3 trillion won. It also moved away from its fairly easy stance concerning asset purchases, and, in accordance with the agreement with the IMF, announced that any future asset purchases and disposal of non-performing loans by KAMCO would be made only for those financial institutions whose rehabilitation plans are approved by the FSC. KAMCO injects new capital into the banks in the form of interest-bearing government-backed securities. Its resources are financed by issuing its own bonds of 32.5 trillion won and by disposing of purchased assets through direct sale or asset-backed securities. The KAMCO bailout funds, along with the Korea Deposit Insurance Corporation (KDIC) constitute the fiscal support base of the financial sector restructuring process.

To facilitate liberalization, in April 1999 Korea abolished the regulatory Foreign Exchange Management Act and introduced instead the Foreign Investment and Foreign Capital Inducement Act. The new act effectively eliminated most restrictions on foreign-exchange transactions and on domestic transactions in foreign currencies for businesses and financial institutions. Overall, the new act has greatly improved the business environment for foreign direct investment. For example, under the act, most restrictions on foreign-exchange transactions and on domestic transactions in foreign currencies for businesses and financial institutions have been eliminated. Domestic businesses now have more financing options, such as credit transactions for exports and imports or medium- and long-term foreign borrowing. Korean exporters are now able to establish their own trade-finance corporations, and payments for goods and services within Korea can be made with foreign currency. Beginning in 2001, all remaining foreign-exchange transactions have been liberalized, allowing individuals to deposit their money into foreign-based banks and to buy foreign securities or real estate. In addition, new regions are to be developed and opened to foreign investors. For large investments that entail "significant development benefits for underdeveloped areas," the Korean government will provide infrastructure and basic facilities. FDI in such areas will enjoy tax exemptions. By the end of 1998, restrictions on foreign investment in the equity of domestic companies, foreign takeovers of management, and foreign land ownership had mostly been eliminated. Also, to facilitate investment and prevent selective treatment, the remaining restrictive regulations related to foreign investment have been streamlined and unified into a single legal framework under the Foreign Investment Promotion Act. Indeed, the investment procedures have been greatly simplified. Foreign investors will need to notify only Korean banks or the Korea Trade-Investment Promotion Agency (KOTRA). The Korea Investment Service Center (KISC), set up within KOTRA, will provide a one-stop service for foreign investors. KISC, which has close links with both the central and regional governments, will provide both pre-investment consulting services and post-investment follow-up services.

Finally, increasing flexibility in the labor market is necessary to solve Korea's economic inefficiency. Thus, enhancing labor-market flexibility has been a key goal of Korea's structural reform. Kim Dae-Jung was instrumental in forging corporatist agreements with business, labor and the government in order to get them to work together to resolve the country's financial woes. Arguably, it was Kim Dae-Jung's long history in the opposition, his well-known pro-labor views and his overall populist credentials that enabled him to get Korea's mobilized and militant working-class constituency to accept the austerity requirements of fiscal stabilization. However, once in place, these agreements placed public pressure on both business and labor to make concessions and provided the basis for subsequent legislation. As Yong Cheol Kim and Moon (2000, 62) note, "in order to persuade labor to join the talks, Kim Dae Jung urged big business to share the burden and pain through corporate restructuring and downsizing. Public pressure made it impossible for labor to refuse to join the council. On 14 January [1998] the Labor–Employer–Government Consultative Council was formally launched to ensure a fair burden sharing in coping with the economic crisis."[77] On February 9, 1998 the council announced a "Social Agreement for the Overcoming of the Economic Crisis," reflecting the grand compromise between labor and business on difficult issues concerning layoffs and restructuring. After the successful tripartite consultative negotiations between labor, business and government, the Labor Standards Act was amended by the National Assembly on February 13, 1998. Under the new accord, business promised to ensure transparency in its management and to take prudent measures in laying off its employees. Specifically, the law now provides legal grounds for employment adjustment. The law permits layoffs if a company has duly considered the interests of its workers. Labor, on the other hand, agreed to the implementation of flexible worker layoffs for the purposes of restructuring, and pledged to make every effort to enhance productivity and cooperate with business on wages and working hours. In return, the government has committed itself to strengthening its support programs by providing vocational training and information on re-employment. To adjust labor supply in accordance with changing market environments, new employment options such as temporary work, part-time employment and work at home are being developed. For example, in order to deal with the expected large-scale layoffs from the restructuring process, the government pledged to strengthen and expand the coverage of unemployment insurance.

The government responded by more than tripling its expenditure on social protection. Outlays on social protection were increased from 2.6 trillion won (0.6 per cent of GDP) in 1997 to 9.1 trillion won (2.0 per cent of GDP) in 1999 (World Bank 1999, 35). The budget allocation for the employment insurance fund, including funds for more training and employment stabilization, tripled from 0.7 trillion won to 2 trillion won (Yong Cheol Kim and Moon 2000, 64). Overall, the government committed some 8.4 trillion won in 1998 to fund public work programs and the extended unemployment insurance coverage. In 1999 a total budget of 16 trillion won was allocated for unemployment policies, of which 6.5 trillion won went to create jobs in the private sector, 2.5 trillion won to create public works jobs for 300,000 people, 0.5 trillion won to support firms that retained employees, 1.1 trillion won to support vocational training and job placement, and 5.4 trillion won to support the social safety net (Kang *et al.* 2001, 109). This caused the government budget for social safety nets to increase sharply.[78]

However, what is important to note is that the government did not simply throw money at the social programs, but took precautions to design a social safety-net program that was effective. Specifically, the government used three main instruments of social protection to help the most vulnerable sectors of society: the unemployed, the poor and the elderly. First, it expanded its nascent unemployment insurance program by including all firms (from the original firms with more than 30 employees), shortened the contribution period required for eligibility, and extended the duration of unemployment benefits. This expanded the eligible workforce from 5.7 million workers at the beginning of 1998 to 8.7 million at the end of the year. Beneficiaries increased tenfold, from around 18,000 in January 1998 to

174,000 in March 1999. Yet this still only constituted 10 per cent of the unemployed workforce. Second, since most of Korea's jobless did not benefit from the expansion of unemployment insurance, the government introduced a temporary public work program in May 1998, enrolling 76,000 workers. By January 1999, the program was providing 437,000 jobs. By the first quarter of 1999, the public work program was benefiting around 2.5 times as many people as the unemployment insurance program. Third, in May 1998 the authorities introduced a temporary livelihood protection program with funding to cover 750,000 beneficiaries. It also introduced a means-tested non-contributory social pension for 600,000 elderly people (World Bank 2000d, 167–77). The Korean case shows that the worst-hit victims of the crisis can be sheltered without compromising macroeconomic reforms.

## Concluding observations

In hindsight, a number of lessons can be drawn from the Korean financial crisis. First, it is clear that a well-functioning financial sector and an effective financial supervisory apparatus is critical – especially in this era of capital mobility. Second, prudence is necessary when opening the capital account. As Mexico before it, Korea opened its capital accounts without having in place the necessary supervisory and prudential structures. Third, Korea's experience illustrates the negative consequences of short-term foreign debts and relying heavily on short-term foreign borrowing to finance long-term domestic projects. Fourth, Korean policy-makers and the *chaebols* bear much responsibility for failing to respond to the economic challenges the country was facing. Instead of making massive investments in redundant projects, they should have first made more efforts to upgrade their firms' economic structure through investments in technology and human resource development – and most importantly, to improve their firms' productivity and profitability. Thus the Korean case underscores the proposition that the private sector can make mistakes in its investment decisions. Indeed, the Korean crisis was as much a case of market failure as of government failure. However, this should mean that in their efforts to reform the *chaebols*, the authorities significantly constrict the *chaebols'* freedom of operation. In this era of globalization, the *chaebols* with their international networks, brand names and marketing expertise have the potential to contribute greatly to the Korean economy. Finally, and as noted earlier, the Korean case suggests that the gap between domestic and international interest rates is not in itself sufficient condition for stabilization of the exchange rate through interest arbitrage. In addition, in a country like Korea, where savings rates are already very high, seeking currency stability through high interest rates with the intention of curtailing consumption and boosting savings is subject to severe limits.

Despite the severity of the crisis in Korea, there was little nostalgia for a return to authoritarian rule. The Korean case illustrates the fact that even weak democracies have the capacity to provide critical leadership and deal with major socioeconomic and political challenges. Indeed, as Mo and Moon (1999a, 158) note, "democracy provided unexpected opportunities for economic reform." Because of his longstanding commitment to democracy, Kim Dae-Jung has enjoyed a great deal of goodwill and support from foreign investors and allies (especially the US government), who wanted him to succeed. Domestically, too, democracy gave legitimacy and credibility to the government's reform efforts. Kim Dae-Jung's apparent success in reforming the Korean economy shows that democracy can be compatible with economic reform.

Yet over the long term Korea will need to forge stable political coalitions in favor of reform. This prospect does not seem likely any time soon. The parliamentary elections held on April 13, 2000 once again resulted in a deeply divided parliament, as no party won a majority. The opposition Grand National Party (GNP) won 133 seats – which gave it a plurality in the 273-member National Assembly, but left it 4 seats short of an absolute legislative majority. Kim Dae-Jung's NCNP – whose name was now changed to Millennium Democratic Party (MDP) – came second, with 115 seats and 35.9 per cent of the popular vote. Kim Jong-pil's United Liberal Party (ULD) came third, winning 17 seats. In such an environment, getting working coalitions committed to reform will be difficult. Morever, the various corruption scandals (although neither Kim Dae-Jung nor his family members have been implicated in any) have certainly diminished the presidency, and the popular disillusionment with politics will make it difficult to maintain the public pressure for reform. Yet economic reforms in Korea will remain (for the foreseeable future) a work in progress. Kim Dae-Jung started the progress. As his term runs out in February 2003, it will be up to others to carry on the work his administration embarked on with such determination.

## Notes

1 Kim Dae-Jung as quoted in *Chosun Ilbo* (cited in DeRosa 2001, 133).
2 In Korea, the distribution of total income has been fairly equitable. This has led to a dramatic improvement in living standards. According to the World Bank (2000a), "life expectancy at birth increased from 53.9 years in 1960 to 71.5 years in 1994. The adult literacy rate, already high by Third World standards in 1970 (88 per cent) reached 98 per cent in 1994. The percentage of total population with access to safe water grew from 66 per cent in 1975–80 to 93 per cent in 1990–96. The infant mortality rate (per 1,000 live births) was reduced from 85 in 1960 to 10 in 1994."
3 South Korea became the twenty-ninth member of OECD on December 12, 1996.

4  For details, see World Bank (2000a) and Bustelo (1999, 163). DeRosa (2001, 129–30) aptly notes that "by the middle of the 1990s, South Korea had established a serious competitive foothold against Japan's export-oriented industries, examples being steel milling, shipbuilding, automobile manufacturing, and consumer electronics. South Korean construction companies had a presence everywhere that development was taking place; somehow it seemed that South Korean companies always managed to be the winning bidder for the big projects like airports, hospitals, and public housing. South Korea was beating Japan and the rest of the industrialized countries at their own game."

5  For example, the 3-year corporate bond yield (the benchmark interest rate) declined from an average of 15 per cent during 1990–95 to 12 per cent in 1996. For details, see World Bank (1999).

6  Data are compiled from the Bank of Korea (1998) and Hahm (1999).

7  In the World Bank classification, a country is "less indebted" when the debt/GNP ratio is less than 48 per cent; "moderately indebted" when the ratio is between 48 per cent and 80 per cent; and "severely indebted" when it is over 80 per cent.

8  Jay Choi (2000, 4) notes that "in Korea, the economic planning minister pronounced, as late as November 1997 – several months after Southeast Asia had already fallen and less than a month before Korea had to seek assistance from the IMF – that Korea would not fall because of strong macroeconomic fundamentals."

9  The emergency financing mechanism (EFM) was established in September 1995. The EFM strengthened the IMF's ability to respond quickly in support of a member country facing an external financial crisis and seeking financial assistance from the IMF in support of a strong economic adjustment program.

10  The "first national shame day" was Korea's annexation by Japan in 1910. The quotations are from Nicholas Kristof, *The New York Times*, November 22, 1997, p. B2. It is important to note that all the three political parties and presidential candidates, Rhee In Je, Lee Hoi-Chang (the ruling party candidate) and the long-time dissident, Kim Dae-Jung (who was slow to embrace the IMF package), all finally acceded to the IMF demands. In fact, because the crisis occurred in the middle of the presidential election campaign, the IMF made a very unusual request for a written endorsement of the IMF program from the three major presidential candidates. All three endorsed the program. Kim Dae-Jung was elected president for a five-year term on December 18, 1997.

11  The concept of "reputational externalities" was developed by Richard Zeckhauser (1986).

12  *Chaebols* are conglomerates of many companies clustered around one holding company. The parent company is usually controlled by one family. That is, the company founder and his family on average own about 10 per cent, and through cross-shareholdings control another 30 per cent to 40 per cent, of the group member firms in the top thirty *chaebols*. In 1998, the top 40 *chaebols* grouped a total of 671 companies.

13  In a televised speech given on 6 January 1995, President Kim Young-Sam stated, "Fellow citizens, globalization is the shortcut which will lead us to building a first-class country in the 21st century. This is why I revealed my plan for globalization and the government has concentrated all of its energy in forging

ahead with it. It is aimed at realizing globalization in all sectors – politics, foreign affairs, economy, society, education, culture and sports. To this end, it is necessary to enhance our viewpoints, way of thinking, system and practices to the world class level . . . we have no choice other than this." (Cited in Samuel S. Kim 2000, 1.)

14 Quote cited in Lie (1998, 43).

15 The large stockholders were mostly big business owners who had been accused of illicit wealth-accumulation.

16 The profitability of commercial banks has been low because the "policy loans" they were obliged to extend were at rates that were lower than prime rates.

17 It is important to note that while "there were a large number of foreign banks – about 80 in the 1990s – they operated under restrictions on branching at least until the late 1980s. This meant that the government-owned commercial banks tended to dominate domestic financial transactions" (Ariff and Khalid 2000, 62).

18 The so-called "policy loans" were offered to private businesses at an interest rate substantially lower (by one-half to one-third) than regular bank loans.

19 Kihwan Kim and Leipziger (1997, 158) note that "the interesting fact about KOTRA is that it was not government financed. It was supported by the exporters themselves, although it was clearly an instrument designed to achieve government objectives."

20 Under *Yushin Honbop* (*Yushin* meaning "revitalizing reforms"), under which the Korean constitution was amended by Park-Chung Hee (in 1972) to strengthen his presidential powers and abolish the limit on presidential tenure.

21 Indeed, the National Investment Fund (NIF) was created in 1974 for the purpose of raising funds. The NIF was funded by the compulsory deposit of savings from pensions, savings and postal savings accounts, and by other purchasers of NIF bonds, such as life insurers.

22 The quotation is from Campos and Root (1996, 91). Also, Amsden (1989, 16) notes that "the sternest discipline imposed by the Korean government on virtually all large size firms – no matter how politically well connected – related to export targets. There was constant pressure from government bureaucrats on corporate leaders to sell more abroad – with obvious implications for efficiency. Pressure to meet ambitious export targets gave the Big Push into heavy industry its frenetic character."

23 Figures are from Haggard and Moon (1990, 218).

24 Figures are from Haggard and Moon (1990, 216).

25 Curb market loans were from outside the legal financial institutions, and were considered illegal by the Korean government. Curb market loans were popular among businesses when regular financing was unavailable or when businesses wanted a quick loan without extensive paperwork and a quick turnaround time. Curb market loans could come from commercial capital, loan sharks or individuals (Yeon-ho Lee 1997, 147).

26 Although there was a ceiling on the number of shares that could be held by a *chaebol* group, the top 30 *chaebol* owned about 30 per cent of the total outstanding shares in the banking sector in 1988. For details see Chung H. Lee (2000).

27 In its effort to distance itself from the Park regime, the Chun government attacked the *chaebols* for gross inefficiency and corruption, and made reforming

the *chaebols* a top priority (Haggard and Moon 1990, 226). However, as Beck (1998, 1019) notes, "when Chun Doo-hwan seized power in 1980, he threatened to prosecute the *chaebols'* owners for illicit wealth accumulation. A few groups were forcibly restructured or dissolved, but in the end the effort failed. Chun's democratically elected successors, Roh Tae-Woo and Kim Young-sam, also pledged to take on the *chaebol*, only to experience similar results."

28  The DLP now controlled 217 of the 299 seats in the National Assembly.

29  President Kim not only won a convincing victory over his principal opponent, Kim Dae-Jung; he was also less indebted for his power to the various factions of the party. Not surprisingly, the twenty-five-member Kim cabinet had new faces who were "progressive outsiders" and "reform-oriented men and women" (Oh 1999, 131).

30  The NBFIs were established in the 1970s to reduce the importance of the informal credit markets. They were allowed greater freedom in their management of assets and liabilities and could apply higher interest rates on deposits and loans than could banking institutions.

31  Although an accurate measurement of the size of the Curb market is difficult, estimates suggest that in the mid-1990s the total lending in the Curb market was between 2 and 5 per cent of the total loans of the formal financial sector. In contrast, in the mid-1970s, the Curb market was estimated to account for more than one-third of all credit extended in the economy. As was noted earlier, Curb market loans are characterized by high interest rates and risks – to satisfy the credit demands of individual households and small and medium-size firms that have been excluded from the formal credit market (Balino and Ubide 1999, 11).

32  Although specialized banks can borrow from the government, deposits constitute their main source of funding. Funding for development banks, which are wholly government-owned, comes mainly from government-guaranteed bonds (Balino and Ubide 1999, 9).

33  The market share of banking institutions for Korean won deposits fell from 71 per cent in 1980 to 32 per cent in 1996, while that of NBFIs increased from 29 per cent to 68 per cent (H. Smith 1998, 73).

34  Specifically, Kim Young Sam's merger of the Economic Planning Board (EPB) and the Ministry of Finance (MOF) into a super-ministry, the MOFE, did not bring policy coherence. While the "MOF segment within the MOFE consistently warned of the danger of foreign exchange and financial crises and urged immediate counter-measures including IMF rescue financing . . . the EPB segment, which dominated the MOFE decision-making machinery, ignored MOF warnings by pointing out the 'fundamental health' of macroeconomic indicators. If the MOF had remained as a separate bureaucratic agency, the liquidity crisis could have been avoided" (Moon and Rhyu 2000, 94).

35  Joining the OECD requires, as a precondition, free capital markets.

36  Before the deregulation, the top 15 *chaebols* were not allowed to own and control life insurance companies, while the next top 15 *chaebols* were allowed to have only up to a 50 per cent ownership of life insurance companies. However, by May 1996, all *chaebol* but the top 5 were allowed to own or control life insurance companies. Also, before the deregulation only the commercial banks could own investment trust companies. However, in early 1996 the restriction was lifted.

37 It is important to note that short-term borrowing rates were lower than long-term rates, and short-term funds could be raised relatively easily through the international money markets. This resulted in domestic banks channeling external short-term funds to long-term loans financing investments by domestic corporations.

38 The economic policy that put the first priority on the competitiveness of the export sector forced the monetary authority to intervene frequently in the market and to maintain stable exchange rates. During the first half of the 1990s, the real effective exchange rate of the Korean won had depreciated, unlike the currencies of the other crisis countries, partly owing to the appreciation of the Japanese yen during the period and the government's policy of supporting the export sector.

39 Kyung-Hwan Kim (2000, 107), notes that "unlike those in Japan, Thailand, or Indonesia, Korean financial institutions had been prohibited from lending to finance real estate purchases except for land for new housing. This regulation was repealed in January 1998, right after the economic crisis began. Due to this and other regulations, Korea's exposure to real estate was relatively small." However, this does not mean that the *chaebols* did not engage in land speculation. E. C. S. Kang (2000, 89) notes that "in the period 1985–95, land prices increased by 250 per cent, with industrial land prices increasing even more, by 310 per cent. This rapid increase in prices was driven largely by investments by the *chaebol*, which could not find a more productive use for their money, much of it borrowed. The *chaebol* bought land to use as collateral and a hedge against inflation. Indeed, they bid up the land prices to offset the interest rates on their bank loans."

40 According to a recent report by the Korea International Trade Association, the foreign-exchange earnings ratio of Korean exports, which is defined as the ratio of value-added created net of export-induced import to the total value added, started to decline continuously from the peak of 67.9 per cent in 1989 to the level of 55.9 per cent in 1997 (Pyo 2000, 20).

41 Bustelo (1999, 167) notes that in Korea, "total labor costs increased at an average annual rate of 8.2 per cent between 1985 and 1995, a period in which labor productivity grew substantially less, at 6.5 per cent."

42 Until the mid-1980s, Korea had enjoyed cheap labor costs compared with competing countries such as Hong Kong, Singapore and Taiwan. However, the rapid rise in wages after 1987 increased unit labor costs, and Korea could no longer count on cheap labor to give the country an edge in international competition. After the democratization of 1987, trade unions were often successful in getting relatively advantageous collective bargaining contracts – and real wages came close to doubling between 1987 and 1997 (Kang *et al.* 2001, 97). During the period 1985–95, unit labor cost in manufacturing increased by 46.0 per cent in Korea, while the corresponding figures were 22.1 per cent in Japan, 25.1 per cent in Taiwan and 4.4 per cent in the United States. The situation became even worse when other countries such as China, Thailand, Malaysia and Indonesia adopted an export-oriented economic strategy. In the process, Korea was sandwiched between the developed countries (with their superior technological base) and the newly-industrializing countries, with their very low wages (Suh 1998, 13). As the dollar became stronger, particularly against the yen,

Korea's export competitiveness suffered, and the country experienced an accelerated increase in its trade deficit.

43  The electronics exports declined from US$43.6 billion in 1995 to US$41.2 billion in 1996, an annual decrease of 5.5 per cent, after 30.4 per cent and 41.1 per cent annual increases in 1994 and 1995 (Yoon 1999, 412).

44  See "Semiconductors: Chips on their Shoulders," *The Economist*, November 1, 1997, p. 62.

45  For example, Samsung spent 4 trillion won building a car-manufacturing plant in Pusan when there was already an excess supply of cars, not only in South Korea, but in the world. With a capacity of 240,000 units per year, it sold only 60,000 units in 1998. Not surprisingly, Samsung Motors lost 156 billion won in the first six months of 1998. Its debt rose to nearly 4 billion won, taking its debt/equity ratio to 555 per cent (Tan 2000, 130–31).

46  Mathews (2001, 161) notes, "why the banks had continued to lend to such a poor risk subsequently became clear: they were being bribed by Hanbo's founder, Chung Tae Soo, to do so. Chung, it turned out, had been indicted twice before for bribery, but somehow had managed to stay in business. Eventually he was forced to default because even the banks, despite the bribes, refused to go on lending to him, and demanded his removal from the company's management. Eventually, the bribery scandals spread, reaching even into the President's office, thus effectively tying the hands of the government at the very moment when strong leadership was called for to stem the mounting crisis."

47  On April 21, the Jinro group faced near-collapse, but was saved from bankruptcy owing to an Anti-Bankruptcy Accord hastily imposed on the creditor institutions by the Korean government to prevent a ripple effect in the economy.

48  Chae-Jin Lee (2000, 190) notes that "the government's crisis management capability during Kim Young Sam's presidency was lacking: when he replaced the chief economic planner (the deputy prime minister) seven times and the senior economic secretary to the president six times in five years, confusion, inconsistency and unpredictability ensued. And rampant corruption, particularly government–business collusion, undermined rational economic decisions."

49  The quotation is from Moon and Rhyu 2000, 91. Also Doowon Lee (2000, 11) notes: "at first, the Korean government repeatedly denied the existence of a crisis. For example, the prime minister assured the National Assembly that the economy was not in trouble. Deputy Prime Minister Kyong-sik Kang mentioned many times that the economy's fundamentals were sufficiently strong and there should be no worry about an economic crisis. In addition, the government refused to reveal the true situation of the economy to the public. A government report inflated the amount of available foreign exchange reserves."

50  Moon and Rhyu (2000, 92) note that "Kim Young Sam failed to ensure bureaucratic and policy stability. Macroeconomic policy instability and the subsequent economic crisis were in fact aggravated by frequent reshuffles of the economic cabinet. During the Kim Young Sam government, deputy prime ministers in charge of finance and the economy were reshuffled seven times for reasons of policy failures such as price instability, current-account deficits and the Hanbo scandal, and their average tenure was less than eight months. It was virtually impossible for the Ministry of Finance and Economy to formulate and implement consistent and coherent economic policy with such a short tenures."

51  KAMCO was first established in 1962 to manage and dispose of bad loans of the state-run Korea Development Bank. Its function has been increasingly expanded over the years, and in November 1997 legislation was passed to entrust KAMCO with the administration of a Non-Performing Asset Management Fund (NPA Fund). The objective of the NPA Fund is to purchase and dispose of non-performing loans of all financial institutions covered by a deposit guarantee as efficiently as possible. In August 1998 the reorganization of KAMCO as a "bad bank" was completed and KAMCO adopted a structure similar to the US Resolution Trust Company.

52  Doowon Lee (2000, 10) notes that "when the Hong Kong stock market collapsed in October 1997, many foreigners thought that Korea would be next."

53  With the collapse of the Thai and Indonesian currencies, a large volume of loans made by Japanese banks to these countries became non-performing. This led the Japanese banks to collect their mature loans from Korea. According to In-June Kim and Rhee (1998, 363), Japanese banks collected short-term lending of some US$9 billion from Korea between October 1997 and December 3, 1997.

54  These deposits were not usable as foreign reserves.

55  See Lindgren *et al.* (1999, 71).

56  The quotes are taken from Nicholas Kristof, "Seoul Plans to Ask the IMF for a Minimum of $20 billion," *The New York Times*, November 22, 1997, p. B2. Also Chae-Jin Lee (2000, 191) notes that "in November 1997, when IMF Managing Director Michel Camdessus secretly visited Seoul and informed South Korean economic officials that South Korea's crumbling finances required the IMF's intervention, they flatly responded, 'you're crazy; our system works' . . . This response betrayed either overconfidence or blind nationalistic pride." Camdessus's secret visit to Seoul is also discussed in Blustein (2001, 127–8).

57  Nicholas Kristof, "Package of Loans Worth $55 Billion Set for South Korea," *New York Times*, December 4, 1997, p. C6.

58  The change in Kim Dae Jung's policy should not be surprising. As Blustein (2001, 197) notes, "there were some powerful advisers within the president-elect's camp who favored breaking the power of the *chaebol*. Indeed, DJ's [Kim Dae Jung's] main economic adviser, You Long Kuen, a provincial governor and former Rutgers's economics professor, had been trying since the election to convince the Treasury and IMF that the populist DJ would prove far more willing than the existing government to endorse those kinds of reforms." Second, as Samuel S. Kim (2000, 245) notes: "faced with a likely financial meltdown in late 1997, President-Elect Kim Dae Jung quickly reversed his earlier stand against the International Monetary Fund (IMF), becoming perhaps the world's most outspoken champion of the controversial institution."

59  That is, in exchange for the interbank loans they held, the foreign banks received equal amounts of bonds, fully guaranteed by the Korean government. In addition, these bonds paid attractive yields, at an average interest rate of 8.2 per cent, which was 2.25 per cent over the London Interbank Offered Rate (LIBOR) for one-year bonds, 2.50 per cent over LIBOR for two-year bonds, and 2.75 per cent over LIBOR for three-year bonds.

60  In Korea, SMEs are defined as companies with fewer than 300 persons and assets of less than 80 billion won. As of 1996, there were 2.64 million SMEs – which accounted for more than 98 per cent of enterprises and 78 per cent of

employment. Of these, nearly 100,000 were in the manufacturing sector, representing 47 per cent of total value added and 42 per cent of total exports. However, the overwhelming majority of manufacturing SMEs employ between 5 and 50 workers (World Bank 1999, 5).

61 Figures from Balino and Ubide (1999, 58). However, it is important to note that since a large number of people gave up searching for another job upon becoming unemployed and thus became part of the economically inactive population, the unemployment rate was a significant understatement of the actual degree of unemployment.

62 Lister (2001, 3) notes that "the incoming administration of President Kim Dae-Jung had no difficulty, in conjunction with the IMF adjustment program and emergency World Bank loans, in articulating sensible reforms to the financial and corporate sectors, the labor market, and state-owned enterprises. The authorities readily adopted principles that had become basic tenets in most of the industrialized world, even though these principles clashed in many respects with traditional way of doing business in South Korea."

63 Mathews (2001, 165) aptly notes that "the clarification of the role of the Bank of Korea, and its separation from any supervisory function, is likely to diminish the scope for bribery and corruption."

64 Until new institutions consisting of a Financial Supervisory Board (FSB) and Financial Supervisory Agency (FSA), together with a Securities and Futures Trade Commission are established, the FSC will act as financial watchdog and to direct reforms of the industrial conglomerates.

65 Deposit protection was amended and, with effect from August 1998, interest on deposits over 20 million won was no longer protected (World Bank 1999, 17).

66 Korea was able to re-enter international capital markets as early as May 1998.

67 Kwan S. Kim (2001, 40), notes that "the rapid rise in unemployment in the first half of 1998 was largely attributable to the bankruptcies of small and medium-sized firms which were hit disproportionately severely by the IMF's high interest rate policy."

68 As the economic recession grew worse and corporate bankruptcy multiplied, the IMF, it seems, finally realized its mistake, and in May 1998 granted permission to the Korean authorities to lower interest rates and to ease the money supply. However, the damage was done.

69 Even with the end of the IMF-supported program, the IMF will continue to have close relations with Korea. Regular consultations under Article IV of the IMF Articles of Agreement will continue to be held on an annual basis. IMF staff missions will also visit Korea because of the annual consultation discussions to maintain a close policy dialogue, and Korea will be subject to the IMF's new policy on post-program monitoring.

70 The quotation is from Sunhyuk Kim (2000, 167). Also Beck (1998, 1030) notes that: "shortly after taking office, President Kim told one reporter, 'if the *chaebols* reform, they will be given incentives; if they don't, they will be at a disadvantage.'"

71 Oh (1999, 231) notes that if Rhee had not split the ruling camp, Lee would probably have been the winner.

72 Faizul M. Islam (2000, 136) asks "how did the South Korean economy recover so quickly? It was due primarily to the newly elected President Kim Dae Jung in December 1997 who introduced and implemented the reforms from the outset.

*Chaebol* and the labor unions who vehemently opposed those changes are surely but slowly yielding to President Jung's reform plans."

73 Mathews (2001, 166) notes that the top five have generally been responsible in their behavior.

74 More specifically, under the "big deals" it was hoped that each of the major *chaebols* would concentrate on only three or four core businesses, swapping other businesses with each other in order to achieve industrial rationalization.

75 Based on an exchange rate of 1,200 won per dollar.

76 Daewoo narrowly averted a default after its domestic creditor banks agreed to restructure its short-term debt.

77 The council was composed of eleven members (two from labor, two from business, two from government, four from political parties and the chairperson).

78 Despite this, Yong Cheol Kim and Moon (2000, 66) note that "the economic crisis penalized every sector of Korean society, but the hardest hit were the workers."

# 5

# The domino that did not fall: why China survived the financial crisis

When the financial crisis unexpectedly hit the high-performing East and Southeast Asian economies in mid-1997, it was widely believed that the People's Republic of China (PRC) would be the next domino to fall. China's extensive intra-regional trade and investment linkages with the rest of Asia, and the fact that the Chinese economy suffers from many of the same debilitating structural problems that long plagued (and ultimately did incalculable damage) to the Republic of Korea (South Korea), Thailand, Malaysia and Indonesia – namely, fragile bank-dominated financial systems, poor prudential surveillance and weak central bank regulation and supervision of commercial banks, a large build-up of non-performing loans due in part to excessive lending to inefficient, over-leveraged state enterprises, and a largely state-owned financial sector that may be almost insolvent – led many observers to conclude that the contagion's virulent spread to China was imminent.

However, the Middle Kingdom beat the odds. Although the Asian flu affected China in both its external trade account and external capital account, nevertheless, like the Great Wall, China not only remained conspicuously insulated from a region-wide financial meltdown of unprecedented severity, but the mighty dynamo fueling its economy has missed only a few beats during the crisis and since.[1] China's ability to sustain a strong gross domestic product (GDP) growth performance of 8.8 per cent in 1997 and 7.8 per cent in 1998 and over 8.0 per cent in 1999,[2] continued success in attracting foreign direct investment (FDI),[3] in running healthy current account surpluses (roughly 3 per cent in 1998–99), and in maintaining the stability of its currency, the RMB (*renminbi*) in the face of plummeting currency devaluations and precipitous asset price deflation elsewhere in the region and beyond, is simply miraculous.[4] In a region where China's intentions are viewed with much suspicion, the PRC's handling of the crisis earned it plaudits. Chuan Leekpai, the Prime Minister of Thailand, on more than one occasion has publicly thanked China for maintaining the value of the *renminbi* and for contributing US$1 billion to the IMF package for Thailand. Similarly,

Singapore's minister for information, the indefatigable George Yeo, while accusing Japan of abdicating its global responsibilities, noted that "the determination of the Chinese government not to devalue the renminbi in order not to destabilize Asia further will long be remembered" (Kelley 1998, 28). Another observer noted that the RMB was a "pillar of stability" in the region (Dassu 1998).

How did China respond to the Asian financial crisis? Why did China come through such a severe region-wide economic contraction relatively unscathed? What explains the resilience of the Chinese economy, and can the PRC continue to remain insulated from the uncertainty that still pervades the region and beyond? What lessons can be learned from China's experience? And what policy measures must China implement to insulate itself further from the seemingly unpredictable (and volatile) international financial and currency markets? The following sections discuss these interrelated issues. The core argument is that China's handling of the crisis, and in particular, the country's ability to withstand the crisis, must be understood within the context of its domestic political economy. While it was arguably in China's interest not to devalue the RMB during the height of crisis, there are forces at work within the economy that may force China to rethink this strategy in the future.

### The economy: underlying strengths

Never in recorded history has an economy grown so rapidly and as extensively as that of post-Mao China. The Third Plenum of the Eleventh Communist Party Congress in December 1978 saw the rise of the late Deng Xiaoping as the paramount leader and the launching of his pragmatic economic program aimed at ostensibly creating a "socialist market economy with Chinese characteristics." Between 1978 and 1995–96, the PRC's economy grew at an unprecedented average rate of 9.5 per cent per year, notching up an all-time high of a 14.2 per cent growth-rate of GDP in 1992. Over the period 1980–1993, the annual growth-rates of agriculture, industry and services were 5.3 per cent, 11.5 per cent and 11.1 per cent respectively. Overall, China's gross national product (GNP) has more than quadrupled since the early 1980s (J. Y. Lin, Cai and Li 1996, 1–17). The additional 20 per cent added to China's GDP on July 1, 1997 when Hong Kong became a Special Administrative Region of the People's Republic was a bonus. China's rapid transformation into a veritable "dragon economy" is reflected in the fact that, based on purchasing-power calculations, it is currently the second largest economy after the United States, a far cry from the bottom rungs of the economic development ladder it occupied less than two decades ago.[5]

Market-oriented policies epitomizing Deng Xiaoping's gradualist strategy of "crossing the river by groping for stepping-stones" have been the catalyst behind China's phenomenal economic growth. The core of this strategy has been "decentralization." In the Chinese context, decentralization has meant, on the one hand, devolving the power of decision-making from the central to local governments, and on the other hand, from planning authorities to state-owned enterprises. It is widely recognized that the devolution of government power and authority from the central to sub-national or local governments (the latter including provinces, prefectures, counties, townships, municipalities and villages) has been the engine behind China's rapid economic expansion. In their seminal paper, Montinola, Qian and Weingast (1995) have called this "Federalism, Chinese Style." That is, the Chinese-style "fiscal federalism" was fundamentally "market-preserving federalism." By devolving regulatory authority from the central to the local governments, the interventionist role of the central government was limited. The theory provides two possible mechanisms for aligning local government's interest with promoting markets. One is through inter-jurisdictional competition under factor and goods mobility to discipline interventionist local governments. That is, decentralized control over the economy by sub-national governments within a common market prevents the central government from interfering in markets, besides reducing their scope for rent-seeking. Another is through linking local government expenditure with the revenue generated to endure that the local governments face the financial consequences of their decisions. Moreover, inter-governmental competition over mobile sources of revenue constrains individual sub-national governments.[6]

It should also be noted that the devolution of authority in the PRC was accompanied by the provision of fiscal incentives, and local governments were encouraged and rewarded by promoting the development of their local economies. For example, the formal budgetary revenue starting in 1980, the "fiscal contracting system" known by the nickname of "eating from separate kitchens" replaced the previous system of "unified revenue collection and unified spending," known as "eating from one big pot." Under the new fiscal system local governments entered into long-term (usually five-year) fiscal contracts with higher-level governments, and many were allowed to retain 100 per cent at the margin to make them "residual claimants." In addition, local governments also received "extra-budgetary funds" that were not subject to sharing, not to mention the "off-budget funds" that were not even incorporated into the budgetary process and thus not recorded.

It is well known that agricultural reform was the first reform success in the PRC. In the countryside, the de-collectivization of agriculture, the restoration of rural markets and the changes in the grain procurement system – indeed, the complete replacement of the decrepit and corruption-ridden agricultural collectivization system with the incentive-based "household responsibility system" in 1979 is seen by many as key to China's economic success.[7] For example, according to Jean Oi (1992), the household responsibility system, which transferred the income rights over agricultural production from collectives to individual households, significantly enhanced the production incentives of peasants, while depriving local governments of a major source of income (see also J. Y. Lin, Cai and Li 1996, 130–8). At the same time, China's fiscal reform granted local governments the right to retain part of the extra tax revenue they raised. In other words, the higher the rate of economic growth, the higher the tax revenue, and the greater the income of local governments. Given such an important stake in economic growth, local governments were motivated to mobilize resources under their jurisdiction to engage in entrepreneurial activities. They established and ran rural enterprises and took the profits to pay for expenditures and reinvestment. Thus, increased fiscal incentives gave rise to a new form of state-led growth in rural China – what Oi calls "local state corporatism." Under this system, local governments "treat enterprises within their administrative purview as one component of a larger corporate whole" (Oi 1992, 99). By causing local governments to function like a large corporation with diversified businesses and facing fairly hard budget constraints, including bearing the risks of their investments in industry, the household responsibility system served as the engine of China's economic development. Oi compellingly argues that local state corporatism explains why China has been able to achieve rapid economic growth without privatization and why state officials have not been resistant to reform.

The Chinese political leadership has long viewed agriculture as the foundation of the economy. This is hardly surprising, given the fact the country has 22 per cent of the world's population, but only 7 per cent of its arable land, and that some 800 million people still live in rural communities. China's economic reforms began in agriculture in the late 1970s. Because this sector had been heavily repressed under central planning, its liberalization had immediate payoffs. Specifically, the adoption of the household responsibility system resulted in an immediate and dramatic increase in agricultural production and productivity – putting an end to China's long history of shortages of farm produce. Between 1981 and 1984 agriculture grew on average by 10 per cent a year, generating higher rural savings and investment, and the release and reallocation of labor for employment in agriculture and in the emerging rural industries (World Bank 1996b, 20–21). The agricultural growth was critical, because by mid-1975 the per capita consumption of grain, cooking oil and meat protein was lower than it had been in the 1950s, and malnutrition and hunger were a growing problem (Dernberger 1999, 609). Indeed, under Maoist collectivism (1952–78) total agricultural factor productivity fell sharply, and rural per capita incomes grew by an average of only 0.5 per cent between 1957 and 1977 – not to mention the estimated 16.5 million to 29.5 million people who perished during the ill-fated Great Leap Forward (J. Y. Lin 1990). In sharp contrast, during the post-Mao era the agricultural sector (measured in terms of farm output) has grown consistently at the impressive rate of 6 per cent per year.

Net rural incomes have risen from less than 150 *yuan* in 1978 to roughly 400 *yuan* in 1985, and reached approximately 2,000 *yuan* by 1997.[8] In real per capita terms, rural incomes increased by 63 per cent between 1985 and 1997 (Nyberg and Rozelle 1999). This has led to a significant improvement in the living standards of China's peasants, who have seen their consumption increase at an annual rate of 7.8 per cent per annum between 1979 and 1992.[9] Agricultural growth has also provided the surplus needed to sustain the rapidly expanding industrial base and the growing urban population (J. Y. Lin, Cai and Li 1996, 1–17).

The initial success of the rural reforms encouraged the government to broaden reforms to include the urban-industrial sectors in 1984, and to gradually dismantle the central planning system. In the industrial sector important reform measures implemented included experiments to grant the state-owned enterprises (SOEs) more autonomy in production and employment decisions ("the contract responsibility system"), the extension of the dual-track system to industrial prices, and the introduction of enterprise taxation. These reforms gave the SOE managers greater autonomy and allowed the firm to keep a larger share of its profits (under the "profit-retention system") for bonuses and self-investment (J. Y. Lin, Cai and Li 1996, 138–46). Under the dual-track pricing system, state firms that fulfilled their existing quotas under the plan were now able to market any surplus without fear of their quota's increasing. Eventually, as the above-quota and marketed share became dominant, the central plan was gradually dismantled – what Barry Naughton (1995) has called "growing out of the plan."

In sharp contrast to what happens in most developing nations, China's handling of surplus, or so-called "floating," rural labor made redundant as the result of gains in agricultural productivity (estimated to be between 120 and 140 million persons), has been impressive. In 1984, as the central government decentralized fiscal power and allowed provincial and local governments to retain and reinvest locally generated revenues, it created a powerful incentive for the development of local businesses. To meet this demand, the government astutely encouraged the development of rural township and village enterprises (TVEs).[10] Although still predominantly collectively-owned, the TVEs had a big advantage over their competitors, the state-owned enterprises. The TVEs operated free from government restraints, were not subject to any planning targets, were responsible for their own profits and losses, and could buy inputs and sell products freely wherever there was a demand, including on export markets.[11] The majority of TVEs are small and medium-sized firms, and their products are generally labor-intensive in nature. Currently, TVEs dominate the building materials and agricultural machinery industries, including textiles and garments, processed foods and beverages, and coal and cement. TVEs account for a growing share of the production of electronics and telecom equipment. The growth and performance of the TVEs has been extraordinary. The TVEs have grown from

1.52 million in 1978 to roughly 23 million in 1996 (Yabuki and Harner 1998, 143–44). Owned as they are by local government, private citizens, and other local enterprises, the TVEs' share in GDP has risen from 13 per cent in 1985 to 31 per cent in 1994. Output has grown by some 25 per cent a year since the mid-1980s, and in 1996 the TVEs accounted for a third of total industrial growth in China, besides creating 130 million jobs between 1980 and 1996, absorbing nearly 30 per cent of the 450 million laborers in the countryside (World Bank 1996b, 50–1; Yabuki and Harner 1998, 144; J. Y. Lin, Cai and Li 1996, 179–81).

Central to China's economic growth has been the liberalization of the foreign trade and investment regime, and the adoption of an ambitious "open-door" strategy. Prior to the introduction of the Deng reforms, China remained a backward and closed economy, with foreign trade amounting to a minuscule 4.7 per cent of GNP. However, the liberalization of the foreign-trade and exchange-rate regimes, followed by further wide-ranging reforms introduced in 1988 (which included increased retention of foreign exchange and easier access to foreign-exchange adjustment centers established in 1986), enabled businesses (i.e. the enterprises) to buy and sell foreign exchange at a depreciated rate known as the "swap rate" and greatly helped to boost exports. China's foreign trade as percentage of its GNP jumped to 10.8 per cent in 1988 (Zheng 2001, 65). By the early 1990s, foreign trade had grown to an unprecedented US$200 billion, or roughly 40 per cent of GNP (Cerra and Dayal-Gulati 1999).

Before 1994, liberalization of foreign-exchange markets followed a dual-track approach, in that there existed an official rate and a "swap rate" (i.e. the market rate). On January 1, 1994 China unified its exchange rate by bringing the official rate into line with the prevailing swap-market rate, resulting in a depreciation in the official rate by about 50 per cent (i.e. the *yuan* was devalued by 50 per cent).[12] China's pre-emptive devaluation, even as it led to a real exchange appreciation for the dollar-pegged currencies in Southeast Asia (significantly undercutting their export competitiveness), created an export boom for China.[13] Moreover, reform measures such as (a) the abolition of the retention quota system for foreign exchange, (b) the revision of the tax system to allow a zero value-added tax (VAT) rating for exports by domestic firms and the newly established foreign-funded enterprises,[14] (c) further relaxation of China's open-door policy towards foreign direct investment, including the provision of special tax incentives to foreign investment in technology-intensive industries, and (d) generous tariff concessions (including lower income-tax rates and tax holidays) to firms operating in the coastal special economic zones only served further to enhance China's international competitiveness, and helped it to expand its export markets greatly. Between 1990 and 1997, Chinese exports to industrialized countries have grown at an average rate of 15.5 per cent per annum, and for the period 1995–1997, which saw a decline in world trade growth, China's exports to the United States grew by 8 per cent, while Japanese exports declined by 2.4 per cent. Overall, since the start of the reform period, China's share of world trade has almost quadrupled.[15]

Although, China's exports have slowed since the Asian financial crisis, China's trade surplus continues to remain at a historically high level. In 1990 China's foreign-exchange reserves were only US$40 billion, compared to Japan's US$100 billion; however, by 1997 they had increased to US$111 billion in comparison to Japan's US$150 billion.[16] By the beginning of 1999, China's foreign-exchange reserves had risen to US$150 billion (equivalent to twelve to fourteen months of imports), thanks to robust trade performance and massive inflows of foreign capital, which have largely taken the form of FDI. While FDI was negligible before 1978, by early 1999 foreign direct investment in joint ventures and wholly foreign-owned companies in China exceeded one-quarter of a trillion US dollars, several times larger than the cumulative FDI since the Second World War in Japan, South Korea and Taiwan combined (Lardy 1999, 3). The bulk of the FDI has been invested in industries in the Special Economic Zones (SEZs) set up in Guangdong, Fujian and Hainan in 1980–81, in Economic and Technological Zones (ETDZs) set up in 1984 and in the Free Trade Zones (FTZs) established in fourteen coastal cities, followed by several more FTZs in Dalian, Guangzhou, Zhangjiang, Tianjin, Shenzhen, and Pudong New Area in Shanghai. While China's large and growing reserves are matched by growing external liabilities, it is important to note that the bulk of these liabilities have long-term maturities, thereby making the external debt manageable. Moreover, China's foreign debt is at a low level compared with that of other Asian countries, with the debt/GDP ratio at 16.0 per cent and the debt-service ratio (i.e. debt service vs percentage of exports) at 8.5 per cent in 1998. As was noted earlier, the debt also has long maturity, with short-term debt making up only 19.7 per cent of total debt in 1996.[17] Given this, it is not surprising that China is amongst a handful of developing economies with an investment-grade rating on its sovereign external debt.

Finally, the evidence is unequivocal: the fruits of post-reform economic development have trickled down to broad segments of the Chinese population. For example, per capita consumption has increased four times for eggs and eight times for poultry, and the per person living space has more than doubled in the urban areas and nearly tripled in the rural areas. Average disposable per capita income has quadrupled since the early 1980s, and Chinese households are saving on average some 40 per cent of their income. Indeed, total household bank deposits measured against the GDP increased from less than 6 per cent in 1978 to more than 60 per cent in 1998. All this has helped to improve dramatically the living conditions of the majority of China's 1.3 billion inhabitants. The number of people living in absolute poverty has been substantially reduced, from over 250 million to about 50 million in two decades. Life expectancy has increased from 64.3 years in the 1970s to 70.8 years in 1996, and infant mortality has dropped from over 50 per thousand in the 1970s to less than 30 per thousand in the 1990s.[18]

By any standards post-reform China's economic achievements are enviable. Yet, to his credit, China's amiable economic czar, Premier Zhu Rongji, and his team of able technocrats have not been lulled into complacency. It seems they have grasped the essential lesson, the so-called "paradox" of the Asian financial crisis: that strong macroeconomic fundamentals, while necessary, are not always sufficient for averting currency crises or providing immunity from virulent contagions. Acutely aware of their economy's underlying structural weaknesses, they remain deeply concerned. As the next section shows, their concerns are not misplaced.

### The economy: underlying weaknesses

An important lesson of Mexico's peso crisis of 1994 and the Asian financial crisis was that a sound banking sector is the single most essential element of a healthy financial system. This is particularly relevant in transitional economies like the PRC, where markets for corporate securities are limited and much of the lending unsecuritized. In such settings the banking sector constitutes the main institutions that can (and must) effectively evaluate and monitor the risks and returns on financial intermediation, including the evaluation of borrowers' creditworthiness, and can enforce financial contracts, loan recovery and the realization of collateral. Given these awesome responsibilities and their potentially far-reaching economic impact (both good and bad), it is critical that governments, including the central bank and related regulatory and supervisory agencies, establish clear legal and institutional guidelines, implement adequate prudential supervision and regulation (including rules to ensure that there is no undue reliance on deposits many times larger than banks' capital or assets that are longer-term and less liquid than liabilities) and accounting and auditing practices that are clearly defined and adhered to. Such transparency is important so that the banks (and other financial institutions) cannot mask problems such as a high proportion of non-performing loans, and, for banks involved in international transactions, that a healthy balance between assets and liabilities denominated in different currencies exists. Asia's financial crisis vividly demonstrated that systemic problems in the banking and financial sector are accidents just waiting to happen – or more appropriately, waiting to "explode" without warning and quickly engulf the economy as a whole.[19]

According to *The Economist*, China has "the worst banking system in Asia."[20] Sorely lacking in professional competence and institutional autonomy, burdened with balance-sheets that conceal many worthless assets, undercapitalized by international standards, unable to offer a wide range of services and products, and subject to political interference, it is arguably the

Achilles' heel of the entire economy. While the central reformers have instituted some important measures to create the institutional structures of a modern financial system, much more financial deepening is necessary to move China away from its present "socialist market economy" status.[21] As during the era of central planning, the central government continues to dominate other economic agents in the marketplace. Although stock markets were established in Shanghai and Shenzhen in 1990, and the activities of domestic (and some foreign)[22] commercial banks and non-banking financial institutions, in particular, insurance companies, trusts and brokerage houses, security firms, and Credit Cooperatives (both rural and urban) have gradually expanded, China's financial markets remain fundamentally bank-dominated – *and virtually all banks in China are state-owned*. In other words, although China has done away with the heavy reliance on budgetary financing of investment characteristic of the pre-reform era, and investment, particularly in the state sector, is now financed primarily by banks, the banking institutions are state-owned. Bank lending is huge in relation to GDP, while alternative channels of intermediation (whether private commercial banks, stock or corporate bond markets or capital markets) remain underdeveloped and plagued by government regulation and interference. Currently, state banks account for approximately nine-tenths of all financial intermediation between savers and investors, a ratio that exceeds that found in almost all other Asian countries.[23] The banks' near total monopoly and the lack of competition in the financial sector have stunted the development of capital markets, resulting in systematic underpricing of loans by banks, not to mention inefficient financial intermediation, almost non-existent credit risk-assessment, and diminishing rates of return for savers who have no real alternative to bank deposits.

Establishing the institutional framework of a modern financial system has been particularly difficult because economic decentralization has not been accompanied by parallel political and institutional reforms. Specifically, the fiscal and administrative devolution gave provincial and local governments broad discretionary authority regarding economic investment and allocation without simultaneously enhancing the banking sector's regulatory and supervisory capabilities.[24] Over time, this dense network of local political machines made of party officials, bureaucrats, managers and bankers, who repay their special commercial privileges with political loyalty and financial kickbacks, greatly undermined the central government's control over macroeconomic aggregates. An overview of this unfolding process is necessary for context.

During the Maoist period China's financial sector was essentially limited to a Soviet-style monobank. The People's Bank of China (PBC), founded in 1949, was the supreme bank in the country. While the PBC served as both a central bank (since 1984) and government treasury (managed foreign-exchange reserves, currency issuance and credit distribution), as well as a commercial bank (receiving deposits from households and enterprises and making loans), in practice the PBC functioned mainly as an accounting body, its major task being to take in household deposits (which were often the only asset households could hold) and to keep track of financial transactions that corresponded to allocations under the annual plan. As Figure 5.1 shows, the PBC directs and supervises all of China's banking system.

**Figure 5.1**   *Structure of China's banking system*

---

**People's Bank of China**
   (Central bank)

1   *Policy banks*
   (about RMB1,380 billion in assets at 1999 year-end)
   • State Development Bank of China
   • Export–Import Bank of China
   • Agricultural Development Bank of China

2   *State-owned commercial banks*
   (RMB9,552 billion in assets at 1999 year-end)
   • Industrial and Commercial Bank of China
   • Agricultural Bank of China
   • Bank of China
   • China Construction Bank

3   *"Share-ownership" commercial banks*
   (about RMB1,680 billion in assets as of 1999 year-end)

   | | |
   |---|---|
   | • Bank of Communication | • Shenzhen Merchants Bank |
   | • CITIC Industrial Bank | • Fujian Industrial Bank |
   | • China Everbright Bank | • Pudong Development Bank |
   | • Huaxia Bank | • Hainan Development Bank |
   | • Minsheng Bank | • Yantai Housing Savings Bank |
   | • Guangdong Development Bank | • Bengbu Housing Savings Bank |
   | • Shenzhen Development Bank | • China Investment Bank |

4   *Urban cooperative banks*
   (RMB1,650 billion in assets at 1999 year-end)
   • there are roughly 160 urban cooperative banks

5   *Non-bank financial institutions*
   • Financial trust and investment corps
   • Finance companies
   • Finance leasing companies
   • Rural credit cooperatives
   • Urban credit cooperatives

---

On January 1, 1984, in an effort to eliminate the PBC's conflict of interest (inherent in its supervisory and commercial roles), and to enhance its ability to formulate and conduct monetary policy independently, it was granted the status of a central bank. As a central bank, the PBC enjoys industry-level status. That is, it controls the money supply, determines interest and deposit rates, and handles foreign-exchange reserves through its division, the State Administration of Exchange Control. It also oversees banks' operations, using the credit plan to control administratively overall lending, and supervises the People's Insurance Company of China. Despite this, the PBC's commercial activities were further devolved and transferred to the more "independent" (yet still state-owned) commercial banks, including a newly established fourth state-owned commercial or "specialized bank," the Industrial and Commercial Bank of China – which took over from the PBC various commercial functions and now is the largest of the four state-owned banks. Together the "big four" state-owned commercial banks account for about 75 per cent of outstanding loans, have 150,000 branches and employ 1.7 million staff.

Since 1986, the State Council has approved the establishment of a number of share-holding company-based commercial banks at both national and regional levels, as well as non-bank financial institutions such as credit cooperatives, insurance companies and international trust and investment corporations (ITICs). These were set up mainly to attract foreign investment, raise funds for local development projects and make investments on China's stock markets. Apart from the China International Trust and Investment Corporation, all the ITICs are controlled by provincial and municipal governments. However, such seemingly prudent decentralization and the separation of powers did not make China's banking system any more "independent," transparent or efficient. On the contrary, while the PBC continued to allocate the total credit target for each specialized bank, and individual targets for their respective branches, it left the monitoring to the provincial and local PBC branches. In fact, horizontal political control over the PBC branches at the provincial, municipal and county levels gave local officials wide discretion over lending decisions. Moreover, the fact that local government officials had to be consulted before the center appoints a local bank governor (not to mention that the governor's promotion and future prospects depend on the local government's evaluation) predictably allowed the various local and regional governments and political bosses quickly to exert considerable pressure on their local branches of the PBC for credit and loans. Last, but not least, the "soft budget" constraints faced by the specialized banks (which do not bear the risks of their loan decisions), and the fact that the PBC sets interest rates that are below market rates, facilitate the quick issuing of loans and easy credit to support an array of SOEs (state-owned enterprises) both healthy and ailing, not to mention the local and regional governments' appetite for speculative investments in real estate and other lucrative ventures.

By 1987, it was painfully clear that the central government was unable to keep the growth of money supply in check, or to prevent "soft lending" (loans made without reference to commercial criteria), and had simply lost control of the money supply. Local banks (which are local branches of the PBC), and the specialized banks, under pressure from local governments, often exceeded lending limits laid down by the central authorities to subsidize the state enterprises and other pet projects (including illicit ones) in their localities. Indeed, it was not unusual for the state enterprises to roll over due loans automatically, or not to repay their loans, and for the banks to finance the deficits of local governments, including issuing loans at below the official interest rates and funding the junkets of public officials. Following Deng Xiaoping's promotional "southern tour" in Spring 1992, during which he emphasized the need to accelerate economic reforms, the lid literally came off the money supply. As the central bank, unable to impose the necessary hard budget constraints on local banks, passively moved to the sidelines, the regional and local governments and their cronies, with both explicit and implicit support from the local banks, embarked on a nationwide credit and investment binge. Many literally plundered the banks to fuel their desire to build even more skyscrapers and high-tech industrial parks in their town, not to mention numerous other wasteful and speculative activities.[25] According to Jingping (1995, 20–1):

> As local governments sought accelerated development, the bank was obliged to provide capital indiscriminately . . . In one county of Hunan Province, for example, the vice county magistrate ordered the president of the local bank branch to turn over the bank's seal so the magistrate could issue letters of credit at will. It was common for local officials to force bankers to provide loans to favored projects.

Predictably, the provincial and local governments' pursuit of an excessive expansionary monetary policy not only fueled rising inflation (that jumped to some 37 per cent in 1987–88), but also official corruption and graft. Indeed, China's experience questions the conventional view that decentralization improves efficiency, or that delegation of greater autonomy to local authorities or firm-level management will eradicate the "soft budget constraints." In fact, official corruption has reached epidemic proportions, and China earned the dubious distinction of being one of the most corrupt countries in Asia, surpassing kleptomaniac states like Myanmar and Suharto's Indonesia (Pei 1999).

Finally, on January 1, 1994, Vice-Premier Rongji stepped in to cool the overheated and unsustainable growth. Besides curtailing the runaway local bank loans and commercial credit by squeezing lending and suspending wasteful projects, he announced a series of bank and financial sector reforms. First, in an effort to loosen (if not break) the grip of the local and provincial leaders, all directors of regional branches of the PBC were now to be appointed directly by Beijing. Second, all projects above a certain scale now had to be approved by the governor of the PBC in Beijing. Third, in an effort to transform the state-owned commercial banks into real commercial banks, they were no longer required to carry out policy loans to the state-owned enterprises.[26] Rather, all bank-financed government investment was now to flow through the three newly created policy banks: the State Development Bank of China (to provide loans for infrastructure and key industrial development), the Agricultural Development Bank of China (to provide rural infrastructure and finances for crop purchases and food reserves), and the Export–Import Bank of China (to provide trade finance for machinery and electronic exports). These three policy banks were now responsible for the provision of preferential loans to projects deemed important according to government policies. It was hoped that the separation of the banks' commercial and policy-lending functions would prevent the transfer of funds earmarked for state projects to other projects. Fourth, the new rules prohibited the PBC from issuing loans to enterprises. And finally, the so-called "icing on the cake," the promulgation of the Central Bank Law and Commercial Bank Law (in March 1995) enhanced the independence of the state-owned commercial banks and their ability to function as real commercial banks. Specifically, these banks were made responsible for their profits and losses, and it was required that they maintain an 8 per cent capital adequacy ratio (none have met the requirement yet). Moreover, the law banned the PBC from financing government budget deficits by printing money (deficits have to be financed by the sale of bonds), and from making loans to the various levels of central and local government agencies. The laws also gave power to the PBC to implement monetary policy and exercise financial supervision over the other financial institutions.

These reform measures have given rise to a new type of banking institution (the so-called "share-ownership commercial banks"),[27] and helped bring the economy to a "soft landing" by reducing inflation to below 7 per cent, and removing some of the structural impediments and inefficiencies in the system. In March 1995, the National People's Congress (NPC) promulgated the Central Bank Law, which provided the PBC with legal authority to exercise financial supervision over other financial institutions. Two months later the NPC passed the Commercial Bank Law on May 10, requiring the state banks to meet capital adequacy standards, besides imposing a much clearer system for classifying loans that brought commercial banking practices closer to those in the West. However, neither the reforms nor the *Central Bank Law*, the *Commercial Bank Law* and the *Negotiable Instrument Law* of 1995 transformed the PBC into a truly independent central bank. That is, although the PBC has become more independent of the local and provincial governments, and, like the US Federal Reserve, can set the reserve requirements of the banks, can buy and sell bonds and set the discount rate and regulate the money supply, it nevertheless still had to operate under the watchful eye of the State Council. As in the past, all important bank decisions regarding the money supply, interest rates or exchange rates still have to be approved by the State Council. In the light of this, Premier Zhu Rongji's claims that politically directed lending will end by the year 2001 sound unduly optimistic.

Rather, the pervasive influence of the State Council, the PBC's huge and procrastinating *nomenklatura*, and its weak supervisory and disclosure framework, not to mention the meddling by recalcitrant political bosses, will continue to prevent it from exercising real discretion. Unlike an auto-nomous central bank, the PBC is in no position to perform independent credit-risk analysis, or to evaluate bank performance on the basis of normal commercial criteria. Nicholas Lardy notes that "China's largest banks are not subject to independent audits. Three of China's four largest banks do not even report their consolidated financial results, meaning that losses can be buried in subsidiary firms. Nonperforming loans are classified by more lenient standards than the international norm, impairing the value of the data in measuring bank performance" (Lardy 1998a, 79). Suffice it to note that weak bank supervision combined with ineffective prudential regulation will continue to make it easier for the obstinate Communist party insiders, influential provincial and local bosses, and those with the ubiquitous *guanxi* connections to determine ingeniously who gets access to credit, besides channeling funds to themselves and their cronies through fraud, corrup-tion and other lending irregularities. Although China's recent high-publicity anti-corruption campaigns have witnessed the arrest of several high-profile businessmen and bank executives, evidence also indicates that criminal financial activities, cronyism and favoritism continue to be rampant, and in fact may have worsened since the new laws were introduced.

At present, China's banking sector as a whole is not commercially viable, and certainly is unable to function effectively in the area of financial inter-mediation. Not only is China's banking system burdened with a huge build-up of non-performing loans conservatively estimated at US$200 billion, or roughly 25 per cent of the country's total GDP; the profitability of the Chinese banks is one of the lowest in Asia. Dobson (1998, 133) notes that "in 1995 China recorded 8.6 per cent of returns on equity and 0.31 per cent on the return on assets. With the exception of Korea and Japan, these figures were lower than in most of the developing countries in Asia." However, under pressure from international financial markets for greater transparency the usually stoic Dai Xianglong, the Governor of PBC, admit-ted (in January 1999) with uncharacteristic candor that the share of non-performing loans in the portfolios of China's four largest state-owned banks had increased from 20 per cent at the year-end of 1994 to 25 per cent at the year-end of 1997 (Lardy 1998a, 83). Yet it is important to note that, given the lack of transparency and full disclosure of the banking system, the total volume of non-performing loans remains unclear. Not only do Chinese authorities not release official data; prior to 1998, Chinese banks used a loan classification system based on actual loan performance that divided non-performing loans into three types: "overdue," "doubtful" and "bad." This approach underestimated non-performing loans, as it did not include highly risky loans that were not yet overdue. In 1998, China adopted the international standard loan classification system, which consists of five categories: normal (pass), special mention, substandard, doubtful and loss (unrecoverable). Reclassification of loans using the international standard was completed in the four large state banks in July 1999. On the basis of the new system, and on the internationally recognized 8 per cent capital adequacy standard, China's four state-owned commercial banks were found to have a negative net worth, and are basically insolvent.

The deterioration of bank balance-sheets is the direct result of what Nicholas Lardy has termed "China's unfinished economic revolution." Specifically, the reforms have not only failed to fundamentally restructure the country's 300,000-odd ailing cash cows – the SOEs (state-owned enterprises)[28] – but have further exacerbated the problem by continuing to maintain the life-support system of this ruinous vestige of Maoist central planning through the provision of large (if not extravagant) doses of subsidies. According to Janos Kornai (1992), the failure of the SOEs is rooted fundamentally in the "soft-budget constraint." That is, while the managers of an SOE may be given reason to desire profit-generating performance levels, they cannot be similarly motivated to act with vigilance against losses so long as they enjoy an unwritten bankruptcy insurance policy from the state. Given such insurance, managers have been tempted to expand into new lines of production if they believe, despite the sizeable risks, that such actions will pay off with profits. The lure of a possible favorable outcome dominates decision-making, because the downside (i.e. potential losses) is cushioned by the state.

Yet, on the other hand, the SOEs are still the primary providers of employment in the urban areas, and care for the basic needs of their workers, from housing and medical expenses to pensions. Concentrated in the "rust-belt" in the north-east, but present in virtually every production sector, ranging from steel mills to coal plants and factories making machines, electronics or chemicals, the majority of these firms are loss-making, and depend on government subsidies for survival. While the SOE sector accounts for a shrinking share of GDP, it continues to absorb a disproportionately large share of bank credit. According to Lardy, direct and indirect subsidies to the SOEs and the banking system may now be costing the country some 10 per cent of its GDP. It is these so-called concessionary indirect "soft credits" or "policy loans" from state banks to SOEs, implicitly guaranteed by the government (as well as granted under preferential terms) that have over time reduced the banks to little more than conduits for cheap credit to the SOEs. It is no surprise that borrowing by the SOEs (measured by the value of loans outstanding) has increased 40-fold between 1978 and the end of 1997.

Yet the unwieldy SOEs' insatiable appetite for subsidized credit is not reflected in their poor performance. Currently, SOEs account for less than 30 per cent of the industrial output, compared to 80 per cent fifteen years ago; yet they consume almost 75 per cent of national industrial investment.[29] Factory-capacity utilization rates for major industrial products of SOEs have fallen below 60 per cent, while the industrial SOEs' profits have declined precipitously from 6 per cent of GDP to less than 1 per cent in the past decade.[30] While asset-stripping (the illegal transfer of state assets to non-state ownership), and the customary practice by the central, provincial and even local governments of conveniently saddling the SOEs with excessive social responsibilities (including the responsibility of providing cradle-to-grave services to the estimated 112.4 million SOE workers),[31] have taken a toll on performance, Lardy notes that the major reason for the SOEs' moribund performance is the lack of fundamental change in ownership and in corporate governance. Besides overproducing an array of unwanted goods, a growing number of SOEs have been losing money. Approximately 50 per cent perennially incur net losses, compared with one-third just a decade ago. As of October 1997 roughly 46 per cent of SOEs were in the red, and the losses of these enterprises made up 57 per cent of the total. Indeed, available data show that a growing number of SOEs have accumulated unmanageable debt-to-equity ratios of between 400 per cent and 700 per cent.[32] In effect, the majority of the SOEs, unable to amortize their debt, through reckless borrowing have zero or negative net worth today. They have not only made themselves technically insolvent, but have also left the banking sector hopelessly burdened with large portfolios of non-performing – indeed, non-redeemable – loans.[33] It is important to note that the bulk of the banks' SOE loans are still performing only because of government guarantees to banks and government subsidies to SOEs. Were these to cease, interest payments for SOEs would cease, rendering the banks illiquid. Asia's financial crisis illustrates the fact that in an economic slowdown the highly leveraged SOEs have the potential to create major liquidity problems for the banks. A domestic banking crisis could push China into a deep recession, and could eventually force the government to devalue the currency. The cost of bank bailouts under such conditions would be astronomical.

Yet if by tomorrow the SOEs were miraculously to honor all their financial obligations, the banks' position would continue to remain weak. This is because, like those of Thailand, Malaysia, South Korea, Japan and Indonesia (to name just a few), Chinese banks have played a lead role in creating "asset bubbles," especially in the volatile real estate and construction sectors (Ramo 1998, 64–75). During the early to mid-1990s, when "a casino mentality"[34] gripped the country, banks and other financial institutions imprudently funded massive property developments throughout China. First-class office spaces, luxury villas, ostentatious townhouses and apartments sprang up almost overnight, not only in major cities like Beijing, Shanghai and

Shenzhen, but also in the many smaller provincial and coastal county towns (Tse 2000). Perhaps nowhere was the transformation as stunning as in Shanghai. The so-called "Shanghai bubble" transformed this once drab city into one of the world's glamor metropolises. By the end of 1995 Shanghai boasted over a thousand skyscrapers (including some one hundred five-star hotels), about 13.5 million square feet of office space in 1997 (an unprecedented five times the 2.7 million square feet in 1994), and a "hot" real-estate market that was adding stock at a faster rate than New York city (Lardy 1998a; Ramo 1998). However, the boom was relatively short-lived. By late 1996 the bubble had burst, in large part because of inefficient allocation of resources and overcapacity. By the first quarter of 1999, some 350 million square meters of office space stood empty, and real-estate prices slid to below 50 per cent (Pomfret 1999, A21). Tse (2000, 167) notes that "between the end of 1994 and the end of 1997, prime central business district office rents (monthly) had fallen from their peak of US$73 per square meter to nearer $28 in the middle of 1998 in Shanghai." For many banks and their sub-sidiaries, such as the free-wheeling ITICs and SOEs, with heavy exposure to real-estate construction and speculation, this has meant a further deterioration in their balance-sheets.[35] However, for an increasing number it has meant bankruptcy. The collapse of the country's second largest financial-trust company, the Guangdong International Trust and Investment Corporation (GITIC), in October 1998 sent an ominous signal. The GITIC had to declare bankruptcy when it was revealed that its debt totaled $4.4 billion, compared to only $2.9 billion in assets. In October 1998, the government announced the closure of GITIC, sending shock waves to Hong Kong, where many banks claimed they had lent to GITIC because the Guangdong provincial government had guaranteed the loans.[36] In early November 1998 two more ITICs, the Dalian International Trust and Investment Corporation and the Guangzhou International Trust and Investment Corporation, failed to make foreign debt repayments on the due date.

### Explaining China's resilience

One of the ironies of Asia's financial crises: why did China, beset with many of the same fatal flaws that sent the dynamo Asian economies crashing like dominoes, survive the crisis with barely a bruise? In other words, what explains China's remarkable immunity to the "Asian flu"?

First, China's economic soft landing amid the general financial turmoil prevented "economic overheating . . . this laid a foundation for resistance to external shocks" (Song 1998, 105). Second, in December 1996 China agreed to Article 8 of the IMF and permitted full convertibility of the yuan for current-account transactions. Thus, unlike the currencies of virtually all other Asian economies directly affected by the financial turmoil, the RMB is not convertible for capital account transactions.[37] Instead, it is only convertible on the current account (that is, an official documentation of a legitimate trade or other approved transaction is required to change money). This partial convertibility of the RMB makes it extremely difficult for speculators to take any short position against the RMB or to place large leveraged bets for or against the currency – since there is no forward market that speculators can use to attack the RMB. As a further precaution against speculators taking short positions on the RMB, on October 30, 1996, the State Administration for Exchange Control (SAEC) issued regulations to prevent foreign exchange under capital accounts from entering exchange settlements under current accounts. Chinese depositors were no longer allowed to convert their RMB deposits and purchase financial assets denominated in foreign currencies, while foreigners were legally barred from purchasing RMB-denominated shares. Also, the PBC, by requiring everyone to buy or sell foreign exchange or foreign-currency-denominated financial assets to enter the exchange market operating through designated banks, has inadvertently gave itself greater flexibility in responding to balance-of-payments problems. This is because the foreign-exchange market is not open to any purchase of foreign exchange for capital account transactions. Large RMB spot transactions require the pre-approval of the State Administration for Foreign Exchange (SAFE). In fact, without the approval of SAFE, trading of foreign currency by businesses and individuals is illegal in China. The SAFE approval requirements and related limitations on foreign participation in PRC equity markets have translated into low levels of portfolio investment. Also, in early July 1997, the Supervisory Commission on Securities Transactions (SCST) prohibited margin trading of overseas futures and foreign exchange in order to eliminate high-risk speculation and violations by Chinese enterprises in overseas markets. Finally, the Chinese authorities significantly intensified enforcement of exchange and capital controls, and moved to reduce circumvention. These measures involved enhanced screening of capital account transactions and increased documentation and verification requirements on current transactions to demonstrate that the transactions are in fact legitimate current transactions rather than disguised capital transactions.

The combination of these measures has made China less vulnerable to contagion and domestic or externally driven speculative attacks. To illustrate a case in point: to stem the outflows of the country's hard currency amid rumors that China would devalue its currency to match the depreciation in other regional currencies, the Chinese government took dramatic measures to intensify enforcement of exchange and capital controls. In early September 1998, SAFE ordered Chinese bank branches to cease trading hard currency from September 30, 1998. After that date, only the headquarters of the banks would be allowed to engage in foreign-currency trading. In October 1998, the central government announced that, as of December 1,

1998, all foreign-exchange swap centers (which acted as the official channel for foreign enterprises to adjust their foreign-exchange requirements) would be closed. In June 1999, the authorities restricted overseas yuan transactions by prohibiting domestic banks from accepting inward remittances in domestic currency. Moreover, in order to prevent smuggling of foreign currencies, the government (in August 1999) implemented a new rule requiring Chinese banks to obtain approval from SAFE before they could be issued exit permits for foreign currency leaving China in amounts exceeding US$4,000 for Chinese citizens and US$10,000 for non-Chinese citizens (Zheng 2001, 59–60).

Third, as the earlier chapters have shown, in the pre-crisis high-performing Asian economies, a mix of pegged exchange rates, heavy sterilization and no capital controls to discourage liquid short-term flows encouraged heavy external borrowing – in particular, of ever-increasing amounts of "hot money" in the form of short-term credits. Within a short period of time such practices not only created an excessive exposure to foreign-exchange risk in both the financial and corporate sectors (the result of growing mismatches in the structure of lending and borrowing), but also had negative effects on foreign direct investment and portfolio investment – which sharply declined in share in total private capital flows. However, in mid-1997 approximately 70 per cent of capital flows to China were in the form of FDI. An estimated US$200 billion, this was at almost twice the level of China's officially reported foreign borrowing (Lardy 1998a). FDI, with their much longer-term maturities and manageable debt-service ratios (given their relatively little exposure to private debt denominated in foreign currency) are far more stable and less susceptible to sudden reversals in direction due to negative monetary shock or investor panic. This, coupled with the fact that Hong Kong accounts for over half China's foreign direct investment, made China less vulnerable to a speculation-led liquidity crisis.[38] In addition, more than 60 per cent of the foreign direct investment is supplied in kind, in the form of equipment and materials. As a result, the capital inflows have not created excess demand or generated substantial inflationary pressure (Jinping 1998, 298–99). Equally important, China's massive geographic size and market potential allowed it to keep capital accounts closed and still enjoy sustained inflows of FDI.

Fourth, China, unlike pre-crisis Thailand, South Korea, Indonesia or Malaysia, was not heavily burdened with short-term debt liabilities. As was noted earlier, approximately 90 per cent of China's external debt is medium- to long-term – the bulk of these debts taking the form of direct investments, mostly in joint ventures, that are highly illiquid and difficult to withdraw quickly.[39] In addition, China (unlike its Asian neighbors) does not have a banking and financial system with substantial foreign debts denominated in foreign currencies. By contrast, nearly all South Korea's external exposure was in so-called portfolio form (mostly bank debts and bonds), some two-thirds of it short-term. Thus, in the case of China, foreign lenders could not call in their loans every three to six months. Such relative stability greatly reduced the possibility of an immediate banking crisis. Also, China has less capitalization through the stock market and less foreign equity investment to be repatriated by nervous investors if market sentiments change. Finally, since the banks in the PRC are state-owned, their bad debts are simply government debts, not private debts. Moreover, the country's bad debts in the banking system are denominated in RMB and not US dollars. Considering the fact that the taxation ability of the central government is about one-half of that in the developed countries, the burden of servicing the government debts as a share of the government budgetary expenditure is still comparable to that of other countries and still manageable. These strengths gave China a greater breathing space to make the necessary policy adjustments during the crisis.

Fifth, China's total foreign trade has been growing rapidly, from US$21 billion in 1978 to US$325 billion in 1997. China's merchandise export volume reached US$182.7 billion in 1997, with a trade surplus of US$40 billion (Zheng 2001, 65). Not surprisingly, China has experienced trade and current-account surpluses since 1994. China's healthy current-account surpluses (some $30 billion) and massive trade surpluses, and a formidable "war chest" in foreign-exchange reserves (totaling some $150 billion in mid-1999 and second in size only to that of Japan) reduced the pressure to devalue the currency or raise interest rates. Moreover, in mid-1997, China had substantial foreign-exchange reserves relative to short-term debts: thus there was no overhang of short-term debt that could not be repaid easily out of foreign-exchange reserves when debt was not rolled over. While there was an outflow of direct foreign investment, the foreign assets remained sufficiently in place that foreign-exchange reserves were not threatened with depletion. During the period January to June 1998, although export growth was slowing, import growth was declining even more.

Sixth, unlike most hard-hit Asian economies, China did not suffer from significant exchange-rate misalignment. As was noted earlier, after depreciating in the early 1990s, the RMB has appreciated considerably in recent years in real terms. Even after the 1997 devaluations of its neighbors, a change of merely 10 per cent could return the RMB to its pre-1994 value in trade-weighted terms.[40] Yet, as will be discussed later, if the other Asian currencies sink lower, China's trade competitiveness will follow, especially in the absence of concomitant productivity growth (Song 1998). Yet it is important to note that China's export growth may not be adversely affected by devaluations elsewhere in Asia. Not only does China export a more diverse range of products, but its labor costs are below the average for the Asian region. Regional devaluations may reduce the labor-cost differential relative to China, but may not eliminate it. In industries such as textiles and garments, Southeast Asia is unlikely to take away significant market share from China.

And, seventh, the sheer size and diversity of the Chinese economy helped it better to withstand the crisis. Because China's domestic market is huge, the Chinese industries (in relative terms) are less dependent on world markets. Exports as a share of GDP are lower for China than for most of the crisis-affected Asian economies. In smaller economies, firms tend to rely excessively on exports and/or concentrate on a relatively narrow range of industries. In contrast, China's size and diversity has allowed for the development of a highly varied export structure. This enabled China to remain competitive in labor-intensive industries, while still developing its high-technology industries.

## The challenges ahead

In China, a key precondition for a financial crisis – a fragile, if not largely insolvent, banking sector – already exists. This makes a domestic banking crisis the most serious threat to macroeconomic stability. Thus the problems in the banking and financial sectors and within the SOEs need to be resolved expeditiously. Specifically, the banks must be further re-capitalized and opened to competition (to increase their holdings of commercially viable, performing loans) and their prudential supervision strengthened. It is very unlikely that a significant portion of the loans to the SOEs will ever be repaid. Given this, the central dilemma facing the Chinese leadership is how to phase out the loss-making SOEs without precipitating massive unemployment. Ultimately the SOEs must be restructured through either hard-budget constraints, downsizing or outright closure. Since such measures have the potential to displace millions of workers who rely on the SOEs not only for employment, but for medical, housing and education benefits, it is important to begin the reform process before a crisis hits.[41] And the notion of a crisis of internal makings is not far-fetched. For example, should the government's willingness to bail out even one Chinese bank come into doubt, or when savers lose confidence in the government's implicit guarantee of their bank deposits, millions of ordinary Chinese could potentially pull their deposits out of banks, including banks that were previously sound but would become unsound as a result. The authorities are well aware that the availability of alternative financial assets would tempt depositors to withdraw their funds from bank savings accounts, thus exposing the insolvency of much of the banking system. The fact that China's banks rely heavily on savings deposits of households (the household share in total domestic saving increased from 24 per cent in 1979 to above 70 per cent in 1997), the resulting bank run would have disastrous consequences (Huang 1999). Among other things, a bank run would force a large number of SOEs to close abruptly.[42]

In the area of SOE reform, prior to the Asian crisis, the Chinese authorities tended to favor the Korean model. That is, there was strong ideological

272

support for retaining state ownership in key strategic industries, and support for *chaebol*-type conglomerates. The leadership believed that taking advantage of economies of scale (through firm mergers and industry consolidation) would increase efficiency to address the problems facing the SOEs. Indeed, the creation of such conglomerates was seen as a short-cut method of reforming (or restructuring) the SOEs. The financial crisis in general, and the massive failures of *chaebols* in particular, vividly demonstrated that "big" is not necessarily "better," and that the Korean model was no panacea.

During the Ninth Party Congress in April 1998 China's leaders candidly acknowledged the daunting economic challenges the country faced. The highlight of the Congress was when Premier Zhu Rongji sternly announced that the problems associated with money-losing SOEs and failing banks will be solved within three years through an accelerated program of "grasping the large and letting go the small." This strategy, which tries to retain some key aspects of the Korean model, implies that the government would select large SOEs in strategic sectors for restructuring, while "dumping," by way of closure, privatization and mergers of smaller enterprises that were either bankrupt or had limited potential. Specifically, the basic thrust is to divest small, non-strategic companies completely and to restructure the larger ones through mergers, public ownership, hard budget constraints, or other means. The prospect of bankruptcy or the shutting down of loss-making firms is not excluded, although the government will probably apply such measures only if all other means have failed. It is hoped that the reforms will establish a modern enterprise system based on a clear separation of the state's ownership of enterprises from their management. However, progress has been slow. Some small and medium-sized firms have undergone *de facto* privatization (or privatization in the form of management buyouts and the sale of shares to employees), and some SOEs have reduced excess capacity and overstaffing. The authorities have also experimented with ways to develop and strengthen the social safety nets in order to protect workers adversely affected by the reforms. Yet formidable challenges remain. As Zheng (2001, 70) notes:

> in a rush to "dump" the losers, local government officials often hastily put their SOEs up for sale, sometimes at bargain-basement rates. It was reported that 1,078 small and medium-sized SOEs located in 13 cities of Heilonggjiang province, with a total of 320,000 employees, were offered for sale at a trade fair in 1998. Some provincial government officials even attempted to give away some of the troubled companies for free. Liaoning province, home to 10 per cent of China's SOEs tried to sell off 1,500 of its unwanted companies through a promotional tour of major southern cities . . . this rush of sales of the SOEs prompted Premier Zhu to order a halt in late 1998. Zhu accused local government officials of misunderstanding the SOE reform.

No doubt, the leadership of the PRC is aware that the creation of a modern financial system is essential if China is to achieve the central goal of its economic reform program: improving the efficiency with which capital is allocated and utilized. Without doubt, the most critical step in improving efficiency of resource allocation and utilization is the creation of a modern banking system. As was noted earlier, the reasons for this are straightforward. First, with their share of financial intermediation totaling some nine-tenths, China's financial system revolves around banks. And second, the development of capital markets obviously depends on a strong commercially-oriented banking system to process payments and act as custodians. Since early 1998, in the area of bank reform, state-owned commercial banks have been deepening their operations and management systems, merging the provincial banks with provincial city branches, and improving loan classification and provisioning regulations. For example, banks have been given freedom to appraise investment projects independently, using international risk-management and prudential norms. Also, the business practices of banks are being improved by the classification of non-performing loans according to international standards, the adoption of international accounting standards, and the publication of consolidated accounts, including the accounts of subsidiaries, so that portfolios can be assessed properly.

Cognizant of the fact that the ratio of non-performing loans in South Korea was 17 per cent on the eve of the crisis, Governor Dai and other reform-minded officials of the PBC were quick to point out that only 5 to 6 per cent of the loans are unrecoverable. However, keeping in mind that the so-called problem loans in China are not clearly recognized on banks' balance-sheets (thereby making the scale of uncovered losses a major source of uncertainty), most analysts (including those in the IMF), are of the view that some 50 per cent of the borrowers are already in default, and that a similar percentage of the loans are non-redeemable.[43] The government has borrowed heavily to recapitalize banks and take non-performing loans off their books. In August 1998, the government provided a one-time capital injection of RMB270 billion (US$33 billion) in a bank recapitalization program (financed by Treasury-bond issues) to bring the banks up to international adequacy standards, in particular, enabling them to meet the 8 per cent capital adequacy ratio required under the Basle Agreement.[44] Clearly, this is a step in the right direction. China needs to create a capital market to supplement the role of banks in the allocation of capital. Bonds can serve as a more effective instrument than bank loans in providing long-term capital for infrastructure and other projects with long gestation periods. Moreover, equity markets can supplement bank financing for enterprises, thereby enabling them to achieve a more balanced financing structure. Yet it is also important to note that much more in the shape of both funds and strengthening of the supervisory and regulatory framework is needed.[45]

Since early 1999, debt-restructuring has become an important priority. Over the past three years, the state banks have written off some RMB126.1 billion (US$15.3 billion) in non-performing loans to SOEs (State Statistical

Bureau 2001). However, these debt write-offs have been very small in comparison to the amount of bad debt currently in the hands of the SOEs. To deal with this problem, between April and October 1999, the four state-owned banks each established an asset management corporation (AMC) – modeled largely after the US Resolution Trust Corporation. The task of the AMCs is to clean up the non-performing loans of the big four state-owned banks by literally taking over the loans, and to assess the credit expansion of banks by asset–liability ratios rather than through the centrally directed credit plan. Each AMC received RMB10 billion from the state budget as registration capital to cover current operating expenses. Since their creation, the AMCs have taken over bad debts from the major state banks, using a variety of restructuring methods to gain the best returns possible. However, restructuring has mainly taken place via debt–equity swaps, although asset sales, asset leasing, debt write-offs and asset rearrangements have also been concurrently employed. Although created to deal with the RMB1 trillion in non-performing loans (which is slightly less than half of the estimated bad loans of Chinese banks), by November 1999 the four AMCs had together purchased RMB1,393.9 billion (US$168.3 billion) worth of bad assets from the state banks. This was followed by arrangements to swap debt for equity in SOEs with bad debts (State Statistical Bureau 2001). However, limited progress has been made in this area – in large part because AMCs do not have the authority to override the concerns of local governments or to effectively restructure SOEs with bad debts, including the right to appoint new managers or liquidate failing enterprises. Not surprisingly, as an IMF (2000) report notes, "the AMCs' activities to date have largely been book-keeping transactions . . . A key element to the success of the AMC strategy will be to ensure restructuring of the enterprises in which the AMCs become stakeholders . . . the AMCs need to be provided with the skills and incentives to discharge their responsibilities, and to ensure that their financial positions are soundly based."[46]

The government has also taken action to turn the four major state-owned banks into independent commercial institutions. Most importantly, these banks are to be given decision-making authority over their financial activities and bear responsibility for their own risks, profits and losses. Finally, the PBC has increased the number of pilot cities for RMB business of foreign banks, approving Shenzhen City to be the second city where the foreign banks are permitted to open RMB business. Foreign banks now enjoy the same status with China-invested banks as members of the national interbank transaction market and are free to choose transaction counterparts to conduct bond dealings and bond repos. Foreign banks are also encouraged to provide consortium loans with China-invested banks. By August 1999, 25 foreign banks have been permitted to run RMB business. In early 2000, the PBC canceled the regional restrictions on foreign banks, allowing them to establish branches in all central cities (Fanzhang and Zhong

2000, 15–22). The authorities have also taken steps to reform the non-bank financial institutions. A number of institutions have been closed down, most notably GITIC, China's second largest trust and investment company. In December 1998, the National People's Congress promulgated the Securities Law to punish illegal financial activities.

Starting in 2000 the Chinese government has introduced a number of additional measures to strengthen risk management. These include:

1 Reducing risk exposure by making loans only against collateral. Banks must assess borrower creditworthiness, and loans to a single borrower must not exceed 10 per cent of bank capital.

2 The reorganization of the PBC's local branches along regional lines to reduce political interference in lending decisions by provincial and municipal authorities. Specifically, the People's Bank of China canceled 30 provincial branch banks and then established nine regional branches – each with jurisdiction over several provinces and municipalities.[47] The nine branches are to be directly supervised by Beijing, which will hold them responsible for implementing monetary policy, collecting financial information, supervising foreign-exchange activities and overseeing clearing and payment settlement in their respective geographic regions. In other words, the People's Bank will now operate more like a central bank, along lines similar to those of the US Federal Reserve System. Moreover, individuals and non-bank organizations may not interfere in bank operations. Commercial banks may not give unsecured loans to related parties or provide secured loans on preferential terms.

3 The establishment of a risk-management system for the banks and the phasing out of mandatory lending quotas.

4 Tightening supervision over banks and other financial institutions such as insurance companies and brokerages.

Despite these reforms, China still has a long way to go. It is important to recognize that the implementation of such an ambitious reform agenda is by no means guaranteed. Specifically, will the political and economic strains of a quasi-Leninist state push the reformers to backtrack? Consider for example the double-entendre: Although, Premier Zhu Rongji in 1998 abolished the so-called "credit plan" (which regulated annual bank lending by quotas and ceilings), and allowed the banks to make loans on the basis of stringent standards of accountability and creditworthiness, in 1999 the government once again ordered these banks to help fund the economic stimulus with loans to SOEs – loans that will very probably never be repaid. Or will the government take the other easy way out: through a competitive devaluation of the currency, rather than via the more prudent (and painful) reforms designed to increase productivity via internally generated efficiencies. Although, during the height of the crisis, Chinese leaders from President Jiang Zemin and Premier Zhu Rongji to Foreign Minister Tang Jiaxuan, Foreign Trade Minister Shi Guangsheng, Finance Minister Xiang Huaicheng and PBC Governor Xianglong, together with other senior officials, repeatedly stated that the *renminbi* would not be devalued, the pressures for competitive devaluation are quite real.

First, although China received much praise for not devaluing the RMB during the crisis, the price paid has been declining international competitiveness and growing balance of payments pressure. The deep currency devaluations elsewhere in Asia, coupled with the overall economic slowdown, and in particular the continuing sluggishness of the Japanese economy, is having an adverse impact on China's export competitiveness.[48] Exports are crucial to China's economic growth and employment – and the crisis-affected countries account for about 60 per cent of China's merchandise exports. While it is true that the fall in the Korean won has had little impact on China's exports, because Korean products are more capital- and technology-intensive, there is little doubt that the commodity mix of China's exports (dominated by labor-intensive products) has been hurt (and will continue to suffer) through competitive devaluations in Indonesia, Thailand, Malaysia and the Philippines.[49] Few economists now believe that the current policy of nominally pegging the value of the RMB to the US dollar is the optimal exchange-rate policy for China. Rather, most agree that a managed float or some kind of basket peg in which non-dollar currencies, in particular the yen, receive a significant weight would be preferable. It is estimated that a modest 5 per cent real depreciation of the RMB would increase China's trade surplus by around US$20 billion (Noland 1999). Will this push China to move to a new exchange-rate policy by devaluing the RMB and re-establishing its competitiveness? An early conventional account has so far proved to be incorrect:

> Although the Chinese government announced that the RMB would not be devalued, there are strong doubts. Chinese leaders and economists agree that an RMB devaluation would have little effect on China's exports, but may cause a regional currency depreciation cycle, which would hurt the recovery of affected economies. But, there is a price to be paid to maintain the RMB value. Though devaluation may do little to improve exports, it would adversely affect imports . . . With a large foreign exchange reserve and trade surplus, the Chinese government probably has enough financial wherewithal to maintain the RMB exchange rate at least until early 2000, if not beyond.[50]

And second, can the Chinese government carry out the necessary "deep" restructuring challenges in the banking and SOE sector without maintaining the growth-rates of the critical 8 to 9 per cent? It should be noted that even respectable growth rates of 6 per cent and 7 per cent may not be sufficient. Even an 8 per cent growth-rate is barely sufficient to maintain the much-cherished cradle-to-grave "iron rice bowl" for those with jobs, let alone to generate employment for the swelling and increasingly impatient urban labor force. Indeed, unemployment has been increasing, and the imperative to maintain aggregate demand to absorb displaced labor and new entrants into the workforce is great. No doubt, for most of 1999, the government was preoccupied with reviving the sluggish economy. It slashed interest rates twice, in January and June, bringing the rate for a one-year deposit down to 2.25 per cent, and embarked on a Keynesian-style 100 billion yuan (US$12 billion) public spending program, funded by issuing a record volume of Treasury Bonds. No doubt, such public works programs will help create employment in the short term. Yet, in order to provide continued stimulus to output growth, public investment must not only remain at a high level, but must continue to grow steadily. Given China's relatively low level of tax revenue and undeveloped bond market, financing further large-scale investment surges will be difficult.

The big question is how China will balance the conflicting concerns. Will Beijing's recognition of its regional responsibility (not to devalue) prompt it to continue to rely on fiscal and monetary tools to stimulate domestic demand, or will domestic economic and political pressures take precedence, forcing devaluation in order to increase exports? While devaluation could re-ignite financial market turmoil and another round of competitive devaluations, it is important to note that RMB devaluation is an easy way to stimulate China's slowing economy. After all, relaxation of lending, by itself, is unlikely to boost the economy, given the large volume of non-performing loans. Also, lower infrastructure and labor costs and the greatly improved regulatory and supervisory banking systems in Southeast Asia and South Korea may result in FDI bypassing China. Indeed, investment capital originating from Hong Kong, Taiwan, Singapore and Japan has fallen sharply. Their combined share of total FDI in China has shrunk to 45 per cent in 1998 from 68 per cent in 1994 (J. Leung 1999, 32).

Finally, another concern is whether China's accession to the WTO in December 2001 will adversely affect the viability of the financial sector. China has committed to eliminating non-tariff barriers and to reducing tariffs significantly, as well as to opening a number of sectors to foreign investment, including the financial sector. Over the long term, the country's adherence to WTO commitments should lead to significant efficiency gains and higher consumer choice. However, during the initial years, accession to the WTO will pose several challenges in key sectors such as agriculture, manufacturing, banking, insurance and telecommunications. Moreover, WTO obligations will require the government to reform further its laws and regulations to (1) honor the immediate obligations of being a WTO member, (2) accord equal treatment to domestic and foreign enterprises as required by the national treatment clause, and (3) improve the legal framework and the supervisory and regulatory systems to cope with a more competitive environment.

The impact of liberalizing foreign entry in the domestic banking sector and the granting of a number of RMB-dealing licenses to foreign banks to encourage competition will not be felt for some time. Foreign banks initially will be allowed only to provide foreign-currency services to Chinese clients. They may provide local-currency services to Chinese enterprises within two years of accession, and the full range of banking services to all Chinese clients within five years of accession. No doubt, foreign bank entry will put tremendous pressure on domestic bank profits. WTO accession will also affect banks through its impact on manufacturing and services. Finally, WTO accession will place unprecedented competitive pressure on the SOEs and their products, as many SOEs are not in a position to compete effectively with foreign firms.

## Notes

1 On the trade account, much-depreciated currencies and plummeting incomes in Southeast Asia hurt China's exports. On the capital account, foreign investment dried up, particularly from Hong Kong, China's main source of foreign investment.

2 See ADB (Asian Development Bank) 1999, 5. It is important to note that the official PRC figure for 1998 GDP measured in current *yuan* is 7.95 trillion. Measured in US dollars, using the IMF's average exchange rate for 1998 (8.28 *yuan* = $1), China's 1998 GDP was $961 billion.

3 In 1997 foreign direct investment rose for the seventh consecutive year to reach US$45.3 billion. This is in addition to the US$16 billion in debt and equity offerings China raised in international markets. Moreover, official holdings of foreign exchange reserves increased in 1997, reaching US$140 billion by year-end, second in size only to Japan. Data compiled from Government of China (GoC, 1998), and Foreign Broadcast Information Service, *China Daily Report*, March 12, 1998.

4 China's nominal exchange rate *vis-à-vis* the US dollar (RMB8.3 to the dollar) has been virtually unchanged since early 1995. Encouraging Chinese currency stability was critical at the height of the Asian crisis, since a devaluation of the yuan could have set off a wave of additional competitive devaluations and a further downward economic spiral in the region. Also, in sharp contrast, by late 1997, in US$ terms, the Indonesian *rupiah* was worth only one-fifth of its June 1997 value, while the Thai *baht* and the Korean *won* lost around half their former values. The Philippines *peso* and the Malaysian *ringgit* fell some 40 per cent below pre-crisis values.

5 For an excellent overview, see Lardy (1994; 1998); Economy and Oksenberg (1999).

6 While it is recognized that decentralization has been key to China's post-reform economic dynamism, it has also brought about serious side-effects – making China inflation-prone as a result of persistent budget deficits and excessive monetary expansion at the local levels. According to Dobson (1998, 131), "the decentralization of decision-making power from the central government to regional and local governments has weakened the central government's capacity

for conducting macroeconomic policy. It has also become difficult for central monetary and fiscal authorities to monitor the performance and behavior of economic agents, creating moral hazard problems in a variety of areas. Speculative and reckless investments by financial subsidiaries of provincial and local governments have increased the risk exposure of the Chinese financial sector."

7   By March 1956, over 90 per cent of peasants were in collectives, and by 1957, almost all were in advanced producers' collectives (Howe 1978). Unlike what happened under the collectivized system, under the household responsibility system farmland is contracted out to individual families, who enjoy autonomy in regard to the production and marketing of crops. After paying (either in cash or kind) taxes to the government and contract fees to the village (which still owns the land), the family is largely free to consume or sell what it produces. Land contracts that in 1995 had been set at fifteen years were extended for another thirty years in 1999 in order to give farming families more stability in planning their production and investment. This was supported by a policy to enlarge private plots and to purchase a fixed proportion (around 20 per cent) of the harvest at above market prices. For an excellent overview, see J. Y. Lin (1992).

8   Guojia Tongi Ju (GTJ), 1998, 345.

9   Data are taken from Nath and Tao (1998) and Guojia Tongji Ju (1993, 46). Also see Brugger and Reglar (1994).

10  TVEs can be classified into two types. The first, the collectively owned enterprises (township-run or village-run enterprises) are owned by the local government and operate like holding companies, reinvesting profits in existing or new ventures, including local infrastructure. The second, and more recently developed, type is much closer to private enterprise, in that most are controlled, if not informally owned, by an individual. Nevertheless, both types maintain close fiscal ties to the local and provincial governments.

11  In contrast, the SOEs had the advantage of captive markets and government support, but also remained subject to heavy government intervention, state pricing and the obligation to provide social support services.

12  At the time the official rate of the RMB was 5.8 RMB per US dollar, versus the 8.7 RMB per dollar at the swap center.

13  For a discussion of how China's pre-emptive devaluation contributed to the Asian financial crisis, see Corsetti, Pesenti and Roubini (1998).

14  The tax change meant that exporters could claim a refund of the VAT paid on inputs.

15  Data compiled from World Bank (1999a; 1996); IMF (1997) and State Statistical Bureau (1997) (*Zhongguo Jinrong Nianjian*).

16  The bilateral trade deficit of the United States with China has grown every year since 1985. The Department of Commerce estimates that the trade gap grew by 15 per cent, reaching an all-time high of US$57 billion, in 1998. This is only a few billion less than the deficit registered with Japan, the United States's largest trade-deficit partner. See Lardy (1999, 1–8); Fung and Lau (1997) and various issues of *Jinrong Shibao*, China's leading financial newspaper.

17  This is sharp contrast to Indonesia with a debt/GDP ratio at 59.7 per cent and a debt-service ratio at 36.8 per cent, with short-term debt making up 25 per cent of the total debt in 1996. Similarly, Thailand in 1996 had a debt/GDP ratio at

50.3 per cent and a debt-service ratio at 11.5 per cent, with short-term debt making up 41.4 per cent of the total debt. World Bank (1998b, 1–20).

18  Data are taken from *China Statistical Yearbook*. (1997). The international poverty line as measured by the World Bank is based on US$1-a-day. A recent World Bank (1998a, 3), study reports that "in absolute terms, the number of poor decreased by more than one-half in China since mid-1980." Also see Hu and Khan (1997), Stiglitz (1998) and Li and Loconto (1998).

19  In Asia, once it became evident that many borrowers lacked the ability to repay their loans, depositors lost confidence in their banks' ability to meet their obligations, resulting in a "run on the banks." This, combined with the fact that most banks were highly leveraged, made them highly vulnerable to sudden bouts of instability.

20  See *The Economist* (1998, 65–7); Lardy (1998; 1998a).

21  Most notably, while the banking and financial reforms have strengthened the system's ability to mobilize savings, they have been largely unsuccessful in promoting the efficient use and allocation of these savings. For details, see Xu (1998).

22  In 1997, two overseas banks, the Hong Kong and Shanghai Banking Corp. and the Industrial Bank of Japan, were allowed to conduct local currency services in the Shanghai Pudong New Zone.

23  According to Lardy (1998), in the mid-1990s banks still accounted for 90 per cent of China's financial intermediation. Also, Yabuki and Harner (1998, 174–6) note that "Chinese banks are massive not only in terms of assets but also in terms of physical presence and people. The banks complicated, multi-tier organizational system extends from Beijing to the lowest districts and townships and villages throughout China. In 1996, the Industrial and Commercial Bank of China employed a total of 565,955 persons, including 121,140 at the township and village level in 38,219 branches, sub-branches and offices nationwide." The Agricultural Bank of China employed 538,780 in 65,870 branches, sub-branches and offices nationwide. The total employment of China's state-owned commercial banks, policy banks and the People's Bank of China at year-end 1996 was 1,915,947 persons in 157,365 branches, sub-branches and offices nationwide. Suffice it to note the enormous scale and scope of the banking operations make efficiency, accountability and risk control exceedingly difficult, it not impossible.

24  Local government is a broad category used here to imply the intermediate levels (county and municipal) as well as township and village government.

25  According to one school of thought, Deng Xiaoping often sided with the local and regional governments because he used them as a counterweight to the more conservative central ministries. For details, see Shirk (1993).

26  As commercial enterprises, these banks will now have to bear the responsibility for any losses incurred in their operations.

27  In the "share-ownership commercial banks," various levels of government, Chinese institutions and, in rare cases, private individuals are permitted to hold shares.

28  Before reforms, China's industrial economy resembled that of the former Soviet Union. SOEs accounted for 78 per cent of all industrial output, almost all urban employment and 91 per cent of investments in fixed assets. Of the estimated 300,000 SOEs, roughly 5,000 to 6,000 are regarded as "large-scale." The rest are either "medium" or "small."

29 This sharp decline is due in large part to the fact that since 1978 Beijing has allowed the non-state sector to compete with SOEs.

30 According to Naughton (1998, 275), "Overall, industrial SOE profits sank to 45 billion yuan in 1997 (after deducting losses), or only 0.6 per cent of GDP."

31 This figure is for 1996 (*China Statistical Yearbook* 1997).

32 Broadman (1999) and World Bank (1997a).

33 According to Steinfeld (1998, 40), "In 1997, total net assets of the banking system were listed officially at RMB317 billion, less than 20 per cent of the estimated value of non-performing loans in the system."

34 I owe this term to Gao Xiqing, vice-chairman of the China Securities Regulatory Commission.

35 Non-bank financial institutions such as the ITICs are sponsored by individual provinces to help them raise capital overseas, bypassing the supervision of central authorities. For many of the ITICs the value of their speculative overseas equities and real-estate investments collapsed during the Asian crisis.

36 GITIC is not the only major financial company to collapse. In early 1999, Hainan Development Bank also collapsed under a mountain of bad debt.

37 Capital-account convertibility can be broadly defined as the freedom from quantitative controls, taxes and subsidies that affect capital-account transactions between residents and non-residents. Examples of such transactions include all credit transactions between residents and non-residents, including trade and non-trade-related credits and deposit transactions, and transactions in securities and other negotiable financial claims.

38 Zheng (2001, 62) notes that "by the end of July 1998, among the 314,533 overseas funded projects registered in Mainland China, 174,880 (55.6 per cent) were tied to Hong Kong investors."

39 Song (1998, 105–6) notes that "China had only a moderate level of foreign debt (US$131 billion) by the end of 1997, compared with its capacity for repayment. Judged by the measures of debt service ratio (12 per cent), liability ratio (14 per cent) and foreign debt ratio (74 per cent) for 1997, China's foreign debt is at a moderate level."

40 Song (1998, 106) notes that "the yuan closed at 8.2796 yuan per US dollar at the end of 1997, representing an appreciation from the rate of 8.7 yuan per US dollar which was in place when the unified system was introduced in 1994."

41 Some have suggested that the government could use fiscal stimulus by spending funds on infrastructure and residential housing to revive domestic demand and soak up unemployment.

42 As Zheng (2001, 68) notes, "about two-thirds of the SOEs are losing money and 90 per cent of the bad loans by China's state banks are with SOEs."

43 Reuters News Service, "Full Text: China's Central Bank Governor's Speech January 27, 1999." Lardy (1998, 115–17), notes that the share of non-performing loans that is accounted for by the most impaired categories of loans has increased. Specifically, the sum of the share of loans that are outstanding to firms that have already gone through bankruptcy and been liquidated without the bank recovering their loans, the so-called "dead loans," and loans that are two years or more overdue (i.e. "doubtful loans") increased by at least half between the end of 1994 and the end of 1997.

44 Because the bond issue has no budgetary implications, it effectively shifts these costs to future years. There is also the question as to whether the sum is large enough to permit a sound separation of good and bad debts.

45 According to "Moody's Investor Service estimates, China needs RMB1,000 billion, or 12 per cent of its GDP, to clean up the bad loans (Rosario 1999, 93).

46 IMF. 2000g. IMF Concludes Article IV Consultation with China, *Public Information Notice*, No. 00/71, September 1.

47 The nine regional "mega-branches" and their jurisdictions include: Shenyang (Liaoning, Jilin and Heilongjiang provinces), Tianjin (Tianjin municipality, Hebei and Shanxi provinces and Inner Mongolia), Jinan (Shandong and Henan provinces), Nanjing (Jiangsu and Anhui provinces), Shanghai (Shanghai municipality, Zhejiang and Fujian provinces), Guangzhou (Guangzhou and Hainan provinces and the region of Guangxi), Wuhan (Jiangxi, Hubei and Hunan provinces), Chengdu (Sichuan, Guizhou and Yunnan provinces and Tibet) and Xi'an (Shaanxi, Gansu and Qinghai provinces and the regions of Ningxia and Xinjiang).

48 In the first three months of 1999, total exports dropped nearly 8 per cent from the same period a year earlier, while imports rose 11.5 per cent. As a result, the first-quarter trade surplus narrowed to US$4.3 billion, down 60 per cent from the preceding year. For details, see J. Leung (1999, 31).

49 China's exports grew by just 0.5 per cent in 1998, compared with 20.9 per cent the year before. Forecasts point to further export declines in 1999–2000.

50 Brookings Institution Policy Brief (1999).

# 6

# Beyond the Asian crisis: the evolving international financial architecture

> We face a world of crisis. If Hong Kong, with its sound fundamentals and prudent financial management, can be brought to the brink of systemic break-down by aggressive cross-border speculation, then something must be wrong with the world financial order (Joseph Yam, chief executive of the Hong Kong Monetary Authority, January 5, 1999).[1]

Shortly after the Mexican peso crisis, the G-7 countries launched an effort to strengthen the international financial system. The goal was to expeditiously formulate and implement measures to prevent (or at least mitigate) the risk of future crises and to cope more effectively with those that still occur. At the Halifax Summit of 1995, the G-7 governments made a number of recommendations to this effect. Most notably, they urged the IMF to intensify its surveillance of its members' policies and to send explicit messages to governments that seem to be avoiding the necessary policy reforms. In addition, the G-7 asked the IMF to set standards for the publication of economic and financial data by member governments and to identify publicly those that complied with the standards. While some progress was made, namely the establishment of the IMF's Special Data Dissemination Standards (SDDS) to help countries better participate in international capital markets, much still remained at the planning stage. As the peso crisis receded from the headlines, and with Mexico making a surprisingly quick recovery, the G-7 and the IMF were content with making "minor repairs" – leaving fundamental reforms to the international financial system for another day.[2]

However, the rapid spread and severity of the Asian crisis, the enormous size of the rescue packages, and the realization that such bailouts could not be continued indefinitely finally forced the G-7 governments to look seriously at ways to strengthen the international financial system. Since then, an ever-growing list of architects have come up with proposal after proposal on how to reform the existing regime and construct a "new international financial architecture." Although there is general agreement on the need to strengthen the global financial system via more intensive surveillance and monitoring of capital markets and country financial sectors (in particular, the banking systems), timely dissemination of financial information under internationally agreed standards, and greater transparency in both public and private sector activity, including greater private-sector burden-sharing in order to eliminate (or at least keep within permissible limits) the problems associated with "asymmetric information" and "moral hazard," there is also much disagreement.[3] This chapter discusses some of the core areas of debate, consensus and disagreements on the new international financial architecture.

## The IMF: critics and reformers

Without doubt, one of the most contentious issues has to do with the future role of the IMF in the international financial system. To critics, the IMF is a Bretton Woods relic incapable of playing a constructive role in the building of the new international financial architecture.[4] While its harshest critics want the IMF altogether abolished, others are prepared to live with a severely restricted institution with limited powers and resources. Still, some others have proposed alternatives to the IMF. Among those calling for the IMF's immediate shutdown is the former US Secretary of State, George Schultz, former Treasury Secretary, William Simon, and the former chairman and CEO of Citicorp/Citibank, Walter Wriston. This trio argue that "the IMF's promise of massive intervention has spurred global meltdown of financial markets . . . the IMF is ineffective, unnecessary and obsolete and should be abolished" (Schultz *et al.* 1998, 7; also see Calomiris and Meltzer 1999). Similarly, Robert Barro (1999, 3), argues that "the IMF can best help the global economy by declaring itself insolvent and going out of business," while the Nobel laureate Milton Friedman blames the IMF's huge bailout packages for "helping to exacerbate the Asian crisis" and calls for its immediate dissolution.[5]

To these critics the IMF's most egregious fault is that its policies (in particular, its large rescue packages) undermine market discipline by promoting *moral hazard*. However, the criticism must be seen in a larger perspective. Specifically, in deciding how much the Fund should lend, they first have to distinguish conceptually between liquidity and solvency crises – a distinction easier to make in theory than in practice. That is, the Fund has to decide whether a country's balance-of-payments position is sustainable in the medium term. If it is not sustainable, then it will be necessary to restructure the country's debts. If it is sustainable, the Fund may decide to lend huge sums to help the country through the crisis. The challenge is in deciding when "huge" becomes "too huge," taking into account the perceived risk of moral hazard. Suffice it to note that these issues are simply too difficult to judge in the abstract, and they have to be dealt with on a crisis by crisis basis.

Second, it must be recognized that some degree of moral hazard is inherent in any rescue package, as foreign creditors will be willing to take on more risks because of the implicit insurance that packages offer. The critical issue is whether the moral hazard implicit in the expectation of official support induces excessively risky lending. This is a difficult judgement, given that it is not clear *ex ante* what level of lending is excessive, and it is impossible to tell what would have been the level of finance available from the markets without packages. Yet, having noted this (as discussed earlier), it is true that bailout packages have allowed errant private creditors (especially big commercial banks) to escape from bad lending decisions at relatively little cost.[6] It is also true that financial intermediaries in Asia enjoyed both explicit and implicit government guarantees in case of default (and therefore undertook excessively risky ventures based on the highest possible return rather than expected values), just as creditors ignored information about weak supervisory structures in debtor countries. Yet the widespread perception that the IMF bailed out all foreign and domestic investors is incorrect. Private creditors (mostly European and Japanese banks) have taken large losses and have had to lengthen the maturities of their claims, and bondholders and equity investors have sustained huge losses in Asia. One recent study has estimated that foreign equity investors as a group suffered potential losses of roughly US$240 billion from the Asian and Russian crises, and the corresponding figures for foreign banks and bondholders were US$60 billion and US$50 billion respectively. Between June 1997 and January 1998, US investors are estimated to have lost about US$30 billion on Asian equities alone.[7]

Third, the moral hazard risk must be balanced against a more deadly financial implosion of the monetary system and systemic risks of spillover and meltdown, and the heavy socioeconomic costs of inaction.[8] By providing emergency assistance to *illiquid but not insolvent* borrowers the IMF prevented costly defaults by avoiding driving previously solvent institutions into bankruptcy and thereby limiting risk to the financial system as a whole. After all, we know from the hands-off strategy during the 1980s debt crisis (where creditors and debtors were left to sort out their problems) that inaction can greatly aggravate the problem. Finally, the assumption that only IMF policy creates moral hazard is simplistic. Financial crises, more often than not, reflect misjudgements or "irrational exuberance," and as Mishkin (1997) carefully argues, "asymmetric information problems" that lead investors and banks to underestimate the risks in emerging markets and then to an overreaction when sentiments begins to change. Given these contexts, Krugman (1999, 200–2) aptly notes that calls to abolish the IMF are akin to declaring that the US Federal Reserve "should no longer be allowed to lend money during bank runs" – an idea that is "irresponsible and with serious negative implications for the global economy".[9]

Sebastian Edwards (1998a) also wants to abolish the IMF. He argues that the Asian financial crisis has revealed that the Fund is a secretive, top-down, meddlesome, highly bureaucratized, profligate behemoth that has great difficulty in responding quickly to crises, and implementing even the most modest reforms. To Edwards, "what is needed is a set of new, small and efficient multilateral institutions" that can "provide information and act quickly to avert crises." Edwards proposes the creation of three new small and efficient entities with defined responsibilities to replace the IMF: (1) a Global Information Agency to provide timely and uncensored information on each country's financial health, including publishing public ratings of domestic financial systems and issuing red alerts when countries fail to provide adequate information; (2) a Contingent Global Financial Facility to provide contingent credit lines to countries that, although solvent, face temporary liquidity problems (to be eligible, these countries would have to meet some minimum standards of disclosure and transparency); and (3) a Global Restructuring Agency to provide conditional lending and policy advice to crisis countries. Edwards' proposal has the potential to create an even larger bureaucracy, with coordination and duplication problems. Imagine a scenario with relatively autonomous agencies – one setting standards for transparency and disclosure and one, with little say over the nature of these standards, conditioning its lending on them. This would make the current coordination problems between the IMF, the World Bank and other multilateral agencies seem minor.

In his provocative book, George Soros (1998; 1998a) has argued that the international financial markets are "coming apart at the seams," creating "a crisis of global capitalism." He claims that since the private sector has proved to be ill-suited to allocate international credit, it is time to create a publicly funded "international credit insurance corporation" as a sister institution to the IMF. Under this system, borrowing countries would underwrite the cost of insurance by paying a fee when floating loans, and lenders could buy insurance against default. The idea is that "good borrowers" (those with transparent financial systems) would be able to borrow at lower rates. The Fund would set limits on how much each country could borrow and insure investors against debt default, while shielding solvent borrowers from insolvency contagions (since the Asian contagion wreaked havoc on solid borrowers). It is not clear how the IMF would determine limits on how much could be loaned, or what the appropriate insurance fee would be. Soros has yet to provide more specifics for his global central bank (although he does not use the term). As it stands now, Soros's idea of an international public insurance corporation seems to be a non-starter.

Claiming that the IMF and the World Bank have become "increasingly duplicative," James Burnham (1999) calls for the merger of the two institutions. On the other hand, the Dean of the Yale School of Management, Jeffrey Garten (1998), advocates the creation of a global central bank with the responsibility for overseeing a new global currency, and with wide-ranging powers to engage in market operations by purchasing government securities of its members when they get into financial difficulties. Its operations would be financed by credit lines from national central banks or drawn from a modest tax on international merchandise transactions and/or selected global financial transactions. Moreover, it would enjoy oversight powers over banks and other financial institutions, establish uniform standards for lending, and be accountable to a committee of governors drawn from the G-7 and eight rotating emerging-market members. Garten (1998, 8) writes:

> A global central bank could provide more money to the world economy when it is rapidly losing steam. For example, it could buy the bonds of the Central Bank of Brazil, thereby injecting hard currency into that country when it most needs the help (like right now). It would have the ability to buy a country's debt at steep discounts, a crucial need now because in countries like Thailand and Venezuela debts are piling up and preventing new lending and new investment.

Garten's global central bank faces two difficult challenges. First, it is not clear if the credits extended by national central banks would be sufficient, and second, the question of how much authority national central banks would cede (or whether they will be willing to cede any at all) to a global central bank, and how this political and economic obstacle would be overcome, remains unresolved. Henry Kaufman (1998) has proposed the creation of a single super-regulator – an "international credit-rating agency" – with broad supervisory and regulatory powers over financial markets and institutions, including the capacity to enforce common prudential standards on financial institutions and monitor the performance of financial institutions and markets. Like Garten's, Kaufman's proposal is short on specifics. It does not spell out the standards or specify how greater transparency and risk-management would be enforced. What is clear is that no national government will be willing to cede so much power and sovereignty to international regulators or supervisors. As Barry Eichengreen (1999, 9), has aptly noted, at a time when there is little interest in creating new supranational bodies with the power to usurp the traditional prerogatives of nation-states, what "such proposals have in common is their impracticality. They have not a snowball's chance in hell of being implemented."

Willem Buiter and Anne Sibert (1999) have proposed adding a "universal debt-rollover option with penalty" (UDROP) to all foreign-currency denominated loans and credits as a way of dealing with the creditor panic problem. It would give the borrower the option of extending a maturing debt for a specified period. The authors argue that the regulatory authorities should mandate the inclusion of this option in all debt instruments in order to solve the adverse selection problem. Its precise terms could, however, be negotiated between the debtors and creditors. Moreover, to prevent the borrower from exercising the option under orderly market conditions, Buiter and Sibert propose requiring a debtor invoking the option to compensate the lender at a penalty rate. The option could be invoked only once. Hence a borrower who was insolvent would not be sheltered from the need to restructure his/her debts at the end of the rollover period. No doubt, in a pure liquidity crisis – where by definition the debtor has no trouble in making debt-service payments in full so long as investor confidence is maintained – UDROP may help ameliorate its effects. Also, if the main cause of crises is creditor panic, then UDROP would reduce crisis incidence, because the cost to a foreign creditor of being last through the exit is less in the presence of UDROP than in its absence. While it is argued that the IMF would activate the UDROP only if the country was suffering from a pure investor panic or if it had demonstrated a credible commitment to adjust, some fundamental problem areas need to be resolved first. As Eichengreen (2000, 45) notes, "does the Fund have the capacity to distinguish these cases? Can its conditionality be effective? Since it will have its own loans to the country, can it solve the potential conflict of interest created by the fact that it is a priority creditor?"

A task force convened by the Council on Foreign Relations (1999) has proposed new rules for IMF lending to address the moral hazard problem. Specifically, the task force recommends that IMF loans be greatly limited. To achieve this, the Fund must return to its traditional practice of lending no more than 100 per cent of quota in a year and 300 per cent of quota over the life of the program – expect under exceptional circumstances that threaten systemic stability. Investors and governments will thereby realize that the assistance on offer is limited and lend and borrow more cautiously. However, while limited lending may limit moral hazard, it might also fail to calm investor panic. For example, the more than US$21 billion that the IMF lent to South Korea was 2,000 per cent of quota – and even this failed to stem panic. It is clear that if IMF lending is to be limited in this way, then other mechanisms will have to be in place to resolve the crisis problem.

The International Financial Institution Advisory Commission (IFIAC), also known as the Meltzer Commission (after its chair, Professor Allan Meltzer) has proposed new rules and procedures to limit the frequency, magnitude and duration of IMF rescue loans.[10] Specifically, the Commission has proposed that while the IMF should lend more freely to countries encountering liquidity crises, it should avoid lending to countries experiencing crises for reasons having to do with flawed fundamentals. This means allowing the Fund to lend only for short periods and only to countries with strong banking systems (those that adequately capitalize their banks and open domestic financial markets to foreign entry), strong fiscal policies, and a willingness to treat obligations to the Fund as senior to other liabilities

(Calomiris 2000). Moreover, the Commission recommends that the IMF lend at penalty rates. This recommendation is based on the presumption that if the problem is simply one of liquidity (rather than fundamentals), countries needing assistance for extended periods to service otherwise unviable loans will be precluded from obtaining funds from the IMF. It also means that if the IMF lends at only penalty rates, then a country with major structural flaws will stand to lose by borrowing from the IMF, since borrowing from the Fund subordinates existing debts, exacerbates the deficit (through the high borrowing costs), and makes it harder to repay private debts. The assumption is that the IMF will receive requests for assistance only from illiquid countries, while those with poor long-term fundamentals will opt to adjust. While the G-7 are generally supportive of the Commission's recommendations, some problem areas need to be resolved. First, given the difficulty in distinguishing between liquidity and structural problems, it is not clear that penalty rates will filter out insolvent countries. Second, even if it makes economic sense to refuse to lend to a country because its problems are clearly structural, can the IMF simply stand aside when a crisis erupts in a country like Russia or some other geo-strategically important country? The reality is that the costs of inaction (and the resultant economic contraction) can be extensive, and too painful for the international community to bear. Indeed, experience has shown that the IMF and other multilateral financial institutions are usually forced to back down and release funds, despite *ex ante* commitments to the contrary.

Finally, Barry Eichengreen (2000, 40) has recently proposed two "new approaches" intended to provide alternatives to IMF bailouts: officially sanctioned stand-stills and collective action clauses. According to Eichengreen, financial crises are either the result of investor panic or problems with the economic fundamentals. First, if the crises are mainly caused by investor panic, then a payments standstill imposed or endorsed by the IMF "could shelter countries from destructive creditor grab races until lenders collect their wits and calm returns to the markets."[11] In other words, when a crisis is due to investor panic, resolving it "requires only a cooling-off period for investors to collect their wits, for the authorities to signal their commitment to sound and stable policies, and for calm to return to the markets." Eichengreen claims that making provisions for an IMF-imposed or IMF-endorsed standstill would provide an alternative to large-scale financial rescues for countries experiencing panic-induced liquidity crises. Second, if a crisis reflects problems with economic fundamentals that prevent a country from servicing its obligations, resolving it will require debt restructuring – with initiatives to facilitate orderly restructuring receiving top priority. Eichengreen notes that "the obvious initiative along these lines is the addition of collective action clauses to loan agreements to make the agreement between the debtor and his creditors easier to reach." He adds that "there may also be a case for an IMF imposed or sanctioned standstill, but only if there is reason to think that the country to which it is applied will satisfy the conditionality the Fund attaches to its support, make good-faith efforts to adjust, and resume debt service on reasonable terms" (2000, 41). For Eichengreen, the key point is that there should be a correspondence between the nature of crises and the nature of the reforms pursued to enhance the official community's capacity to contain and resolve them. Eichengreen's proposal clearly outlines that which measure is more attractive depends, therefore, on which type of crisis is more frequent. While neither proposal is without its problems, some initiative along these lines is essential if the international financial architecture is to be reformed to limit reliance on IMF bailouts and to ameliorate the moral hazard problem.

### The IMF: what future role?

Despite the at times heated discussions on what should constitute the new international financial architecture, there is an emerging consensus that the world needs some sort of a global institution to mitigate the recurrent financial crises. For better or worse, that global institution is the IMF. Despite the fact that the IMF made mistakes in dealing with the Asian crisis (and undoubtedly will make more mistakes in the future), this should not invalidate the rationale for having a universally representative institution to oversee the implementation of collectively agreed rules. Moreover, given its institutional resources, administrative capacity, worldwide membership, broad experience and technical and policy competence, the IMF can play an important role in coordinating global economic integration and crisis management. This reality has not been lost on the G-7 governments.

Although the precise nature and extent of the IMF's future role remains unclear, there is no doubt that the institution is currently playing a major role in shaping the new financial architecture. The United States, the G-7 and the G-22 group of nations (the G-7 and G-22 are the major shareholders of the IMF and World Bank) have publicly acknowledged that the IMF is an "indispensable institution" and want the Fund to play a central role in constructing the new international financial architecture.[12] Even the usually reserved US Treasury Secretary, Larry Summers (1999), noted that "events have reaffirmed that the IMF is indispensable. All of us involved with global finance would be breathing less easily this holiday season if the IMF had not taken the steps that it did in response to the crises in Asia and elsewhere."[13]

At the Halifax Summit in June 1995, the G-7 leaders called for a doubling of the SDR 17 billion available to the IMF under the General Arrangements to Borrow (GAB) to respond to financial crises. The New Arrangements to Borrow (NAB) were approved by the IMF's Executive Board in early 1997 and came into effect in mid-1998. In October 1998, the United States

Congress approved some $18 billion in much-needed new funding for the IMF. Indeed, under the NAB, the 25 participating countries agreed to provide up to SDR 34 billion in supplementary resources to the IMF.[14] The Fund has also taken steps to increase its own resources. A 45 per cent quota increase, raising the Fund's total quotas to SDR 210 billion, took effect in January 1999.

With this strong backing, the IMF has already begun to implement measures to "reform the way the International Monetary Fund does business as well as enhance its capacity to respond to future crises more effectively" (IMF 2001). Although progress will be incremental, some measures are already in the process of implementation. *First*, it is clear that the advisory body of the IMF will be more involved in shaping policy and follow-up. In September 1999, the Interim Committee of the IMF (its principal advisory body) was transformed into the International Monetary and Financial Committee (IMFC). The committee's membership consists of IMF governors (typically finance ministers or central bank governors) of those countries that have been appointed or elected to the IMF's 24-member Executive Board. As was the case with the Interim Committee, the IMFC advises and reports to the IMF's Board of Governors, on IMF-related issues, including the international monetary and financial system. The transformation of the Interim Committee involved more than just a name change. Its advisory role was strengthened with the introduction of a deputies' process. IMFC deputies from the finance ministries and central banks now regularly meet before IMFC meetings to allow for greater debate and consensus-building among IMF members on all key issues.

*Second*, in recognition of the fact that banking system weaknesses have been a significant feature of financial crises, a key element in the architecture reforms is the development of frameworks to strengthen banking systems and to promote more effective risk-management capacity within them. In this context, a number of initiatives are under way to strengthen the supervisory arrangements applicable to banking systems. The Fund, along with the World Bank, the regional development banks and the Basle Committee for Banking Supervision (BIS) has taken the lead. Following on the request by G-7 leaders at the Lyons Summit in 1996, the Basel Committee developed "25 Core Principles for Effective Banking Supervision." These principles cover seven broad headings, including preconditions for effective supervision, licensing and structure, prudential regulations, methods of ongoing supervision, information requirements, powers of supervision and cross-border banking (Basel Committee 1997; 1999; 1999a). Comparable principles were subsequently developed for securities supervision by the International Organization of Securities Commissions (IOSCO), and for insurance supervision by the International Association of Insurance Supervisors (IAIS).

To assist emerging-market economies to develop the necessary supervisory expertise, the IMF has been given the key task of helping to improve the banking system of its members. This involves carrying out more intensive surveillance of the financial sectors of member countries, as well as helping members develop their financial sector supervisory and regulatory frameworks in conformity with international standards.[15] Priority has been given to reforming the banking sector in emerging market economies by developing standards (in line with the international standards for Banking Supervision as outlined in the Basle Committee's Core Principles for Banking Supervision) in banking supervision, accounting and disclosure, auditing and valuation of bank assets, and in corporate governance. In addition, the Basel Committee has developed proposals for reforms to the Capital Accord, designed to strengthen the capital adequacy arrangements for banks. In May 1999, the IMF and the World Bank launched a joint Financial Sector Assessment Program (FSAP) to identify strengths, risks and vulnerabilities in national financial systems and to ascertain their development and technical assistance needs. These assessments, which feed into the IMF's regular surveillance process, are conducted by teams composed of staff from the IMF and from other international bodies, as well as national supervisors and central banks. Conducted in more than two dozen countries so far, the FSAP program aims to cover another two dozen countries each year, "with a bias towards those that are important to the health of the global financial system" (IMF 2001, 3). The IMF and the World Bank plan to conduct FSAP assessments of all member countries at least once in the next five years.

*Third*, there is now agreement that the IMF, in collaboration with other institutions such as the World Bank and the Bank for International Settlements,[16] should closely monitor developments in global capital markets, which involves – keeping a watchful eye on the risks of potential large reversals of capital flows and the contagion effects; on the rapid accumulation of short-term debts; on unhedged exposure to currency fluctuations; and on the impact of selective capital-account liberalization. Moreover, in order to prevent a private debt problem rapidly turning into a sovereign debt problem, guidelines on good practices in public debt management are currently being developed by the IMF and the World Bank with international debt-management experts. Similarly, measures are also being developed to make capital flows less volatile and the exchange-rate regimes more realistic, and to make domestic asset prices better reflect the actual underlying returns and risks.[17]

*Fourth*, the Fund has been actively encouraging member countries to adopt the IMF's Code of Good Practices on Fiscal Transparency, and to disseminate reliable, timely and comprehensive fiscal and monetary data – both to the IMF and to market participants by subscribing to the Fund's General Data Dissemination System (GDDS) and the Special Data Dissemination Standard (SDDS). The SDDS has already been amended to include data on reserve-related contingent liabilities, and to provide better coverage of the foreign liquidity position of the corporate and government sectors. Countries subscribing to the SDDS will need to be in full compliance by March 2000. The Fund has also prepared and published several rounds of Reports on the Observance of Standards and Codes with the aim of building up over time a comprehensive analysis of individual country progress.

*Fifth*, the IMF executive board now more fully recognizes that not only do its bailouts, in creating moral hazard, weaken market discipline, but also that continued reliance on bailouts is unlikely to be acceptable on either efficiency or equity grounds.[18] In response to the charges that the IMF's policies encourage moral hazard, the Fund is considering ways to increase private-sector involvement in crisis prevention, and especially in "burden-sharing" (rather than "bailing in"), thereby limiting the "exit-option" that removes private-sector credit from a distressed economy at the very time the organs of the official governmental and multilateral financial community, such as the Fund, are being called upon to inject large doses of public resources. While there is general agreement that private-sector involvement should as far as possible be *market-oriented and voluntary*, as noted earlier, the precise mechanisms are evolving slowly. To date, the range of options being considered include: (a) modifying the terms of international sovereign bond contracts so that creditors have a greater opportunity and incentive to reach a settlement with the debtor; (b) eliminating the regulatory bias to short-term inter-bank credit lines, including assigning higher capital risk weights to banks' short-term debt claims; (c) encouraging debtor countries to put in place private contingent credit lines so that liquidity support is available in periods of financial difficulty; (d) encouraging the use of creditor committees and improving insolvency law to provide greater scope for involving creditors in the resolution process in debtor default situations; and (e) the possible use of debt standstills in a period of financial crisis. A debt standstill aim would be to freeze temporarily the repayment of debt in order to stem the extent of capital outflows, to ease pressure on the domestic economy and to provide time for the implementation of a program to resolve the crisis.

*Sixth*, the Fund has introduced several innovations that will enable it to play the role of crisis manager more effectively than in the past. Following the Mexican peso crisis, it created the Emergency Financing Mechanism in 1996 to respond more quickly to crisis situations. Following the Korean crisis (at the end of 1997), the Fund created another financial instrument, the Supplemental Reserve Facility (SRF), which enabled it to provide finance beyond the normal quota-based access limits to handle any crisis situation (i.e. South Korea) where a loss of confidence created a very large financing gap. As is appropriate in such situations, the period for which financing is made available is very short (12–18 months and extendable by another year), and at a much higher interest rate than regular Fund financing. Overall, the

SRF is intended for use by member countries already in crisis or facing exceptional balance-of-payments outflow due to short-run speculative attacks.[19] The short maturity and higher-than-normal interest rate reflect the extraordinary nature of SRF borrowing and the expectation that the borrowing country will take immediate steps to calm financial markets and reverse the outflow of capital.

In April 1999, the IMF's Executive Board agreed to provide Contingent Credit Lines (CCL) to member countries. The CCL is intended as a precautionary measure for countries with fundamentally strong policies, but at risk of possible contagion or a crisis of confidence unconnected with economic fundamentals. Loans under the CCL will have the same maturity as loans under the SRF, but will not be subject to IMF general access limits. To be eligible for a contingent line of credit, a country must receive a positive assessment from the Fund at its previous Article IV consultation. The critical innovation with the CCL is that it would enable the IMF, for the first time, to use its financing in a preventive mode and to help good performers. Thus it seeks to prevent crises by providing a financial incentive for countries to pursue appropriate policies and undertake needed reforms ahead of time. In addition, the IMF Executive Board has approved measures to encourage early repayment of IMF loans and to discourage excessive borrowing by charging higher interest rates on big loans. It is hoped that "these measures will reduce reliance on the Fund as a source of longer-term financing and help it maintain a strong liquidity position in the event of widespread crises" (IMF 2001, 5).

*Seventh*, the IMF, along with other multilateral financial institutions, in consultations with donor and recipient country members has begun the task of designing programs that take better account of the broader structural and institutional environment within which they are implemented, with greater focus on reforms to reduce trade barriers and unproductive or "market-distorting" expenditures, to promote core labor standards and to mitigate the social costs of economic adjustments. *Eighth*, there is broad consensus that the IMF (an institution with tremendous clout in the global economy), not to mention an institution that is underwritten by the world's taxpayers, should not operate behind a wall of secrecy. The IMF has been instructed to move "significantly towards openness and transparency" by the G-7. Specifically, the Fund is now to release a broad array of information on its policies, programs and objectives, including a more comprehensive summary of countries' accounts with the Fund and all outstanding loans. The establishment of an expanded IMF web-site (www.imf.org), has already increased accessibility.

*Ninth*, the IMF surveillance systems have been widely criticized for not providing early warning of problems in Mexico and later in Asia. However, one has to bear it in mind that the IMF can only go so far in the area of transparency. If everything that is shared with the IMF immediately becomes public, governments will be less willing to reveal sensitive information. Similarly, if every warning issued by the IMF becomes public, it runs the risk of precipitating precisely the crises that it seeks to avert. Yet there is now increasing agreement that IMF surveillance must be strengthened as an instrument of crisis-prevention. To this effect, the Fund introduced (in mid-1997) the practice of issuing Public Issuance Notices (PINs), which summarize the main features of the IMF Executive Board discussion on Article 4 reports (which traditionally have been treated as confidential), provided a country requests such a release. Some 80 per cent of member countries now issue PIN reports, which share with the public the IMF Executive Board's assessment of the annual "economic health check" carried out under Fund surveillance. In addition, public users can access a wealth of institutional information and data, including members' financial positions *vis-à-vis* the Fund, numerous letters of intent, Policy Framework papers, speeches by management, the IMF publications database and full texts of hundreds of IMF publications. Yet, important as these reforms are, they are generally considered to be "easy." As the next sections show, a number of important issues remain to be resolved.

### The IMF: an international lender of last resort?

More than a century ago, Walter Bagehot (1999, original 1873) explained that a financial system requires a lender of last resort to assist financial institutions in a liquidity crisis.[20] Bagehot distinguished between liquidity and solvency, and provided rules that separated the two. He argued that in a crisis, the lender of last resort should lend freely, at a penalty rate, on the basis of collateral that is marketable in the ordinary course of business when there is no panic.[21] The collateral requirement separates insolvent from illiquid financial institutions, in particular, banks (banks are vulnerable to runs because they issue highly liquid short-term liabilities). The penalty rate eliminates subsidies, reduces moral hazard, and reduces reliance on the lender. In a national setting, governments (usually a central bank) generally opt for providing lender of last resort facilities, because the public costs of a banking panic are large, and because the private sector is unable to fulfill this role, since lenders cannot quickly determine how a given shock will affect individual institutions. To limit moral hazard and the use of these facilities, the authorities impose supervisory and regulatory standards, and require, through partial deposit insurance and capital adequacy standards, that the private sector should share the cost of risk-taking. Moreover, since a domestic lender of last resort usually has regulatory authority over the commercial banks to which it lends, it can actually increase the supply of domestic money through is operations (for example, by emitting additional currency to buy government securities). Analysts credit the development of lender of last resort facilities with reducing the frequency and severity of national banking crises.[22]

If a lender of last resort is necessary in a domestic context, isn't an analogous institution necessary at the *international* level to resolve collective action problems? Despite quota increases and the creation of instruments such as the New Arrangements to Borrow, the Fund's resources are still minuscule when compared to the sheer volume of private global capital flows. Moreover, the IMF still cannot lend freely (since it cannot create hard currencies) nor quickly (since it must get member approval of and borrower agreement to its conditional loan programs). Also, as Kenen (2001, 60) notes, "the IMF does not lend freely in a Bagehot-like manner, against good collateral. Instead, it disburses large-scale financing in tranches to make sure that policy commitments are being fulfilled." Deepak Lal argues that the IMF should not serve as a lender of last resort, because it cannot distinguish between an illiquid bank and an insolvent bank. Lal (1998, 17) notes:

> The IMF can lend only after lengthy negotiations with a country's government and with the approval of its board. It has no way of sorting out the "good" from "bad" loans, for instance made by foreign banks to residents in the country, and to liquidate the latter. The lender of last resort function for the money center banks involved in foreign lending must therefore continue to be provided by their parent central bank.

Indeed, some prefer that the IMF should stop pretending to be a lender of last resort and get out of the lending business – allowing private markets to distribute liquidity to solvent financial institutions. For example, Schwartz (1999) and Calomiris (1998) argue that official financial support for countries in crisis allows private creditors to get their funds out fully or with reduced losses. They contend that IMF lending in the Mexican crisis (which was used to bail out foreign lenders) set the stage for the Asian crisis, because these lenders expected to be bailed out if things went wrong. More generally, they claim that the presence of an international lender (such as the IMF) gives rise to serious problems of moral hazard – which would only be exacerbated if the Fund were to become a true lender of last resort. Allan Meltzer (1998) agrees, reiterating that when there is a lender of last resort, lenders have less need to assess and monitor foreign borrowers, which potentially leads to an increase in risky behavior and, consequently, more financial crises. Meltzer argues that the IMF should be replaced by a "true lender of last resort." That is, unlike the IMF, a true lender of last resort must employ Bagehot's classic rule: *never to subsidize borrowers*. At best, a lender of last resort must lend freely, to temporarily illiquid but solvent financial institutions, at penalty rates and matched by the borrower's best collateral. At worst, the IMF should restrict itself to providing very short-term, essentially unconditional liquidity support for a limited number of relatively strong emerging-market economies that would have pre-qualified for IMF assistance.

In response, Stanley Fischer (1999), at that time the first deputy managing director of the IMF, argues that the Fund's powers must be enhanced so it can function as a *"true international lender of last resort."* Underpinning Fischer's claim is the view that there are market failures, that capital flows are very volatile, that investors are subject to financial panics, and that crises are contagious. In such a world, an international lender of last resort could not only help mitigate the effects of such instability, but, by its very existence, mitigate the instability itself. Fischer notes that although "the IMF is not an international central bank, it has already undertaken important lender of last resort functions," such as using its own funds to design financial stabilization programs and organizing international rescue packages, including preventing panic-induced declines in the aggregate money supply and contagious spillovers. While the IMF lacks the powers of a central bank, and does not have the resources to cover all potential foreign-exchange obligations, it nevertheless has the capacity to act as a lender to individual countries in specified circumstances. For Fischer, the major function of the lender of last resort in modern economies is that of a "crisis manager" – a role that does not require large amounts of capital – indeed, "the lender of last resort need not have the power to create money as long as it can provide credit to the market or to institutions in trouble."[23] He notes that "panics caused by a demand for currency are rare." More generally, panics take the form of a bank run (possibly enhanced by contagion), in which deposits shift from those banks and financial institutions deemed unsound to those thought to be healthy. In these cases, creating additional money may be unnecessary. At least in principle, the liquidity can simply re-circulate from the institutions gaining money back to those losing it.

Fischer (1999) claims that, more than anything, it is the IMF's inability to act as a reliable lender of last resort that increases moral hazard and investor volatility. In this era of globalization, where adjustment occurs rapidly through the capital account, crises tend to be more systemic and localized. These crises requires a lender of last resort because, although lending may have caused the crises, lending is also required to end them. Without a body like the IMF, an *ad hoc* consortium of countries led by the G-7 would have to be pulled together during times of crises. If past experience is any guide, this consortium would neither act in a timely manner, nor as effectively as the IMF. No doubt, leading the consortium would be the *leader of last resort*, the United States. The idea that the United States should act as the world's central banker would hardly be acceptable at home or abroad. To Fischer, the IMF is the only institution that can coordinate large and rapid injections of credit when fast-moving global financial panics hit sovereign nations.

To date, the international community has steered a middle course between these two views – acknowledging that financial markets are not perfect and that the IMF has a significant role to play in dealing with international crises, especially those that may pose a risk to the stability of the international financial system. As was noted earlier, the G-7 and other IMF shareholders have increased the Fund's financial resources, including its ability to provide liquidity in times of crisis, so that it can continue to serve as an informal lender of last resort. However, the Fund, on its part, must now make certain that its prescribed standards on improving financial disclosure, supervision and regulation are implemented in both the public and private sectors. Most importantly, the Fund must find ways to limit the moral hazard problem. For a start, it should make it clear that it will extend liquidity only to governments that put proper measures in place to prevent excessive risk-taking. In addition, it can reduce the incentives for risk-taking by restricting the ability of governments to bail out stockholders and large uninsured creditors of domestic financial institutions. Indeed, the new provision that only countries that meet specified standards will be eligible to borrow IMF funds under the CCL provides incentives for countries to adopt the necessary international standards. Equally encouraging is the fact that the IMF is now required to become more selective in its lending – providing funds only when there is a liquidity crisis – that is, when private lenders are unwilling to lend. Already, the Fund's lending under the SRF incorporates Bagehot's classic prescription that crisis lending should be at a penalty rate. The fact that SRF short-term loans made to Korea, Russia and Brazil were subject to penalty rates and to strict but necessary policy conditionality (which serves as a further element of the penalty) is an indication that the IMF is serious about limiting moral hazard.

### Capital account liberalization or capital controls?

In 1944, the Bretton Woods conference recognized the fundamental link between capital controls and international trade. Indeed, one of the main purposes of the IMF (which was created at the conference) was to assist in the elimination of foreign-exchange restrictions that hampered the growth of global trade.[24] However, the maintenance of capital controls was not viewed as inconsistent with this objective, partly because capital controls were considered necessary for supporting the system of fixed exchange rates and thus fostering trade. In the ensuing years, dramatic changes in information and communications technology fundamentally transformed the financial services industry and made highly mobile capital a fact of life. Today private capital flows to emerging markets comprise a wide range of instruments, including bank deposits, equities, direct investments, corporate bonds and government securities, among others. In recognition of this, over the past two decades the IMF has steadfastly promoted the liberalization of cross-border capital flows.[25] Just before the outbreak of the financial crisis in Asia, the Interim Committee of the IMF (at its semi-annual meeting in April 1997) proposed that the organization's Articles of Agreement (the basic constitution of international financial relations among the 182 member nations) be amended to include currency convertibility for capital transactions. This view was reiterated in the following months by senior Fund officials, who stated that capital account liberalization should become one of the IMF's fundamental objectives (Fischer 1998; 2000).

Many countries that have current account convertibility (i.e. that allow foreigners and local residents to buy and sell the currency for trade purposes) do not have capital account convertibility (i.e. they do not allow the purchase and sale of the currency for portfolio investments). Capital account convertibility can benefit a country by encouraging capital inflows and by permitting domestic residents to enjoy the benefits of international portfolio diversification. However, capital account convertibility also brings with it the possibility of much more volatile capital flows that can destabilize domestic financial markets and the exchange rate. The Asian countries hardest hit by the crisis had all pursued diverse approaches to opening up their capital accounts. Indonesia liberalized outflows in the 1980s and inflows only gradually. In 1989 it eliminated controls on foreign borrowing by banks (but reintroduced them two years later because of concerns about excessive borrowing). Indonesia continued, however, to liberalize inflows to corporations, allowing borrowing for trade finance, sales of securities to non-residents and foreign investment in the domestic stock market. South Korea took a more gradualist approach. It liberalized outflows in the early 1980s, and inflows into its securities markets in the early 1990s. In 1992, for example, non-residents were given limited access to the Korean stock market, and the types of securities that resident firms could issue abroad were expanded. Thailand attracted foreign inflows by offering tax incentives to foreign investors, including setting up a special facility in 1993 – the Bangkok International Banking Facility (BIBF) – in order to enable domestic banks and financial institutions to borrow from abroad to finance local investment projects and allow foreign investment in Thai securities markets.[26] Not surprisingly, in 1996 almost 60 per cent (or US$100 billion) of total capital flows to developing countries went to Asia (IMF 1999).

During the height of the Asian crisis, the Malaysian government dramatically challenged the prevailing wisdom and imposed capital controls – bringing the issue to the forefront of economic policy debates. In a broad sense, capital controls are measures that discourage capital flows – both in and out of a country. Capital controls encompass a wide range of, often country-specific, measures, although they all attempt to restrict the movement of capital across national boundaries, or between residents and non-residents. Capital controls may affect: (1) foreign direct investment of residents and non-residents; (2) portfolio investments by non-residents; (3) borrowing and lending between residents and non-residents through financial institutions; and (4) other capital transactions, such as controls over resident holdings of foreign-currency deposits or personal transfers and real-estate investments. Capital controls have mainly taken two general forms: *direct* or *administrative* controls and *market-based* or *indirect* controls. Direct controls restrict capital movement and/or the associated payments and transfers of funds through outright prohibitions, explicit quantitative limits, or an approval procedure – which may or may not be rule-based. Administrative controls typically seek to affect the volume of the relevant cross-border financial transactions directly. A common characteristic of such controls is that they impose administrative obligations on the banking system to control flows. Market-based controls discourage capital movements and the associated transactions by making them more costly to undertake. Such controls may take various forms, including: (1) explicit taxation of cross-border flows, in forms such as taxes and levies on external financial transactions; (2) indirect taxation of cross-border flows, in forms such as non-interest-bearing reserve or deposit requirements – under which residents may be required to deposit at zero interest rates a proportion of capital inflows at the central bank; and (3) a multiple exchange-rate system, where different exchange rates apply to different types of transactions. Depending on their specific type, market-based controls may affect either the price or both the price and the volume of a given transaction.

### The Malaysian capital controls

In the region, Malaysia was the most open of the economies, following an approach to economic development that included the liberalization of capital movements. By the mid-1990s Malaysia was home to one of the world's most highly capitalized stock and open financial markets. By 1996, Malaysia's capital account was generally opened. Portfolio inflows were free of restrictions on all types of Malaysian financial instruments (bonds, equities, money market, derivative instruments and bank deposits), while portfolio outflows were also free except for resident corporations with domestic borrowing.[27] Although, prior to the crisis, Bank Negara Malaysia (the country's central bank) did not maintain an official parity for the ringgit, cross-border activities in ringgit were treated liberally, including the use of ringgit in trade and in financial transactions with non-residents.[28] Offshore trading of ringgit securities was also tolerated. Local banks were allowed to provide forward cover against ringgit to non-residents, facilitating arbitrage between domestic and offshore markets. As a result, an active offshore market in ringgit had developed (mainly in Singapore), with the bulk of cross-currency hedging of ringgit taking place in this market rather than onshore. Finally, inward foreign direct investment flows were actively encouraged through tax and other incentives, and non-residents were completely free to repatriate their investments through a system of external accounts (Bank Negara Malaysia 1998).

However, like its neighbors, Malaysia was also susceptible to regional contagion. Institutional investors could not but be concerned about the virtual pegging of the ringgit to the US dollar, which left Malaysia vulnerable to changes in the value of external currencies. Furthermore, the persistent current-account deficit fueling the economic boom and a high investment rate that exceeded the domestic savings rate did not go unnoticed. Finally, the excessive expansion in bank credit to non-productive sectors contributed to speculative price bubbles in real estate and stock markets, and the growing maturity mismatches between assets and liabilities left the financial sector exposed and vulnerable.

Yet, on the eve of the crisis, the Malaysian economy enjoyed stronger fundamentals than her neighbors – partly because of the early set of regulations and restrictions on capital flows that it had instituted in 1989 and 1994. The GDP growth of Malaysia averaged 8.9 per cent in the period 1990–95 and 8.6 per cent and 7.7 per cent respectively in 1996 and 1997. In fact, in the first quarter of 1997, Malaysia enjoyed a robust 8 per cent growth-rate – one of the highest in the region (Bank Negara Malaysia 1998; 1999). Also, as Athukorala (1998, 85) notes, "the Malaysian economy had experienced virtually full employment for the previous six years and modest inflation (4.5 per cent). The country's foreign currency sovereign credit rating was an A+, in the same league as Hong Kong." Second, Malaysia enjoyed a succession of budget surpluses – which helped to lower public debt, contain inflation, boost savings and encourage private-sector growth. Indeed, Malaysia's savings as a share of GNP were only exceeded by Singapore among the regional economies. Third, although, the external current-account deficit was high when the crisis began, it was financed largely by foreign direct investment. Specifically, the government's explicit policy to limit short-term borrowing, encourage foreign direct investment inflows, and rely on equity capital prevented the corporate sector from building up excessive unhedged foreign-exchange exposures and high debt/equity ratios. Fourth, in sharp contrast to Thailand and Indonesia, Malaysia had a reasonable level of foreign-exchange reserves (an estimated US$22 billion) relative to its short-term debt, making it far less vulnerable to a run on its reserves. The bulk of short-term foreign capital came through the banking system rather than borrowing. As a result Malaysia's debt-service ratio stood at only 6.1 per cent of exports at the end of 1996 (Bank Negara Malaysia 1999). Clearly, Malaysia's low foreign debt placed it in a relatively good position to confront the crisis. Fifth, Malaysia could avoid requesting assistance from the IMF because of the lower exposure of the Malaysian banking sector to foreign liabilities. Finally, since Malaysia had already experienced a banking crisis in the mid-1980s, the government had implemented a substantial reform program in the late 1980s. Thus, compared to the other crisis-hit countries, Malaysia already had in place a relatively well-developed regulatory, legal and accounting framework for the financial system. For example, all foreign borrowings had to be approved by Bank Negara, and they were approved only when there was a natural hedge. This prevented the corporate sector from building up large unhedged foreign exchange exposures and very high debt-equity ratios. Indeed, owing to its tighter controls on foreign borrowing, Malaysia was also less exposed to short-term foreign debt – which was encouraged by a pegged exchange rate in Thailand and Indonesia.

In spite of these obvious strengths, with the onset of the crisis the ringgit came under significant depreciation pressure along with other regional currencies.[29] Much of this pressure occurred through previously unrestricted currency trading in the offshore ringgit market. As offshore currency traders took short positions in ringgit in anticipation of a depreciation, Bank Negara Malaysia's immediate response was to intervene in the foreign-exchange markets to defend the ringgit against speculative attacks. To punish speculators who were shorting the ringgit, offshore ringgit interest rates increased relative to domestic interest rates (Bank Negara Malaysia 1999). But, this was to no avail. As Cheong (1998, 237) notes, "currency speculators and hedge funds in the major foreign exchange markets in London, New York, Hong Kong and Singapore mounted increasingly larger onslaughts against the ringgit . . . large foreign banks which had monitored the market movements of the currency speculators and hedge funds joined in the attacks with prospects of huge forex profits."

On July 14, 1997, after about a week of trying to uphold the ringgit's value and spending an estimated RM9 billion (US$3.5 billion) in external reserves, Bank Negara Malaysia ceased its intervention. The ringgit was allowed to free-float clean for the first time in twenty-two years, as "Bank Negara appeared to be unwilling to commit the rest of its US$24.6 billion in external reserves in the face of a seemingly unlimited supply of offshore ringgit for sale" (Cheong 1998, 237). In August 1997, the Malaysian authorities temporarily broke the link between the domestic and offshore rates by imposing limits on ringgit non-trade-related swap transactions with non-residents, besides imposing limits on banks non-commercial-related offer-side swap transactions (i.e. forward order/spot purchases of ringgit) by foreign customers. As a result, wide spreads emerged between domestic and offshore interest rates.[30] However, the breaking of the direct arbitrage link did not prevent outflows. Rather, outflows continued through various unrestricted channels to take advantage of the large interest differentials created by the swap limits. The flow of ringgit funds offshore led to further increases in domestic rates, accelerating the economic contraction (some 5 per cent in the first half of 1998), and exacerbating the difficulties in the corporate and banking sectors.[31]

Malaysia's initial response to the crisis was to mimic faithfully the IMF prescription of tight fiscal and monetary policies – referred to as a case of "virtual IMF policy without the IMF loans" (Jomo 2001a, xl). Interest rates were raised (from 6 per cent in June 1997 to 35 per cent in July 1997) to stem the decline of the ringgit, and in early December 1997 a drastic cut (18 per cent) in government spending was announced to improve the current-account balance (Boorman *et al.* 2000, 12). However, by the end of 1997 it was clear that these measures had failed to produce the expected results. Instead, the contractionary measures transformed the financial crisis into a nationwide crisis. As Yusof, Hew and Nambiar (2000, 70), note, "the effect of the tight macroeconomic policy stance, therefore, proved very destructive." However, the "virtual IMF policies" cannot be held solely responsible. The Malaysian government's policy responses made the situation worse. First, Mahathir's diatribes against international currency traders and hedge fund managers, in particular, George Soros, only served further to undermine market sentiment. Second, the government's repeated threat to use repressive measures against commentators making unfavorable reports about the Malaysian economy only gave credence to the impression that the government was hiding important economic information from the markets. Third, in early September 1997 the Malaysian government unveiled a plan to use funds from the Employees Provident Fund (totaling some RM60 billion), to prop up share prices by buying stocks from selected Malaysian shareholders only at premium prices. Besides the well-connected cronies, the "selected" also included Mahathir's eldest son, the publicly-listed corporation set up by his party cooperative (KUB), and the country's largest conglomerate, Renong – controlled by Mahathir and his close confidante, Daim Zainuddin. As Gomez and Jomo (1999, 189) note, the government's generous financial package "was understandably seen as a bailout facility designed to save cronies." Moreover, the mid-October 1997 budget announcement for 1988 was seen by foreign financial interests as further evidence of official denial of the gravity of the crisis and its causes. In the ensuing several months policy inconsistency, culminating in political conflicts within the ruling UMNO party (especially between Prime Minister Mahathir and Deputy Prime Minister Anwar Ibrahim) generated market uncertainty. When it became clear (by late 1997) that Mahathir and Daim had literally taken over economic policy-making from the reform-oriented Anwar, there was a sharp exacerbation of economic problems.

Not surprisingly, the ringgit fell precipitously after mid-July 1997, reaching RM4.88 to the US dollar in early January 1998. This was the ringgit's lowest level ever, representing a collapse by almost half within less than six months from a high of RM2.47 in mid-July 1997. Similarly, the Kuala Lumpur Stock Exchange (KLSE) Composite Index dropped from over 1,300 in the first quarter of 1997 to less than 500 in January 1998. On 7 January 1998, a National Economic Action Council (NEAC) was established to develop a plan to deal more effectively with the crisis. Made up of senior cabinet members, technocrats and executives from the private sector, the NEAC unveiled its "alternative action plan" – the National Economic Recovery Plan (NERP) – in July 1998. Among other things, the NERP recommended a relaxation of the tight fiscal policy; fiscal stimulus to boost the domestic economy; improvement in corporate governance; and, without doubt, the most controversial: selective capital controls.

The Malaysian economy contracted every quarter in 1998, with the biggest contraction (10.9 per cent) in the third quarter. On September 1, 1998, 14 months after the outbreak of the crisis, and after substantial capital outflows had already taken place, the Malaysian government imposed controls on *capital outflows and restrictions on exchange rate transactions* in an effort to (to use Prime Minister Mahathir Mohamed's words), stop "rogue foreign speculators from trying to destroy the Malaysian economy" (Mahathir 1999). On September 2, the leading opponent of capital controls, finance minister Anwar, was dismissed from cabinet.[32] The government now had a free hand to introduce the control measures. Specifically, the measures were designed to insulate monetary policy from external volatility and facilitate a low-interest-rate policy and to contain speculative capital movements. Thus a series of measures were introduced for containing ringgit speculation and the outflow of capital by eliminating the offshore ringgit market (which was viewed as the source of the speculative pressures on the ringgit) and restricting the supply of ringgit to speculators in order to prevent them from taking positions against the currency. Bank Negara Malaysia was given the task of repatriating all ringgit held offshore, including ringgit deposits in overseas banks, by October 1, 1998. In addition, Bank Negara approval was required to transfer funds between external accounts (freely allowed previously), and licensed offshore banks were prohibited from trading in ringgit assets. Similarly, residents were prohibited from granting ringgit credit facilities to non-resident corresponding banks and stockbroking companies (Bank Negara Malaysia 1998). Also, a "temporary" (one-year) prohibition was instituted (effective September 1, 1998) against repatriation of earnings by foreign investors on portfolio investments held in the country for less than one year.[33] In addition, exporters were required to turn in foreign-currency earnings to the central bank in exchange for ringgit at the new pegged exchange rate of 3.80 to the US dollar – a rate that represented a 10 per cent appreciation relative to the level that the ringgit had been trading at. Finally, the authorities imposed tight limits on transfers of capital abroad by residents, and Malaysian citizens were prohibited from taking as little as US$100 out of the country – the law being enforced by random searches at the airport and other exit points.[34]

## Assessing the efficacy of the reforms

As Yusof, Hew and Nambiar (2000, 85) note, "the earlier indictment that capital controls would be disastrous for Malaysia has been proved to be incorrect." Nevertheless, the effectiveness of the Malaysian controls in realizing their intended objectives remains the subject of controversy. Ethan Kaplan and Dani Rodrik (2001) present empirical evidence on the aggregate effects of the Malaysian controls. Were they a success? they ask. According to the authors, that depends on the counterfactual. Contrasting Malaysia's performance with that of the other Asian countries during the year *after* controls were imposed suggests that the controls were not successful. On the other hand, if economic performance is compared during the *preceding* 12 months, Malaysia looks like a considerable success – even controlling for differences in the external environment across the two periods. To the authors, the latter is the right comparison, because the preceding 12-month period is the time when IMF-supported programs – the presumed alternative for Malaysia – began to be implemented by the other crisis-affected Asian countries. Moreover, financial indicators in Malaysia worsened before the imposition of the controls, suggesting that the main crisis was yet to come. Thus Kaplan and Rodrik conclude that, compared to the performance of Thailand, Korea and Indonesia while they were under IMF programs, Malaysia's non-IMF policies produced faster economic recovery, lower inflation, smaller declines in employment and inflation-adjusted wages and a more rapid turnaround in the stock market.

There is no doubt that the controls did provide a measure of certainty at a time of unprecedented financial turbulence. The reduction of the ringgit's internationalization and the elimination of most potential sources of access to ringgit by non-residents effectively eliminated the offshore ringgit market. For example, the offshore bank in Singapore had to dispense with the ringgit, thereby eliminating external restrictions on the velocity of circulation. This, coupled with the restrictions on non-residents' repatriation of portfolio capital and on residents' outward investments, contributed much to the containment of capital outflows. In conjunction with other macroeconomic and financial policies, the controls helped to stabilize the exchange rate. Since the introduction of the controls, there have been no signs of speculative pressures on the exchange rate, despite the marked relaxation of fiscal and monetary policies to support weak economic activity. Finally, it can be argued that Malaysia had the last laugh, since its decision to revitalize the economy via fiscal expansion and a more easy monetary policy was later advocated by the IMF for Indonesia, South Korea and Thailand.

On the other hand, those critical of the Malaysian controls, including the IMF, point out that they were introduced well into the crisis, after a substantial amount of capital had already left the country, and thus their effects on portfolio outflows were limited. For example, Boorman *et al.* (2000, 10) note that "Malaysia's capital controls introduced in September 1998, after market conditions had stabilized and capital outflows abated, hardly provide a test of the usefulness of capital controls in handling a crisis." Critics like Boorman also note that several rating agencies downgraded Malaysia's credit and sovereign risk ratings immediately following the imposition of capital controls. Malaysia's risk premium in international markets also increased, raising the costs of foreign-currency funding to Malaysian corporations and banks. Thus, for the critics, the Malaysian controls have been somewhat of a missed opportunity. They claim that rather than utilizing the so-called "breathing space" to implement more fundamental policy reforms, in particular, the correction of macroeconomic imbalances and the strengthening of its fragile and highly leveraged financial sector, the Malaysian government has done very little. They note, for example, that Prime Minister Mahathir, besides sacking reform-oriented policy-makers (such as Anwar Ibrahim), has followed policies, including further loosening non-performing loan classification regulation and setting minimum lending targets for banks, that will only serve to exacerbate the underlying structural problems. Second, it has been argued that the controls were designed to bail out the regime's cronies. According to Johnson and Mitton (2001, 4) capital controls created a "screen for cronyism" that made it easier for strong politicians to support favored firms. They add that "only firms connected to Prime Minister Mahathir experienced a disproportionate increase in stock prices in September 1998." Namely, following the imposition of capital controls, the stock of politically connected firms rose by about 20 per cent more than other similar, but unconnected firms. In addition, among politically connected firms, those that benefitted the most had not previously reduced their cost of capital by listing overseas. That is, they stood to gain more from official support. Similarly, Jomo (2001, 3) notes:

> The window of opportunity offered by capital controls has been abused by certain powerfully-connected business interests, not only to secure publicly funded bail-outs at public expense, but even to consolidate and extend their corporate domination, especially in the crucial financial sector. Capital controls have been part of a package focused on saving friends of the regime, usually at the public's expense.

Yet the arguments of supporters and critics notwithstanding, a balanced assessment of the pro and cons of the Malaysian controls requires that we take into account a number of key policy measures introduced by the Malaysian government that had nothing to do with the controls, but that enabled the government to curtail the deterioration in the financial sector and assist in the recovery. *First*, the government's announcement of a guarantee of bank deposits early in the crisis (January 1998) was perceived to be credible in view of the country's legal and regulatory framework. This prevented the type of bank runs and "flight to quality" experienced in Indonesia, Thailand and Korea. In March, the authorities adopted a strategy to safeguard the soundness of the financial system. Key measures included the upgrading of capital adequacy, prudential guidelines and disclosure standards for banking institutions, as well as a merger program for finance companies. *Second*, in June 1998, the government established Pengurusan Danaharta Nasional Berhad (or Danaharta), an asset-management and recovery agency designed to acquire non-performing loans from banks and manage their impaired assets. Initially invested with RM1.5 billion in capital provided by the Finance Ministry, Danaharta was authorized to issue up to RM15 billion (face value) in bonds. Moreover, legislation vested the agency with special power over borrowers, including insulation of the agency from undisclosed claims made after the initial purchase of assets; the ability to appoint special administrators without having to go to court; and the power to abrogate underlying contracts when the agency foreclosed on collateral. Indeed, the legal power vested in Danaharta helped ensure that banks were left with a manageable level of problem loans, that acquired assets were rehabilitated, and that non-performing loans would be dealt with promptly. The use of independent auditors to determine the value of assets acquired by Danaharta avoided the subsidies required in Indonesia and Korea, besides ensuring that the agency did not become a tool for indirect bailouts of existing shareholders – which would have undermined the incentives for private sector recapitalization.

*Third*, in July 1998, the government established Danamodal Nasional Berhad (or Danamodal) to manage bank restructuring and recapitalization. Capital injections from Danamodal were designed to enable institutions to restore their capital adequacy ratio to 9 per cent. To support its mission, Danamodal raised RM10.7 billion – RM3 billion in paid-up capital from Bank Negara and RM7.7 billion through the issuance of bonds to financial institutions. The selection of candidates for recapitalization was initially guided by Bank Negara's watchlist-based stress tests of banking institutions. Institutions requesting capital injections were required to submit recapitalization plans and were subject to monthly reporting of performance against a list of targets. Moreover, Danamodal exercised control over management by appointing at least two members to the boards of directors – one of whom had to be an executive director or chairman of the board. Indeed, Danamodal succeeded early in restoring the capital levels of domestic banks, whereas the capital standards were not fully met in Indonesia and Thailand, which employed a more decentralized process. Clearly, Danamodal's mandate inspired confidence that all domestic financial institutions in Malaysia would be recapitalized to the required standards and that necessary operational restructuring would be imposed through the exercise of control over their management. Moreover, the requirement that institutions seeking Danamodal's capital would have to sell non-performing loans in excess of the specified proportion to Danaharta gave banks the incentive to deal with their bad assets in a timely manner.

*Fourth*, also in July 1998, the government established the Corporate Debt Restructuring Committee (CDRC) to help mediate voluntary out-of-court restructuring of large debt involving a number of major creditors, following the London Rules model. Specifically, CDRC's aim was to minimize losses to creditors and company shareholders through coordinated debt workouts that avoided placing viable companies into liquidation or receivership, and to have banking institutions play a greater role in the financial rehabilitation of the corporate sector. Thus, debt-restructuring under CDRC was reserved for viable businesses only, and not those in receivership or liquidation. Moreover, aggregate bank loans had to be RM50 million or more, with at least three lending institutions participating, and the creditor committees representing the interests of at least 75 per cent of the total debt of all creditors. Overall, Danaharta, Danamodal and CDRC worked in tandem to allow banks to reduce their non-performing loans, corporations to reduce their debts and both to strengthen their capital bases.

And *fifth*, Malaysia was also fortunate to experience a cyclical recovery in its key manufacturing industry, namely electronics – which saw a major resurgence in exports in the first quarter of 1999. Moreover, as an oil exporter, the sharp increases in oil prices three times in the period 1998–2000 greatly helped Malaysia overturn the current-account deficit. Of course, these developments were driven by forces that had nothing to do with capital controls.

### The broader debate on capital controls

Malaysia's heterodox policy response to the crisis, besides bringing sharp rebuke from the Fund and the United States Treasury, also re-ignited an old debate on the appropriate sequencing of financial sector reforms – specifically, on the appropriate timing for liberalizing the capital account. No doubt, economic theory has long recognized the negative effects of exchange and capital controls. The efficient market hypothesis and conventional neoclassical accounts support capital market liberalization largely on "efficiency arguments." In a nutshell, it is argued that open capital accounts can foster a more efficient allocation of resources, provide opportunities for risk diversification and help promote financial development. To quote Fischer (1998, 2–3):

> free capital movements facilitate an efficient global allocation of savings and help channel resources into their most productive uses, thus increasing economic growth and welfare. From the individual country's perspective, the benefits take the form of increases in the pool of investible funds and in the access of domestic residents to foreign capital markets. From the viewpoint of the international economy, open capital accounts support the multilateral

trading system by broadening the channels through which countries can finance trade and investment and attain higher levels of income. International capital flows expand the opportunities for portfolio diversification and thereby provide investors in both industrial and developing countries with the potential to achieve higher risk-adjusted rates of returns.

It is argued that by taxing foreign money required to purchase foreign-made goods and services, exchange controls cut the quantity imported and/or raise the domestic relative price of imports. Moreover, exchange and capital controls raise transaction and other trade-related costs, and give rise to negative market perceptions, which in turn make it costlier and more difficult for the country to access foreign funds. Costs associated with international transactions increase because exchange controls tend to undermine the development of liquid (and efficient) foreign-exchange markets, besides postponing necessary adjustments in policies and hampering private-sector adaptation to modern financial instruments and changing international circumstances. Both types of controls foster evasion, rent-seeking, and the development of a parallel or black market in foreign exchange, including corruption, besides prolonging the survival of unsustainable domestic policies. In addition, controls will inevitably generate a huge bureaucracy to enforce the rules, besides reducing trade by limiting the transfer of technology, portfolio diversification, managerial expertise and skills through foreign direct investment. These problems make capital controls poor candidates for permanent solutions.

Similarly, controls on repatriation of profits and dividends discourage direct foreign investment, reduce international trade and limit domestic business opportunities. In the presence of capital controls, financial intermediation is less efficient, since savings are not allocated to the most efficient uses, and the range of available financial products and services tends to be narrow and of poorer quality. Also, as capital controls tend to create a wedge between domestic and external financial markets, the resultant differentials between domestic and international interest rates may create problems. That is, the wedge may create incentives for circumvention – meaning that the effectiveness of controls will then depend on the size of this incentive relative to the cost of circumvention.[35] It has been argued that the amount of foreign currency and currency-related derivative trading has risen so rapidly that it is almost impossible to impose effective controls on them. Coupled with the sheer volume of international financial transactions in global markets, controls only provide new incentives for evasion. Moreover, as Stanley Fischer (2001, 10–11) notes, "controls on capital outflows can be used to help maintain a pegged exchange rate, given domestic policies are consistent with maintenance of the exchange rate. However, such controls tend to lose their effectiveness and efficiency over time. Capital inflow may for a time be useful in enabling a country to run an independent monetary policy when the exchange rate is softly pegged, and may influence the composition of capital inflows, but their long-term effectiveness to those ends is doubtful." Finally, it is well understood that capital controls cannot substitute for sound macroeconomic policies. Countries with serious macroeconomic imbalances and no credible prospects for correction in the short-run, however, have regularly been unable to address large-scale capital outflows by using capital controls. Indeed, in some cases, controls have reduced pressures on the authorities to introduce needed policy reform.[36] And, as Eichengreen (1999) notes, capital controls are ineffective in the sense that they do not prevent speculative attacks and exchange-rate adjustment from occurring, even if they buy time before this happens.

On the other hand, it is also recognized that there are situations in which capital-account restrictions improve economic welfare by compensating for financial market imperfections, including those resulting from informational asymmetries. In the case of herd behavior, foreign investors may suddenly react to the actions of others whom they believe to have access to better information. In such circumstances, capital flows become volatile and are easily reversed. Policy implementation arguments hold that capital controls may help reconcile conflicting policy objectives when the exchange rate is fixed or heavily managed. Also, since unimpeded capital inflows can lead to real exchange-rate appreciation and current-account deficits, capital controls can act as a shield to protect monetary and financial stability in the face of persistent capital flows. This is particularly true when there are concerns about (1) the inflationary consequences of large inflows, or (2) inadequate assessment of risks by banks or the corporate sector in the context of a heavily managed exchange rate – which, by providing an implicit exchange-rate guarantee, encourages a build-up of unhedged foreign-currency positions.

Thus, it is argued that regulating short-term capital inflows – on the basis of prudential requirements on financial institutions – and regaining maneuvering room for monetary policy is highly beneficial. Specifically, it is often pointed out that Asian economies that did not experience a severe crisis during the Asian crisis had controls on capital flows. For example, China had extensive capital controls. Singapore had not internationalized its currency, given the restrictions on the usage of the Singaporean dollar and on borrowing outside Singapore. India's policy towards foreign capital in the 1990s differentiated between different types of flows. While there was considerable liberalization of the regime for foreign direct investment, liberalization of portfolio flows began gradually in 1993. Most importantly, debt flows have not been liberalized, and short-term debt is tightly controlled for all Indian residents, including banks. Also, unlike many other emerging market countries, India also restricts capital outflows. Thus, it is argued that India's cautious approach insulated it from the destabilizing forces of highly volatile capital flows.

On the other hand, it is argued that in countries where the capital account was liberalized prematurely, without adequate preparation and strengthening of the financial system to build in an appropriate reflection of risk, there have been huge inflows of capital, especially short-term borrowing, that made these countries extremely vulnerable to a sudden change in investor sentiment. Specifically, in South Korea, Thailand and Indonesia, a key source of vulnerability had been the large capital inflows in the earlier part of the 1990s – particularly, unhedged short-term foreign borrowing. This had made these three crisis countries vulnerable to capital outflows and exchange-rate depreciation. Capital inflows had also fueled a rapid credit expansion that led to asset-price inflation and financing of low-quality investments. The credit expansion also reflected weaknesses in lending practices, ineffective market discipline, deficiencies in prudential regulation and supervision, and close links among governments, banks and corporations. Finally, capital controls are sometimes justified on the grounds that it is necessary to ensure that scarce domestic savings are used to finance investments at home rather than investments abroad. In such cases, controls usually take the form of rules on investments by resident individuals or institutions in foreign assets. At times such controls are used to ensure adequate (and lower-cost) financing for the government. Conversely, controls may also be used to limit foreign ownership of domestic firms.

Before the Asian crisis, the general perception in the international financial community was that liberalization of capital movements was an essential element of economic liberalization – almost a touchstone of commitment to market reforms. However, the Asian financial crisis forcefully demonstrated that capital flows carry both benefits and costs. First, the highly competitive and globalized financial world has created individual market participants that are huge enough to mobilize, often with the help of leverage, financial resources larger than the GDP of smaller economies. Thus, they can build up dominating positions in the markets of smaller economies and influence short-term market movements either singly or through acting in concert. This means that for countries with poorly developed financial markets, free cross-border movement of capital is incompatible if these countries try to maintain separate currencies and their own exchange arrangements. Second, there has been growing awareness that rapid liberalization and the associated expansion of credit and increase in the mobility of cross-border capital can give rise to significant risks, unless liberalization is preceded or accompanied by measures to promote more effective risk-management. One of these risks is the potential for large capital inflows to be poorly invested, resulting in a misallocation of resources – which in turn can reduce the growth capacity of an economy and distort asset prices.

Thus a number of distinguished economists (who on principle are supportive of the idea of free capital mobility) have nevertheless cautioned that controls help limit *volatile short-term capital flows*, thereby avoiding balance-of-payments crises and limiting exchange-rate volatility. Equally important, it provides governments greater independence in determining the interest-rate policy. In 1978, James Tobin (later a Nobel laureate in economics) proposed "throwing sand in the wheels of short-run capital flows" by imposing a uniform tax (dubbed the Tobin tax) on all foreign-exchange transactions to reduce the destabilizing speculation in international financial markets. Admittedly, the Tobin tax would be a small percentage levy (in the order of about 0.1 per cent to 0.5 per cent) on all foreign-exchange transactions. Tobin (1978) argued that such a tax would greatly lessen the profit margins on short-term currency trading (so called "round-tripping"), while having minimal effects on the returns to long-term international investments.[37] In a similar vein, MIT's Rudiger Dornbusch (1986) noted that since financial markets are very liquid and react quickly to shocks (while the real economy is slow to react, owing to price and wage rigidities and investment irreversibility), this "differential speed of adjustment" may induce excess exchange-rate volatility (over-shooting, bubbles, etc.), with negative effects on real economic activity. Dornbusch proposes the adoption of measures such as dual exchange-rate systems to protect the real economy from the fluctuations in the financial markets. Similarly, Radelet and Sachs (1998, 36) have concluded:

> the rapid push towards fully open capital markets among the developing countries would seem to be misguided. There is certainly no strong empirical evidence that economic growth in middle-income developing countries depends on unfettered access to short-term capital flows from abroad. The policy goal – should be to support long-term capital flows especially foreign direct investment, and equity portfolio flows, but to limit short-term international flows mainly to the financing of short-term trade transactions.

Angered by the "unnecessary destruction" caused by the Asian financial crisis, the Columbia University economist Jagdish Bhagwati (1998, 7; also 1998a; 1998c) – an uncompromising advocate of free trade – accused the "Wall Street–Treasury Department Complex" (which he claims commands tremendous influence over the IMF and the World Bank) for preaching the virtues of unfettered capital flows without highlighting the costs associated with "the inherently crisis-prone nature of freer capital movements" – in particular, that large influxes of capital can lead to overcapacity and speculative bubbles. Bhagwati notes that for a long time it has been taken for granted that capital flows are analogous to trade flows. – i.e. that wherever they occur and in whatever form, they invariably benefit long-term economic development. However, he cautions that between the processes of trade liberalization and financial liberalization there lies a great difference. Specifically, Bhagwati (1998, 10–11), notes that there is a "difference between trade in widgets and dollars ... many assumed that free capital mobility among all nations was exactly like free trade in their goods and services ... that the gains might be problematic because of the costs of crises was not considered ... [and it is this] original version of the myth which has steadily propelled the IMF into its complacent and dangerous moves toward the goal of capital account convertibility." Thus, trade liberalization should not be linked to capital liberalization – as the former is not subject to herd behavior, market panics and speculation. While Bhagwati (1998, 8) cautions that countries should "not jump to capital controls," he notes that "it has become apparent that crises attendant on capital mobility cannot be ignored." Bhagwati's (1998a, A-38) advice includes:

> For many developing countries today, including India and China, the question is not whether to impose capital controls but whether to drop them. To them, I say: Cease moving towards free capital flows until you have political stability, sustained prosperity and substantial macroeconomic expertise. Concentrate instead on internal reforms such as privatization and external reforms such as freer trade. Allow "targeted convertibility" for dividends, profits and invested capital for direct foreign investment. It brings capital and skills and is more stable than short-term capital flows. For the countries that had already freed capital flows substantially and are currently afflicted by panic-driven outflows, my advice is the opposite: Do not jump into capital controls.

On August 28, 1998 (just three days before Malaysia imposed controls), the iconoclastic MIT economist Paul Krugman posted on his web-site a provocative article justifying the use of controls on capital outflows to combat speculative attacks (Krugman 1998a). Specifically, Krugman argued that emergency controls on capital outflows may be a prudent choice at times of severe speculative attacks from domestic and foreign speculators. While some viewed Krugman's piece as providing intellectual cover for Malaysia's use of controls, Krugman clarified his position a week later in an article (1998) aptly titled, "Saving Asia: It's Time to Get Radical" – arguing that since earlier prescriptions, in particular protecting the currency through sharp rises in interest rates ("the IMF model"), or allowing a sharp depreciation of the exchange rate (advocated by Sachs and others), have not worked – *"temporary controls on capital"* is the least bad choice, if not the only choice, left to a country desperately trying to halt a financial meltdown.[38] In "A Letter to Malaysia's Prime Minister" Krugman (1998c), argues that Malaysia has little choice but to introduce capital controls. He (1998, 75–6) provocatively notes:

> think about China right now: a country whose crony capitalism makes Thailand look like Switzerland and whose bankers make Suharto's son look like J. P. Morgan. Why hasn't China been nearly as badly hit as its neighbors? Because it has been able to cut, not raise, interest rates in this crisis, despite maintaining a fixed exchange rate: and the reason it is able to do that is that it has an inconvertible currency, a.k.a. exchange controls. Those controls are often evaded, and they are the source of lots of corruption, but they still give China a degree of policy leeway that the rest of Asia desperately wishes it had.

Yet Krugman also adds that such temporary and "curative" controls must serve as an aid to reforms, and should be dismantled once the economy recovers. A host of other distinguished analysts have echoed similar sentiments. Harvard University's Dani Rodrik (1998a) uses a GDP per capita growth equation and a simple index of capital-account openness with a sample of some 100 developed and developing countries for 1975–89, and finds that there was no significant relationship between liberalizing capital flows and economic growth. He issues an indictment of the IMF's push for unconditional capital market liberalization, arguing that since asymmetric information problems are endemic to financial markets it is time for "the IMF to accept temporary capital controls in the countries that are otherwise following its recipes, so that they, too, can revive their economies." Princeton University's Alan Blinder (1999, 50–63) (also a former vice-chairman of the Federal Reserve) suggested that emerging economies should not "rush to open capital markets [since] unfettered international financial mobility is not the best system for all countries." Berkeley's Barry Eichengreen and Charles Wyplosz (1996) point out that most foreign-exchange transactions have little to do with economic fundamentals, and only contribute to destabilizing and reducing social welfare. Thus they make a case for the Tobin tax as a tool to lower welfare-reducing short-term capital flows without affecting welfare-enhancing long-term flows. For Eichengreen (1999) capital controls can be used as a third line of defense following the first line of defense (banks' own risk-management practices), and the second line of defense (regulatory supervision). Eichengreen (1999, 49–50; 2000a) argues that, since building effective regulatory and supervisory institutions for financial markets may take a long time, countries with underdeveloped domestic financial markets and inadequate auditing and accounting standards should impose a tax on short-term capital inflows, because, "under these circumstances, banks gambling for redemption or otherwise unable to manage the riskiness of their portfolios will tend to fund themselves excessively abroad, and foreigners will tend to accommodate them. Holding-period taxes on all capital inflows are the only effective way of containing this problem." For Eichengreen, Chilean-style controls on *capital inflows* is an appropriate way to stop the "boom and bust cycles" associated with volatile short-term capital flows.

Similarly, Joseph Stiglitz (1999, 6) (at that time, the Chief Economist at the World Bank) argued that developing countries needed to put some limits on capital inflows in order to moderate the excessive boom–bust pattern in financial markets. He noted that "it has become increasingly clear that financial and capital market liberalization – done hurriedly, without first putting into place an effective regulatory framework – was at the core of the problem. It is no accident that the two large developing countries that survived the crisis – and continued remarkably strong growth in spite of a difficult global economic environment – were India and China, both countries with strong controls on these capital flows." Stiglitz's (1999, 6) solution is clear: "volatile markets are an inescapable reality. Developing countries need to manage them. They will have to consider policies that help stabilize the economy. . . . These could include sound bankruptcy laws and Chilean-style policies that put some limits on capital flows."[39] And last, but not least, Morris Goldstein (1999) recommends that the IMF advise all emerging economies with fragile domestic financial sectors and weak prudential regulations to implement Chilean-style capital restrictions until they can successfully intermediate such flows. Such advice seems prudent. Edwards' (2001) careful empirical analysis suggests "quite strongly that the positive relationship between capital account openness and productivity performance only manifests itself after the country in question has reached a certain degree of economic development . . . a plausible interpretation is that countries can only take advantage, in net, of a greater mobility of capital once they have developed a somewhat advanced domestic financial market." It should be noted that all four authors recognize that taxes on short-term capital inflows are not a panacea, and indeed can be counter-productive if authorities use the measures as an excuse to delay implementing financial-sector reforms. They all agree that banks and non-bank financial intermediaries must manage their balance-sheets' risks prudently by adopting proper credit-risk analysis and avoiding dependence on short-term foreign-denominated debt. Equally importantly, implicit government guarantees must be avoided so as to discourage excessive short-term capital inflows.

### A sort-of "emerging consensus"

While it is difficult to gauge to what extend these criticisms, including the Malaysian controls, forced the IMF to "reevaluate" its policies on capital liberalization and capital controls, there is little doubt that there has been a re-thinking within the IMF on these issues. It should be noted that at present the IMF's Articles of Agreement do not give the Fund any mandate in the area of restrictions on capital-account transactions. In 1997, the IMF's Interim Committee had directed that the Fund should explore the possibility of amending the Article to include liberalization of capital movements as one of the "objectives" of the Fund. However, developing country opposition and the financial crisis in Asia clearly put the issue on the back burner. Nevertheless, on the basis of my interviews with senior Fund officials, two broad perspectives can be discerned. To some, full financial liberalization is still the least bad alternative, because imposing capital controls and limiting capital mobility is no solution to the structural problems underlying many emerging economies. Hence they maintain that there should not be any retreat from current levels of capital account liberalization, and second, that if there is, then the Fund should have authority to approve it in advance.

Also, the proponents of financial liberalization point out that the restoration of capital inflows will be crucial in ensuring an early recovery. After all, one reason Mexico recovered so quickly from the peso crisis was the large foreign investor participation in its export sector. Moreover, capital controls may insulate economies, thereby eroding the incentive to reform. However, others believe in a more gradualist approach. They argue that in order to compensate for financial market imperfections and the reality that adequate domestic regulation in emerging markets will take many years at best, some controls on volatile short-term capital could be permitted to allow "some temporary breathing space in which to adopt and implement sound economic policies and reforms" (IMF 2000a, 32). They add that the Fund should allow for a transitional arrangement during which countries would be urged (via a carrot-and-stick approach) to take concrete steps to strengthen their banking and financial systems.

The IMF has now qualified its earlier advocacy with an approach that favors a gradual, orderly, "properly sequenced and managed" capital-account liberalization – where long-term flows (such as FDI and term loans) are favored over short-term equity flows. As regards control on capital inflows, there is greater acceptance of the need to deter large-scale short term capital inflows with the help of indirect price-based policy tools such as the reserve requirements used by Chile. In the case of capital outflows, the Fund remains opposed to controls, considering them unworkable, especially if they are introduced during a crisis. The Fund's unorthodox position is nicely summed up by Stanley Fischer (1998, iii–iv):

> Malaysia's decision to impose controls on capital outflows – and support for the idea among some academics – raises the question of whether such controls will once again become widespread. The IMFs position has long been that capital account liberalization should proceed in an orderly way: countries should lift controls on outflows only gradually as the balance of payments strengthens; liberalization of inflows should start at the long end and move to the short end only as banking and financial systems are strengthened. We have not opposed Chilean-style, market-based measures to regulate capital inflows at the short end, but they must be considered case-by-case (Chile has recently eased its controls).

Thus, the Funds's position means neither a return to pervasive capital controls nor a rush towards unconditional capital liberalization. Rather, it seems to have adopted a policy that recognizes that controls over inflows, particularly those designed to influence their composition, might be justified, but only in countries with appropriate prudential policies. An important lesson of the Asian financial crisis is that capital-market liberalization must be undertaken with care. The problem in Asia was not that they liberalized their capital accounts, but that the sequencing was wrong and that liberalization was only partial. Most of these countries liberalized short-term capital inflows before foreign direct investment, when they should have done it the other way around. Also, if the domestic financial systems are weak, poorly regulated and subject to institutional distortions, rapid capital-account liberalization can lead to excessive short-term borrowing and lending and a build-up of excessive debt burdens – quickly turning liquidity problems into solvency problems. Hence, an orderly and sequenced liberalization until the requisite regulatory institutions are in place is critical.

Finally, the IMF's admittedly qualified support of the market-based Chilean controls on capital inflows should not be interpreted to mean that it views these as a model to be applied more broadly. The Chilean controls, or the *encaje*, in effect between May 1992 and May 1998 required anyone borrowing abroad to pay a premium of between 20 per cent and 30 per cent of the loan, to be held at the central bank without interest, for one year. The penalty rate for early withdrawal was 3 per cent. The rationale for the Chilean tax was threefold: (1) to prevent overvaluation of the peso, which would have negatively affected the country's export-oriented growth; (2) to encourage more long-term capital inflows for developmental purposes; and (3) to discourage residents from relying too heavily on short-term borrowing, thereby reducing the problem of maturity mismatch (that is heavy short-term borrowing and long-term lending). When short-term flows dried up in 1998, the premium was reduced to zero. However, what is important to note is that Chile's unremunerated reserve requirement (URR) on most capital flows was a market-based and non-discriminatory form of capital control with many desirable macroeconomic effects. Studies of the Chilean case suggest that, while the controls had limited success in reducing the overall size of capital inflows, they were effective in altering the composition of inflows away from short-term money in favor of longer-term funds (Edwards 2001). However, the Chilean control "worked because it was comprehensive and an integral part of broader macroeconomic reforms." Specifically, the Chilean authorities closed all possible loopholes – even to the extent that domestic banks were prevented from writing offshore derivative swap contracts with foreign holders of long-term Chilean debt. Most importantly, Chile could do this because of its strong macroeconomic fundamentals. Its regulation of the financial sector is well developed. Chile has in place a modern system of prudential banking regulation, effective loan-recovery mechanisms and high transparency, disclosure and accountability standards, and an autonomous central bank. Suffice it to note that these preconditions are sadly absent in most emerging economies.[40]

### What exchange-rate regimes?

In 1944, delegates from 44 countries met at Bretton Woods, New Hampshire, to reform the international monetary system. The delegates hoped to design a system that would combine the benefits of both flexible and fixed exchange-rate systems. The result was a system of fixed, but adjustable, nominal exchange rates. Under the system, the US dollar was fixed in terms of gold (initially at US$35 per ounce), and the US Treasury bought and sold gold to maintain this official price. In turn, every other member country was to anchor its currency to the dollar (and indirectly to gold) and keep its exchange rate within a 1 per cent range on either side of the parity by buying or selling US dollars in the foreign-exchange market. Only in the face of a significant and long-lasting deficit or surplus in its balance of payments was a country allowed to adjust the parity of its currency. In fact, to maintain fixed exchange rates when countries suffered balance-of-payments deficits and were losing international reserves, the IMF would loan deficit countries the needed funds. If the IMF loans proved insufficient to prevent currency depreciation, the country was allowed to devalue its currency by setting a new, lower exchange rate. Thus, the goal was to enjoy the stability associated with fixed exchange rates while simultaneously retaining the ability to move the nominal exchange rate when necessary to restore equilibrium in the balance of payments.

This system essentially collapsed in August 1971, when the United States suspended its promise to exchange gold for dollars at the official rate.[41] The current international financial system is a hybrid of a fixed and a flexible exchange-rate system. That is, rates fluctuate in response to market forces, but are not determined solely by them. Today, countries can choose from among three basic regimes in linking their economies into the international system. *First*, a flexible or "floating" exchange rate where governments let their currency float freely in the exchange markets against all other currencies. Under this system, the price of one currency relative to another is determined by the market without any intervention by central banks. That is, any current-account deficit has to be financed entirely by capital inflows (a financial account surplus) and vice versa, without any change in official reserves. Therefore, under a floating currency, a growing current-account deficit will generally be self-correcting, as the value of the currency declines in response to an outflow of funds that are seeking protection from a potential currency decline. Indeed, at the macro level, the key argument in favor of a flexible exchange rate is that it allows a country to retain independent and discretionary monetary policy as a tool for responding to shocks, particularly shocks to aggregate demand. However, a flexible regime is not cost-free. A flexible exchange rate and a discretionary monetary policy usually means some loss of credibility – which can lead to an inflation bias. At the microeconomic level, greater exchange-rate variability creates uncertainty and discourages international trade and investment. Although a floating currency introduces volatility that makes business more difficult for exporters and for those companies that compete with imports from overseas, the pain caused to them is much less than the grief of widespread bankruptcies when an overvalued fixed currency fall in a sharp devaluation.

In reality, however, few countries have truly flexible exchange-rate systems. Calvo and Reinhart (2000) have termed the unwillingness to let exchange rates be completely determined in markets "the fear of floating." This fear is based on the fact that under a pure flexible exchange-rate system, the volatility in capital flows causes corresponding volatility in the exchange rate. A volatile exchange rate, in turn, means that relative prices in the economy are volatile – which can be extremely disruptive to real economic activity.[42] Thus, even when the exchange rate is flexible in this sense, the government may (usually through the central bank) buy foreign exchange to push up the value of the foreign currency and depreciate the home currency, or sell foreign exchange to push down its value and appreciate the home currency, in order to smooth short-term fluctuations in demand and supply, and thus also short-term exchange-rate changes. Such intervention is referred to as a "dirty float," while the "managed float" means the absence of a specific target for the exchange rate.

*Second*, the general unwillingness to let exchange rates float has pushed countries towards "intermediate" exchange-rate regimes, in which official intervention is used to keep the exchange rate within predetermined bands. Thus, an intermediate regime, or "pegged" exchange rate, are those that can be adjusted or changed through such mechanisms as the "adjustable peg" (or fixing the exchange rate, but without any open-ended commitment to resist devaluation or revaluation in the presence of a large balance-of-payments deficit or surplus), or pursuant to some pre-determined parameters such as "target zones" (a margin of fluctuation around some central rate) or "crawling bands" (a pre-announced policy of devaluing a bit each week) and other hybrid systems. Pegged exchange-rate regimes imply an explicit or implicit commitment by the policy authorities to limit the extent of fluctuation of the exchange rate to a degree that provides a meaningful nominal anchor for private expectations about the behavior of the exchange rate and the requisite supporting monetary policy. Thus, in a pegged regime, it is incumbent on the pegging country to set a monetary policy that always appears to currency traders to be consistent with the pre-announced conversion rate. The best method of upholding this commitment is to run a monetary policy that is similar to that in the anchor country in terms of inflation rates and credit expansion. That is, a central bank trying to maintain an exchange-rate peg has to focus on the interest-rate differential between the short-term rate in its domestic currency and the prevailing short-term rate in the anchor currency. If the home currency comes under selling pressure, an increase in the interest-rate differential can attract buyers by convincing them that higher domestic interest rates will keep domestic inflation in check, prevent a devaluation, and result in excess returns to the domestic currency relative to the anchor currency. However, over the long term, the pegging central bank must keep domestic inflation rates close to inflation in the anchor currency. By harmonizing the inflation rates, the central bank prevents the real exchange rate from appreciating to unsustainable levels at the pegged nominal exchange rate.[43] A pegging regime is more resistant to speculative attack if banks and other institutions hold an amount of foreign-exchange reserves that is at least as great as the quantity of short-term debt that is denominated in foreign currencies. For example, Taiwan was relatively immune to the Asian crisis owing to its large holdings of foreign-exchange reserves. However, many other emerging markets are net borrowers in foreign currencies, and they attract foreign funds by establishing a peg and promising a stable exchange rate. As was noted earlier, the most prudent way to keep this promise is to run a monetary policy that closely mimics that of the anchor country.

And, *third*, countries can adopt fixed (but potentially adjustable) exchange rates.[44] There are several advantages to a fixed exchange rate. A fixed exchange rate can provide a nominal anchor that helps the country to achieve price stability. Pegging to a low-inflation currency can provide a credible anchor for restraining domestic inflation expectations as long as expectations that the fixed exchange rate will not be abandoned are credible. In addition, a fixed exchange rate encourages an inflow of foreign capital, and by appearing to eliminate exchange-rate volatility can keep interest rates lower than they would otherwise be. However, a fixed exchange rate also brings with it the problem that the real exchange rate can become overvalued – either because the domestic price level increases more rapidly than that of competing countries or because of a relative decline in the nominal value of competing currencies. Foreign lenders may be induced by higher interest rates to continue financing a growing current-account deficit; but eventually the fear of devaluation tends to overcome the high interest incentive. At that time, lenders may no longer extend loans or roll over debt, and domestic residents convert funds and take them out of the country. Finally, fixed rates lacking credibility leave countries open to speculative attacks on their currencies. More broadly, by serving as a so-called "lightning rod" for concerns about debt and banking problems as well as macroeconomic policies, they may trigger crises that greatly amplify the costs of adjustment.

Exchange rates can be fixed through multilateral arrangements, although these require more coordination and negotiation than unilateral pegs. Two multilateral systems are multilateral pegs and currency unions. In a multilateral peg, the distinction between the anchor currency and the pegging currency becomes blurred, because the participating countries are obliged to take monetary policy measures to defend the exchange-rate peg. The best example of a multilateral peg is the European Monetary System prior to the adoption of a single currency in January 1999. In contrast, a currency union consists of an arrangement to merge several currencies to fix the exchange rates and unify their monetary policy-making permanently. The European Monetary Union, undertaken in 1999, is a prime example. A rigidly fixed exchange rate is where governments can fix the price of their currency against a specific foreign currency or a basket of foreign currencies. Fixed rates can be managed by *currency boards*, albeit a currency board differs from a unilateral peg in that the home country no longer sets its own monetary policy. Instead, the size of the monetary base is determined by monetary policy in the anchor country and capital flows.

Specifically, while the typical fixed or pegged exchange-rate regime allows the monetary authorities some discretion in their conduct of monetary policy because they can still adjust interest rates or print money, under a currency board the commitment to the fixed exchange rate is strong, because the conduct of monetary policy is taken completely out of the hands of the central bank and the government. A currency board combines three elements: an exchange rate that is fixed to an "anchor currency," automatic convertibility (that is, the right to exchange domestic currency at this fixed rate whenever desired), and a long-term commitment to the system, which is often set out directly in the central bank law. Therefore, unlike a central bank, a currency board issues funds that are fully backed (100 per cent) by reserves of a hard currency such as the US dollar, and the domestic currency is freely convertible into the hard currency. The exchange rate is fixed by law, not just by a currency market intervention, and monetary policy is targeted strictly on maintaining balance-of-payments equilibrium with the fixed exchange rate. Such an arrangement leaves no room for adjustments in the real exchange rate through changes in the nominal exchange rate. Accordingly, adjustments to changing conditions must be made by other means, including domestic prices and costs and economic activity and employment.

A currency-board arrangement has important advantages over a monetary policy strategy that just uses an exchange-rate target. First, the money supply can expand only when dollars are exchanged for domestic currency at the central bank. That is, the increased amount of domestic currency is matched by an equal increase in foreign-exchange reserves. The currency board arrangement leaves no room for policies that are inconsistent with the fixed exchange rate, because the only policy is a commitment to adjust the monetary base in tandem with flows of foreign-exchange reserves in and out of the central bank. As a consequence, the home country's central bank can no longer act as a lender of last resort to the domestic banking sector. Second, the currency board involves a stronger commitment by the central bank to the fixed exchange rate, and may therefore be effective in bringing down inflation and in reducing the likelihood of a successful speculative attack against the currency.

Currency-board arrangements are the strongest form of exchange-rate peg, short of a currency union or outright dollarization. To take the idea to its logical conclusion, an extreme form of a fixed exchange rate is the abandonment of a national currency and the adoption of a powerful foreign currency such as the US dollar for domestic use – hence, the term "dollarization." While a currency board can be abandoned, allowing a change in the value of the currency, a change of value is impossible with dollarization – that is, one US dollar is always worth one dollar whether it is held in the United States or outside. A country that has official dollarization (such as Panama since 1904), besides adopting the US dollar as legal tender, has also eliminated the monetary policy-making role of its central bank. Without a national currency to manage, the country's monetary policy is, in effect, put into the hands of the United States Federal Reserve. Limited or unofficial dollarization occurs when US dollars circulate alongside a country's national currency, or where private agents use the dollar as a substitute for the domestic currency. Under both these arrangements, the domestic currency continues to serve to some degree as a medium of exchange, store of value and unit of account. Limited dollarization exists in many countries, especially in Latin America.[45] Figure 6.1 provides a rough overview of major exchange-rate regimes.

Thus the shift from fixed to more flexible exchange rates has been gradual, dating from the breakdown of the Bretton Woods system of fixed exchange rates in the early 1970s. With the collapse of the Bretton Woods par value system and the widespread adoption of floating exchange rates by the major advanced economies in the early 1970s, most developing countries initially continued to peg their currencies either to a key currency (mainly the US dollar), or to a basket of currencies, including the IMF's special drawing right (SDR).[46] However, starting in the late 1970s, a number of developing countries moved away from these arrangements. At first, the shift was mainly away from single-currency pegs to pegs defined in terms of baskets of currencies. However, since the early 1980s, there has been a market shift towards more flexible exchange-rate arrangements. For example, in 1975, 87 per cent of developing countries had some type of pegged exchange rate, while only 10 per cent had flexible exchange rates. By 1985, the proportions were 71 per cent and 25 per cent respectively (Caramazza and Aziz 1998; Mussa *et al.* 2000). Among other factors, the trend toward greater exchange-rate flexibility has been associated with more open and outward-oriented policies on trade and investment, and increased emphasis on market-determined exchange and interest rates. At the latest count (Autumn 2001), the IMF member countries have distributed themselves rather evenly along the spectrum from free floats to the irrevocably fixed rates of a currency union. At the flexible end, 50 countries, including many economically or geographically large nations like the United States, Japan, Australia and India, allow their currencies to float independently. However, several members of this group (Japan, Canada, and Brazil, for instance) intervene fairly frequently in an effort to offset disorderly market forces. Another group of 45 countries embrace some form of limited flexibility: 26 "manage" their float, while 19 allow the exchange rate to fluctuate within a specified band

**Figure 6.1**   *Major exchange-rate regimes*

---

*Fixed corner*

1   *Monetary union:* participating members replace their national currencies with a new common currency and establish a common central bank (e.g. Euroland) to manage monetary policy for the union as a whole. This includes the special case of the adoption of a foreign currency as legal tender, such as official dollarization (e.g. Panama).

2   *Currency board:* rigidly linking the value of domestic money to that of a foreign currency and tying the domestic monetary base firmly to the level of foreign-exchange reserves (e.g. Hong Kong). Argentina also uses this arrangement, exchanging one peso for one US dollar.

3   *A truly fixed peg:* a commitment to buy or sell however much foreign currency is necessary at a given exchange rate, with a firm and lasting intention of maintaining the policy.

*Intermediate regimes*

4   *Adjustable peg:* fixing the exchange rate, but without any open-ended commitment to resist devaluation or revaluation in the presence of a large balance-of-payments deficit or surplus (e.g. European countries under the European Monetary System).

5   *Crawling peg:* a pre-announced policy of adjusting the exchange rate bit by bit over time (e.g. Indonesia before the 1997 crisis). Costa Rica uses a crawling peg system.

6   *Basket peg:* fixing not to a single currency, but to a weighted average of other major currencies (e.g. Thailand before the 1997 crisis).

7   *Target zone or band:* a margin of fluctuation around a central rate (e.g. Israel).

*Flexible corner*

8   *Managed floating or Dirty float:* the monetary authority of the country does not adopt a particular exchange-rate target; nevertheless, it intervenes occasionally in the foreign-exchange market to influence the movements of the exchange-rate. The monetary authority, however, does not specify or pre-commit to any particular value for the exchange rate, thereby allowing the exchange-rate to fluctuate subject to intervention, but without an explicit exchange-rate target (e.g. Japan). It also intervenes or alters interest-rates at discretion to affect the level or path of the exchange rate.

9   *Free floating:* no official intervention undertaken in the foreign-exchange market, or altering of interest rates for the purpose of affecting the level or path of the nominal exchange-rate. Economic policies (especially monetary policy) pursued with benign indifference to the exchange rate (such a system does not exist in its pure form, but the United States comes close).

---

or to move gradually (i.e. "crawl") along a specified path. A further 44 are still trying to maintain a traditional exchange-rate peg. Finally, 45 countries have sought additional stability by joining a currency union or by taking a major world currency as their own.

However, it is important to note that, although the high-performing Asian economies kept their exchange rates in the "flexible" category, in practice most operated a tightly managed policy. Against the single exception of Korea, Thailand and Indonesia maintained regimes virtually pegged in nominal terms against the US dollar.[47] Such regimes were chosen for two reasons: first, to ensure price stability, and second, to make foreign finance available at a cheaper rate by means of bank loans, and portfolio and foreign direct investment with reduced interest rates spreads. Moreover, exchange-rate pegs had a twofold positive effect on interest rate spreads, by both curbing inflation expectations and sustaining market confidence. However, such a regime is fragile. The peg does not necessarily provide monetary and fiscal discipline, and can lead to an overvalued currency and a widening of current-account imbalances. As the Asian crisis vividly illustrated, a pegged rate can encourage excessive foreign-currency borrowing, as the perceived exchange-rate risk is deceptively small. As was noted earlier, the US dollar pegs resulted in massive competitive losses in many East Asian countries after 1995, when the dollar began to appreciate against other major currencies. The choice of the US dollar as the anchor for a pegged exchange-rate regime could be appropriate for a small open economy when at least the following conditions are satisfied: (1) its trade and investment structure is aimed primarily at the dollar area; and (2) its export competitors are also located in the dollar area – in such conditions, a country's competitiveness would tend to be stable irrespective of any fluctuation in the dollar. From January 1995 to April 1997 the dollar's nominal exchange rate appreciated by 25 per cent against the yen and by 17 per cent against the then euro-equivalent (IMF 1999). This appreciation affected the East Asian economies, whose export markets and export competitiveness were diverse in terms of currency. The increasing overvaluation of the East Asian currencies in effective terms provoked growing current-account imbalances.

Furthermore, fixed exchange-rate strategies increased systemic risks by providing an implicit guarantee to domestic companies and international investors – giving them a strong (but misleading) signal of confidence. Pegging against the dollar lent credibility to the central bank's commitment to maintain the currency's external stability. On the one hand, in the context of weak and underdeveloped domestic financial sectors, it encouraged domestic companies to take full advantage of the efficiency gap between foreign and domestic financial operators and to borrow directly from foreign banks in US dollars without hedging their liabilities. On the other hand, it prompted foreign banks to lend indiscriminately, especially at shorter maturities, without carefully checking for country risk and debtor creditworthiness.

Thus fixed nominal pegs against the US dollar (combined with other inappropriate policy measures) brought on the crisis sooner and made it more widespread. In fact, the Asian crisis dramatically validated Mundell's (1968) famous "open economy trilemma" – the so-called "impossible trinity" or "incompatibility triangle" – whereby fixed exchange-rate regimes are incompatible with free capital mobility and independent national monetary policies.[48]

The choice of exchange rate has important consequences for an economy, since the exchange rate is one of the most important price signals in the market of tradeable goods and services under an open economy. Thus, the correct choice is crucial to ensuring financial and macroeconomic stability. While all the various regimes have their strengths and weaknesses, until the outbreak of the Asian financial crisis the conventional view among economists was that, for emerging economies, the limited flexibility of a crawling band or managed float offered a good middle ground between the confidence and stability of fixed exchange rates and the flexible monetary policy of floating rates.[49] However, an important lesson of the Mexican and Asian financial crises is that fixed but adjustable exchange-rate pegs (be it soft pegs, bands or crawling pegs) tend to crumble too easily under speculative attacks. Specifically, although adhering to a pegged exchange-rate regime can be a successful strategy for controlling inflation, it also has fatal flaws.[50] According to Eichengreen (1999), pegged exchange-rate regimes are inherently crisis-prone. As Mishkin (1999a, 19) notes, "under a pegged exchange rate regime, when a successful speculative attack occurs, the decline in the value of the domestic currency is usually larger, more rapid and more unanticipated than when a depreciation occurs under a floating exchange rate regime." No doubt, in each case – Mexico in 1994, Thailand, Indonesia and Korea in 1997, Russia and Brazil in 1998 and Argentina and Turkey in 2000 – the defense of an exchange rate pegged at untenable levels was at the heart of the crises.[51] The worst-hit country (Indonesia) saw its currency decline to less than one-quarter of its pre-crisis value in a matter of weeks. In fact, all the crisis-affected Asian countries were forced to abandon their *de facto* exchange-rate pegs, and the subsequent floats of their currencies were associated with very sharp declines and fluctuations in their values. In contrast, "emerging market economies that maintained greater flexibility in their exchange rate regimes generally fared better. For example, Chile, Mexico, Peru, South Africa and Turkey all seem to have benefitted from the flexibility of their exchange rates during the recent international financial crisis" (Mussa *et al.* 2000, 38).

Why don't pegs work as well as they used to do, and why don't countries abandon them? Most analysts agree that financial globalization and high capital mobility have rendered the operation of intermediate arrangements (in particular, the adjustable peg regime) problematic because rapid flows of large and liquid international capital markets make its exceedingly difficult

**Table 6.1** *Official exchange-rate regimes in selected Asian countries*

| Country | Date | Regime |
|---|---|---|
| Indonesia | November 1978–June 1997 | Managed floating |
| | July 1997–December 2000 | Independently floating |
| South Korea | March 1980–October 1997 | Managed floating |
| | November 1997–December 2000 | Independently floating |
| Malaysia | January 1986–February 1990 | Limited flexibility |
| | March 1990–November 1992 | Fixed |
| | December 1992–September 1998 | Managed floating |
| | September 1998–December 2000 | Pegged arrangement |
| Thailand | January 1970–June 1997 | Fixed |
| | July 1997–December 2000 | Independently floating |

for authorities to support a peg. Specifically, when capital inflows accelerate, if the exchange rate is prevented from rising, inflationary pressures build up and the real exchange rate will appreciate through higher domestic inflation. To avoid such consequences, central banks usually attempt to "sterilize" the inflows by using offsetting open-market operations to try to mop up the inflowing liquidity. However, sterilization only provides short-term relief.[52] Since open-market operations have only a limited impact in offsetting the monetary consequences of large capital inflows, in particular, the more speculative short-term capital inflows – in the face of a sudden reversal of sentiment and currency depreciation – even the most competent central bank will find it difficult to know when to abandon the defense of its currency, or when to call the speculators' bluff. In any case, both strategies carries enormous costs. As Eichengreen (1999, 104), aptly notes: "pegged rates create one-way bets for speculators, making sitting ducks of the central banks and governments seeking to operate them." Table 6.1 provides a rough classification of the exchange rate regimes in the four crisis-hit countries before and after the financial crisis.

It is now generally agreed that countries can only with great difficulty maintain intermediate exchange-rate regimes in the face of open capital markets. Although there are a number of developing countries still engaged in intermediate exchange-rate arrangements, the middle has greatly shrunk. What should be done next? It is now argued that only polar extremes – floating or fixed exchange rates supported by very strong commitment mechanisms ("hard pegs") can be sustained for extended periods. Indeed, in the context of increased integration with international capital markets, it seems that there are two credible choices left: a country can either let its exchange rate float freely or adopt a truly fixed arrangement such as hard pegs. In fact, this vanishing middle ground for exchange-rate regimes has been identified in the literature as the "hollowing of the middle" in the spectrum of exchange-rate regimes (Williamson 2000). In a provocative article, aptly titled, "Exchange Rate Regimes: Is the Bipolar View Correct?," Stanley Fischer (2001) notes:

> In recent years, fixed or pegged exchange rates have been a factor in every major emerging market financial crisis – Mexico at the end of 1994; Thailand, Indonesia and Korea in 1997; Russia and Brazil in 1998; Argentina and Turkey in 2000; and Turkey again in 2001. Emerging market countries without pegged rates – including South Africa, Israel, Mexico and Turkey in 1998 – have been able to avoid such crises. No wonder many policymakers now warn against the use of pegged but adjustable rates (soft pegs) in countries open to capital flows. This belief that intermediate regimes between hard pegs and free floating are unsustainable is known as the bipolar view, or two-corner solution. Willingly or otherwise, a growing number of countries have come to accept it. The proportion of IMF members with intermediate arrangements fell during the 1990s, while the use of hard pegs and more flexible arrangements rose. Proponents of the bipolar view – myself included – have perhaps exaggerated their argument for dramatic effect.

Yet Fischer (2001) recognizes that developing countries that are not yet very exposed to international capital flows still face a wide range of intermediate exchange regime options, in particular "crawling bands with wide ranges." Mussa and his co-authors (2000) go a step further in defending intermediate regimes by making a distinction between the sustainability and the desirability of pegs. The fact that soft pegs may not be sustainable for many countries need not imply that they cannot play a positive role for a limited period of time, for example, as a nominal anchor during stabilization from high inflation.[53] More explicitly, Williamson (2000) proposes "monitoring bands" as a viable intermediate regime. Such a system operates within a wide band, ensuring full flexibility of exchange rates. However, once the exchange rate goes outside the band (on either side), the central bank would be allowed to intervene. To Williamson, the key difference between a crawling band and a monitoring band is that the latter does not involve an obligation to defend a publicly announced margin – the major culprit in provoking speculative attacks.

Given the competing views, what is appropriate is difficult to say. As Frankel (1999) has noted, "no single currency regime is right for all countries or at all times." Indeed, the optimal regime ultimately depends on a wide range of factors peculiar to a country, such as size, openness, labor mobility, fiscal capacity, the size of reserves, and the strength of the banking system, among others. For example, floating exchange rates allow a country to pursue an independent monetary policy. Since such a regime allows the exchange rate to move in response to market forces, it generates an exchange-rate risk, compelling firms and investors to hedge their currency exposures. Nevertheless, floating exchange rates remain at the mercy of the markets and, in particular, susceptible to herding and contagion. Rapid capital movements can quickly overwhelm emerging markets with limited absorptive capacities. Floating rates can be subject to sharp fluctuations, forcing currencies to "overshoot the economic fundamentals" – thereby pushing a currency far below its underlying economic value – leaving rising inflation, trade deficits, and eroding export competitiveness in its wake. Finally, as Hausmann, Panizza and Stein (1999) have shown, emerging markets in Latin America that have attempted to allow their exchange rates to float have experienced greater interest-rate volatility than fixed-rate regimes. For this reason, Calvo and Reinhart (2000) argue that floating exchange rates can have destabilizing effects on emerging markets.

On the other hand, a fixed exchange-rate regime reduces transaction costs. As was noted earlier, it can provide a useful anchor for price stability by linking weak and emerging economies to the large, powerful economies, *inter alia* bringing about reductions in the transaction costs of international trade and investment. However, a fixed exchange rate can generate moral hazard among foreign investors if the regime is perceived to be credible. Under such conditions, the regime can take the form of an implicit guarantee and a source of moral hazard by promoting unhedged currency borrowing and skewing capital flows toward the short end. Moreover, private capital flows can overwhelm a fixed exchange rate, forcing costly devaluations and revaluations, the costs including raising the current-account deficit and reducing foreign reserves. A "successful defense" of a fixed rate can often be costly, requiring a country to raise interest rates and/or slow its economy to avoid speculative attacks.

The experiences of Hong Kong and Argentina illustrate that even the rigid pegs of a currency board arrangement are not free from speculative attacks or banking collapse. Currency-board pressures in both these countries (especially Argentina) have exacted very high costs in terms of economic growth.

For example, under Argentina's 1991 convertibility law, the peso/dollar exchange rate was fixed at one to one. The meant that the public could go to the Argentine central bank and exchange a peso for a dollar, or vice versa, at any time. In the early years Argentina's currency board performed successfully. Inflation, which had been running at an 800 per cent–1,000 per cent annual rate in 1990, fell to less than 5 per cent by the end of 1994. Similarly, economic growth averaged almost 8 per cent as an annual rate from 1991 to 1994 – one of the highest in the world. However, in the aftermath of the Mexican peso crisis, concern about the health of the Argentine economy resulted in the public pulling money out of the banks (deposits fell by some 18 per cent), and exchanging pesos for dollars. This caused a contraction in the country's money supply, resulting in a sharp drop in economic activity. What is important to note is that because the Argentine central bank had no control over monetary policy under the currency board system, it was relatively helpless to counteract the contractionary monetary policy stemming from the public's behavior. Moreover, because the currency board did not allow the central bank to create pesos and lend them to the banks, it had very little capacity to act as a lender of last resort. However, with the assistance of the IMF, the World Bank and the Inter-American Development Bank (which altogether lent over US$5 billion to Argentina), the country was able to shore up its banking system, and thereby its currency board system.

Although Argentina was able to maintain its fixed exchange rate *vis-à-vis* the US dollar, the situation became increasingly precarious over time. Brazil (Argentina's main competitor) has a floating exchange rate that made the *real* increasingly competitive against the Argentine peso. The result was a growing trade deficit in Argentina – which in turn placed significant pressure on the peso, leading to extremely high interest rates in Argentina. In turn, the high interest rates produced a mushrooming government deficit because of the higher interest on the national debt and a lower tax base as the economic downturn took its toll. Finally, unable to control the interest-rate differentials between peso-denominated and dollar-denominated debt, Argentina abandoned the system in January 2002.[54] Thus, at the end of the day, a currency board system can be credible only if the central bank holds sufficient official foreign-exchange reserves at least to cover the entire narrow money supply. In this way, financial markets and the public can be assured that every domestic currency bill is backed by an equivalent amount of foreign currency in the official coffers. This was not the case in Argentina.

The two primary benefits of dollarization include the elimination of exchange-rate volatility (against the dollar) and exchange-rate crises. While total dollarization almost eliminates the possibility of a currency devaluation and transaction costs associated with international trade and finance with the United States, dollarized economies face similar problems to those associated with currency board systems. Namely, dollarization is subject to the usual disadvantages of an exchange-rate target. Besides losing several important instruments of control over policy (for example, no domestic institution can act as the lender of last resort, increased the exposure of the economy to shocks from the anchor country), there is also complete loss of seigniorage – or the revenue that a government receives by issuing money.[55] It is recognized that dollarization may be feasible only for small, open economies highly vulnerable to international shocks, and with strong international trade and financial ties to the United States.[56] In addition, a dollarized economy with a weak banking system may not be able to efficiently channel the capital inflow that inevitably accompanies dollarization, leading to unsustainable lending booms and financial disintermediation. Finally, while a country's decision to dollarize its economy does not require the permission of the United States government or the Federal Reserve, it should be noted that the chief policy-makers at both the Fed and the US Department of the Treasury have stated that the policies of the United States will not be altered to adapt to the economic considerations of countries that choose to dollarize.

As of June 1999, the IMF reported that 67 countries had pegged their currency, 8 adhered to a currency board arrangement and the remaining 73 followed more flexible arrangements, such as managed or independent floating. Even among the more homogeneous group of 29 OECD countries, 6 had pegged their currencies, 12 followed arrangements of independent or managed floating and 11 had just formed a monetary union in which they agreed to adopt a common currency, the euro – which became legal tender in January 2002. In accordance with the IMF's Articles of Agreement, which leave the choice of its exchange-rate system to each country, the Fund does not have an official position on its member countries' exchange-rate regimes. Furthermore, the IMF generally avoids being doctrinaire on the exchange-rate regime when deciding whether to support a country's program. Rather, the Fund maintains that it sees advantages in both fixed and flexible exchange-rate systems – depending on a country's economic circumstances. Indeed, the Fund has taken different approaches in different situations. In Ecuador (early in 2000), the IMF supported dollarization, when a few months earlier it was against the idea. In Turkey, the Fund supported a crawling peg to stabilize triple-digit inflation in early 2000, albeit the strategy did not succeed. Nevertheless, the Fund's deputy managing-director, Stanley Fischer (1999, 10), noted that "the virulence of the recent crises is likely to shift the balance towards the choice of more flexible exchange rate systems, including crawling pegs with wide bands."

However, if the IMF is to play an important role in shaping the new international financial architecture and building a financial and monetary system with fewer vulnerabilities, it will have to guide countries effectively in adopting exchange-rate regimes that are right for them. That is, the IMF must offer timely assessment of whether the prevailing exchange-rate regime is broadly consistent with the country's external and domestic policy goals. Most importantly, the IMF should not provide large-scale assistance to countries that are intervening heavily to support an exchange-rate peg if this peg is inconsistent with underlying policies. Rather, the IMF should do more to encourage exchange-rate flexibility for countries that liberalize their capital accounts. Of course, flexibility does not necessarily mean free floating. As Fischer (1999) notes, bands of fluctuation allow much flexibility if they are wide enough to ensure that the equilibrium exchange rate is included in the band. For countries that decided to retain a fixed exchange-rate system, they should, as a precondition, be requested to make the regime sustainable.

## A new approach to sovereign debt restructuring

Recently Anne Krueger (2002), the new first deputy managing-director of the IMF, made a bold proposal: that under certain conditions, a government's international debt repayments should be temporarily suspended while negotiations take place on restructuring the debt. To Krueger, the establishment of an effective sovereign debt restructuring mechanism (SDRM) will not only fill a glaring weakness in the emerging international financial architecture by ensuring the timely and orderly restructuring of unsustainable sovereign debts, but also put debtors and creditors, rather than the IMF, in the driver's seat regarding debt negotiations.

No doubt, currently sovereign borrowers often find it very difficult to get their creditors to agree collectively to a restructuring that reduces the net present value of their obligations to a manageable level. Even if such a restructuring would be in the interests of creditors as a group, some may prefer to "free-ride," hoping that they will ultimately be repaid in line with their original contracts. Similarly, a debtor country may all too often delay a necessary restructuring until the last possible moment, draining its reserves and increasing the eventual cost of restoring sustainability. Creditors also suffer when fears about some being unfairly favored over others block agreement on a restructuring. Indeed, creditors often "rush to the exits" because they fear that restructuring will be disorderly. This can leave all parties concerned with no option but to accept a disruptive and potentially contagious unilateral default – or a bailout of private creditors that contributes to moral hazard. Moreover, the citizens of the defaulting country experience greater hardship than they need to, and the international community via the IMF has a tougher task helping pick up the pieces.

The proposed SDRM (modeled on corporate bankruptcy law) would allow countries to seek legal protection from creditors that stand in the way of restructuring, and in exchange debtors would have to negotiate with their creditors in good faith. Specifically, a formal SDRM would be built on four principles: (1) creditors would not be allowed to disrupt negotiations by having recourse to their own national courts; (2) debtor countries would need to provide assurances that they are negotiating in good faith and treating all creditors equally; (3) private creditors would need to be encouraged to lend new money by receiving some guarantee that they would be repaid ahead of existing private creditors; and (4) once agreement on a restructuring had been reached by a large enough majority of creditors, the rest would have to be bound to accept the terms. Countries would come to the IMF and request a temporary standstill on their debts (probably lasting a few months) while the country negotiates a rescheduling or restructuring. Extensions would require IMF approval. Moreover, the plan may also require the imposition of temporary exchange controls to stop money from fleeing the country. For Krueger, the primary objective in creating such a formal mechanism is to create incentives for debtors and creditors to reach agreement on their own, so that the mechanism would rarely need to be used.

Krueger makes it clear that the key step would be to enable a majority of creditors (across the broad range of credit instruments) to make the terms of restructuring binding on the rest. That is, all creditors would be obliged to comply with a plan approved by a large enough majority. This would eliminate the free-rider problem, thereby making early agreement more likely, and reducing the threat of unilateral legal action by creditors after a sovereign default. How would decisions made by the debtor and a majority of creditors be made binding on all creditors? For Kreuger, the solution is the wider use of collective action clauses (which would allow a majority of creditors to impose a deal on the remaining minority), thereby helping to resolve some debt problems. However, Krueger is fully aware that collective action clauses will solve only part of the problem. Thus she calls for a universal treaty rather than piecemeal changes to national legislation. Such a treaty would set up an international judicial panel to arbitrate disputes.

Krueger's proposal, if comprehensively implemented, would represent a significant improvement over existing arrangements. The new mechanism would create a more efficient debt-restructuring process by allowing countries to resolve debt-problems in an orderly way. Yet the challenges to creating an effective SDRM remain daunting. First, debt-restructuring has become more complicated over the past two decades, in part because of the growing use of bonds and complicated derivatives. Bondholders are more numerous, anonymous and difficult to coordinate than banks. They also have a bigger incentive to sue debtors for repayment. And, second, although the IMF has officially endorsed Krueger's proposal, an amendment to the IMF's articles would be required before this proposal can move to the implementation stage. Even if the Fund's articles are amended (not an easy task), questions regarding what financing the IMF should provide after the restructuring, or to what type of debt the stay should apply, still need to be resolved.

### Notes

1 Cited in DeRosa (2001, 114).
2 Kenen (2000, 1–2). Also Grunberg (1999, 432) notes that "the Halifax summit only endorsed tougher data disclosure standards . . . the consequences of the inaction at Halifax are seen now" – meaning the Asian crisis.
3 "Moral hazard" refers to a situation where someone can reap the rewards from their actions when things go well, but does not suffer the full consequences when things go badly. Hence investors do not have to exercise due diligence, since they would expect a bailout in the case of default; or, for that matter, debtor countries can choose to pursue risky economic policies with the expectation that they will not have to pay the full costs of their debts; and investors will not lose the full amount invested if a financial crisis occurs. In the case of

the Mexican peso crisis, it was argued, the IMF, by cushioning the losses of imprudent lenders and borrowers with generous "bailout packages," only encouraged reckless behavior in the future. "Asymmetric information" emerges when one party to a financial contract does not have the same information as the other party.

4   The IMF (along with the World Bank) was established at Bretton Woods in 1944 to supervise the operation of the system of fixed exchange rates. This system ended in 1971.

5   Friedman (1999, 4). For similar arguments, see also Schwartz (1998).

6   For example, the Mexican rescue package allowed holders of Mexican government securities (*tesobonos*) to get out with little cost.

7   For details, see Institute of International Finance (1999) and Kho and Stulz (1999).

8   The collapse of a relatively small US hedge fund, Long-Term Capital Management, in August 1998, and the threat of its bringing down a much wider circle of financial institutions, is illustrative. The Federal Reserve stepped in in time to prevent the contagion.

9   Suffice it to note that the moral hazard argument can be applied on a variety of levels, including the IMF, governments and companies. That is, if we do not need the IMF internationally, should we then not have lenders of last resort domestically – more specifically, should we abolish our national deposit insurance schemes?

10  For details, see International Financial Institution Advisory Commission (2000) and Meltzer (1998, 1999).

11  A standstill agreement is where creditors agree to "stand still" – that is, not to request a debt repayment at the contractual maturity date.

12  For details, see G-7 (Group of Seven) (2000); G-22 (Group of Twenty-Two) (1998).

13  The United States is the one of the IMF's major financial backers, with a quota or "membership fee" that accounts for roughly 18 per cent of the total IMF funds. The quota also determines its "drawings," or voting power and borrowing capacity.

14  The establishment of the NAB did not replace the GAB, which remained in force. However, the NAB became the arrangement of first recourse. The GAB was activated during the summer of 1998 to help finance the IMF's loan of SDR 8.5 billion to Russia. This was the first time in 20 years that the GAB had been activated. Following its entry into force, the NAB was activated in December 1998 to help finance the IMF's loan of SDR 13 billion to Brazil.

15  None the less, it was recognized that Basle Committee on Banking Supervision will continue to take responsibility for formulating banking and supervision standards, while the IMF's primary role will be to monitor the adoption and implementation of these standards during its regular Article IV surveillance work.

16  The Bank for International Settlements, an international institution based in Basle, Switzerland, acts as a kind of central bankers' bank.

17  There was recognition that the monitoring of international capital flows had to be improved. This meant that much better data had to be made available. The Bank for International Settlements (BIS) (which provided some of the best data

on short-term international capital flows), was available only twice a year, with a six-month lag. Hence a foreign-exchange crisis could arrive and depart well before these data could even provide a warning sign. It was agreed that the BIS move towards a quarterly data system, with a one-month lag.

18   After all, when foreign investors escape without "taking a hit," it is taxpayers who end up footing the bill to service IMF debts.

19   Of course, there is no assurance that the IMF would be able to mobilize the resources needed to meet the requirements if it should be called upon for assistance under the SRF. The inadequacy of resources has in the past forced the Fund to deal with crises by trying to arrange finance from different sources, including multilateral agencies such as the World Bank and bilateral assistance from member countries.

20   Bagehot, of course, was thinking of the Bank of England's acting as the lender of last resort to avert the liquidity crises afflicting the city of London in the early nineteenth century. Bagehot argued that the lender of last resort should provide cash without limit to solvent borrowers at a penal rate of interest.

21   That is, the collateral should be valued at pre-panic prices.

22   Still, episodes like the US Savings and Loan crisis indicate that good supervision and regulation do not eliminate the need for a lender of last resort.

23   In theory, the IMF has the means to create unlimited resources through the allocation of special assets known as special drawing rights (SDRs). Members could vote it the power to create such liquidity in an emergency, although they have not done so to date.

24   In fact, the IMF Articles of Agreement (Article VI, section 3) signed at Bretton Woods explicitly permitted capital controls. Also, one of the architects of those articles, John Maynard Keynes, was a strong proponent of capital controls.

25   Earlier, the maintenance of capital controls was not viewed as inconsistent with the objective of the elimination of foreign-exchange restrictions, partly because capital controls were considered necessary for supporting the system of fixed exchange rates.

26   In hindsight, the BIBF ended up unintentionally serving as a conduit for local firms vastly to expand their loans from foreign banks. Much of this money went into the real-estate sector, creating over-supply. When these investments went sour, bad loans proliferated. The worst part was that most of these loans were denominated in foreign currency, with usually no hedging against currency depreciation. The results were disastrous.

27   That is, corporate residents with domestic borrowing were required to seek prior approval to remit funds in excess of 10 million ringgit per corporate group per year for overseas investment, including extension of loans to non-residents.

28   In principle, the exchange-rate value of the currency was determined by the market, though Bank Negara Malaysia acknowledged intervening to smooth fluctuations that it considered excessive.

29   On July 14, 1997, the Malaysian government floated the ringgit after finding the existing *de facto* exchange regime to be unsustainable. With the flotation, the ringgit dropped from RM2.50 to the US dollar prior to the crisis to its lowest level of RM4.88 to the dollar on January 7, 1998.

30   As of August 1998, the offshore ringgit market was offering deposit interest rates exceeding 20–40 per cent, compared with 11 per cent in Malaysian banks.

By that time the ringgit had depreciated to around RM4.20 per US dollar from around RM3.75 in April 1998.

31 For example, on January 12, 1998, the Kuala Lumpur Stock Exchange (KLSE) saw its composite index crash to a low of 477.57 points, which wiped out almost RM580 billion or 65 per cent of the total market capitalization recorded when the index was at a high of 1271.57 points in February 1997 (Yusof, Hew and Nambiar 2000, 67).

32 Anwar was also accused of being an IMF stooge and blamed for the economic recession.

33 In February 1999, a system of taxes on outflows replaced the prohibition on repatriation of capital. Specifically, the old measure was replaced with exit levies on the repatriation of portfolio capital that decline with the holding period of the investment.

34 The Malaysian case is quite different from controls on *capital inflows* as implemented in Chile between 1991 and 1998. Specifically, Chile imposed various restrictions on inflows, including a requirement that a portion of any money borrowed abroad be deposited for a year at the central bank, without interest. As was noted earlier, in the case of Malaysia, on February 4, 1999, the 12-month holding restriction on the repatriation of portfolio capital was replaced with a declining scale of exit levies.

35 Firms, for example, may evade controls on capital flows by falsifying invoices for traded goods.

36 The argument is that high capital mobility limits discretionary policy and forces governments to adopt "good" or market-conforming policies, including sound financial supervision policies.

37 Tobin (1978) argued that since the order of magnitude for the tax would be around 0.1 per cent, or US$1,000 per million dollars sold, it would be a negligible cost for long-term investors. However, for speculators flipping currencies weekly or daily, it would amount to a tax of 10 per cent to 50 per cent on their investment. Criticism of the Tobin tax has focused mainly on its technical feasibility. With over US$1 trillion changing hands daily in foreign-exchange markets, imposing such a tax would be greatly challenging. Also, to be effective, the tax would have to be uniformly adopted worldwide. That is, if it were to be adopted in only a few countries, it would probably lead the taxed agents to shift to untaxed locations.

38 See Krugman (1998, 74–80; 1998b; 1998c). In a later article, Krugman (1999a, 56–7), argued that "Sooner or later we will have to turn the clock at least part of the way back: to limit capital flows for countries that are unsuitable for either currency unions or free floating."

39 Also see Stiglitz (2000).

40 No doubt, there is evidence indicating that capital controls involving taxes and reserve requirements can change the composition of capital inflows in favor of long-term investment, and thereby decrease the likelihood of large, sudden outflows. However, Calvo and Reinhart (2000) caution that these results may depend on the accounting classification of capital flows. Furthermore, Edwards (2001, 1999) argues that when analyzing the maturity of a country's foreign debt, the relevant concept is residual maturity (measured by the value of a country's liabilities that are held by foreigners and mature within a year), rather

than contractual maturity. Using data from Chile, Edwards shows that short-term capital controls had a limited effect on Chile's residual maturity of foreign debt and that Chile had higher residual maturity than Mexico (a country without capital controls) at the end of 1996.

41 Many elements contributed to the fall of Bretton Woods system, but an important one concerned the liquidity of the system. Under the agreement, the US Treasury fixed the price of the US dollar in terms of gold by buying and selling gold on the market. In other words, the United States promised to exchange US dollars for gold at the official price of US$35 per ounce. The system collapsed when other countries no longer believed that the United States could keep its promise to exchange US dollars for gold at the official price. In the 1960s, US reserves of gold steadily declined, while the amount of US liabilities to foreigners increased. That is, there were more and more US dollars in circulation for every ounce of gold, putting more strain on the capacity of the United States to honor the agreement. Other countries that had accumulated US dollars became afraid that the dollar would be devalued in terms of gold, and began to convert their holdings of dollars into gold. In August 1971, President Nixon suspended the convertibility of dollars into gold – ending the Bretton Woods system.

42 In support of their argument, Calvo and Reinhart (2000) conduct an empirical analysis comparing the announced exchange-rate regime of countries with their actual exchange-rate behavior. Their findings indicate that countries classified as letting their exchange rate float, in general do not. Thus it seems that very few, if any, countries are in reality willing to take this approach.

43 Speculators often bet that central banks that have allowed substantial appreciation of the real exchange rate through relatively high domestic inflation will choose to break the peg and devalue, rather than let the domestic economy stagnate for a prolonged period with a high, uncompetitive real exchange rate.

44 All so-called fixed exchange rates are potentially adjustable unless the country literally gives up its currency.

45 There are two ways a country's economy can become dollarized. A *de facto* dollarization can occur when citizens lose faith in their national currency and turn away from it towards the dollar. This has occurred in many Latin American countries. Second, dollarization occurs when a foreign government makes a conscious decision to replace its own currency with the US dollar.

46 The end of convertibility of the dollar into gold in the summer of 1971 was a first step toward the breakdown of the Bretton Woods system – which collapsed with the floating of major currencies in early 1973. A major reason why most developing countries continued to peg their currencies was because many restricted the convertibility of their currencies for current transactions, thereby essentially obliging them to peg (either explicitly or implicitly) to a convertible foreign currency.

47 As has been noted, by the early 1980s all the crisis-hit countries had moved away from the old policy of pegging against the US dollar towards more flexible exchange-rate regimes of basket pegging or managed "dirty float." But the extensive intervention policies of the central banks meant that exchange rates were *de facto* pegged to the dollar. In Korea, although the exchange rate was not fixed, its undervaluation in a managed float system and relatively high interest rates at home had increased the attractions of foreign borrowing. Yen-denominated loans

became especially attractive in the couple of years before the crisis, because the continuing decline in the value of the yen against the US dollar lowered the real cost of yen loans to borrowers.

48  A basic principle of open macroeconomics is that one can only have two of the three following features: a fixed exchange rate, full capital mobility, and monetary policy independence. Any pair is possible; however, any attempt to achieve all three inevitably results in a currency crisis. The reason for the inconsistency is well documented. Full capital mobility implies that the interest rate is determined by financial conditions out of reach of the domestic monetary authorities. A fixed exchange rate implies that the central bank must stand ready to buy or sell its own currency in unlimited quantities: thus, the money supply is fully demand-determined, and monetary independence is lost. Viewed in this context, the policies adopted by Asian countries in the 1990s can be seen as challenging the impossible trinity. For example, capital inflows stimulated the domestic economy, but often to the level of overheating. Moreover, the interest rate could not be raised to dampen domestic overheating, because higher interest rates would invite more capital inflows. In the case of Thailand, easy monetary policy played a big role in creating the bubble. However, in the absence of capital controls, monetary policy was bound by the world market, and offshore markets made it very easy to move funds in and out of Thailand. To recover independence, a country can either give up the fixed exchange rate target or recover control of its interest rate and demand for money by preventing capital movements.

49  More specifically, prior to the Asian crisis, the mainstream economic literature argued that the desire to satisfy several objectives – flexibility versus commitment, inflation stabilization versus competitiveness, and insulation from monetary shocks versus insulation from real shocks – made the compromise solutions between hard pegs and pure floats inevitable.

50  A number of authors have argued that fixed, but adjustable, nominal exchange rates provide an effective device for guiding a disinflation program and maintaining macroeconomic stability. According to this view, a prerequisite for a successful exchange-rate-based stabilization program is that the country in question have its public finances in order. Mexico adopted this strategy in 1988 – the year the exchange-rate-based stabilization program known as the *Pacto de Solidaridad* was implemented. See Edwards and Santaella (1993).

51  All these countries had *de jure* or *de facto* exchange-rate pegs or otherwise substantially limited the movement of their exchange rates.

52  First, sterilization prevents domestic interest rates from falling in response to the inflows. And, second, given the relatively small size of the domestic market compared with international capital flows, sterilization tends to become less effective over time.

53  Of course, this assumes that these countries will find a way to "exit" safely from the peg without a crisis.

54  It should also be noted that Argentina's fixed exchange-rate system was made even more unstable by a full capital account convertibility. This not only allowed domestic residents to convert pesos to dollars at a fixed exchange rate of one peso per dollar, but also allowed an unlimited export of those dollars.

55  Seigniorage is the revenue (or the profit) a country earns by issuing currency. For example, when the US Federal Reserve issues dollars it buys US Treasury

securities in exchange. So when the Treasury makes payments on these securities they go to the Federal Reserve. In turn, the Federal Reserve uses a small portion of these payments to help finance its operations and sends the rest back to the Treasury Department.

56 Both the US Federal Reserve and the Treasury have stated that the policies of the United States will not be altered to adapt to the economic exigencies of countries that choose to dollarize. So foreign governments considering full dollarization must do so with the understanding that US monetary policy will remain focused on domestic issues.

# 7

# Conclusion:
# post-crisis Asia – economic
# recovery, September 11, 2001
# and the challenges ahead

To the extent that Asia is recovering, no one can claim the credit. The amazing thing to me – if you leave Indonesia out – is how similar the performances are, regardless of the policies. Korea took the IMF's advice and it's bouncing back. Thailand took the IMF's advice and it's starting to come back. Malaysia defied the IMF and did everything the IMF told it not to – it's coming back fast. Everybody's contemplating success for their policies: Mahathir said he did it, the IMF said they did it. The truth is the natural resilience of economies did it (Paul Krugman, August 25, 1999).[1]

In the aftermath of East Asia's spectacular economic collapse in mid-1997 even the most optimistic predictions gave at least a decade before Asia could fully recover.[2] Yet, in early 2000, an IMF study triumphantly noted that "the financial crises that erupted in Asia beginning in mid-1997 are now behind us and the economies are recovering strongly" (IMF 2000a). Indeed, the economic recovery between the second quarter of 1999 and the last quarter of 2000 was simply astounding. South Korea, Thailand, Malaysia and the Philippines notched growth-rates equal to or above those just before the crisis. South Korea made the biggest gain, its GDP growing by a whopping 10.7 per cent in 1999 and 11.2 per cent in the first half of 2000, from a contraction of −6.7 per cent in 1998. Also, by October 2000, Korea had already surpassed its pre-crisis per capita income peak.[3] In September 1999, the IMF-prescribed programs for South Korea (and Thailand) were brought to an end after being in effect for two years. South Korea also stopped drawing from the IMF, and in August 2000 completed repayment of a US$19.5 billion IMF loan, almost three years ahead of schedule. By March 2000, South Korea had accumulated substantial enough reserves (from US$9 billion at the end of 1997 to about US$83 billion) to provide it with reasonable insulation against shocks. In October 2001, Korea's foreign-exchange reserves stood at US$100.4 billion, and in November 2001, the international rating agencies restored the country's sovereign rating to investment grade.

The recovery in Hong Kong, China has been equally impressive. The first-quarter growth in 2000 was 14.3 per cent, followed by 10.8 per cent in the second quarter. GDP growth in Singapore of 5.4 per cent in 1999 was partly due to rising productivity levels. Moreover, Singapore experienced a rapid growth of its information technology industry – no doubt benefiting from the government's policy of transforming the island republic into a "wired" economy. Malaysia, the Philippines and Thailand grew at 5.4, 3.2 and 5.2 per cent respectively in the first quarter of 2000 (ADB 2000). Only Indonesia continues to lag behind. However, considering the fact that Indonesia experienced a dramatic output contraction of −13.2 per cent in 1998, its real GDP growth of 0.23 per cent in 1999 was a significant milestone (ADB 2000). Moreover, the rupiah strengthened to about 7,450 per US dollar in mid-2000. Also, inflation, which peaked at 82 per cent in September 1998, has declined to about 1.7 per cent in December 1999.[4] At the end of June 2000, Indonesia's gross external reserves stood at US$27.4 billion (ADB 2000b, 31). The more recent figures show that in the first quarter of 2000 real GDP growth in Indonesia reached 3.0 per cent.

Other indicators of the region-wide recovery included the steady return of capital. For example, portfolio equity investment flows have stabilized and turned positive with US$8 billion in aggregate inflows in 1999–2000. FDI flows have been also positive, largely owing to sharply depreciated asset values and exchange rates and also to the relaxation of foreign ownership rules, which has encouraged mergers and acquisitions. The latter factor has been most pronounced in South Korea. In fact, South Korea, almost closed to foreign direct investment before the crisis, received US$15.5 billion in outside investment in 1999, five times the 1996 inflow. By early 2000, the current accounts of South Korea, Indonesia, Thailand and Malaysia were all positive, foreign-currency liabilities, especially those with short maturities, had fallen, and the exchange-rate misalignments have largely been corrected. By mid-May 2000, the value of local currencies (in nominal terms) had stabilized, although they still bought 20 to 35 per cent fewer US dollars than before the crisis in South Korea, Malaysia, the Philippines and Thailand, and 50 per cent fewer dollars in Indonesia. Overall, these positive developments reduced the region's external vulnerabilities substantially.

What explains this remarkable economic recovery? There are several interrelated factors. *First*, the massive financial injection, totaling some US$35 billion, provided by the IMF in 1998–99, and some US$85 billion committed (although not all of this actually materialized) by other multilateral and bilateral sources helped to restore investor confidence and stop any further economic hemorrhage, and in particular the massive currency depreciation. In South Korea, an increase in foreign equity participation in the financial sector has provided an additional source of inflows. Balance-of-payments surpluses have allowed the crisis-hit countries to accumulate additional international reserves and let currencies appreciate gradually. *Second*, it is important to recognize that financial crises do not necessarily destroy the capacity for economic growth. Although the Asian financial crisis exacted a heavy toll in terms of lost output and socioeconomic dislocations, it did not destroy the industrial and manufacturing infrastructure and the productive capacities of these economies. The significant investments these countries made in physical plant and equipment served them well as the global economy picked up. *Third*, domestic fiscal stimulus and a rebuilding of inventories combined with favorable external developments provided Asia's sagging export sector with a much-needed boost. Specifically, the global output growth of 3 per cent greatly stimulated the initially suppressed demand for goods and services produced in Asia. Most importantly, as the negative effects of the global electronics downturn that occurred from 1996 through to 1998 were gradually reversed, this boosted the South Korean, Malaysian, Thai and Singaporean economies, which depend heavily on the manufacture and exports of electronics, including information-technology-related products. The Korean recovery was also helped substantially by the external demand for cars and semi-conductors. Moreover, in all four countries service-sector output grew strongly, owing to growth in telecommunications, wholesale and retail trade, and financial services.

Prior to the global economic slowdown (which began ostensibly in the last quarter of 2000, compounded by the uncertainty produced by September 11, 2001), the US economy played an important role in supporting global demand – accounting for more than 50 per cent of the growth of global demand. While this was reflected in record US current-account deficits, these deficits proved to be an important buffer against global recession. Japan, on the other hand, has failed to live up to expectations as the engine behind the regional economies. Although positive growth in Japan in the first half of 1999 began to stimulate recovery in the region, it was short-lived.[5] The return to negative growth (0.5 per cent in 2001) weakened the stimulus to regional exports that otherwise would have been created by the stronger yen. Moreover, the Japanese government's growth stimulus from the 1999 fiscal package has petered out. The growth forecast for 2002 has been marked down to 0.5 per cent, reflecting in part the global economic slowdown, but also the continuing weakness of consumer confidence and underlying problems with the financial system. While the Japanese government has the resources to introduce another fiscal stimulus plan, given the high level of public debt, at 125 per cent of GDP, there is little scope for reflationary fiscal policies. Indeed, given Prime Minister Koizumi's plans to curb government spending, the economy is not likely to be stimulated by fiscal policy. Japan is therefore unlikely to provide much support to the regional economies this year through demand for their exports. Although it is expected that the growing intra-Asian trade and demand from the European Union will help to fill the void, there is little doubt that Japan's recovery is crucial (at least, in the short term) to the region's recovery. Over the long term, Japan's importance as a market for Asian exports and a source of long-term direct capital to the region will gradually diminish.

*Fourth*, the Asian crisis was not a current-account, but a capital-account crisis. Conventional current-account crises are caused by the deterioration of domestic macroeconomic fundamentals, such as price inflation, fiscal deficits and low rates of saving. A capital-account crisis is characterized by massive international capital inflows, usually large enough to surpass the underlying current-account deficit, and composed mainly of short-term borrowing denominated in foreign currencies. This leads to currency and maturity mismatches, which adversely affect the balance-sheets of domestic financial institutions. There is thus a dual financial crisis – a currency crisis due to currency mismatch that leads to international liquidity problems, and a domestic banking crisis resulting in credit contraction. During the Asian crisis, the swing of international capital from inflows to outflows amounted to more than 20 per cent of GDP in Thailand. Currency depreciation further worsened the balance-sheets of corporations by inflating the value of liabilities in domestic currency terms, thereby precipitating a currency and banking crisis. Further, there was an imbalance between high levels of short-term foreign debt and low foreign-exchange reserves. However, as investor panic (both foreign and domestic) that partly triggered the crisis abated, capital once again started to return – with FDI dominating the composition of net private flows, representing about 82 per cent of the total (World Bank 2000c, 154). This allowed the economies to rebuild their official international reserves, reduce their external liabilities, and strengthen their currencies and external current-account positions.

*Fifth*, prudent monetary and fiscal policy – some domestically inspired and some promoted by the IMF – have acted as important catalysts for recovery. For example, in South Korea, Thailand and Malaysia, money-market interest rates have been broadly unchanged since mid-1999, at levels significantly below those observed before the crisis.[6] Lower interest rates helped reduce the pressure on heavily indebted corporations and contain the non-performing loans problem.[7] with regard to fiscal policy, in Korea a supplementary budget adopted in August 1999 provided a much-needed additional stimulus, while targeting a consolidated central government deficit of 5 per cent of GDP for 1999. And *sixth*, luck has played an important role in Asia's recovery, just as it compounded underlying problems in 1997. In particular, while the El Niño and La Niña weather phenomena devastated agricultural production in 1997–98, the favorable weather conditions in 1999 and the first half of 2000 have helped Indonesia and the Philippines to reap bumper crops of rice and other basic agricultural commodities. In addition to creating agricultural employment, this has also eased burdens on the overstretched social safety nets and enabled vulnerable households better to meet their consumption needs.

### The global economic slowdown and September 11, 2001

Most Asian countries experienced a sharp economic slowdown beginning in the last quarter of 2000. The problems of a deteriorating external environment due in large part to the downturn in the US economy were exacerbated by the September 11 terrorist attacks. Countries that are closely linked to the global economy through trade and capital flows were more adversely affected than those where these linkages are weaker. In particular, Asian countries with heavier dependence on manufacturing, in particular the production and export of electronics, saw a larger decline in growth. For example, South Korea's manufacturing sector grew only by 1.5 per cent in the first three quarters of 2001, compared to an average growth of more than 18 per cent between 1999 and 2000. Similarly, in Malaysia the manufacturing sector actually shrank by 4 per cent in the first three quarters of 2001, whereas the average growth rate was 17.4 per cent in the preceding two years. Singapore's manufacturing shrank by 9 per cent in the first three quarters of 2001, from an average growth of more than 14 per cent in the preceding two years (ADB 2001, 4). To varying degrees, the decelerating export demand has been accompanied by softening domestic demand. Indeed, slowing growth and the sharp decline in stock prices have adversely affected both consumer confidence and business investment. The impact of the economic slowdown has been reflected in the growth-rates. In the first three quarters of 2001, Indonesia, South Korea, Malaysia, the Philippines and Thailand taken together grew only by 2.5 per cent. This represents a sharp deceleration from the 7.8 per cent growth they achieved in the first three quarters of 2000 (ADB 2001, 4). Even resilient Singapore saw its GDP decline by 0.6 per cent in the first three quarters of 2001, compared to 9.5 per cent growth in the corresponding period in 2000. The impact of the global slowdown on China has been moderate, partly because of its lower dependence on information technology exports, and partly because of a series of substantial fiscal stimulus measures that have been implemented over the last four years. Thus, China posted a growth of 7.6 per cent in the first three quarters of 2001 (ADB 2001, 4).

Another negative impact was the result of the sharp rise in oil prices in the first six months of 2001. Although prices have since leveled off, the potential oil-price instability (compounded by the uncertainty in the Middle East) remains a major concern. However, the price-rise was something of a mixed blessing. It has worked in favor of net exporters of oil such as Indonesia and Malaysia, but against net importers, such as South Korea, Taiwan, the Philippines and Thailand.[8] Korea is more vulnerable to rising international crude oil prices than most other Asian countries. Clearly, Korea's current-account balance would deteriorate significantly if oil prices were to rise sharply.

Third, the rebounds in East Asian equity markets in 1999 declined gradually in 2000, but were further sharply eroded following the September 11 attacks. In local currency terms, as of end-September 2000, Korean, Indonesian and Thai equities had fallen by almost 40 per cent, while losses in the Philippines were just under 35 per cent since early 2000 (ADB 2000b, 4). The drop in equity markets has been influenced by external and domestic factors. Externally, rising US interest rates triggered downward adjustments in global equity markets, while increased capital outflows have contributed to the decline in stock prices. Overall, all this has had an adverse impact on regional markets. Another factor that has influenced regional equity markets is the worldwide corrections in prices of information-technology stocks since the second quarter of 2000. Since the information technology sector in the affected Asian countries has expanded in recent years, this has also increased their exposure to fluctuations in information-technology stock prices.[9]

### The challenges ahead

The palpable concern that the drop in equity markets and the currency depreciations would trigger another crisis have since subsided – in large part because gross domestic product growth picked up in much of Southeast and East Asia in the first quarter of 2002. Taken together, Indonesia, Malaysia, the Philippines, Singapore, Thailand, the PRC and Korea grew by 5.3 per cent, representing an improvement from the 3.8 per cent growth achieved in the last quarter of 2001 and the 4.3 per cent growth for the entire year 2001. This resurgence in growth is driven primarily by a rise in global demand for the region's exports. This positive development notwithstanding, it is important to recognize that the crisis-affected countries are now more resilient to shocks than before. First, almost all the crisis-affected countries now run current-account surpluses. Second, foreign-exchange reserves have improved significantly, and more than cover the entire short-term external debt. In fact, the short-term to total debt ratios and total external debt to GDP ratios are now lower than those seen at the height of the 1997 crisis. Third, the magnitude of net private capital outflows is nowhere near as large as it was in 1997 and 1998. Fourth, the composition of capital being withdrawn is also different. In 1997–98 the main problem was the non-renewal of short-term credit by banks and investor panic. Now the problem is scheduled debt repayments and slowdown or withdrawal of foreign direct investment and portfolio capital. Fifth, the ratio of money supply to foreign-exchange reserves (another indicator of the vulnerability of a country to a currency crisis) has improved, and capital adequacy ratios and the profitability of banks are slowly recovering. Finally, as was noted earlier, the 1997 crisis was primarily a capital-account crisis that was exacerbated by pegged – and ultimately unsustainable – exchange rates. Currently, most Southeast and East Asian countries have adopted more flexible exchange-rate regimes. This should enable them to adjust to external shocks more smoothly.

Yet the crisis-affected countries still face some daunting challenges. For example, in order to deal with the social costs of the crisis and then the subsequent economic slowdown, governments responded with a series of fiscal stimuli measures to boost the economy. For example, between August 1998 and August 1999 the Thai government launched three fiscal stimulus packages, including tax and tariff reductions, to boost domestic demand. Consequently, it ran a large deficit which, on a cash-balance basis, reached a cumulative 79.4 billion baht in the first half of fiscal year 1999/2000 (ending September 30). The overall public-sector deficit, including interest costs of financial sector restructuring for the fiscal year 1999/2000 was around 7 per cent of GDP. Total public debt was estimated at about 2.6 trillion baht (US$67.7 billion) in 1999, equivalent to around 56 per cent of GDP (ADB 2000c, 37–38). Thus rising deficits in combination with very substantial financial sector restructuring costs have contributed to a rapid increase in public-sector debt since the onset of the crisis. Although China, South Korea, Malaysia, Singapore and Thailand introduced the stimuli measures in their 2001 budgets, the sharp downturn following September 11 forced them to announce supplementary spending packages. As a result, fiscal deficits have further increased in each country. Bringing these deficits to a manageable level remains a major challenge.

Since weaknesses in the financial and corporate sectors were at the heart of the crisis, reforming them has been a top priority. There are broadly two phases in resolving financial system distress: containment and restructuring. The containment or distress-resolution phase occurs with the onset of a financial crisis, when there is a major loss of confidence in the financial system. The aim during this phase is quickly to stabilize the financial system and prevent a credit crunch. The usual strategy is to provide large-scale liquidity support to the financial institutions and to limit losses by closing down unviable banks. The countries are now beyond the containment stage. Now in the restructuring and rehabilitation phase, the governments of Indonesia, Korea, Malaysia and Thailand have all intervened in non-viable financial institutions and re-capitalized some of the viable, but weak institutions, and have begun to take steps to improve prudential regulation and supervision. Yet inadequate regulation, weak supervision of financial institutions, poor accounting standards and disclosure rules, outmoded laws, and weak corporate governance continue to pose problems. Moreover, since financial restructuring has involved the governments' injecting a large amount of capital into or nationalizing troubled banks, this has resulted in the state's owning a high proportion of the banking sector. Although governments are committed to privatizing the nationalized banks and divesting state ownership, the process has been slow – owing in large part to unstable market conditions and political sensitivity in selling bank assets to foreign buyers. Of greater concern is the fact that most banks remain heavily burdened with large volumes of non-performing loans, many of which may ultimately have a relatively low recovery rate.

Governments have pursued various approaches to corporate restructuring. One popular voluntary method has involved mergers and acquisitions (M&As). The number of M&As, particularly those that are cross-border, has increased sharply. That is, total cross-border M&As, defined as acquisitions of more than 50 per cent of equity by foreign investors, increased from some US$3 billion in 1996 to about US$22 billion in 1999. The largest rise was in Korea, accounting for roughly US$13 billion of M&As in 1999 (ADB 2001, 123). While M&As have been triggered by important policy changes, including the liberalization of investment in non-traded sectors and changes in competition policy, it is important to note that much of the M&A activity has been concentrated in such activities as wholesale and retail trade, real estate and financial services. Overall, progress in corporate restructuring has been modest. There are several reasons for this. First, asset disposition has been slow, owing to the difficulty in valuing assets, thin markets for selling assets, and fear of selling them too cheaply. Secondly, many banks not only have insufficient capacity to absorb losses without facing a serious threat of closure, but in most countries operate with a full government guarantee on their liabilities, reducing any real incentive to undertake fundamental restructuring. Third, most banks have a limited technical capacity to restructure, while their long-standing links with corporations have complicated the restructuring process. Finally, the needed restructuring and asset sales have been hampered by disagreement between creditors over loss-sharing, and weak insolvency procedures, including creditors' reluctance to write down losses, have prolonged the liquidation of unviable companies.

Compared to their peak levels during the crisis, non-performing loan ratios have fallen in most of the crisis-hit countries. However, caution should be exercised in interpreting this decline. The reductions in non-performing loan ratios have been brought about by the transfer of such loans from banks' balance sheets to the government-owned asset-management companies (AMCs). While this has enabled banks to resume lending and support recovery, the real test of restructuring also hinges on the progress made in asset-disposal by AMCs.

Finally, the financial crisis left widespread socioeconomic distress in its wake, with massive job losses and bankruptcies. The resultant sharp rise in inflation (in the context of a considerably weakened labor market) exacted a heavy toll in terms of falling real wages and incomes. The combined effects of higher unemployment, inflation and the absence of a meaningful social safety net pushed hundreds of thousands, if not millions, of people into poverty. While the various social support systems introduced in Thailand, Malaysia, South Korea and Indonesia helped to protect the most vulnerable sectors of society, much more needs to be done. In the immediate term, given that the scope for expansionary macroeconomic policies is greatly limited, it is imperative to develop a means-tested social assistance that provides minimum income support to the most needy. Only Korea has come close to developing such a system. In the long term, sustained economic growth and continuing investments in health, education and social services are a must.

### A new East Asian regionalism?

Does East Asia's long-term salvation lie in a new East Asian regionalism? Obviously many East Asian governments think so. The single greatest push for East Asian regionalism has been the Asian financial crisis. The commonly held view in Asia (especially Korea and the ASEAN countries) was that they were let down by the West (in particular, the United States and Japan) during the crisis. In their view, since Western banks and financial institutions from the G-7 countries had created and exacerbated the crisis by suddenly pulling their funds from the region, it was only appropriate for Western governments to provide assistance. The fact that G-7 governments either declined individually to take part in the rescue operations (as was the case of the United States and Japan with Thailand), or required excessively stringent demands through the IMF, only served to aggravate the feelings of let-down and betrayal. At the same time it was widely believed that the United States (through the IMF) was not only dictating flawed policy responses to the crisis, but also that these self-serving policies had worsened the crisis by pushing Asian economies into a deeper economic recession. As Bergsten (2000, 24) notes:

> The single greatest catalyst for the new East Asian regionalism, and the reason it is moving most rapidly on the monetary side, is the financial crisis of 1997–98. Most East Asians feel that they were both let down and put upon by the West. In their view, western banks and other lenders created much of the crisis by pulling out. The leading financial powers then either declined to take part in the rescue operations, as the United States did in Thailand, or built the much-bally-hooed "second lines of defense" so deviously that they could never be used. At the same time, the IMF and the United States dictated much of the Asian response to the crisis.

Whatever the merits of such thinking, it is clear that Asian governments now agree that they must reduce their dependence on the G-7 countries and multilateral financial institutions like the IMF and the World Bank. Perhaps, most significantly, the celebrated APEC (Asia Pacific Economic Cooperation) has been severely compromised. APEC's failure at its Vancouver Leaders' Meeting in November 1997 to support Japan's proposal for an Asian Monetary Fund and its endorsement of the centrality of the IMF to the resolution of the crisis alienated many Asian governments from the organization. However, one cannot conclude that Asian countries are rejecting multilateralism and global economic integration. Rather, it seems that they want their own institutions and a bigger say in regional economic matters. More diplomatically, Asian countries claim that a regionally focused facility might be able to design more appropriate conditionality than the IMF because of the former's presumably superior regional expertise and its closer geographical proximity to its member countries.

### The Asian Monetary Fund

The idea of the Asian Monetary Fund (AMF) dates back to August 1997, when Thailand approached the Japanese government for financial assistance. In response, Japan, along with several member countries of ASEAN, proposed setting up a separate monetary fund to provide emergency financing to countries affected by the economic crisis. The proposal was enthusiastically welcomed, as the ASEAN nations were only too eager to see Japan take on a greater leadership role (i.e. in the economic sphere) in the region. Moreover, there was an anticipation that the conditionality attached to AMF resources would not be nearly as strict as that imposed by the IMF. However, in its public relations campaign, ASEAN claimed that the AMF would not only promote regional cooperation and trust, but that there was a real economic rationale for such a body. Specifically, since trade tends to be regional, the affected region loses disproportionately from trade disruptions caused by currency crises. Thus it made sense that the regional governments work in unison to prevent the spread of financial crises. It was also argued that the AMF, like the Arab Monetary Fund and the Latin American Reserve Fund, would complement the IMF (Sussangkarn 2000).

By the end of September 1997, it seemed that the AMF would be a reality. The Japanese government pledged an initial US$50 billion, while an additional US$50–60 billion was to be raised through contributions from the PRC, Taiwan, Hong Kong and Singapore (Yoshitomi and Shirai 2000, 67–9). It was argued that the AMF and its financing arm, the Regional Financing Facility, would provide sufficient liquidity that could be quickly mobilized to forestall speculative attacks on the region's currencies. Also, unlike the IMF assistance, funds from the AMF were to be unconditional, taking into account the individual needs of the member countries. As expected, the United States and the European Union were unequivocal in their objections. First, they argued that unconditional financial assistance would increase the risk of moral hazard, and second, that an independent AMF would undermine the IMF, because of the potential conflicts in their policy guidelines for member states. In the end "Japan decided to give up the proposal in November 1997, owing to the opposition by the United States and the IMF on the grounds that such an arrangement would enhance the problems of moral hazard and double-standards" (Yoshitomi and Shirai 2000, 68). Wade and Veneroso (1998b, 19), more bluntly note that "the United States Treasury pulled out all the stops to kill the proposal, and it died."

Although the proposal for the AMF did not get off the ground, the ASEAN finance ministers at the November 1997 APEC Summit in Vancouver agreed to establish a cooperative arrangement of regional surveillance (called the Manila Framework Group) through a better coordination between the member states' finance ministries and central banks. The Framework included the following initiatives: (1) a cooperative financing arrangement that would supplement IMF resources, (2) enhanced economic and technical cooperation, particularly in strengthening domestic financial systems and regulatory capacities, and (3) a mechanism for regional surveillance to complement the IMF's global surveillance. To enhance cooperation further, the ASEAN finance ministers (on October 4, 1998), formed the ASEAN Surveillance Process (ASP) to promote closer consultations on economic policies. The ASP has two major elements: (1) to monitor global, regional and national economic and financial developments, and (2) to provide a forum where ASEAN finance ministers can share information and jointly develop collective action programs to counter potential threats to any member country and the region.[10]

On October 3, 1998, Japan formally proposed a "New Initiative to Overcome the Asian Currency Crisis." The most ambitious element was the "Miyazawa Initiative." Under this initiative, Japan pledged US$30 billion to support the crisis-hit countries. Half the pledged amount was to be dedicated to short-term capital needs during the process of implementing economic reforms. The rest was earmarked for medium- and long-term reforms. By February 2000, US$21 billion had been committed, with US$13.5 billion for medium- and long-term reforms. Korea has been the largest recipient (US$8.4 billion), followed by Malaysia (US$4.4 billion), and Indonesia and Thailand with US$2.9 billion each, and the Philippines (US$2.5 billion). The initiative has supported economic adjustment, financial and corporate restructuring, social safety nets, infrastructure and export financing. In the second phase of the initiative, Japan has partially guaranteed sovereign debt issues, enabling countries to use limited public resources to mobilize private capital, thereby promoting private debt markets (World Bank 2000b, 152–3).

## Conclusion: after September 11, 2001

### The Chiang Mai initiative

About a decade ago, Malaysian Prime Minister Mahathir Mohamad proposed the creation of an exclusive "East Asian Economic Group" (EAEG) comprising the ASEAN countries, China, Japan and South Korea. Concerned as he was about the emerging trade blocs in Europe and North America, Mahathir's undeclared objective was to persuade the mentioned countries to shift their economic strategies along the lines of his own "look East" policy – with Japan as the economic focal point. While the EAEG proposal received lukewarm support from Asian countries (including Japan), it was vigorously opposed by the United States, Australia and New Zealand, because they felt that the EAEG would undermine the incipient Asia–Pacific Economic Cooperation (APEC) forum.[11]

However, the organization that actually expanded (with strong American backing) was the broad-based APEC (Asia-Pacific Economic Co-operation). However, in the aftermath of the Asian financial crisis, the ASEAN countries hastily created the "ASEAN+3" (comprising the 10 member countries of ASEAN, plus China, Japan and South Korea) as envisaged earlier by Mahathir. Since December 1997, informal ASEAN+3 summits have been convened on an annual basis. They have already set up a "vision group" to explore ideas for cooperation, and have been holding regular meetings of their finance ministers.

However, the central task of ASEAN+3, besides setting up the vision group, has been to establish a surveillance mechanism to try to anticipate and head off future financial crises. Top-level discussion has also taken place regarding common currency baskets and joint intervention arrangements – to replace both the discredited dollar pegs of the past and the costly free floats imposed by the crisis.[12] Most dramatically, at the thirty-third annual meeting of the Board of Governors of the Asian Development Bank meeting in Chiang Mai, Thailand in June 2000, the finance ministers of ASEAN+3 committed their countries to even greater regional cooperation under the new "Chiang Mai Initiative." Specifically, they announced their agreement to share foreign-exchange reserves (through a region-wide system of currency swaps and repurchase arrangements) in order to defend their currencies against speculative attacks. The finance ministers reasoned that providing countries under pressure with short-term hard-currency liquidity would act as a firewall against future financial crises. To show their commitment, the ASA (ASEAN Swap Arrangement) was endowed with US$1 billion effective November 17, 2000. While the repurchase agreements (repos) are designed to allow ASEAN members with collateral like US Treasury Bills to swap them for hard currency, and then repurchase them at a later date, it is hoped that hard-currency lines of credit can be made available to members without strict linkages to repos. Indeed, under the initiative,

ASA is to be made available for two years and is renewable upon the mutual agreement of the members. Each member is allowed to draw a maximum of twice its committed amount from the facility for a period of up to six months, with the possibility of a further extension, which is not to exceed six months. In addition to ASA, members are encouraged to establish bilateral swap arrangements. In April 2001 Japan signed a bilateral swap arrangement with Malaysia, Thailand and Korea totaling some US$6 billion. While the maximum amount that can be withdrawn under the bilateral swap will be determined by the two countries, in the spirit of regional cooperation all member states will be fully consulted when deciding the size of the disbursements.

Moreover, in keeping with the signed Chiang Mai Initiative, ASEAN+3 have committed themselves to work towards cooperation. In March 2001, the ASEAN Task Force on the ASEAN Currency and Exchange Rate Mechanism was established, with the ambitious task of working towards harmonizing the macroeconomic and exchange-rate policies of the member countries. Moreover, there is agreement to work towards a common market and a single Asian currency unit on the euro model. Even the IMF has given its blessing to this goal. In fact, the fund has expressed support for any regional initiative as long as it is complementary with the policy of the IMF. The IMF recently noted that "regional initiatives can be helpful in supporting sustained economic growth and stable financial relations among participating countries. In this vein, the recent Chiang Mai Initiative among ASEAN members and China, Korea and Japan is an important example of enhanced regional cooperation through which countries in temporary financial difficulties will be able to obtain foreign exchange from their neighbors through swap and repurchase arrangements" (IMF 2000d, 9). In this context, some have argued that the Chiang Mai Initiative is like the European Monetary System (EMS) arrangement. However, this seems to be a bit of an exaggeration. After all, the exchange rate mechanism (ERM) of the EMS provided for automatic and unlimited support of bilateral pegs. That is, the arrangement conveyed an essential message to the markets: any attempt at tearing apart any one currency from the others is bound to face strong official resistance, since the central bank is committed to put up unlimited amounts of its currency as a defense. In contrast, the amounts to be swapped within the Chiang Mai arrangement are limited and unlikely to be commensurate with the amounts that markets can mobilize.

In the end, how all these initiatives will actually work in practice remains to be seen. However, what once seemed a pipe-dream is now no longer that. The growth of cross-border trade is driving Asian economies inexorably towards closer cooperation. Suffice it to note that, the demands for regional arrangements to ensure currency stability and more efficient regional exchange transactions will grow. The Asian financial crisis vividly underscored the fact that Asian countries have a vested interest in cooperating with one another to minimize the systemic risk now inherent under globalization.

## Notes

1 Cited in DeRosa (2001, 186–7).
2 The Asian Development Bank (ADB) defines East Asia as the 10 Association of Southeast Asian Nations (ASEAN), including Brunei Darussalam, Cambodia, Indonesia, Laos, Malaysia, Myanmar, the Philippines, Singapore, Thailand and Vietnam), plus China and South Korea.
3 International credit-rating agencies such as Moody's, Standard and Poor and Fitch IBCA have raised their credit ratings for South Korea, Malaysia and Thailand. Most importantly, in all three countries the capital inflows have been mostly non-debt-creating. Thus these countries have been able further to reduce their external liabilities. With short-term liabilities being redeemed, the maturity profile of the external debt has improved significantly.
4 Although the rupiah now seems to be less vulnerable and volatile than before, trading levels during the last week of February represent a depreciation of about 67 per cent in US dollar terms from its end-June 1997 level.
5 In the second half of 1999, Japan's GDP growth fell to 0.9 per cent and to a negative 0.3 per cent in the third and fourth quarters respectively. For details, see ADB (2000c, 5).
6 In Indonesia, a market-led decline in short-term interest rates resumed in the late 1999 as political uncertainty eased, but interest-rate levels continue to exceed those elsewhere in the region.
7 Short-term nominal interest rates have come down sharply and are now either below their pre-crisis level or close to it.
8 In the case of Indonesia, the net effect of higher oil prices on the government's fiscal position is unlikely to be substantial, as increased government revenues will be partially offset by the higher costs of the government fuel subsidy.
9 Prices of IT stocks tend to be more volatile and more closely correlated internationally than those of traditional non-IT stocks.
10 In addition to the usual monitoring of exchange rates and macroeconomic aggregates, the ASP also monitors sectoral and social policies, including provisions for capacity-building, institutional strengthening and sharing of information.
11 Although some Japanese officials viewed the EAEG proposal favorably, the Japanese government had to oppose it publicly in the face of strong opposition from the United States.
12 Although the finance ministers of ASEAN+3 met for the first time in Manila in April 1999, top-level discussions have been taking place since mid-1997.

# Bibliography

Abidin, Mahani Zainal. 2000. Malaysia's Alternative Approach to Crisis Management, *Southeast Asian Affairs 2000*. Singapore: Institute of Southeast Asian Studies, pp. 184–202.

Adams, Charles, Robert E. Litan and Michael Pomerleano (eds.). 1999. *Managing Financial and Corporate Distress: Lessons from Asia*. Washington, DC: Brookings Institution Press.

ADB (Asian Development Bank). 1999. *Asian Development Outlook: 1999*. New York: Oxford University Press.

——, 2000. *Asia Recovery Report 2000*. October. (http://aric.adb.org).

——, 2000a. Asia's Recovery: A Regional Update in *Asian Recovery Report 2000*. May. (http://aric.abd.org).

——, 2000b. *Asian Development Outlook 2000: May Update*. Manila: ADB.

——, 2000c. *Asian Development Outlook 2000: October Update*. Manila: ADB.

——, 2001. *Asia Economic Monitor 2001*. September. Manila: ADB.

——, 2002. *Asia Economic Monitor 2002*. July. Manila: ADB.

Adelman, Irma and Erinc Yeldan. 2000. Is this the end of Economic Development? *Structural Change and Economic Dynamics*, vol. 11, pp. 95–109.

Agenor, Pierre-Richard, Marcus Miller, David Vines and Axel Weber (eds.). 1999. *Asian Financial Crisis: Causes, Contagion and Consequences*. New York: Cambridge University Press.

Ahuja, Vinod, Benu Bidani, Francisco Ferreira and Michael Walton. 1997. *Everybody's Miracle: Revisiting Poverty and Inequality in East Asia*. Washington, DC: World Bank.

Alba, Pedro, Amar Bhattacharya, Stijn Classens, Swati Ghosh and Lernardo Hernandez. 1999. Volatility and Contagion in a Financially Integrated World: Lessons from the East Asia's Recent Experience, in Gordon de Brouwer and Wisarn Pupphavesa (eds.), *Asia Pacific Financial Deregulation*. New York: Routledge, pp. 9–66.

——, Leonardo Hernandez and Daniela Klingebiel. 1999. *Financial Liberalization and the Capital Account: Thailand 1988–1997*. World Bank: Washington, DC.

Alexander, Arthur. 1998. Japan in the Context of Asia, *SAIS Policy Forum Series, Report No. 2*, September. School of Advanced International Studies.

Alm, James, Robert H. Aten and Roy Bahl. 2001. Can Indonesia Decentralize Successfully? Plans, Problems and Prospects, *Bulletin of Indonesian Economic Studies*, vol. 37, no. 1, April, pp. 83–102.

Altbach, E. 1997. The Asian Monetary Fund Proposal: A Case Study of Japanese Regional Leadership *Japan Economic Institute Report 47A*, December.

Amsden, Alice. 1989. *Asia's Next Giant: South Korea and Late Industrialization*. New York: Oxford University Press.

Anwar, Dewi Fortuna. 1999. The Habibie Presidency, in Geoff Forrester (ed.), *Post-Soeharto Presidency: Renewal or Chaos?* Singapore: Institute of Southeast Asian Studies, pp. 33–47.

Ariff, Mohamed and Ahmed M. Khalid. 2000. *Liberalization, Growth and the Asian Financial Crisis*. Cheltenham, UK: Edward Elgar.

Arphasil, Prakarn. 2001. Financial Liberalization and Financial Crisis: The Case of Thailand, in Masayoshi Tsurumi (ed.), *Financial Big Bang in Asia*. Aldershot, UK: Ashgate Publishing, pp. 167–87.

Aspe, Pedro. 1993. *Economic Transformation the Mexican Way*. Cambridge, MA: MIT Press.

Asra, Abuzar. 1989. Inequality Trends in Indonesia 1968–81: A Re-Examination, *Bulletin of Indonesian Economic Studies*, vol. 25, no. 2, pp. 100–10.

Athukorala, Prema-Chandra. 1998. Malaysia, in Ross H. McLeod and Ross Garnaut (eds.), *East Asia in Crisis: From Being a Miracle to Needing One*. London: Routledge, pp. 85–104.

——, 1998a. *Trade Policy Issues in Asian Development*. New York: Routledge.

Azis, Iwan. 1999. Do We Know the Real Causes of the Asian Crisis?, in Barry Herman (ed.), *Global Financial Turmoil and Reform: A United Nations Perspective*. Tokyo: United Nations University Press, pp. 75–92.

Backman, Michael. 1999. *Asian Eclipse: Exposing the Dark Side of Business in Asia*. Wiley: Singapore.

Baer, Werner, William R. Miles and Allen B. Moran. 1999. The End of the Asian Myth: Why Were the Experts Fooled?, *World Development*, vol. 27, no. 10, pp. 1735–47.

Bagehot, Walter. 1999 (originally published 1873). *Lombard Street: A Description of the Money Market*. New York: Wiley.

Baig, Taimur and Ilan Goldfajn. 1999. Financial Market Contagion in the Asian Crisis, *IMF Staff Papers*, vol. 46, no. 2, June, pp. 167–95.

Bailey, Martin N. and Eric Zitzewitz. 1998. Extending the East Asian Miracle: Microeconomic Evidence From Korea, *Brookings Papers on Economic Activity: Microeconomics*, pp. 249–308.

Balino, Tomas J. T. and Angel Ubide. 1999. The Korean Financial Crisis of 1997 – A Strategy of Financial Sector Reform, *IMF Working Paper*, March, WP/99/28.

Bank Negara Malaysia. 1999. *Quarterly Bulletin 1999*, First Quarter, vol. 14, no. 1. Kuala Lumpur, Malaysia: The Bank.

——, 1998. *Quarterly Bulletin 1998*, Third Quarter, vol. 13, no. 3, Kuala Lumpur, Malaysia: The Bank.

——, 1998a. *Annual Report*. Kuala Lumpur, Malaysia: The Bank.

Bank of Korea. 1998. *Statistics of the Korean Economy* (www.bok.or.kr).

Barro, Robert J. 1998. Malaysia Could Do Worse than this Economic Plan, *Business Week*, November 2, p. 26.

——, 1999. How the IMF Starts Fires It's Supposed to Put Out, *Hoover Digest*, no. 3, pp. 1–4.

Basel Committee on Banking Supervision. 1997. *Core Principles for Effective Banking Supervision*. Basle: Bank for International Settlements.

——, 1999. *Sound Practices for Banks? Interactions with Highly Leveraged Institutions*. Basle: Bank for International Settlements. January.

——, 1999a. *A New Capital Adequacy Framework*. Basle: Bank for International Settlements. June.

Beck, Peter M. 1998. Revitalizing Korea's *Chaebol Asian Survey*, vol. xxxviii, no. 11, November, pp. 1018–35.

——, 2000. Korea's Embattled *Chaebol*: Are They Serious About Restructuring?, in *The Two Koreas in 2000: Sustaining Recovery and Seeking Reconciliation*. Washington, DC: The Korea Economic Institute of America, pp. 16–24.

Bedeski, Robert. 1994. *The Transformation of South Korea: Reform and Reconstruction in the Sixth Republic under Roh Tae Woo 1987–1992*. London: Routledge.

Bennett, Michael. 1995. Banking Deregulation In Indonesia, *University of Pennsylvania Journal of International Business Law*, vol. 16, no. 443.

Berg, Andrew. 1999. The Asia Crisis: Causes, Policy Responses and Outcomes, *IMF Working Paper*, no. WP/99/138.

—— and Eduardo Borensztein. 2000. The Pros and Cons of Full Dollarization, *IMF Working Paper*, WP/00/50. March.

Bergsten, Fred. 1998. A New Strategy for the Global Crisis, *International Economics Policy Briefs*. Washington, DC: Institute for International Economics. September.

——, 2000. East Asian Regionalism: Towards a Tripartite World, *The Economist*, July 15, pp. 24–6.

Berthelemy, Jean-Claude and Tommy Koh (eds.). 1998. *The Asian Crisis: A New Agenda for Euro-Asian Cooperation*. Singapore: World Scientific Publishing.

Betcherman, Gordon and Rizwanul Islam (eds.). 2001. *East Asian Labor Markets and the Economic Crisis: Impacts, Responses and Lessons*. Washington, DC: World Bank.

Bhagwati, Jagdish. 1996. The Feuds over Free Trade, paper presented at the Institute for Southeast Asian Studies, Singapore, September 18.

——, 1998. The Capital Myth: The Difference Between Trade in Widgets and Dollars, *Foreign Affairs*, vol. 77, no. 3, May–June, pp. 7–12.

——, 1998a. Yes to Free Trade, Maybe to Capital Controls, *The Wall Street Journal*, November 16, p. A-38.

——, 1998b. Poverty and Reforms: Friends or Foes?, *Journal of International Affairs*, vol. 52, no. 1, Autumn.

——, 1998c. Free Thinker: Free Trader Explains Why He likes Capital Controls, *Far Eastern Economic Review*, October 15, p. 14.

Bhattacharya, Amar and Mari Pangestu. 1997. Indonesia: Development Transformation and the Role of Public Policy, in Danny M. Leipziger (ed.), *Lessons from East Asia*. Ann Arbor, MI: University of Michigan Press, pp. 387–442.

Bhattacharya, Anindya. 2000. The Asian Financial Crisis: An Evaluation of Market Intervention Policies by Hong Kong Regulations, in J. Jay Choi (ed.), *Asian Financial Crisis: Financial, Structural and International Dimensions*. New York: Elsevier Publishing Inc., pp. 293–303.

Bird, Graham. 1998. Convertibility and Volatility: The Pros and Cons of Liberalizing the Capital Account, *Economic Notes*, vol. 27, no. 2, pp. 141–56.

BIS (Bank for International Settlements). 1998. *The Maturity, Sectoral and Nationality Distribution of International Bank Lending*. January. Basle, Switzerland: The Bank.

——, 1999. *69th Annual Report*. Basle, Switzerland: The Bank.

Blecker, Robert A. 1999. *Taming Global Finance: A Better Architecture for Growth and Equity*. Washington, DC: Economic Policy Institute.

Blinder, Alan. 1999. Eight Steps to a New Financial Order, *Foreign Affairs*, vol. 78, no. 5, September/October, pp. 50–63.

Blustein, Paul. 1998. Is Malaysia's Reform Working? Capital Controls Appear to Aid Economy, *Washington Post*, November 21, p. GO1.

——, 2001. *The Chastening: Inside the Crisis that Rocked the Global Financial System and Humbled the IMF*. New York: Public Affairs.

Bogetic, Zeljko. 2000. Full Dollarization: Fad or Future?, *Challenge*, vol. 43, no. 2, March/April, pp. 17–48.

Boomgaard Peter and Ian Brown. 2000. *Weathering the Storm: The Economies of Southeast Asia in the 1930s Depression*. Singapore: Institute of Southeast Asian Studies.

Boorman, Jack, Timothy Lane, Mariane Schulze-Ghattas, Ales Bulir, Atish Ghosh, Javier Hamann, Alexander Mourmouras and Steven Phillips. 2000. Managing Financial Crises: The Experience in East Asia, *IMF Working Paper*, no. WP/00/107.

Booth, Anne. 1998. *The Indonesian Economy in the Nineteenth and Twentieth Century: A History of Missed Opportunities*. New York: St Martin's Press.

——, 1999. Development: Achievement and Weakness, in Donald K. Emmerson (ed.), *Indonesia Beyond Suharto: Polity, Economy and Society*. Armonk, NY: M. E. Sharpe, pp. 109–35.

——, 1999a. The Social Impact of the Asian Crisis: What Do We Know Two Years On?, *Asian-Pacific Economic Literature*, vol. 13, no. 2, November, pp. 16–29.

Bordo, Michael and Barry Eichengreen. 1993. *A Retrospective on the Bretton Woods System: Lessons for International Monetary Reform*. Chicago: The University of Chicago Press.

Bordo, Michael and Harold James. 2000. The International Monetary Fund: Its Present Role in Historical Perspective, *NBER Working Paper*, no. 7724, June.

Borensztein, Eduardo and Jong-Wha Lee. 1999. Credit Allocation and Financial Crisis in Korea, *IMF Working Paper*, No. 99/20. Washington, DC: IMF.

Borsuk, Richard. 1999. Markets: The Limits of Reform, in Donald Emmerson (ed.), *Indonesia Beyond Suharto: Polity, Economy and Society*. Armonk, NY: M. E. Sharpe.

Bosworth, Barry. 1998. The Asian Crisis in Context, *International Finance*, vol. 1, no. 2, December, pp. 289–310.

Boskin, Michael. 1998. How the Tigers Lost their Tail, *Hoover Digest*, no. 2, pp. 1–5.

BoT (Bank of Thailand). 1992. *Fifty Years of the Bank of Thailand: 1942–1992*. Bangkok: Bank of Thailand.

——, 1994. *Annual Report 1993*. Bangkok: Bank of Thailand.

——, 1995. Thailand's Current Account Deficit, *Economic Focus*. vol. 1, no. 1, October–December.

——, 1995a. *Annual Report 1994*. Bangkok: Bank of Thailand.

357

——, 1996a. Analyzing Thailand's Current Account Deficit, *Economic Focus*, vol. 1, no. 1, January–March, pp. 1–27.

——, 1996b. Analyzing Thailand's Short-Term Debt, *Economic Focus*, vol. 1, no. 3, July–September, pp. 1–26.

——, 1996c. Economic Performance in 1996 and Outlook in 1997, *Bank of Thailand Quarterly Bulletin*, vol. 36, no. 4, December.

——, 1998. *Financial Institutions and Markets in Thailand*. Economic Research Department. November. Bangkok: Bank of Thailand.

——, 1998a. Focus on the Thai Crisis *Economic Focus*, vol. 2, no. 2, April–June, pp. 1–42.

——, 1998b. Asset Price Inflation: Developments and Policy Issues *Economic Focus*, vol. 2, no. 1, January–March, pp. 1–22.

——, 1998c. Economic Performance in 1998 and Outlook for 1999, *Quarterly Bulletin*, vol. 38, no. 4, pp. 7–32.

Bowie, Alasdair and Danny Unger. 1997. *The Politics of Open Economies: Indonesia, Malaysia, the Philippines and Thailand*. New York: Cambridge University Press.

Bresnan, John. 1993. *Managing Indonesia: The Modern Political Economy*. New York: Columbia University Press.

——, 1999. The United States, the IMF, and the Indonesian Financial Crisis, in Adam Schwarz and Jonathan Paris (eds.), *The Politics of Post-Suharto Indonesia*. New York: Council on Foreign Relations Press.

Bridges, Brian. 1999. Europe and the Asian Financial Crisis: Coping with Contagion, *Asian Survey*, vol. xxxix, no. 3, May/June, pp. 456–67.

——, 2001. *Korea After the Crash: The Politics of Economic Recovery*. London: Routledge.

Broadman, Harry G. 1999. The Chinese State as Corporate Shareholder, *Finance and Development*, vol. 36, no. 3, September, pp. 52–5.

Brookings Institution Policy Brief. 1999. *The Economic Debacle in Northeast Asia: Economic, Political and Social Legacies*. Washington, DC: The Brookings Institution.

Brown, Stephen, William Goetzmann and James Park. 1998. *Hedge Funds and the Asian Currency Crisis of 1997*. New Haven, CT: International Center for Finance, Yale School of Management. May.

Brugger, Bill and Stephen Reglar. 1994. *Politics, Economy and Society in Contemporary China*. Stanford, CA: Stanford University Press.

Bueno de Mesquita, Bruce, James D. Morrow and Hilton Root, 1999. IMF Loans Must be Linked to Reforms, *Los Angeles Times*, April 9, p. 27.

Buiter, Willem and Anne Sibert. 1999. UDROP: A Small Contribution to the New International Financial Architecture, *International Finance*, no. 2, pp. 227–39.

Bunbongkarn, Suchit. 1999. Thailand's Successful Reforms, *Journal of Democracy*, vol. 10, no. 4, pp. 54–68.

Burnham, James B. 1999. The IMF and World Bank: Time to Merge, *The Washington Quarterly*, vol. 22, no. 2, pp. 101–11.

Bustelo, Pablo. 1999. South Korea in 1997–98, in Holger Henke and Ian Boxill (eds.), *The End of the Asian Model?* Philadelphia: John Benjamins Publishing Company, pp. 163–78.

——, 2000. Novelties of Financial Crises in the 1990s and the Search for New Indicators, *Emerging Markets Review*, vol. 1, pp. 229–51.

Callahan, W. A. and D. McCargo. 1996. Vote-Buying in Thailand's Northeast, *Asian Survey*, vol. 36, no. 4, April. pp. 376–91.

Calomiris, Charles. 1998. The IMF's Imprudent Role as Lender of Last Resort, *Cato Journal*, vol. 17, pp. 275–95.

——, 2000. When Will Economics Guide IMF and World Bank Reforms?, *Cato Journal*, vol. 20, no. 1, Spring/Summer, pp. 85–103.

—— and Allan Meltzer. 1999. Fixing the IMF, *The National Interest*, no. 56, Summer, pp. 88–96.

Calvo, Guillermo. 1996. Capital Inflows and Macroeconomic Management: Tequila Lessons, *International Journal of Finance and Economics*, vol. 1, July, pp. 207–23.

—— and E. G. Mendoza. 1997. Capital Flows and Capital-Market Crises: The Simple Economics of Sudden Stops, unpublished paper. University of Maryland.

—— and Carmen Reinhart. 2000. Fixing for your Life, *Working Paper 8606*. National Bureau of Economic Research, November.

——, Leonardo Leiderman and Carmen Reinhart. 1993. Capital Inflows and Real Exchange Rate Appreciation in Latin America: The Role of External Factors, *IMF Staff Paper 40* (March), pp. 108–51.

Camdessus, Michel. 1995. Press conference of the Managing Director of the IMF, Washington, DC, February. (www.imf.org).

——, 1998. The IMF's Role in Today's Globalized World: Address to the IMF-Bundesbank Symposium, Frankfurt, Germany, 2 July. (www.imf.org).

Campos, Jose E. and Hilton Root. 1996. *The Key to the Asian Miracle: Making Shared Growth Credible*. Washington, DC: The Brookings Institution.

Capie, Forrest. 1998. Can There Be an International Lender-of-Last-Resort?, *International Finance*, vol. 1, no. 2, December, pp. 311–25.

Caprio, Gerard. 1997. Safe and Sound Banking in Developing Countries: We're Not in Kansas Anymore, *Research in Financial Services: Private and Public Policy*, no. 9. pp. 79–97.

——, Patrick Honohan and Joseph E. Stiglitz (eds.). 2001. *Financial Liberalization: How Far, How Fast?* New York: Cambridge University Press.

Caramazza, Francesco and Jahangir Aziz. 1998. Fixed for Flexible? Getting the Exchange Rate Right in the 1990s, *IMF Economic Issues*, no. 13.

Cargill, Thomas and Elliot Parker. 2001. Financial Liberalization in China: Limitations and Lessons of the Japanese Regime, *Journal of Asia Pacific Economy*, vol. 6, no. 1, pp. 1–21.

Cathie, John. 1997/98. Financing Contagion in East Asia and the Origins of the Economic and Financial Crisis in Korea, *Asia Pacific Business Review*, vol. 4, nos. 2/3, Winter/Spring, pp. 18–28.

Cerra, Valerie and Anuradha Dayal-Gulati. 1999. China's Trade Flows: Changing Price Sensitivities and the Reform Process, *IMF Working Paper 99/1*.

Cha, Baekin. 1999. Financial Sector Reform in Korea after the Asian Financial Crisis, *Seoul Journal of Economics*, vol. 12, no. 41, pp. 457–83.

Cha, Dong-Se. 2001. The Korean Economy in the New Millennium: Reform or Revival, in O. Yul Kwon and William Shepherd (eds.), *Korea's Economic Prospects: From Financial Crisis to Prosperity*. Cheltenham, UK: Edward Elgar, pp. 39–59.

Chan, Anthony S. 2001. Restarting Economic Growth in Indonesia, in Anthony L. Smith (ed.), *Gus Dur and the Indonesian Economy*. Singapore: Institute of Southeast Asian Studies.

Chan, Vei-Lin and Sheng-Cheng Hu. 2000. Financial Liberalization in Taiwan, *Review of Pacific Basin Financial Markets and Policies*, vol. 3, no. 2, pp. 429–49.

Chanda, Nayan. 1998. Rebuilding Asia, in Dan Biers (ed.), *Crash of '97: How the Financial Crisis is Reshaping Asia.* Hong Kong: Review Publishing Company, pp. 8–17.

Chang, Ha-Joon. 1998. Korea: The Misunderstood Crisis, *World Development*, vol. 26, no. 8, pp. 1555–61.

——, 2000. The Hazard of Moral Hazard: Untangling the Asian Crisis, *World Development*, vol. 28, no. 4, pp. 775–88.

——, 2002. The Stiglitz Connection, *Challenge*, vol. 45, no. 2, March/April, pp. 77–96.

—— and Hong-Jae Park. 1999. An Alternative Perspective on Post-1997 Corporate Restructuring in Korea, December, unpublished manuscript.

——, Gabriel Palma and D. Hugh Whittaker (eds.). 2001. *Financial Liberalization and the Asian Crisis*. New York: Palgrave Publishers.

——, Hong-Jae Park and Chul Gyue Yoo. 1998. Interpreting the Korean Crisis: Financial Liberalization, Industrial Policy and Corporate Governance, *Cambridge Journal of Economics*, vol. 22, pp. 735–46.

Chang, Li Lin and Ramkishen S. Rajan. 1999. East Asian Cooperation in Light of the Regional Crises: A Case of Self-Help or No-Help, *Australian Journal of International Affairs*, vol. 53, pp. 261–81.

Chang, Roberto. 2000. Dollarization: A Scorecard, *Federal Reserve Bank of Atlanta: Economic Review*, vol. 85, no. 3, pp. 1–11.

—— and Andres Velasco. 1998. Financial Crises in Emerging Markets: A Canonical Model, *Working Paper*. Federal Reserve Bank of Atlanta, March.

Chen, Chyong L. 2000. Why Has Taiwan Been Immune to the Asian Financial Crisis?, *Asia Pacific Financial Markets*, vol. 7, pp. 45–68.

Chen, Edward K. Y. 2000. The Asian Financial Crisis of 1997–8: A Case of Market Failure, Government Failure or International Failure?, in Brigitte Granville (ed.), *Essays on the World Economy and its Financial System*. London, The Royal Institute of International Affairs, pp. 49–65.

Cheong, Ong Hong. 1998. Coping with Capital Flows and the Role of Monetary Policy: The Malaysian Experience, 1990–95, in C. H. Kwan, Donna Vandenbrink and Chia Siow Yue (eds.), *Coping with Capital Flows in East Asia*. Singapore: Institute of Southeast Asian Studies, pp. 220–43.

*China Statistical Yearbook*. 1997. State Statistical Bureau. Beijing: China Statistical Publishing House.

——, 1998. State Statistical Bureau. Beijing: China Statistical Publishing House.

Cho, Dongchul. 1998. Coping with Capital Flows and Monetary Policy Framework: The Case of Korea, in C. H. Kwan, Donna Vandenbrink and Chia Siow Yue (eds.), *Coping with Capital Flows in East Asia*. Singapore: Institute of Southeast Asian Studies, pp. 79–110.

Cho, Soon. 1994. *The Dynamics of Korean Economic Development*. Washington, DC: Institute for International Economics.

Cho, Yoon Je. 2001. The Role of Poorly Phased Liberalization in Korea's Financial Crisis, in Gerard Caprio, Patrick Honohan and Joseph E. Stiglitz (eds.), *Financial Liberalization: How Far, How Fast?* New York: Cambridge University Press, pp. 159–87.

—— and Joon-Kyung Kim. 1995. Credit Policies and the Industrialization of Korea, *World Bank Discussion Paper*, no. 409. Washington, DC: World Bank.

Choe, Chongwoo and Imad A. Moosa. 1999. Financial System and Economic Growth: The Korean Experience, *World Development*, vol. 27, no. 6, pp. 1069–82.

Choi, Byung-Sun. 1993. Financial Policy and Big Business in Korea: The Perils of Financial Regulation, in Stephan Haggard, Chung H. Lee and Sylvia Maxfield (eds.), *The Politics of Finance in Developing Countries*. Ithaca, NY: Cornell University Press.

Choi, Dosoung, Frank C. Jen and H. Han Shin. 2000. Causes and Consequences of the Korean Financial Crisis, *Review of Pacific Basin Financial Markets and Policies*, vol. 3, no. 1, pp. 1–26.

Choi, Jay J. 2000. The Asian Financial Crisis: Moral Hazard in More Ways Than One, in Jay J. Choi (ed.), *Asian Financial Crisis: Financial, Structural and International Dimensions*. New York: Elsevier Science Inc., pp. 3–14.

Choi, Seoung-No. 1996. *The Analysis of the 30 Korean Big Business Groups for 1996*. Seoul: Korea Economic Research Institute.

Chopra, Ajai, Kenneth Kang, Meral Karasulu, Hong Liang, Henry Ma and Anthony Richards. 2001. From Crisis to Recovery in Korea: Strategy, Achievements, and Lessons, *IMF Working Paper*, WP/01/154. Washington, DC: IMF.

Chou, Catherine. 1999. Indonesia's Banks: Survival of the Fittest, *Occasional Paper*. Manila: ADB.

Chow, Peter C. Y. and Bates Gill. 2000. *Weathering the Storm: Taiwan, its Neighbors and the Asian Financial Crisis*. Washington, DC: The Brookings Institution Press.

Chowdhry, Bhagwan and Amit Goyal. 2000. Understanding the Financial Crisis in Asia, *Pacific Basin Finance Journal*, vol. 8, pp. 135–52.

Christensen, Scott R. and Ammar Siamwalla. 1993. *Beyond Patronage: Tasks for the Thai State*. Bangkok: Thailand Development Research Institute.

Christensen, Scott R., David Dollar, Ammar Siamwalla and Pakron Vichyanond. 1997. Thailand: The Institutional and Political Underpinnings of Growth, in Danny M. Leipziger (ed.), *Lessons from East Asia*. Ann Arbor, MI: The University of Michigan Press, pp. 345–85.

Christoffersen, Peter and Vihang Errunza. 2000. Towards a Global Financial Architecture: Capital Mobility and Risk Management Issues, *Emerging Markets Review*, no. 1, pp. 3–20.

Citrin, Daniel and Stanley Fischer. 2000. Strengthening the International Financial System: Key Issues, *World Development*, vol. 28, no. 6, pp. 1133–42.

Clad, James. 1989. *Behind the Myth: Business Money and Powers in Southeast Asia*. London: Unwin.

Claessens, Stijn and Thomas Glaessner. 1998. Internationalization of Financial Services, in Asia, *World Bank Working Paper*, no. 1911. Washington, DC: World Bank.

——, Swati Ghosh and David Scott. 1999. Korea's Financial Sector Reforms, in *Korea and the Asian Economic Crisis: One Year Later*. Washington, DC: Korea Economic Institute of America, pp. 83–110.

——, Simeon Djankov and Lixin Colin Xu. 2000. Corporate Performance in the East Asian Financial Crisis, *The World Bank Research Observer*, vol. 15, no. 1, February, pp. 23–46.

Clifford, Mark. 1994. *Troubled Tiger: Businessmen, Bureaucrats and Generals in South Korea*. Armonk, NY: M. E. Sharpe.

—— and Pete Engardio. 2000. *Meltdown: Asia's Boom, Bust and Beyond*. Paramus, NJ: Prentice Hall.

Cole, David C. and Betty F. Slade. 1996. *Building a Modern Financial System: The Indonesian Experience*. New York: Cambridge University Press.

—— and ——. 1998. Why Has Indonesia's Financial Crisis Been So Bad?, *Bulletin of Indonesian Economic Studies*, vol. 34, no. 2, pp. 61–6.

—— and ——. 1998a. The Crisis and Financial Sector Reform, *ASEAN Economic Bulletin*, vol. 15, no. 3, pp. 338–46.

—— and Yung Chul Park. 1983. *Financial Development in Korea, 1945–78*. Cambridge, MA: Harvard University Press.

Collins, Susan and Barry Bosworth. 1996. Economic Growth in East Asia: Accumulation Versus Assimilation, *Brookings Papers on Economic Activity*, no. 2, pp. 135–203.

—— and ——. 1998. Capital Flows to Developing Countries: Implications for Saving and Investment, *Brookings Papers on Economic Activity*, no. 1, pp. 43–180.

Combs, Gifford. 2000. The Role of International Finance in Korean Economic Reconstruction and Reunification, *NBR Analysis*, vol. 10, no. 5, The National Bureau of Asian Research Publications.

Cooper, Richard. 1999. The Asian Crises: Causes and Consequences, in Alison Harwood, Robert Litan and Michael Pomerleano (eds.), *Financial Markets and Development: The Crises in Emerging Markets*. Washington DC: The Brookings Institution, pp. 17–28.

Corbo, Vittorio and Sang-mok Suh (eds.). 1992. *Structural Adjustment in a Newly Industrialized Country: The Korean Experience*. Baltimore, MD: The Johns Hopkins University Press.

Corden, Max. 1999. *The Asian Crisis: Is There a Way Out*. Singapore: Institute of Southeast Asian Studies.

Corsetti, Giancarlo. 1998. Interpreting the Asian Financial Crisis: Open Issues in Theory and Policy, *Asian Development Review*, vol. 16, no. 2, pp. 18–63.

——, Paolo Pesenti and Nouriel Roubini. 1998. What Caused the Asian Currency and Financial Crisis: A Macroeconomic Overview, *NBER Working Paper* 6833, National Bureau of Economic Research, Cambridge, MA.

Council on Foreign Relations, 1999. *Safeguarding Prosperity in a Global Financial System: The Future International Financial Architecture*. Report of an Independent Task Force. New York: Council on Foreign Relations.

CPER (Centre for Economic Policy Research). 1998. *Financial Crises in Asia*. Conference Report, No. 6. London: Center for Economic Policy Research.

Crafts, Nicholas. 1999. East Asian Growth Before and After the Crisis, *IMF Staff Papers*, vol. 46, no. 2, June, pp. 139–66.

Crispin, Shawn. 2001. Old Boys' Reunion, *Far Eastern Economic Review*, January 18, pp. 17–20.

Crouch. Harold. 1996. *Government and Society in Malaysia*. Ithaca, NY: Cornell University Press.

Culp, Christopher, Steve H. Hanke and Merton Miller. 1999. The Case for the Indonesian Currency Board, *Journal of Applied Corporate Finance*, vol. 11, no. 4, Winter.

Cumings, Bruce. 1984. The Origins and Development of the Northeast Asian Political Economy: Industrial Sectors, Product Cycles and Political Consequences, *International Organization*, vol. 38, no. 1, pp. 1–40.

Dae-Jung, Kim. 1998. Economic Reform in Korea: Establishment of a Democratic Market Economy, *Korea and World Affairs*, vol. 22, no. 2, pp. 279–83.

——, 1999. To Open a New Millennium of Hope and Prosperity, *Korea Observer*, vol. xxx, no. 3, Autumn, pp. 527–39.

Daquila, Teofilo. C. 1999. Japan–Asia Economic Relations: Trade, Investment and the Economic Crisis, *East Asia: An International Quarterly*, Autumn, pp. 88–114.

Dassu, M. 1998. China and the Asian Crisis: Pillar of Stability or Next Country at Risk?, *International Spectator*, vol. 33, no. 3, July–September, pp. 29–40.

De Brouwer, Gordon. 1999. *Financial Integration in East Asia*. New York: Cambridge University Press.

—— (ed.). 2002. *Financial Markets and Policies in East Asia*. London: Routledge.

Dekle, Robert and Cheng Hsiao. 1999. The Real Effects of Capital Inflows on Emerging Markets, University of Southern California, mimeo.

Demirguc-Kunt, Asli and Enrica Detragaiche. 1998. Financial Liberalization and Financial Fragility, *World Bank Working Paper*, no. 1917, May.

Dernberger, Robert F. 1999. The People's Republic of China at 50: The Economy, *The China Quarterly*, no. 159, September.

DeRosa, David. F. 2001. *In Defense of Free Capital Markets: The Case Against a New International Financial Architecture*. Princeton, NJ: Bloomberg Press.

Diamond, D. and P. Dybvig. 1983. Bank Runs, Liquidity and Deposit Insurance, *Journal of Political Economy*, vol. 91, no. 3, June, pp. 401–19.

Diamond, Larry and Doh Chull Shin (eds.). 2000. *Institutional Reform and Democratic Consolidation in Korea*. Stanford, CA.: Hoover Institution Press.

Dick, Howard. 2001. Survey of Recent Developments, *Bulletin of Indonesian Economic Studies*, vol. 37, no. 1, April, pp. 7–42.

Dixon, Chris. 1998. *The Thai Economy*. London: Routledge.

Djiwandono, Soedradjad J. 1997. The Banking Sector in an Emerging Market: The Case of Indonesia, in Charles Enoch and John H. Green (eds.), *Banking Soundness and Monetary Policy: Issues and Experiences in the Global Economy*. Washington, DC: IMF.

——, 1998. Indonesian Financial Sector Reforms: Development and Lessons, in Jean-Claude Berthelemy and Tommy Koh (eds.), *The Asian Crisis: A New Agenda for Euro-Asian Cooperation*. Singapore: World Scientific Publishers, pp. 1–24.

——, 1999. *The Banking Industry Facing the 21st Century*. Bank of Indonesia. (www.bi.go.id/intl/speeches/century.htm).

——, 1999a. The Rupiah: One Year After its Float, in Geoff Forrester (ed.), *Post-Soeharto Indonesia: Renewal or Chaos?* Singapore: Institute of Southeast Asian Studies, pp. 144–52.

Dobson, Wendy. 1998. *Fiscal Frameworks and Financial Systems in East Asia: How Much Do They Matter?* Toronto: University of Toronto Press.

Dohyung, Kim. 1999. IMF Bailout and Financial and Corporate Restructuring in the Republic of Korea, *The Developing Economies*, vol. 37, no. 4, December, pp. 460–513.

Dollar, David and Mary Hallward-Driemeier. 2000. Crisis, Adjustment and Reform in Thailand's Industrial Firms, *The World Bank Research Observer*, vol. 15, no. 1, February, pp. 1–22.

Dominguez, Jorge and James McCann. 1996. *Democratizing Mexico: Public Opinion and Electoral Choices*. Baltimore, MD: Johns Hopkins University Press.

Doner, Richard F. 1991. *Driving a Bargain: Japanese Firms and Automobile Industrialization in Southeast Asia*. Berkeley, CA: University of California Press.

Dooley, Michael P. 1996. A Survey of the Literature on Controls over International Capital Transactions, *IMF Staff Papers*, vol. 43, no. 4, December.

——, 1996a. The Tobin Tax: Good Theory, Weak Evidence, Questionable Policy, in M. ul-Haq, I. Kaul and I. Grunberg (eds.), *The Tobin Tax: Coping with Financial Volatility*. New York: Oxford University Press, pp. 83–106.

——, 1997. A Model of Crises in Emerging Markets, *NBER Working Paper*, no. 6300.

Dornbusch, Rudiger. 1986. Special Exchange Rates for Capital Account Transactions, *World Bank Economic Review*, vol. 1, September, pp. 3–26.

——, 1997. The Folly, the Crash, and Beyond: Economic Policies and the Crisis, in Sebastian Edwards and Moises Naim (eds.), *Mexico 1994: Anatomy of an Emerging-Market Crash*. Washington, DC: Carnegie Endowment for International Peace.

——, 1997a. Brazil's Incomplete Stabilization and Reform, *Brookings Papers on Economic Activity*, vol. 1, 1997, pp. 367–401.

——, 1998. On the Edge, in Dan Biers (ed.), *Crash of '97: How the Financial Crisis is Reshaping Asia*. Hong Kong: Review Publishing Company, pp. 106–9.

——, Yung Chul Park and Stijn Claessens. 2000. Contagion: Understanding How it Spreads, *The World Bank Research Observer*, vol. 15, no. 2, August, pp. 177–97.

Drysdale, Peter (ed.). 2000. *Reform and Recovery in East Asia: The Role of the State and Economic Enterprise*. New York: Routledge.

Dueker, Michael and Gyuhan Kim. 1999. A Monetary Policy Feedback Rule in Korea's Fast-Growing Economy, *Journal of International Financial Markets, Institutions and Money*, vol. 9, pp. 19–31.

Dyker, David A. 2000. The Structural Origins of the Russian Economic Crisis, *Post-Communist Economies*, vol. 12, no. 1, pp. 5–24.

Eatwell, John and Lance Taylor. 1999. *Global Finance at Risk: The Case for International Regulation*. New York: The New Press.

Economist. 1994. Economy: Bapindo Scandal Highlights Crisis in Banking Industry, *Economist Intelligence Unit – Country Report*, August 5.

——, 1996. *Damage Control*. July 13, p. 77.

——, 1998. The Worst Banking System in Asia, *Economist*, May 2, pp. 65–7.

——, 1998. Economics Focus: Why Did Asia Crash?, *Economist*, January 10–16.

Economy, Elizabeth and Michel Oksenberg, 1999. *China Joins the World: Progress and Prospects*. New York: Council on Foreign Relations Press.

Edison, Hali J. and Cornelia H. McCarthy. 1999. Perspectives on the Financial Crisis in Asia, *Journal of International Money and Finance*, vol. 18, no. 4, pp. 495–500.

Edwards, Sebastian. 1995. *Crisis and Reform in Latin America: From Despair to Hope*. New York: Oxford University Press.

——, 1998. The Morning After: The Mexican Peso in the Aftermath of the 1994 Currency Crisis, *NBER Working Paper*, no. 6516.

——, 1998a. Abolish the IMF, *Financial Times*, 1998, November 13, p. A1.

——, 1999. On Crisis Prevention: Lessons from Mexico and East Asia, in Alison Harwood, Robert Litan and Michael Pomerleano (eds.), *Financial Markets and Development: The Crisis in Emerging Markets*. Washington DC: The Brookings Institution Press.

——, 2001. Capital Mobility and Economic Performance: Are Emerging Economies Different?, *NBER Working Paper*, no. 8076.

—— and Moises Naim (eds.). 1997. *Anatomy of An Emerging-Market Crash: Mexico 1994*. Washington, DC: Carnegie Endowment for International Peace.

—— and Julio Santaella, 1993. Devaluation Controversies in the Developing Countries: Lessons from the Bretton Woods Era, in Michael Bordo and Barry Eichengreen (eds.), *A Retrospective on the Bretton Woods System: Lessons for International Monetary Reform*. Chicago: University of Chicago Press.

Eichengreen, Barry. 1991. Historical Research on International Lending and Debt, *Journal of Economic Perspectives*, vol. 5, no. 2, Spring, pp. 149–69.

——, 1999. *Toward A New International Financial Architecture: A Practical Post-Asia Agenda*. Washington, DC: Institute for International Economics.

——, 2000. Can the Moral Hazard Caused by IMF Bailouts be Reduced? *Geneva Reports on the World Economy, Special Report*, 1. Geneva: International Center for Monetary and Banking Studies.

——, 2000a. Taming Capital Flows, *World Development*, vol. 28, no. 6, pp. 1105–16.

——, 2000b. Strengthening the International Financial Architecture: Where Do We Stand?, *ASEAN Economic Bulletin*, vol. 17, no. 2, August, pp. 175–92.

——, and Andrew Rose. 1998. Contagious Currency Crises: Channels of Conveyance, in Takashito Ito and Anne Kreuger (eds.), *Changes in Exchange Rates in Developing Countries*. Oxford: Blackwell.

——, and Charles Wyplosz. 1996. Taxing International Financial Transactions to Enhance the Operation of the International Monetary System, in M. Ul-Haq, I. Kaul and I. Grunberg (eds.), *The Tobin Tax: Coping with Financial Volatility*. Oxford: Oxford University Press.

——, Andrew Rose and Charles Wyplosz. 1995. Speculative Attacks on Pegged Exchange Rates: An Empirical Exploration with Special Reference to the European Monetary System, *Federal Reserve Bank of San Francisco Working Paper*, no. 95–104. San Francisco: Federal Reserve Bank of San Francisco.

Eklof, Stefan. 1999. *Indonesian Politics in Crisis: The Long Fall of Suharto, 1996–98*. Copenhagen: Nordic Institute of Asian Studies.

Emmerson, Donald. 1999. Exit and Aftermath: The Crisis of 1997–98, in Donald Emmerson (ed.), *Indonesia Beyond Suharto: Polity, Economy and Society*. Armonk, NY: M. E. Sharpe.

Enoch, Charles. 2000. Interventions in Banks During Banking Crises: The Experience of Indonesia, *IMF Policy Discussion Paper*, PDP/00/2. Monetary and Exchange Affairs Department.

—— and Anne-Marie Gulde. 1998. Are Currency Boards a Cure for All Monetary Problems?, *Finance and Development*, vol. 35, no. 4, December.

——, Barbara Baldwin, Olivier Frecaut and Arto Kovanen. 2001. Indonesia: Anatomy of a Banking Crisis – Two Years of Living Dangerously, 1997–99, *IMF Working Paper*, no. WP/01/52, May. Monetary and Exchange Affairs Department.

Faison, Seth. 1999. China Points Finger at Culprit of the Week, *New York Times*, January 13, p. A8.

Fanzhang Huang and Xu Zhong, 2000. Carrying Forward Financial Reform in China, *Journal of Asian Economics*, vol. 11, pp. 15–22.

*FEER* (*Far Eastern Economic Review*). 1997. Interview of Prime Minister Mahathir Mohamad October, p. 32.

Feldstein, Martin. 1994. The Effects of Outbound Foreign Direct Investment on the Capital Stock, *NBER Working Paper*, no. 4668. Cambridge, MA: National Bureau of Economic Research.

——, 1998. Refocusing the IMF, *Foreign Affairs*, vol. 77, no. 2, March/April, pp. 20–33.

Feridhanusetyawan, Tubagus. 1998. Social Impact of the Indonesian Economic Crisis, *Indonesian Quarterly*, vol. 26, no. 4, pp. 325–64.

Fernald, John, Hali Edison and Prakash Loungani. 1999. Was China the First Domino? Assessing links between China and other Asian Countries, *Journal of International Money and Finance*, vol. 18, pp. 515–35.

Fernandez-Arias, Eduardo. 1996. The New Wave of Private Capital Inflows: Push or Pull?, *Journal of Development Economics*, 48, March, pp. 389–418.

French-Davis, Ricardo. 2002. *Economic Reforms in Chile: From Dictatorship to Democracy*, Ann Arbor, MI: University of Michigan Press.

Fields, Karl J. 1995. *Enterprise and the State in Korea and Taiwan*. Ithaca, NY: Cornell University Press.

Fischer, Dominique. 2000. Indonesia's Real Estate Disturbance: An Ineluctable Outcome, in Koichi Mera and Bertrand Renaud (eds.), *Asia's Financial Crisis and the Role of Real Estate*. Armonk, NY: M. E. Sharpe, pp. 219–41.

Fischer, Stanley. 1982. Seigniorage and the Case for a National Money, *Journal of Political Economy*, vol. 90, April, pp. 295–313.

——, 1993. The Role of Macroeconomic Factors on Growth, *Journal of Monetary Economics*, vol. 32, no. 3, pp. 395–415.

——, 1994. International Capital Flows, the International Agencies and Financial Stability, *Bank of Japan Monetary and Economic Studies,* vol. 12, no. 1, pp. 17–27.

——, 1998. The Asian Crisis: A View from the IMF, address at the Midwinter Conference of the Bankers Association for Foreign Trade, Washington, DC, January 22.

——, 1998a. In Defense of the IMF, *Foreign Affairs*, July/August, vol. 77, no. 4, pp. 103–6

——, 1998b. Reforming World Finance: Lessons from a Crisis, *IMF Survey*, October 19 (special supplement), pp. iii–iv.

——, 1998c. Capital Account Liberalization and the Role of the IMF, in *Should the IMF Pursue Capital Account Convertibility?* Essays in International Finance, no. 207, May. Princeton, NJ: Department of Economics, Princeton University.

——, 1998d. The Asian Crisis and the Changing Role of the IMF, *Finance and Development*, vol. 35, no. 2, June, pp. 1–8.

——, 1999. On the Need for an International Lender of Last Resort, available via (www.imf.org/external.no/speeches/1999/010399.htm).

——, 2000. Proposals and IMF Actions to Reduce the Frequency of Crises, in Eric S. Rosengren and John S. Jordan (eds.), *Building an Infrastructure for Financial Stability*. Conference Series, no. 44, Boston: Federal Reserve Bank of Boston.

——, 2001. Exchange Rate Regimes: Is the Bipolar View Correct?, *Finance and Development*, vol. 38, no. 2, June, pp. 18–21.

FitzGerald, Valpy. 1999. Global Capital Market Volatility and the Developing Countries: Lessons from the East Asian Crisis, *IDS Bulletin*, vol. 30, no. 1, pp. 19–32.

Flatters, Frank. 2000. Thailand and the Crisis: Roots, Recovery and Long-Run, in Wing Thye Woo, Jeffrey Sachs and Klaus Schwab (eds.), *The Asian Financial Crisis: Lessons for a Resilient Asia*. Cambridge, MA: MIT Press, pp. 257–74.

——, 2000a. Thailand, the International Monetary Fund, and the Financial Crisis: First In, Fast Out?, in Peter C. Y. Chow and Bates Gill (eds.), *Weathering the Storm: Taiwan, Its Neighbors and the Asian Financial Crisis*. Washington, DC: The Brookings Institution Press, pp. 71–110.

Flood, Robert and Peter Garber. 1984. Collapsing Exchange Rate Regimes: Some Linear Examples, *Journal of International Economics*, vol. 17, pp. 1–13.

—— and Nancy P. Marion. 1999. Perspectives on the Recent Currency Crisis Literature, *International Journal of Finance and Economics*, vol. 4, no. 1, pp. 1–26.

Forrester, Geoff (ed.). 1999. *Post-Soeharto Indonesia: Renewal or Chaos?* Singapore: Institute of Southeast Asian Studies.

Frankel, Jeffrey. 1999. No Single Currency Regime is Right for All Countries or At All Times, *NBER Working Paper*, no. 7338. September.

—— and S. J. Wei, 1994. Yen Bloc or Dollar Bloc? Exchange Rate Policies of the East Asian Economies, in Takatoshi Ito and Anne Krueger (eds.), *Macroeconomic Linkage*. Chicago: University of Chicago Press.

Fratzscher, Marcel. 1998. Why are Currency Crises Contagious? A Comparison of the Latin American Crisis of 1994–95 and the Asian Crisis of 1997–98, unpublished paper.

Frieden, Jeffrey. 1991. *Debt, Development and Democracy: Modern Political Economy of Latin America, 1965–1985*. Princeton, NJ: Princeton University Press.

Friedman, Milton. 1999. How Asia Fell, *Hoover Digest*, no. 2, 1999, pp. 1–4.

Friedman, Thomas. 1999. *The Lexus and the Olive Tree: Understanding Globalization*. New York: Farrar, Straus and Giroux.

Fung, K. C. and Lawrence Lau. 1997. *China's Foreign Economic Relations*. Stanford, CA: Asia Pacific Research Center, Stanford University, May.

Furman, Jason and Joseph Stiglitz. 1998. Economic Crises: Evidence and Insights from East Asia, *Brookings Papers on Economic Activity*, 2, pp. 1–135.

G-7 (Group of Seven). 1998. Declaration of G-7 Finance Ministers and Central Bank Governors (www.imf.org/external/np/g7/103098dc.htm).

——, 2000. Strengthening the International Financial Architecture: Progress to Date, *Treasury News* LS-758, July 8. Washington, DC: US Department of Treasury, Office of Public Affairs.

G-22 (Group of Twenty-Two). 1998. *Report of the Working Group on Strengthening Financial Systems*, Washington, DC: Group of Twenty-Two.

Garnaut, Ross. 1998. The Financial Crisis: A Watershed in Economic Thought about East Asia, *Asia Pacific Economic Literature*, vol. 12, no. 1, May, pp. 1–11.

Garran, Robert. 1998. *Tigers Tamed: The End of the Asian Miracle*. Honolulu, HI: University of Hawaii Press.

Garten, Jeffrey. 1998. In This Economic Chaos, a Global Bank Can Help, *International Herald Tribune*, 25 September, p. 8.

Geertz, Clifford. 1963. *Agricultural Involution: The Process of Ecological Change in Indonesia*. Berkeley, CA: University of California Press.

Gil-Diaz, Francisco and Agustin Carstens. 1997. Pride and Prejudice: The Economics Profession and Mexico's Financial Crisis, in Moises Naim and Sebastian Edwards (eds.), *Mexico 1994: Anatomy of an Emerging-Market Crash*. Washington, DC: Carnegie Endowment for International Peace.

Gilpin, Robert. 2000. *The Challenge of Global Capitalism: The World Economy in the 21st Century*. Princeton, NJ: Princeton University Press.

Glassburner, Bruce. 1978. Political Economy and the Soeharto Regime, *Bulletin of Indonesian Economic Studies*, vol. xiv, no. 3, pp. 24–51.

Glick, Reuven. 1998. Thoughts on the Origins of the Asia Crisis: Impulses and Propagation Mechanisms, *Pacific Basin Working Paper Series*, no. PB98-07. Federal Reserve Bank of San Francisco, Economic Research Department.

—— and Michael Hutchison. 1999. Banking and Currency Crises: How Common are Twins?, *Pacific Basin Working Paper Series*, no. PB99-07. Federal Reserve Bank of San Francisco, Economic Research Department.

GoC (Government of China). 1998. State Statistical Bureau. *Economic Statistical Communique*. Beijing: China Statistical Publishing House, March 4.

GoI (Government of Indonesia). 1999. Government of Indonesia Announces Sweeping Reforms to the Bank System, press release (www.bi.go.id.Intl/press.html).

Goldfajn, Ilan and Timur Baig. 1998. Financial Market Contagion in the Asian Crisis, *International Monetary Fund Working Paper* WP/98/155.

Goldstein, Morris. 1999. *Safeguarding Prosperity in a Global Financial System*. Washington, DC: Institute for International Economics.

——, Graciela L. Kaminsky and Carmen M. Reinhart. 2000. *Assessing Financial Vulnerability: An Early Warning System for Emerging Markets*. Washington, DC: Institute for International Economics.

Gomez, Edmund Terence and K. S. Jomo. 1999. *Malaysia's Political Economy: Politics, Patronage and Profits*. New York: Cambridge University Press.

Goodhart, Charles. 1988. *The Evolution of Central Banks*. Cambridge, MA: MIT Press.

Gopinath, Deepak. 1999. Slouching Towards a New Consensus, *Institutional Investor*, September.

Gordon, Lincoln. 2001. *Brazil's Second Chance: En Route Toward the First World*. Washington, DC: Brookings Institution Press.

GoT (Government of Thailand). 1997. Letter of Intent to the International Monetary Fund November 25. (www.img.org/external/np/loi/112597.htm).

——, 1998. Letter of Intent to the IMF, February 24. (www.imf.org/external/np/loi/022498.HTM).

——, 1998a. Letter of Intent to the IMF, May 26 (www.imf.org/external/np/loi/052698.HTM).

——, 1998b. Letter of Intent to the IMF, August 25 (www.imf.org/external/np/loi/082598.htm).

Gould-Davies, Nigel and Ngaire Woods. 1999. Russia and the IMF, *International Affairs*, vol. 75, no. 1, pp. 1–22.

Grabel, Ilene. 1996. Marketing the Third World: The Contradictions of Portfolio Investment in the Global Economy, *World Development*, vol. 24, no. 11, pp. 1761–76.

Granville, Brigitte (ed.). 2000. *Essays on the World Economy and its Financial System*. London: The Royal Institute of International Affairs.

Greenspan, Alan. 1997. The Globalization of Finance, *Cato Journal*, vol. 17, no. 3, pp. 1–7.

Greenwood, John. 2000. The Real Issues in Asia, *Cato Journal*, vol. 20, no. 2, pp. 141–57.

Greider, William. 1997. *One World, Ready or Not: The Manic Logic of Global Capitalism*. New York: Simon and Schuster.

Grenville, Stephen A. 1998. The Asian Economic Crisis, *Reserve Bank of Australia Bulletin*, Sydney: Reserve Bank of Australia, April, pp. 9–20.

——, 1999. Capital Flows and Crises, *Asian-Pacific Economic Literature*, vol. 13, no. 2, November, pp. 1–15.

Griffith-Jones, Stephany. 1996. The Mexican Peso Crisis, *CEPAL Review*, no. 60, December, pp. 155–75.

Gruben, William and John Welch, 1996. Distortions and Resolutions in Mexico's Financial System, in Laura Randall (ed.), *Changing Structure of Mexico: Political, Social and Economic Perspectives*. Armonk, NY: M. E. Sharpe, pp. 63–76.

Grunberg, Isabelle. 1999. Discussion: Financial Markets, in Barry Herman (ed.), *Global Financial Turmoil and Reform: A United Nations Perspective*. New York: United Nations University Press, pp. 431–5.

Guojia Tongji Ju. 1993. *Zongguo tongji nianjian* (Statistical Yearbook of China 1993). Beijing: Zhongguo Tongji Chubanshe.

——, 1998. *Zhongguo tongji nianjian* (China Statistical Yearbook 1998). Beijing: Zhongguo Tongji Chubanshe.

Habir, Ahmad D. 1999. Conglomerates: All in the Family, in Donald Emmerson (ed.), *Indonesia Beyond Suharto: Polity, Economy and Society*. Armonk, NY: M. E. Sharpe.

Haggard, Stephan. 2000. *The Political Economy of the Asian Financial Crisis*. Washington, DC: Institute for International Economics.

—— and Andrew MacIntyre. 1998. The Political-Economy of the Asian Economic Crisis, *Review of International Political Economy*, vol. 53, no. 1, Autumn, pp. 381–92.

—— and Chung-In Moon. 1990. Institutions and Economic Policy: Theory and a Korean Case Study, *World Politics*, vol. 42, January, pp. 210–37.

—— and Jongryn Mo. 2000. The Political Economy of the Korean Financial Crisis, *Review of International Political Economy*, vol. 7, no. 2, Summer, pp. 197–218.

Hahm, Joon-Ho. 1999. Financial System Restructuring in Korea: The Crisis and its Resolution, in Seiichi Masuyama, Donna Vandenbrink and Chia Siow Yue, *East Asia's Financial Systems: Evolution and Crisis*. Singapore: Institute of South East Asian Studies, pp. 109–43.

—— and Frederic S. Mishkin. 2000. The Korean Financial Crisis: An Asymmetric Information Perspective, *Emerging Markets Review*, vol. 1, pp. 21–52.

Hale, Christopher D. 2001. Indonesia's National Car Project Revisited: The History of Kia-Timor Motors and its Aftermath, *Asian Survey*, vol. 41, no. 4, July/August, pp. 629–45.

Hamilton-Hart, Natasha. 2001. Anti-Corruption Strategies in Indonesia, *Bulletin of Indonesian Economic Studies*, vol. 37, no. 1, April, pp. 65–82.

Hammond, Alistair. 1997. Million Indonesian Construction Workers to Lose Jobs in 98, *Bloomberg News*, December 19, available in LEXIS, News Library.

Hanson, Philip. 1999. The Russian Economic Crisis and the Future of Russian Economic Reform, *Europe-Asia Studies*, vol. 51, no. 7, pp. 1141–66.

Harianto, Farid and Mari E. Pangestu. 1999. Changes in Corporate Governance Structure in Indonesia, in Gordon de Brouwer and Wisarn Pupphavesa (eds.), *Asia Pacific Financial Deregulation*. New York: Routledge, pp. 173–82.

Hausmann, Ricardo, Ugo Panizza and Ernesto Stein. 1999. Why Do Countries Float and the Way They Float, *Working Paper* 418, Inter-American Development Bank, May.

Henderson, Callum. 1998. *Asia Falling*. New York: McGraw-Hill.

Heo, Uk and Sunwoong Kim. 2000. Financial Crisis in South Korea: Failure of the Government-led Development Paradigm, *Asian Survey*, vol. 40, no. 3, May/June, pp. 492–507.

Higgins, Benjamin. 1968. *Economic Development: Problems, Principles and Policies*. New York: W. W. Norton.

Hill, Hal. 1996. *The Indonesian Economy Since 1966*. New York: Cambridge University Press.

——, 1999. *The Indonesian Economy in Crisis: Causes, Consequences and Lessons*. Singapore: The Institute of Southeast Asian Studies.

Hollinger, William. 1996. *Economic Policy under President Soeharto: Indonesia's Twenty-Five Year Record*. Washington, DC: The United States–Indonesia Society.

Hong, Kiseok and Jong-Wha Lee. 2000. Korea: Returning to Sustainable Growth, in Wing Thye Woo, Jeffrey Sachs and Klaus Schwab (eds.), *The Asian Financial Crisis: Lessons for a Resilient Asia*. Cambridge, MA: The MIT Press, pp. 203–26.

Hong, Wontack. 1998. Financing Export-Oriented Catching-Up in Korea: Credit Rationing, Sustained High Growth and Financial Chaos, *International Economic Journal*, vol. 12, no. 1, Spring, pp. 140–55.

Horiuchi, Akiyoshi. 2000. Japan's Bank Crisis and the Issue of Governance, in Peter Drysdale (ed.), *Reform and Recovery in East Asia: The Role of the State and Economic Enterprise*. New York: Routledge, pp. 28–58.

Howe, Christopher. 1978. *China's Economy: A Basic Guide*. New York: Basic Books.

Hu, Xiaobo. 2000. The State, Enterprises and Society in Post-Deng China, *Asian Survey*, vol. 40, no. 4, July/August, pp. 641–57.

Hu, Zuliu and Moshin S. Khan, 1997. Why is China Growing so Fast?, *IMF Working Paper*, no. 96/75, IMF Research Department.

Huang, Yiping. 1999. Challenges for China's Financial Reform, paper presented at China Update Conference, The Australian National University.

Hufbauer, Gary. 1999. Cleaning Up the Financial Wreckage: An Eight-Point Program for Indonesia, *Policy Paper*, Washington, DC: Institute for International Economics.

Huntington, Samuel. 1991. *The Third Wave: Democratization in the Late Twentieth Century*. Norman, OK: University of Oklahoma Press.

Illarionov, Andrei. 1999. The Roots of the Economic Crisis, *Journal of Democracy*, vol. 10, no. 2, pp. 68–82.

IMF (International Monetary Fund). 1995. *International Capital Markets: Developments, Prospects and Policy Issues*, Washington, DC: IMF.

——, 1997. *People's Republic of China: Recent Economic Developments, Staff Country Report*, no. 97/71, Washington, DC: IMF.

——, 1997a. *IMF Approves Stand-by Credit for Thailand*, press release no. 97/37 (www.imf.org/external/np/sec/pr/1997/pr9737.htm).

——, 1997b. Camdessus Commends on Indonesia's Impressive Economic Policy Program, *IMF Survey*, vol. 26, no. 20, November 3.

——, 1997c. Indonesian Measures Welcomed as Important Step in Stabilizing Southeast Asian Financial Markets, *IMF Survey*, vol. 26, no. 21, November 17.

——, 1997d. IMF Approves SDR 15.5 Billion Stand-By Credit for Korea, *Press Release*, no. 97/55, December 4.

——, 1997e. Letter of Intent: Indonesia – Memorandum of Economic and Financial Policies, November 5, 1997, accessed on June 10, 2000: www.imf.org/external/np/loi/103197.htm.

——, 1998a. Statement by the Managing Director on the IMF Program with Indonesia, *News Brief*, no. 98/2, January 15.

——, 1998b. Indonesia: Memorandum of Economic and Financial Policies. January 15. (www.imf.org/external/np/loi/011598.htm).

——, 1998c. Indonesia: Supplementary Memorandum of Economic and Financial Policies, April 10. (www.imf.org/external/np/loi/041098.htm).

——, 1998d. Indonesia: Second Supplementary Memorandum of Economic and Financial Policies, June 24. (www.imf.org/external/np/loi/062498.htm).

——, 1998e. Letter of Intent: South Korea, Memorandum on the Economic Program, February 7. (www.imf.org/external/np/loi/020798.htm).

——, 1999. *World Economic Outlook, 1999*. Advance copy available on the Internet (www.imf.org).

——, 1999a. *World Economic Outlook: May 1999*. Washington, DC: IMF.

——, 2000. *Thailand: Selected Issues. IMF Staff Country Report*, no. 00/21. Washington, DC: International Monetary Fund.

——, 2000a. Recovery from the Asian Crisis and the Role of the IMF, *IMF Issues Brief*, June.

——, 2000b. *IMF Survey*, vol. 29, no. 2, January 24.

——, 2000c. *World Economic Outlook: May 2000*. Washington, DC: IMF.

——, 2000d. Recovery from the Asian Crisis and the Role of the IMF, *IMF Issues Briefs*, June.

——, 2000e. IMF Completes Final Review of Korea Program, *News Brief*, no. 00/72, August 23.

——, 2000f. Republic of Korea: Economic and Policy Developments, *IMF Staff Country Report*, no. 00/11.

——, 2000g. IMF Concludes Article IV Consultation with China, *PIN*, no. 00/71, September 1.

——, 2001. Reforming the International Financial Architecture: Progress Through 2000, *IMF Issues Brief*, March 9. (www.imf.org/external/np/exr/ib/2001/030901.htm).

——, 2001a. Resolving and Preventing Financial Crises: The Role of the Private Sector, *IMF Issues Brief*, March 26. Washington, DC: IMF.

——, 2001b. IMF Concludes Article IV Consultation with Korea, *PIN*, no. 01/8, February 1.

——, 2002. IMF Concludes 2001 Article IV Consultation with Korea, *PIN*, No. 02/09. Washington, DC: IMF. (www.imf.org/external/np/sec/pn/2002/pn0209.htm).

Indrawati, Sri Mulyani. 2001. Fiscal Issues and Decentralization, in Anthony L. Smith (ed.), *Gus Dur and the Indonesian Economy*. Singapore: Institute of Southeast Asian Studies.

Institute of International Finance. 1999. *Report of the Working Group on Financial Crises in Emerging Markets*. Washington, DC: The Institute, January.

International Financial Institution Advisory Commission. 2000. *Report*. Washington, DC: International Financial Institution Advisory Commission.

Islam, Azizul. 1999. The Dynamics of Asian Economic Crisis and Selected Policy Implications, in Barry Herman (ed.), *Global Financial Turmoil and Reform: A United Nations Perspective*. Tokyo: United Nations University Press, pp. 49–74.

Islam, Faizul M. 2000. The Asian Five: from Financial Crisis to Economic Recovery, in J. Jay Choi (ed.), *Asian Financial Crisis: Financial, Structural and International Dimensions*. New York: Elsevier Publishing Inc., pp. 123–46.

Islam, Iyanatul and Anis Chowdhury. 2000. *The Political Economy of East Asia: Post-Crisis Debates*. Melbourne: Oxford University Press.

Ito, Takatoshi. 1999. Capital Flows in Asia, *NBER Working Paper*, no. 7134. National Bureau of Economic Research.

—— and Tokuo Iwaisako, 1996. Explaining Asset Bubbles in Japan. Bank of Japan, *Monetary and Economic Studies*, vol. 14, no. 1, July, pp. 143–93.

James, Harold. 1996. *International Monetary Cooperation Since Bretton Woods*. New York: Oxford University Press.

Jansen, Karel. 1997. *External Finance in Thailand's Development: An Interpretation of Thailand's Growth Boom*. London: Macmillian.

Jingping, Ding. 1995. *China's Domestic Economy in Regional Context*. Washington, DC: The Center for International and Strategic Studies.

Jinping, Zhao. 1998. Management of Capital Inflows in China's Opening Economy, in C. H. Kwan, Donna Vandenbrink and Chia Siow Yue (eds.), *Coping with Capital Flows in East Asia*. Singapore: Institute of Southeast Asian Studies, pp. 293–319.

Johnson, C. 1998. Survey of Recent Developments, *Bulletin of Indonesian Economic Studies*, vol. 32, no. 2, pp. 3–60.

Johnson, Robert. 1997. What Asia's Financial Crisis Portends, *New York Times*, December 5.

Johnson, Simon and Todd Mitton. 2001. Cronyism and Capital Controls: Evidence from Malaysia National Bureau of Economic Research, *NBER Working Paper*, 8521. October.

Johnston, Barry, Salim M. Durbar and Claudia Echeverria. 1997. Sequencing Capital Account Liberalization: Lessons from the Experiences in Chile, Indonesia, Korea and Thailand, *IMF Working Paper*, no. WP/97/157.

Jomo, Kwame Sundaram. 1986. *A Question of Class: Capital, the State and Uneven Development in Malaya*. Singapore: Oxford University Press.

—— (ed.). 1995. *Privatizing Malaysia: Rents, Rhetoric, Realities*. Boulder, CO: Westview Press.

——, 1997. *Southeast Asia's Misunderstood Miracle: Industrial Policy and Economic Development in Thailand, Malaysia and Indonesia*. Boulder, CO: Westview Press.

——, 2001. Capital Controls, *National Bureau of Economic Research (NBER) Working Paper*, 8517, May.

—— (ed.). 2001a. *Malaysian Eclipse: Economic Crisis and Recovery*. New York: Zed Books.

Jones, David Martin. 1997. *Political Development in Pacific Asia*. Cambridge, UK: Polity Press.

Jones, Leroy and I. Sakong. 1980. *Government, Business and Entrepreneurship in Economic Development: The Korean Case*. Cambridge, MA: Harvard University Press.

Judd, Kenneth L. and Young Ki Lee (eds.). 2000. *An Agenda for Economic Reform in Korea: International Perspectives*. Stanford, CA: Hoover Institution Press.

Kahler, Miles (ed.). 1998. *Capital Flows and Financial Crises*. Ithaca, NY: Cornell University Press.

Kamin, Steven B. 1999. The Current International Financial Crisis: How Much is New?, *Journal of International Money and Finance*, vol. 18, no. 4, pp. 501–14.

Kaminsky, Graciela and Carmen Reinhart. 1999. The Twin Crises: The Causes of Banking and Balance-of Payments Problems, *American Economic Review*, June, pp. 423–500.

—— and Sergio Schmukler, 1999a. What Triggers Market Jitters: A Chronicle of the Asian Crisis, *Journal of International Money and Finance*, vol. 18, no. 4, pp. 537–60.

Kanaya, Akihiro and David Woo. 2000. The Japanese Banking Crisis of the 1990s: Sources and Lessons, *IMF Working Paper*, no. WP/00/7. January.

Kane, Edward J. 2000. Capital Movements, Banking Insolvency and Silent Runs in the Asian Financial Crisis, *Pacific Basin Finance Journal*, vol. 8, pp. 153–75.

Kang, Elliot C. S. 2000. Segyehwa Reform of the South Korean Developmental State, in Samuel S. Kim (ed.), *Korea's Globalization*. New York: Cambridge University Press, pp. 76–101.

Kang, Moon-Soo. 1999. Financial System Restructuring in the Republic of Korea: The Crisis and its Resolution, *Asia–Pacific Development Journal*, vol. 6, no. 1, June, pp. 35–53.

Kang, Soon-Hie, Jaeho Keum, Dong-Heon Kim and Donggyun Shin. 2001. Korea: Labor Market Outcomes and Policy Responses after the Crisis, in Gordon Betcherman and Rizwanul Islam (eds.), *East Asian Labor Markets and the Economic Crisis: Impacts, Responses and Lessons*. Washington, DC: World Bank, pp. 97–139.

Kaplan, Ethan and Dani Rodrik. 2001. Did the Malaysian Capital Controls Work?, *National Bureau of Economic Research (NBER) Working Paper*. February.

Kapur, Devesh. 1998. The IMF: A Cure or a Curse?, *Foreign Policy*, no. 111, Summer, pp. 114–29.

Karl, Terry and Philippe Schmitter. 1991. What Democracy is . . . and is Not, *Journal of Democracy*, vol. 2, no. 3, Summer, pp. 75–86.

Kaufman, Henry. 1998. Preventing the Next Financial Global Crisis, *The Washington Post*, January 28, p. A17.

Kaufman, Robert, Carlos Bazdresch and Blanca Heredia. 1994. Mexico: Radical Reform in a Dominant Party System, in Stephan Haggard and Steven B. Webb (eds.), *Voting for Reform: Democracy, Political Liberalization and Economic Adjustment*. New York: Oxford University Press.

Kawai, Masahiro, Ira Lieberman and William Mako. 1999. Evolving Patterns of Capital Flows and the East Asian Economic Crisis, in Gordon de Brouwer and Wisarn Pupphavesa (eds.), *Asia Pacific Financial Deregulation*. New York: Routledge, pp. 89–126.

——, 2000. Financial Stabilization and Initial Restructuring of East Asian Corporations: Approaches, Results and Lessons, in Charles Adams, Robert Litan and

Michael Pomerleano (eds.), *Managing Financial and Corporate Distress: Lessons from Asia*. Washington, DC: The Brookings Institution Press.

Kelley, Paul. 1998. Great Stumble Forward, *The Weekend Australian*, April 25–26.

Kenen, Peter B. 2000. The New International Financial Architecture: Reconstruction, Renovation or Minor Repair, *International Journal of Finance and Economics*, vol. 5, no. 1, pp. 1–14.

——, 2001. *The International Financial Architecture: What's New? What's Missing?*, Washington, DC: Institute for International Economics.

Kenward, Lloyd. 1999. What Has Been Happening at Bank Indonesia?, *Bulletin of Indonesian Economic Studies*, vol. 35, no. 1, pp. 121–7.

——, 1999a. Assessing Vulnerability to Financial Crisis: Evidence from Indonesia, *Bulletin of Indonesian Economic Studies*, vol. 35, no. 3, pp. 71–95.

Kho, Bong-Chan and Rene Stulz. 1999. Banks, the IMF and the Asian Crisis, *NBER (National Bureau of Economic Research) Working Paper Series*, no. 7361, September.

Kim, Byung-Kook. 2000. The Politics of Crisis and a Crisis of Politics: The Presidency of Kim Dae-Jung, in Kongdan Oh (ed.), *Korea Briefing: 1997–1999*. Armonk, NY: M. E. Sharpe, pp. 35–74.

Kim, Daesik and Jaeha Park. 2000. Korean Financial Crisis and Reform, in J. Jay Choi (ed.), *Asian Financial Crisis: Financial, Structural and International Dimensions*. New York: Elsevier Science Inc., pp. 79–122.

Kim, Eun-Mee. 1997. *Big Business, Strong State: Collusion and Conflict in South Korean Development, 1960–1990*. Albany, NY: State University of New York Press.

——, 2000. Reforming the *Chaebols*, in Larry Diamond and Doh Chull Shin (eds.), *Institutional Reform and Democratic Consolidation in Korea*. Stanford, CA: Hoover Institution Press, pp. 171–98.

Kim, Hong Nack. 2000. The 2000 Parliamentary Election in South Korea, *Asian Survey*, vol. 40, no. 6, November/December, pp. 894–913.

Kim, Ilpyong J. and Uk Heon Hong. 2000. The Republic of Korea: The Taming of the Tiger, *International Social Science Journal*, March, no. 163, pp. 61–77.

Kim, In-June and Yeongseop Rhee. 1998. The Korean Currency Crisis and the IMF Program: An Insider's View, *Seoul Journal of Economics*, vol. 11, no. 4, pp. 351–80.

Kim, Kihwan. 2000. The Korean Financial Crisis: Causes, Response and Lessons, in Joseph R. Bisignano, William C. Hunter and George G. Kaufman (eds.), *Global Financial Crises: Lessons from Recent Events*. Boston: Kluwer Academic Publishers, pp. 201–8.

—— and Danny M. Leipziger. 1997. Korea: A Case of Government-Led Development, in Danny M. Leipziger (ed.), *Lessons from East Asia*. Ann Arbor, MI: The University of Michigan Press, pp. 155–212.

Kim, Kwan S. 2001. Market Liberalization and the Problem of Governance in South Korea, in Xiaoming Huang (ed.), *The Political and Economic Transition in East Asia: Strong Markets, Weakening State*. Washington, DC: Georgetown University Press, pp. 27–54.

Kim, Kyung-Hwan. 2000. Korea: Could a Real Estate Price Bubble have Caused the Economic Crisis?, in Koichi Mera and Bertrand Renaud (eds.), *Asia's Financial Crisis and the Role of Real Estate*. Armonk, NY: M. E. Sharpe, pp. 99–114.

Kim, Samuel S. 2000. Korea and Globalization (*Segyehwa*): A Framework for Analysis, in Samuel S. Kim (ed.), *Korea's Globalization*. New York: Cambridge University Press, pp. 1–28.

——, 2000a. Korea's *Segyehwa* Drive: Promise versus Performance, in Samuel S. Kim (ed.), *Korea's Globalization*. New York: Cambridge University Press, pp. 242–81.

Kim, Sunhyuk. 2000. The Politics of Reform in South Korea: The First Year of the Kim Dae Jung Government, 1998–1999, *Asian Perspective*, vol. 24, no. 1, pp. 163–85.

Kim, Yong Cheol and Chung-in Moon. 2000. Globalization and Workers in South Korea, in Samuel S. Kim (ed.), *Korea's Globalization*. New York: Cambridge University Press, pp. 54–75.

Kim, Youn-Suk and Hyeng Keun Koo. 1999. Asia's Contagious Financial Crisis and Its Impact on Korea, *Journal of Asian Economics*, vol. 10, pp. 111–21.

——, 2001. The IMF Policy and Its Effects on Korean *Chaebols*, *Review of Asian and Pacific Studies*, no. 21, pp. 1–14.

Kindleberger, Charles. 1978. *Manias, Panics and Crashes: A History of Financial Crises*. New York: Basic Books.

King, Dan. 1999. Thailand, in Ian Marsh, Jean Blondel and Takashi Inoguchi (eds.), *Democracy, Governance and Economic Performance: East and Southeast Asia*. Tokyo: United Nations University Press, pp. 203–29.

King, Dwight. 2000. Corruption in Indonesia: A Curable Cancer, *Journal of International Affairs*, vol. 53, no. 2, Spring, pp. 603–24.

Kingsbury, Damien. 1998. *The Politics of Indonesia*. New York: Oxford University Press.

Kirk, Donald. 1999. *Korean Crisis: Unraveling of the Miracle in the IMF Era*. New York: St Martin's Press.

Kong, Tat Yan. 2000. Power Alternation in South Korea, *Government and Opposition*, vol. 35, no. 3, Summer, pp. 370–91.

Kornai, Janos. 1992. *The Socialist System: The Political Economy of Communism*. Princeton, NJ: Princeton University Press.

Kristov, Nicholas. 1998. Has the IMF Cured or Harmed Asia?, *The New York Times*, April 23, p. C3.

Krueger, Anne. 2002. *A New Approach to Sovereign Debt Restructuring*. Washington, DC: International Monetary Fund.

——, and Jungho Yoo. 2001. Chaebol Capitalism and the Currency–Financial Crisis in Korea, *NBER Conference Paper*, March.

Krugman, Paul. 1979. A Model of Balance of Payments Crises, *Journal of Money, Credit and Banking*, vol. 11, pp. 311–25.

——, 1994. The Myth of Asia's Miracle, *Foreign Affairs*, vol. 73, no. 6, November/December.

——, 1996. Are Currency Crises Self-Fulfilling? *NBER Macroeconomics Annual*. MIT Press, pp. 345–78.

——, 1998. Saving Asia: It's Time to Get Radical, *Fortune*, vol. 138, no. 5, September 7, pp. 74–80.

——, 1998a. The Confidence Game: How Washington Worsened Asia's Crash, *The New Republic*, October 5, pp. 23–5.

——, 1998b. Malaysia's Opportunity, *Far Eastern Economic Review*, no. 161, September 17, p. 32.

——, 1998c. A Letter to Malaysia's Prime Minister, *Fortune*, vol. 138, no. 6, September 28, pp. 35–6.

——, 1999. The Indispensable IMF, in Lawrence J. McQuillan and Peter C. Montgomery, *The International Monetary Fund: Financial Medic to the World*. Stanford, CA: Hoover Institution Press.

——, 1999a. The Return of Depression Economics, *Foreign Affairs*, vol. 78, no. 1, January/February, pp. 56–74.

Kusumanto, Bambang. 2001. Indonesia's Economic Policy under the Wahid Administration, in Anthony L. Smith (ed.), *Gus Dur and the Indonesian Economy*. Singapore: Institute of Southeast Asian Studies.

Kwack, Sung Yeung. 1998. Factors Contributing to the Financial Crisis in Korea, *Journal of Asian Economics*, vol. 9, no. 4, pp. 611–24.

Kwan, C. H. 1995. *Economic Interdependence in the Asia–Pacific Region*. London: Routledge.

——, 1998. Asia's Currency Crisis and Its Implications for the Japanese Economy, in C. H. Kwan, Donna Vandenbrink and Chia Siow Yue (eds.), *Coping with Capital Flows in East Asia*. Singapore: Institute of Southeast Asian Studies, pp. 25–53.

——, 2000. Asia in Search of a New Exchange Rate Regime, in Brigitte Granville (ed.), *Essays on the World Economy and its Financial System*. London: The Royal Institute of International Affairs, pp. 127–52.

Kwon, O. Yul and William Shepherd (eds.). 2001. *Korea's Economic Prospects: From Financial Crisis to Prosperity*. Cheltenham, UK: Edward Elgar.

Lal, Deepak. 1998. Don't Bank on It, Mr. Blair, *The Spectator*, 26 September, pp. 17–19.

Lall, Sanjay. 1990. *Building Industrial Competitiveness in Developing Countries*. New York: OECD Development Center.

——, 1999. *Raising Competitiveness in the Thai Economy*. Geneva: International Labor Office, Working Paper.

Lamfalussy, Alexandre. 2000. *Financial Crises in Emerging Markets*. New Haven, CT: Yale University Press.

Landers, Peter and Dan Biers. 1998. This Will Hurt, in Dan Biers (ed.), *Crash of '97: How the Financial Crisis is Reshaping Asia*. Hong Kong: Review Publishing Company, pp. 98–108.

Lane, Timothy and Steven Phillips. 2001. IMF Financing and Moral Hazard, *Finance and Development*, vol. 38, no. 2, June, pp. 50–2.

——, Atish R. Ghosh, Javier Hamann, Steven Phillips, Marianne Schulze-Ghattas and Tsidi Tsikata. 1999. *IMF-Supported Programs in Indonesia, Korea and Thailand: A Preliminary Assessment*. Washington, DC: International Monetary Fund.

Laothamatas, Anek. 1996. A Tale of Two Democracies: Conflicting Perceptions of Elections and Democracy in Thailand, in R. H. Taylor (ed.), *The Politics of Elections in Southeast Asia*. New York: Cambridge University Press.

La Porta, Rafael, Florencio Lopez-de-Silanes and Andrei Shleifer. 1998. Law and Finance, *Journal of Political Economy*, 106, pp. 1113–55.

Lardy, Nicholas R. 1994. *China in the World Economy*. Washington, DC: Institute for International Economics.

——, 1998. *China's Unfinished Economic Revolution.* Washington, DC: The Brookings Institution Press.

——, 1998a. China and the Asian Contagion, *Foreign Affairs*, vol. 77, no. 4, July/August, pp. 78–88.

——, 1999. China's WTO Membership, *Brookings Policy Brief #47* (The Brookings Institution: Washington, DC: April, pp. 1–8).

Lauridsen, Laurids. 1998. Thailand: Causes, Conduct, Consequences, in K. S. Jomo (ed.), *Tigers in Trouble: Financial Governance, Liberalization and Crises in East Asia.* New York: Zed Press.

Lee, B. 1998. *Growth Factors of the Korean Economy and the Role of Industrial Policy.* Seoul: Korean Economic Research Institute.

Lee, Chae-Jin. 2000. South Korean Foreign Relations Face the Globalization Challenges, in Samuel S. Kim (ed.), *Korea's Globalization.* New York: Cambridge University Press, pp. 170–96.

Lee, Chung H. 2000. Chaebol, Financial Liberalization and Economic Crisis, unpublished paper. University of Hawaii at Manoa.

Lee, Doowon. 2000. South Korea's Financial Crisis and Economic Restructuring, in Kongdan Oh (ed.), *Korea Briefing: 1997–1999.* Armonk, NY: M. E. Sharpe, pp. 9–34.

Lee, Eddy. 1998. *The Asian Financial Crisis: The Challenge for Social Policy.* Geneva: International Labor Office.

Lee, Jisoon. 1999. An Understanding of the 1997 Korean Economic Crisis, *EXIM Review*, vol. 19, no. 2, July, pp. 41–87.

Lee, Soo-Won and Ann Orr. 1999. The Financial Restructuring and Reform Program in the Republic of Korea: Progress and Constraints, in Barry Herman (ed.), *Global Financial Turmoil and Reform: A United Nations Perspective.* Tokyo: United Nations University Press, pp. 93–108.

Lee, Yeon-ho. 1997. *The State, Society and Big Business in South Korea.* London: Routledge.

——, 2000. The Failure of the Weak State in Economic Liberalization: Liberalization, Democratization and the Financial Crisis in South Korea, *The Pacific Review*, vol. 13, no. 1, pp. 115–31.

Leipziger, Danny M. 1997. *Lessons from East Asia.* Ann Arbor, MI: University of Michigan Press.

Leung, James. 1999. The Downward Spiral, *Asian Business*, June, p. 31.

Leung, Suiwah. 1999. *Vietnam and the East Asian Crisis.* Cheltenham: Edward Elgar.

Levinsohn, James, Steven Berry and Jed Friedman. 1999. Impacts of the Indonesian Economic Crisis: Price Changes and the Poor, *NBER Working Paper*, 7197. June.

Li, Conghua and Pat Loconto. 1998. *China: The Consumer Revolution.* New York: John Wiley and Sons.

Liddle, William R. 1996. *Leadership and Culture in Indonesian Politics.* Sydney: Allen and Unwin.

——, 2000. Indonesia in 1999: Democracy Restored, *Asian Survey*, vol. 40, no. 1, January–February, pp. 32–42.

Lie, John. 1998. *Han Unbound: The Political Economy of South Korea.* Stanford, CA: Stanford University Press.

Lieberman, Ira. 1999. Korea's Corporate Reforms, in *Korea Approaches the Millennium.* Washington, DC: The Korea Economic Institute of America.

Liebhold, David. 1998. Rough Road Ahead, *Asian Business*, vol. 30, no. 2, February.

Lim, Linda, Y. C. 1998. Whose Model Failed? Implications of the Asian Economic Crisis, *The Washington Quarterly*, vol. 21, no. 3, pp. 25–36.

——, 1999. The Asian Economic Crisis, *Asian Update*. Asia Society Publications.

Lin, Justin Yifu. 1990. Collectivization and China's Agricultural Crisis in 1959–61, *Journal of Political Economy*, vol. 98, no. 6, December, pp. 1228–52.

——, 1992. Rural Reforms and Agricultural Growth in China, *American Economic Review*, 82, no. 1 March, pp. 34–51.

——, Fang Cai and Zhou Li. 1996. *The China Miracle: Development Strategy and Economic Reform*. Hong Kong: The Chinese University Press.

Lin, Wuu-Long and Anna Kuo. 2000. An Overview of the East Asian Financial Crisis, *Review of Pacific Basin Financial Markets and Policies*, vol. 3, no. 1, pp. 107–20.

Lincoln, Edward J. 1998. Japan's Financial Problems, *Brookings Papers on Economic Activity*, no. 2, pp. 347–85.

Lindgren, Carl-Johan, Tomas Balino, Charles Enoch, Anne-Marie Gulde, Marc Quintyn and Leslie Teo. 1999. Financial Sector Crisis and Restructuring: Lessons from Asia, *IMF Occasional Paper*, 188. Washington, DC: International Monetary Fund.

Lipsey, Robert. 2001. Foreign Direct Investors in Three Financial Crises, *NBER Working Paper*, no. 8084.

Lister, James M. 2001. South Korea: Accomplishments and Challenges, *Korea's Economy: 2001*. Washington, DC: The Korea Economic Institute of America, pp. 1–6.

Litan, Robert E. 1998. A Three-Step Remedy for Asia's Financial Flu, *Brookings Policy Brief Series*, no. 30, February, pp. 1–10.

——, Paul Masson and Michael Pomerleano (eds.). 2001. *Open Doors: Foreign Participation in Financial Systems in Developing Countries*. Washington, DC: The Brookings Institution Press.

Little, Jane. 1997. Anatomy of a Currency Crisis, *Federal Reserve Bank of Boston Regional Review*, vol. 7, no. 4, Autumn, pp. 8–13.

Liu, Ligang, Marcus Noland, Sherman Robinson and Zhi Wang. 1998. Asian Competitive Devaluations, *Institute for International Economics, Working Paper*, 98–2.

Lloyd, Grayson and Shannon Smith. 2001. *Indonesia Today: Challenges of History*. Singapore: Institute of Southeast Asian Studies.

Lowe-Lee, Florence. 2000. Economic Trends, *Korea Insight*, vol. 2, no. 9, September.

Lowenstein, Roger. 2000. *When Genius Failed: The Rise and Fall of Long-Term Capital Management*. New York: Random House.

MacDonald, Scott. 1998. Transparency in Thailand's 1997 Economic Crisis: The Significance of Disclosure, *Asian Survey*, vol. 38, no. 7, July, pp. 688–702.

MacIntyre, Andrew (ed.). 1994. *Business and Government in Industrializing Asia*. Ithaca, NY: Cornell University Press.

McKinnon, Ronald. 1973. *Money and Capital in Economic Development*. Washington, DC: The Brookings Institution.

McLeod, Ross. 1999. Indonesia's Crisis and Future Prospects, in Karl D. Jackson (ed.), *Asian Contagion: The Causes and Consequences of a Financial Crisis*. Boulder, CO: Westview Press.

McQuillan, Lawrence and Peter C. Montgomery (eds.). *The International Monetary Fund: Financial Medic to the World*. Stanford, CA: Hoover Institution Press.

Mahathir, Mohamad. 1999. *A New Deal for Asia*. Subang Jaya: Pelanduk Publications.

Mahmood, Moazam and Gosah Aryah. 2001. The Labor Market and Labor Policy in a Macroeconomic Context: Growth, Crisis and Competitiveness in Thailand, in Gordon Betcherman and Rizwanul Islam (eds.), *East Asian Labor Markets and the Economic Crisis: Impacts, Responses and Lessons*. Washington, DC: World Bank, pp. 245–92.

Makin, Tony. 1999. The Great East Asian Capital Flow Reversal: Reasons, Responses and Ramifications, *The World Economy*, vol. 22, no. 3, May, pp. 407–19.

Mallaret, Thierry, Natalia Orlova and Valdimir Romanov. 1999. What Loaded and Triggered the Russian Crisis, *Post-Soviet Affairs*, vol. 15, no. 2, pp. 107–29.

Mann, Catherine. 1999. Market Mechanisms to Reduce the Need for IMF Bailouts, *International Economics Policy Briefs*. Washington, DC: Institute for International Economics.

Martinez, Guillermo Ortiz. 1998. What Lessons Does the Mexican Crisis Hold for Recovery in Asia?, *Finance and Development*, vol. 35, no. 2, June, p. 3.

Masson, Paul R. 1998. Contagion Effects: Monsoonal Effects, Spillovers and Jumps between Multiple Equilibria, *IMF Working Paper*, no. 98/142, September.

——, 1999. Contagion: Macroeconomic Models with Multiple Equilibria, *Journal of International Money and Finance*, vol. 18, no. 4, pp. 587–602.

Mathews, John A. 2001. Fashioning a New Korean Model out of the Crisis: The Rebuilding of Institutional Capabilities, in Ha-Joon Chang, Gabriel Palma and D. Hugh Whittaker (eds.), *Financial Liberalization and the Asian Crisis*. New York: Palgrave Publishers, pp. 156–74.

Mattione, Richard. 2000. Japan: The World's Slowest Crisis, in Wing Thye Woo, Jeffrey Sachs and Klaus Schwab (eds.), *The Asian Financial Crisis: Lessons for a Resilient Asia*. Cambridge, MA: MIT Press.

Maxfield, Sylvia. 2000. Capital Mobility and Democratic Stability, *Journal of Democracy*, vol. 11, no. 4, October, pp. 95–106.

Meltzer, Allan H. 1998. Asian Problems and the IMF, *The Cato Journal*, vol. 17, no. 3, pp. 267–74.

——, 1999. What's Wrong with the IMF: What Would be Better?, *The Independent Review*, vol. iv, no. 2, Autumn, pp. 201–15.

Mera, Koichi and Bertrand Renaud. 2000. *Asia's Financial Crisis and the Role of Real Estate*. Armonk, NY: M. E. Sharpe.

Mietzner, Marcus. 1999. From Soeharto to Habibie: The Indonesian Armed Forces and Political Islam during the Transition, in Geoff Forrester (ed.), *Post-Soeharto Indonesia: Renewal or Chaos?* Singapore: Institute of Southeast Asian Studies, pp. 65–102.

Mikitani, Ryoichi and Adam S. Posen (eds.). 2000. *Japan's Financial Crisis and its Parallels to U.S. Experience*. Washington, DC: Institute for International Economics.

Miller, Merton H. 1998. The Current Southeast Asia Financial Crisis, *Pacific-Basin Finance Journal*, no. 6, pp. 225–33.

Mills, Edwin. 1995. *Growth and Equity in the Indonesian Economy*. Washington, DC: The United States–Indonesia Society. Background paper, no. 1.

Min, Byung S. 1999. South Korea's Financial Crisis in 1997: What Have We Learned?, *ASEAN Economic Bulletin*, vol. 16, no. 2, August, pp. 175–87.

Mishkin, Frederic S. 1997. The Causes and Propagation of Financial Instability: Lessons for Policymakers, in C. Hakkio (ed.), *Maintaining Financial Stability in a Global Economy*. Federal Reserve Bank of Kansas City, pp. 55–96.

——, 1999. Lessons from the Asian Crisis, *Journal of International Money and Finance*, vol. 18, pp. 709–23.

——, 1999a. Lessons from the Asian Crisis, *NBER Working Paper Series*, no. 7102.

Mo, Jongryn. 2001. Political Culture and Legislative Gridlock: Politics and Economic Reform in Pre-crisis Korea, *Comparative Political Studies*, vol. 34, no. 5, June, pp. 467–92.

——, and Chung-In Moon. 1999. Epilogue: Democracy and the Origins of the 1997 Korean Economic Crisis, in Jongryn Mo and Chung-In Moon (eds.), *Democracy and the Korean Economy*. Stanford, CA: Hoover Institution Press, pp. 171–98.

—— and ——, 1999a. Korea After the Crash, *Journal of Democracy*, vol. 10, no. 3, pp. 150–64.

MOFE (Ministry of Finance and Economy). 1998. *Challenge and Chance: Korea's Response to the New Economic Reality*. Seoul: MOFE.

Monetary Authority of Singapore (MAS). 2001. *MAS Quarterly Bulletin*. Singapore. June.

Montes, Manuel F. 1998. Global Lessons of the Economic Crisis in Asia, *Asia Pacific Issues*, no. 38, March. East–West Center, Hawaii.

Montgomery, John. 1997. The Indonesian Financial System: Its Contribution to Economic Performance and Key Policy Issues, *IMF Working Paper*, WP/97/45. Washington, DC: International Monetary Fund.

Montiel, Peter and Carmen Reinhart. 1997. The Dynamics of Capital Movements to Emerging Economies during the 1990s, photocopy.

Montinola, Gabriella, Yingyi Qian and Barry Weingast. 1995. Federalism, Chinese Style: The Political Basis for Economic Success in China, *World Politics*, vol. 48, no. 1, October, pp. 50–81.

Moon, Chung-In and Sang-young Rhyu. 2000. The State, Structural Rigidity, and the End of Asian Capitalism, in Richard Robison, Mark Beeson, Kanishka Jayasuriya and Hyuk-Rae Kim (eds.), *Politics and Markets in the Wake of the Asian Crisis*. London: Routledge, pp. 77–98.

Moreno, Ramon. 1999. Did a Boom in Money and Credit Precede East Asia's Recent Currency Crisis?, *Federal Reserve Bank of San Francisco Economic Review*, no. 1, pp. 25–34.

——, Gloria Pasadilla and Eli Remolona. 1998. Asia's Financial Crisis: Lessons and Policy Responses, *Pacific Basin Working Paper Series*, no. PB98-02, Federal Reserve Bank of San Francisco, Economic Research Department.

Motohashi, Kazuyuki. 1998. Structural Aspects of the Asian Financial Crisis, *Asia–Pacific Review*, vol. 5, no. 3, pp. 27–50.

Muhammad. Mar'ie. 1997. Statement by the Hon. Mar'ie Muhammad at the 1997 World Bank/IMF Annual Meeting in Hong Kong, September 23, *IMF press release*, no. 25.

Mundell, Robert. 1963. Capital Mobility and Stabilization Policy under Fixed and Flexible Exchange Rates, *Canadian Journal of Economics and Political Science*, vol. 29, pp. 475–85.

——, 1968. *International Economics*. New York: Macmillan.

Muscat, Robert, J. 1994. *The Fifth Tiger: A Study of Thai Development Policy*. Armonk, NY: M. E. Sharpe.

Mussa, Michael. 2000. Monetary Policy to Resist Excessive Depreciation, in Joseph R. Bisignano, William C. Hunter and George G. Kaufman (eds.), *Global Financial Crises: Lessons from Recent Events*. Boston: Kluwer Academic Publishers, pp. 77–88.

—— and Miguel Savastano. 1999. The IMF Approach to Economic Stabilization, *IMF Working Paper*, WP/99/104. July.

——, Paul Masson, Alexander Swoboda, Esteban Jadresic, Paolo Mauro and Andrew Berg. 2000. *Exchange Rate Regimes in an Increasingly Integrated World Economy*. Washington, DC: IMF.

Nabi, Ijaz and Jayasankar Shivakumar. 2001. *Back from the Brink: Thailand's Response to the 1997 Economic Crisis*. Washington, DC: World Bank.

Naim, Moises. 1997. Mexico's Larger Story, in Sebastian Edwards and Moises Naim (eds.), *Anatomy of an Emerging-Market Crash: Mexico 1994*. Washington DC: The Carnegie Endowment for International Peace.

Naisbitt, John. 1995. *Megatrends Asia*. London: Nicholas Brealy.

Nasution, Anwar. 1999. The Financial Crisis in Indonesia, in Seiichi Masuyama, Donna Vandenbrink and Chia Siow Yue (eds.), *East Asia's Financial System: Evolution and Crisis*. Singapore: Institute of Southeast Asian Studies.

——, 2001. Meltdown of the Indonesian Economy: Causes, Impacts, Responses and Lessons, in Anthony L. Smith (ed.), *Gus Dur and the Indonesian Economy*. Singapore: Institute of Southeast Asian Studies.

Nath, Raghu and Qingjiu Tao. 1998. Economic Transition Strategies of China, paper presented at conference, "China, India and Russia: Progress in Challenges of Economic Transition," Michigan State University, East Lansing, October 23–25.

Naughton, Barry. 1995. *Growing Out of the Plan: Chinese Economic Reform, 1978–1993*. Cambridge: Cambridge University Press.

——, 1998. China's Economy: Buffeted from Within and Without, *Current History*, September, pp. 273–8.

Neiss, Hubert. 1998. In Defense of the IMF's Emergency Role in East Asia, *International Herald Tribune*, October 9, p. 22.

Nellor, David C. L. 1998. The Role of the International Monetary Fund, in Ross H. McLeod and Ross Garnaut (eds.), *East Asia in Crisis: From Being a Miracle to Needing One*. New York: Routledge, pp. 245–65.

Nidhiprabha, Bhanupong. 1998. Adverse Consequences of Capital Inflows and Thailand's Optimal Policy Mix, in C. H. Kwan, Donna Vandenbrink and Chia Siow Yue (eds.), *Coping with Capital Flows in East Asia*. Singapore: Institute of Southeast Asian Studies, pp. 192–219.

——, 1999. Economic Crises and the Debt-Deflation Episode in Thailand, in H. W. Arndt and Hal Hill (eds.), *Southeast Asia's Economic Crisis: Origins, Lessons and the Way Forward*. Singapore: Institute of Southeast Asian Studies, pp. 67–80.

—— and Peter G. Warr. 2000. Thailand's Experience with Reform in the Financial Sector, in Peter Drysdale (ed.), *Reform and Recovery in East Asia: The Role of the State and Economic Enterprise*. New York: Routledge, pp. 99–119.

Noble, Gregory and John Ravenhill. 2000. The Good, the Bad and the Ugly? Korea, Taiwan and the Asian Financial Crisis, in Gregory Noble and John Ravenhill (ed.), *The Asian Financial Crisis and the Architecture of Global Finance*. New York: Cambridge University Press.

Noland, Marcus. 1999. Asian Economic Recovery. Washington, DC: Institute for International Economics, Policy Paper (www.iie.org).

——, 2000. The Philippines in the Asian Financial Crisis: How the Sick Man Avoided Pneumonia, *Asian Survey*, vol. 40, no. 3, May/June, pp. 401–12.

——, 2001. Economic Reform in South Korea: Achievements and Future Prospects, *Policy Briefs*, Institute for International Economics, Washington, DC.

Nyberg, Albert and Scott Rozelle, 1999. Accelerating China's Rural Transformation, *World Bank Working Paper Series*, Washington DC.

Oberdorfer, Don. 1997. *The Two Koreas: A Contemporary History*. Reading, MA: Addison-Wesley.

Obstfeld, Maurice. 1986. Rational and Self-Fulfilling Balance of Payments Crises, *American Economic Review*, vol. 76, pp. 72–81.

——, 1994. The Logic of Currency Crises, *NBER Working Paper*, no. 4640.

——, 1996. Models of Currency Crises with Self-Fulfilling Features, *European Economic Review*, vol. 40, nos. 3–5, pp. 1037–47.

——, 1998. The Global Capital Market: Benefactor or Menace, *Journal of Economic Perspectives*, vol. 12, no. 4, Autumn.

OECD (Organization for Economic Cooperation and Development). 1998. *OECD Economic Surveys, 1997–98: Mexico*. Paris: OECD.

——, 1998a. *OECD Economic Surveys, 1997–98: Korea*. Paris: OECD.

——, 1999. *Structural Aspects of the East Asian Crisis*. Paris: OECD.

——, 1999a. *Asia and the Global Crisis: The Industrial Dimension*. Paris: OECD.

Oh, John Kie-Chiang. 1999. *Korean Politics*. Ithaca, NY: Cornell University Press.

Oi, Jean. 1992. Fiscal Reform and the Economic Foundations of Local State Corporatism in China, *World Politics*, vol. 45, October.

——, 1999. *Rural China Takes Off: Institutional Foundations of Economic Reform*. Berkeley, CA: University of California Press.

Pangestu, Mari. 1996. *Economic Reform, Deregulation and Privatization: The Indonesian Experience*. Jakarta: Center for Strategic and International Studies.

—— and Miranda Swaray Goeltom. 2001. Survey of Recent Developments, *Bulletin of Indonesian Economic Studies*, vol. 37, no. 2, pp. 141–71.

Park, Daekeun and Changyong Rhee. 1998. Currency Crisis in Korea: How Was It Aggravated?, *Asian Development Review*, vol. 16, no. 1, pp. 149–80.

Park, Sang Yong. 1999. Financial Reform and its Impact on Corporate Organization in Korea, in Gordon de Brouwer and Wisarn Pupphavesa (eds.), *Asia Pacific Financial Deregulation*. New York: Routledge, pp. 207–31.

Park, Yung Chul and Kim, D. W. 1994. Korea: Development and Structural Change of the Banking System, in H. Patrick and Y. Park (eds.), *The Financial Development of Japan, Korea and Taiwan: Growth, Repression and Liberalization*. New York: Oxford University Press, pp. 188–221.

Passell, Peter. 1998. Economic Scene: In Indonesia, Slowdown on a Risky Bet, *New York Times*, February 19.

Peek, Joe and Eric Rosengren, 1998. Japanese Banking Problems: Implications for Southeast Asia, paper presented at the Second Annual Conference of the Central Bank of Chile, held in Santiago, Chile, September 3–4.

Pei, Minxin. 1999. Will China become another Indonesia?, *Foreign Policy*, Autumn, pp. 94–109.

Perkins, Dwight Heald and Wing Thye Woo. 2000. Malaysia: Adjusting to Deep Integration with the World Economy, in Wing Thye Woo, Jeffrey D. Sachs and Klaus Schwab (eds.), *The Asian Financial Crisis: Lessons for a Resilient Asia.* Cambridge, MA: MIT Press, pp. 227–55.

Phongpaichit, Pasuk. 1996. The Thai Economy in the Mid-1990s, *Southeast Asian Affairs: 1996.* Singapore: Institute of Southeast Asian Studies, pp. 369–81.

——, 1997. *Thailand: Economy and Politics.* London: Oxford University Press.

——, 1998. *Thailand's Boom and Bust.* Chiang Mai, Thailand: Silkworm Books.

——, 1999. The Political Economy of the Thai Crisis, *Journal of the Asia Pacific Economy*, vol. 4, no. 1, pp. 193–208.

——, 2000. *Thailand's Crisis.* Chiang Mai, Thailand: Silkworm Books.

—— and Chris Baker. 2001. Thailand's Crisis: Neo-Liberal Agenda and Local Reaction, in Ha-Joon Chang, Gabriel Palma and D. Hugh Whittaker (eds.), *Financial Liberalization and the Asian Crisis.* New York: Palgrave Publishers, pp. 82–101.

——, and Sungsidh Piriyarangsan. 1994. *Corruption and Democracy in Thailand.* Bangkok: Silkworm Books.

Pincus, Jonathan and Rizal Ramli. 1998. Indonesia: From Showcase to Basket Case, *Cambridge Journal of Economics*, vol. 22, no. 6, pp. 723–34.

Pomfret, John. 1999. China set to Tackle Economic Woes, *The Washington Post*, January 16, p. A21.

Posen, Adam S, 1998. *Restoring Japan's Economic Growth.* Washington, DC: Institute for International Economics.

Prachuabmoh, Nukul. 1998. *Analysis and Evaluation of Facts Behind Thailand's Economic Crisis* (Nukul Report). Bangkok: Thailand Development Research Institute. English translation by Nation Multimedia Group, Bangkok.

Prakash, Aseem. 2001. The East Asian Crisis and the Globalization Discourse, *Review of International Political Economy*, vol. 8, no. 1, Spring, pp. 119–46.

Prawiro, Radius. 1998. *Indonesia's Struggle for Economic Development: Pragmatism in Action.* Kuala Lumpur: Oxford University Press.

Pyo, Hak K. 2000. Excess Competition, Moral Hazard and Industrial Trauma in Korea, 1997–8, in Uri Dadush, Dipak Dasgupta and Marc Uzan (eds.), *Private Capital Flows in the Age of Globalization: The Aftermath of the Asian Crisis.* Northampton, MA: Edward Elgar, pp. 13–26.

Radelet, Steven. Indonesia's Long Road to Recovery, unpublished paper, March. Harvard Institute for International Development.

——, 2000. Indonesia: Long Road to Recovery, in Peter C. Y. Chow and Bates Gill (eds.), *Weathering the Storm: Taiwan, its Neighbors and the Asian Financial Crisis.* Washington, DC: The Brookings Institution Press, pp. 39–70.

——, and Jeffrey Sachs. 1997. Asia's Re-emergence, *Foreign Affairs*, vol. 76, no. 6, November/December, pp. 44–59.

—— and ——, 1998. The East Asian Financial Crisis: Diagnosis, Remedies and Prospects, *Brookings Papers on Economic Activity*, vol. 1.

—— and ——, 1998a. Onset of the East Asian Financial Crisis, *NBER Working Paper*, no. 6680, April.

Rajan, Ramkishen and Iman Sugema. 2000. Government Bailouts and Monetary Disequilibrium: Common Fundamentals in the Mexican and East Asian

Currency Crises, *North American Journal of Economics and Finance*, vol. 11, pp. 123–35.

Ramage, Douglas E. 1995. *Politics in Indonesia: Democracy, Islam and the Ideology of Tolerance*. New York: Routledge.

Ramo, Joshua Cooper. 1998. The Shanghai Bubble, *Foreign Policy*, Summer, pp. 64–75.

Reisen, Helmut. 1999. Domestic Causes of Currency Crises: Policy Lessons for Crisis Avoidance, *IDS Bulletin*, vol. 30, no. 1, pp. 120–31.

Renaud, Bertrand. 2000. How Real Estate Contributed to the Thailand Financial Crisis, in Koichi Mera and Bertrand Renaud (eds.), *Asia's Financial Crisis and the Role of Real Estate*. Armonk, NY: M. E. Sharpe, pp. 183–207.

Richburg, Keith B. 1998. Cashing In On Years in Power, *Washington Post*, May 22, p. A40.

Ries, Philippe. 1998. *The Asian Storm: Asia's Economic Crisis Examined*. Boston: Tuttle Publishing.

Rodan, Garry, Kevin Hewison and Richard Robison (eds.). 1997. *The Political Economy of Southeast Asia*. New York: Oxford University Press.

Rodrik, Dani. 1998. Who Needs Capital-Account Convertibility, in *Should the IMF Pursue Capital-Account Convertibility?* Essays in International Finance, no. 207, Department of Economics, Princeton University.

——, 1998a. The Global Fix, *The New Republic*, November 2.

Rohwer, Jim. 1995. *Asia Rising: Why America Will Prosper as Asia's Economies Boom*. New York: Simon and Schuster.

Root, Gregory, Paul Grela, Mark Jones and Anand Adiga. 2000. Financial Sector Restructuring in East Asia, in Charles Adams, Robert Litan and Michael Pomerleano (eds.), *Managing Financial and Corporate Distress: Lessons From Asia*. Washington, DC: The Brookings Institution Press.

Rosario, Louise. 1999. Trouble Spots: China, *The Banker*, October, p. 93.

Rosen, Daniel, Ligang Liu and Lawrence Dwight. 1998. Financial Fallout, *The China Business Review*, vol. 25, no. 2, March/April, pp. 44–60.

Rosul, Mochammad. 1998. Coping with Capital Flows and the Monetary Policy Framework: The Case of Indonesia, in C. H. Kwan, Donna Vandenbrink and Chia Siow Yue (eds.), *Coping with Capital Flows in East Asia*. Singapore: Institute of Southeast Asian Studies, pp. 244–71.

Rubin, Robert. 1998. Strengthening the Architecture of the International Financial System, public statement delivered at the Brookings Institution, April 14. Also published in *Treasury News* (April 14, 1998).

Sabirin, Sjahril. 1999. Recent Developments in the Indonesian Economy, presentation to Banque de France, March (mimeo).

Sachs, Jeffrey. 1997. Personal View, *Financial Times*, 30 July.

——, 1997a. The IMF is a Power unto Itself, *Financial Times*, December 11.

——, 1997b. IMF Orthodoxy Isn't What Southeast Asia Needs, *International Herald Tribune*, November 4, p. 8.

——, 1997c. The Wrong Medicine for Asia, *New York Times*, November 3.

——, 1998. Stop Preaching, *Financial Times*, November 5.

——, 1998a. The IMF and the Asian Flu, *The American Prospect*, no. 37 (http://epn.org/prospect/37/37sachsfs.html).

——, 1998b. Alternative Approaches to Financial Crises in Emerging Markets, in Miles Kahler (ed.), *Capital Flows and Financial Crises*. Ithaca, NY: Cornell University Press, pp. 247–62.

——, 1999. Time to End Backroom Poker Game, *Financial Times*, November 15, p. 19.

—— and Felipe Larrain. 1999. Why Dollarization is more Straitjacket than Salvation, *Foreign Policy*, Autumn, pp. 80–93.

——, Aaron Tornell and Andres Velasco. 1996. Financial Crises in Emerging Markets: The Lessons from 1995, *Brookings Papers on Economic Activity*, vol. 1.

Sadli, Mohammad. 1999. The Indonesian Crisis, in H. W. Arndt and Hal Hill (eds.), *Southeast Asia's Economic Crisis: Origins, Lessons and the Way Forward*. Singapore: Institute of Southeast Asian Studies.

Sahasakul, Chaipat. 1999. Thailand's Financial Reforms: Problems and Prospects, in Gordon de Brouwer and Wisarn Pupphavesa (eds.), *Asia Pacific Financial Deregulation*. New York: Routledge, pp. 277–90.

Salant, S. and D. W. Henderson. 1978. Market Anticipations of Government Policies and the Price of Gold, *Journal of Political Economy*, vol. 86, no. 4, pp. 627–48.

Salim, Emil. 2001. Comments on Indonesia's Economic Reform, in Anthony L. Smith (ed.), *Gus Dur and the Indonesian Economy*. Singapore: Institute of Southeast Asian Studies.

Sandee, Henry. 1999. The Impact of the Crisis on Village Development in Java, *Bulletin of Indonesian Economic Studies*, vol. 35, no. 1, pp. 141–2.

Sanger, David. 1998. Risking IMF Aid, Suharto Dismisses Central Banker, *New York Times*, February 18.

Sarel, Michael. 1997. Growth and Productivity in ASEAN Countries, *IMF Working Paper*, no. WP/97/97.

Sarno, Lucio and Mark P. Taylor. 1999. Moral Hazard, Asset Price Bubbles, Capital Flows and the East Asian Crisis: The First Tests, *Journal of International Money and Finance*, vol. 18, no. 4, pp. 637–57.

Sato, Shuhei. 1998. Asian Financial Crisis, *Japan and the World Economy*, vol. 10, pp. 371–5.

Sazanami, Yoko and Seiji Yoshimura. 1999. Restructuring East Asian Exchange Rate Regimes, *Journal of Asian Economics*, vol. 10, pp. 509–23.

Schultz, George P., William Simon and Walter Wriston. 1998. Who Needs the IMF?, *Hoover Digest*, no. 2, pp. 7–9.

Schwartz, Anna. 1998. Time to Terminate the ESF and the IMF, *CATO Institute Foreign Policy Briefing, No. 48*. August 26. Washington: CATO Institute.

——, 1999. Is there a Need for an International Lender of Last Resort?, *Cato Journal*, vol. 19, no. 1, Spring/Summer, pp. 1–6.

Schwarz, Adam. 2000. *A Nation in Waiting: Indonesia's Search for Stability*. Boulder, CO.: Westview Press.

—— and Jonathan Paris (eds.). 1999. *The Politics of Post-Suharto Indonesia*. New York: Council on Foreign Relations Press.

Scott, Kenneth. 1999. Corporate Governance and East Asia: Korea, Indonesia, Malaysia and Thailand, in Alison Harwood, Robert E. Litan and Michael Pomerleano (eds.), *Financial Markets and Development*. Washington, DC: The Brookings Institution, pp. 335–65.

Searle, P. 1999. *The Riddle of Malaysian Capitalism*. Sydney: Allen and Unwin.

Sender, Henry. 1994. Space Race: Jakarta's Real Estate Market Headed for Trouble?, *Far Eastern Economic Review*, August 4, pp. 55–6.

——, 1997. The devil to pay, *Far Eastern Economic Review*, June 5, pp. 50–8.

—— and Alkman Granitsas. 1998. Broken Wings: Peregrine's Collapse Raises Troubling Questions, *Far Eastern Economic Review*, 22 January, pp. 52–3.

—— and Charles Lee. 1998. Rotten to the core, *Far Eastern Economic Review*, 2 April, pp. 14–16.

Shale, Tony. 1993. Top-Level Shakeout Needed to Mend the Financial System, *Euromoney*, June, p. 55

Sharma, Shalendra D. 1998. Asia's Economic Crisis and the IMF, *Survival: The IISS Quarterly*, vol. 40, no. 2, pp. 27–52.

——, 2000. How Effective are Capital Controls: A Review of the Chilean *Encage: 1991–1998*, *Stanford Journal of International Relations*, vol. 11, no. 1, Spring/Summer, pp. 55–65.

Shenon, Philip. 1998. For the First Family of Indonesia, an Empire Now in Jeopardy, *New York Times*, January 16.

Shirazi, Javad K. 2000. Financial Sector Restructuring: Progress and Issues, in Dominique Dwor-Frecaut, Francis Colaco, and Mary Hallward-Driemeier (eds.), *Asian Corporate Recovery: Findings from Firm-Level Surveys in Five Countries*. Washington, DC: World Bank.

Shirk, Susan. 1993. *The Political Logic of Economic Reform In China*. Berkeley, CA: University of California Press.

Siamwalla, Ammar. 1998. *Can a Developing Democracy manage its Macro-Economy: The Case of Thailand*. Bangkok: Thailand Development Research Institute.

——, Pakorn Vichyanond and Yos Vajragupta. 1999. Foreign Capital Flows to Thailand: Determinants and Impact, Thailand Development Research Institute, Mimeo.

Simandjuntak, Djisman S. 1999. An Inquiry into the Nature, Causes and Consequences of the Indonesian Crisis, *Journal of Asia–Pacific Economy*, vol. 4, no. 1, pp. 171–92.

Singh, Ajit. 1999. Asian Capitalism and the Financial Crisis, in Jonathan Michie and John Grieve Smith (eds.), *Global Instability: The Political Economy of World Economic Governance*. London: Routledge, pp. 9–36.

—— and Bruce A. Weisse. 1999. The Asian Model: A Crisis Foretold, *International Social Science Journal*, no. 160, June, pp. 203–15.

Singh, Bilveer. 2000. *Succession Politics in Indonesia: The 1998 Presidential Elections and the Fall of Suharto*. New York: St Martin's Press.

Sirithaveeporn, Wichit. 1997. Cutting Out–In Loans by BIBF's Not Easy, *Bangkok Post*, January 16 (internet edition).

Smith, Anthony (ed.). 2001. *Gus Dur and the Indonesian Economy*. Singapore: Institute of Southeast Asian Studies.

Smith, Heather. 1998. Korea, in Ross H. McLeod and Ross Garnaut (eds.), *East Asia in Crisis: From Being a Miracle to Needing One*. New York: Routledge, pp. 66–84.

——, 2000. The State, Banking and Corporate Relationships in Korea and Taiwan, in Peter Drysdale (ed.), *Reform and Recovery in East Asia: The Role of the State and Economic Enterprise*. New York: Routledge, pp. 59–98.

Soesastro, Hadi. 2000. Governance and Crisis in Indonesia, in Peter Drysdale (ed.), *Reform and Recovery in East Asia: The Role of the State and Economic Enterprise.* New York: Routledge, pp. 120–45.

—— and Chatib Basri. 1998. Survey of Recent Developments, *Bulletin of Indonesian Economic Studies*, vol. 34, no. 1, April, pp. 3–54.

Sohn, Chan-Hyun and Junsok Yang (eds.). 1998. *Korea's Economic Reform Measures under the IMF Program.* Seoul: Korea Institute for International Economic Policy.

Solomon, Robert. 1999. *Money on the Move: The Revolution in International Finance Since 1980.* Princeton, NJ: Princeton University Press.

Song, Ligang. 1998. China, in Ross H. McLeod and Ross Garnaut (eds.), *East Asia in Crisis: From Being a Miracle to Needing One.* New York: Routledge, pp. 105–19.

Soros, George. 1998. *The Crisis of Global Capitalism.* Boston: Little Brown.

——, 1998a. Towards a Global Open Society *Atlantic Monthly*, vol. 281, no. 1, pp. 20–32.

Srinivasan, T. N. 1998. Strengthening the International Financial Architecture, *Asian Development Review*, vol. 16, no. 2, pp. 1–17.

State Statistical Bureau. 1997. *Zhongguo Jinrong Nianjian 1997.* (Almanac of China's Finance and Banking 1997), Beijing: Almanac of China's Finance and Banking Editorial Department.

——, 1999. *Zhongguo tongji nianjian.* (China Statistical Yearbook). Beijing: Zhongguo tongji chubanshe.

——, 2001. *Zhongguo tongji nianjin* (China Statistical Yearbook). Beijing: Zhongguo tongji chubanshe.

Steinfeld, Edward S. 1998. The Asian Financial Crisis: Beijing's Year of Reckoning, *The Washington Quarterly*, vol. 21, no. 3, pp. 37–51.

——, 1998a. *Forging Reform in China: The Fate of State-Owned Industry.* New York: Cambridge University Press.

Stiglitz, Joseph. 1998. Second Generation Strategies for Reform for China, address given at Beijing University, July 20 (the World Bank website: www.worldbank.org).

——, 1999. Bleak Growth Prospects for the Developing World, *International Herald Tribune*, April 10–11, p. 6.

——, 2000. Capital Market Liberalization, Economic Growth and Instability, *World Development*, vol. 28, no. 6, pp. 1075–86.

——, and Shahid Yusuf (eds.). 2001. *Rethinking the East Asian Miracle.* New York: Oxford University Press.

Suehiro, Akira. 1989. *Capital Accumulation in Thailand.* Tokyo: Center for East Asian Cultural Studies.

——, 1992. Capitalist Development in Postwar Thailand: Commercial Bankers, Industrial Elite and Agribusiness Groups, in Ruth McVey (ed.), *Southeast Asian Capitalists.* Ithaca, NY: Cornell University Press.

Suh, Sang-Mok. 1998. The Korean Economic Crisis, unpublished paper. Asia/Pacific Research Center, Stanford University.

Summers, Lawrence. 1999. The Right Kind of IMF for a Stable Financial System, presentation at the London School of Business, UK, December 14 (www.ustreas.gov/press/release/ps294.htm).

——, 1999a. Building an International Financial Architecture for the 21st Century, *Cato Journal*, vol. 18, no. 3, Winter, pp. 321–9.

——, 2000. International Financial Crises: Causes, Prevention and Cures, *American Economic Review: Papers and Proceedings*, vol. 90, no. 2, pp. 1–16.

Suryadinata, Leo. 2001. Chinese Politics in Post-Suharto's Indonesia: Beyond the Ethnic Approach, *Asian Survey*, vol. 41, no. 3, May/June, pp. 502–24.

Sussangkarn, Chalongphob. 2000. East Asian Monetary Cooperation, unpublished paper, Thailand Development Research Institute.

Tan, Gerald. 2000. *The Asian Currency Crisis*. Singapore: Times Academic Press.

——, 2000a. *ASEAN: Economic Development and Cooperation*. Singapore: Times Academic Press.

Taylor, Lance. 1997. The Revival of the Liberal Creed – the IMF and the World Bank in a Globalized Economy, *World Development*, vol. 25, no. 2, pp. 145–52.

——, 1998. Capital Market Crises: Liberalization, Fixed Exchange Rates and Market-Driven De-stabilization, *Cambridge Journal of Economics*, vol. 22, no. 6, pp. 663–76.

Tesoro, Jose Manuel. 1998a. Gearing for Trouble: Suharto Will Spend To Avert Potential Unrest, *Asiaweek*, January 16.

——, 1998b. A Quick Fix? Maybe Not, *Asiaweek*, March 6.

Thurow, Lester. 1998. Asia: The Collapse and the Cure, *The New York Review of Books*, vol. 14, no. 2, February 5, p. 22.

Tobin, James. 1978. A Proposal for International Monetary Reform, *Eastern Economic Journal*, 4, July–October, pp. 153–9.

Tse, Raymond Y. C. 2000. China: A Real Estate Boom in a Protected Transition Economy, in Koichi Mera and Bertrand Renaud (eds.), *Asia's Financial Crisis and the Role of Real Estate*. Armonk, NY: M. E. Sharpe, pp. 159–82.

Tsurumi, Masayoshi (ed.). 2001. *Financial Big Bang in Asia*. Aldershot, UK: Ashgate Publishing.

Un-chan, Chung. 1999. A Proposal to Transform Korea's Capitalism, *Korea Focus*, vol. 7, no. 1, January–February, pp. 15–27.

UNDP (United Nations Development Program). 1997. *Human Development Report 1997*. New York: Oxford University Press.

——, 1999. *The China Human Development Report*. New York: Oxford University Press.

Vajragupta, Yos and Pakorn Vichyanond. 1999. Thailand's Financial Evolution and the 1997 Crisis, in Seiichi Masuyama, Donna Vandenbrink and Chia Siow Yue (eds.), *East Asia's Financial System: Evolution and Crisis*. Singapore: Institute of Southeast Asian Studies.

Van Wijnbergen, S. 1990. Capital Controls and the Real Exchange Rate, *Economica*, vol. 57, pp. 15–28.

Vatikiotis, Michael. 1993. *Indonesian Politics Under Suharto: Order, Development and Pressure for Change*. New York: Routledge.

——, 1998. The Party's Over: Political Fallout from the Southeast Asian Currency Crisis, *Public Policy*, vol. 2, no. 1, pp. 1–15.

Vines, Stephen. 2000. *The Years of Living Dangerously: Asia – From Financial Crisis to the New Millennium*. New York: Texere LLC.

Wade, Robert. 1990. *Governing the Market: Economic Theory and the Role of Government in East Asian Industrialization*. Princeton, NJ: Princeton University Press.

——, 2001. From Miracle to Cronyism: Explaining the Great Asian Slump, in Ha-Joon Chang, Gabriel Palma and D. Hugh Whittaker (eds.), *Financial Liberalization and the Asian Crisis*. New York: Palgrave Publishers, pp. 63–81.

—— and Frank Veneroso. 1998. The Asian Crisis: The High-Debt Model vs. The Wall Street–Treasury–IMF Complex, *New Left Review*, March/April.

—— and ——, 1998a. The Gathering Support for Capital Controls, *Challenge*, November/December, pp. 14–26.

—— and ——, 1998b. The Resources Lie Within, *The Economist*, 7 November, pp. 19–21.

Walker, Scott. 2000. A Tale of Two Tigers and a Giant: Comparing the Responses of Japan, Korea and Taiwan to the Asian Financial Crisis, *Asia Perspective*, vol. 24, no. 2, pp. 27–58.

Wanandi, Sofyan 1999. The Post-Soeharto Business Environment, in Geoff Forrester (ed.), *Post-Soeharto Indonesia: Renewal or Chaos?* Singapore: Institute of Southeast Asian Studies, pp. 128–43.

Wang, Hongying. 1999. The Asian Financial Crisis and Financial Reforms in China, *The Pacific Review*, vol. 12, no. 4, pp. 537–56.

Wang, Y. 2000. The Asian Financial Crisis and its Aftermath: Do we Need a Regional Financial Arrangement?, *ASEAN Economic Bulletin*, vol. 17, no. 3, pp. 205–17.

Warr, Peter G. 1998. Thailand, in Ross H. McLeod and Ross Garnaut (eds.), *East Asia in Crisis*. London: Routledge.

—— and Bhanupong Nidhiprabha. 1996. *Thailand's Economic Miracle: Stable Adjustment and Sustained Growth*. Washington, DC: World Bank.

Weber, Max. 1947. *The Theory of Social and Economic Organization*. New York: The Free Press.

Weingast, Barry. 1995. The Economic Role of Political Institutions: Market-Preserving Federalism and Economic Development, *Journal of Law, Economics and Organization*, vol. 2, no. 1, pp. 1–31.

Whitt, Joseph. 1999. The Role of External Shocks in the Asian Financial Crisis, *Federal Reserve Bank of Atlanta Economic Review*, second quarter, pp. 18–31.

Wibulswasdi, Chaiyawat. 1995. Strengthening the Domestic Financial System, in Bank of Thailand's Economic Research Department: *Papers on Policy Analysis and Assessment*.

Williamson, John. 2000. *Exchange Rate Regimes for Emerging Markets: Reviving the Intermediate Option*. Washington, DC: Institute for International Economics.

——, 2000a. The Role of the IMF: A Guide to the Reports, *International Economics Policy Briefs*, no. 00–5. Washington, DC: Institute for International Economics.

Winters, Jeffrey. 1996. *Power in Motion: Capital Mobility and the Indonesian State*. Ithaca, NY: Cornell University Press.

——, 2000. The Financial Crisis in Southeast Asia, in Richard Robison, Mark Beeson, Kanishka Jayasuriya and Hyuk-Rae Kim (eds.), *Politics and Markets in the Wake of the Asian Crisis*. London: Routledge, pp. 34–52.

Wise, Carol and Riordan Roett (eds.). 2000. *Exchange Rate Politics in Latin America*. Washington, DC: Brookings Institution Press.

Witcher, Karene and Jay Solomon. 1998. Jakarta Takes Over Much of the Bank System, *Asian Wall Street Journal*, August 24.

Witteveen, H. J. 1999. The Volatility of Private Capital Flows to the Developing Countries: Lessons from the Asian Crisis, *IDS Bulletin*, vol. 30, no. 1, pp. 19–32.

Wolf, Charles. 1998. What Caused the Crash?, *Hoover Digest*, no. 2, pp. 1–5.
——, 2000. Have You Heard About the Incredible Recovery?, *Los Angeles Times*, July 23, p. M2.
Wong, Richard Y. C. 1999. Lessons from the Asian Financial Crisis, *Cato Journal*, vol. 18, no. 3, Winter, pp. 391–8.
Woo-Cumings, Meredith. 1999. The State, Democracy and the Reform of the Corporate Sector in Korea, in T. J. Pempel (ed.), *The Politics of the Asian Economic Crisis*. Ithaca, NY: Cornell University Press, pp. 116–42.
——, 2001. Miracle as Prologue: The State and the Reform of the Corporate Sector in Korea, in Joseph Stiglitz and Shahid Yusuf (eds.), *Rethinking the East Asian Miracle*. New York: Oxford University Press, pp. 343–78.
Woo, Wing-Thye, Bruce Glassburner and Anwar Nasution. 1994. *Macroeconomic Policies, Crises, and Long-Term Growth in Indonesia: 1965–90*. Washington, DC: World Bank.
World Bank. 1993. *The East Asian Miracle: Economic Growth and Public Policy*. New York: Oxford University Press.
——, 1995. *Trends in Developing Economies: 1995*. Washington, DC: World Bank.
——, 1996. *The Chinese Economy: Fighting Inflation and Deepening Reforms*. Washington, DC: World Bank.
——, 1996a. *Global Economic Prospects and the Developing Countries*. Washington, DC: World Bank.
——, 1996b. *World Bank Development Report, 1996*. New York: Oxford University Press.
——, 1997. *Indonesia: Sustaining High Growth with Equity*. Washington, DC: World Bank.
——, 1997a. *China's Management of Enterprise Assets: The State as Shareholder*. Washington, DC: World Bank.
——, 1997b. *Country Briefs: Thailand*. Washington, DC: World Bank.
——, 1998. *The World Development Report, 1998/99*. New York: Oxford University Press.
——, 1998a. *East Asia: The Road to Recovery*. Washington, DC: World Bank.
——, 1998b. *Global Development Finance*. Washington, DC: World Bank.
——, 1998c. *Indonesia in Crisis: A Macroeconomic Update*. Washington, DC: World Bank.
——, 1999. *Republic of Korea: Establishing a New Foundation for Sustained Growth*. Washington, DC: World Bank.
——, 1999a. *China: Weathering the Storm and Learning the Lessons*. Washington, DC: World Bank.
——, 2000. *Global Economic Prospects, 2000*. Washington, DC: World Bank
——, 2000a. *World Development Report, 1999/2000*. Washington, DC: World Bank.
——, 2000b. *East Asia: Recovery and Beyond*. Washington, DC: World Bank.
——, 2000c. *Global Development Finance 2000*. Washington, DC: World Bank.
——, 2000d. *World Development Report 2000/2001*. New York: Oxford University Press.
Xu, Xiaoping. 1998. *China's Financial System under Transition*. New York: St Martin's Press.
Yabuki, Susumu and Stephen Harner. 1998. *China's New Political Economy*. Boulder, CO: Westview Press.

Yam, Joseph. 1998. *Coping with Financial Turmoil*. Hong Kong: Hong Kong Monetary Authority.

——, 1998a. *Review of the Currency Board Arrangements in Hong Kong*. Hong Kong: Hong Kong Monetary Authority.

Yanagita, Tatsuo. 2000. International Monetary Fund Conditionality and the Korean Economy in the Late 1990s, in Peter C. Y. Chow and Bates Gill (eds.), *Weathering the Storm: Taiwan, its Neighbors and the Asian Financial Crisis*. Washington, DC: The Brookings Institution Press, pp. 19–38.

Yang, Ya-Hwei. 1998. Coping with the Asian Financial Crisis: The Taiwan Experience, *Seoul Journal of Economics*, vol. 11, no. 4, pp. 423–45.

Yoo, Jang-Hee and Chul Woo Moon. 1999. Korean Financial Crisis during 1997–1998: Causes and Challenges, *Journal of Asian Economics*, vol. 10, pp. 263–77.

Yoon, Bong Joon. 1999. The Korean Financial Crisis, the Chaebol and Economic Reform, *Korea Observer*, vol. 30, no. 3, Autumn, pp. 411–41.

Yoon-je, Cho. 1999. Asian Financial Crisis and the Future of the Korean Economy, *Korea Focus*, vol. 7, no. 1, January–February, pp. 1–14.

Yoshitomi, Masaru and Kenichi Ohno. 1999. Capital-Account Crisis and Credit Contraction, *ADBI Working Paper, no. 2*. Tokyo: Asian Development Bank Institute.

—— and Sayuri Shirai. 2000. Policy Recommendations for Preventing Another Capital Account Crisis, *ADB Technical Background Paper*, July 7. Manila: Asian Development Bank.

Young, Alwyn. 1992. A Tale of Two Cities: Factor Accumulation and Technical Change in Hong Kong and Singapore, *NBER Macroeconomics Annual*, pp. 13–54.

Yusof, Zainal Aznam, Denis Hew and Gomathy Nambiar. 2000. Capital Controls: A View from Malaysia, in Brigitte Granville (ed.), *Essays on the World Economy and its Financial System*. London: The Royal Institute of International Affairs. pp. 66–92.

Zalewski, David. 1999. Brothers, Can You Spare $58 Billion? Regulatory Lessons from the South Korean Currency Crisis, *Journal of Economic Issues*, vol. 33, no. 2, June, pp. 359–66.

Zeckhauser, Richard. 1986. The Muddled Responsibilities of Public and Private America, in Winthrop Knowlton and Richard Zeckhauser (eds.), *American Society: Public and Private Responsibilities*. Cambridge, MA: Ballinger, pp. 45–77.

Zheng, Shiping. 2001. Institutional Adaptation under Pressure: China's Changing Economic Environment, in Xiaoming Huang (ed.), *The Political and Economic Transition in East Asia: Strong Market, Weakening State*. Washington, DC: Georgetown University Press, pp. 55–79.

# Index